Open Source
Security Tools

BRUCE PERENS' OPEN SOURCE SERIES

http://www.phptr.com/perens

- *C++ GUI Programming with Qt 3*
  Jasmin Blanchette, Mark Summerfield

- *Managing Linux Systems with Webmin: System Administration and Module Development*
  Jamie Cameron

- *Understanding the Linux Virtual Memory Manager*
  Mel Gorman

- *Implementing CIFS: The Common Internet File System*
  Christopher Hertel

- *Embedded Software Development with eCos*
  Anthony Massa

- *Rapid Application Development with Mozilla*
  Nigel McFarlane

- *The Linux Development Platform: Configuring, Using, and Maintaining a Complete Programming Environment*
  Rafeeq Ur Rehman, Christopher Paul

- *Intrusion Detection with SNORT: Advanced IDS Techniques Using SNORT, Apache, MySQL, PHP, and ACID*
  Rafeeq Ur Rehman

- *The Official Samba-3 HOWTO and Reference Guide*
  John H. Terpstra, Jelmer R. Vernooij, Editors

- *Samba-3 by Example: Practical Exercises to Successful Deployment*
  John H. Terpstra

Open Source
Security Tools

Practical Applications for Security

Tony Howlett

Prentice Hall
Professional Technical Reference
Upper Saddle River, NJ 07458
www.phptr.com

Visit Prentice Hall on the Web: www.phptr.com

Library of Congress Cataloging-in-Publication Data

Howlett, Tony.
   Open source security tools : practical applications for security / Tony Howlett
      p. cm.
   Includes index.
   ISBN 0-321-19443-8 (pbk. : alk. paper)
    1. Computer security. 2. Computer networks—Security measures. 3. Open source software. I. Title.

  QA76.9.A25H6985 2004
  005.8—dc22

                                         2004009479

Printed in the United States of America

First Printing, July 2004

ISBN 0-321-19443-8

Pearson Education Ltd.
Pearson Education Australia Pty., Limited
Pearson Education South Asia Pte. Ltd.
Pearson Education Asia Ltd.
Pearson Education Canada, Ltd.
Pearson Educación de Mexico, S.A. de C.V.
Pearson Education—Japan
Pearson Malaysia S.D.N. B.H.D.

Contents

Preface

Open source software is such an integral part of the Internet that is it safe to say that the Internet wouldn't exist as we know it today without it. The Internet never would have grown as fast and as dynamically as it did without open source programs such as BIND, which controls the domain name system; Sendmail, which powers most e-mail servers; INN, which runs many news servers; Major Domo, which runs many of the thousands of mailing lists on the Internet; and of course the popular Apache Web server. One thing for sure is that the Internet is a lot cheaper due to open source software. For that, you can thank the Free Software Foundation, BSD UNIX, Linux and Linus Torvalds, and the thousands of nameless programmers who put their hard work and sweat into the programs that run today's Internet.

While open source programs cover just about every aspect of computer software—from complete operating systems and games to word processors and databases—this book primarily deals with tools used in computer security. In the security field, there are programs that address every possible angle of IT security. There are open source firewalls, intrusion detection systems, vulnerability scanners, forensic tools, and cutting-edge programs for areas such as wireless communications. There are usually multiple choices in each category of mature, stable programs that compare favorably with commercial products. I have tried to choose the best of breed in each major area of information security (in my opinion, of course!). I present them in a detailed manner, showing you not just how to install and run them but also how to use them in your everyday work to have a more secure network. Using the open source software described in this book, you can secure your enterprise from both internal and external security threats with a minimal cost and maximum benefit for both the company and you personally.

I believe combining the concepts of information security with open source software offers one of the most powerful tools for securing your company's infrastructure, and by extension the entire Internet. It is common knowledge that large-scale virus infections and worms are able to spread because many systems are improperly secured. I believe that by educating the rank-and-file system managers and giving them the tools to get the job done, we can make the Internet more secure, one network at a time.

Audience

The audience for this book is intended to be the average network or system administrator whose job duties are not specifically security and who has at least several years of experience. This is not to say that security gurus won't get anything out of this book; there might be areas or tools discussed that are new to you. And likewise, someone just getting into IT will learn quite a bit by installing and using these tools. The concepts discussed and techniques used assume a minimal level of computer and network proficiency.

There is also a broad group of readers that is often overlooked by the many open source books. These are the Windows system administrators. The info-security elite often has a certain disdain for Windows-only administrators, and little has been written on quality open source software for Windows. However, the fact remains that Windows servers make up the lion's share of the Internet infrastructure, and ignoring this is doing a disservice to them and the security community at large. While overall the book is still tilted towards Linux/UNIX because most open source programs are still Linux/UNIX-only, I have tried to put Windows-based security tools in every chapter. I've also included helpful hints and full explanations for those who have never run a UNIX machine.

Contents

This book covers most of the major areas of information security and the open source tools you can use to help secure them. The chapters are designed around the major disciplines of information security and key concepts are covered in each chapter. The tools included on the book's CD-ROM allow for a lab-like environment that everyone can participate in. All you need is a PC and this book's CD-ROM to start using the tools described herein.

This book also contains some quick tutorials on basic network terminology and concepts. I have found that while many technicians are well-schooled in their particular platforms or applications, they often lack an understanding of the network protocols and how they work together to get your information from point A to point B. Understanding these concepts are vital to securing your network and implementing these tools properly. So while this book may seem slanted towards the network side of security, most of the threats are coming from there these days, so this is the best place to start.

Coverage of each security tool is prefaced by a summary of the tool, contact information, and various resources for support and more information. While I give a fairly detailed look at the tools covered, whole books can and have been written on many of the programs discussed. These resources give you options for further research.

Helpful and sometimes humorous tips and tricks and tangents are used to accent or emphasize an area of particular importance. These are introduced by Flamey the Tech, our helpful yet sometimes acerbic mascot who is there to help and inform the newbies as well as keeping the more technical readers interested in sections where we actually make some minor modifications to the program code. He resembles the denizens you may encounter in the open source world. In exploring the open source world, you will meet many diverse, brilliant, and sometimes bizarre personalities (you have to be a least a little bent to spend as much unpaid time on these programs as some of us do). Knowing the proper etiquette and protocol will get you a lot farther and with fewer flames. On a more serious note, many of the tools in this book can be destructive or malicious if used in the wrong ways. You can unintentionally break the law if you use these tools in an uninformed or careless manner (for example, accidentally scanning IP addresses that aren't yours with safe mode off). Flamey will always pipe up to warn you when this is a possibility.

Open Source Security Tool Index

Immediately following this Preface is a listing of all the tools and the pages where they are covered. This way you can skip all the background and go straight to installing the tools if you want.

Chapter 1: Information Security and Open Source Software

This chapter offers an introduction to the world of information security and open source software. The current state of computer security is discussed along with a brief history of the open source movement.

Chapter 2: Operating System Tools

This chapter covers the importance of setting up your security tool system as securely as possible. A tool for hardening Linux systems is discussed as well as considerations for hardening Windows systems. Several operating system-level tools are reviewed too. These basic tools are like a security administrator's screwdriver and will be used again and again throughout the course of this book and your job.

Chapter 3: Firewalls

The basics of TCP/IP communications and how firewalls work are covered here before jumping into installing and setting up your own open source firewall.

Chapter 4: Port Scanners

This chapter delves deeper into the TCP/IP stack, especially the application layer and ports. It describes the installation and uses for a port scanner, which builds up to the next chapter.

Chapter 5: Vulnerability Scanners

This chapter details a tool that uses some of the earlier technology such as port scanning, but takes it a step further and actually tests the security of the open ports found. This security Swiss army knife will scan your whole network and give you a detailed report on any security holes that it finds.

Chapter 6: Network Sniffers

This chapter primarily deals with the lower levels of the OSI model and how to capture raw data off the wire. Many of the later tools use this basic technology, and it shows how sniffers can be used to diagnose all kinds of network issues in addition to tracking down security problems.

Chapter 7: Intrusion Detection Systems

A tool that uses the sniffer technology introduced in the previous chapter is used here to build a network intrusion detection system. Installation, maintenance, and optimal use are also discussed.

Chapter 8: Analysis and Management Tools

This chapter examines how to keep track of security data and log it efficiently for later review. It also looks at tools that help you analyze the security data and put it in a more usable format.

Chapter 9: Encryption Tools

Sending sensitive data over the Internet is a big concern these days, yet it is becoming more and more of a requirement. These tools will help you encrypt your communications and files with strong encryption as well as create IPsec VPNs.

Chapter 10: Wireless Tools

Wireless networks are becoming quite popular and the tools in this chapter will help you make sure that any wireless networks your company uses are secure and that there aren't wireless LANs you don't know about.

Chapter 11: Forensic Tools

The tools discussed in this chapter will help you investigate past break-ins and how to properly collect digital evidence.

Chapter 12: More On Open Source Software

Finally, this chapter will give you resources for finding out more about open source software. Various key Web sites, mailing lists, and other Internet-based resources are identified. Also, I give a number of ways to become more involved in the open source movement if you so desire.

Appendix A: Common Open Source Licenses

Contains the two main open source licenses, the GPL and BSD software licenses.

Appendix B: Basic Linux/UNIX Commands

Contains basic navigation and file manipulation commands for those new to UNIX and Linux.

Appendix C: Well-Known TCP/IP Port Numbers

Contains a listing of all the known port numbers as per IANA. Note that this section is not intended to be comprehensive and is subject to constant update. Please check the IANA Web site for the most current information.

Appendix D: General Permission and Waiver Form

Contains a template for getting permission to scan a third-party network (one that is not your own). This is intended to be used as an example only and is not intended as a legal document.

Appendix E: Nessus Plug-ins

Contains a partial listing of plug-ins for the Nessus Vulnerability Scanner discussed in Chapter 5. This listing will not be the most current since the plug-ins are updated daily. The Nessus Web site should be consulted for plug-ins added after January 12, 2004.

CD-ROM Contents and Organization

The CD-ROM that accompanies this book has most of the open source security tools on it for easy access and installation. The disk is organized into directories labeled by tool. If there are separate files for Windows and Linux, they will be in their own directories. The directory "Misc" has various drivers and other documentation such as RFCs that will be of general use through your reading.

Using the Tools

Whenever possible, the tools in this book are provided in RedHat Package Manager (RPM) format. Of course, you don't have to be running RedHat Linux to use RPM. The RedHat folks originally designed it, but now it comes with most Linux versions. The RedHat Package Manager automates the installation process of a program and makes sure you have all the supporting programs and so forth. It is similar to a Windows installation process where you are guided through the process graphically and prompted where necessary. Using the RPM is almost always preferable to doing a manual installation. When you need to set custom install parameters or if a RPM file is not available for your distribution, I describe how to install the program manually. If the RPM file is provided, simply download the file or copy it from the CD-ROM that comes with this book and click on it. Your version of RPM will take care of the rest.

If you use any of the other variations of UNIX (BSD, Solaris, HP/UX, and so on), they will probably work with the tools in this book, but the installation instructions may be different. You can run most of the tools in this book on alternative versions of UNIX or Linux. Staying within the Linux family will certainly make compatibility more likely with the actual tools on the CD-ROM. If you have to download a different version of the program, some of the features discussed may not be supported. But if you are a Solaris aficionado or believe that BSD is the only way to go, feel free to use it as your security workstation. Just be aware that the instructions in this book were designed for a specific implementation and you may have to do some additional homework to get it to work. The platforms supported are listed at the beginning of each tool description.

Reference Installation

Most of the tools in this book were tested and reviewed on the following platforms:

- Mandrake Linux 9.1 on a HP Vectra series PC and a Compaq Presario laptop.
- Windows XP Pro and Windows 2000 Pro on a Compaq Prosignia series desktop and Compaq Armada laptop.

Input or Variables

In code and command examples, italics are used to designate user input. The words in italics should be replaced with the variables or values specific to your installation. Operating system-level commands appear like this:

```
ssh -1 login hostname
```

Due to page size limits, code lines that wrap are indented with a small indent.

I hope you enjoy and learn from this book. There are many, many more tools that I couldn't include due to space limitations, and I apologize in advance if I didn't include your favorite tool. I had room to cover only *my* favorites and tried to pick the best of breed in each category. I'm sure some will differ with my choices; feel free to e-mail me at tony@howlett.org, and perhaps those will make it into a future edition.

Acknowledgments

This book wouldn't be possible without the tireless efforts of programmers all around the world, making great open source software. I'd name a few but would certainly leave too many out. Thanks for your great software! I'd like to thank my business partner, Glenn Kramer, for assisting with proofing this book (as well as minding the business while I was busy trying to make deadlines) and my Nessus Command Center (NCC) project mates, Brian Credeur, Lorell Hathcock, and Matt Sisk. Finally, my love and gratitude goes to my lovely wife, Cynthia, and daughters, Carina and Alanna, who sacrificed countless hours without husband and daddy to make this book happen.

Open Source Security Tools Index

Tool Name	On CD?	Linux/ UNIX?	Windows?	Page Number
ACID	Yes	Yes	No	249
AirSnort	Yes	Yes	No	344
Autopsy Forensic Browser	Yes	Yes	No	369
Bastille Linux	Yes	Yes	No	28
dd	Yes	Yes	No	366
Dig	No	Yes	No	37
Ethereal	Yes	Yes	Yes	183
Finger	No	Yes	No	39
Forensic Toolkit	Yes	No	Yes	375
Fport	No	No	Yes	357
FreeS/WAN	Yes	Yes	No	306
GnuPG	Yes	Yes	No	295

Tool Name	On CD?	Linux/ UNIX?	Windows?	Page Number
Iptables	Yes	Yes	No	62
John the Ripper	Yes	Yes	Yes	312
Kismet Wireless	Yes	Yes	No	334
lsof	Yes	Yes	No	360
NCC	Yes	Yes	No	266
Nessus	Yes	Yes	No	131
NessusWX	Yes	No	Yes	149
NetStumbler	Yes	No	Yes	324
Nlog	Yes	Yes	No	112
Nmap	Yes	Yes	Yes	96
NPI	Yes	Yes	No	259
OpenSSH (client)	Yes	Yes	No	43
OpenSSH (server)	Yes	Yes	No	301
PGP	No	Yes	Yes	287
Ping	No	Yes	Yes	30
PuTTY	Yes	No	Yes	49
Sam Spade	Yes	No	Yes	46
Sleuth Kit	Yes	Yes	No	368
SmoothWall	Yes	No	No	75
Snort	Yes	Yes	No	201
Snort for Windows	Yes	No	Yes	217
Snort Webmin	Yes	Yes	No	216
StumbVerter	Yes	No	Yes	337

Tool Name	On CD?	Linux/ UNIX?	Windows?	Page Number
Swatch	Yes	Yes	No	236
Tcpdump	Yes	Yes	No	167
Traceroute	No	Yes	Yes	32
Tripwire	Yes	Yes	No	226
Turtle Firewall	Yes	Yes	No	71
Whois	No	Yes	Yes	35
Windump	Yes	No	Yes	181

Information Security and Open Source Software

When Tom Powers took a new job as system administrator at a mid-sized energy company, he knew his computer security skills had been a critical factor for being hired. The company had been hacked several times in the last year and their home page had been replaced with obscene images. Management wanted him to make their company information more secure from digital attacks in addition to running the computer network day to day.

After only his first day on the job, he knew he was in for a challenge. The company lacked even the most basic security protections. Their Internet connection, protected only by a simple ISP router, was wide open to the world. Their public servers were ill-maintained and looked like they hadn't been touched since they were installed. And his budget for improving this situation was practically nothing.

Yet within four months Tom had stabilized the network, stopped any further attacks, locked down the public access points, and cleaned up the internal network, as well as adding services that weren't there before. How could he do all this with such limited resources? He knew the basic principles and concepts of information security and found the right software tools to get the job done. He developed a plan and methodically carried out the following steps using security tools to improve company security.

Securing the Perimeter

First, Tom had to establish some basic defenses to protect his network from the outside so he could direct his time to securing the servers and the inside of the network. He built a firewall for their Internet connections using a program called Turtle Firewall (covered in Chapter 3). Using this software and an old server that wasn't being used for anything else, he configured this machine to allow connections only from the inside of the network outwards; all incoming connections not requested from the inside were blocked. He made some exceptions for the public servers operated by his new employer that needed access from the outside. He was even able to set up a Virtual Private Network (VPN) through the firewall so that his users could connect securely from the outside (see Chapter 3). Now he was able to repel most of the basic attacks coming from the Internet and focus on closing up the other holes in the network.

Plugging the Holes

Tom knew that he needed to assess his network for security holes and figure out where the intruders were getting in. Even though the firewall was now protecting the internal work-stations from random incursions, the public servers, such as Web and mail, were still vulnerable to attack. His firewall was also now a target, so he needed a way to ensure it was secure from all attacks. He installed a program called Bastille Linux on his firewall server to make sure it was configured securely (Chapter 2). He then ran a program called Nmap from both outside and inside his network (Chapter 4). This reported what application ports were "visible" from the outside on all his public IP addresses. The internal scan let him know if there were any unusual or unnecessary services running on his internal machines.

Next, he used a program called Nessus to scan the network from the outside and inside again (Chapter 5). This program went much deeper than Nmap, actually checking the open ports for a large number of possible security issues and letting him know if machines were improperly configured on his internal network. The Nessus program created reports showing him where there were security holes on the Web and mail servers and gave him detailed instructions on how to fix them. He used these reports to resolve the issues and then ran the Nessus program again to make sure he had eliminated the problems.

Establishing an Early Warning System

Even though he had sealed up all the holes he knew about, Tom still wanted to know if there was unusual activity happening on his LAN or against his public IP addresses. He used a network sniffer called Ethereal to establish a baseline for different types of activity on his network (Chapter 6). He also set up a Network Intrusion Detection System (NIDS) on a server, using a software package called Snort (Chapter 7). This program watched his network 24/7, looking for suspicious activity that Tom could define specifically, telling him if new attacks were happening, and if people on the inside were doing something they shouldn't be.

Building a Management System for Security Data

Tom was initially overwhelmed with all the data from these systems. However, he set up a database and used several programs to manage the output from his security programs. One called Analysis Console for Intrusion Database (ACID) helped him sort and interpret his NIDS data (Chapter 8). A program called Nessus Command Center (NCC) imported all his Nessus security scan data into a database and ran reports on it (Chapter 8). Tom also had a program called Swatch keeping an eye on his log files for any anomalous activity (Chapter 8). These programs allowed him to view the reports from a Web page, which consolidated all his security monitoring jobs into a half-hour a day task. For a guy like Tom, who was wearing many hats (technical support, programmer, and of course security administrator), this was a crucial time saver.

Implementing a Secure Wireless Solution

Another of Tom's assignments was to set up a wireless network for his company. Tom knew wireless network technology to be rife with security issues, so he used two programs, NetStumbler and WEPCrack, to test the security of his wireless network, and deployed a wireless network that was as secure as it could be (Chapter 10).

Securing Important Files and Communications

One of the things that worried his company's management was the use of e-mail to transfer potentially sensitive documents. As Tom knew, sending information via regular e-mail was akin to sending it on a postcard. Any one of the intermediaries handling a message could potentially read it. He replaced this way of doing business with a system using PGP software, which allowed users to send encrypted files whenever sending confidential or sensitive information and to secure important internal files from unauthorized prying eyes (Chapter 9).

Investigating Break-ins

Finally, with his network as secure as it could be, he checked each server for any remains of past break-ins, both to make sure nothing had been left behind and to see if he could determine who had done the dirty work. Using system-level utilities such as wtmp and lsof, and a program called The Coroner's Toolkit, Tom was able to identify the probable culprits responsible for the past break-ins (Chapter 11). While his evidence wasn't hard enough to turn in to authorities for criminal prosecution, he blocked the offending IP addresses at his new firewall so they couldn't come back to haunt him. He also used this information to file an abuse complaint with their Internet provider.

Tom had accomplished an impressive turnabout in his first few months on the job. And the most amazing thing of all was that he had been able to do it with almost no budget. How did he do this? His training in the information security field helped him develop his plan of attack and carry it out. He was able to leverage this knowledge to install low-cost but effective security solutions by using open source software to build all his systems. Using these packages, Tom was able to turn a poorly secured network into one that could rival the security of much larger networks. And he did this with no staff and a minimal amount of money.

You too can use open source software to secure your company or organization. This book will introduce you to dozens of software packages that will help you accomplish this as well as educate you on the proper policies and procedures to help keep your information secure. As I emphasize many times in this book, software tools are a great help, but they are only half the equation. A well-rounded information security program is also comprised of polices and procedures to maximize the benefits of the software. So, before you start installing software, let's first discuss the basics of information security and the background of open source software.

The Practice of Information Security

The discipline of information security (often shortened to **info-security**) has many different elements, but they all boil down to the main goal of keeping your information safe. They can be distilled into three areas that are the foundation for all information security work: confidentiality, integrity, and availability. The acronym **C.I.A.** is often used to refer to them (no relation to the government agency). This triad represents the goals of information security efforts (see Figure 1.1). Each one requires different tools and methods and protects a different area or type of information.

Confidentiality

The confidentiality segment of info-security keeps your data from being viewed by unauthorized individuals. This can be information that is confidential to your company, such as engineering plans, program code, secret recipes, financial information, or marketing plans. It can be customer information or top-secret government data. Confidentiality also refers to the need to keep information from prying eyes within your own company or organization. Obviously, you don't want all employees to be able to read the CEO's e-mail or view the payroll files.

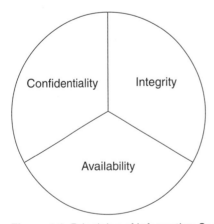

Figure 1.1 Principles of Information Security

There are multiple ways to protect your private data from getting out. The first way is to deny access to it in the first place. But sometimes that is not possible, as in the case of information going over the Internet. In that case, you have to use other tools, such as encryption, to hide and obscure your data during its journey.

Integrity

The integrity factor helps to ensure that information can't be changed or altered by un-authorized individuals. It also means that people who are authorized don't make changes without the proper approval or consent. This can be a subtle distinction. If a bank teller is secretly debiting someone's account and crediting another, that is an integrity problem. They are authorized to make account changes but they didn't have approval to make those ones. Also, data integrity means your data is properly synchronized across all your systems.

Availability

Having your information secure doesn't do you much good if you can't get to it. With denial of service attacks becoming more common, a major part of your info-security goals is not only keeping the bad guys from accessing your information, but making sure the right people can access it. Many computer criminals are just as satisfied to destroy your data or take your Web site offline. The availability element also includes preparing for disasters and being able to recover cleanly when they do occur.

In this example, Tom knew he had to apply each of these principles to completely secure his company's network. He found the software tools that would tackle each area. He was going to need all the help he could get. From the news and trade articles he had read, he knew the chilling statistics.

The State of Computer Crime

Computer crime has become an epidemic that affects every computer user from Fortune 500 CEO to the home user. According to the FBI's annual study on computer crime, conducted in connection with the Computer Security Institute (CSI), over 90 percent of U.S. companies have fallen victim to some form of computer crime. Eighty percent of those surveyed had experienced some financial loss associated with those attacks. Losses of $445 million were attributed to computer crime in 2001, up from $337 million in 2000. And it is certain that many more attacks go unreported. Many companies do not want to publicize that their computer systems were broken into or compromised and therefore avoid going to the authorities because they fear bad publicity could hurt their stock prices or business, especially firms in industries like banking that rely on the public trust.

As the FBI's National Infrastructure Protection Center (NIPC) predicted, computer attacks in 2002 were more frequent and more complex, often exploiting multiple avenues of attack like the Code Red worm did in 2001. They had expected hackers to concentrate on routers, firewalls, and other noncomputer devices as these are less visible and offer fuller access to a corporate LAN if exploited. They had also predicted that the time between the release of a known exploit and tools to take advantage of it would shrink, giving companies less time to respond to a potential threat. Sure enough, the average time from announcement of a security vulnerability and publishing exploit code has dropped from months to weeks. For example, the Blaster worm debuted a mere six weeks after the Microsoft Remote Procedure Call (RPC) vulnerabilities were discovered in early 2003.

The Computer Emergency Response Team (CERT), which is run jointly by Carnegie Mellon University and the federal government, tracks emerging threats and tries to warn companies of newly discovered exploits and security holes. They found that reports of computer security incidents more than doubled in 2001 over the previous year, from 21,756 to 52,658. They have been recording over 100 percent increase in attacks each year since 1998. In 2003, the number of incidents rose 70 percent even though the overall number of new vulnerabilities, defined as weaknesses in hardware or software that allow unauthorized entry or use, dropped (see Figure 1.2). This is due to the emergence of worms that spread quickly across the Internet affecting many systems with a single virus.

This exponential growth in both the number of attacks and the methods for making those attacks is a troubling trend as businesses connect their enterprises to the Internet in record numbers. Unfortunately, many businesses have chosen to stick their heads in the sand and ignore the information security problem. A common excuse for not properly securing their computer network is "Why would a hacker come after my company? We don't have anything they want." In years past, they would have been right. Old-school hackers generally only went after large institutions with data that was valuable to them or someone else.

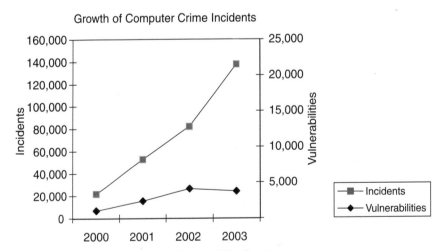

Figure 1.2 CERT Incident and Vulnerability Graph

However, a sea change in the computer security equation has made everyone a target, even small business users. In fact, small- and medium-sized companies now comprise over 50 percent of the attacks reported by the FBI. This change has been caused by several factors, which are described in the following sections.

The Advent of the Internet

When only a few networks were connected to the Internet, companies primarily had to worry about the risk of someone gaining access to a computer console or a virus being introduced by a floppy disk. Protecting against this kind of physical threat is something businesses have been doing for years. Locks on doors, alarm systems, and even armed guards can protect the computers and systems from physical access. Anti-virus software and passwords served as the only necessary technical security precaution for firms in the pre–World Wide Web age.

With the Internet, hackers can attack from thousands of miles away and steal critical company assets, bypassing any and all physical barriers. They can then sink back into the anonymity that the Internet provides. They can come from foreign countries with no extradition treaties with the United States. They leave few clues as to who they are or even what they did. When you are connected to the Internet, you are literally no more than a few keystrokes away from every hacker, cracker, and ne'er-do-well on the network. Password protection and anti-virus software is not enough to keep intruders out of your virtual office.

Ubiquitous, Inexpensive Broadband

Not too long ago, dedicated Internet connections were the sole domain of large companies, educational institutions, and the government. Now, you can get DSL or cable modem access for your business or home use for less than $100 per month. Companies are getting online by the thousands, and this is a good thing overall for business. However, having a dedicated connection exposes them to more risk than their previous dial-up or private line connections. First of all, broadband is quite different from just dialing up via a modem from a network standpoint. Usually when you dial up, you are connected only while you are using it. With always-on broadband, hackers can work away, trying to get in, taking as much time as they need. They especially like working during the late night hours, when system administrators who might notice something awry have gone home.

Having access to a site with dedicated broadband access is very attractive to hackers. They can use that bandwidth and leverage it to attack other sites. If a hacker's goal is to take down a hugely popular site like Yahoo or Amazon by sheer brute force, they need a lot of bandwidth. Most of these sites have bandwidth that is measured in gigabits, not megabits. In order to flood those sites, they need a huge bandwidth pipe, which the average hacker can't afford. However, if they break into other machines on the Internet with broadband connections, they can use these machines to attack their real target. If they can "own" enough sites, they suddenly have a very big gun to wield. This is known as a **distributed denial of service** (DDOS) attack. It has the added benefit of throwing the authorities off their trail because all of the attacks are coming from unsuspecting victims, rather than the attackers themselves. These victim machines are known as **zombies**, and hackers have special software they can load to make these computers or servers "awake" on special commands that only they can issue. These programs are often very hard to find and eradicate because the host computer shows no ill effects while the zombie software is dormant. The one thing that the hacker hordes want is your bandwidth; they could generally care less who you are.

Another reason hackers want to break into machines is to store their tools and other ill-gotten loot. These exploited machines are called **storage lockers** by the hackers, who often traffic in illicit files. The files might be pornography, pirated software or movies, or other hacker tools. Rather than store these on their own machines, where they might be found and used against them in court, they prefer to hide them on unsuspecting victim's servers. A broadband connection is nice because they have lots of bandwidth for uploading and downloading files. A small company is even better because it is likely they don't have a large IT staff monitoring their Internet connection and probably don't have very sophisticated security measures in place. They can give the hacked server IP address out to their buddies and use them for informal swap meets. Again, these kinds of intrusions are hard to find because the computer acts normally, although you might notice a slowdown in performance or download speeds while it is being used for these unauthorized activities.

Attack of the Script Kiddies

Another thing that has changed the targets for computer crime is simply a rise in the number of participants, especially at the low end of expertise. These hacker novices are called **Script Kiddies** because they often use point-and-click hacking tools or "scripts" found on the Web rather than their own knowledge. Hackers used to be part of an elite community of highly skilled (albeit morally challenged) individuals who were proficient in writing code and understood computers at their most fundamental level. They even had an informal Hacker Ethics code, which, although eschewing the idea of privacy, stated that no harm should be done to computers invaded. The hacker experience was primarily about learning and exploring. However, that community soon splintered and was watered down by newcomers. Now one can find hundreds of Web sites that can teach you how to hack in a matter of minutes. Many so-called hackers are teenagers with little knowledge of coding. Rather than seeking knowledge, they are intent on joyriding hacked computers, bragging rights, and outright vandalism. And with the influx of new bodies to the hacking community, like any thief or criminal, they look for the easiest "mark." These inexperienced criminals attack the systems of smaller companies, those with fewer defenses and less-experienced administrators who are not as likely to notice their neophyte mistakes. Most of them wouldn't dare taking on the Pentagon or the CIA's computers, which have impressive digital defenses and significant prosecutorial powers. Few small companies can afford to investigate, much less prosecute, a computer intrusion even if they do notice it. And since most Script Kiddies' main goal is not learning but mischief, they often cause more damage than an experienced computer criminal would.

Worms, Auto-rooters, and Other Malware

Finally, a major reason that the fundamental computer security scene has changed is that much hacking nowadays is automated and random. Script kiddies can use tools that scan IP addresses at random to look for weak or exploitable machines. They will often let these programs run all night, harvesting potential victims for them. There are packages, called **auto-rooters**, that gain "root" or admin privileges on a machine. These tools not only do the reconnaissance for them, but also actually carry out the act of breaking into the machine and placing their Trojan horse or other malicious software (**malware**) in place. The result is that with a single click of a mouse, someone with no more computer experience than a six-year old can "own" dozens of machines in a single evening.

With the advent of Internet worms like Nimda in 2001, even the human element has been taken out of the picture. These autonomous cousins to the computer virus roam the Internet, looking for computers with a certain set of security holes. When they find one, they insert themselves into that computer, perform whatever function they were programmed to do, and then set that machine up to search for more victims. These automated hacking machines have infected far more networks than have human troublemakers. They also spread incredibly fast. It is estimated that the Code Red worm spread to over 300,000 servers within a few days of its release.

Info-Security Business Risks

So it's clear that the playing field has changed. Before, few small companies really had to worry about their data security; now firms of all sizes are forced to spend time and money to worry about it—or risk the consequences. What are these risks? Few companies stop to think about all the possible risks that they are exposed to from an information security standpoint. You should understand all these risks, recognize which ones apply to your organization, and know what the value or dollar cost of each one is. This will help you make a business case for better computer security and justify the expenditures you need.

Data Loss

While computer viruses have kept this threat current since the 1980s, few managers stop to think what it would really cost them to lose part or all of their data. Without proper backups, which many small firms lack, the loss of critical data can be catastrophic. Years of accounting, payroll, or customer data can be wiped out. Orders can be lost. If the data belongs to customers, the company could be liable for its loss. Certain professions, such as legal or accounting, can be subject to regulatory fines or punishment for loss of such data. And this doesn't include the loss of business and productivity while employees restore the data or have to revert to paper records. Even when they have backups, the time and hassle involved to get systems back up and running is considerable. The bottom line is that few businesses can survive long without their computerized records and systems. Does your company have a written Disaster Recovery Plan that covers data and systems? If not, you could be in for a nasty surprise in the event of an unexpected outage.

Denial of Service

Many of today's hackers are more high-tech vandals than computer geniuses. They take joy in knocking down servers or denying service for any reason, and sometimes for no reason at all. Often the denial of service is accidental or incidental to the hacker's real goal. The Code Red and Nimda worms brought many networks to their knees just from trying to respond to all the attempts at infection. With the reliance of today's business on the Internet, this can be like shutting off the electricity. E-mail communication comes to a halt. A company Web site might go down. For a company that does a considerable amount of business over the Internet, this could mean a total stoppage of work.

How many companies know the hourly or daily cost to their business of a loss of Internet access? In certain industries or companies, it is very large due to their reliance on information technology. Few companies these days are without some dependence on Internet access. Depending on how much the business relies on the Internet, a denial of service attack can either be a minor annoyance or a major blow to a company's business. Try calculating the cost for your company based on the number of employees unable to work, the number of orders processed online, and so on.

Embarrassment/Loss of Customers

Being offline can make a company look very bad. Not being able to communicate via e-mail or missing critical messages can be embarrassing at best. If their Web site is offline, customers will immediately begin asking questions. For public companies, it could mean a loss of stock value if the news gets out. Witness the drop in stock prices of Yahoo and Amazon after well-publicized denial of service attacks. Millions or even hundreds of millions of dollars of stockholder value can disappear in an instant. For businesses like financial intuitions or e-commerce companies that depend on people feeling safe about putting their financial information online, a single Web defacement can wipe out years of goodwill. CD Universe, an online CD retailer who had their credit card database stolen, never recovered from that attack. Cloud Nine Communications, an ISP in England, was down for a week due to a concerted and lengthy denial of service attack and eventually had to close its doors. There are now gangs of hackers who go on mass Web site defacement binges, sometimes hitting hundreds of sites per night. The admission to these hacker clubs is racking up a certain number of Web site defacements. Do you want your Web site to become a notch on their scorecard?

Liability

In this litigious age, making a small mistake can result in a lawsuit costing millions. Imagine the results if your entire customer database is stolen and then traded on the Internet. Class action suits have resulted from such events. With the huge rise in identity theft, laws are being passed that require companies to exercise the proper standard of care when dealing with a customer's personal or financial data. One industry that has been particularly affected by legislation is healthcare. The Health Insurance Portability and Accountability Act of 1996 (HIPAA) requires any company dealing with patient information to properly secure that data from unauthorized use. The privacy provisions of the act affecting computer networks went into effect in 2003. There are civil and criminal penalties for violators, so it is no longer just a money issue. Executives and managers could go to jail if found in violation.

Also, hackers are always looking for unsecured computers to launch their distributed denial of service attacks from. If your company's computers are used in such an attack and victims can't find the original perpetrator, they might come after you, charging that you were negligent in securing your network. After all, companies tend to have deeper pockets than most hackers.

Another area to be concerned about is liability for copyright violations. Copying of pirated movies, music, and software over the Internet has reached a fever pitch. Media companies are fed up and are starting to go after violators directly by tracking down the IP addresses of the downloaders and sending lawyers after them. InternetMovies.com, a Hawaii-based Web site, had their ISP service disconnected when their ISP was served with a lawsuit for alleged pirated files found on their network. Pirates who want to distribute their wares are resorting to storing them on third-party computers, often compromised servers on corporate networks. If your company is unknowingly running one of these servers or has such files stored on it, you could be disconnected from the Internet, liable for fines, or sued. Stories like these can often help you persuade reluctant executives to implement stricter personnel policies when it comes to information security, such as banning file sharing software or implementing stronger password requirements.

Disclosure of Corporate Secrets and Data

It is hard to put a dollar value on this risk because it varies from firm to firm. For example, the value of the recipe for Coca-Cola or Colonel Sander's fried chicken could reach into the billions. At a smaller company, detailed plans for a proprietary device or formula may be invaluable. In some cases, much of the value of the company may be locked up in this important data. For example, a biotech company may have their research for their latest gene patents on their corporate network.

Customer lists are always valuable to competitors, especially in very competitive markets. Hewlett-Packard was served with a shareholder lawsuit after sensitive discussions between their executives were released to the public during a contentious merger.

However, even at companies where there are no secret plans or recipes, this risk exists. For instance, think of the damage of releasing the corporate payroll file to the rank-and-file workers. This happens all the time, usually due to snoopy or vindictive employees. The discord and subsequent loss of morale and perhaps employee exodus due to being disgruntled over pay differences can be huge. Often, all this could be avoided if the system administrator had simply secured the system properly.

Tampering with Records

Sometimes an intruder is not intent on stealing or destroying data but rather just making changes to existing records, hopefully without being detected. This can be one of the most difficult kinds of computer crime to detect because the systems keep functioning just as they were before. There is no system crash or performance drain to point to an intrusion. There is no defaced Web site to raise an alarm. Obviously, for banks and government agencies, this can be a very serious problem. But every company has to worry about someone getting into the payroll system and changing pay amounts. Schools and universities have to deal with students trying to change grades. Often it is up to the accounting auditors to find evidence of foul play. However, with the right system security, these problems can be avoided up front.

Loss of Productivity

This is a much more subtle risk and often very hard to avoid. It can range from bandwidth being used by employees to download music or movies, thereby slowing down other workers, to employees surfing objectionable or nonwork Web sites. While these are employee policy issues, the system administrator is often called on to fix them with technology such as content filters and firewalls. And many of these unauthorized programs, such as Napster, Kazaa, and instant messengers, in addition to being productivity drainers, can create security holes in a company's network defenses.

Given all these risks, you would think that companies would be falling over themselves to put the proper protections in place. Yes, the largest companies have implemented significant defenses, but most small- and medium-sized companies have little in the way of network security. At best, a company will install a firewall and anti-virus software and consider that enough to protect them. Unfortunately, it is often not enough.

A whole industry has sprung up to offer solutions to these problems. There are commercial hardware and software solutions such as firewalls, intrusion detection systems, and vulnerability scanners. However, most of these products are priced so high that only larger firms can afford them. A simple firewall costs several thousands of dollars. Commercial intrusion detection systems and vulnerability testing solutions can run into the tens of thousands or more. In addition to the up-front costs, there are often yearly maintenance fees to support the software. And many of the software solutions require high-end computers to run on. They also often require pricey database software such as Oracle for reporting features. Given these costs, proper computer security is often seemingly out of reach for the small- and medium-sized firms. And as you have seen, the risk is just as great for these businesses as the Fortune 500, and perhaps even more so, since their financial resources to withstand such an attack will be much more limited than a large firm.

So what's a harried, overworked, underfunded system administrator to do? Well, there is a solution that can provide companies with quality computer security for little or no cost: *open source software*.

Open Source History

The open source software movement has its roots in the birth of the UNIX platform, which is why many people associate open source with UNIX and Linux systems, even though the concept has spread to just about every other computer operating system available. UNIX was invented by Bell Labs, which was then the research division of AT&T. AT&T subsequently licensed the software to universities. Because AT&T was regulated, it wasn't able to go into business selling UNIX, so it gave the universities the source code to the operating system, which was not normally done with commercial software. This was an afterthought, since AT&T didn't really think there was much commercial value to it at the time.

Universities, being the breeding grounds for creative thought, immediately set about making their own additions and modifications to the original AT&T code. Some made only minor changes. Others, such as the University of California at Berkley, made so many modifications that they created a whole new branch of code. Soon the UNIX camp was split into two: the AT&T, or System V, code base used by many mainframe and minicomputer manufacturers, and the BSD code base, which spawned many of the BSD-based open source UNIX versions we have today. Linux was originally based on MINIX, a PC-based UNIX, which has System V roots.

The early open sourcers also had a philosophical split in the ranks. A programmer named Richard Stallman founded the Free Software Foundation (FSF), which advocated that all software should be open source. He developed a special license to provide for this called the General Public License (GPL). It offers authors some protection of their material from commercial exploitation, but still provides for the free transfer of the source code. Berkley had developed its own open source license earlier, the BSD license, which is less restrictive than the GPL and is used by the many BSD UNIX variants in the open source world.

These two licenses allowed programmers to fearlessly develop for the new UNIX platforms without worry of legal woes or having their work being used by another for commercial gain. This brought about the development of many of the applications that we use today on the Internet, as well as the underlying tools you don't hear as much about, such as the C++ compiler, Gcc, and many programming and scripting languages such as Python, Awk, Sed, Expect, and so on.

However, open source didn't really get its boost until the Internet came to prominence in the early 1990s. Before then, developers had to rely on dial-up networks and Bulletin Board Systems (BBSs) to communicate and transfer files back and forth. Networks such as USENET and DALnet sprung up to facilitate these many specialized forums. However, it was difficult and expensive to use these networks, and they often didn't cross international boundaries because of the high costs of dialing up to the BBSs.

The rise of the Internet changed all that. The combination of low-cost global communications and the ease of accessing information through Web pages caused a renaissance of innovation and development in the open source world. Now programmers could collaborate instantly and put up Web sites detailing their work that anyone in the world could easily find using search engines. Projects working on parallel paths merged their resources and combined forces. Other splinter groups spun off from larger ones, confident that they could now find support for their endeavors.

Linux Enters the Scene

It was from this fertile field that open source's largest success to date grew. Linus Torvalds was a struggling Finnish college student who had a knack for fiddling with his PC. He wanted to run a version of UNIX on it since that is what he used at the university. He bought MINIX, which was a simplified PC version of the UNIX operating system. He was frustrated by the limitations in MINIX, particularly in the area of terminal emulation, since he needed to connect to the school to do his work. So what became the fastest growing operating system in history started out as a project to create a terminal emulation program for his PC.

By the time he finished with his program and posted it to some USENET news groups, people began suggesting add-ons and improvements. At that point, the nucleus of what is today a multinational effort, thousands of people strong, was formed. Within six months he had a bare-bones operating system. It didn't do much, but with dozens of programmers contributing to the body of code, it didn't take long for this "science project" to turn into what we know as the open source operating system called Linux.

Linux is a testament to all that is good about open source. It starts with someone wanting to improve on something that already exists or create something totally new. If it is any good, momentum picks up and pretty soon you have something that would take a commercial company years and millions of dollars to create. Yet it didn't cost a dime (unless you count the thousands of hours invested). Because of this, it can be offered free of charge. This allows it to spread even farther and attract even more developers. And the cycle continues. It is a true meritocracy, where only the good code and good programs survive.

However, this is not to say that there is no commercial motive or opportunity in open source. Linus himself has made quite a bit of money by his efforts, though he would be the first to tell you that was never his intention. Many companies have sprung up around Linux to either support it or to build hardware or software around it. RedHat and Turbo Linux are just a few of the companies that have significant revenues and market values (albeit down from their late 1990s heights). Even companies that were known as proprietary software powerhouses, such as IBM, have embraced Linux as a way to sell more of their hardware and services.

This is not to say that all software should be free or open source, although some of the more radical elements in the open source world would argue otherwise. There is room for proprietary, closed source software and always will be. But open source continues to gain momentum and support. Eventually it may represent a majority of the installed base of software. It offers an alternative to the commercial vendors and forces them to continue to innovate and offer real value for what they charge. After all, if there is an open source program that does for free what your commercial program does, you have to make your support worth the money you charge.

Open Source Advantages

You and your company can use open source both to cut costs and improve your security. The following sections touch on the myriad of reasons why open source security tools might make sense for you and your company.

Cost

It's hard to beat free! Although open source does not necessarily always mean free, most open source software is available at no charge. The most common open source license is the GNU GPL license, which is a free software license. Other open source software might be shareware or even charge up front, like the commercial servers available from RedHat. But either way, open source is usually available for a fraction of the cost of commercial alternatives. This helps greatly in justifying new security projects within your company. When all that is needed is a little of your time and maybe a machine to run the software, it is a lot easier to get approval for a new solution. In fact, depending on your authority level, you may be able to go ahead and implement it without having to make a business case for it. If you want to take it a step further, after successful installation, you can bring the results to your boss and demonstrate that you saved the company thousands of dollars while making the network more secure (and that may improve your job security!).

Extendability

By definition, open source software is modifiable and extendable, assuming you have the programming skills. Many open source programs have scripting languages built in so that you can write small add-on modules for them without having to be a programming guru. Nessus, the open source vulnerability scanner does this with their NASL scripting language (this is demonstrated later in this book, and you'll learn how to write some custom security tests too). Snort, the open source intrusion detection system mentioned earlier, lets you write your own alert definitions. This means that if there is something specific to your company that you need to test for, you can easily write a custom script to look for it. For example, if you have a database file called customer.mdb that is specific to your company and that should only be used by certain departments, you could write a Snort rule that looks for that file traversing the network and alerts you.

And of course if you are a real programming guru, you can get involved in contributing to the core code and gain both valuable experience and recognition within the open source community. This could also be helpful in terms of your job marketability.

Security

There are some people, mostly those involved with commercial software concerns, who advocate that closed source software is inherently more secure since hackers do not have the internal workings of the software easily available to them. This school of thought relies on the security premise of obfuscation—keeping the design of your product secret. However, this logic breaks down when you look at the facts. Windows is the largest proprietary software product in the world, yet the number of security holes announced in the Windows platforms is about the same as those found in Linux and other open source platforms. The truth is that whether the source code is open or closed doesn't make programmers write more secure programs.

Independence

Discovery and remediation of security issues in software can be much faster with open source programs. Commercial companies often have strong monetary motivations for not admitting to security flaws in their products. Multiple security holes found in a product, especially if it is a security product, could hurt sales to new customers. If it is a publicly traded company, the stock price could fall. Additionally, developing security patches and distributing them to customers are expensive endeavors, ones that usually don't generate any revenue. So getting a company to confirm a security issue with its software can be a major effort. This means days or weeks can go by while customer systems are still vulnerable. Frustration with this process has prompted some security researchers to adopt a policy of releasing new security vulnerabilities directly to the public rather than privately to the company.

Once a security hole is known to the public, a company will often go through a complicated development and testing process before releasing a patch to the public, ensuring that there aren't any liability issues and that the patch can be released for all platforms at once. So more time may go by while you have a known security hole that hackers can exploit.

Open source software projects have no such limitations. Security patches are usually available within hours or days, not weeks. And of course you don't have to wait for an official patch; if you understand the code well enough, you can write your own or design a workaround while you wait for one.

The general thinking in the open source community is that the best overall security comes from a critical review by a large body of people who don't have a vested interest in not finding any holes. This is the same measure of quality that cryptographic researchers apply to their work. The open source concept, while not guarantying that you will get more secure software, means you don't have to take a company's word that a product is secure, and then wait for them to come up with a solution for any security holes.

User Support

Commercial software products usually have support lines and a formal channel to go through for help. One of the main reasons many people shy away from open source solutions is that they feel like they have to pay for a product to get decent support. However, the support you often get for your money is not that great. If the software company is small, you might have to wait hours or days for a return call. If the vendor is large, you will probably be shunted into a call queue. When you finally get connected, it will be with an entry-level technical person who can't do much more than enter your problem into a knowledge base to see if anyone has had the problem before and then parrot back a generic solution. Usually you have to get to a level two or three technician before you get someone who truly understands the product and can help you with complicated problems. Not to mention that companies don't like to admit their products have bugs; they will tend to blame it on everything else beside their product (your operating system, your hardware, and so on).

Add to that, many companies are now charging separately for support. The price you pay over several years for support of the software can exceed the initial purchase price of it. These charges create a nice steady stream of revenue for the company even if you never upgrade. Most software companies, if they aren't already doing it, are moving in this direction. Toll-free numbers for software technical support are becoming a thing of the past.

Open source products often have terrific support networks, albeit somewhat non-traditional. Open source support is less organized but often more helpful and more robust. There will rarely be a phone number to call, but there are usually several options to get answers on the software. On a smaller project, it might be as simple as e-mailing the developer directly. The larger packages usually have a mailing list you can post questions to. Many have several different lists depending on your question (user, developer, specific modules, or platforms). Many now have chat rooms or IRC channels where you can ask questions, ask for new features, or just sound off in real time.

The neat thing is that you are usually talking to people who are very familiar with the software, possibly even the actual developers. You can even ask them for new features or comment on recently added ones. You will end up talking to some of the brightest and most experienced people in the industry. I've learned a lot by just following the conversations on the mailing lists.

Most questions I've posed to these lists have been answered in a few hours or less. The answers are usually insightful and informative (and sometimes witty). You will often get several different opinions or solutions to your problem, all of which may be right! Besides getting very detailed answers to your questions, you can talk about the state of the art in that particular area or engage in philosophical debates about future versions, and so forth (if you have a lot of extra time on your hands). And of course, if you are knowledgeable about the software, you are free to chime in with your own answers to questions.

Keep in mind that these folks usually aren't employees of a company producing the software and might sometimes seem a bit harsh or rude. Asking simple questions that are answered fully in the INSTALL pages or in a FAQ might earn you a rebuke. But it will also usually get you the answer or at least a pointer to where you can find it. Sometimes the flame wars on the lists crowd out the real information. However, I'll take impassioned debate over mindless responses any day.

Finally, if you really do feel like you have to pay for support, there are companies that do just that for open source platforms. Numerous Linux companies offer supported versions of that open source operating system. Many of the more popular applications also have companies providing support for them. You can buy a prepackaged Snort IDS box from several companies that will support you and provide regular updates. This way you can have the same vaulted support that commercial products offer but still keep all the benefits of an open source platform.

Product Life Span

With commercial software, you are at the mercy of the corporation that owns the product you select. If it's a large company like Microsoft, then you are probably in good shape. However, even Microsoft has tried to get into market segments and then decided they wanted out and dropped product lines. Smaller companies could go out of business or get bought or merged. In this day and age, it is happening more and more. If the company that buys them has competing products, more than likely they will get rid of one of the lines. If they decide to drop your product, then you are out of luck for future support. With a closed source product, you have no way of asking any questions or making any necessary up-grades to it once the company decides they don't want to play anymore.

Open source projects never die a final death. That's not to say that they don't go dormant. Projects go by the wayside all the time as the participants graduate or move on to a new stage of life. This is more prevalent in the smaller programs and tools. The larger ones (which comprise the majority of programs mentioned in this book) always have someone willing to step up and grab the reins. In fact, there are sometimes power struggles in the hierarchy for control of a project. However, if someone doesn't like the direction it is going, there is nothing to stop him or her from branching off and taking the product where he or she wants it to go. Even in the smaller ones, where there is a single developer who might not be actively developing it anymore, you can simply pick up where they left off. And if you need to fix something or add a feature, the code is wide open to let you do that. With open source software, you are never at the mercy of the whims of the market or a company's financial goals.

Education

If you want to learn about how security software works or polish your programming skills, open source software is a great way to do it. The cost is low, so you don't have to worry about dropping a couple of thousand dollars on training or programs. If you are doing this yourself, all you need is a machine to run it on and an Internet connection to download the software (or the CD-ROM included with this book). If you are doing it for a company, it is the cheapest training course your company will ever approve. Plus, your company has the added benefit that you will be able to use the technology to improve the company's com-puter security without spending a lot of money. Talk about a win-win situation!

Of course, budding programmers love open source software because they can get right into the guts of the program and see how it works. The best way to learn something is to do it, and open source software offers you the ability to see all the code, which is usu-ally fairly well documented. You can change things, add new features, and extend the base code—all things that are impossible with closed source software. The most you can ever be with a closed source program is an experienced user; with open source, you can be an innovator and creator if you want.

The mailing lists and chat rooms for open source projects are excellent places to ask questions and make friends with people who can really mentor your career. Getting involved with an open source project is probably the quickest way to learn about how software is developed. Which leads into my next point.

Reputation

After you've cut your teeth, gotten flamed a few times, and become a regular contributing member of an open source package, you will notice that you are now the go-to guy for all the newbies. Building a reputation in the open source world looks great on a resume. Being able to say you were integrally involved in the development of an open source product speaks volumes about your dedication and organization skills, not to mention your programming skills. Designing an open source software package makes for a great graduate research project. And of course, once you get good enough, you may end up producing your own open source software and building quite a following. More than a few authors of open source software have gone on to parley their user base into a real company making real money. So whether your efforts in open source are just a hobby, as most are, or become your sole aim in life, it can be very rewarding and a lot of fun.

When Open Source May Not Fit Your Needs

I've said a lot about how great open source software is. You'd think it was going to solve all the world's problems with the way I have gone on about it. However, there are instances when it is just not appropriate. There aren't many of them, but here they are.

Security Software Company

If you work for a company that is designing proprietary, closed source security software, then open source software is not appropriate as a base of code to start from. This is not to say you can't play around with open source software to get ideas and learn the art, but be very careful about including any code from an open source project. It could violate the open source licenses and invalidate your work for your company. If your company can work with the license that's included with the open source software, then you may be okay. Also, some companies are beginning to open source some part of their software. These "hybrid" licenses are becoming more common. If you do decide to do this, you will want to make sure you clearly understand the open source license and have your legal department research it thoroughly.

This doesn't mean that you can't use open source software within your company. If you are a network administrator, you can use an open source firewall, for example. Many closed source software companies do this, as hypocritical as it sounds. You just can't use the code to create a product that won't be open sourced.

100 Percent Outsourced IT

Another case where open source may not fit is if your IT department is not technically capable of handling program installations, compilations, and so on. While most open source software is fairly easy to use, it does require a certain level of expertise. If your IT department consists of the administrative assistant who does it in his or her spare time, or you outsource your entire IT department, then it probably doesn't make sense, unless your contractor has experience in that area.

Restrictive Corporate IT Standards

Finally, you may be faced with corporate standards that either require you to use specific vendors or outright forbid open source. This is becoming less and less common as companies are realizing that locking into a single vendor is silly. Ignored for a long time by the big boys, open source is coming on strong in corporate America. Companies like IBM, once the champion of closed source and proprietary products, are embracing and even promoting open source. The old adage of "no one ever got fired for buying (insert blue-chip vendor of choice)" is no longer valid in most companies. An updated version of the proverb might be "no one ever got fired for saving the company money with a solution that worked." Certainly, however, going out on limb with a new concept can be more risky than the status quo.

Windows and Open Source

It used to be that open source software was primarily developed only for UNIX-based operating systems. Many developers consider Windows and the company behind it as being the antithesis of what open source software stands for. And the company hasn't denied the charge; in fact, Microsoft has commissioned studies that show open source in a bad light, and heavily markets against the Linux operating system, which is starting to encroach on its market share in the server arena. However, no matter what the Microsoft attitude is towards the concept, Windows users have been busy creating programs for it and releasing them as open source. There are ports of most of the major tools in the UNIX and Linux world for Windows. These programs are sometimes not full versions of their UNIX brethren, but there are also open source programs that are released only on the Windows platform, such as the wireless sniffer NetStumbler that is reviewed in Chapter 10.

Many times, technical personnel will be limited in what operating systems they can run on their company's LAN. Even if they have carte blanche, they may just not be able to dedicate the time to loading and learning one of the open source operating systems I recommend in the next chapter. So for each area mentioned in this book, I try to present both a UNIX and a Windows option (they are often the same program). Like it or not, Windows is the dominant operating system on most desktops, and ignoring this would be doing a disservice to a large body of technical professionals who could benefit from open source software.

Open Source Licenses

Many people assume that open source means software free of all restrictions. Indeed, in many cases there is no charge for the software. However, almost all open source software is covered by a license that you must agree to when using the software, just as you do when using a commercial product. Generally this license is much less restrictive than a traditional closed source license; nonetheless, it does put limits on what you can do with the software. Without these limits, no programmer would feel safe releasing the results of his or her hard work into the public domain. When using open source software, make sure you are in accordance with the license. Also be sure that any modifications or changes you make also comply. This is the important part: If your company spends a lot of time customizing an open source program for its own use, you should be aware that you will have some responsibilities under the open source license.

There are two main types of open source licenses: the GNU General Public License and the BSD license. As long as you understand them thoroughly, you should be able to confidently use most open source software without fear of running afoul of any copyright issues. There are some unusual open source licenses coming out for things like artwork created in games and so forth. These "hybrid" licenses are a little murkier to deal with, and you should definitely be careful when using them, because you could be incurring charges or be in violation of their copyright without knowing it.

The goal of both major open source licenses is not so much to protect the existing software, but to control the uses of derivative code from that software. After all, it is usually free and the original developer shouldn't care if you make a million copies of it and distribute them to your friends. It's when you start making changes to the software and want to distribute it that you have to be careful. The two major open source licenses and their similarities and differences are described next.

The GNU General Public License

The GNU General Public License (GPL) is probably the more commonly used open source license. It is championed by the Free Software Foundation, which promotes the creation and proliferation of free software using this license. The actual GNU project works on certain specific software projects and puts their stamp of approval on them. These projects are usually core tools and libraries, such as the Gcc compiler and other major works. Anyone can use the GPL license for software as long as you use it verbatim and without changes or additions. Many developers use it because it has been vetted by a team of lawyers and has withstood the test of time. It is so common that if someone says that something is "GPL'd," generally people understand that to mean that it has been released open source under the GPL license.

The GPL is more complicated than the other major open source license, the BSD license. It has a few more restrictions on the use of the code by the licensee, which makes it more appropriate for companies that are making a commercial product. Generally, if you are licensing something under the GPL, it is understood that it is free software. A vendor, however, may charge for packaging, distribution, and support. This is the area that a lot of companies make money from what is supposedly a free package. Witness the retail packages of various flavors of Linux and commercial versions of the Apache Web servers and Sendmail communication package. However, if you download or load from a CD-ROM something that is covered under the GPL and didn't put a credit card number in somewhere, you can reasonably assume that you don't owe anyone any money for it.

The real beauty of the GPL from a developer's standpoint is that it allows the original author of the program to maintain the copyright and some rights while releasing it for free to the maximum number of people. It also allows for future development, without worry that the original developer could end up competing against a proprietary version of his or her own program.

In its basic form, the GPL allows you to use and distribute the program as much as you want with the following limitations.

- If you distribute the work, you must include the original author's copyright and the GPL in its entirety. This is so that any future users of your distributions fully understand their rights and responsibilities under the GPL.
- You must always make a version of the source code of the program available when you distribute it. You can also distribute binaries, but you must also make the source code easily available. This gets back to the goal of the open source concept. If all that is floating around is the binaries of a free program and you have to track down the original designer to get access to the source, the power of free software is greatly diminished. This ensures that every recipient of the software will have the full benefit of being able to see the source code.
- If you make any changes to the program and release or distribute it, you must also make available the source code of those modifications in the same manner as the original code, that is, freely available and under the GPL. The key phrase here is "and release or distribute it." If you don't release it, then you are not obligated to release the source code. If you are making custom changes to the code for your company, they might be worried about giving out the results of your efforts. As long as you don't release it publicly or intend to sell it, it can remain proprietary.

  However, it usually makes good sense to go ahead and release the new code with the GPL. This not only generates lots of good will with the open source community, but it will also ensure that your changes are compatible with future versions of the program and are fully tested. You can use this logic to convince your company that they can get the experience and free labor of all the other programmers on the project by doing this. It will generally not hurt a company competitively to release this kind of code unless that program is part of the core business of the company, in which case open source software may not make sense anyway. And finally, it won't hurt your reputation and leverage with the other developers on the project and elsewhere in the software community.

Appendix A has the entire text of the GPL. You can get it in different text formats from www.gnu.org/licenses/gpl.html.

The BSD License

The BSD license is the open source license under which the original University of California at Berkley version of UNIX was released. After they won their lawsuit with AT&T over the original license, they released the software into the public domain with the permissive BSD license. The primary difference from the GPL is that the BSD license does not include the requirement of releasing future modifications under the same license. Based on this, several companies went on to release commercial versions of UNIX based on the BSD code base. BSDI is one such company. Some say that this goes against the idea of open source, when a company can take an improved version and charge for it, while others feel that it encourages innovation by giving a commercial incentive. Either way, it spawned a whole family of UNIX versions, including FreeBSD, NetBSD, and OpenBSD, from the free side of the house, and others such as BSDi on the commercial side. Appendix A has the full text of the BSD license. You can also access it at www.opensource.org/licenses/bsd-license.php.

Now that you understand the background of info-security and open source software, we are going to get into the specifics: installing, configuring, and using actual software packages. The following chapters review programs that can help you secure your network and information in a variety of ways. The chapters are loosely organized into different info-security subjects, and most of the most major areas of information security are covered. Also, many tools can have multiple uses. For example, even though Snort is covered in the chapter on intrusion detection systems, it can be used in forensic work too. And certainly if your interest is in a tool for particular area, you can skip right to that section.

Operating System Tools

Most of the tools described in this book are application programs. As such, they require an underlying operating system to run on. If you think of these programs as your information security toolkit, then your operating system is your workbench. If your OS is unstable, your security work will suffer; you will never be able to truly trust the data coming from it. In fact, your OS might introduce even more insecurity into your network than you started with. In computer security jargon, having a secure OS to build on is part of what is known as a **Trusted Computing Base** (TCB). The TCB consists of the entire list of elements that provides security, the operating system, the programs, the network hardware, the physical protections, and even procedures. An important base of that pyramid is the operating system. Without that, you are building your Trusted Computing Base on quicksand.

Chapter Overview

Concepts you will learn:
- Introduction to Trusted Computing Base
- Guidelines for setting up your security tool system
- Operating system hardening
- Basic use of operating system-level tools

Tools you will use:
Bastille Linux, ping, traceroute, whois, dig, finger, ps, OpenSSH, and Sam Spade for Windows

Many attacks on computers are directed at the operating system. Modern operating systems have ballooned to such size that it is extremely difficult for any one person to completely understand what is going on "under the hood." XP, the most current version of Windows, contains over 50 million lines of code. While it is supposed to be the most secure version of Windows yet (according to Microsoft), new security bugs are found in it almost daily. The more complexity you add to a product, the more likely it is to give unexpected results when given unexpected input. Hackers count on these unexpected results.

It used to be that a computer had a limited number of possible inputs—the application programs that were either designed by or approved by the computer vendor. Now, with the Internet and Java- and Active X-enabled Web browsers, all kinds of traffic and code can come at a computer that the designers never allowed for. The sheer volume of programs combined with the types of traffic coming from the Internet means that operating systems are getting less secure, not more secure, as times goes on, especially when you use them "straight out of the box."

Add to this vendors' tendency to try to make computers as ready as possible so users can simply "plug and play." While some might argue that this is a good thing for the masses of computer illiterates, it is certainly not a good thing from a security standpoint. Most security features are turned off by default, many programs and services are loaded automatically, whether the user will need them or not, and many "extras" are thrown onto the system in an effort to outdo the competition. While Microsoft Windows has been the worst offender in this area, consumer versions of Linux aren't much better, and even server-level operating systems are guilty of this sin. A standard installation of RedHat Linux still loads far too many services and programs than the average user needs or wants. Windows Small Business Server 2000 loads a Web server by default. And while Windows XP improved on the past policy of "everything wide open," there are still insecurities in the product when using the default installation.

Making sure your security tool system is secure is important for several reasons. First of all, if a front-line security device such as a firewall is breached, you could lose the protection that the firewall is supposed to provide. If it's a notification device, for example, an intrusion detection system, then potential intruders could invade the box and shut off your early warning system. Or worse yet, they could alter the data so that records of their activities are not kept. This would give you a false sense of security while allowing the intruders free reign of your network.

There are hacker programs designed to do just this. They alter certain system files so that any data coming out of the machine can be under the control of the hacker. Any computer that has been infected with one of these programs can never be trusted. It is often more cost effective to reformat the drive and start over.

Finally, if unauthorized users commandeer your security box, they could use the very security tools you are using against you and other networks. An Internet-connected machine with these tools loaded could be very valuable to someone intent on mischief.

Ensuring that the base operating system of your security machine is secure is the first thing you should do, before you load any tools or install additional programs. Ideally, you should build your security tool system from scratch, installing a brand new operating system. This way you can be sure that no programs or processes will interfere with your security tools. Also, this guarantees that the base operating system is secure from any previous tampering or malicious programs. If for some reason you have to install your tools on an existing installation of an operating system, make sure you follow the directions later in this chapter for OS hardening and securing your system. Later in this chapter I review Bastille Linux, a tool for doing this on a Linux platform. There are free utilities available from Microsoft for hardening Windows. You can also use the tools described in Chapter 5 to scan an existing system for vulnerabilities.

Your choice of operating system for your security tool system determines how you go about securing it. I recommend an open source operating system such as Linux or BSD, but Windows will work fine as long as you properly secure it first. I used Mandrake Linux to install and run the Linux-based tools recommended in this book, and most Linux distributions and BSD or UNIX operating system can use these tools.

There are many open source operating systems available as mentioned in Chapter 1. Most of them are UNIX-based, although they all have a graphical interface available called X-Windows, and window managers such as KDE and GNOME. These interfaces will be familiar to anyone who has used Microsoft Windows, but there are a few differences.

I do not advocate that one operating system is intrinsically better than the others as far as security goes. It is all in the way you use it and configure it; hence the lengthy section that follows on hardening the OS installation. I used Linux because it is the one I have the most experience with, and I felt that it was compatible with most systems being used. With over 50 million users worldwide and dozens of variants, Linux has the widest variety of programs, and most of the open source security tools I mention in this book are designed specifically for it.

The first tool discussed automates locking down a Linux system. This will ensure you are working with a workstation that is as secure as it can be initially. There are also some basic tips on how to properly secure the Windows operating system for use as a security workstation. Finally, you will use some tools at the operating system level. There are certain system-level functions that you will use regularly in your security applications, and several of these are included in the tools section.

This chapter is not intended to be a definitive guide on securing any of these operating systems, but it gives you an overview of the basics and some tools to use.

Hardening Your Security Tool System

Once you have installed your operating system, you need to **harden** it for use as a security system. This process involves shutting off unneeded services, tightening permissions, and generally minimizing the parts of the machine that are exposed. The details of this vary depending on the intended uses of the machine and by operating system.

Hardening used to be an intensive manual process whereby you walked through each possible setting and modified it. Many books have been written on the subject of hardening each different operating system. However, you don't have to read a whole other book to do this if you are using the Linux operating system—there are now tools that will do this for you automatically on a Linux system. This both saves time and makes it much less likely that you will miss something.

Bastille Linux: An OS Hardening Program for Linux

Bastille Linux

Author/primary contact:	Jay Beale
Web site:	www.bastille-linux.org
Platforms:	Linux (RedHat, Mandrake, Debian), HP/UX
License:	GPL
Version reviewed:	2.1.1
Important e-mails:	
General inquiries:	jon@lasser.org
Technical inquires:	jay@bastille-Linux.org
Mailing lists:	

Bastille Linux announcement:
http://lists.sourceforge.net/mailman/listinfo/bastille-Linux-announce
Bastille Linux development:
http://lists.sourceforge.net/mailman/listinfo/bastille-Linux-discuss

System requirements:
Perl 5.5_003 or greater
Perl TK Module 8.00.23 or greater
Perl Curses Module 1.06 or greater

This first security tool is an operating system hardening tool called Bastille Linux. Contrary to what the name sounds like, it isn't a stand-alone operating system, but rather a set of scripts that goes through and makes certain system settings based on prompts from you. It greatly simplifies the hardening process and makes it as easy as answering some questions. It can also set up a firewall for you (that's covered in the next chapter). Bastille Linux can run on Mandrake, RedHat, Debian, and HP/UX, which is not even Linux. Jay Beale, the developer, is continuing to release support for other Linux distributions.

Installing Bastille Linux

Bastille is written using a toolkit called Curses (finally an appropriate name for a programming language!).

1. You first need to download and install the Perl Curses and TK modules, which Bastille depends on. They can be obtained from this chart on the Bastille site:

   www.bastille-Linux.org/perl-rpm-chart.html.

2. RedHat users: You also need to install a package called Pwlib, which you can obtain from the same chart. Run RPM to install it from the command line with the parameters given in the chart there.

3. Once you've installed the required modules, download the Bastille RPM or get it from the CD-ROM that accompanies this book. Click on it, and Bastille should install automatically.

Now you are ready to run Bastille to harden or lock down your operating system.

Flamey the Tech Tip:

Run Bastille on Nonproduction Systems First!

Always run these tools for the first time on nonproduction or test systems. These programs might turn off services needed for a Web server or mail server to function and cause an outage. Once you've fully tested the effect and verified that it's stable, you can run them in your production environment.

Running Bastille Linux

1. If you didn't select to start X-Windows at boot time when installing your OS, type `startx` at a command prompt and the X-Windows graphical interface will display.
2. Start Bastille in Interactive mode by clicking on the Bastille icon located in /usr/ bin/bastille. You can also type `bastille` from a terminal window opened in X.
3. If you don't want to use Bastille in X-Windows or can't for some reason, you can still run Bastille from the command line using the Curses-based user interface. Type

```
bastille c
```

at any command prompt. Both interfaces will give you the same result.

You can also run Bastille in what is called Non-Interactive mode. This runs Bastille automatically, without asking any questions, from a predesignated configuration file. Every time you run Bastille, a configuration file is created. You can then use it to run Bastille on other machines in Non-Interactive mode. This technique is useful for locking down multiple machines quickly. Once you have a configuration file that does the things you want, simply load Bastille on additional machines and copy the configuration file onto those machines (or have them access the file over the network). Then type `bastille non-interactive` *config-file* (*config-file* is the name and location of the configuration file you want to use).

Most of the time, however, you will run Bastille in Interactive mode. In this mode you answer a series of questions on how you will use the machine. Based on the answers, Bastille shuts down unneeded services or restricts the privileges of users and services. It asks you things like, "Do you intend to use this machine to access Windows machines?" If not, it shuts off the Samba server, which allows your machine to interact with Windows machines. Samba could introduce some potential security holes into your system, so it is a good idea to turn it off if you don't need it. If you do have to run some servers (SSH, for example), it will attempt to set them up with limited privileges or use a **chrooted jail**. This means that if the server has to run with root access, it has a limited ability to affect other parts of the system. This blunts the effects of any successful attacks on that service.

Each question is accompanied by an explanation of why this setting is important, so you can decide if it is appropriate to your installation. There is also a More detail button that has additional information. Bastille takes the novel approach of trying to educate the administrator while it is locking down the system. The more information you have, the better armed you will be in your network security duties.

You can skip a question if you aren't quite sure and come back to it later. Don't worry; it gives you a chance at the end to finalize all the settings. You can also run Bastille later after you have researched the answer and change the setting at that time. Another nice thing that Bastille does is gives you a "to do" list at the end of the hardening session for any items that Bastille doesn't take care of.

Now you have a secure Linux computer from which to run your security tools. If you are new to a UNIX-based operating system, you will want to familiarize yourself with the common commands and navigation. If you have ever used DOS, many of the commands will be familiar although the syntax is somewhat different. One of the most significant differences between Windows and Linux and other UNIX-based operating systems is that the file system is case sensitive. Appendix B contains a cheat sheet of the most commonly used Linux and UNIX commands. Take some time to practice moving around the operating system and make sure you can do simple things like change directories, copy files, and so on.

There are several operating system commands you will be using frequently in your security work. They are not truly separately security programs but rather operating system utilities that can be used to generate security information. They are used so much in later chapters and in security work in general that I want to discuss them in detail here.

---

ping: A Network Diagnostic Tool

ping
Author: Mike Muus (deceased)
Web site: http://ftp.arl.mil/~mike/ping.html
Platforms: Most UNIX platforms and Windows
Licenses: Various

UNIX manual pages:
Type `man ping` at any command prompt.

If you've been around Internet systems for any time at all, you've probably used ping. But there are some unique uses for ping in security applications as well as various considerations for how pings are handled by certain security programs. **Ping** stands for Packet

Internet Groper (which sounds a little politically incorrect) and is a diagnostic tool now built into most TCP/IP stacks. Many people think that ping is like submarine radar: a ping goes out, bounces off a target, and comes back. While this is a good general analogy, it doesn't accurately describe what happens when you ping a machine. Pings use a network protocol called **ICMP** (Internet Control Message Protocol). These messages are used to send information about networks. Ping uses ICMP message types 8 and 0, which are also known as Echo Request and Echo Reply, respectively. When you use the ping command, the machine sends an echo request out to another machine. If the machine on the other end is accessible and running a compliant TCP stack, it will reply with an echo reply. The communications in a ping basically look like this.

System A sends a ping to System B: Echo Request, "Are you there?"

System B receives the Echo Request and sends back an Echo Reply, "Yes, I'm here."

In a typical ping session this is repeated several times to see if the destination machine or the network is dropping packets. It can also be used to determine the **latency**, the time that it takes packets to cross between two points.

You may also get these other types of ICMP messages back when you ping a host. Each has its own meaning and will be explained in later chapters.

- Network unreachable
- Host unreachable

You can tell a lot more about a host with a ping than just if it is alive or not. As you will see, the way a machine responds to a ping often identifies what operating system it is running. You can also use ping to generate a DNS lookup request, which gives the destination's host name (if it has one). This can sometimes tell you if this machine is a server, a router, or perhaps someone on a home dial-up or broadband connection. You can ping an IP address or a fully qualified domain name. Table 2.1 lists additional switches and options for the ping command that you might find useful.

Table 2.1 ping Options

Options	Descriptions
-c *count*	Sends count number of pings out. The default on Linux and UNIX systems is continuous pings. On Windows, the default count is four pings.
-f	Ping flood. Sends as many packets as it can, as fast as it can. This is useful for testing to see if a host is dropping packets, because it will show graphically how many pings it responds to. Be very careful with this command, as it can take down a machine or network quite easily.

(continues)

Table 2.1 ping Options (*continued*)

Options	Descriptions
-n	Don't perform DNS on the IP address. This can speed up a response and rule out DNS issues when diagnosing network issues.
-s *size*	Sends packets of *size* length. This is good for testing how a machine or router handles large packets. Abnormally large packets are often used in denial of service attacks to crash or overwhelm machines.
-p *pattern*	Sends a specific pattern in the ICMP packet payload. This is also good for testing how a machine responds to unusual ICMP stimuli.

traceroute (UNIX) or tracert (Windows): Network Diagnostic Tools

traceroute (UNIX) or tracert (Windows)
Author/primary contact: Unknown Web sites: www.traceroute.org   www.tracert.com Platforms: Most UNIX and all Windows platforms Licenses: Various UNIX manual pages: Type man traceroute at any UNIX command prompt.

This command is similar to ping, but it provides a lot more information about the remote host. Basically, traceroute pings a host, but when it sends out the first packet, it sets the TTL (Time to Live) setting on the packet to one. This setting controls how many hops a packet will take before dying. So the first packet will only go to the first router or machine beyond yours on the Internet, and then a message acknowledging that the packet has "expired" will return. Then, the next packet is set with a TTL of 2, and so on until it reaches your target. This shows the virtual path (the route) that the packets took. The name of each host along the way is resolved, so you can see how your traffic traverses the Internet. It can be very interesting to see how a packet going from Houston to Dallas might bounce from the East Coast to the West Coast, traveling thousands of miles before reaching its target a fraction of a second later.

This tool comes in handy when you are trying to track down the source or location of a perpetrator you have found in your log files or alerts. You can traceroute to the IP address and learn a number of things about it. The output might tell you if they are a home user or inside a company, who their ISP is (so you can file an abuse complaint), what type of service they have and how fast it is, and where geographically they are (sometimes, depending on the descriptiveness of the points in-between). Listings 2.1 and 2.2 show examples of traceroutes.

Listing 2.1 traceroute Example 1

```
Tracing route to www.example.com
over a maximum of 30 hops:

1    <10 ms   <10 ms   <10 ms 192.168.200.1

2    40 ms   60 ms   160 ms 10.200.40.1

3    30ms   40ms    100ms   gateway.smallisp.net

4    100 ms   120 ms   100 ms iah-core-03.inet.genericisp.net
     [10.1.1.1]

5    70 ms   100 ms    70 ms dal-core-03.inet.genericisp.net
     [10.1.1.2]

6    61 ms   140 ms    70 ms dal-core-02.inet.genericisp.net
     [10.1.1.3]

7    70 ms   71 ms    150 ms dal-brdr-02.inet.genericisp.net
     [10.1.1.4]

8    60 ms   60 ms   91 ms 192.168.1.1

9    70 ms   140 ms    100 ms sprintds1cust123.hou-pop.sprint.com
     [192.168.1.2]

10   101 ms   130 ms   200 ms core-cr7500.example.com
     [216.34.160.36]

11   180 ms   190 ms   70 ms acmefirewall-hou.example.com
     [216.32.132.149]

12   110 ms   110 ms   100 ms www.example.com [64.58.76.229]

Trace complete.
```

In Listing 2.1, the DNS names have been changed to generic names, but you get the general idea. From this simple command, you can tell that the IP address in question belongs to a company called Acme, that it is probably a Web server, it is inside their firewall or on the DMZ, their ISP is Sprint, and they are in Houston. Many network administrators and large ISPs use geographical abbreviations or initials to name their routers, so by looking at the DNS name and following the trail of routers, you can deduce that hou-pop.sprint.com is a Sprint router in Houston.

Listing 2.2 traceroute Example 2

```
Tracing route to resnet169-136.plymouth.edu [158.136.169.136]

over a maximum of 30 hops:



1    <1 ms   <1 ms   <1 ms 192.168.200.1

2    12 ms    7 ms    8 ms 10.200.40.1

3    26 ms   28 ms   11 ms iah-edge-04.inet.qwest.net
     [63.237.97.81]

4    37 ms   15 ms   12 ms iah-core-01.inet.qwest.net
     [205.171.31.21]

5    51 ms   49 ms   47 ms dca-core-03.inet.qwest.net
     [205.171.5.185]

6    52 ms   55 ms   65 ms jfk-core-03.inet.qwest.net
     [205.171.8.217]

7    73 ms   63 ms   58 ms jfk-core-01.inet.qwest.net
     [205.171.230.5]

8    94 ms   67 ms   55 ms bos-core-02.inet.qwest.net
     [205.171.8.17]

9    56 ms   56 ms   60 ms bos-brdr-01.ip.qwest.net
     [205.171.28.34]

10   64 ms   63 ms   61 ms 63.239.32.230

10   67 ms   59 ms   55 ms so-7-0-0-0.core-rtr1.bos.verizon-gni.net
     [130.81.4.181]

11   56 ms   61 ms   62 ms so-0-0-1-0.core-rtr1.man.verizon-gni.net
     [130.81.4.198]

12   58 ms   59 ms   57 ms so-0-0-0-0.core-rtr2.man.verizon-gni.net
     [130.81.4.206]
```

```
13   59 ms   57 ms   64 ms  a5-0-0-732.g-rtr1.man.verizon-gni.net
     [130.81.5.126]

15   74 ms   62 ms   61 ms  64.223.133.166

16   68 ms   67 ms   68 ms  usnh-atm-inet.plymouth.edu
     [158.136.12.2]

17   80 ms 2968 ms   222 ms  xhyd04-3.plymouth.edu [158.136.3.1]

18   75 ms 2337 ms   227 ms  xspe04-2.plymouth.edu [158.136.2.2]

19   74 ms   65 ms   72 ms  resnet169-136.plymouth.edu
     [158.136.169.136]



Trace complete.
```

From the traceroute example in Listing 2.2 you can tell that the IP in question is probably being used by a student at Plymouth State University in Plymouth, New Hampshire. How can you tell this? First of all, the final domain name is a giveaway. If you follow the traceroute, it goes from bos (Boston) to man (Manchester), then to plymouth.edu. The .edu means that it's a university. This was an educated guess, but you can verify it by going to the plymouth.edu Web site. Also, the resolved host name is resnet169-136. The name suggests it is the network for their student residences.

As you can see, sometimes reading traceroutes is like being a detective, more of an art than a science, but over time you will learn more and get better at recognizing what each abbreviation means.

Traceroute gives lots of information to use to follow up on this IP if it was the source of an intrusion or attack. In the example in Listing 2.1, you could look up the company Web site to find a main number. You can call their ISP and complain. Larger ISPs usually have a main e-mail or contact to use for complaints, and will usually enforce their terms of service with the customer. Or you can use the next command, whois, to find specific technical contacts for the company or organization.

whois: A DNS Query Tool	
whois	
Author/Primary contact:	N/A
Web site:	N/A
Platforms:	Most UNIX platforms
Licenses:	Various
UNIX manual pages:	Type man whois at any UNIX command prompt.

The whois command is useful when trying to track down a contact for someone causing trouble on your network. This command queries the primary domain name servers and returns all the information that Internic (or whoever their name registrar is) has. Internic used to be the quasi-government agency that was responsible for keeping track of all the domain names on the Internet. Internic became a commercial company called Network Solutions, and was then acquired by VeriSign. Now that name registration has been opened up for competition, there are literally dozens of official name registrars. However, you can still usually find out who owns a domain by using the whois command.

This command is useful for attacks coming both from within companies or within ISP networks. Either way, you can track down the person responsible for that network and report your problems to them. They won't always be helpful, but at least you can try. The syntax is:

```
whois domain-name.com
```

The variable `domain-name.com` is the domain name you are looking for information on. Listing 2.3 shows the kinds of information returned that might be returned.

Listing 2.3 whois Results

```
Registrant:
Example Corp (EXAMPLE.DOM)
   123 Elm, Suite 123
   New York, NY 10000
   US
   212-123-4567
   Domain Name: EXAMPLE.COM

   Administrative Contact:
    Jones, Jane (JJ189)    jane.jones@example.com
     123 Elm, Ste 123
     New York, NY 10000
     212-123-4567

   Technical Contact:
    John Smith  (JS189)    john.smith@example.com
     123 Elm, Ste 123
     New York, NY 10000
     212-123-4567


   Record expires on 06-Oct-2006.
   Record created on 05-Oct-2002.
   Database last updated on 30-Apr-2004 21:34:52 EDT.

   Domain servers in listed order:

   NS.EXAMPLE.COM        10.1.1.1
   NS2.EXAMPLE.COM       10.1.1.2
```

As you can see, you can contact the technical person in charge of that domain directly. If that doesn't work, you can always try the administrative person. The whois command usually displays an e-mail address, a mailing address, and sometimes phone numbers. It tells when the domain was created and if they've made recent changes to their whois listing. It also shows the domain name servers responsible for that domain name. Querying these numbers with the dig command (described next) can generate even more information about the remote network's configuration.

Unfortunately, whois is not built into the Windows platforms, but there are plenty of Web-based whois engines, including the one located on Network Solutions Web site at:

> www.networksolutions.com/cgi-bin/whois/whois

Flamey the Tech Tip:

Don't Drop Your Corporate Drawers on *whois*!

If you administer domains of your own, you should make sure your whois listing is both up to date and as generic as possible. Putting real e-mail addresses and names in the contact information fields gives information that an outsider can use either for social engineering or password-cracking attacks. Also, people might leave the company, making your record outdated. It is better to use generic e-mail addresses, such as **dnsmaster@example.com** or **admin@example.com**. You can forward these e-mails to the people responsible, and it doesn't give out valuable information on your technical organization structure.

---

dig: A DNS Query Tool

dig
Author/primary contact: Andrew Scherpbeir
Web site:
http://www-search.ucl.ac.uk/htdig-docs/author.html
Platforms: Most UNIX Platforms
Licenses: Various
UNIX manual pages: Type `man dig` at any UNIX command prompt.

The dig command queries a name server for certain information about a domain. Dig is an updated version of the nslookup command, which is being phased out. You can use it to determine the machine names used on a network, what the IP addresses tied to those machines are, which one is their mail server, and other useful tidbits of information. The general syntax is:

```
dig @server domain type
```

where *server* is the DNS server you want to query, *domain* is the domain you are asking about, and *type* is the kind of information you want on it. You will generally want to query the authoritative DNS for that domain; that is, the one listed in their whois record as being the final authority on that domain. Sometimes the company runs this server; other times its ISP runs the server. Table 2.2 lists the kinds of records you can ask for with the type option.

Listing 2.4 shows an example of results of the dig command. As you can see, their whole domain zone file has been downloaded. This yields valuable information, such as the host name of their mail server, their DNS server, and other important machines on their network. If you run a DNS server, you should be able to configure it to respond only to these kinds of request from authorized machines.

Listing 2.4 Output from `dig @ns.example.com AXFR`

```
; <<>> DiG 9.2.1 <<>> @ns.example.com.com example.com ANY
;; global options: printcmd
;; Got answer:
;; ->>HEADER<<- opcode: QUERY, status: NOERROR, id: 54042
;; flags: qr aa rd; QUERY: 1, ANSWER: 6, AUTHORITY: 0, ADDITIONAL: 4

;; QUESTION SECTION:
;example.com    IN   ANY

;; ANSWER SECTION:
example.com.   86400   IN   MX    10 mail.example.com.
example.com.   2560    IN   SOA   ns.example.com
hostmaster.example.com. 1070057380 16384 2048 1048576 2560
example.com.   259200  IN   NS    ns.example.com.
example.com.   259200  IN   NS    ns2.example.com.
example.com.   86400   IN   A     10.1.1.1

;; ADDITIONAL SECTION:
nat1.example.com.   86400   IN   A   10.1.1.2
ns.example.com.     86400   IN   10.1.1.3
ns2.example.com.    86400   IN   A   10.1.1.4
sql.example.com     86400   IN   A   10.1.1.5
www.example.com     86400   IN   A   10.1.1.6


;; Query time: 107 msec
;; SERVER: 64.115.0.245#53(ns.example.com)
;; WHEN: Wed Dec 31 18:39:24 2003
;; MSG SIZE rcvd: 247
```

Table 2.2 dig Record Types

Options	Descriptions
AXFR	Attempts to get the whole file for the domain or "zone" file. Some servers are now configured not to allow zone file transfers, so you may have to ask for specific records.
A	Returns any "A" records. "A" records are individual host names on the network, such as webserver.example.com and firewall1.example.com.
MX	Returns the registered mail host name for that domain. This is useful if you want to contact an administrator (try administrator@mailhost.example.com or root@mailhost.example.com).
CNAME	Returns any CNAMED hosts, also known as aliases. For example: fido.example.com = www.example.com.
ANY	Returns any information it can generate on the domain. Sometimes this works when AXFR doesn't.

---

finger: A User Information Service

finger
Author/primary contact: Unknown
Web site: Various including:
   www.infonet.st-johns.nf.ca/adm/finger.html
   www.developer.com/net/cplus/article.php/627661
Platforms: Most UNIX and Windows platforms
Licenses: Various
UNIX manual pages:
Type `man finger` at any command prompt.

Finger is an old UNIX command that isn't used much anymore, but it is still running on many machines as a legacy service. It was originally designed when the Internet was a friendlier place and users didn't mind people halfway across the world knowing their schedule, office numbers, and other information. Most competent system administrators turn this daemon off now because it has been associated with many security holes. However, you'd be surprised how many servers still run it. Many routers come with it (I can't figure out why, except maybe the vendor implemented a TCP stack that included it), and some UNIX operating systems still enable it by default on installation, and people forget or don't know how to turn it off.

The finger command lets you query the remote system for information on its users. The syntax is:

```
finger user@hostname.example.com
```

Replace the variables *user* with the username you are trying to find out about and *hostname.example.com* with the fully qualified host name. You can also use an IP address. Listing 2.5 shows the results of a finger query run on the user bsmith on server1.example.com.

Listing 2.5 *finger* Query Results
```
Login name: bsmith In real life: Bob Smith
Directory: /home/bsmith Shell: /bin/bash
Last Login: 7/03/04 0800:02
No unread mail
Project: Writing a book

Plan:  I'll be on vacation in Europe from September 1-15th.
```

As you can see, there quite a bit of information on Bob available through finger, including the last time he logged on, if he has any new e-mail, and any personal information he entered. He was also kind enough to let us know when he will be out of the office. This could be used by hackers to divine information about Bob for use in social engineering. It also can help them to learn his log-on habits and schedule so they could attempt to crack his account when he is out of town.

Another crafty use of finger is to send the command without a user name. This generates a list of all the users currently logged on. Listing 2.6 shows the results of what this query might look like on the fictitious example.com. You can see who is logged on and what their real names are. You can also see if they have been idle (perhaps they forgot to log out) and for how long. Finally, it lists what station they are coming from (whether they are local or remote) and the hostname or IP of where they are logging on from if it is not local. You can see one user is logged on multiple times with one session idle. A malicious viewer of this data might decide to attempt to hijack this idle session.

You could also run full finger queries on any of those users that looked worth pursuing further. Using the command `finger -l @hostname.example.com` generates a full finger query on every user logged in at that moment.

Listing 2.6 *finger -l* with No Username
```
[hostname.example.com]


User    Real Name    What   Idle TTY Host   Console Location

bsmith  Bob Smith            2 lab1-30 (cs.example.edu)
```

```
ajohnson Andrew Johnson        2 lab1-10 (dialup.genericisp.com)
bjones   Becky Jones           co lab3-22

atanner Allen H Tanner         0:50 co lab3-9

atanner Allen H Tanner         co lab3-1

atanner Allen H Tanner         4:20 co lab3-8

cgarcia Charles Garcia         3 lab1-10
```

---

ps: A UNIX Process Query Command

ps
Author/primary contact: Unknown
Web sites: Various, including
                         www.nevis.columbia.edu/cgi-bin/man/sh?man=ps
Platforms: Most UNIX platforms
Licenses: Various
UNIX manual pages:
Type man ps at any UNIX command prompt.

The ps command, short for process, shows you all the processes running on a system. This can be very useful to determine if there is some daemon or process running that shouldn't be. It can also be used to debug many of the tools in this book. Table 2.3 lists some useful ps switches.

Table 2.3 ps Switches

Switches	Descriptions
A	Shows all users' processes.
a	Shows users' processes for all processes with a tty.
u	Shows the name of the process user.
x	Displays processes with controlling ttys.

Listing 2.7 shows the output from a ps command with the -aux switch.

Listing 2.7 *ps -aux* Output

```
USER      PID  %CPU %MEM   VSZ  RSS  TTY    STAT  START   TIME  COMMAND
root        1  0.1  0.7  1288  484  ?       S    18:00   0:04  init [3]
root        2  0.0  0.0     0    0  ?      SW    18:00   0:00  [keventd]
root        3  0.0  0.0     0    0  ?      SW    18:00   0:00  [kapmd]
root        5  0.0  0.0     0    0  ?      SW    18:00   0:00  [kswapd]
root        6  0.0  0.0     0    0  ?      SW    18:00   0:00  [bdflush]
root        7  0.0  0.0     0    0  ?      SW    18:00   0:00 [kupdated]
root        8  0.0  0.0     0    0  ?      SW<   18:00   0:00  [mdrecoveryd]
root       12  0.0  0.0     0    0  ?      SW    18:00   0:00  [kjournald]
root      137  0.0  0.0     0    0  ?      SW    18:00   0:00  [khubd]
root      682  0.0  1.0  1412  660  ?       S    18:01   0:00  /sbin/cardmgr
rpc       700  0.0  0.8  1416  532  ?       S    18:01   0:00  portmap
root      720  0.0  1.2  1640  788  ?       S    18:01   0:00  syslogd -m 0
root      757  0.0  1.8  1940 1148  ?       S    18:01   0:00  klogd -2
root      797  0.0  0.8  1336  500  ?       S    18:01   0:00  gpm -t ps/2 -m
xfs       869  0.0  5.8  5048 3608  ?       S    18:01   0:00  xfs -port -1
daemon    884  0.0  0.8  1312  504  ?       S    18:01   0:00  /usr/sbin/atd
root      928  0.0  2.0  2660 1244  ?       S    18:01   0:01  /usr/sbin/SSHd
root      949  0.0  1.5  2068  948  ?       S    18:01   0:00  xinetd -stayalive
root      951  0.0  0.7  1292  496  ?       S    18:01   0:00  /sbin/dhcpcd -h m
root     1078  0.0  1.0  1492  628  ?       S    18:01   0:00  crond
root     1132  0.0  3.4  3808 2152  ?       S    18:01   0:02  nessusd: waiting
root     1134  0.0  1.9  2276 1224  ?       S    18:01   0:00  login -- tony
tony     1394  0.0  2.6  2732 1624  tty1    S    18:29   0:00  -bash
tony     1430  0.0  2.6  2744 1636  tty1    S    18:29   0:00  bash
tony     1805  0.0  1.2  2676  796  tty1    R    18:56   0:00  ps -aux
```

You can see each process running on the system with its process ID. This is important if you want to kill the service or take some other action. The –u switch shows the user at the far left. This readout shows various system processes owned by root. It also shows a user running the ps command. If you see some mysterious service running, you should investigate it further. This listing shows what might be a suspicious service: the nessusd daemon, which is the vulnerability scanner you will use in Chapter 5. However, this is your security tool system, so it is all right for it to be running here.

You can also pipe the ps command into a grep command to search for specific services running. For example, the command

```
ps -ax |grep snort
```

will tell you if Snort is running on your system and its associated process ID (PID). So, as you'll find with many of the operating system level tools in this book, the ps command can be useful for all kinds of system administration activities, not just security.

OpenSSH Client: A Secure Terminal Service

OpenSSH Client
Author/primary contact: Tatu Ylönen
Web site: www.openSSH.com
Platforms: Most UNIX platforms, Windows, OS/2
License: BSD

Other Web sites:
www.uni-karlsruhe.de/~ig25/SSH-faq/
www.SSH.com
http://kimmo.suominen.com/SSH/

SSH is such a useful tool that there is a separate section on it in Chapter 9 as a server-side tool. However, I highly recommend using the client whenever possible for interactive logins in lieu of Telnet or some other nonsecure method. You will be using it so much I want to give some basic details and syntax of the client here. SSH (secure shell) is a remote access tool that allows you to log into a remote system securely. A major Achilles' heel of most networks is the fact that inter-system communications are generally passed over a network in plain text. So you can harden the individual machines all you want, but if you log into them remotely with an insecure terminal program, thieves could still grab your log-on credentials off the network with a sniffer. They can then log on as you without breaking a sweat. One of the most popular remote access tools, Telnet, suffers from this deficiency. SSH fixes this problem by encrypting all the communications from the first keystroke.

SSH is an open source program that is available on almost every platform, and it comes by default with most Linux-based operating systems. There is a commercial version, available at the www.ssh.com Web site, which is also open source. The one I review here is OpenSSH, the free version that comes with most Linux distributions and is on the CD-ROM that comes with this book. While there are a few differences, most of the commands and syntax should work and the two are interoperable.

In order to access a remote system with SSH, you need an SSH client on your end and there must be an SSH server running on the remote side. While SSH isn't as widespread as Telnet, it is catching on. Cisco is finally installing SSH on it routers, although it still leaves the Telnet server enabled by default while SSH is optional.

SSH is released under an open source license that is similar in effect to the BSD license. Make sure you are using version 3.6 or newer; some earlier versions had flaws in their implementation of cryptographic protocols and are susceptible to being cracked. In fact, it is a good idea to make sure you have the latest version available, as the code is constantly being improved and the algorithms are being tweaked.

SSH has a number of really interesting uses other than just logging into a remote system securely. It can be used to tunnel almost any service through an encrypted channel between servers (this application is discussed more in later chapters). Basic SSH syntax to log in remotely is:

```
ssh -l login hostname
```

Replace *login* with your login name on that remote system and *hostname* with the host you are trying to SSH into. You can also use:

```
ssh login@hostname
```

So, to log onto the Web server called web.example.com using my login of tony, I would type

```
ssh tony@web.example.com
```

I can also use `ssh -l tony web.example.com` to log into the server using SSH. If you simply type `ssh web.example.com`, the server will assume the same user name as your system login.

Table 2.4 lists some more SSH options.

Table 2.4 More SSH Options

Options	Descriptions
-c *protocol*	Uses a specific cryptographic protocol. Replace protocol with blowfish, 3des, or des, depending on the cryptographic algorithm you want to use. Note that your version of SSH must support these algorithms.
-p *port#*	Connects to a specific port number rather than the default SSH port of 22.
-P *port#*	Uses a specific port that is not part of the standard list of proprietary ports. This usually means a port number above 1024. This can be useful if you have a firewall that knocks down communications on lower port numbers.
-v	Displays verbose output. This is useful for debugging.
-q	Reports in quiet mode, opposite of verbose.
-C	Uses compression on the encrypted traffic. This can be useful for extremely slow connections like dial-up, but you better have a powerful processor to do the compression or it will slow you down more than it will speed you up.
-1	Forces SSH to use only SSH protocol version 1. This is not recommended for the reasons mentioned in the -C option, but it may be required if the server you are connecting to isn't upgraded to version 2.
-2	Forces SSH to use SSH protocol version 2 only. This may keep you from connecting to some servers.

Considerations for Hardening Windows

While not the subject of this book, it's important if you're using a Windows system to lock the system down as much as possible so you can establish that Trusted Computing Base discussed earlier. Windows is notorious for running all kinds of network-aware services. Some vendors of Windows PCs even load small Web servers on them so their technical support staff can "come in" and help you out interactively if you call in. Needless to say, this is horribly insecure and hacks have been published for many of these little "helpful" tools. Most people are unaware of all these programs running in the background.

One thing you can do if you are running one of the newer versions of Windows (NT, 2000, or XP) is to go to the Services window located under Administrative Tools in the Control Panel menu. This lists all the processes running on your computer (similar to the UNIX ps command). You can scroll down through this list and see all the little programs that Windows helpfully starts up for you. Most of these are services that are required for the basic operation of Windows. However, some of them you don't need and are just taking up processor cycles, slowing down your computer, and possibly creating a security hole. You can shut them down by clicking on the service and selecting Stop. Make sure you also set the start-up type to Manual or Disabled, or they will just start up again when you reboot.

Flamey the Tech Tip:

Be Sure You Know What You're Turning Off!

You need to be very careful when shutting things down like this. If you don't explicitly know what the service is and that you don't need it, then don't shut it off. Many processes depend on others, and shutting them down arbitrarily might cause your system to stop functioning properly.

There are some excellent guides created by the National Security Agency (www.nsa.gov) for secure configuration of Windows operating systems. Guides are currently available for Windows 2000 and NT, and more are being added as they become available. You can download them from http://nsa1.www.conx-ion.com/index.html.

The Center for Internet Security (www.cisecurity.org) publishes a benchmark and scoring tools for Windows 2000 and NT as well. You can use these tools to help configure your Windows machines securely.

Many books and Internet resources cover this subject in more depth. You can also use some of the tools discussed later in this book, such as the port scanner and vulnerability scanner, to scan and secure Windows systems as well. However you do it, make sure you harden your system before you begin installing tools on it.

While Windows has some of the network diagnostic and query tools that UNIX has, such as ping and traceroute, it does not offer some of the other services, such as whois and dig, right out of the box. There is, however, an add-on security tool, Sam Spade for Windows, that adds this functionality to your Windows system and improves on the existing ones.

Sam Spade for Windows: A Network Query Tool for Windows

Sam Spade for Windows
Author/primary contact: Steve Atkins
Web site: www.samspade.org
Platforms: Windows 95, 98, ME, NT, 2000, XP
Version reviewed: 1.14
License: GPL
Other resources:
See the Help file included with the installation.

This wonderful Swiss army knife for Windows machines fixes the dearth of real network tools in the Windows OS. No longer can UNIX system administrators gloat over their Windows counterparts who don't have neat things like dig, whois, and other valuable tools. In fact, Sam Spade for Windows even adds a few that the UNIX guys don't have. It is an invaluable tool for finding out information on networks. Like the fictional detective of the same name, Sam Spade can find out just about anything about a network.

Installing and Using Sam Spade for Windows

Start by visiting the Samspade.org Web site and downloading the program, or get it from the CD-ROM that comes with this book. Then simply double-click on the file and let the install program take care of everything for you. Once you've installed Sam Spade, fire it up and you will get the main console screen (see Figure 2.1).

Sam Spade has an easy-to-use interface. You enter the IP address or host name you want to run tests on in the upper-left field, and then click the icons below it to run different tests against that target. Each test runs in a window of its own, and all the output is stored in a log file that you can save for later use and documentation. You must set up a default name server under the Options menu so that any tests that rely on DNS will function. You can also enter this number in the menu bar to the far right.

Flamey the Tech Tip:

Be a Responsible Sam Spade

Running Sam Spade on your own network or one you are responsible for is fine. However, be very careful when running these tools against networks outside your control. While most of these tests are benign, some could put a heavy load on a server or set off intrusion monitors. So make sure you have

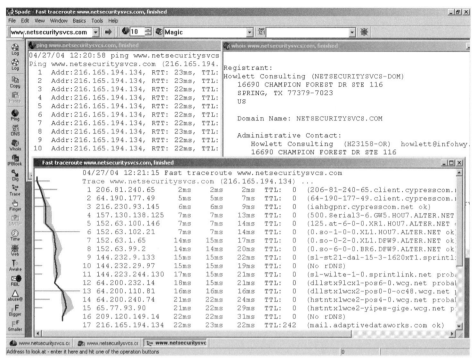

Figure 2.1 Sam Spade Main Screen

permission before running these tools on outside networks. Not only is it in a gray area legally, but it's also just good manners. You wouldn't want some other system administrator running these against your network without your permission, would you?

Table 2.5 lists the main functions of Sam Spade and describes what they do. Table 2.6 lists other useful tests located under the Tools menu.

Table 2.5 Sam Spade Main Functions

Functions	Descriptions
Ping	This is the same as the built-in Windows and UNIX ping, except you can easily configure the number of pings and the output is a little more verbose.
Nslookup	Similar to the UNIX command of the same name.

(continues)

Table 2.5 Sam Spade Main Functions (*continued*)

Functions	Descriptions
Whois	Similar to the UNIX command of the same name.
IPBlock	This command checks the ARIN database for an IP address or set of IP addresses and generates some useful information on it. This data includes the organization that owns those IPs, where they were allocated from an ISP, and different contacts, including a contact to report abuse if they registered one. See Figure 2.2 for an example of the output.
Trace	Similar to the traceroute command. However, additional information is generated, such as any reverse DNS entry and a graphical display of the latency between hops.
Finger	Similar to the UNIX finger command.
Time	Checks the time clock on the remote system. This is good for ensuring that your server's time clocks are synchronized.

Table 2.6 Sam Spade Tools Menu Tests

Tests	Descriptions
Blacklist	Checks to see if your mail server is listed in any of the e-mail black hole lists (databases that contain the addresses of known spammers). If your address somehow gets in there (by leaving your server open to mail relays, for example), then some people won't be able to get mail from you.
Abuse	Looks up the official abuse contact for a set of IP addresses so you can register a complaint if you are having a problem with one of their addresses.
Scan Addresses	Performs a basic port scan of a range of addresses. This very simple port scanner identifies open network ports. If you are going to need to scan addresses, I recommend you use one of the fully featured port scanners reviewed in Chapter 4. Also, keep in mind that port scanning can be considered hostile activity by outside networks.
Crawl website	Takes a Web site and "crawls" it, identifying each link and page and any other forms or files it can reach. This is useful for finding all the pages that a Web site references and for looking for files that you weren't aware were there.

```
04/27/04 12:31:03 IP block www.netsecuritysvcs.com
Trying 216.165.194.134 at ARIN
Trying 216.165.194 at ARIN

OrgName:    Crescent Consulting
OrgID:      CRES
Address:    701 North Post Oak Rd., Suite 350
City:       Houston
StateProv:  TX
PostalCode: 77024
Country:    US

NetRange:   216.165.192.0 - 216.165.223.255
CIDR:       216.165.192.0/19
NetName:    HTE8
NetHandle:  NET-216-165-192-0-1
Parent:     NET-216-0-0-0-0
NetType:    Direct Allocation
NameServer: NAME.BLUEGATE.COM
NameServer: NAME2.CRESCENTTECHNOLOGY.COM
Comment:    ADDRESSES WITHIN THIS BLOCK ARE NON-PORTABLE
RegDate:    2001-01-22
Updated:    2003-01-15

TechHandle: CH156-ARIN
TechName:   Crescent Hostmaster
TechPhone:  +1-713-682-7400
TechEmail:  hostmaster@crescentb.com

# ARIN WHOIS database, last updated 2004-04-26 19:15
# Enter ? for additional hints on searching ARIN's WHOIS database.
```

Figure 2.2 Sam Spade IP Block Output

There are several other tools that are not the subject of this book, such as Check cancels for USENET News and Decode URLs, that you may find useful if you are developing a Web site. Sam Spade can give you UNIX-like capabilities in terms of network discovery. The next tool, PuTTY, gives you the capabilities of SSH, another UNIX-based program for secure remote terminal access on Windows.

PuTTY: An SSH Client for Windows

PuTTY
Author/primary contact: Sam Tatham
Web site: www.chiark.greenend.org.uk/~sgtatham/putty
Platforms: Windows 95, 98, ME, NT, 2000, XP
Version reviewed: .54b
License: MIT (similar to BSD license)
Other resources:
See Help file or Web site.

One of these days Microsoft will get with the program and begin including a built-in SSH client with Windows. In the meantime, PuTTY is an excellent SSH client for Windows, and it also includes an enhanced, encryption-enabled Telnet client. You can use PuTTY to securely communicate with any server running the SSH protocol.

Installing and Running PuTTY

Download the file from the Web site or get it from the CD-ROM that comes with this book and double-click on it to install it. PuTTY has a pretty clean interface and should be able to emulate almost all terminals. You can configure the port number you come in on if the SSH server is using a nonstandard port number. You can also fiddle with all the settings by using the menus on the left.

You can log all your sessions to a text file, which can be quite useful (I used PuTTY to log all of the terminal session listings in this book). You can also mess with the configuration ad infinitum, including which encryption protocols it will accept. It will even warn

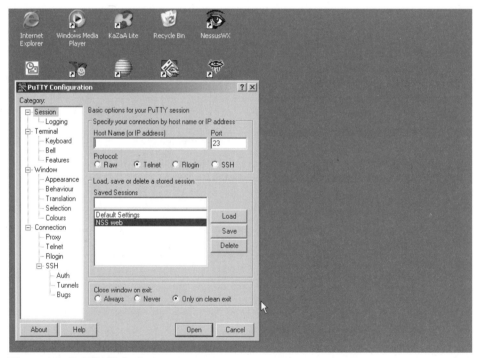

Figure 2.3 PuTTY Main Screen

you if it is attempting to connect to a SSH server that uses one of the weak versions of SSH that may be vulnerable to cracking.

When connecting to a server for the first time, PuTTY will warn you that it is adding that server's fingerprint and key to your database. This is normal—just make sure the certificate looks appropriate, accept it, and it won't appear in future connections to that server.

Firewalls

So now that you have a fairly secure operating system and know a few basic tricks, let's get into using some more complex security tools. This chapter describes how to configure and run a secure open source firewall. If you already have a firewall, you may still want to read this chapter if you need a refresher or primer on how firewalls function. This will come in handy in later chapters that discuss port scanners and vulnerability scanners.

A **firewall** is a device that acts as the first line of first defense against any incoming attacks or misuses of your network. It can deflect or blunt many kinds of attacks and shield your internal servers and workstations from the Internet. A firewall can also prevent internal LAN machines from being accessed from outside your network. With the growing use of random scanners and automated worms and viruses, keeping your internal machines shielded from the Internet is more important than ever. A properly configured firewall will get you a long way towards being safe from outside attacks. (Protecting yourself from inside attacks is a different thing altogether and is a subject of Chapters 4 through 7.)

Chapter Overview

Concepts you will learn:

- Basic concepts of TCP/IP networking
- How firewalls operate
- The philosophy of firewall configuration
- Business processes for firewalls
- Sample firewall configurations

Tools you will use:

Iptables, Turtle Firewall, and SmoothWall

It's pretty much a given these days that firewalls are an essential part of any secure infrastructure. There are many very viable commercial alternatives available: Cisco, NetScreen, SonicWALL, and Checkpoint are just a few of the vendors making high-end, commercial firewall solutions. These products are built to handle large corporate networks and high traffic volumes

Linksys (now owned by Cisco), D-Link, and NETGEAR are some of the vendors making low-end consumer-grade firewalls. These devices generally don't have much configurability or expandability; they basically act as a packet filter, blocking incoming TCP and UDP connections and as a NAT appliance. They are usually marketed for DSL and cable-type connections and may buckle under heavier loads.

The higher end firewalls will do just about anything you want them to do. However, that comes at a price: most of them start at several thousand dollars and go up from there. And they often require you to learn a new syntax or interface in order to configure them. Some of the newer models, like SonicWALL and NetScreen, are going to a Web-based configuration interface, but that usually comes at the expense of less depth in the configuration options.

The little known and rarely advertised secret of some commercial firewalls is that they have open source software just underneath the hood. What you are really paying for is the fancy case and the technical support line. This may be worth it for companies that need the extra support. However, if you are going to have to learn yet another interface, and if they are using the same technologies that are available to you for free, why not create your own firewall with the open source tools provided in this book and save your firm thousands of dollars? Even if you don't want to throw out your commercial firewall, learning more about firewall basics and what happens behind the scenes will help you keep your firewall more securely configured.

Before we dive into the tools, I want to go over the basics of what a firewall does and how it works with the various network protocols to limit access to your network. Even if you are not planning to use open source software for your firewall, you can still benefit from knowing a little more about what is really going on inside that black box.

Network Architecture Basics

Before you can truly understand network security, you have to first understand network architecture. Although this book is not intended to serve as a network primer, this section is a quick review of network concepts and terms. I will be referring to these terms often and it will help you to have a basic understanding of the TCP/IP protocol. If you are already well-schooled in network topologies, then you can skip over this section and jump straight into the tools.

As you may know, every network design can be divided into seven logical parts, each of which handles a different part of the communication task. This seven-layered design is called the **OSI Reference Model**. It was created by the International Standards Organizations (ISO) to provide a logical model for describing network communications, and it

OSI Layer Number	Layer Name	Sample Protocols
Layer 7	Application	DNS, FTP, HTTP, SMTP, SNMP, Telnet
Layer 6	Presentation	XDR
Layer 5	Session	Named Pipes, RPC
Layer 4	Transport	NetBIOS, TCP, UDP
Layer 3	Network	ARP, IP, IPX, OSPF
Layer 2	Data Link	Arcnet, Ethernet, Token Ring
Layer 1	Physical	Coaxial, Fiber Optic, UTP

Figure 3.1 The OSI Reference Model

helps vendors standardize equipment and software. Figure 3.1 shows the OSI Reference Model and gives examples of each layer.

Physical

This layer is the actual physical media that carries the data. Different types of media use different standards. For example, coaxial cable, unshielded twisted pair (UTP), and fiber optic cable each serve a different purpose: coaxial cable is used in older LAN installations as well as Internet service through cable TV networks, UTP is generally used for in-house cable runs, while fiber optic is generally used for long-haul connections that require a high load capacity.

Data Link

This layer relates to different pieces of network interface hardware on the network. It helps encode the data and put it on the physical media. It also allows devices to identify each other when trying to communicate with another node. An example of a data link layer address is your network card's MAC address. (No, the MAC address doesn't have anything to do with Apple computers; it's the Medium Access Control number that uniquely identifies your computer's card on the network.) On an Ethernet network, MAC addresses are the way your computer can be found. Corporations used many different types of data link standards in the 1970s and 80s, mostly determined by their hardware vendor. IBM used Token Ring for their PC networks and SNA for most of their bigger hardware, DEC used a different standard, and Apple used yet another. Most companies use Ethernet today because it is widespread and cheap.

Network

This layer is the first part that you really see when interacting with TCP/IP networks. The network layer allows for communications across different physical networks by using a secondary identification layer. On TCP/IP networks, this is an IP address. The IP address on your computer helps get your data routed from place to place on the network and over the Internet. This address is a unique number to identify your computer on an IP-based network. In some cases, this number is unique to a computer; no other machine on the Internet can have that address. This is the case with normal publicly routable IP addresses. On internal LANs, machines often use private IP address blocks. These have been reserved for internal use only and will not route across the Internet. These numbers may not be unique from network to network but still must be unique within each LAN. While two computers may have the same private IP address on different internal networks, they will never have the same MAC address, as it is a serial number assigned by the NIC manufacturer. There are some exceptions to this (see the sidebar Follow the MAC), but generally the MAC address will uniquely identify that computer (or at least the network interface card inside that computer).

Flamey the Tech Tip:
Follow the MAC

MAC addresses can help you troubleshoot a number of network problems. Although the MAC address doesn't identify a machine directly by name, all MAC addresses are assigned by the manufacturer and start with a specific number for each vendor. Check out www.macaddresses.com for a comprehensive list. They are also usually printed on the card itself.

By using one of the network sniffers discussed in Chapter 6, you can often track down the source of troublesome network traffic using MAC addresses. Mac addresses are usually logged by things like a Windows DHCP server or firewalls, so you can correlate MAC addresses to a specific IP address or machine name. You can also use them for forensic evidence—amateur hackers often forge IP addresses, but most don't know how to forge their MAC address, and this can uniquely identify their PCs.

Transport

This level handles getting the data packet from point A to point B. This is the layer where the TCP and UDP protocols reside. TCP (Transmission Control Protocol) basically ensures that packets are consistently sent and received on the other end. It allows for bit-level error correction, retransmission of lost segments, and fragmented traffic and packet reordering. UDP (User Datagram Protocol) is a lighter weight scheme used for multimedia traffic and short, low-overhead transmissions like DNS requests. It also does error detection and data multiplexing, but does not provide any facility for data reordering or ensured data arrival. This layer and the network layer are where most firewalls operate.

Session

The session layer is primarily involved with setting up a connection and then closing it down. It also sometimes does authentication to determine which parties are allowed to participate in a session. It is mostly used for specific applications higher up the model.

Presentation

This layer handles certain encoding or decoding required to present the data in a format readable by the receiving party. Some forms of encryption could be considered presentation. The distinction between application and session layers is fine and some people argue that the presentation and application layers are basically the same thing.

Application

This final level is where an application program gets the data. This can be FTP, HTTP, SMTP, or many others. At this level, some program handling the actual data inside the packet takes over. This level gives security professionals fits, because most security exploits happen here.

TCP/IP Networking

The TCP/IP network protocol was once an obscure protocol used mostly by government and educational institutions. In fact, it was invented by the military research agency, DARPA, to provide interruption-free networking. Their goal was to create a network that could withstand multiple link failures in the event of something catastrophic like a nuclear strike. Traditional data communications had always relied on a single direct connection, and if that connection was degraded or tampered with, the communications would cease. TCP/IP offered a way to "packetize" the data and let it find its own way across the network. This created the first fault-tolerant network.

However, most corporations still used the network protocols provided by their hardware manufacturers. IBM shops were usually NetBIOS or SNA; Novell LANs used a protocol called IPX/SPX; and Windows LANs used yet another standard, called NetBEUI, which was derived from the IBM NetBIOS. Although TCP/IP became common in the 1980s, it wasn't until the rise of the Internet in the early 90s that TCP/IP began to become the standard for data communications. This brought about a fall in the prices for IP net-working hardware, and made it much easier to interconnect networks as well.

TCP/IP allows communicating nodes to establish a connection and then verify when the data communications start and stop. On a TCP/IP network, data to be transmitted is chopped up into sections, called **packets**, and encapsulated in a series of "envelopes," each one containing specific information for the next network layer. Each packet is stamped with a 32-bit sequence number so that even if they arrive in the wrong order, the transmission can be reassembled. As the packet crosses different parts of the network each layer is opened and interpreted, and then the remaining data is passed along according to those instructions. When the packet of data arrives at its destination, the actual data, or payload, is delivered to the application.

It sounds confusing, but here is an analogy. Think of a letter you mail to a corporation in an overnight envelope. The overnight company uses the outside envelope to route the package to the right building. When it is received, it will be opened up and the outside envelope thrown away. It might be destined for another internal mailbox, so they might put in an interoffice mail envelope and send it on. Finally it arrives at its intended recipient, who takes all the wrappers off and uses the data inside. Table 3.1 shows how some network protocols encapsulate data.

As you can see, the outside of our data "envelope" has the Ethernet address. This identifies the packet on the Ethernet network. Inside that layer is the network information, namely the IP address; and inside that is the transport layer, which sets up a connection and closes it down. Then there is the application layer, which is an HTTP header, telling the Web browser how to format a page. Finally comes the actual payload of packet—the content of a Web page. This illustrates the multi-layered nature of network communications.

There are several phases during a communication between two network nodes using TCP/IP (see Figure 3.2). Without going into detail about Domain Name Servers (DNS)

Table 3.1 Sample TCP/IP Data Packet

Protocol	Contents	OSI Layer
Ethernet	MAC address	Datalink
IP	IP address	Network
TCP	TCP header	Transport
HTTP	HTTP header	Application
Application Data	Web page	Data

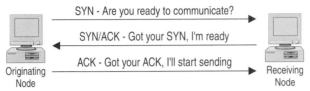

Figure 3.2 TCP Three-Way Handshake

and assuming we are using IP addresses and not host names, the first thing that happens is that the machine generates an ARP (Address Resolution Protocol) request to find the corresponding Ethernet address to the IP it is trying to communicate with. ARP converts an IP address into a MAC address on an Ethernet network. Now that we can communicate to the machine using IP, there is a three-way communication between the machines using the TCP protocol to establish a session. A machine wishing to send data to another machine sends a SYN packet to synchronize, or initiate, the transmission. The SYN packet is basically saying, "Are you ready to send data?" If the other machine is ready to accept a connection from the first one, it sends a SYN/ACK, which means, "Acknowledged, I got your SYN packet and I'm ready." Finally, the originating machine sends an ACK packet back, saying in effect, "Great, I'll start sending data." This communication is called the **TCP three-way handshake**. If any one of the three doesn't occur, then the connection is never made. While the machine is sending its data, it tags the data packets with a sequence number and acknowledges any previous sequence numbers used by the host on the other end. When the data is all sent, one side sends a FIN packet to the opposite side of the link. The other side responds with a FIN/ACK, and then the other side sends a FIN, which is responded to with a final FIN/ACK to close out that TCP/IP session.

Because of the way TCP/IP controls the initiation and ending of a session, TCP/IP communications can be said to have **state**, which means that you can tell what part of the dialogue is happening by looking at the packets. This is a very important for firewalls, because the most common way for a firewall to block outside traffic is to disallow SYN packets from the outside to machines inside the network. This way, internal machines can communicate outside the network and initiate connections to the outside, but outside machines can never initiate a session. There are lots of other subtleties in how firewalls operate, but basically that's how simple firewalls allow for one-way only connections for Web browsing and the like.

There are several built-in firewall applications in Linux: these are known as **Iptables** in kernel versions 2.4x, **Ipchains** in kernel versions 2.2x, and **Ipfwadm** in kernel version 2.0. Most Linux-based firewalls do their magic by manipulating one of these kernel-level utilities.

All three applications operate on a similar concept. Firewalls generally have two or more interfaces, and under Linux this is accomplished by having two or more network cards in the box. One interface typically connects to the internal LAN; this interface is called the **trusted** or **private** interface. Another interface is for the public (WAN) side of your firewall. On most smaller networks, the WAN interface is connected to the Internet. There also might be a third interface, called a **DMZ** (taken from the military term for Demilitarized Zone), which is usually for servers that need to be more exposed to the Internet so that outside users can connect to them. Each packet that tries to pass through the machine is passed through a series of filters. If it matches the filter, then some action is taken on it. This action might be to throw it out, pass it along, or masquerade ("Masq") it with an internal private IP address. The best practice for firewall configuration is always to deny all and then selectively allow traffic that you need (see the sidebar on firewall configuration philosophy).

Firewalls can filter packets at several different levels. They can look at IP addresses and block traffic coming from certain IP addresses or networks, check the TCP header and determine its state, and at higher levels they can look at the application or TCP/UDP port number. Firewalls can be configured to drop whole categories of traffic, such as ICMP. ICMP-type packets like ping are usually rejected by firewalls because these packets are often used in network discovery and denial of service. There is no reason that someone outside your company should be pinging your network. Firewalls will sometimes allow echo replies (ping responses), though, so you can ping from inside the LAN to the outside.

Security Business Processes

At some point, preferably before you start loading software, you should document in writing a business process for your firewall(s). Not only will this be a useful tool for planning your installation and configuration, but it may also help if you have to justify hardware purchases or personnel time to your boss. Documenting your security activities will make you look more professional and emphasize the value you add to the organization, which is never a bad thing. It also makes it easier for anyone who comes after you to pick up the ball.

This plan documents the underlying processes and procedures to make sure that you get a business benefit from the technology. Installing a firewall is all well and good, but without the proper processes in place, it might not actually give the organization the security it promises. The following steps outline a business process for firewall implementation and operation.

    1. Develop a network use policy.

       There may already be some guidelines in your employee manual on proper computer use. However, many computer use polices are intentionally vague and don't specify which applications count as misuse. You may have to clarify this with your manager or upper management. Are things like instant messengers allowed? Do you want to follow a stringent Wcb and e-mail only outbound policy? Remember that it is safer to write a rule for any exceptions rather than allowing all types of activity by default. Getting the answers to these questions (hopefully in writing) is crucial before you start writing rules.

2. Map out services needed outward and inward.

If you don't already have a network map, create one now. What servers need to be contacted from the outside and on which ports? Are there users who need special ports opened up for them? (Hint: technical support staff often need FTP, Telnet, and SSH.) Do you want to set up a DMZ for public servers or forward ports to the LAN from the outside? If you have multiple network segments or lots of public servers, this could take longer than the firewall setup itself. Now is the time to find out about these special requests, not when you turn on the firewall and it takes down an important application.

3. Convert the network use policy and needed services into firewall rules.

This is when you finally get to write the firewall rules. Refer to your list of allowed services out, required services in, and any exceptions, and create your firewall configuration. Be sure to use the "deny all" technique described in the sidebar to drop anything that doesn't fit one of your rules.

4. Implement and test for functionality and security.

Now you can turn on your firewall and sit back and wait for the complaints. Even if your rules conform exactly to policy, there will still be people who didn't realize that using Kazaa to download movies was against company policy. Be ready to stand your ground when users ask for exceptions that aren't justified. Every hole you open up on your firewall is a potential security risk.

Also, once your firewall is operating to your users' satisfaction, make sure that it is blocking what it is supposed to be blocking. By using two tools discussed later in this book together, you can run tests against your firewall: A port scanner on the outside and a network sniffer on the inside will tell you which packets are getting through and which ones aren't. This setup can also be useful for troubleshooting applications that are having problems with the firewall.

5. Review and test your firewall rules on a periodic basis.

Just because your firewall is working great today doesn't mean it will be tomorrow. New threats may evolve that require new rules to be written. Rules that were supposed to be temporary, just for a project, may end up being left in your configuration. You should review your rules periodically and compare them with the current business requirements and security needs. Depending on the size and complexity of your configuration and how often it changes, this may be as infrequently as once a year for firewalls with a small rule set (20 or fewer rules), or once a month for very complex firewalls. Each review should include an actual test using the scanner/sniffer setup mentioned above using the tools in Chapters 4, 5, and 6 to verify that the rules are indeed doing what they are supposed to be.

Designing and using a business process such as this will help ensure you get a lot more out of your firewall implementation, both professionally and technically. You should also develop plans for the other technologies discussed in this book, such as vulnerability scanning and network sniffing.

Flamey the Tech Tip:

"Deny all!" When It Comes to Firewall Rules

There are two ways set up a firewall: You can start with an "allow all" stance and then add the behavior you want blocked, or start with a "deny all" statement and then add what you want to allow (permissible user behavior). The overwhelmingly preferred method is starting with "deny all." By beginning with this statement, you automatically block all traffic unless it is specifically allowed in the configuration. This method is both more secure and easier to maintain securely than the other route.

Most commercial firewalls use this philosophy. The idea behind it is that if you have to define what is bad behavior, you will be continually behind as the Internet changes and evolves. You cannot predict what form the next new attack might take, so you will be vulnerable until it is published and you can add a new line to your firewall configuration. By using the "deny all" approach, you categorically deny anything that isn't known good activity.

The "allow all" type of configuration might make sense in a extremely permissive environment where the overhead of adding lines for allowed items overrides the value of the information on the network, for example, on a nonprofit or purely informational site. But for most sites the "deny all" approach is much safer. However, just because you use this approach doesn't mean your network is totally secure. Attacks can still come in via any holes you've created, such as for the Web and e-mail. Also, keep in mind that even when the "deny all" statement is used, you have to be careful not to negate it with an overly permissive statement higher up in your configuration.

Iptables: A Linux Open Source Firewall

Iptables

Author/primary contact:	Paul "Rusty" Russell
Web site:	www.netfilter.org
Platforms:	Most Linux
License:	GPL
Version reviewed:	1.2.8
Resources:	
Netfilter mailing lists:	
Netfilter-announce	General announcement list for news of new releases and updates. Subscribe at:
https://lists.netfilter.org/mailman/listinfo/netfilter-announce	

Netfilter-users	General questions about using Netfilter/Iptables. Post general discussion topics and questions here. Subscribe at:
https://lists.netfilter.org/mailman/listinfo/netfilter-users	
Netfilter-devel	Development and contributor discussions. Subscribe at:
https://lists.netfilter.org/mailman/listinfo/netfilter-devel	

This section describes how to configure a firewall with Iptables, which is the firewall/packet filter utility built into most Linux systems with kernel version 2.4 and later. This utility lets you create a firewall using commands in your operating system. Iptables evolved from earlier attempts at firewalls on Linux. The first system, called Ipfwadm, could be used to create a simple set of rules to forward or deny packets based on certain criteria. Ipchains was introduced in kernel 2.2 to overcome the limitations of Ipfwadm. Ipchains worked pretty well and was modular in architecture. However, with the growing number of people using their firewalls for multiple functions (for example, proxy server and NAT device), Ipchains also became insufficient. Iptables represents an update to these programs and allows for the multiple uses that today's firewalls are expected to perform. (Note that the concepts and terms for Iptables are pretty much the same for Ipchains.)

Iptables is a powerful but complex tool, and is usually recommended for users who are familiar with firewalls and the art of configuring them (see the sidebar on writing shell scripts). If this is your first firewall, I suggest using one of the autoconfiguration tools discussed later in the chapter to create your firewall configuration, at least at first. These tools use Iptables (or its predecessor, Ipchains) to create a firewall by using your input. However, it is good to have a basic understanding of what is going on "under the hood" with Iptables before start configuring with one of the graphical tools.

Installing Iptables

Most Linux systems on kernel 2.4 or higher will have Iptables built right in, so you don't have to install any additional programs. (If your system is earlier than kernel 2.4, it will use Ipchains or Ipfwadm. These are similar systems, but they are not reviewed in this book.) You can issue Iptables statements from the command line or via a script (see the sidebar). To double-check that Iptables is installed, type iptables - L and see if you get a response. It should list your current rule set (which is probably empty if you haven't configured a firewall yet).

If your system doesn't have Iptables or if you want to get the latest version of the code, go to www.netfilter.org and download the RPM for your operating system. You can also get it from the CD-ROM that comes with this book.

If you don't have a Webmin RPM on your installation disks, check www. webmin.com to see if there is a version of Webmin available for your operating system. Webmin is required for the Turtle Firewall, and there are specific versions for each distribution and operating system. If there isn't one for your particular operating system, then you can't use Turtle Firewall, but the list of supported systems is quite large. Click on the RPM file in X-Windows and it will install automatically.

Using Iptables

The idea behind Iptables and Ipchains is to create pipes of input and process them according to a rule set (your firewall configuration) and then send them into pipes of output. In Iptables, these pipes are called **tables**; in Ipchains, they are called **chains** (of course!). The basic tables used in Iptables are:

- Input
- Forward
- Prerouting
- Postrouting
- Output

The general format of an Iptables statement is

```
iptables command rule-specification extensions
```

where *command*, *rule-specification*, and *extensions* are one or more of the valid options. Table 3.2 lists the Iptables commands, and Table 3.3 contains the Iptables rule specifications.

Table 3.2 Iptables Commands

Commands	Descriptions
-A *chain*	Appends one or more rules to the end of the statement.
-I *chain rulenum*	Inserts chain at the location *rulenum*. This is useful when you want a rule to supercede those before it.
-D *chain*	Deletes the indicated chain.
-R *chain rulenum*	Replaces the rule at *rulenum* with the provided *chain*.
-L	Lists all the rules in the current chain.
-F	Flushes all the rules in the current chain, basically deleting your firewall configuration. This is good when beginning a configuration to make sure there are no existing rules that will conflict with your new ones.

Commands	Descriptions
-Z chain	Zeros out all packet and byte counts in the named chain.
-N chain	Creates a new chain with the name of *chain*.
-X chain	Deletes the specified chain. If no chain is specified, this deletes all chains.
-P chain policy	Sets the policy for the specified chain to *policy*.

Table 3.3 Iptables Rule Specifications

Rule Specifications	Descriptions	
-p protocol	Specifies a certain protocol for the rule to match. Valid protocol types are icmp, tcp, udp, or all.	
-s address/mask!port	Specifies a certain address or network to match. Use standard slash notation to designate a range of IP addresses. A port number or range of port numbers can also be specified by putting them after an exclamation point.	
-j target	This tells what to do with the packet if it matches the specifications. The valid options for target are:	
	DROP	Drops the packet without any further action.
	REJECT	Drops the packet and sends an error packet in return.
	LOG	Logs the packet to a file.
	MARK	Marks the packet for further action.
	TOS	Changes the TOS (Type of Service) bit.
	MIRROR	Inverts the source and destination addresses and sends them back out, essentially "bouncing" them back to the source.

(continues)

Table 3.3 Iptables Rule Specifications (*continued*)

Rule Specifications	Descriptions
SNAT	Static NAT. This option is used when doing Network Address Translation (NAT). It takes the source address and converts it into another static value, specified with the switch --to-source.
DNAT	Dynamic NAT. Similar to above but using a dynamic range of IP addresses.
MASQ	Masquerades the IP using a public IP.
REDIRECT	Redirects the packet.

There are other commands and options but these are the most common operations. For a full listing of commands, refer to the Iptables man page by typing `man iptables` at any command prompt.

Creating an Iptables Firewall

The best way to learn is to do, so let's walk through a couple of commands to see how they are used in practical application. Here is an example of how to create a firewall using Iptables. You can enter these commands interactively (one at a time) to see the results right away. You can also put them all into a script and run it at boot time to bring your firewall up at boot time (see the sidebar on writing scripts). Remember to type them exactly as shown and that capitalization is important.

Writing Shell Scripts

Often you will need to automate a process or have a single command initiate a number of statements. In the firewall example, you will generally want to have all your firewall commands executed when your system boots. The best way to do this is to write a shell script. A **shell script** is a simple text file that contains a command or list of commands. The shell editor executes the commands when it is invoked by a user typing the name of the script.

1. To create a shell script, first open a text editor such as vi or EMACS and type in your command(s).
2. Make sure you put a line at the very top that looks like this:

```
#! /bin/bash
```

This tells the script which shell to use to execute the command. You must have that shell on your OS, and the commands you put in your script will have to be valid commands for that shell. This example is for the bash shell location on Mandrake Linux. You can use a different shell, for example, Tcsh or Csh. Just put the path to it on this line. Then save your file.

3. Make the file executable so the shell can run it as a program. You do this with the `chmod` command. Type:

```
chmod 700 script_name
```

where you replace `script_name` with your file name. This makes the permissions on the file readable, writable, and executable.

To run the script, type the file's name in the command line. (In the bash shell, you need to add a `./` before the file name to run the script from your local directory.) When you press Enter, the commands in your script should run.

You have to be in the same directory as the file or type the path in the command line statement when you run it. Alternatively, you could add the directory for the script to your PATH statement so it will run from anywhere or put the script in one of your PATH directories.

The example in the following procedure assumes that your local LAN subnet is 192.168.0.1 - 192.168.0.254, that the eth1 interface is your local LAN connection, and that the eth0 interface is your Internet or WAN connection.

1. Start by eliminating any existing rules with a Flush command:

```
iptables -F FORWARD
```

This flushes all rules for the FORWARD chain, which is the main "funnel" for any packets wanting to pass through the firewall.

2. Flush the other chains:

```
iptables -F INPUT
iptables -F OUTPUT
```

This flushes any rules to your local machine and your output chain.

3. Put your standard "deny all" statement right up front.

```
iptables -P FORWARD DROP
iptables -A INPUT -i eth0 -j DROP
```

4. To accept fragmented packets in Iptables, this must be done explicitly.

```
iptables -A FORWARD -f -j ACCEPT
```

5. There are two types of common attacks that you should block right away. One is what is known as **spoofing**, which is when someone forges the IP packet headers to make it look like an outside packet has in internal address. By doing this, someone could route onto your LAN even if you have private IP addresses. The other type of attack is done by sending a stream of packets to the broadcast address of the LAN to overwhelm the network. This is called a **smurf** attack (although I'm not sure what this has to do with little blue cartoon characters). You can block these types of attacks with two simple statements.

```
iptables -A FORWARD -s 192.168.0.0/24 -I eth0 -j DROP
iptables -A FORWARD -p icmp -i eth0 -d 192.168.0.0/24 -j
    DENY
```

The first statement drops any packets coming from the Internet interface eth0 with the internal address 192.168.0.0/24. By definition, no packets should be coming from the untrusted interface with an internal, private source address. The second statement drops any packets of protocol ICMP coming from the outside address to the inside.

6. You generally do want to accept incoming traffic based on connections initiated from the inside, for example, someone surfing a Web page. As long as the connection is ongoing and it was initiated internally, then it is probably okay. You can, however, limit the type of traffic allowed in. Let's say that you only want to allow employees Web and e-mail access. You can specify the types of traffic to allow through and only if it is on an already-initiated connection. You can tell if it is an existing connection by seeing that the ACK bit has been set, that is, that the TCP three-way handshake has occurred. The following statements allow HTTP and Web traffic based on this criteria.

```
iptables -A FORWARD -p tcp -i eth0 -d 192.168.0.0/24 --
    dports
www,smtp --tcp-flags SYN,ACK -j ACCEPT

iptables -A FORWARD -p tcp -i eth0 -d 192.168.0.0/24 --
    sports
www,smtp --tcp-flags SYN,ACK -j ACCEPT
```

The -dport statement says to only allow e-mail and Web, and the –tcp flags statement says you only want packets with the ACK field set.

7. To be able to accept incoming connections from the outside only on certain ports, such as e-mail coming into your mail server, use a statement like this:

```
iptables -A FORWARD -m multiport -p tcp -i eth0 -d
    192.168.0.0/24
--dports smtp --syn -j ACCEPT
```

The -m multiport flag tells Iptables that you will be issuing a match statement for ports. The -syn statement tells it to allow SYN packets, which means to initiate TCP connections. And the -dports flag allows only the SMTP mail traffic.

8. You can allow outgoing connections to be initiated by your users, but only on the protocols you want them using. This is where you can prevent your users from using FTP and other nonessential programs. The all-zero IP address is shorthand for saying "any address."

```
iptables -A FORWARD -m multiport -p tcp -i eth0 -d
    0.0.0.0 --dports www,smtp --syn -j ACCEPT
```

9. You need to allow certain incoming UDP packets. UDP is used for DNS, and if you block that your users won't be able to resolve addresses. Because they don't have a state like TCP packets, you can't rely on checking the SYN or ACK flags. You want to allow UDP only on port 53, so you specify domain (a built-in variable for port 52) as the only allowable port. You do that with these statements.

```
iptables -A FORWARD -m multiport -p udp -i eth0 -d
    192.168.0.0/24  --dports domain -j ACCEPT

iptables -A FORWARD -m multiport -p udp -i eth0 -s
    192.168.0.0/24  --sports domain -j ACCEPT

iptables -A FORWARD -m multiport -p udp -i eth1 -d
    0.0.0.0 --dports domain -j ACCEPT

iptables -A FORWARD -m multiport -p udp -i eth1 -s
    0.0.0.0 --sports domain -j ACCEPT
```

10. The first two statements allow the incoming UDP datagrams, and the second two allow the outbound connections. You also want to do this for ICMP packets. These are the network information packets discussed in Chapter 2. You want to allow all types of internal ICMP outwards, but only certain types such as echo-reply inwards. This can be accomplished with the following statements.

```
iptables -A FORWARD -m multiport -p icmp -I eth0 -d
192.168.0.0/24 --dports 0,3,11 -j ACCEPT

iptables -A FORWARD -m multiport -p icmp -I eth1 -d
0.0.0.0
    --dports 8,3,11 -j ACCEPT
```

11. Finally, you want to set up logging so you can look at the logs to see what is being dropped. You will want to view the logs from time to time even if there isn't a problem, just to get an idea of the kinds of traffic being dropped. If you see dropped packets from the same network or address repeatedly, you might be being attacked. There is one statement to log each kind of traffic.

```
iptables -A FORWARD -m tcp -p tcp -j LOG
iptables -A FORWARD -m udp -p udp -j LOG
iptables -A FORWARD -m udp -p icmp -j LOG
```

That's it! This will provide you with firewall protection from the most common attacks from the Internet.

IP Masquerading with Iptables

When the Internet was originally designed, several large blocks of addresses were set aside for use on private networks. These addresses will not be routed by the Internet and can be used without worrying that they will conflict with other networks. The private address ranges are:

> 10.0.0.0 – 10.255.255.255
>
> 192.168.0.0 – 192.68.255.255
>
> 172.16.0.0 – 172.31.255.255

By using these addresses on your internal LAN and having one external, routable IP on your firewall, you effectively shield your internal machines from outside access. You can provide this additional layer of protection easily with Iptables using **IP masquerading**. The internal IP header is stripped off at the firewall and replaced with a header showing the firewall as the source IP. The data packet is then sent out to its destination with a source IP address of the public interface of the firewall. When it comes back, the firewall remembers which internal IP it goes to and re-addresses it for internal delivery. This process is also known as **Network Address Translation** (NAT). You can do this in Iptables with the following statements.

```
iptables -t nat -P POSTROUTING DROP
iptables -t nat -A POSTROUTING -o eth0 -j MASQUERADE
```

The MASQUERADE flag can be abbreviated to MASQ. One of the improvements of Iptables over previous systems like Ipchains and Ipfwadm is the way that it handles secondary tasks like NAT.

So now you know how to build a basic firewall. This is just a simple configuration; the possible variations are endless. You can forward certain ports to internal servers so they don't have to have a public IP address. You can put another network card in your firewall box and make it a DMZ interface for servers with public addresses. There are entire books on advanced firewall configuration and many mailing lists. One of the better lists is firewall-wizards. To subscribe to this list, send an e-mail with "subscribe" in the body to:

> firewall-wizards-request@honor.icsalabs.com

The firewall-wizards list hosts discussions about all levels of firewall configuration and is vendor agnostic, that is, all firewall brands are discussed, from open source to commercial.

If you want to build a quick firewall without entering all those Iptables statements and remembering the syntax, there is tool that builds the firewall statements using a graphical interface—so it's all done for you in the background.

**Turtle Firewall: An Iptables-Based Firewall with a
Graphical User Interface**

Turtle Firewall

Author/primary contact: Andrea Frigido
Web site: www.turtlefirewall.com/
Platforms: Most Linux-compatibles that support Iptables
License: GPL 2.0
Contact information: andrea@friweb.com
System requirements: Linux operating system with kernel 2.4 or newer
                            Perl with expat library
                            Webmin server

This neat little contraption, called Turtle Firewall, was created by Andrea Frigido. Turtle is basically a set of Perl scripts that do all the dirty work for you to set up an Iptables firewall. This program makes it much easier to see your rules and to make sure you are getting the statements in the right order. It runs as a service, so you don't have to worry about initializing your firewall with a shell script. It uses the Linux Webmin service, which is a little Web server that allows you to make configuration changes to your server via a Web browser. While this might introduce some insecurity into your system by running a Web server on the firewall, it may be worth it for the ease of configuration it brings. Many commercial vendors now use a Web browser interface for configuration. A big benefit of this application is that you can reach the configuration screen from any Windows or UNIX machine.

For support, Andrea offers a commercial support option. For a mere 100 euros (don't ask me to convert that to dollars exactly, but when this book was printed it was about $100.00), you can get 30 days of e-mail support so you can get help setting it up. It also might be worth subscribing if you have a problem with an existing installation that you can't solve on your own.

Installing Turtle Firewall

Installing and setting up Turtle Firewall is very easy because it uses the Webmin administration module, which is available on most Linux platforms.

1. If you did not install the Webmin administration module during your OS installation, you will need to in order to use Turtle Firewall. Locate and run the RPM, which should be on most Linux distributions disks. Click on the RPM file and it will install automatically.
2. Once that is done, you should be able to log into your firewall's configuration screen by putting its IP address in your browser window and pressing Enter.

3. Now you are ready to install Turtle Firewall. Download the packed distribution from www.turtlefirewall.com or get it from the CD-ROM that comes with this book and unzip it.

4. Change to the turtlefirewall directory and type:

```
./setup
```

This runs an installation script that puts the Perl modules and other things that are needed in the right places.

5. Log into the Webmin server using a Web browser pointed at the IP address or host name the server is using. The Webmin interface will display.

6. Click the Module Index tab, and the Turtle Firewall Main screen displays (see Figure 3.3).

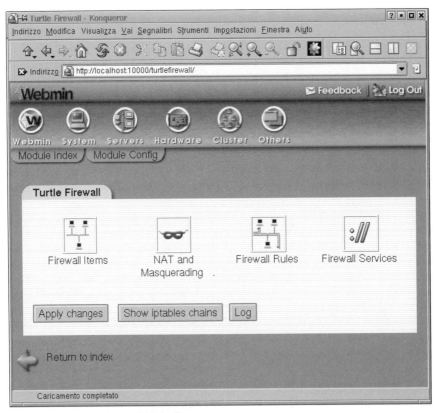

Figure 3.3 Turtle Firewall Main Screen

7. Click on the Firewall Items icon to begin configuring your firewall.

First you will need to define some basic things about your firewall (see Figure 3.4). Turtle Firewall uses the concept of zones to define trusted and untrusted networks. A **trusted zone** connects to a network with employees or people who should generally be trusted on it, such as your internal network. An **untrusted zone** is a network that could have anything on it, from employees to customers, vendors, or even people with malevolent intentions. Turtle calls them "good" and "bad," but it is basically the same thing as trusted and untrusted.

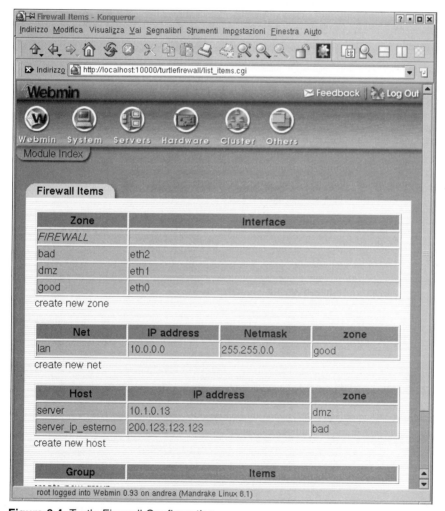

Figure 3.4 Turtle Firewall Configuration

Turtle also has an entry for a DMZ or "Demilitarized Zone" segment. A DMZ segment is used to put servers that need unfettered access to the untrusted zone. Put the interfaces for your good, bad, and DMZ (if any) interfaces here.

8. Next you need to define your internal network IP addresses in the Net box. Put the IP address range with subnet mask for your internal LAN to be protected by the firewall in the box provided (see Figure 3.4).

9. Next, define any internal or DMZ hosts that will need special consideration, such as your mail server or Web server. Do this in the Hosts box (see Figure 3.4).

10. Finally, you can define any special hosts that you want to treat differently, such as administrators, in the Group area. Now your firewall is up and running in basic mode.

There are probably some additional restrictions or permissions you will want to add, for example, the ability for someone from the outside to use SSH to get in. You can do this by writing a rule on the Firewall Rules tab. Click on that tab, and it will graphically walk you through writing a new firewall rule. You will notice the format is similar to Iptables (see Figure 3.5).

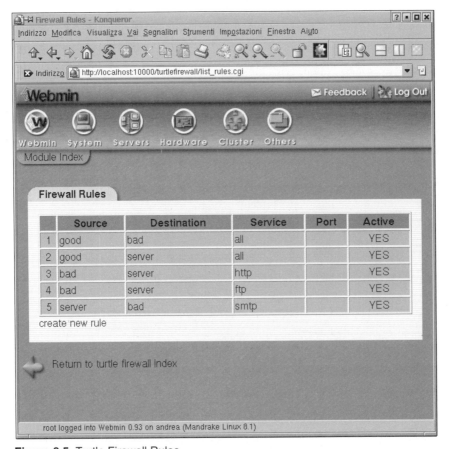

Figure 3.5 Turtle Firewall Rules

If you want to implement the Iptables Masquerade function using private IP addresses for your internal LAN, click on the NAT and Masquerading icon on the main screen. Here you can define what zone will be masqueraded (see Figure 3.6). Generally, it will be your "good" or trusted interface. You can also set up hosts to be "NAT'ed" here. Putting a host to be your virtual IP makes it act as the front for your real host, and the firewall will forward all packets through the virtual host to the real host. This provides an extra level of protection for your internal servers.

SmoothWall Express: A Complete Multi-Function Firewall

SmoothWall Express
Authors/primary contacts: Lawrence Manning, Richard Morrell, Jon Fautley, and Tom Ellis (original authors)
SmoothWall Limited (current contact)
Web site: www.smoothwall.org
Platform: Linux
License: GPL
Version reviewed: 2.0
Web forums:
http://community.smoothwall.org/forum/
IRC chat channels:
Use IRC server irc.smoothwall.org 6667.
Join the channel #help for SmoothWall questions and general chat.
Mailing lists:
For general/installation support, subscribe at:
http://lists.smoothwallusers.org/mailman/listinfo/gpl

The two programs discussed previously, Iptables and Turtle Firewall, offer an inexpensive way to set up a simple firewall. But if you need a DHCP server, you have to set that up separately. And if you want to be able to SSH into the machine, that is another program to install. SmoothWall is an open source firewall that offers a robust firewall package with all those features and more built in. It is designed by a company that offers both a free GPL version and a commercial version with some additional features and enhanced support. This is another example of how a product can take advantage of the power of open source and also reap commercial gains for a company. The free version is called Smooth-Wall Express and is currently on version 2.0; the commercial version is called Smooth-Wall Corporate Server version 3.0.

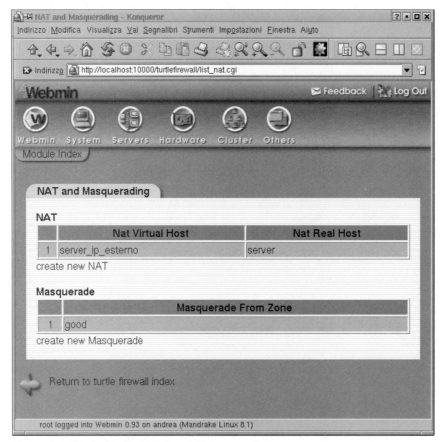

Figure 3.6 Turtle Firewall NAT and Masquerading

SmoothWall Express contains several options beyond Iptables that most companies would want in a fully functional firewall. Granted, you can cob most of these together with other programs and Iptables, but SmoothWall offers it all in one program in an easy to install package. Some of these features are:

- VPN support: SmoothWall integrates an IPsec VPN with firewall capabilities. This allows people on the outside to securely access the local area network via an encrypted tunnel. This can be a fixed remote office or a roaming salesperson (nonstatic IP VPN is only supported in the corporate edition).
- DHCP client and server: The client allows the firewall to get a dynamic IP address for its WAN interface. This is common practice on DSL and cable modem ISP service. It also allows the firewall to act as a DHCP server for the internal LAN, handing out IP addresses according to a preset policy. Again, you can add these

things to an Iptables firewall, but then you have two separate programs to install and manage.

- SSH and Web access to firewall: Secure access via command line and a Web browser. The Turtle Firewall gives this capability for Iptables but doesn't allow SSH access. SmoothWall has both built in with no additional software to install.

- Web proxy server: The ability to set up a Web proxy so that all Web sites are accessed through a firewall. This provides some level of Web security, since any exploits would have to run on the firewall and not the local machine. It can also allow for further protection through a content filtering option available from SmoothWall Limited.

- Web caching server: This feature stores the most popular Web pages for local access so that access times are improved and bandwidth usage is lowered.

- Intrusion detection: SmoothWall offers some basic network intrusion detection capabilities.

- Graphs and reports: SmoothWall allows you to run some simple reports on firewall activity and generate graphs based on this data.

- Support for additional connection types: SmoothWall supports many types of interfaces including dial-up, cable, ADSL, ISDN, and Ethernet. Some of these interfaces require additional software and configuration when supported under Ipchains.

One major difference between SmoothWall and the programs mentioned earlier is that SmoothWall needs to run on a dedicated machine. When you install SmoothWall, it wipes everything off the hard disk and installs its own operating system. This is basically a stripped down and hardened version of Linux, but you don't have to know anything about it to run your SmoothWall firewall. This means you won't be able to run any other tools on that machine or use it for anything else (at least not without a lot of hassle and the potential of breaking the SmoothWall software), so it may not be the right fit for everyone. But if you are looking for a cheap and quick way to set up a turnkey firewall with a lot of features, SmoothWall may be right for you.

SmoothWall Hardware Requirements

As mentioned earlier, SmoothWall needs a dedicated machine to run on. The good news is that the requirements for this machine are quite low since it will be running only the firewall software. The minimum specifications required for SmoothWall are a Pentium-class Intel-compatible PC running at 200Mhz or higher with at least 32MB of RAM and 512MB of disk space. A more optimal configuration would be a 500Mhz processor with 64MB of RAM and 2GB of disk space. These specifications should be easy to meet on all but the oldest machines. You will also need a CD-ROM drive and at least one network card (typically two, if the WAN interface is Ethernet).

SmoothWall Express Versus SmoothWall Corporate

If you have a little money to spend and are considering other commercial alternatives, you might look at the SmoothWall Corporate edition. This firewall has all the benefits of the Express version with the following important differences:

- Enhanced IDS support
- Connection fail-over capabilities
- VPN roaming support (dynamic IPs)
- Additional graphs and reports
- Enhanced graphical user interface
- Certificate authentication support for VPN

You can see a complete list of the differences at

> http://download.smoothwall.org/archive/docs/promo/CorporateServer_vs_
> Express_Comparison_20040113.pdf.

Pricing for the commercial version is quite reasonable (check the Web site for the latest prices). The cost is significantly less than what you'd pay to buy a server to run it on. SmoothWall also makes other software products for network monitoring and content filtering. Check out their full product line at www.smoothwall.net.

Installing SmoothWall

Caution: Remember, installing SmoothWall will erase any data on the hard disk and put its own operating system on it. Do not run this installation on a computer on which you have data or programs you need.

1. You must first create a bootable CD-ROM disk. To do this, use CD-writing software, such as Nero or Easy CD Creator, and create a disk from the .iso image file from the SmoothWall directory on the CD-ROM that accompanies this book. The disk it creates will be bootable.
2. Set your PC to boot from the CD-ROM first. Otherwise, it will search the hard drive and load the operating system it finds there. You usually do this in the BIOS settings of a PC accessed at boot-up before the OS loads. Many PCs use the F2 function key to enter this mode.
3. Boot the machine from the CD-ROM. A title screen displays some basic licensing and disclaimer information. Click on OK.

    You have the choice of loading from the CD-ROM or HTTP. Remember, do not enter this mode unless you are ready for all the data on that hard disk to be erased and replaced with the SmoothWall software.

    Choose CD-ROM, and the installation will begin.

You will see it formatting the disk and then probing your machine for its network interfaces. It should auto-detect any network interface cards (NICs). It lets you accept or skip each one and set them up as firewall interfaces. For example, if you have two NICs on your computer but only want to use one as a firewall interface on the firewall, you would define that here.

4. Define the attributes of each selected interface. Assign them an IP address and subnet mask. After this, SmoothWall installs some additional driver files and asks you to eject the CD-ROM. You have finished installing the program and will automatically enter setup mode.

5. In setup mode, you will be asked for a hostname for the SmoothWall. You can use the hostname to access the machine instead of using its LAN IP address.

6. Next it asks if you want to install the configuration from a backup. This nifty feature allows you to easily restore your firewall to its original configuration if the system crashes (assuming you made a backup, which is covered later in this section). Don't select this unless you are in the process of restoring from a backup.

7. Assuming you chose to set up a new firewall (not from backup) in the previous step, you will be prompted to set up several network types:

   • ISDN: Leave this set to Disable if you aren't using ISDN. If you are, then add the parameters appropriate for your IDSN line.

   • ADSL: This section is necessary only if you are using ADSL and actually have the ADSL modem in your computer. Leave this on Disable if you aren't using ADSL service or if the provider gives you an external modem to plug into. Otherwise, click on the settings for your ADSL service.

   • Network configuration: SmoothWall divides its zones into three categories:

     • Green: Your internal network segment to be protected or your "trusted" network.

     • Red: The external network to be firewalled off from the LAN. The "untrusted" network, usually the Internet or everything that is not your LAN.

     • Orange: This is an optional segment that can contain machines that you generally trust but need to be exposed to the Internet (the DMZ mentioned earlier). This protects your internal LAN, should one of the servers be compromised, since DMZ nodes don't have access to the LAN by default, and also allows these machines to be accessed by the outside world.

   Select the configuration that is appropriate for your network. Most simple networks will use Green (Red is for modems or ISDN), or Green and Red if you have two NIC cards in the machine.

8. Now it is time to set up the DHCP server. If you want your firewall to be responsible for handing out and managing dynamic IP addresses on your LAN, enable this feature. Otherwise leave it turned off. You can set the range to be assigned, and the DNS and lease times for the addresses given out.

9. You now set several passwords for different levels and methods of access. The "root" password is accessible from the console and command line interface and acts just like UNIX root in that you have total control over the box. You then assign a password for the "setup" user account. This user can also access the system from the console and command line. This user has more limited powers than "root" and can only run the setup utility program.

10. Finally, set up a Web interface user account. This isn't a UNIX-type account and can't be accessed from the command line. It is strictly used to control access to features from the Web interface.

11. Now reboot the machine and your SmoothWall firewall should be up and running. You can log into the machine from the console using either the root or setup user. You can also SSH into the box from a remote location and get the command line interface. However, one of the truly nice things about this program is that there is a powerful and easy-to-use GUI accessible from any Web browser that makes administering the firewall a snap.

Administering the SmoothWall Firewall

The easiest way to manage the SmoothWall firewall is using the Web interface. This gives you a powerful tool for administering and adding other functionality to your firewall. You can access this interface two ways: via port 81 for normal Web communications or via port 441 for secured Web communications using SSL. Either way, you put the IP address or URL with the port number in the location window of a Web browser. For example, if your firewall LAN interface card has IP address 192.168.1.1, you would enter the following into the Web browser

```
http://192.168.1.1:81/
```

for normal Web communications, or

```
https://192.168.1.1:441/
```

for secure Web access.

This will display the SmoothWall opening screen. To access any of the other screens you will need to enter your user name and password. The default user name is **admin** and the password is the one you entered for the Web interface during the setup process. There are several main menus accessible from the main page (see Figure 3.7)

Each menu has a number of submenus underneath it.

- Control: This is the firewall homepage and contains copyright and uptime information.
- About Your Smoothie: This has a number of useful submenus:
  - Status: This shows you the status of the various services on the SmoothWall.
  - Advanced: This screen contains detailed information about your system.

Figure 3.7 SmoothWall Main Menu

- Graphs: This is one of the cooler features in SmoothWall. This enables you to create bandwidth graphs so you can analyze your network traffic on different interfaces at different times of the day and on different days. You can use this as a quick way to find network problems. If you notice huge bandwidth increases on the weekend or late at night without any known reason, you know that something is amiss (see Figure 3.8).
- Services: This is where you configure various basic and optional services on the SmoothWall (see Figure 3.9).
  - Web Proxy: If you want to be able to set up your SmoothWall to act as a proxy for anyone surfing the Web, this function can be set up here.
  - DHCP: The built-in DHCP server is configured here.
  - Dynamic DNS: If your ISP assigns you a dynamic IP address but you still want to allow services in from the outside, you can set up the SmoothWall to update a DNS record automatically with its new IP address. It can be configured to use any one of several online services such as dyndns.org and dhs.org.
  - Remote Access: This section controls access to your SmoothWall from anywhere but the console. You can enable SSH (it is disabled by default) and control what specific addresses can get access.
  - Time: This configures the time settings on the machine. This can be very important if you are comparing its log files to other servers. You can set it up to get time from a public time server, which makes logs more accurate.

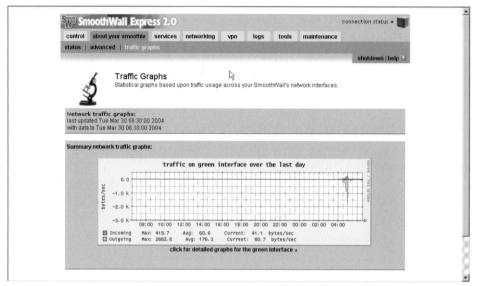

Figure 3.8 SmoothWall Traffic Graph

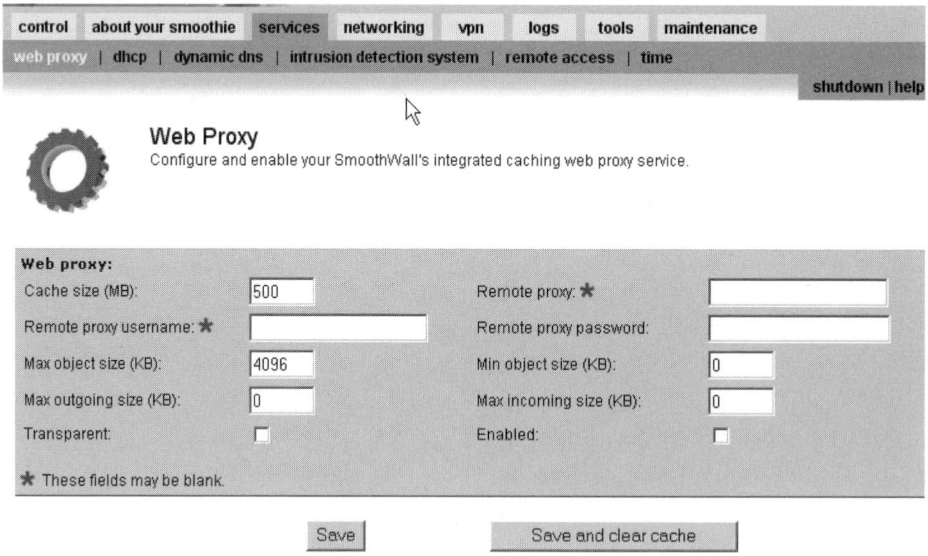

Figure 3.9 SmoothWall Services Screen

- Networking: This is where you configure anything associated with the firewall and network functions of the SmoothWall. This includes adding, deleting, or modifying the rule sets and other functions:
  - Port Forwarding: You can forward a specific port or series of ports to an internal protected host.
  - Internal Service Access: Click here if you need access to an internal service from the outside.
  - DMZ Pinhole: This lets you set up access from a host on your DMZ to a host on your LAN. This is normally not allowed as part of the function of a DMZ.
  - PPP Settings: If you are using the SmoothWall to connect to the Internet via dial-up, you set the various phone settings here such as number, modem commands, and so on.
  - IP Block: This is a nice feature that allows you to easily block an IP or range of IP addresses from your network without having to write any rules.
  - Advanced: Several miscellaneous network settings such as Universal Plug and Play (UpnP) support are found here.
- VPN: Here is where you configure the SmoothWall to act as a VPN for secure remote access from another network. The details are covered later in this chapter.
- Logs: Access to all the log files kept by the SmoothWall is facilitated through this screen. The interface allows you to easily scan different types of log files such as system and security.
- Tools: There are several standard network tools here including ping, traceroute, and whois. They also include a nifty Java-based SSH client so you can access SSH servers from your Web browser.
- Maintenance: This section is used for system maintenance activity and has several submenus.
  - Maintenance: This section keeps track of any patches to your SmoothWall operating system. It is important to keep the SmoothWall OS patched. Just like any operating system, there are security holes discovered from time to time that are fixed in the patches. New features or compatibility are added periodically as well.
  - Password: You can change any of the logins and passwords for the system here (assuming you have the old passwords).
  - Backup: You can make a backup of your SmoothWall configuration so that in the event of a crash you can easily restore it. You should make a backup as soon as you get the SmoothWall configured to your liking to save your settings.
  - Shutdown: This will safely shut down SmoothWall.

Creating a VPN on the SmoothWall Firewall

You can use SmoothWall to set up a secure connection to another network by creating a VPN tunnel with IPsec encryption.

1. To configure the VPN function on the firewall, click on the VPN item from the main menu. There are two submenus located there (see Figure 3.10).
   • Control: This is the main screen where you can start and stop your configured VPN sessions as well as get status information on them.
   • Connections: Here is where you configure new VPN connections. It gives you a pretty simple way to create new VPN connections. On SmoothWall Express (the free GPL version), both ends must have a static, public IP address. To create a new connection profile, go to the Connections tab off of the main VPN tab (see Figure 3.11).
2. Enter a name for this connection. Be sure to use a name that makes it obvious what is being connecting.
3. Define the "left" and "right" sides of the connection. (These names have nothing to do with direction, but are just used as references to differentiate the ends of a VPN. The local side is typically on the left.) Input the IP address and subnet for your local SmoothWall on the left side, and the IP address and subnet of the remote SmoothWall on the right side.

Figure 3.10 SmoothWall VPN Control Screen

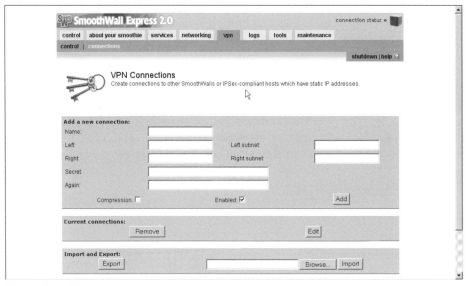

Figure 3.11 VPN Connections Screen

4. Below that you enter the shared secret that is used to create the encryption. This secret has to be the same on both firewalls being connected. It should be protected and not passed through insecure means (for example, e-mail). Make your secret at least 20 characters long and comprised of lowercase, uppercase, and special characters to make your VPN as strong as it can be.

5. You can also click on the compression box to make your VPN data stream smaller. But keep in mind that this will eat processor cycles and might slow your VPN down more than the gain from less bandwidth.

6. Make sure you click on the Enable box and then click on Add to add your VPN connection. You will now see it on the main VPN Control page and it will come up immediately if the link it is associated with is up.

7. You can also export the VPN settings to another SmoothWall to make for easier configuration and avoid data entry error on configuring additional VPN endpoints. Simply click on Export and it will create a file called vpnconfig.dat. You can then take this to your remote machine and go to the same page and select import. SmoothWall will automatically reverse the entries for the remote end. Your VPN is now ready to go. Repeat this process for as many additional sites as you want to add.

Additional Applications with the SmoothWall

This section is only a cursory overview of the basic functions of the SmoothWall. There are other advanced functions covered in the documentation that accompanies SmoothWall.

For details on setting up the other special services, such as the Web proxy or dynamic DNS, consult the administration manual. All three documentation files are contained in the SmoothWall directory on this book's CD-ROM in PDF format. If you have a spare machine to dedicate to your firewall, SmoothWall Express lets you go beyond simple firewall functionality and provides a full security appliance for your network.

Windows-Based Firewalls

None of the firewalls described in this chapter run on Windows. Regrettably, there is a lack of quality of firewall open source software for Windows. Because Windows code is itself not open, it isn't easy for programmers to write something as complex as a firewall, which requires access to operating system–level code. With the addition of a basic firewall in Windows XP, there is even less motivation for coders to develop an open source alternative. This is unfortunate, because the firewall included with XP is fine for individual users, but it isn't really up to the task of running a company gateway firewall. There are commercial options available for Windows from companies such as Checkpoint. However, even they are moving away from a purely Windows-based solution because of the underlying security issues with Windows. If you need to use a Windows-based firewall solution, you will probably have to go to a commercial firewall, as there isn't a good open source firewall for Windows. This underscores the limitations and issues with closed source operating systems.

Port Scanners

A firewall helps protect your network from the most basic attacks and is a mandatory tool for any network attached to the Internet. Now that you have protected your network's front door, we will examine tools to help you check your locks and windows to make sure that the openings in your network are secure.

Looking at the OSI model of network communications again, you see that once a basic network connection has been established between two machines, an application uses that connection to perform whatever function the user requests. The application could be to download a Web page, send an e-mail, or log in interactively using Telnet or SSH.

Chapter Overview

Concepts you will learn:
- TCP/UDP ports
- TCP fingerprinting
- How port scanning works
- Port scanning configuration
- Port scanning techniques

Tools you will use:
Nmap, Nmap for Windows, and Nlog

The Internet Assigned Numbers Authority (IANA) assigns TCP/UDP port numbers. This little known but important organization keeps track of the many different standards and systems that make the Internet run. Among its duties are handing out IP addresses and

OSI Layer Number	Layer Name	Sample Protocols
Layer 7	Application	DNS, FTP, HTTP, SMTP, SNMP, Telnet
Layer 6	Presentation	XDR
Layer 5	Session	Named Pipes, RPC
Layer 4	Transport	NetBIOS, TCP, UDP
Layer 3	Network	ARP, IP, IPX, OSPF
Layer 2	Data Link	Arcnet, Ethernet, Token Ring
Layer 1	Physical	Coaxial, Fiber Optic, UTP

delegating who is responsible for top-level domain names. The IANA wields considerable power, albeit mostly behind the scenes. Few people outside the engineering departments of communications companies even know IANA exists, but it controls a big part of the Internet "real estate." The IANA is also responsible for keeping a list of which services can be found on what network ports, assuming the application or operating system is compliant with these standards. Of course, it behooves all companies making software to closely adhere to these standards; otherwise, their products may not work with other Internet-connected systems. Table 4.1 lists some of the most commonly used TCP ports for server applications.

A full list of port numbers appears in Appendix C. You can also find the most current list at the IANA Web site (www.iana.org). Almost every major application has a port number assigned to it. Port numbers range from 1 to 65,535 for both TCP services and UDP services. Port numbers 0 to 1,023 are considered reserved for common applications. These services usually run as root or a privileged user and are called the **well-known** port numbers. Port numbers from 1,024 to 65,535 can be registered with the IANA for specific applications. These usually map to a specific service, but vendors don't abide as strictly by these registrations as they do the reserved numbers.

Finally there are **ephemeral** port numbers, which the operating system chooses at random from the numbers above 1,024, usually high up in the range. These are used for machines that connect on an ad-hoc basis to other machines. For example, your machine would connect on a Web server on port 80 to download a Web page. The server would see a connection coming in from a machine on some random port above 1,024. This way the server knows it is probably a user and not another application connecting to it. It also uses the ephemeral port number to track the specific user and session. For example, if you

Table 4.1 Common Server Ports

Common Port Number	Protocol	Service
21	FTP	File Transfer Protocol (control port)
22	SSH	Secure Shell
23	Telnet	Telnet
25	SMTP	Mail service
53	DNS	Domain name resolution
79	Finger	Finger
80	HTTP	Web service
135–139	NetBIOS	Windows network communications
443	SSL	Secure Web service

were to open two browsers at the same time, your computer would create two separate port numbers to connect on for each browser session, and the server would track them as separate connections.

Just because a packet is labeled for port 80, nothing is stopping it from having data other than Web traffic. The port number system depends on a certain "honesty" from the machines it is communicating with, and that's where the trouble can come in. In fact, many applications such as instant messaging and peer-to-peer software programs, which might normally be blocked at a company's firewall, will flout this convention and sneak through on port 80. Most firewalls will allow traffic on port 80 because they are configured to allow Web access for users behind the firewall.

When a port is exposed on a computer, it receives all traffic being sent to the port, legitimate nor not. By sending malformed packets or packets with too much or incorrectly formatted data, people can sometimes crash the underlying application, redirect the flow of code inside the application, and gain access to that machine illicitly. This is called a **buffer overflow**, and these make up a large percentage of the security holes that exist today.

Buffer overflows happen when application programmers don't properly code their programs to handle data that "overflows" the memory space allotted to input variables. When the program receives input that exceeds the allotted buffer, it can override internal program control and thereby give a hacker access to system-level resources.

This used to be a very technical task that only the most experienced code hackers could attempt. But you don't have to be a high-level programmer to perform this kind of break-in anymore. There are programs available that automatically perform these buffer overflows with point-and-click ease.

Almost all programs of any size usually have some of these errors inside them. Modern software that runs into the millions of lines of code is just too complex to keep this from happening. Maybe once whole generations of programmers have been retrained to automatically write secure code, this problem will lessen or go away. Until then, you have to keep a close eye on what applications or ports are showing on your network. These ports are potential "windows" into your servers and workstations through which hackers can launch their malicious code into your computers. Since this is where most security exploits happen, it is very important to understand what is going on at this level on your various servers and machines. You can do this easily and accurately with a type of software called a **port scanner**.

Overview of Port Scanners

Port scanners, simply enough, poll a set of TCP or UDP ports to see if an application answers back. If it receives a response, this means there is some application listening on that port number. There are a possible 65,535 TCP ports, and the same number of ports are available for the UDP protocol. Port scanners can be configured to scan all possible ports, or just the commonly used ones (those below 1,024), to look for servers. A good reason to do a complete scan of all possible ports is that network-aware Trojan horses and other nasty software often run on uncommon ports high up in the range in order to avoid detection. Also, some vendors don't stick as closely to the standards as they should and put server applications on high port numbers. A full scan will cover all the possible places that applications can be hiding, although this takes more time and eats up a little more bandwidth.

Port scanners come in many different flavors, from very complex with lots of different features to those with minimal functionality. In fact, you can perform the functions of a port scanner yourself manually. You can use Telnet to do this, one port at a time. Simply connect to an IP address and add the port number like this:

```
telnet 192.168.0.1:80
```

This command uses Telnet to connect to the machine. The number after the colon (on some implementations of Telnet you just leave a space between the IP address and the port number) tells Telnet to use port 80 to connect instead of the standard Telnet port of 22. Rather than the normal Telnet prompt you get on the defaultTelnet port, you'll connect to the Web server if one is running on that machine. When you press Enter you will get the first response from a Web server to a browser. You'll see the HTTP header information, which is normally processed by your browser and hidden from view. It will look something like the output shown in Listing 4.1.

Listing 4.1 HTTP Response to a TCP connection

```
GET / HTTP

HTTP/1.1 400 Bad Request
Date: Mon, 15 Mar 2004 17:13:16 GMT
Server: Apache/1.3.20 Sun Cobalt (Unix) Chili!Soft-ASP/3.6.2
mod_ssl/2.8.4 OpenSSL/0.9.6b PHP/4.1.2 mod_auth_pam_external/0.1
FrontPage/4.0.4.3 mod_perl/1.25
Connection: close
Content-Type: text/html; charset=iso-8859-1

<!DOCTYPE HTML PUBLIC "-//IETF//DTD HTML 2.0//EN">
<HTML><HEAD>
<TITLE>400 Bad Request</TITLE>
</HEAD><BODY>
<H1>Bad Request</H1><P>
Your browser sent a request that this server could not understand
Request header field is missing colon separator.<P>
<PRE>
/PRE>
<P>
</BODY></HTML>
```

You can do this with any open port, but you won't always get anything intelligible back. Basically this is what port scanners do: they attempt to establish a connection and look for a response.

Some port scanners also try to identify the operating system on the other end. They do this by performing what is called **TCP fingerprinting**. Although TCP/IP is a standard for network communications, every vendor implements it slightly differently. These differences, although they don't normally interfere with communications, show up in the response they give to any stimulus such as a ping or an attempted TCP connection. Thus, the digital signature of a ping response from a Windows system looks different from the response from a Linux system. There are even differences between versions of operating systems. See Listing 4.2 for an example of the TCP fingerprint for Windows ME, 2000, and XP.

Listing 4.2 Windows TCP Fingerprints

```
# Windows Millennium Edition v4.90.300
# Windows 2000 Professional (x86)
# Windows Me or Windows 2000 RC1 through final release
# Microsoft Windows 2000 Advanced Server
# Windows XP professional version 2002 on PC Intel processor
# Windows XP Build 2600
# Windows 2000 with SP2 and long fat pipe (RFC 1323)
# Windows 2K 5.00.2195 Service Pack 2 and latest hotfixes
# XP Professional 5.1 (build 2600).. all patches up to June 20,
2004
# Fingerprint Windows XP Pro with all current updates to May 2002
Fingerprint Windows Millennium Edition (Me), Win 2000, or WinXP
TSeq(Class=RI%gcd=<6%SI=<23726&>49C%IPID=I%TS=0)
T1(DF=Y%W=5B4|14F0|16D0|2EE0|402E|B5C9|B580|C000|D304|FC00|FD20|FD
  68|FFFF%ACK=S++%Flags=AS%Ops=NNT|MNWNNT)
T2(Resp=Y|N%DF=N%W=0%ACK=S%Flags=AR%Ops=)
T3(Resp=Y%DF=Y%W=5B4|14F0|16D0|2EE0|B5C9|B580|C000|402E|D304|FC00|
  FD20|FD68|FFFF%ACK=S++%Flags=AS%Ops=MNWNNT)
T4(DF=N%W=0%ACK=O%Flags=R%Ops=)
T5(DF=N%W=0%ACK=S++%Flags=AR%Ops=)
T6(DF=N%W=0%ACK=O%Flags=R%Ops=)
T7(DF=N%W=0%ACK=S++%Flags=AR%Ops=)
PU(DF=N%TOS=0%IPLEN=38%RIPTL=148%RID=E%RIPCK=E|F%UCK=E|F%ULEN=134%
  DAT=E)
```

What looks like unintelligible gibberish at the bottom is the unique settings that Windows uses when it connects via TCP. By comparing the TCP response received from a machine to a database of known TCP fingerprints, you can make a reasonable guess at the operating system on the other end.

This method isn't perfect. Sometimes the port scanner program gets it wrong because some operating system vendors cannibalize or reuse parts of other systems (UNIX systems in particular) when building a TCP stack. This causes the port scanner to think it is the OS they borrowed the TCP stack from. Also, there are odd operating systems like switches, printers, and network appliances that may not be in the signature database.

If people are scanning your network with less than honorable intentions in mind, this provides them with valuable information. Knowing the operating system and version can be a good starting point for figuring out what angles and exploits to try. This is a very good reason to regularly scan your network to see what ports are showing open on your systems. Then you can go through and close up unnecessary ports and lock down those that must stay open.

Considerations for Port Scanning

When planning to do port scanning of any network, keep in mind that this activity is very network intensive. Scanning tens of thousands of ports in a short amount of time puts lot of traffic on the network. If your scanning machine is very fast and it is scanning on an older 10Mbps network, this can significantly affect the network's performance. Over the Internet, it is less of an issue because the scanning will be limited by the size of the connections in between; however, you could still degrade the performance of a busy Web server or mail server. In extreme cases, you might even take machines down.

When using these tools in any fashion, always make sure you have the permission of the owner of the hosts you are scanning. The legality of port scanning is a gray area (you are not actually breaking in, just performing network interrogation). However, your boss might not care about the fine points if you take the corporate network down. And before you decide to go out and scan a few of your favorite Web sites just for fun, keep in mind that your ISP may have something in your Internet terms of service contract prohibiting this kind of activity. Web site operators routinely file abuse complaints against the ISPs of repeat offenders. So unless you want to get fired or have your ISP connection terminated, get written permission from either your superior (when doing it for a company) or your client/volunteer (if doing against a third party). Appendix D has a standard letter agreement for getting permission from an intended scan target that is a good starting point to cover your bases legally.

Even when you have permission, you should consider what the effect of scanning will be on the target network. If it's a heavily used network, you should do your scans at night or during low usage periods. Some scanners have the ability to throttle back the rate they throw packets onto the network so that it doesn't affect the network as much. This will mean your scan will take longer but will be much more network friendly.

Certain devices, such as firewalls and some routers, are now smart enough to recognize port scans for what they are. Iptables can be configured to do this using the multiport option and setting the priority flag. The machines can respond to port scans by slowing down the rate of response for each successive poll. Eventually your scan could spool out into forever. Sometimes you can trick the machine on the other end by randomizing the order the ports are scanned or by stretching out your ping rate. Some devices will fall for this, but others won't. You just have to experiment to find out what works.

Uses for Port Scanners

Once you have permission to scan, you need to consider what your goal is in scanning your network.

Network Inventory

Not sure exactly how many machines you have running? Want to know the IP addresses of all your servers? Ports scanners offer a quick way to scan a range of addresses and find all the live machines on that segment. You can even use the Nlog tool (discussed later in this chapter) to log this into a database and create useful reports.

Network/Server Optimization

A port scanner will show you all the services currently running on a machine. If it is a server machine, it is likely that there are many programs running, but you may not be aware that some of these services are running. They may not be needed for the primary function of the machine. Remember, the more services that are running, the more insecure it is. And all these programs can slow down the performance of a heavily loaded server. Things like extraneous Web servers, FTP servers, or DNS servers can take processor cycles away from the main function of the box. Port scanning your servers and then going through and optimizing them can give you an immediate increase in speed and response times.

Finding Spyware, Trojan Horses, and Network Worms

Regular Web surfers will often pick up little programs from Web sites that try to track their behavior or send custom pop-up ads to their computer. These programs are known as **spyware** because they often try to track the user's activities and may report this data back to a central server. These programs are usually benign, but enough of them can dramatically slow down a user's performance. Also, they are often not well written and can interfere and crash other programs. They also can present opportunities for hackers looking for weak spots.

Another class of network-aware software that you definitely don't want on your network is the **Trojan horse**. These programs are specifically designed for those intent on breaking into networks. Just like the Trojan horse of Greek lore, these programs allow hackers and crackers a back door into your network, usually advertising their presence via an open network port. Trojan horses can be notoriously hard to track down even if you are using anti-virus software. They don't always set off anti-virus scanners, and sometimes the only thing that shows they are there is an open network port. Once inside a computer, most Trojan horses try to communicate outwards to let their creator or sender know they've infected a machine on these ports. Table 4.2 lists the most prevalent Trojan horses and their port numbers. Many of the port numbers are easily recognizable from the clever arrangements of numbers (for example, NetBus is 54,321, and Back Orifice is 31,337, which stands for "elite" in the numbers used for letters in hacker code). Trojan horses tend to run on high number ports with unusual, unrecognizable port numbers, although some really wily Trojans try to run on low-level reserved ports to masquerade as a conventional service.

Network Worms are a particularly nasty type of virus. They are often network-aware and open up ports on the host computer. Network Worms use the network to spread and as such sometimes show up on network scans. A port scan can be a valuable backup to anti-virus protection against these threats.

Table 4.2 Major Trojan Horse Ports

Port Number	IP Protocol	Trojan Horses Known to Use These Ports
12456 and 54321	TCP	NetBus
23274 and 27573	TCP	Sub7
31335	TCP	Trin00
31337	TCP	Back Orifice
31785–31791	TCP	Hack 'a' Tack
33270	TCP	Trinity
54321	UDP	Back Orifice 2000
60000	TCP	Deep Throat
65000	TCP	Stacheldraht

Looking for Unauthorized or Illicit Services

Regulating what employees run on their computers is a tough task. While you can limit their access to floppy and CD-ROM drives using domain security polices, they can still download software easily from the Web. Also, employees like to run instant messaging services such as ICQ or AOL Instant Messenger to communicate with friends, relatives, and other people outside your network. If you allow these services, you should be aware of the security risks that they present to your enterprise. In addition to the employee productivity and bandwidth they eat up, instant messaging networks are often used to spread viruses. They also are known for having bugs that allow users to access files on the local machine. Even if you don't allow them officially, they can be hard to track down. A regular port scan will turn up many of these services by showing the open ports they use.

There are even more noxious applications that your users may try to run, such as peer-to-peer file transfer software. This software allows users to network with thousands of other users worldwide to share files such as music, movies, and software programs. These programs can consume your bandwidth because of the size of the files transferred (often hundreds of megabytes). This can also potentially expose your company to legal liability for copyright violations. The large media companies as well as software concerns are pursuing illegal file sharing more aggressively these days, and companies present a much bigger target than individuals. Also, this use can open up the inside of your network to outsiders. These programs can make part of users' hard drive accessible by other users of the software, often without explicitly notifying them. And there are many hacks and exploits for these programs that allow malicious users to do far more. The bottom line is that you don't want employees using peer-to-peer software on your enterprise network. And with a good port scanner like the one discussed next, you can identify any users of such software and shut them down.

Nmap: A Versatile Port Scanner and OS Identification Tool

Nmap

Author/primary contact: Fyodor
Web site: www.insecure.org/nmap
Platforms: FreeBSD, HP/UX, Linux, Mac OS X, OpenBSD,
                          Solaris, Windows 95, 98, 2000, and XP
License: GPL
Version reviewed: 3.5-1
Mailing lists:
Nmap hackers:
Send message to nmap-hackers-subscribe@insecure.org
Nmap developers:
Send message to nmap-dev-subscribe@insecure.org

Nmap is arguably the best port scanner out there, bar none. It is primarily written by a guy called "Fyodor" (a pseudonym). His software is used in many other programs and has been ported to just about every major operating system. It is a prerequisite for the Nessus vulnerability scanner described in Chapter 5. There are also several add-ons available, including the Nlog program discussed later in this chapter. Suffice it to say, Nmap should be in every security administrator's toolkit. The following are some of the main advantages of Nmap.

- It has lots of options. Simple port scanners are available with tools like Sam Spade (see Chapter 2). However, Nmap has a huge number of options, which gives you almost unlimited variations on how you can scan your network. You can turn down the frequency of probe packets if you are nervous about slowing down your network or turn them up if you have bandwidth to spare. Stealth options are one thing that Nmap has in spades. While some criticize these features as being needed only by hackers, there are legitimate uses. For example, if you want to check to see how sensitive your intrusion detection system is, Nmap lets you do that by running scans at various stealth levels. Nmap also goes beyond mere port scanning and does OS identification, which comes in handy when trying to figure out which IP is on which machine. This section discusses most of the major options, but there are so many they can't all be covered here.

- It's lightweight, yet powerful. The code for Nmap is pretty small and it will run on even the oldest machines (I routinely run it on a Pentium 133 with 16 MB of RAM, and I'm sure it would run on something older). In fact, it even runs on some PDAs now. It packs a lot of punch in a small bundle and it has no problem scanning very large networks.

- It's easy to use. Even though there are numerous different ways to run it, the basic default SYN scan does everything you want for most applications. There are both command line modes and graphical interfaces for both UNIX and Windows to satisfy both the geeks and the GUI-needy. It is also very well documented and supported by a large body of developers and online resources.

Installling Nmap on Linux

If you are running Mandrake, RedHat, or SUSE, you can get the files from the CD-ROM that accompanies this book, or download the binary RPM. To download the files from the Web, type this at the command line:

```
rpm -vhU http://download.insecure.org/nmap/dist/
   nmap-3.50-1.i386.rpm
rpm -vhU http://download.insecure.org/nmap/dist/
   nmap-frontend-3.50-1.i386.rpm
```

You will need two packages: the actual Nmap program with the command line interface and the graphical front end for X-Windows. The preceding commands will download the RPMs and run them. You may want to update the command to reflect the file for the latest version (see the Web site for the exact file name). Once you have run both RPMs, you should be ready to go.

If that doesn't seem to work or if you have a different distribution, you will have to compile it manually from the source code (see the sidebar on compiling). This is a little more complicated but not too difficult. It is good to learn how to do this as you will be doing it with other security tools in this book. You will be seeing these commands often, in this format or one very similar to it.

Compiling from Source Code: A Quick Tutorial

Many major UNIX programs are written in C or C++ for both speed and portability. This makes it easy for programmers to distribute one version of the source code and allow users to compile it for their particular operating system. Most UNIX systems come with a C compiler built in. The open source C compiler used by Linux is called **Gcc** (for Gnu C Compiler). When you want to build a binary program from some source code, you invoke Gcc (assuming the program is written in C code).

1. From the directory where you untarred the program source code, type:

   ```
   ./configure program_name
   ```

   This runs a program that checks your system configuration with what the program will need and sets what are called **compile-time parameters**. You can often specify certain settings, such as to leave out parts of programs or to add optional elements by using the configure program. When configure runs, it creates a configuration file called **makefile** that Gcc, in conjunction with the make program, will tell the compiler how and in what order to build the code.
2. Run the make command to compile the program:

   ```
   make program_name
   ```

   This takes the source code and creates a binary file compatible with your configuration. Depending on the program and the speed of your computer, this may take some time.
3. Finally, run the following command:

   ```
   make install
   ```

   This command installs the binary so you can run it on your computer.

This process may differ slightly from program to program. Some programs do not use a configure script and have a makefile all ready to go. Others may have slightly different syntax for the make commands. In most open source programs, there should be a file called INSTALL in the main directory. This is a text file that should contain detailed instructions for installing the program and any compile-time options you may want to set. Sometimes this information is contained in a file called README.

Here is the entire process using Nmap as an example.

1. To compile Nmap from source, run the following commands from the nmap directory.

   ```
   ./configure
   make
   make install
   ```

Note that you must have root privileges to run the make install command, so be sure you change to root before running the final command by typing su root and then entering the root password. It is not a good idea to run the first two commands as root because they could cause damage to your system if there are bugs or malicious code in the programs. You will need to run this set of commands for each source file, the main Nmap program, and the Nmap front-end program (unless you only intend to use it via the command line).

2. Once you have either run the RPM or compiled the program, you are ready to using Nmap. Start the graphical client by typing:

   `nmapfe`

   If you don't have /usr/local/bin in yourPATH statement, type:

   `s/usr/local/bin/nmapfe.`

   The main interface screen will display (see Figure 4.1).

   Tip: You can also create a link to the binary on your desktop so you can just double-click on it to start the program.

Installing Nmap for Windows

Nmap for Windows is maintained by Jens Vogt. He has ported it to the Windows OS and has done an admirable job of keeping up with the UNIX releases, although it is a version behind as off this writing (version 3.0) and is considered to be in beta format (what open source project isn't?). It isn't quite as fast as the UNIX version but it has the same major features.

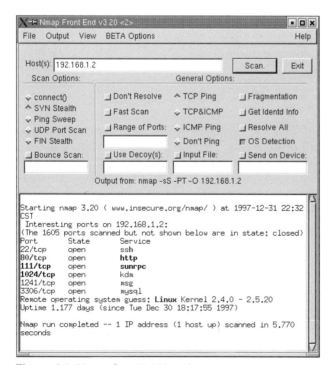

Figure 4.1 Nmap Graphical Interface

1. Get the file from the CD-ROM that comes with this book, or download the simple executable setup file for NMapWin from:

http://download.insecure.org/nmap/dist/nmapwin_1.3.1.exe

2. You will need to install the WinPcap executable if you don't already have this driver loaded. If you aren't sure, then you probably don't have it since it is not a standard item included with any version of Windows. The WinPcap libraries allow Nmap to have lower-level access to your network card so it can capture unaltered packets in a standard cross-platform fashion. Fortunately, the NmaPWin install package provides these files. The WinPcap install file is in files/nmapwin/winpcap.

There are two versions of WinPcap. It is preferable to run the newer version, WinPcap 3.1Beta. If you are running a multiple processor system, you must use the WinPcap 3.X branch or turn off all but one of your processors. If that doesn't work, try the older one or get one for a version that will work with your system from the WinPcap site at

http://winpcap.polito.it/

WinPcap is used for many other Windows programs, including the open source IDS and Sniffer programs discussed in later chapters, so it is important to get this software working.

NOTE: WinPcap does not currently run properly over a dial-up connection under Windows NT, 2000, or XP. If you want to use a port scanner over a dial-up connection (not a good idea anyway, given the limited bandwidth to send probe packets out), you will have to find a different solution.

3. Once WinPcap is installed, you need to reboot your system in order to get all the drivers working. Then fire up NMapWin and you are ready to start scanning.

Scanning Networks with Nmap

When Nmap starts up, the graphical client presents a pretty straightforward interface (see Figure 4.2). There is a spot at the top to put your IP address or IP address range and you can click on Scan to start a scan.

Table 4.3 shows the different formats IP addresses can be entered in. They can also be pulled from a file by selecting the Input item under File on the main menu and selecting a text file with data in proper Nmap format (see Figure 4.2).

Flamey the Tech Newbie Lesson:
Understanding Netmasks and Slash Notation

You will often see IP networks referred to with either a netmask or a slash and a number at the end of it. Both of these are ways of defining the size of the network. To understand them, you need to understand a little of how an IP address is structured. A standard IPv4 address is made up of 32 bits. It is usually represented in four sections, with four octets of 8 bits each. Each octet is usually converted from a set of 8 binary bits to a decimal number when written to make it easy to read. So when you see 192.168.1.1, the computer sees it as:

11000000 10101000 00000001 00000001

A **netmask** is usually a set of four numbers that tells you where the local network ends and the wide area network begins. It usually looks something like this:

255.255.255.0.

A quick way to figure out the size of a network represented by a netmask is to subtract each octet from 256 and multiply those numbers together. For example, the netmask of 255.255.255.248 describes an 8 IP network because

$$(256 - 255) * (256 - 255) * (256 - 255) * (256 - 248) = 8.$$

A netmask of 255.255.255.0 describes a 256 IP network because

$$(256 - 255) * (256 - 255) * (256 - 255) * (256 - 0) = 256.$$

And finally, a netmask of 255.255.0.0 describes a network of 65,536 IP addresses because

$$(256 - 255) * (256 - 255) * (256 - 0) * (256 - 0) = 65536.$$

Slash notation is a little tougher to grasp but it uses the same concept. The number after the slash tells how many bits describe the wide area network. Subtract that number from 32 and that is number of bits that describe the local network. For example, the notation 192.168.0.0/24 describes a network starting at 192.168.0.0 that is 256 IP addresses big. (This is the same size as the one above with a netmask of 255.255.255.0.)

The 32 bits in an IP address minus the 24 bits for the network prefix leaves 8 bits turned on (equal to 1) for the local network size. An 8-bit binary number of 11111111 converted into decimal is 256. If binary math gives you the fits, then just use this little cheat sheet to help you remember.

Slash Notation	Network Size
/24	256 IP addresses
/25	128 IP addresses
/26	64 IP addresses
/27	32 IP addresses
/28	16 IP addresses
/29	8 IP addresses
/30	4 IP addresses
/31	2 IP addresses
/32	1 IP address

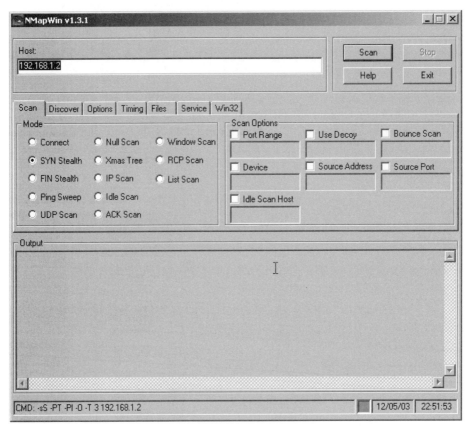

Figure 4.2 Screen Shot of NMapWin

Table 4.3 IP Address Formats

Format	Example
Single IP address	192.168.0.1
IP addresses separated by commas	192.168.0.1,192.168.0.2
IP ranges separated by dashes	192.168.0.1-255
Using standard slash notation	192.168.0.1/24 (a class C network of 256 addresses)

Nmap Command Line Operation

You can run Nmap from the command line either in UNIX or Windows. The general format is:

```
nmap parameters ip-range
```

with any additional settings replacing *parameters*. Throughout the rest of this chapter, any settings or options for the GUIs will have the equivalent command line settings in parentheses with the name of the option, for example, SYN (-sS) and Bounce Scan (-n FTP_HOST).

Nmap Scan Types

There are many different kinds of scans you can run with Nmap. Table 4.4 lists some of the ones you'll probably use most often. The command line parameters are also given if you want to use that interface.

Table 4.4 Nmap Scan Types and Command Line Parameter s

Scan Types (Command Line Parameters)	Descriptions
SYN (-sS)	This is the default scan and is good for most purposes. It is quieter than a TCP Connect scan, that is, it won't show up on most simple logs. It works by sending a single TCP SYN packet to each possible port. If it gets a SYN ACK packet back, then Nmap knows there is a service running there. If it doesn't get a response, it assumes the port is closed.
	The SYN scan does not complete the TCP handshake by sending an ACK back to the machine; as far as the scanee is concerned, it never sees a valid connection. However, the remote system will hold this "half socket" open until it times out from not receiving a response. Some servers and IDS programs are smart enough to catch this now, but the SYN scan will be invisible to most machines.
TCP Connect (-sT)	This works much like the SYN scan, except it completes the full TCP handshake and makes a full connection. This scan is not only noisy but also puts more load on the machines being scanned and the network. However, if stealth or bandwidth is not an issue, a Connect scan is sometimes more accurate than the SYN scan. Also, if you don't have administrator or root privileges on the Nmap machine, you won't be able to run anything other than a Connect scan because the specially crafted packets for other scans require low-level OS access.

(continues)

Table 4.4 Nmap Scan Types and Command Line Parameters *(continued)*

Scan Types (Command Line Parameters)	Descriptions
Ping Sweep (-sP)	This does a simple ping of all the addresses to see which ones are answering to ICMP. If you don't really care about what services are running and you just want to know which IP addresses are up, this is a lot faster than a full port scan. However, some machines may be configured not to respond to a ping (for example, machines running the new XP firewall) but still have services running on them, so a ping sweep is not as accurate as a full port scan.
UDP Scan (-sU)	This scan checks to see if there are any UDP ports listening. Since UDP does not respond with a positive acknowledgement like TCP and only responds to an incoming UDP packet when the port is closed, this type of scan can sometimes show false positives. However, it can also reveal Trojan horses running on high UDP ports and hidden RPC services. It may be quite slow, since some machines intentionally slow down responses to this kind of traffic to avoid being overwhelmed. Machines running Windows OS, however, do not implement this slowdown feature, so you should be able to use UDP to scan Windows hosts normally.
FIN Scan (-sF)	This is a stealthy scan, like the SYN scan, but sends a TCP FIN packet instead. Most but not all computers will send a RST packet back if they get this input, so the FIN scan can show false positives and negatives, but it may get under the radar of some IDS programs and other countermeasures.
NULL Scan (-sN)	Another very stealthy scan that sets all the TCP header flags to off or null. This is not normally a valid packet and some hosts will not know what to do with this. Windows operating systems are in this group, and scanning them with NULL scans will produce unreliable results. However, for non-Windows servers protected by a firewall, this can be a way to get through.
XMAS Scan (-sX)	Similar to the NULL scan except all the flags in the TCP header are set to on (hence the name—it lights up like a Christmas tree). Windows machines won't respond to this due to the way their TCP stack is implemented.

Scan Types (Command Line Parameters)	Descriptions
Bounce Scan (-n FTP_HOST)	This tricky scan uses a loophole in the FTP protocol to "bounce" the scan packets off an FTP server and onto an internal network that would normally not be accessible. If you have the IP address of an FTP server that is attached to the local LAN, you may be able to breach the firewall and scan internal machines. It's a good idea to test to see if your network is vulnerable to this exploit. Most current FTP servers have fixed this security hole. Note: You must input a valid FTP server that would have access to the network in addition to the IP addresses to be scanned.
RPC Scan (-sR)	This special type of scan looks for machines answering to RPC (Remote Procedure Call) services. RPC, which allows remote commands to be run on the machine under certain conditions, can be a dangerous service. Since RPC services can run on many different ports, it is hard to tell from a normal scan which ones might be running RPC. This scan will probe the ports found open on a machine with commands to show the program name and version if RPC is running. It's not a bad idea to run one of these scans every so often just to find out if and where you have these services running.
Windows Scan (-sW)	This scan relies on an anomaly in the responses to ACK packets in some operating systems to reveal ports that are supposed to be filtered. Operating systems that are known to be vulnerable to this kind of scan include some versions of AIX, Amiga, BeOS, BSDI, Cray, DG/UX, Digital UNIX, FreeBSD, HP/UX, IRIX, MacOS, NetBSD, OpenBSD, OpenStep, OpenVMS, OS/2, QNX, Rhapsody, SunOS 4.X, Tru64 UNIX, Ultrix, VAX, and VxWorks.
Idle Scan (-sI zombie_host: probe_port)	This type of scan is a new feature for Nmap version 3.0. It is a superstealthy method whereby the scan packets are bounced off an external host. You don't need to have control over the other host but it does have to be up and meet certain requirements. You must input the IP address of your "zombie" host and what port number to use. While this scan is very hard to track back to the original scanner, it is probably not very useful to most administrators scanning their own networks. It is one of the more controversial options in Nmap since it really only has a use for malicious attacks.

Nmap Discovery Options

You can also adjust the way Nmap does its network discovery and determines which hosts are alive. Table 4.5 lists several different choices.

Nmap Timing Options

Nmap offers you the capability of speeding up or slowing down the frequency at which it sends out its scan packets. If you are worried about too much network traffic (or trying to be stealthy), you can crank the level down. Just keep in mind that the longer you spread them out, the longer your scan will take. This can increase scan times exponentially on large networks. On the other hand, if you are in a hurry and don't mind some extra network traffic, you can turn it up. You can see the different levels and packet frequencies in Table 4.6. You can also set a custom frequency on the Windows version or using the command line options.

Table 4.5 Nmap Discovery Options

Options	Descriptions
TCP + ICMP (-PB)	This is the default setting. Nmap normally uses both ICMP and TCP packets to determine a host's status. This is the most reliable and accurate way since it usually gets a response from one of the two methods if something is there. However, it's also the noisiest way and is likely to end up being logged by some device on the scanned network.
TCP Ping (-PT)	This uses only the TCP method to find hosts. Many firewalls and some routers will drop ICMP packets and may also log them. If you are trying to be stealthy, this is your best option. However, with some of the more exotic scan types (FIN, XMAS, NULL) you may end up missing hosts.
ICMP Ping (-PE)	This uses only ICMP packets for network discovery. This is not a good choice if you are scanning from outside the network firewall because most of your packets will probably be dropped. However, inside a network it is fairly reliable, although you may miss your firewall and some network devices that don't respond to ICMP.
Don't Ping (-P0)	If you set with this option, Nmap will not attempt to learn which hosts are up first and will instead send its packets to every IP in the specified range, even if there isn't a machine behind them. This is wasteful both in terms of bandwidth and time, especially when scanning large ranges. However, this may be the only way to scan a well-protected network that doesn't respond to ICMP.

Table 4.6 Nmap Frequency Settings

Frequency Level	Command Line Parameter	Packet Frequency	Comments
Paranoid	-F 0	Once every 5 minutes	Don't use this option on scans of more than a few hosts or your scan will never finish.
Sneaky	-F 1	Once every 15 seconds	
Polite	-F 2	Once every 4 seconds	
Normal	-F 3	As fast as the OS can handle	Default setting
Aggressive	-F 4	Same as Normal but the packet timeout is shortened to 5 minutes per host and 1.25 seconds per probe packet	
Insane	-F 5	.75 second timeout per host and .3 seconds per probe packet	This method won't work well unless you are on a very fast network and using a very fast Nmap server. Even then, you may still lose data.

Other Nmap Options

Table 4.7 lists a number of other miscellaneous options for Nmap that control things like DNS resolution, OS identification, and other features that don't fit into one of the other categories.

There are more options for fine-tuning your scans available using the command line interface. Read the Nmap man pages for more details.

Running Nmap as a Service

By default, Nmap is run as a service in the Windows version. This means that it is running in the background all the time and can be called by other programs or run by a script or cron job. In Windows, the Nmap service is manageable and configurable under the

Table 4.7 Miscellaneous Nmap Options

Options	Descriptions
Don't Resolve (-n)	Normally, Nmap tries to resolve DNS names for any IP it scans. This can cause the scan to take a lot longer, so if you are not worried about knowing the host names you can turn this off. Keep in mind, however, that host names are useful to know, especially when scanning on a DHCP network where IP addresses can change.
Fast Scan (-F)	This option only tries to scan ports in the Nmap common ports files. By default, these are commonly known server ports under 1,024. You can edit this file and add ports to the list. It can make for a much faster scan but it won't find Trojan horses or services running on higher ports.
Port Range (-p *port_range*)	By default, Nmap scans all 65,535 possible TCP ports. However, if you just want it to scan a certain range, you can set this by using this switch and replacing *port_range* with the range you want to look for. You could use this to scan for just a single type of server, such as port 80 for Web servers, or you might just want to scan the upper ranges to look for odd services and potential Trojan horses.
Use Decoy (-D *decoy_address1, decoy_address2…*)	This option makes it look like the host(s) you enter are decoys scanning the machine as well. The scanned machine will see traffic from several sources and it will be hard to tell which one is the real scanning host. This is another extreme stealth option and not necessary for most legitimate uses. It also puts a lot more traffic on the network and can submit your decoy hosts to being blocked from accessing the scanned machine. This could bring you ire from the people whose hosts you are using as decoys.
Fragmentation (-f)	This option fragments the scan packets as they go out. This is a stealth feature that can be used to avoid having your scan detected. They will be assembled on the other end by the machine receiving them, but the fragmented packets might fool intrusion detection systems and firewalls, which often look to match a specific pattern signature.

Options	Descriptions
Get Identd Info (-I)	The Identd service runs on some machines and provides additional information on that host when queried. It can provide data beyond what the port scan provides, such as operating system type. However, it usually only runs on UNIX systems. Nmap will also automatically do an OS identification using TCP fingerprints as well, so this feature is less useful than it used to be. If you don't have UNIX systems on your network, it is not worth running with this option.
Resolve All (-R)	This option tries to resolve every address in the range, even when they are not answering. This can be useful, for example, in an ISP network, where a whole range of host entries may be assigned to potential IP addresses for a dial-up pool, but only a certain number may be used at a given time.
OS Identification (-O)	This option is set by default. As mentioned earlier, every TCP stack is slightly different. By comparing the exact "fingerprint" of the replies to a database of known TCP fingerprints, Nmap can usually identify the OS it is talking to with a fair amount of accuracy. It can even narrow it down to version ranges. Occasionally, something will come up that it doesn't know, and then it prints out the TCP response at the bottom of the report. If you find one of these unidentified signatures, you can help build the OS fingerprint database when you get an unidentified TCP signature. If you know what it is for sure, cut and paste it into an e-mail to the Nmap development group. They will add it to the database so when someone else scans that type of machine, it will be properly identified. You can find all the TCP fingerprints Nmap knows in the file nmap-os-fingerprints in the Data directory of the Nmap installation.
Send on Device (-e interface_name)	This forces the scan packets to go out a specific interface. This is really needed only on a machine with multiple network cards or if Nmap doesn't recognize your network interface automatically.

Services Tool. To do this, from the Control Panel menu select Administrative Tools, and then Services. You will see Nmap listed as a service; you can click on it and configure its properties.

This option is useful if you want to have Nmap run scans on a regular basis. You can set Nmap to scan your network once a week or once a month and report the results to you. Or you might just have it scan your servers to see if anything substantive has changed. If you are not going to be using this feature, I suggest you disable the service in Windows to conserve resources and for better security. You can do this by clicking on the Nmap service in the service viewer and changing the Start-up Type to Manual rather than Automatic. This change will take place the next time you reboot the machine. You can also manually stop the service by clicking on the Stop button.

Flamey the Tech Tip:

Friendly Nmap Scanning

As mentioned earlier, Nmap can cause problems on networks if used incorrectly or indiscriminately. Here are a few tips to keep your Nmap scanning safe.

- Select where you scan from carefully. Scanning from inside a network will generate a lot more information than scanning outside the firewall. Doing both and comparing the results is often useful, but it is less vital if a server shows an open port inside your network than if it shows one open from outside the firewall.
- You may want to run your scans early in the morning or late at night. That way, you minimize the chances of slowing down vital servers or user machines.
- If you are worried about overwhelming your network, put an older 10Mbps network card in your scanning machine or connect it via a 10Mps hub. That way the maximum traffic it can put on the wire is 10Mbps, which is unlikely to overwhelm a 100Mbps network.

Output from Nmap

Nmap produces a report that shows each IP address found, the ports that were discovered listening on that IP, and the well-known name of the service (if it has one). It also shows whether that port was open, filtered, or closed. However, just because Nmap gets an answer back on port 80 and prints "http," this does not mean that a Web server is running on that box, although it's a good bet. You can always verify any suspicious open ports by telneting to that IP address on the port number specified and seeing what response you get. If there is a Web server running there, you can usually get it to respond by entering the command GET / HTTP. This should return the default index home page as raw HTML (not as a pretty Web page), but you will be able to verify that a server is running there. You can do similar things with other services such as FTP or SMTP. In the UNIX version, Nmap also color codes the ports found according to what they are (see Table 4.8)

As you can see from Figure 4.3, this output lets you scan a report and quickly determine whether there are any services or ports you should be concerned with. This doesn't mean you should ignore any unusual numbers that aren't highlighted or bolded (in UNIX versions). Trojan horses and chat software often show up as unknown services, but you can look up a mystery port in the list of common ports in Appendix C or cross-reference it against a list of known bad ports to quickly determine if the open port is anything to be concerned about. If you can't find it anywhere, you have to wonder what strange service is running on that machine that doesn't use a well-known port number.

Table 4.8 Nmap Output Color Coding

Colors	Descriptions
Red	This port number is assigned to a service that offers some form of direct logon to the machine, such as Telnet or FTP. These services are often the most attractive to hackers.
Blue	This port number represents mail service such as SMTP or POP. These services are also often the subject of hackers' attacks.
Bold black	These are services that can provide some information about the machine or operating system such as finger, echo, and so on.
Plain black	Any other services or ports identified.

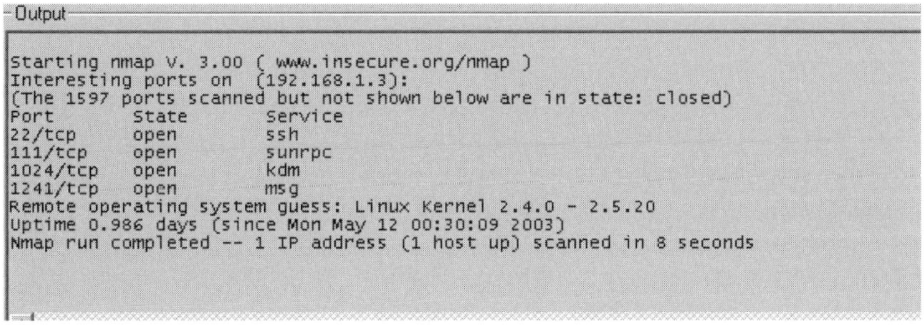

```
Output

Starting nmap V. 3.00 ( www.insecure.org/nmap )
Interesting ports on  (192.168.1.3):
(The 1597 ports scanned but not shown below are in state: closed)
Port        State      Service
22/tcp      open       ssh
111/tcp     open       sunrpc
1024/tcp    open       kdm
1241/tcp    open       msg
Remote operating system guess: Linux Kernel 2.4.0 - 2.5.20
Uptime 0.986 days (since Mon May 12 00:30:09 2003)
Nmap run completed -- 1 IP address (1 host up) scanned in 8 seconds
```

Figure 4.3 Nmap Output

You can save Nmap logs as a number of formats, including plain text or machine-readable, and import them into another program. However, if these options aren't enough for you, Nlog, the next tool discussed, can help you make sense of your Nmap output. Running it on very large networks may be a lifesaver, because poring over hundreds of pages of Nmap output looking for bad guys can quickly drive you blind, crazy, or both.

Nlog: A Tool for Sorting and Organizing Nmap Output

Nlog
Author/primary contact: H.D. Moore
Web site: www.secureaustin.com/nlog/
Platforms: Most Linux
License: No license (GPL-like)
Version reviewed: 1.6.0

The Nlog program helps you organize and analyze your Nmap output. It presents them in a customizable Web interface using CGI scripts. Nlog makes it easy to sort your Nmap data in a single searchable database. On larger networks, this kind of capability is vital to making Nmap useful. Austinite H. D. Moore put together these programs and made them available, along with other interesting projects, at his Web site www.secureaustin.com.

Nlog is also extensible; you can add other scripts to provide more information and run additional tests on the open ports it finds. The author provides several of these add-ons and instructions on how to create your own. Nlog requires Perl and works on log files generated by Nmap 2.0 and higher.

Installing Nlog

Follow these steps to install and prepare Nlog.

1. Get the files from the CD-ROM that accompanies this book or download the files from the Nlog Web site.
2. Unpack the Nlog files using the tar -zxvf command. It will unzip and neatly organize all the files for Nlog in a directory called nlog-1.6.0 (or other numbers, depending on the version number).
3. You can use the installer script provided to automatically install and prepare the program. Note that you need to edit the program before you run it. Go to the Nlog directory and, using a text editor program such as vi or EMACS, open the file installer.sh and enter the variables where indicated for your system.

Flamey the Tech Tip:

Newbie Lesson on Using UNIX Text Editors

Throughout this book you will need to edit text files to set program variables, install configurations, and for other reasons. There are many good text editors for UNIX including vi, EMACS, and Pico. Each of these has their strengths and weakness, but in this book I will assume the use of EMACS because it's the most X-Windows friendly, easy to use, and is available on most systems. On Mandrake Linux, you can find EMACS located in X-Windows on your Start menu under the Programming menu. You can also start EMACS from a command line by typing `emacs` or `emacs filename` to edit a specific file.

Be careful when using text editors on executable or binary files. Any changes made to these files could break the program they support. You can tell if it is a binary file because it will generally contain a bunch of gibberish rather than plain text. Generally, you use text editors to only modify text files.

EMACS gives you a familiar menu at the top to select actions for the file such as save and close. You can use the mouse to move around the screen and select menus or text. You can also use a number of shortcut keystrokes. A few of the most useful ones are listed below. Note: CTRL means pressing the control key while pressing the other key, and where two key combinations are listed, do one after the other.

EMACS Quick Keys	Functions
CTRL+x, CTRL+c	Closes EMACS. It prompts you to save your current file if you haven't already.
CTRL-g	Escape. If you are in a key sequence you can't get out of, this will return you to the main buffer.
CTRL+x, k	Closes the current file.
CTRL+x, s	Saves the current file.
CTRL+x, d	Opens a directory listing that you can click on to open files and perform other functions.
CTRL+a	Moves the cursor to the beginning of the line.
CTRL+e	Moves the cursor to the end of the line.
CTRL+s	Searches for text entered.

There are lots of other key combinations and macros for advanced users. For more information on EMACS, visit the following sites:

EMACS home page: www.gnu.org/software/emacs/
EMACS Quick Reference: http://seamons.com/emacs/

Edit the following parameters with the correct values for your installation.

```
CGIDIR=/var/www/cgi/
HTMLDIR=/var/www/
```

Put the path to your CGI directory. The above represents the correct values on a default Mandrake installation. Make sure you enter the correct ones for your system. For other Linux systems, find the path to this directory by using the locate command. This useful command will find any files with the text you insert after it.

4. Save the file, then run it by typing:

```
./install.sh
```

The installation script automatically copies the CGI files to your CGI directory and the main HTML file to your HTML directory. It also changes the permissions on those files so they can be executed by your Web browser.

5. For the final step, go into the /html directory and edit the nlog.html file. In the POST statement, change the reference to the cgi files to your cgi files, which should be the same one used above (/var/www/cgi/). Save the file and you are ready to go.

Using Nlog

This section describes how to use Nlog.

1. The first thing you must do is create a Nlog database file to view. You do this by converting an existing Nmap log file. Make sure you save your Nmap logs with the machine-readable option (-m on the command line) to be able to use them in Nlog. You can then use a script provided with Nlog to convert the Nmap log into the database format that Nlog uses. To convert a Nmap machine readable log, run the log2db.pl script using this command:

```
Ip2db.pl logfile
```

Replace *logfile* with your log file name and location.

2. To combine multiple log files into a single database, use the following commands.

```
cat * > /PATH/temp.db
cat * > /PATH/temp.db | sort -u > /PATH/final.db
```

3. Replace /PATH with the path to your Nmap files and final.db with the name you want to use for the combined Nmap database. This sorts the files into alphabetical order and eliminates any duplicates.

4. Start your Web browser and go to the Web directory (/var/www/ from the previous section).

5. Select the Nmap database file you want to view and click Search (see Figure 4.4).

6. You can now open your Nmap database and sort it based on the following criteria.

- Hosts by IP address
- Ports by number
- Protocols by name
- State (open, closed, filtered)
- OS match

You can also use any combination of these criteria. For example you could search for any Web servers (http protocol) on Windows systems with a state of open.

Nlog Add-ons

As mentioned earlier, Nlog is easily extensible and you can write add-ons to do other tests or functions on any protocols or ports found. In fact, there are several included with the program. If there is an add-on available, there will be a hypertext line next to the port and you can click on it to run the subprogram. Table 4.9 lists the built-in extensions.

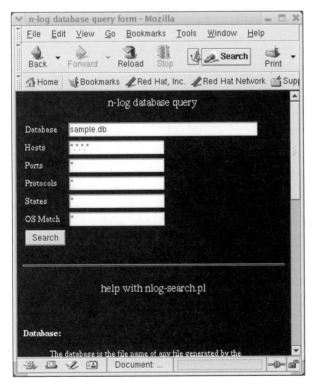

Figure 4.4 Nlog Screen Shot

Table 4.9 Nlog Built-in Extensions

Extensions	Descriptions
Nlog-rpc.pl	This add-on takes any RPC services that are found and attempts to find out if there are any current RPC attachments and exports for that service.
Nlog-smb.pl	For any nodes running NetBIOS (which most Windows machines will be), this script tries to retrieve shares, user lists, and any other domain information it can get. It uses the user name and login specified in the nlog-config.ph file.
Nlog-dns.pl	This script runs a standard nslookup command on the IP address. (See Chapter 2 for more information on nslookup.)
Nlog-finger.pl	This runs a query against any finger service found running to see what information is sent.

Creating Your Own Nlog Extensions

If you examine these add-on scripts, you will see that they are just basic Perl programs. If you are experienced with Perl, you can write your own extensions to execute just about any function against your scanned hosts. For example, you can retrieve and display the HTTP header for any Web servers found so you can more easily identify it. You don't need to go overboard with this, because programs like Nessus (discussed in Chapter 5) can do much more comprehensive testing, but if you just need a banner or some small bit of information, then using Nlog is a good solution.

Nlog comes with a sample custom add-on called nlog-bind.pl. This script is designed to poll a DNS server and tell you what version of BIND (the Berkley Internet Naming Daemon DNS service) it is running. However, this script is not finished; it is provided as an exercise to create your own add-ons. The sample script is in /nlog*/extras/bind/. The following procedure guides you through finishing the script. You can use that format to create any custom script of your own.

1. Compile the script using the Gcc compiler with the following command from that directory:

   ```
   gcc -o bindinfo binfo-udp.c
   ```

   This creates a binary file called bindinfo in that directory.
2. Copy this binary file to the directory where you are keeping your nlog scripts.
3. Change the permissions on it to make it executable. (Remember that you have to be root to issue this command.)

   ```
   chmod 700 bindinfo
   ```

4. Open your nlog-config.ph file in a text editor.

5. Add this line:

```
$bindinfo = "/path/to/bindinfo";
```

Replace *path/to/bindinfo* with the location where you put the binary file.

6. Save this file.

7. Now edit nlog-search.pl. This is the Perl script that creates your search results page.

8. Find the section that looks like this:

```
1: # here we place each cgi-handler into a temp var for
   readability.
2:
3: $cgiSunRPC = "sunrpc+$cgidir/nlog-rpc.pl+SunRPC";
4: $cgiSMB   = "netbios-ssn+$cgidir/nlog-smb.pl+NetBIOS";
5: $cgiFinger = "finger+$cgidir/nlog-finger.pl+Finger";
6:
7: $qcgilinks ="$cgiSunRPC $cgiSMB $cgiFinger";
```

9. Between lines 5 and 6, add a line that looks like:

```
$cgiBIND = "domain+$cgidir/nlog-bing.pl+BIND";
```

10. Edit line 7 to look like this:

```
$qcgilinks = "$cgiSunRPC $cgiSMB $cgiFinger $cgiBIND";
```

Line 7 is also where you would add, in a similar fashion, links to any other scripts you had created.

11. Copy the nlog-bind.pl file from this directory into your cgi-bin directory (/var/www/cgi on Mandrake Linux), and change the permissions (chmod) so the application can read it.

Now when your Nmap scans find port 53 open (which is generally a DNS server), you can click on the link that Nlog creates and find out what version of BIND it is running. You can write additional scripts to extend Nlog by following the logic in this example.

Interesting Uses for Nlog and Nmap

So now you can port scan with Nmap and sort and analyze the results with Nlog. So what do you do with these new toys? Well, there are some interesting applications for port scanners. Here are some real examples for you to try on your network (or someone else's, with their permission, of course!). You may be surprised at what you find.

Scan for the Least Common Services If you have a service or port number that is only showing up on one or two machines, chances are that it is not something that is standard for your network. It could be a Trojan horse or a banned service (for example, Kazaa, ICQ, or MSN). It could also be a misconfigured machine running an FTP server or other type of public server. You can set Nlog to show the number of occurrences of each and sort them by the least often occurring. This will generate a list for you to check out. You probably won't want to include your companies' servers in this scan as they will have lots of one of kind services running. However, it wouldn't hurt to scan these servers separately either to fine-tune or eliminate extraneous services.

Hunt for Illicit/Unknown Web Servers   Chances are that if you run one or more Web servers for your company, you will see the HTTP service showing up a few times on your network. However, it is also likely that you will see it on machines where you don't expect it. Some manufacturers of desktop computers are now loading small Web servers by default on their systems for use by their technical support personnel. Unfortunately, these Web servers are often barebones programs with security holes in them. You will also find Web servers running on printers, routers, firewalls, and even switches and other dedicated hardware. You may need these servers to configure the hardware, but if you aren't using these servers, you should shut them off. These mini-servers are often configured with no password protection by default and can offer a hacker a foothold onto that machine. They can also offer access to the files on the machines if an intruder knows how to manipulate them. Scan for these hidden Web servers, and either turn them off or properly protect them. You should also search for ports other than 80 that are commonly used for HTTP. Table 4.10 has a short list of port numbers for Web service.

Scan for Servers Running on Desktops   Going a step further with the last exercise, restrict the IP range to only those that are nonserver machines and set a port range from 1 to 1,024. This will find desktop machines running services that are normally done

Table 4.10 Common Alternate Web Server Ports

Common Port Number	Protocol
81	Alternate Web
88	Web
443	Https, Secure Web
8,000–8,002	Web
8,080	Web
8,888	Web

by servers, such as mail, Web, and FTP. Unless there is a good reason for this (for example, PCAnywhere), your desktop machines should not be running these types of services.

Hunt for Trojan Horses To hunt for Trojan horses on your network, run a scan of your network and translate it into the Nlog database format. Open the Nlog search page, select the ports, and set the range from 30,000 to 65,400. This is the favored range for Trojan horses because it is out of the range of normal services and so they usually will go unnoticed—that is, unless you are port scanning your network. However, just because there are some services running on high-level ports doesn't always mean you have Trojan horses, but it is worth paying attention to services running on these high port numbers. Once you've narrowed it down to the machine and port numbers, you can rule them out by checking the services running on those machines or by telneting to those port numbers and seeing if you get a service banner.

Check Your External Network Exposure Put your Nmap box outside your network, either on a dial-up or home broadband connection, and try scanning your company's public IP addresses. By doing this you will see what services are accessible from the Internet (and thereby to any port scanner–wielding person). This is the most vulnerable part of your network, and you should take extra care to secure any services that are public-facing by using a vulnerability scanner, such as the one described in the next chapter. It will also show if your firewall is properly filtering ports that it is forwarding to internal LAN addresses.

So you've seen all the cool things you can do with a port scanner like Nmap. These programs are useful for finding out what you have running and where your exposures might be. But how do you know if those exposed points might be vulnerable? Or if services that are supposed to be open are safe and secure? That goes beyond the function of a port scanner and into the realm of a vulnerability scanner, which is discussed next.

Vulnerability Scanners

Now that you have secured your perimeter with a firewall and port-scanned your interior and exterior networks, what can you do next to make your network more secure? Firewalls prevent people from easily accessing your internal LAN from the outside. Port scanning shows you what services are running and lets you eliminate those that you don't need. However, what about the services you have to keep? You have to run Web and mail servers to communicate to the outside world. You may have to run other applications as well, such as FTP, SSH, Telnet, and custom database applications. How do you know if these services are secure? To understand your risks, you have to understand the threats and how they can be used to gain illicit access to your company's information and resources.

Chapter Overview

Concepts you will learn:
- Typical application-level vulnerabilities
- Vulnerability scanning setup and configuration
- How to do safe and ethical vulnerability scanning
- Sample scan configurations
- What vulnerability scanning *doesn't* do

Tools you will use:

Nessus and NessusWX

What exposes your systems to vulnerability most of the time? Applications. Looking at the OSI Reference Model, you'll see that the application layer is at the top of the network communication stack, which makes it is the most complex and variable layer. You can use a vulnerability scanner to run tests against various applications on your system to see if there are holes that can be exploited. The vulnerability scanner can also use lower-level tools such as a port scanner to identify and analyze potential applications and protocols running on the system.

OSI Layer Number	Layer Name	Sample Protocols
Layer 7	Application	DNS, FTP, HTTP, SMTP, SNMP, Telnet
Layer 6	Presentation	XDR
Layer 5	Session	Named Pipes, RPC
Layer 4	Transport	NetBIOS, TCP, UDP
Layer 3	Network	ARP, IP, IPX, OSPF
Layer 2	Data Link	Arcnet, Ethernet, Token Ring
Layer 1	Physical	Coaxial, Fiber Optic, UTP

Identifying Security Holes in Your Systems

The thing to remember about computer security is that it is like any other kind of security. The average computer troublemaker is going to pick the targets of opportunity and ease. Yes, there are master system crackers who go after particular targets and work on them for months or even years using physical, social, and technical means. And like physical security, if someone really wants to break into your computer and they have enough money, time, and resources to dedicate to it, then they probably will succeed. However, unless you are working for a bank, government institution, or Fortune 500 company, you probably don't have to worry about these über-hackers coming after you. What you do have to worry about is the rank-and-file computer criminals and the automated worms and viruses. Your job is to make sure your network has fewer security holes than the next guy's so that they will pass you over when looking for a system to crack. Just like a car with an alarm, The Club, and an Immobilizer—only a really dedicated car thief is going to try to steal it.

Just a very small percentage of computer criminals actually research and develop their own attack methods. Most hackers operate by using published and known security holes and tools to figure out how to get into your computers. These can be found in any number of Web sites, and hacking tools are available for downloading to exploit these holes.

Of the major Internet outages caused by computer crime, all of them have come from the exploitation of security holes that been known for some time before the incident. Usually the outbreak comes months or even years after the underlying vulnerability became known. The Code Red outbreak in 2001 used a vulnerability that had had a patch available for over a year; the same with the Nimda worm. The SQL Slammer worm that went after SQL databases in February of 2003 also had had a fix available for six months before it hit. The fact is that most computer break-ins use methods and vulnerabilities that are well known and have had patches or solutions available for them. The use of so-called zero-day exploits and unpublished security holes is relatively rare.

Why don't people keep up with these things and patch their systems? If they did, then there would be a lot less computer crime and books like this probably wouldn't exist. However, for a myriad of valid reasons, there continue to be plenty of systems with plenty of vulnerabilities.

- Not enough time or staff. Companies cut costs and eliminate IT staff during tight times (IT doesn't generate income). They may opt to outsource the IT function altogether. And while this is often a cost-effective option, the external companies managing LANs often don't have a company's security on their mind as job one. Their job is to keep a network up. Keeping users happy often comes before security.
- Concern about system stability. It's a well-known fact that when systems vendors issue patches, they sometimes fix one thing and break two others. For mission-critical systems, finding the time and resources to properly test a patch is often not worth the benefit of upgrading.
- Too many patches to keep up with. If you are a subscriber to Windows Update, the Microsoft patch service, you probably get a notice at least once a week to upgrade or patch your system. For busy system administrators, this can be too much to handle on top of their normal system administration duties. Indeed, studies have been done that show that the personnel cost of patching software often exceeds its initial purchase price.
- Ignorance. Many company system administrators are simply not aware that a problem exists or that a patch is available. Now with Microsoft's automatic update this has become a little less of a problem for Windows systems, but the problem persists for other vendors and more obscure software. Even with Windows, there are several different patch managers and none of them talk to each other. This is one of the reasons that SQL Slammer got out of hand so fast—the standard Windows update service didn't look for it.

Another thing that makes hackers' jobs easy is that there are usually several different ways into a system. In fact, with lots of services running, there might be a dozen or more potential windows for entry on an Internet-connected server. If one type of attack doesn't work, they can always try another. The following sections describe some of the potential ways that someone with the right knowledge can cause havoc on your company's system. Some of them may not apply to your network, but chances are that you will have at least two or three of these potential sources of vulnerability.

Buffer Overflows

As I mentioned in Chapter 4, buffer overflows are by far the most popular way to exploit a system. The first documented use of a buffer overflow was the original Internet worm released by Robert Morris on November 2, 1988. It was called the Morris worm after its author, and was designed only to prove the point that it could be done. It worked by exploiting a bug in the finger program and propagating itself from one machine to another. It used poor configuration in Sendmail and rsh to replicate itself. It was supposed to copy itself only to a few systems. However, Morris made a mistake in the coding of the worm and it rapidly spread all over the Internet, which was then only a few thousand systems. It brought major universities and other institutions to their knees as they tried to cope with the rapidly spreading bug. It was the dawn of a new age for computer hackers and opened the eyes of many who thought that the Internet was a safe and friendly place. Since then, buffer overflows have been found in just about every major program and are used frequently by those seeking unauthorized access to systems.

How do you protect yourself from buffer overflows? Well, unless you feel like debugging every piece of software you have (which assumes you have access to the source code as well!), you have to wait for someone to discover the bug and report it and then for the software company to issue a patch. Unfortunately, keeping up with patches and which ones apply to you can be a full-time task—not to mention testing and applying them. Many companies just opt not to bother, yet even companies that are diligent in the patching process often are behind by sheer virtue of scheduling downtime. Even Microsoft had some of its own systems taken down during the SQL Slammer outbreak because some of its SQL servers weren't updated with the patch that they themselves released! One good way to know if you have buffer overflow conditions on your applications is to test them with vulnerability scanning software. This will detect most known buffer overflows that exist on your system and help keep you up to date on patches that are needed to remedy these conditions.

Router or Firewall Weaknesses

These devices are the first line of defense against outsiders coming onto your corporate network. However, due to the increasing complexity of the devices and sophistication of attackers, they can be poor defense mechanisms if they aren't configured correctly. Learning the Cisco IOS router language is a career in itself. If a company doesn't have a Cisco technician on staff, it is probable that their Cisco routers are not configured optimally for security. And firewalls can be even more difficult to configure. As you learned in Chapter 3, one wrong configuration line can negate the protection a firewall offers. A harried technician trying to set up access for employees or outside parties will often err on the side of more access rather than better security in the effort to get the job done.

Even when the rule sets are well written, routers often run weak or dangerous services. Many routers still rely on Telnet for interactive logins rather than a secure application such as SSH. This opens the door for sniffer attacks to grab login and password combinations. Some routers still run finger and other information-leaking services as well.

And even though firewalls are supposed to be the most secure devices, they are not immune to attacks. Some firewalls sit on top of regular operating systems, such as Windows or UNIX, and thus can be vulnerable to all the normal OS-level exploits. Even if the firewall operating system is proprietary, exploits have been found in them. Many firewalls use a Web server to interface with users, and that can be exploited via holes in the Web interface as well. Securing these frontline defenses is critical and should be one of your first priorities.

Also, firewalls tend to provide a security that is "crunchy on the outside, chewy inside" (analogy courtesy of Bill Cheswick). This means that they are hard to penetrate coming from the outside, but offer almost no protection if you are being attacked from within. You should make sure your systems internally are at least minimally secure and not depend on the firewall for all your network security.

Web Server Exploits

Almost every company has to run a Web server these days—not having a Web site is like not having a telephone or fax number. However, Web servers are notorious for having bugs and security holes in them. The very idea of a Web server—that a user can pull files from the server without any authentication at all—sets up the potential for security gaps. The large number of holes is due to the ever-expanding number and types of protocols and commands that Web servers have to deal with. When Web pages just consisted of HTML, it was much easier to control things. But now Web servers have to interpret ASP, PHP, and other types of traffic that contain executable code, and as Web applications get more complex, these issues will only increase.

Some Web servers are more secure than others, but they have all had their problems. And a hacked Web server can mean more than just embarrassment from a defaced Web page if that server also accesses a database and other internal systems, which is common these days.

Mail Server Exploits

E-mail has become vital for companies to communicate in the electronic age. However, mail servers have traditionally been a favorite target of attackers. The original mail transfer agent, Sendmail, was riddled with vulnerabilities and continues to cause security professionals fits. And Microsoft's flagship mail server, Exchange, is not much better. Web and mail servers usually represent a company's most exposed points.

DNS Servers

The servers that control and maintain your company's domain names offer hackers an enticing target. Berkley Internet Naming Domain (BIND), which is the primary DNS server, has consistently been in the list of top ten exploited services. DNS is an older program and its structure lends itself to potential holes (one monolithic binary rather than a more modular architecture). DNS often is run as root, which makes it all the more dangerous if it is co-opted. Also, because DNS is hard to set up and little understood, it often is misconfigured and ill secured. The firewall settings for DNS are often not properly configured, with most system administrators allowing unfiltered access in and out.

While Web, mail, and other services have more visibility and get more attention from the IT staff, DNS holes offer the quickest and easiest way to take your company off the Internet map. Even if you have IP connectivity to the world, without valid DNS service for your domains no one will be able to reach your Web servers and no mail will go through. In fact, DNS has been cited as the weakest point in the whole Internet infrastructure and a potential target for cyberterrorism attacks. Rather than crack into your servers or break through your firewalls, an attacker can simply launch a denial of service against your DNS service, effectively taking your firm off the air. Or worse, using a type of attack called DNS cache poisoning, Web surfers bound for your site will be redirected to a site the hacker chooses.

Database Exploits

More company Web sites are offering external access into their databases. For example, you might allow customers to place and check the status of orders online, allow employees to get information on benefits programs via the Web, or let vendors access your system to automatically update ship times. All of these functions usually access an internal company database. This takes Web sites beyond the one-dimensional, online brochures they were in the early days of the Internet and makes them an extension of your systems to external users. However, doing this opens up a big potential source of vulnerabilities. These are often systems that have not been hardened for external use. In other words, they assume that the users will be benign and not do overtly hostile things. Web front-end software such as ColdFusion and PHP have been found to be lacking in proper authentication controls and contain bugs such as buffer overflows. Specially crafted URLs can send SQL or other database commands straight into the heart of your system. The SQL Slammer worm that spread quickly worldwide in early 2003 using weaknesses in Microsoft's SQL Server showed how this can happen.

User and File Management

This area is one of the stickiest in info-security. You have to provide your users with the access to the systems and programs that they need to do their work. However, a key principle of good security is that of **least privilege**, the concept of giving users the minimum access that they need to do their job—and no more. Finding that level is the tricky part. Give them too little access and you will be barraged by help desk calls and complaints;

give them too much access and you weaken the security of your system. Most administrators will err on the side of more relaxed access rules because it means less work for them.

Unfortunately, user-friendly systems like Windows also lean in this direction by setting up many permissions at their weakest level: poor security by default. Windows has some built-in accounts and shares that it uses for system-level operations that have more access than they really need. One example is the IPC (Inter-Process Communication) share, a default share on Windows that can be used by any user to gain information about that machine or domain. The default guest account can be used in a similar way. You can disable or limit these accounts, but you have to do it manually after installation. To Microsoft's credit, these types of default accounts have been limited in Windows XP, but the accounts still exist (they are necessary for the simple peer-to-peer networking that Windows allows). And UNIX systems aren't much better. The lack of granularity in account management, that is, there is only root and non-root, makes it hard to keep from handing out root-level access to many people.

And of course, keeping your user account list current can be a daily task with larger networks. Idle or unused accounts are considered valuable targets for hackers because they can use them without worry of the real owner suspecting foul play.

A good vulnerability scanner will check for default and easy-to-guess passwords, such as the standard "administrator/administrator" login and password combination on Windows systems. The scanner will also take a set of credentials and see how far it can get with them. It can check for idle accounts and users that have never changed their passwords (on Windows systems). This can help you see where the chinks in your armor might be in terms of user account management.

Manufacturer Default Accounts

In trying to make life easier for you, vendors often make your security job much harder. Many hardware manufacturers ship their hardware with standard default logins and user accounts to enable easier set up. Some of them also put in accounts for technicians and service representatives. You are supposed to immediately change these passwords when you install the equipment or software, but many people don't. The result is that many machines can be accessed simply by someone trying any number of default user account and password combinations. Routers, switches, phone systems, and other types of hardware are more likely to have these kinds of vulnerabilities than UNIX or Windows systems. However, there are exceptions. There is a whole protocol that is based on the idea of default passwords. SNMP (Simple Network Management Protocol) was designed to enable software to automatically poll devices and determine basic information about them (for example, the up/down status). In some cases, SNMP lets you even perform simple configuration operations. It was a good idea in concept, and many companies have designed network management systems around this protocol. However, in implementation, manufacturers defaulted to using two main accounts, "public" and "private," as their community strings or passwords. Using these passwords, anyone on the network can poll your devices to find out the status.

SNMP also allows basic commands to be sent to the devices, such as resetting a router or dropping an interface. Very few users of SNMP bother to change their default community strings because it would be a hassle to do that on every machine. The result is that a hacker with a simple tool such as snmpwalk, which is available on the Internet for free, can gather information on your network, map it out, and possibly even take it down if you are running SNMP with these default community strings. To add fuel to this fire, recent exploits of the SNMP protocol using a buffer overflow allows hackers to take over the remote machine entirely. Many people who don't even use SNMP are running it on their machines because manufacturers often turn it on by default to allow for easy network identification.

Another software-based example is the default **sa** account built into Microsoft's SQL server. This account is used by inter-system processes, but it can also be accessed by a script or worm, as demonstrated with the disruption caused by the SQL Slammer worm. There are sites on the Internet that list all the major hardware manufacturers and software vendors and any default passwords that may exist. And of course, there are automated programs that can try them all very quickly without a lot of effort.

Blank or Weak Passwords

While it may seem insane to have accounts with blank passwords, many networks do just that. And believe it or not, some even do this with the administrator account. It is also unexpectedly common to see login/password combinations of administrator/administrator, which is the default installation of Windows. It is not uncommon for worms and hacking programs to automatically check for this condition. If they find it, they have hit the gold mine: full administrator access to the system. Also, when users are setting passwords, they can simply leave their passwords blank. This allows anyone who has a user list to walk through the list, trying for blank password accounts. You can set your password policies to not allow this condition as well as to strengthen the length and complexity of the passwords. Requiring passwords to be changed on a regular basis and getting rid of accounts that have never logged in is also a good idea. Vulnerability scanning will check for these conditions.

Unneeded Services

Like a vestigial tail, there are often applications running on our machines that no longer serve any useful purpose. These services may be part of an earlier set of libraries that the programmers built on and never bothered to take out. This is one of the downsides of ever-increasing processing power and memory capacity. Programmers used to carefully ration every byte they used and would never allow unnecessary lines in their code. However, in this age of bloat-ware and gigabyte-sized operating systems, it is often easier to leave legacy services in rather than risk breaking some other program that depends on them. The incredible thing is that these services are often turned on by default. Table 5.1 lists services that no longer have a use and can generally be safely turned off.

Table 5.1 Useless Services

Services	Common Port Numbers	Functions
chargen	19	Sends a stream of standard characters when polled. Not only isn't this service used anymore, but it can also be used to generate a denial of service by having it continually spit out character streams.
daytime	13	Returns the time of day. Not really needed for any modern system functions.
discard	9	Discards whatever is sent to it silently. Mainly used for testing purposes.
echo	7	Replies back with whatever was sent to it. Like chargen, echo can be used in denial-of-service attacks by sending it a steady stream of data to echo.
finger	79	Much has been said about this service earlier. Very useful to hackers.
qotd (quote of the day)	17	Sends out a little quote or phrase that the system administrator sets up when you log on.

Information Leaks

When hackers or crackers are looking to get into a system, they start by doing some basic reconnaissance. They try to find out as much about your system and network before trying break in. Just like burglars casing a neighborhood, they look for the electronic equivalent of lights off, newspapers stacking up, loose windows, and so on. They do this with a number of tools, like port scanners and other hacking tools available on the Internet. Unfortunately, many operating systems are all too eager to help out these illicit information gatherers. Like chatty doormen, they give out vital system information without so much as an ID card.

Windows is particularly guilty of these transgressions. Because it was designed to be a plug-and-play network system, it offers all kinds of information to any system that polls it with the right commands. As mentioned earlier, incorrectly configured DNS servers can also expose a lot of information about your network configuration. Finally, an amazing amount of information can be gleaned from using public search engines such as Google. People often leave things in public directories of Web servers, thinking that just because they aren't linked from a Web page they won't show up in search engines. This is not true and you should definitely make a practice of regularly "Googling" your company's name and URLs to see if anything interesting comes up.

With this data, an outside user can generate user lists, shared drives and directories, system names, employee names, and other information. They can then leverage this data to perform brute force hacking by trying different password combinations using automated programs. Or they can use it in a social engineering attack (see the sidebar on system cracking).

Anatomy of a System Crack

Here is an example of how a cracker would use some of the methods listed in this chapter to methodically try to gain illicit access. Let's say the hacker wanted to break into Example.com and gain access to employee data.

1. First, he would start by staking out the objective. With a quick visit to Example.com's Web site to view the whois information, he could determine what IP ranges are used. He could also get the name of some of their system administrators from the technical contact section in whois.
2. Next, he would perform a port scan on the IP addresses found to see what systems are answering and what services they are running.
3. Using a more complex tool, like the vulnerability scanner in this chapter, the would-be hacker can gather even more information on the systems and which ones are vulnerable to what attacks.
4. By using the port scanner or vulnerability tester, the hacker could determine that one of the servers allowed NetBIOS null sessions that could generate a list of all the users on the system. Also, the hacker found that the Web server was vulnerable to a buffer overflow condition and was vulnerable to a Windows exploit that allowed access to any of the directories on that server.
5. The hacker could then search on the Internet using keywords for tools to exploit these weaknesses. In all likelihood, he could find a tool to give him administrator-level access using the buffer overflow hole.
6. Even if the systems had no vulnerabilities that allowed direct access, the hacker could use the information gathered thus far for brute force attacks on the password file or social engineering. He could masquerade as a system administrator and call a user and ask for her password. Or he could call the help desk, claiming to be a user who had forgotten his password and get the help desk to change the password to one of the hacker's choosing. The variations are as limitless as the deviousness of the cracker's mind.

Denial of Service

If they can't gain access to your system, many computer criminals are just as happy to take down your system so that nobody else can use it. This is especially true of high-profile sites or political targets. In the case of large e-commerce operations, this can cost millions of dollars per hour of downtime. Denial of Service (DoS) can come in many forms, from simply swamping the main routers with traffic to actually taking advantage of a weakness in a program to crash that service and therefore the server. The former is hard to protect against, but the latter are very preventable by identifying and then fixing or eliminating the condition that allows the DoS attack.

Vulnerability Scanners to the Rescue

As you can see, modern computer networks have multiple potential areas of insecurity. How do you protect all these avenues of attack? You might start to feel like a single guard trying to protect a giant castle with multiple windows, doors, and other ways to get in. You can't be everywhere at once. You could spend all day, every day, just checking for these security holes manually. Even if you tried to automate it with scripts, it would seem to take dozens of programs. Well, fortunately for you and your sanity, there are packages out there called **vulnerability scanners** that will automatically check all these areas and more.

Nessus: A Vulnerability Scanner with Built-in Port Scanner

Nessus

Author/primary contact:	Renaud Deraison
Web site:	www.nessus.org
Platforms:	Linux, BSD UNIX
License:	GPL
Version reviewed:	2.0.10a
Other resources:	

See the mailing lists in the section "Robust Support Network."

Nessus is a truly amazing program. It is a great example of how well open source projects can work. It is robust, well documented, well maintained, and top of its class. Nessus has consistently been rated in the top of all vulnerability scanners, commercial or noncommercial. This is amazing when you consider its counterparts cost thousands of dollars and are created by large companies. It continues to impress and improve, and most importantly, to protect thousands of companies' networks. There are some design features that make Nessus unique and superior to other vulnerability scanners.

Depth of Tests

Nessus currently offers over 2,000 individual vulnerability tests that cover practically every area of potential weakness in systems. Very few scanners out there can compete with this level of testing, and new tests are being added daily by a worldwide network of developers. The speed of release of new tests for emerging vulnerabilities is usually measured in days if not hours. Its plug-in based architecture allows new tests to be added easily. Here is a list of all the categories of tests that Nessus runs.

- Backdoors
- CGI abuses
- Cisco
- Denial of Service
- Finger abuses
- FTP
- Gaining a shell remotely
- Gaining root remotely
- General
- Miscellaneous
- Netware
- NIS
- Port scanners
- Remote file access
- RPC
- Settings
- SMTP problems
- SNMP
- Untested
- Useless services
- Windows
- Windows: User management

You can turn off whole categories of tests if they don't apply or if you are worried they could be dangerous to your systems, or you can deactivate individual tests if you have a concern about a specific one. For example, you may prefer to disable the untested category, which contains tests that haven't been fully tested yet (caveat emptor). See Appendix E for a complete list of all the security checks. Keep in mind, though, that this list is only complete as of the date listed and will be changing constantly as new plug-ins are added.

Client-Server Architecture

Nessus uses a client-server architecture to run its security checks. The server runs the tests and the client configures and controls the sessions. The fact that the client and server can be separated offers some unique advantages. This means that you can have your scanning server outside your network, yet access it from inside your network via the client. This also allows other operating systems to be supported via different clients. There are currently UNIX and Windows clients available, with projects to create additional ones ongoing. There is also now a Web client interface available, which makes Nessus truly platform independent (at least on the client end).

Independence

Because Nessus is open source and the plug-ins are written by a diverse group of individuals in the security community, you don't have to worry about any conflicts of interest that may arise with commercial companies. For example, if the provider of a commercial vulnerability scanner has a large contract with a major OS provider, they may be less critical and slower to release tests for their products. An open source project like Nessus has no financial motivation not to develop and release tests right away. And because of its extendability, you can always write your own rather than wait for the official one.

Built-in Scripting Language

To supplement the plug-in architecture, Nessus has its own scripting language called **Nessus Attack Scripting Language** (NASL). This easy-to-learn utility language allows you to quickly and easily write your own custom security plug-ins without having to know C or all of the internal workings of the main program. (There is an example of writing a custom plug-in with NASL later in this chapter.)

Integration with Other Tools

Nessus can be used by itself or with several other open source security tools. Some of these are discussed in this chapter, and all of them are best-of-breed tools. You can use Nmap, the best port scanner in the world, for the port scanning part of the job, rather than the built-in one. The Nessus port scanner is faster and a little more efficient with memory, but Nmap allows for a lot more options and settings as you learned in Chapter 4. Almost all of the Nmap settings are configurable from within the Nessus client. Nessus also works with Nikto and Whisker, tools that run more complex tests on Web servers; CGI programs; and Hydra, a tool for running brute-force password attacks against common services. The functionality of these tools is written right into Nessus, so you can make configuration changes from a single interface.

Smart Testing

Nessus can be set up so that it doesn't automatically run all of the vulnerability tests on every host. Based on the results of a port's scan or other input such as past vulnerability tests, Nessus will run only tests appropriate to that machine. So if the server is not running a Web server, it won't run Web server-related tests. Nessus is also smart in that it doesn't automatically assume that Web servers will run on port 80, but rather checks all the possible ports for signs of a Web server. Nessus will even find multiple instances of services running on different ports. This is especially important if you are inadvertently running a Web server or other public service on an unusual port.

Knowledge Base

Nessus can save all scan results in a database called the Knowledge Base. This allows it to use the results of past scans to intelligently figure out what tests to run. You can use this to avoid doing a port scan every time you run Nessus, because it will remember what ports it found open last time on each host and test only those. It can also remember what hosts it saw last time and test only new hosts. I don't recommend you do this every time, because you may miss new ports that open up on machines or new vulnerabilities that show up on previously scanned boxes. However, it can allow you to run scans more often with less bandwidth and processor power as long as you do a complete scan on a regular basis.

Multiple Report Formats

Nessus has some of the best reporting capabilities in the open source field. Although it's not perfect, it can output your scan data in just about any format. Basic HTML and HTML with pie charts and graphs are two of the more popular formats. These reports include summary data and are suitable for posting to an internal Web site with little or no editing. Other report formats supported include XML, LaTeX, and good old plain text. The Windows client offers additional report formats. There are additional tools available, discussed in the coming chapters, that allow you to do further manipulation of the data.

Robust Support Network

Nessus has an extensive support network for getting help, both on basic installation and use as well as more complex programming and customization. There are no fewer than five Nessus mailing lists, each dedicated to a different area. Subscribers to the lists will notice that Renaud himself frequently answers many of the questions. Try getting this kind of support from a commercial company! There is an archive of all the past posts so you can check to see if your question has ever been answered. The following are the main Nessus mailing lists.

- nessus: A general discussion list about Nessus, of course!
- nessus-devel: Talks about the development of the upcoming versions.
- nessus-cvs: Shows the CVS commits made on the Nessus tree.
- nessus-announce: A low-traffic moderated list that is dedicated to the announcements of the availability of new releases.
- plug-ins-writers: A list dedicated to the writing of new Nessus plug-ins. If you want to write your own security checks, you should subscribe to it.

To subscribe to any of the above lists, send an e-mail to majordomo@list.nessus.org with the following text in the body of the e-mail:

```
Subscribe listname
```

Replace *listname* with the name of the list you want to subscribe to. To unsubscribe, do the same but write Unsubscribe *listname* in the body.

Nessus has quite a bit of documentation on its Web site, including detailed instructions on installation, basic operation, and tutorials on how to write your own security checks in NASL. To my knowledge, no one has yet attempted to completely cover all the features and settings on the Nessus client in a single document. This section tries to do just that.

Nessus provides you with a quick and easy way to test your network and systems for almost every kind of vulnerability, so let's install it.

Installing Nessus for Linux Systems

There are two prerequisites you must have before installing Nessus, and two others that are nice to have installed beforehand to take full advantage of the add-on capabilities.

1. The two prerequisites are the Gimp Tool Kit (GTK) and libpcap. If you installed Nmap in Chapter 4, you should already have these programs installed. If not, you can download GTK from:

   ```
   ftp://ftp.gimp.org/pub/gtk/v1.2
   ```

   and libpcap from:

   ```
   www.tcpdump.org
   ```

2. The two programs that are optional but recommended are OpenSSL and Nmap. Nessus can use Nmap as its port scanner and OpenSSL for secure communications between the server and client.

There are three ways to install Nessus on UNIX systems, ranging from very simple to slightly more complicated. This is one case where I recommend the more extensive install process in order to have more control over your installation.

The easiest way to install Nessus is to run the auto-installer script remotely. You can do this by typing:

```
lynx -source http://install.nessus.org | sh
```

This initiates the installation script and loads the program on your computer. However, I don't really recommend doing this as it could open your computer up to an attack if that URL was ever compromised. Follow these steps for a safer way to do it.

1. Download the auto-install script manually from install.nessus.org and run it with the following command:

   ```
   sh nessus-installer.sh
   ```

If the auto-install script doesn't work properly for you, you must compile it manually.

NOTE: I recommend that you follow all these steps even if the auto-install "script" (this is a bit of a misnomer since the file actually contains the whole program and all of its elements) seems to work, because with a complex program like Nessus it is sometimes hard to tell what is being done and where it is bombing out if things go wrong with the script. At least when you do the process manually you have a better idea of what happens during the install process.

2. To install Nessus manually, you must first get the following four Nessus files, either from the CD-ROM or from the Nessus Web site, and install them in this order. If you do them out of order, Nessus won't work properly.

- Nessus-libraries: These are the core libraries needed for Nessus to run.
- Libnasl: This is the module for NASL, the built-in scripting language.
- Nessus-core: This is the main Nessus program.
- Nessus-plug-ins: This module contains all the plug-ins that do the security checks. To make sure you have all the latest plug-ins, you should run the nessus-update-plugins script after installation to grab any new ones.

3. Change into the nessus-libraries directory (using the `cd` command), then type the standard compile sequence of:

```
./configure
make
make install
```

There may be special instructions at the end of each compilation process. For example, nessus-libraries will want to you add /usr/local/lib to a file called ld.so.conf in /etc and then type `ldconfig`. This revises your libraries' directories so your operating system can find where your special Nessus directories are. Make sure you follow these instructions before going to the next step.

4. Do the same for libnasl. At the end of compilation, it will want you to make sure that /usr/local/sbin is in your PATH directory. This is the statement that contains a path to look for executables every time a command is typed. The install program should do it automatically for you, but check this by typing:

```
echo $PATH
```

This prints your PATH statement to the screen. If it doesn't have /usr/local/sbin and /usr/local/bin in there, you can add it by editing the bash.rc file in /etc (the correct path for Mandrake Linux using the bash shell). Other distribution locations may vary slightly.

5. Repeat this process for the other two modules.

When you are done, you will have installed Nessus. However, you will still need to do a few things to set it up before you can use it.

Setting Up Nessus

The first thing you need do to get Nessus ready to run is create a certificate that Nessus will use for SSL communications.

1. Type:

```
nessus-mkcert
```

This runs a utility that creates a secure certificate for your installation. You can also use third-party certificates signed by a certificate authority like VeriSign with Nessus.

If you get "file not found" error, make sure both /usr/local/bin and /usr/local/sbin are in your PATH statement (as described in the installation procedure).

Answer the questions as they come up. You will want to register the certificate to your organization. If you are not sure what values to put in, accept the defaults provided.

2. Next, you need to create some user accounts so that you can log into Nessus. Because of the client-server architecture, you have to log into the server with the client before running any scans. Nessus can have any number of users with rules for each user, which you designate in this setup phase. If you are going to be the only person using Nessus, then you just need to set up one user with no rules, though you can limit the IP addresses that it can log on from if you want to. If you have multiple users, this functionality can help you track who is using your Nessus server.

To create a new user, type:

```
nessus-adduser
```

This walks you through creating a new user account.

3. Run this command each time you need to create a new user. You must have at least one user set up to be able to use Nessus.

Now you are finally ready to run Nessus.

1. Make sure you are running X-Windows (the graphical environment) and start up a shell.

2. From the command line, type:

```
nessusd &
```

This starts the Nessus server process. The & (ampersand) indicates to run the program in the background so you can type another command.

3. The next command to type is:

```
nessus
```

This starts the client piece of Nessus and displays the graphical interface.

You are now ready to start using Nessus.

Nessus Login Page

The first thing you will see is the login page for Nessus (see Figure 5.1). Because of the client-server architecture, you must first log in to a Nessus server before you can begin using Nessus. If you will be running the client and server on the same machine, the correct login parameters are:

- Server: Localhost
- Port:1241
- Login: The login you created when you set up Nessus
- Password: The password you created when you set up Nessus

You can also run the client on a separate machine from the server. In this case, just replace `localhost` with the IP address or host name of your Nessus server. This gives you the ability to log in from home and access the Nessus servers at work so you can start scans late at night. Or you may have your Nessus server in a data center where it has access to lots of bandwidth and need to access it from your desk inside your firewall. This flexibility is a big advantage of Nessus over some of the competitive scanners and increases its scalability for larger organizations. You can also perform other local functions on the client without logging into a Nessus server. You can bring up scans run previously to view and manipulate them. You can configure the scan options, but you can't access the plug-ins or preferences section without being logged into a server (because these are saved on the server side).

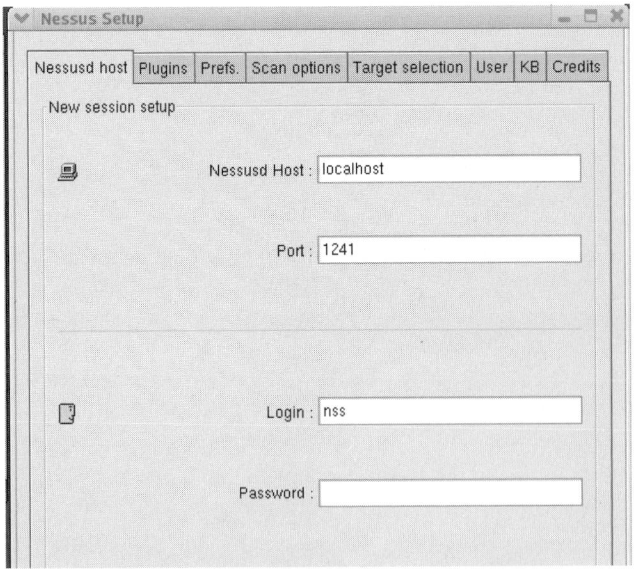

Figure 5.1 Nessus Login Screen

Nessus Plugins Tab

Once you are logged in, you can access the other tab sections. The Plugins tab is where you can selectively enable or disable certain groups of plug-ins as well as individual plug-ins (see Figure 5.2). Each category is listed, and when you click on a category the individual plug-ins in that category appear in the lower section. By deselecting the box to the right of an item, you can disable that category or plug-in.

Plug-ins that may cause a problem with a service or can crash servers are highlighted with a triangular exclamation symbol (see Figure 5.2). Nessus also has buttons that make it easy to quickly enable all plug-ins, enable all but dangerous plug-ins, disable all plug-ins, or load a custom plug-in. You can use the Filter button to sort the plug-ins by Name, Description, Summary, Author, ID number, or Category. I recommend that you generally run Nessus with dangerous plug-ins disabled, unless you have prepared for a true denial of service test and are willing to risk crashing some of your servers.

Nessus Preferences Tab

Most of the server-side Nessus options are configured on the Preferences tab (see Figure 5.3). The following sections and subsections cover these options.

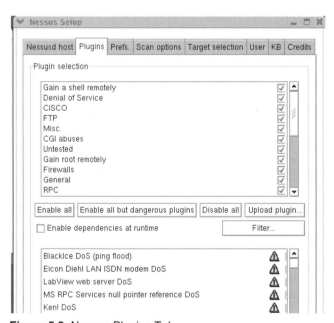

Figure 5.2 Nessus Plugins Tab

Figure 5.3 Nessus Preferences Tab

Nmap   You use these Nmap settings to customize the configuration of how the port scan part of the test runs. Many of these correlate directly to the Nmap settings discussed in Chapter 4, so refer there for details on what each option means.

- TCP scanning technique: Set the kind of port scan you want, for example SYN, FIN, or Connect.
- Timing policy: See the "Nmap Timing Options" section in Chapter 4.

You can also enter a location for an Nmap results file so that Nessus will use that data rather than run a new scan.

Ping the remote host   This selection lets you ping the machines on the target network to determine first if they are alive, or just scan all the IPs in the target range. By default, Nessus tries ICMP and TCP pings on both the Web and secure socket layers ports. If a host is online, it should respond to one of these polls. This is the setting I recommend using most of the time, because you don't want to waste time and bandwidth running the tests against dead addresses. However, if you are scanning from outside a firewall, you may want to run Nessus without pinging the hosts so you don't risk missing anything. You can also configure the number of tries it makes before considering a nonresponding host dead. The default of 10 is probably too high for most high-speed networks. Unless you are scanning from a dial-up connection, turn the retries rate down to 3 to speed up the scan process, especially on large target networks. You can also set whether dead hosts should appear in the report. Usually you don't want these to be included because they will skew your overall scan statistics, reporting that there are more hosts scanned on your network than there really are. However, this can be useful when you want to know each IP that was contacted.

Login configurations This section is where you set up login accounts if you want Nessus to test some services at a deeper level. The standard Nessus scan tests the network as if it had no additional knowledge about it other than just the IP addresses. However, if you specify an account and password for a certain service, Nessus will run additional tests on it. For example, if you enter a Windows domain login (SMB account), it will further test your Windows domain security as a logged-on user. By default, it tests only for an anonymous FTP server using the account of "anonymous" and the standard password of an e-mail address. You can have it test FTP, HTTP, IMAP, NNTP, POP2, POP3, and SNMP services with valid logins.

There is a special section for testing HTTP login forms. You can give it the specific URL and form fields to be filled in. By default, it will test an index directory for blank user and password fields.

Brute-force login (Hydra) This section lets you take advantage of the add-on program Hydra, which tests the integrity of your system's passwords. You give it a file of logins and passwords and it will attempt to go through the whole list on each service you designate. I don't recommend you use this option unless you are prepared to deal with the aftermath of a brute-force attack, which may leave many users locked out of their accounts as the scanner maxes out the number of login attempts they are allowed. A better way to test your password strength would be to run your password file through a password cracker offline. However, it might be useful to test a single service that isn't used much, such as FTP or Telnet. With Hydra, you can attempt brute force on the following services: Cisco IOS standard and enable passwords, FTP, HTTP, ICQ, IMAP, LDAP, NNTP, PCNFS, POP3, Rexec, SMB (Windows Domain), SOCKS 5, Telnet, and VNC.

SMB use host SID to enumerate local users This section gives a range of User ID (UID) numbers to try to get additional information about the user names in the domain. The default uses UIDs 1,000–1,020, which always encompasses at least the administrator and guest users accounts on Windows networks. Nessus will try administrator and guest with passwords as blank and the same as the login.

Services This section has to do with testing SSL services. You can specify certificates to check and get reports on the level of encryption your Web servers will accept. This can locate servers that are still accepting older 40-bit encryption, which is now considered insecure for highly sensitive data.

Web mirroring   This setting lets you adjust how deeply into a Web site the scanner will read looking for any flaws or security holes. You can also change the default start directory.

Misc. Information on the News Server   If there is a Network News (NNTP) server located on any of the IPs in the target range, Nessus checks the settings and restrictions set on postings. This ensures that your news servers aren't susceptible to spamming or other misuse.

Test HTTP dangerous methods   The Integrist test checks to see if any Web servers ' on the network will allow dangerous commands such as PUT and DELETE. This is disabled by default because the test could delete your home page if your server responds to these commands.

Ftp writable directories   This checks for FTP servers that allow write access to anonymous users (which is not a good idea at all). The default setting checks the permissions listed by the file system and responds if one shows as being writable. You can also have it ignore what the file system says and try to write a file anyway to test that there are no writable directories. Again, like the Integrist test above, be careful with this option because you could end up overwriting files on your FTP server.

SMTP settings   These settings are used for additional testing of a mail system. Nessus does this by attempting to send bogus e-mail messages to see how the system responds. Nessus.org is used as the default domain the test mail would be coming from, though this is configurable here. Many mail servers won't respond if the mail server name isn't real. You may want to change this address if you are an outside consultant and want your client to know where the dummy e-mails are coming from. However, don't use your own domain if you are scanning from within a company; this will confuse your mail server to see e-mail coming from itself and may produce unreliable test results.

Libwhisker options   These options are for use with the add-on Whisker program, which tests the integrity of your Web servers. Refer to the Whisker documentation program for explanations of these settings. These options are disabled by default.

SMB use domain SID to enumerate users   This Windows domain test tries to identify users based on their Security ID (SID). In typical Windows domains, SID 1,000 is the administrator, and several other standard designations are used for system accounts such as guest. Nessus polls this range of SIDs to try to extrapolate user names.

HTTP NIDS evasion   This section lets you use various techniques to avoid detection by a network intrusion detection system (NIDS) by crafting and mal-forming special URLs for attacks on Web servers. You need the Whisker add-on program to take advantage of these. The various tests try to send strange URLs to your Web servers to see if they will allow a user to do things that they aren't supposed to be able to do using CGI scripts. For a complete description of these tests, see the Whisker documentation or the article at www.wiretrip.net/rfp/libwhisker/README.

These methods are disabled by default because they tend to create a lot of network traffic and may generate many false positives. However, if you do run a NIDS on your network and want to see if it's really working, you can run these tests to see if it picks up your scans.

NIDS evasion   This section is similar to the HTTP NIDS evasion section, except that Nessus does strange things to the actual TCP packets to avoid pattern-matching NIDS rather than just the URL requests. Most modern NIDS will catch these tricks, but if you have an older system or one that hasn't been patched in a while, it is worth trying these to see if your NIDS catches them. Once again, this will cause your reports to contain data that may be suspect, so it's not recommended for normal vulnerabilities testing.

Scan Options Tab

Unlike the individual tests on the Preferences tab, this tab contains settings that affect the overall scan (see Figure 5.4).

Port range   This controls which ports are scanned during the port scan phase of the test. The default is 1–15,000, which should catch most normal services. However, you should open it up to scan all 65,535 TCP and UDP ports if you want to search for Trojan horses and other services operating on unusual high ports. You should do a full port scan of the machines on your network on regular basis, either monthly or quarterly depending on the network size.

Consider unscanned ports as closed   This option causes Nessus to declare unscanned ports as closed. If you didn't set your port range wide enough in the last option, you may miss something, but it makes your scan run faster and puts less traffic on the network.

Number of hosts to test at the same time   This sets the number of hosts that Nessus tests concurrently. On a large network, you may be tempted to crank this setting way up and run all of them at once. However, at some point this becomes counterproductive and your scan will actually take longer or may not finish at all if it gets bogged down on one particular host. In fact, on average servers (under 2Ghz) machines, I recommend changing this to 10 hosts from the default setting of 30. This seems to be the optimal setting for most scans. However, if you have a super-server and have a very large network, you can try turning it up as high as you can get away with.

Number of checks to perform at the same time   Nessus has the ability to multitask not only how many hosts it scans at once but also the tests. The default setting of 10

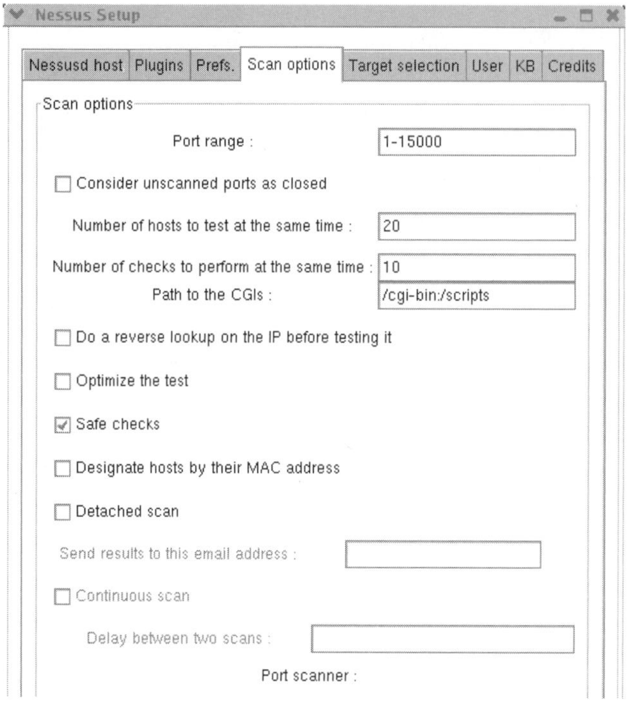

Figure 5.4 Nessus Scan Options Tab

seems to work well; however, you can do more or fewer depending on your how much horsepower your Nessus server has.

Path to the CGIs   This is the default location where Nessus will look for CGI scripts on the remote system to test them. If you have an unusual configuration on a machine, you should change this to the correct path so that Nessus will test your CGIs.

Do a reverse lookup on the IP before testing it   This setting attempts to do a reverse DNS lookup and determine every IP's hostname before testing them. This will considerably slow down your scan and is disabled by default.

Optimize the test   Nessus, by default, attempts to be smart about the tests it runs and won't run tests that don't apply to a particular host. You can disable this here so Nessus will run every test on every host regardless of what the port scan finds.

Safe checks   This setting is always on by default. It means Nessus won't perform any unsafe checks that may crash or otherwise harm a server. It will depend on banners or other information to determine if a host has a particular vulnerability. I recommended to always keep this on, even though it will result in more false positives.

Designate hosts by their MAC address   Enable this option if you want Nessus to show hosts in the report by their MAC address rather than IP address, which is the default. If you have a good database of MAC addresses on your network and you have a hard time correlating IP addresses to specific hosts because of DHCP, this may create a more useful report for you.

Detached scan   This feature allows Nessus to run scans without being connected to the client. This is usually done to run scans at unusual times without human intervention. It can be set up to e-mail the scan report to a specific address when it is done.

Continuous scan   This feature starts a new scan on a regular basis. You can use this to set up an automatic scan of your network on a scheduled basis. Set the "Delay between two scans" timing in seconds (86,400 for a daily scan, 604,800 for weekly scans, and approximately 2,592,000 for monthly scans). There are better ways to do this, such as using the Nessus Command Center (NCC) tool described in Chapter 8. However, if you don't want to set up the Web server and database required by NCC, this feature is a quick and easy way to do a regular scan.

Port scanner   This has several global settings for the port scanner portion of the test.

- tcp connect() scan: This uses the built-in port scanner in Nessus rather than Nmap. The benefit of using this is that it is much less memory-intensive and faster. However, it is noisier on the network and will leave logs on most machines it scans. Also, you don't have as much control over the settings as you do with Nmap.
- Nmap: This uses Nmap and the assorted settings configured on the Preferences tab for the port scan.
- SYN Scan: This feature was implemented in version 2.0. It offers a built-in SYN scan as well as the tcp connect scan mentioned above. This eliminates some of the noise of the scan but still doesn't give you the granular control that Nmap does.
- Ping the remote host: This pings hosts in the target range to make sure they are alive before performing any tests on them.
- scan for LaBrea Tar-pitted hosts: La Brea tar-pitted hosts are set up to detect ports scans and cause them to spool out into infinity. This can slow down or crash your scan. This setting tries to detect hosts with this protection and avoid them.

Target Selection Tab

This tab is where you set your targets to scan (see Figure 5.5). The following list describes the ways you can designate scan targets.

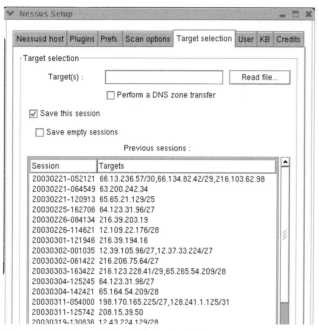

Figure 5.5 Nessus Target Selection Tab

- Single IP address: 192.168.0.1
- IP addresses separated by commas: 192.168.0.1,192.168.0.2
- IP ranges separated by a dash: 192.168.0.1-192.168.0.254
- Standard slash notation: 192.168.0.1/24 (a class C network of 256 addresses)
- A host name: myhost.example.com
- Any combination of the above separated by commas: 192.168.0.1-192.168.0.254, 195.168.0.1/24,192.168.0.1-192.168.0.254

There are several options you can set on this tab.

Read file   Click here to read your targets from a file. This must be a standard text file with addresses formatted as in the above example.

Perform a DNS zone transfer   This attempts to pull a zone file for the domain represented by the target IPs. This doesn't work on private (nonroutable) IP addresses.

Save this session   Keeps a record of the targets and settings so they can be restored at a future date. By default, this is turned on.

Save empty sessions   This saves sessions even when they contain no data, for example, an IP range with no live hosts in it.

Previous sessions   This lists all your previously run sessions and allows you to reload them by clicking on the listing.

User Tab

This tab shows all the users you have set up to use the Nessus server and any rules associated with those users (for example, only able to log on from a specific IP address). These are set up when you create the user with the nessus-adduser script, but you can also edit or add rules for any users from this tab at any time.

KB (Knowledge Base) Tab

This tab contains the configuration and controls for the Nessus Knowledge Base (see Figure 5.6). This is one of the most useful features Nessus offers. It is disabled by default, so you need to select the Enable KB saving check box to turn it on. The Knowledge Base keeps track of all the scans you have done. Then when you want to run that scan again, Nessus uses that data to be intelligent about which hosts it scans and what tests are run on those hosts. Each setting is described below.

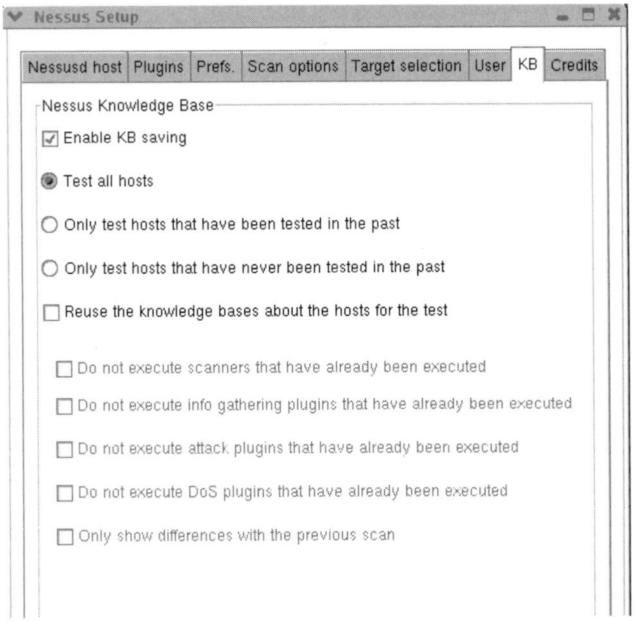

Figure 5.6 Nessus Knowledge Base Tab

Test all hosts   This is the default setting. Knowledge Base data will be saved but each host will be tested in full.

Test only hosts that have been tested in the past   This setting has Nessus test only hosts that it has tested in the past in the target range. This means it will not scan for any new hosts. This reduces network traffic a little, but Nessus won't test any machines on your network that have been added since your last scan.

Test only hosts that have never been tested in the past   This is the opposite of that last setting; it looks only for new hosts on the target network. This is useful for doing a quick check for new machines on your network without scanning your existing machines.

Reuse the knowledge bases about the hosts for the test   This eliminates running certain tests based on what it found and the options you set.

- *Do not execute scanners that have already been executed.* This skips the port scanning portion of the test, relying on the results of past port scans.
- *Do not execute info gathering plug-ins that have already been executed.* Nessus won't run any information-gathering plug-ins that were run on previous scans. Any new information-gathering plug-ins that have been released and you have loaded since the last scan will be run.
- *Do not execute attack plug-ins that have already been executed.* This does the same as the last setting, but for attack plug-ins.
- *Do not execute DoS plug-ins that have already been executed.* This does the same as the previous two settings, but applies to Denial of Service plug-ins.
- *Only show differences with the previous scan.* This will run a diff scan; its report shows the differences between the last two scans. This can be useful to see what has changed on your network since the last scan. This can also be done with the Nessus Command Center, described in Chapter 8.

Max age of a saved KB (in secs)   This setting prevents the server from using a scan Knowledge Base that is older than the entry. The default setting is 86,400 seconds, which is one day. You can set this up to 60 days, which is 5,184,000 seconds. Setting it for any longer is not useful, as you will be relying on data that is too old.

The Knowledge Base features can make your scanning quicker and easier. However, you should use the features selectively and always run a full scan on a regular basis (monthly is recommended).

Nessus Scan in Process Options

Once your scan is underway, Nessus displays a screen showing the status of your scan. You can see each host being tested and how far along in the process it is. It also shows you

Figure 5.7 Nessus Scan in Progress Screen

the plug-in that is running at the moment. Most of these fly by very quickly, but sometimes it will get stuck on a particular plug-in. You can stop the testing on that host only by clicking on the Stop button on the right side (see Figure 5.7). You can also click the Stop the whole test button at the bottom to stop all the testing and just report the results thus far.

NessusWX: A Windows Client for Nessus	
NessusWX	
Author/primary contact:	Victor Kirhenshtein
Web site:	www.securityprojects.org/nessuswx
Platforms:	Windows 98, NT, 2000, XP
License:	GPL
Version reviewed:	1.4.4
Other resources	nessuswx.nessus.org

NessusWX is a Windows client for Nessus. It represents the client end only of the program. Unfortunately, Nessus doesn't yet offer an all-Windows solutions for vulnerability testing. Tenable Network Security makes a commercial Windows Nessus port called

NeWT, but if you can't afford that you will have to use a UNIX-based Nessus server for your NessusWX client to attach to.

NessusWX is far more than just a clone of the UNIX client. Besides giving you access to your Nessus server from your Windows machine, NessusWX adds some features that are missing from the UNIX client. It also implements some of the other settings in a more logical and easier to use manner. If fact, some consider NessusWX a superior way to use Nessus. Just keep in mind that you will still need to have a UNIX Nessus server to connect to in order to run your scans. Also, because NessusWX is a separate programming effort, its features will sometimes be a little behind those of the native UNIX platform. Here are a few nice extras you get with NessusWX.

- MySQL support: You can import your Nessus scan into a MySQL database, either by directly importing it during the scan or saving it in MySQL format for later handling.
- Additional reporting formats: NessusWX lets you save your Nessus reports as a PDF file. Support for Microsoft Word format and other file formats is coming.
- Report manipulation: You can do some neat things, like marking certain alerts as false positives so they don't show up in the report. This can be useful if your boss gets upset when seeing a report with several security holes and you have to explain that they are false positives and not really valid.
- Cleaner user interface: In my opinion, the NessusWX user interface is a little easier to use than Nessus, and the options and preferences are presented in simplified manner. However, if you are accustomed to using the UNIX interface, this could confuse you because some things look quite a bit different. But overall it is an improvement over the sometimes jumbled and redundant options on the UNIX client.

Installing NessusWX

NessusWX is easy to install. Use the file from the CD-ROM or download the binary, self-extracting file from nessuswx.nessus.org/index.htm#download.

You can also get packages with the source code if you care to monkey around with it and see if you can improve on it. But if you are not intending on doing that, there is no real reason to get the sources. Simply click on the file and the install program will guide you through the process.

Using the NessusWX Windows Client

The NessusWX interface looks different from the native UNIX client (see Figure 5.8). You won't see the same tabs described earlier, but all the configuration options discussed are available in this version. The NessusWX client makes it clearer which settings are client controlled and which are server controlled. The server-controlled settings are the ones found in the nessus.rc text file and constitute global settings, whereas the client-side set-

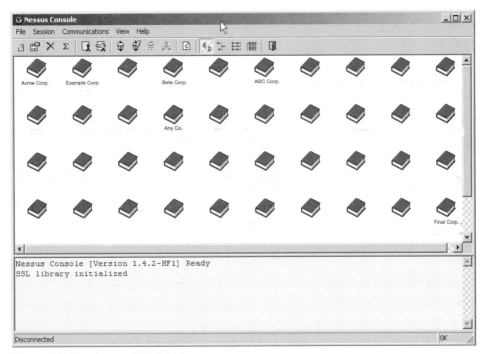

Figure 5.8 The NessusWX Interface

tings are mostly related to specific scans. You can see the contents of the nessus.rc file and edit it by choosing Server Preferences from the Communication menu.

Another nice thing about the Windows client is that you can interactively create scan configurations (called **sessions**) and then connect to a Nessus server. This means you can do your configuration offline without connecting to the server. However, to start a scan or view and configure the server-side preferences you need to be connected and log in. To do this, on the Communications tab click on Connect. You can also use the Quick Connect option and set a default server to always log in to. It will also remember your password and login so that you don't have to enter it each time, which is nice (though certainly less secure!).

Creating a Session Profile

The first thing you want to do is create a session profile. This is a target or collection of targets that you want to scan.

1. From the Profile menu choose New. Enter a name for the scan session in the dialog box that displays. This name appears at the top of the scan report, so you may want to name it something sufficiently descriptive.

2. You will then see the Session Properties window (see Figure 5.9). Be sure to click Apply after entering data on each tab.

3. Click Add to specify the addresses to scan. Notice the easy-to-use format for entering different ranges. You can also opt to import a list of targets by entering the name of a text file that contains them.

4. Click Remove to delete hosts from the status screen as they complete or choose not to show the executing plug-ins as they run.

5. Next, click on the Options tab (see Figure 5.10) to set your scan options. These settings are much the same as the scan options in the UNIX client.

6. The Port scan tab is where you configure the port scan portion of the test (see Figure 5.11). The default setting is only the common server ports (1–1,024) rather than the 1–15,000 setting on the UNIX client. Of course, you can change these to whatever you want. There are two other settings available, Well-known services or Specific range. The latter lets you set any port range you want.

7. Once you are logged in, the Plugins tab offers you the ability to selectively enable or disable individual plug-ins or whole groups of plug-ins. You can actually configure some of the plug-in parameters right from the client. Things like the default password used, default directories, and so forth can be set here, which isn't possible on the UNIX client.

8. There is also a Comments tab. This neat addition lets you document different scans so that you can remember later when you look at them what you were trying to do.

9. Click OK to close the window.

Figure 5.9 NessusWX Session Properties Screen

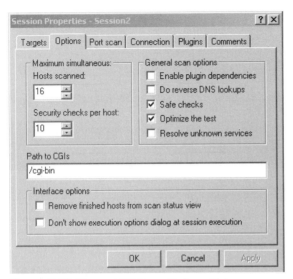

Figure 5.10 NessusWX Scan Options Tab

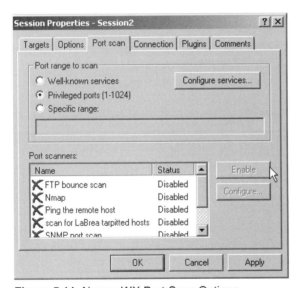

Figure 5.11 NessusWX Port Scan Options

10. Once you have all your scan settings configured, double-click on the icon for the scan profile you want to use and then click Execute. The scan should start and bring up a status screen while the scan executes (see Figure 5.12).

You will notice that the Scan Status screen for NessusWX is more detailed than the UNIX client. It shows things such as the percentage done with the port scan. The UNIX client shows this only as a bar, which isn't accurate. It also shows

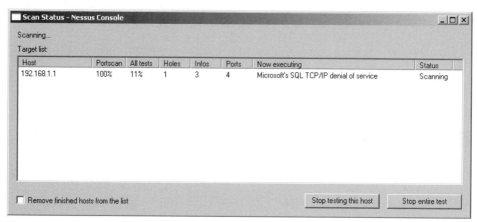

Figure 5.12 NessusWX Scan in Process Screen

how far the tests are from being done and a running total of open ports, information alerts, security warnings, and security holes found for each host. And, just like
the UNIX client, you can stop scanning individual hosts or the whole test.

NessusWX Reports

To get, create, and view NessusWX reports, right click on any scan profile and select
Results. Several options on this screen allow you to control the output of the reports. You
can choose whether the report is sorted by host or by vulnerability. You can select to leave
false positives out of the report and to include the scan configuration so you can remember
what settings were used to obtain these results. You can also have it show only reports on
open ports, and low, medium, or high severity alerts by deselecting the check boxes for
each one. This gives you more flexibility on how the report will look. This is important if
you are presenting these reports to nontechnical management, auditors, customers, or
other outsiders.

Report options in NessusWX include .nsr, which is the older native Nessus format,
.nbe, html, plain text, and .pdf format. All of the results are stored in a database, so you
can easily retrieve old scans. You can also compare results from one scan to another by
using the diff option. The basic HTML report has some nice additions from the UNIX
HTML reports. It adds the profile name, so you know what was scanned. It also timestamps it and gives other statistics, such as how long the scan took. In addition, the scan
can be ordered by IP address, as mentioned earlier, which greatly assists in finding a particular host, as anyone who has tried to sort through the randomly ordered UNIX scan
report can attest to. Unfortunately, it doesn't have the embedded HTML links that the
UNIX reports do, which would greatly improve the ease of navigation through the report.
(Hopefully someone is working on merging the best of the UNIX and Windows reports.)
Or you scan it all into a database and create your own reports using NCC, which is
described in Chapter 8.

Sample Nessus Scanning Configurations

With so many settings to choose from, it can be rather bewildering to know what to do for your first scan. It does take time to learn the intricacies of all the options, but here are a few sample configurations that should produce good results for the most common network configurations.

Sample Configuration 1: External scan of multiple IP addresses; no firewall   This is the simplest possible configuration and requires the fewest changes in the default Nessus configuration.

- Preferences: Leave everything wide open; no stealth is really needed. A SYN scan will reduce the amount of network traffic, however.
- Scan options: Depending on the number of hosts, you may want to use the built-in SYN scan. Scans of more than a few hosts may take a long time with Nmap.
- Leave all other options on the defaults.

Sample Configuration 2: External scan of a network with a single external IP address on the firewall   This is a little more complex and requires some stealth to get scan packets past the firewall.

- Preferences: Use Nmap to scan SYN and fragment packets. With a single IP, memory and timing are not an issue.
- Scan options: Don't ping the host, because most firewalls will drop your ping and you won't get any results.
- Leave all other options on the defaults. If you don't get anything back, try scanning without the port scan enabled.

Sample Configuration 3: External scan of a network with multiple public IP addresses on the firewall and DMZ

- Preferences: Use Nmap to scan SYN and fragment packets.
- Scan options: Ping hosts to eliminate dead IPs on the DMZ. For target networks larger than 20 hosts, use the built-in SYN scan.
- Leave all other options on the defaults. If you don't get anything back, try scanning without the port scan.

Sample Configuration 4: Multiple external IP addresses with a Network Intrusion Detection System

- Preferences: You may want to try some of the NIDS evasion techniques. Also, you can use exotic scan types such as FIN and XMAS if the public servers are not Windows machines. You can also try stretching out the timing on the scan packets, though this will make your scan take quite a bit longer.

- Scan options: Don't do a port scan at all, since this will surely tip off your NIDS.
- Plug-ins: You may want to disable some of the noisier plug-ins, such as the backdoors.

Sample Configuration 5: Internal scan behind the firewall With this kind of scan you are much less concerned about stealth (since you are already inside the firewall) and more concerned about the kind of data you generate.

- Preferences: A simple SYN scan will do since you aren't concerned with getting through a firewall. You don't need to fragment packets, as this will slow down your scan (twice the number of packets). If you are on a Windows network, enter your domain login information so that Nessus can check your Windows users settings. You may want to do one scan with the login credentials and one without to see what someone with no user information could get by just plugging into your LAN.
- Scan options: Use the built-in SYN scan for large numbers of hosts. Ping the remote hosts to cut quickly through dead IP addresses.
- Plug-ins: You may want to disable some of plug-in categories that don't apply to an internal scan, such as default UNIX accounts (if you don't have internal UNIX machines), and vice versa for the Windows plug-ins if you have an all UNIX environment. Cisco and firewalls don't really apply, unless you have internal LAN segments with firewalls. If you don't use Novell's Netware, you can turn this off. Disable others as applicable to your internal LAN environment.

Flamey the Tech Coders Corner:
Writing Your Own Nessus Scripts

As mentioned earlier, it is possible to customize and extend Nessus for your own specific needs because it is open source. It is even easier to add to Nessus than other open source programs because it has its own built-in scripting language, called Nessus Attack Scripting Language (NASL). NASL allows you to quickly and easily write new tests for your Nessus scans without delving into the Nessus engine or other complicated programming.

Note: You should at least have a working knowledge of programming though, specifically the C programming language, before jumping into NASL. NASL is very C-like without a lot of things such as structures and declaring variables. This makes it easy to quickly write a new script to test for some condition.

A NASL script looks much like any other program, with variables, if statements, and functions you can call. Thankfully, Renaud and his team created many functions you can use to easily do the work instead of having to figure out on your own how to craft a packet or check for an open port.

Each script has two sections. The first is the register section, which Nessus uses for documentation purposes. Here you tell Nessus what kind of script this is and provide a little information on it for users to know what it does. The second section is the attack section. This is where you actually execute your code against the remote machine and do something with the results.

For this example, let's say you are having a real problem with Yahoo Messenger on your network. Running Nessus or a port scanner turns up the open ports, but you want to be notified specifically when the Yahoo port shows up.

You can write a custom Nessus script using NASL to do just that. Machines with the Yahoo messenger program running show port 5,101 open, so using the NASL function get_port_state(), you can quickly and easily look for machines running this program and report it. Here is the sample code to accomplish this in NASL. All the lines with # in front of them are comments and are not read by the NASL interpreter.

```
# This is the register section.
# Check for Yahoo Messenger
#
if(description)
{
#This is the register section and contains information for Nessus
 script_name(english:"Looks for Yahoo Messenger Running");
 script_description(english:"This script checks to see if Yahoo
 Messenger is running");
 script_summary(english:"connects on remote tcp port 5101");
 script_category(ACT_GATHER_INFO);
 script_family(english:"Misc.");
 script_copyright(english:"This script was written by
Tony Howlett");
exit(0);
}


# This is the attack section.
# This checks to see if port 5101 is open on the remote system.
# If it is, return the warning
port=5101;
if(get_port_state(port))
{

 report = "Yahoo Messenger is running on this machine!";
 security_warning(port:5101, data:report);

}

# The end.
```

That's all there is to it! This simple script assumes two things: first, that the remote machine was port scanned at least up through port 5,101 as get_port_ state function will erroneously return true on port 5,101 if the state is unknown. It also assumes that a machine with port 5,101 open is running Yahoo when it may be some other application. If you want, you could code some additional logic to verify this, by grabbing a banner or some piece of the response and examining its characteristics.

This is a very simple example and much, much more can be done with NASL. Refer to the online references for NASL for more information on all the functions you can use and additional syntax. There is an excellent tutorial written by Renaud himself located at www.nessus.org/doc/nasl.html.

Considerations for Vulnerability Scanning

Now that you fully understand all the options, you are ready to start scanning. But before you let loose with the packets, here are a few words on responsible scanning. While I have mentioned some of these issues in Chapter 4, there are additional considerations for vulnerability testing. Port scanning is a fairly innocuous activity, although it is annoying when you see the activity showing up in your logs. Vulnerability testing, however, can be quite a bit more disruptive, crashing servers, taking down Internet connections, or even deleting data (for example, the Integrist test). Many of the Nessus tests are specifically designed to cause a denial-of-service attack. Even with the safe checks option turned on, the tests can cause problems with some systems. There are several morals to this story.

Scan with Permission

You should *never* scan a network that is not under your direct control or if you don't have explicit permission from the owner. Some of the activity initiated by Nessus could be legally considered hacking (especially with the denial-of-service checks turned on). Unless you want to take the chance of being criminally charged, sued civilly, or having a complaint lodged against you by your ISP, you should always scan with permission. Non-company outsiders such as consultants should make sure to obtain written permission with all the legal disclaimers necessary. There is a sample waiver form in Appendix D. Internal personnel should make sure they have authority to scan all the machines in the range they are scanning. Coordinate with other departmental personnel as necessary, such as firewall administrators and security staff.

Make Sure All Your Backups Are Current

You should always make sure your backups are current anyway, but it is doubly important when vulnerability scanning, just in case the scan causes a problem with a server. Doing a Nessus scan right after you run backups will ensure that you can restore the most current version. But also make sure you aren't running your scan during a backup. Not only could you cause a corruption of your backup data, but both processes will slow to a crawl.

Time Your Scan

Along the lines of the last comment, make sure you coordinate your scan to get the results you want with minimal impact on other employees. Scanning the mail server at 8:00 a.m. when everyone is getting their e-mail will probably not make you very popular with the staff. Schedule scans on always-up servers for off-hours, and be sure to avoid overlapping with other system administration and general activity levels (scanning an accountant's network on April 14th is not a good idea). If you are scanning internal machines, you will probably want to do it during the day unless you can arrange for everyone to leave their machines on at the end of the day. The best time to do it during business hours is generally around the lunch hour, as a minimal number of people will be using the network.

Don't Scan Excessively

Schedule your scans as often as you feel is necessary, but don't automatically think that nightly scans are going to make your network more secure. If you can't interpret and respond to scan reports on a daily basis, then don't do the scan; all it will do is put additional traffic on your network. Base your frequency on the capability of your staff to deal with the results. I recommend doing it at least once a month, but if you have a particularly busy network, you may want to do it weekly. Similarly, if you have a very small external network, you may feel comfortable with quarterly scans. Daily scans are probably excessive unless you have dedicated staff to handle the remediation work. If you have that much need for up-to-the minute protection, then use an intrusion detection system to supplement your vulnerability testing.

Place Your Scan Server Appropriately

If you want a true test of your external vulnerability (from the Internet), you should make sure your Nessus server is located outside your firewall. This can be on a home Internet connection, at a data center that is outside your company network, or at another company (perhaps you can negotiate a trade to use another company's facilities for scanning and let them use yours for the same). Remember, because of the Nessus client-server architecture, you can still control your scans from inside your firewall. Just make sure you enable the SSL support so communications between your client and the server are encrypted.

   If you are scanning your internal network, your server will have to be located inside your firewall. Loading Nessus on a laptop can facilitate doing scans from both inside and outside your network without requiring multiple machines.

What Vulnerability Testing Doesn't Find

While vulnerability testing is a valuable tool in your security arsenal, you shouldn't think of it as a silver bullet. There are still situations and areas that a vulnerability testing program won't help you with. You have to develop additional systems and procedures to lessen your exposure in these areas. The following include security issues that won't be found by vulnerability testing.

Logic Errors

Logic errors are security holes that involve faulty programming logic inside a program. These are generally undiscovered or unpatched bugs where the program does not perform as it was supposed to, for example, a Web login page that doesn't authenticate properly or one that allows users to get more privileges than they should have. Well-known logic errors in major programs might be included in the Nessus vulnerability tests, but most of them are too obscure to be noticed except by a dedicated hacker.

Undiscovered Vulnerabilities

Vulnerability testers rely on published reports of vulnerabilities. Usually once a vulnerability is announced, an add-on or plug-in for the system is written. With open source programs, this might take only a few days. However, during that time there may be a window of vulnerability because your scanner won't be finding that security hole if it exists. Of course, you could quickly write your own tests using NASL while you wait for the official one to come out.

Custom Applications

Vulnerability testing programs typically only address published commercial and open source programs. If you have a program that was developed for internal use only, a vulnerability tester probably won't test anything on it. If it uses standard protocols or subprograms such as HTTP, FTP, or SQL, then some of the tests may apply. There are additional programs specially designed to test code for its security that you should run on these applications. The good news is that with an open source vulnerability tester like Nessus, you can write tests custom designed for your in-house application.

People Security

All the testing in the world won't help you if you have poor or nonexistent security policies for your employees. As demonstrated in the sidebar, hackers denied technical means to gain access to your network can revert to social engineering, that is, trying to talk someone into giving them access. This can be surprisingly easy, because the hacker takes advantage of the basic human nature of people generally wanting to help others, especially people perceived as fellow employees. There is only one way to combat this kind of hacking, and it doesn't involve any technical systems. Having good security policies, educating employees about them, and enforcing them will lessen your exposure to these kinds of attacks.

Attacks That Are in Progress or Already Happened

Vulnerability testing only shows you potential security holes in your system; it won't tell if those holes have been exploited or alert you if an attack is taking place. (Catching attacks as they happen is the realm of intrusion detection systems and is covered in Chapter 7.) Programs like Nessus are purely preventative in nature, and they are effective only if you take action to fix problems when they are found. Vulnerability scanners won't fix them for you, although Nessus is very helpful in giving you detailed instructions on how to fix any issues found. And as Ben Franklin said, "An ounce of prevention is worth a pound of cure."

Network Sniffers

You can now properly secure and harden your systems and test your network for security vulnerabilities using proactive tools that help to keep your network healthy and secure. Now we will look at some tools that help you to act and react if you have a computer attack or security issue on your network in spite of all your preparations. Network sniffers fit into this category along with intrusion detection systems and wireless sniffers.

Chapter Overview

Concepts you will learn:
- Network sniffer fundamentals
- Ethernet history and operation
- How to do safe and ethical network sniffing
- Sample sniffer configurations
- Network sniffer applications

Tools you will use:
Tcpdump, WinDump, and Ethereal

Simply put, a **network sniffer** listens or "sniffs" packets on a specified physical network segment. This lets you analyze the traffic for patterns, troubleshoot specific problems, and spot suspicious behavior. A **network intrusion detection system** (NIDS) is nothing more than a sophisticated sniffer that compares each packet on the wire to a database of known bad traffic, just like an anti-virus program does with files on your computer.

Sniffers operate at a lower level than all of the tools described thus far. Referring to the OSI Reference model, sniffers inspect the two lowest levels, the physical and data link layers.

OSI Layer Number	Layer Name	Sample Protocols
Layer 7	Application	DNS, FTP, HTTP, SMTP, SNMP, Telnet
Layer 6	Presentation	XDR
Layer 5	Session	Named Pipes, RPC
Layer 4	Transport	NetBIOS, TCP, UDP
Layer 3	Network	ARP, IP, IPX, OSPF
Layer 2	Data Link	Arcnet, Ethernet, Token Ring
Layer 1	Physical	Coaxial, Fiber Optic, UTP

The physical layer is the actual physical cabling or other media used to create the network. The data link layer is where data is first encoded to travel over some specific medium. The data link layer network standards include 802.11 wireless, Arcnet, coaxial cable, Ethernet, Token Ring, and many others. Sniffers are generally specific to the type of network they work on. For example, you must have an Ethernet sniffer to analyze traffic on an Ethernet LAN.

There are commercial-grade sniffers available from manufacturers such as Fluke, Network General, and others. These are usually dedicated hardware devices and can run into the tens of thousands of dollars. While these hardware tools can provide a much deeper level of analysis, you can build an inexpensive network sniffer using open source software and a low-end Intel PC.

This chapter reviews several open source Ethernet sniffers. I chose to feature Ethernet in this chapter because it is the most widely deployed protocol used in local area networks. The chances are that your company uses an Ethernet network or interacts with companies that do.

It used to be that the network world was very fragmented when it came to physical and data link layer transmission standards; there was no one dominant standard for LANs. IBM made their Token Ring topology standard for their LAN PCs. Many companies that used primarily IBM equipment used Token Ring because they had no other choice. Arcnet was popular with smaller companies because of its lower cost. Ethernet dominated the university and research environment. There were many other protocols, such as Apple's AppleTalk for Macintosh computers. These protocols were usually specific to a particular manufacturer. However, with the growth of the Internet, Ethernet began to become more and more popular. Equipment vendors began to standardize and focus on low-cost Ethernet cards, hubs, and switches. Today, Ethernet has become the de facto standard for local area networks and the Internet. Most companies and organizations choose it because of its low cost and interoperability.

A Brief History of Ethernet

Bob Metcalfe invented Ethernet in 1973 while at the Xerox Palo Alto Research Center. (This same innovative place also fostered the invention of the laser printer and the graphical user interface, among other things.) Bob and his team developed and patented a "multipoint data connection system with collision detection" that later became known as Ethernet. Bob went on to form a company specifically dedicated to building equipment for this new protocol. This company eventually became 3Com, one of the largest network companies in the world. Luckily, Ethernet was released into the public domain so other companies could build to the specification. This was not true of Token Ring and most of the other network protocols of the day. If Ethernet had been kept proprietary or limited to only one company's hardware, it probably wouldn't have developed into the dominant standard it is today. It was eventually adopted as an official standard by the International Electrical and Electronic Engineers (IEEE), which all but assured it wide acceptance by corporate and government users worldwide. Other standards have been developed based on Ethernet, such as Fast Ethernet, Gigabit Ethernet, and Wi-Fi.

Ethernet handles both the physical media control and the software encoding for data going onto a network. Since Ethernet is a broadcast topology, where every computer can potentially "talk" at once, it has a mechanism to handle collisions—when data packets from two computers are transmitted at the same time. If a collision is detected, both sides retransmit the data after a random delay. This works pretty well most of the time. However, this is also a downside to the Ethernet architecture. All computers attached to an Ethernet network are broadcasting on the same physical wire, and an Ethernet card on the network sees all the traffic passing it. The Ethernet card is designed to process only packets addressed to it, but you can clearly see the security implication here.

Imagine if the way the postal system worked was that a bag containing all the mail was dropped off at the end of the street and each resident picked through it for their mail and then passed it along. (It might be interesting to see who subscribed to *Playboy* and who was getting the past due notices.) This fictional system is not very secure nor does it make efficient use of everyone's time, but that is essentially how Ethernet was designed.

Nowadays, most Ethernet networks are switched to improve efficiency. This means that instead of each Ethernet port seeing all the traffic, it sees only traffic intended for the machine plugged into it. This helps alleviate some of the privacy and congestion issues, but plenty of broadcast traffic still goes to every port. Broadcast traffic is sent out to every port on the network usually for discovery or informational purposes. This happens with protocols such as DHCP, where the machine sends out a broadcast looking for any DHCP servers on the network to get an address from. Machines running Microsoft Windows are also notorious for putting a lot of broadcast traffic on the LAN.

Other broadcast types are often seen on Ethernet LANs. One is **Address Resolution Protocol** (ARP); this is when a machine first tries to figure out which MAC address relates to which IP address (see the sidebar on MAC addresses in Chapter 3). Ethernet networks use an addressing scheme called **Medium Access Control** (MAC) addresses. They are 12-digit hexadecimal numbers, and are assigned to the card at the factory. Every manufacturer has its own range of numbers, so you can usually tell who made the card by looking at the MAC address. If a machine has an IP address but not the Ethernet address, it will send out ARP packets asking, "Who has this address?" When the machine receives a reply, it can then send the rest of the communication to the proper MAC address. It is this kind of traffic that make Ethernet LANs still susceptible to sniffer attacks even when they use switching instead of broadcasting all traffic to every port. Additionally, if hackers can get access to the switch (these devices are often poorly secured), they can sometimes turn their own ports into a "monitor" or "mirror" port that shows traffic from other ports.

Considerations for Network Sniffing

In order to do ethical and productive sniffing, you should follow the following guidelines.

Always Get Permission

Network sniffing, like many other security functions, has the potential for abuse. By capturing every transmission on the wire, you are very likely to see passwords for various systems, contents of e-mails, and other sensitive data, both internal and external, since most systems don't encrypt their traffic on a local LAN. This data, in the wrong hands, could obviously lead to serious security breaches. In addition, it could be a violation of your employees' privacy, depending on your company policies. For example, you might observe employees logging into their employee benefits or 401(k) accounts. Always get written permission from a supervisor, and preferably upper management, before you start this kind of activity. And you should consider what to do with the data after getting it. Besides passwords, it may contain other sensitive data. Generally, network-sniffing logs should be purged from your system unless they are needed for a criminal or civil prosecution. There are documented cases of well-intentioned system administrators being fired for capturing data in this manner without permission.

Understand Your Network Topology

Make sure you fully understand the physical and logical layout of your network before setting up your sniffer. Sniffing from the wrong place on the network will cause you either to not see what you are looking for or to get erroneous results. Make sure there is not a router between your sniffing workstation and what you are trying to observe. Routers will only direct traffic onto a network segment if it is addressed to a node located there. Also, if you are on a switched network, you will need to configure the port you are plugged into to be a "monitor" or "mirror" port. Various manufacturers use different terminology, but basically you need the port to act like a hub rather than a switch, so it should see all the traffic on that switch, not just what is addressed to your workstation. Without this setting, all your monitor port will see is the traffic addressed to the specific port you are plugged into and the network's broadcast traffic.

Use Tight Search Criteria

Depending on what you are looking for, using an open filter (that is, seeing everything) will make the output data voluminous and hard to analyze. Use specific search criteria to narrow down the output that your sniffer shows. Even if you are not exactly sure what you are looking for, you can still write a filter to limit your search results. If you are looking for an internal machine, set your criteria to see only source addresses within your network. If you are trying to track down a specific type of traffic, say FTP traffic, then limit the results to only those on the port that application uses. Doing this will make your sniffer results much more usable.

Establish a Baseline for Your Network

If you use your sniffer to analyze your network during normal operation and record the summary results, you will then have a baseline to compare it to when you are trying to isolate a problem. The Ethereal sniffer discussed in this chapter creates several nice reports for this. You will also have some data to track your network utilization over time. You can use this data to decide when your network is becoming saturated and what the primary causes are. It might be a busy server, more users, or a change in the type of traffic. If you know what you started with, you can more easily tell what and where your culprit is.

Tcpdump: An Ethernet Traffic Analyzer

Tcpdump
Author/primary contact: University of California, Lawrence Berkeley
Laboratories
Web site: www.tcpdump.org
Platforms: Most Unix
License: BSD
Version Reviewed: 3.8.1
Mailing lists:
tcpdump-announce@tcpdump.org
This list is for announcements only.
tcpdump-workers@tcpdump.org
This list is for discussion of code. It will also receive announcements, so if you subscribe to this list you don't need to subscribe to the other one.
Both lists are archived, so you can search the old postings. The code discussion list is also available in a weekly summary digest format.

There are many sniffers available, both free and commercial, but Tcpdump is the most widely available and inexpensive. It comes with most UNIX distributions, including Linux and BSD. In fact, if you have a fairly current Linux distribution, chances are you already have Tcpdump installed and ready to go.

Installing Tcpdump

Tcpdump does exactly what its name implies: it dumps the contents of the TCP/IP packets passing through an interface to an output device, usually the screen or to a file.

1. In order for Tcpdump to work, it must be able to put your network card into what is called **promiscuous mode**. This means that the network card will intercept all traffic on the Ethernet wire, not just that addressed to it. Each operating system processes traffic from the Ethernet card in a different fashion. To provide a common reference for programmers, a library called **pcap** was created. On UNIX this is known as **libpcap** and on Windows as **WinPcap**. These low-level drivers can modify the way the card would normally handle traffic. They must be installed before you can install Tcpdump.

     If Tcpdump is already on your system, then you already have this driver installed. If not, they are provided on the CD-ROM that accompanies this book in the misc directory, or you can get them from the Tcpdump Web site. Make sure you install them *before* you install Tcpdump.

     Note: Libpcap also requires the Flex and Bison scripting languages, or Lex and Yacc as a substitute. If you don't have these, get them from your OS distribution disks or online and install them so libpcap will install successfully.

2. Install libpcap by unpacking it and issuing the standard compilation commands:

   ```
   ./configure
   make
   make install
   ```

   If you get a warning something like "Cannot determine packet capture interface" during the compilation process, then your network card doesn't support promiscuous mode operation and you will have to get another card to use Tcpdump. Most cards these days should support this mode of operation.

3. Once libpcap is installed, unpack the Tcpdump package and change to that directory.

4. Run the same compilation commands:

   ```
   ./configure
   make
   make install
   ```

   Now you are ready to use Tcpdump.

Running Tcpdump

There are a number of filter operations you can perform on the output to look for a specific type of traffic or lessen the overall amount of output. Indeed, on a busy network, unfiltered Tcpdump output will cause your screen to scroll faster than you can read it! However, for a quick demo of the power of Tcpdump, invoke it from the command line by simply typing:

```
tcpdump
```

You will see all the TCP traffic passing your machine's Ethernet card, unfiltered. It might look something like the example in Listing 6.1.

Listing 6.1 Tcpdump Example

```
12:25:38.504619 12.129.72.142.http > 192.168.1.3.3568: . ack
  1418369642 win 31856 <nop,nop,timestamp 72821542 25475802> (DF)

12:25:38.504758 192.168.1.3.3568 > 12.129.72.142.http: . ack
  1 win 40544 <nop,nop,timestamp 25486047 72811295> (DF)

12:25:38.507753 192.168.1.3.4870 > 65.83.241.167.domain:
  11414+ PTR? 142.72.129.12.in-addr.arpa. (44) (DF)

12:25:38.561481 65.83.241.167.domain > 192.168.1.3.4870:
  11414 NXDomain*- 0/1/0 (113)

12:25:38.562754 192.168.1.3.4870 > 65.83.241.167.domain:
  11415+ PTR? 3.1.168.192.in-addr.arpa. (42) (DF)

12:25:38.609588 65.83.241.167.domain > 192.168.1.3.4870:
  11415 NXDomain 0/1/0 (119)


12:25:38.610428 192.168.1.3.4870 > 65.83.241.167.domain:
  1416+ PTR? 167.241.83.65.in-addr.arpa. (44) (DF)

12:25:38.649808 65.83.241.167.domain > 192.168.1.3.4870:
  11416 1/0/0 (69)

12:25:43.497909 arp who-has 192.168.1.1 tell 192.168.1.3

12:25:43.498153 arp reply 192.168.1.1 is-at 0:6:25:9f:34:ac

12:25:43.498943 192.168.1.3.4870 > 65.83.241.167.domain:
  11417+ PTR? 1.1.168.192.in-addr.arpa. (42) (DF)
```

```
12:25:43.533126 65.83.241.167.domain > 192.168.1.3.4870:
  11417 NXDomain 0/1/0 (119)

12:25:44.578546 192.168.1.1.8783 > 192.168.1.255.snmptrap:
  Trap(35) E:3955.2.2.1 192.168.1.1 enterpriseSpecific[specific-
  trap(1)!=0] 43525500 [|snmp]
```

This might look a little confusing at first, but if you break it down it starts to make more sense. The first number is a timestamp, broken down into fractions of a second, because on a busy network there will be many packets per second on the wire. The next number is the source IP address of the packet followed by > (a greater than sign), and then the destination address. Finally, there may be some comments and other data. You can see several different kinds of traffic in this example, including DNS traffic (domain), ARP, and SNMP.

By default, Tcpdump runs until stopped by you pressing Control+C or another interrupt signal. When Tcpdump stops, it prints a summary of all the traffic it saw. The summary statistics include:

- Packets received by filter. This is the count of packets processed by the Tcpdump filter. It is not a count of all the TCP packets on the wire unless you ran Tcpdump without any filter criteria.
- Packets dropped by kernel. The number of packets that were dropped due to a lack of resources on your system. This feature may not be supported on all systems. Even when it is, it may not be accurate if there is a lot of saturation on the network or your sniffer machine is very slow.

TCP/IP Packet Headers

This section describes the contents of a TCP/IP packet header so you can understand what you see in the Tcpdump display. The layout of the TCP/IP packet is specified in RFC 793 for the TCP portion and RFC 791 for the IP portion. You can find the full text of these RFCs online at www.rfc-editor.org. Figure 6.1 is a graphical representation of TCP and IP headers. Both header types are at least 20 bytes long and are usually shown in 32-bit (4-byte) sections with the addresses, options, and other settings for the session.

Let's look at the IP portion first, since this is the lowest layer of the network model. The IP protocol header contains the delivery address for the packet and its sender. Since each address is 32 bits (4 octets of 8 bits each), the source and destination IP address takes up 8 bytes. The first part of the header contains various switches and options for the packet. The first line contains several switches that identify the IP version. Most networks uses IP version 4 (IPv4), but a newer 128-bit IP system called IP version 6 (IPv6) has been circulating for several years and has been gradually gaining acceptance. IPv6 is supposed to solve the IP address space problem by allowing up to 128 bits for the address portion.

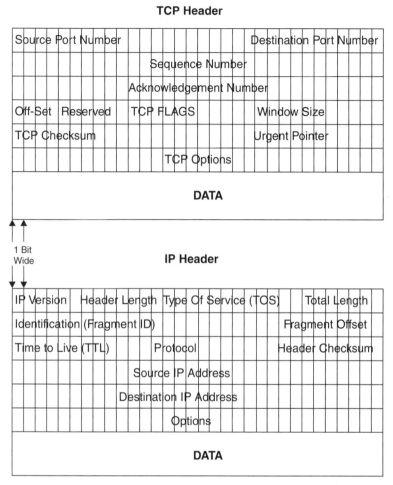

Figure 6.1 TCP/IP Header

This should create enough addresses to solve any foreseeable address space needs. IPv6 also resolves the security and verification issues with IPv4. But for now, you will mostly see IPv4 packets. Then there are the Header Length and the Type Of Service settings (TOS), which allow for differentiating in the priority of packets. The last part of this line is the total length of the header, which is normally the same from packet to packet (20 bytes), but can vary for newer protocols like IPv6.

The next two lines deal with identification of the packet and a checksum to make sure that it is valid. Finally, there are the source and destination IP addresses, and an options field that can be variable length or padded with zeros and any data.

The TCP header takes care of establishing a TCP session and higher-level functions. It is usually 20 bytes long and starts with a source port number of 16 bits and a destination port number of 16 bits. This is why the port numbers can only go up to 65,535—because the port number field in TCP/IP is a 16-bit binary number and 2^{16} power equals 65,536, or 0–65,565. (It is interesting how all these seemingly arbitrary numbers always have a basis in something.)

The port numbers, as mentioned earlier, identify which program the packets need to be directed to on the remote machine and identify the session on the local machine. The next line contains a sequence number. This is used to reassemble the packets in the right order at the other end, even if they arrive in a different order. This is one of the fault-tolerant aspects of TCP sessions. After that, there is an acknowledgment number, also 32 bits long, which allows for verification that it is coming from the right machine. The next line contains a 4-bit section called the data offset, which gives how many 32-bit lines or "words" are in this header (typically 4) and 6 bits that are reserved for future use. After that there is a 6-bit section called the TCP Flags; the last half of that line is used to confer the window size, which tells the recipient how many bits the sender is willing to accept. The Flags are pretty important, as this is where different TCP control bits are set that control how the packet is handled. Each type of TCP communication is designated by one bit, with one being on, or set, and zero being off. Table 6.1 lists the six fields of the TCP Flag section and describes their use. Note: Each "field" is one bit wide, simply a one or zero, on or off.

Table 6.1 TCP Flag Fields

TCP Flags	Full Names	Descriptions
URG	Urgency pointer	Indicates the TCP priority of the packets.
ACK	Acknowledgment	Designates this packet as an acknowledgment of receipt.
PSH	Push	Flushes queued data from buffers.
RST	Reset	Resets a TCP connection on completion or being aborted.
SYN	Synchronization	Synchronizes a connection.
FIN	Finished	Finishes a transmission.

Normally only one or two of these fields are on (the bits set to one), but as you saw in Chapter 4, there is nothing to stop you from sending a packet with all these bits flipped on (XMAS scan) or flipped off (NULL scan) to try to confuse a remote system.

Next are the TCP checksum and an urgent pointer. Then there is a line with any TCP options for the packet. These might include additional checksums, timestamps, or other optional information. This line is padded out to 32 bits with zeros if the options don't fill all the space. Finally the actual payload, the data of the packet, follows. This may seem like a lot of administrative overhead for sending one packet (approximately 48 bytes for every packet), but it does ensure a relatively stable connection on networks that are not always reliable end to end (like the Internet). And indeed, because of the TCP overhead, some protocols that are not connection-sensitive use UDP, which is a connectionless protocol that lowers the amount of overhead.

On a standard Tcpdump session with normal verbosity, you will see a timestamp followed by the TCP sequence number. Then it shows parts of the IP stack, including the source and destination with a > (greater than sign) between them, meaning this packet is going from here to there. At the end is the info field, which tells what the packet is doing. You can use the `-v` or `-vv` option to get more detail from Tcpdump about the header (see the next section).

Usually, you will want to run Tcpdump with some of the options or filters set to narrow down and focus the output. The general form of the Tcpdump statement is:

    tcpdump *options expressions*

Replace *options* or *expressions* with one or more of the valid variables. Table 6.2 lists the Tcpdump options.

Table 6.2 Tcpdump Options

Options	Descriptions
-a	Attempts to convert addresses to names. This puts a higher load on the system and may cause packet loss.
-c *count*	Stops Tcpdump after *count* number of packets are processed.
-C *filesize*	Limits the output files to *filesize* number of bytes.
-d	Dumps the packet-matching code in a human-readable form and then stops.
-dd	Dumps the packet-matching code as a C program fragment.

(continues)

Table 6.2 Tcpdump Options (*continued*)

Options	Descriptions
-ddd	Dumps the packet-matching code as decimal numbers.
-e	Prints the link-level header on each dump line. This is the MAC address on an Ethernet network.
-E *algo:secret*	Uses Tcpdump's built-in ability to decrypt packets encrypted with IPsec ESP on the fly. Of course, you must have the shared secret to use this option. The *algo* options include des-cbc, 3des-cdc, blowfish-cbc, r3c-cbc, cast 128-cbc, and none. The default is des-cbc. The value of *secret* should be the ESP secret key in ASCII text form. For more information on IPsec, see Chapter 9.
-F *file*	Uses the filename *file* as input rather than taking input live from the wire. This is useful for analyzing events after the fact.
-i *interface*	Reads from *interface* when there are multiple network interfaces on the sniffer machine. By default, Tcpdump uses the lowest numbered valid interface. On Linux boxes, you can also use the parameter any to capture packets on all network interfaces.
-n	Doesn't convert addresses to names.
-N	Doesn't print the upper-level domain name element of host names. This is useful if you need to provide a sanitized version of the output and don't want to reveal whose network it is on.
-p	Doesn't put the interface into promiscuous mode. Only used when you are troubleshooting traffic to your sniffer box.
-q	Prints quick output. Less protocol information is printed so the lines are shorter.
-T *type*	Forces packets selected by the filter in the expression to be interpreted by *type*.
-t	Doesn't print a timestamp on each line.

Options	Descriptions
-tt	Prints an unformatted timestamp on each line.
-ttt	Prints the delta time between packets.
-tttt	Prints a timestamp in a default format preceded by the date on each line.
-v	Uses slightly more verbose output. Includes the time-to-live, identification, total length, and options fields of each packet.
-vv	Provides more verbose output. NFS and SMB packets are fully decoded.
-vvv	Provides even more verbose output. This may seriously slow down your sniffer.
-w *filename*	Writes the packets to the file *filename* rather than displaying them on the screen. This way, unattended sniffing can be saved and analyzed later. For example, if you had some strange things happening on your network, you could leave Tcpdump running overnight to capture any odd traffic. Just make sure you write a good filter, or you could have a very large file when you come back in the morning.
-x	Displays each packet (minus the link-level header) in hex.
-X	Displays packet contents in both hex and ASCII.

Tcpdump Expressions

The Tcpdump expressions select which packets from the datastream are displayed. This is where the work of Tcpdump is really done. Only items that match the expression are dumped; if no expression is given, then all packets will be displayed. A Tcpdump expression consists of one more directives, called **primitives**. These consist of an ID followed by a qualifier. Table 6.3 lists the three different kinds of qualifiers, and Table 6.4 lists the allowable primitive combinations.

There are also more complex expressions that can be constructed using Boolean arithmetic operators such as and, or, not, greater than, and less than. See the Tcpdump man page for examples and usage.

Table 6.3 Tcpdump Qualifiers

Qualifiers	Descriptions
type	Specifies what the ID name or number refers to. Possible types are host, net, and port. For example, host foo, net 128.3, or port 20.
dir	Specifies the direction of traffic from a particular ID. Possible directions are src; dst; src or dst; and src and dst (**src** stands for source address and **dst** stands for destination address).
proto	Lets you specify the protocol to filter out. Possible protos are ether, fddi, tr, ip, ipv6, arp, rarp, decnet, tcp, and udp. If no proto is specified, then all protocols consistent with the rest of the expression are allowed. You can use this to find out which machine is doing excessive arps or to filter out udp requests, which can be extensive on many networks since DNS requests use udp.

Table 6.4 Allowable Primitive Combinations

Combinations	Descriptions
dst host *host*	Shows only traffic addressed to *host*, which may be either an IP address or hostname.
src host *host*	Shows only traffic coming from *host*.
host *host*	Shows traffic either originating or destined for *host*.
ether dst *ehost*	Shows traffic destined for a specific Ethernet name, *ehost*, which can be either a name or a number (MAC address).
ether src *ehost*	Shows traffic originating from *ehost*.
ether host *ehost*	Shows traffic either originating from or destined for *ehost*.
gateway *host*	Shows any traffic that used *host* as a gateway. In other words, it was forwarded from *host*. This happens when the IP source or destination address doesn't match the Ethernet address of *host*. You can use this when you want to track all traffic going through your Internet gateway or some specific router.

Combinations	Descriptions
dst net *net*	Filters traffic that is destined for a specific network, *net*, specified in 0.0.0.0 notation. Similar to ether dst *ehost*, except it can be much broader than a single host.
src net *net*	Filters for a source network, *net*.
net *net*	Same as the previous two statements except it allows traffic either from or to the *net* network.
net *net* mask *netmask*	Matches traffic from or to *net* network with a netmask of *netmask*. Used for specifying the exact size of a network in increments smaller than a class C. You can also use src or dst with this statement to specify the direction of the traffic.
net *net/len*	Matches traffic with network addresses of *net* and *len* bits in the netmask. Similar to the last statement.
dst port *port*	Filters TCP and UDP traffic with a destination port value of *port*. You can also specify either TCP or UDP here to only catch traffic of that type. Otherwise, both types are shown.
src port *port*	Same as the last statement, except this captures traffic with a source port of *port*.
less *length*	Shows packets with a length of less than *length*. This can also be stated as len <= *length*.
greater *length*	Same as the statement above except it captures only traffic of length greater than the *length* value.
ip proto *protocol*	Captures traffic that is of a specific protocol type. Allowable names are icmp, icmpv6, igmp, igrp, pim, ah, esp, vrrp, udp, and tcp. The names tcp, udp, and icmp must be put between backslashes in order to keep them from being read as keywords. For example: ip proto protocol /tcp/.
ip6 proto *protocol*	Similar to the above statement but for IPv6 packets and types.
ip6 protochain *protocol*	Finds IPv6 packets that have a protocol header of *protocol*.

(continues)

Table 6.4 Allowable Primitive Combinations (*continued*)

Combinations	Descriptions
ip protochain *protocol*	Same as above but for IPv4 packets.
ip broadcast	Identifies only traffic that is broadcast, that is, has all zeros or all ones in the destination fields.
ether multicast	Registers true (displays) if the packet is an Ethernet multicast packet.
ip multicast	Registers true if the packet is an IP multicast packet.
ip6 multicast	Registers true if the packet is an IPv6 multicast packet.
ether proto *protocol*	Displays any traffic that is of Ethernet type *procotol*. Allowable protocol names are ip, ipv6, arp, rarp, atalk, aarp, decnet, sca, lat, mopdl, moprc, iso, stp, ipx, or netbeui. These names are also identifiers, so they must be escaped by using backslashes.
decnet src *host*	Captures DECnet traffic with a source address of *host*.
decnet dst *host*	Same as the above statement but filters on destination address of *host*.
decnet *host*	Filters for DECnet addresses with either the source or destination equal to *host*.
ip	A shorter version of the ether proto statement described earlier. Traps traffic matching the Ethernet protocol of IP.
ip6	Shorter version of the ether proto statement for trapping traffic matching the Ethernet protocol of IPv6.
arp	Shorter version of the ether proto statement for trapping traffic matching the Ethernet protocol of arp.
rarp	Shorter version of the ether proto statement for trapping traffic matching the Ethernet protocol of rarp.
atalk	Shorter version of the ether proto statement for trapping traffic matching the Ethernet protocol of AppleTalk.

Combinations	Descriptions
aarp	Shorter version of the ether proto statement for trapping traffic matching the Ethernet protocol of aarp.
decnet	Shorter version of the ether proto statement for trapping traffic matching the Ethernet protocol of DECnet.
iso	Shorter version of the ether proto statement for trapping traffic matching the Ethernet protocol of iso.
stp	Shorter version of the ether proto statement for trapping traffic matching the Ethernet protocol of stp.
ipx	Shorter version of the ether proto statement for trapping traffic matching the Ethernet protocol of ipx.
netbeui	Shorter version of the ether proto statement for trapping traffic matching the Ethernet protocol of netbeui.
vlan *vlan_id*	Captures packets based on the 802.1Q VLAN standard. It can be used by itself or by specifying *vlan_id*.
tcp	An abbreviated form of the statement ip proto tcp.
udp	An abbreviated form of the statement ip proto udp.
icmp	An abbreviated form of the statement ip proto icmp.
iso proto *protocol*	Captures OSI packets with a protocol type of *procotol*. Allowable OSI protocol types are clnp, esis, and isis.
clnp	An abbreviated form of the above statement using clnp for *protocol*.
esis	An abbreviated form of the iso proto *protocol* statement using esis for *protocol*.
isis	An abbreviated form of the iso proto *protocol* statement using isis for *protocol*.

Tcpdump Examples

The following are several practical examples of ways to use Tcpdump.

View All Traffic to and from a Particular Host   If you want to monitor only traffic to and from a specific host, you can filter everything else out with the simple "host" expression. For example, to monitor a host with the IP address 192.168.1.1, the statement would look like this:

```
tcpdump -n host 192.168.1.1
```

Watch Only Traffic Coming in or out on a Certain Port   If you want to track usage of a certain application, you can use Tcpdump to trap all traffic for a particular TCP/UDP port. If the application you are trying to monitor is Telnet (port 23), you could do this with the following Tcpdump expression:

```
tcpdump -n port 23
```

View All Traffic to and from a Particular Host but Eliminate Some Kinds of Traffic   Say you want to monitor a single host as in the first example but want to filter out SSH traffic (if you were ssh'd into that host, unfiltered Tcpdump output would show your own connection traffic). You can do this by adding the port expression with a Boolean operator "not" statement. Here is the command:

```
tcpdump -n host 192.168.1.1 and not port 22
```

Find a Rogue Workstation   If you are having network problems and suspect a rogue computer is swamping your network, you can use Tcpdump to quickly track down the culprit. Whether it's a bad network card or a trojanized PC causing a denial of service attack, Tcpdump will help shed some light on your problem. First try just running it wide open to see what is generating the most traffic. Use the -a and -e options to generate names and MAC addresses.

```
tcpdump -ae
```

Notice that you can concatenate the two letters with one dash. If this causes the output to scroll off the screen too fast, use the -c 1000 option to only count 1,000 packets and then stop.

Monitor a Specific Workstation   If you want to log the traffic from a specific workstation to analyze later, you can do this easily with Tcpdump (just make sure that you have the legal right to do so). Use the Tcpdump statement from the first example with a -w switch to write to a file. If you use DHCP on your network, you may be better off using SMB (Windows) names. For example:

```
tcpdump -w logfile host 192.168.1.1
```

where logfile is the file it will log to. You may also want to use the -c or -C options to limit your output file size.

Look for Suspicious Network Traffic   If you are worried about what is happening on your network after hours, you can leave Tcpdump running to flag traffic you might deem questionable. You could run it with the `gateway 192.168.0.1` flag set, where you replace the IP address with that of your own Internet gateway. Assuming your home network was in the IP Range of 192.168.0.0 through 192.168.0.254, this would flag any traffic coming or going from your Internet gateway. If you have an internal mail server and don't want to log that traffic since that would be valid traffic, you could add the statement:

```
and host != 192.168.0.2
```

where the IP address is the address of your mail server. The exclamation point also acts as the Boolean "not" statement. This would flag any incoming traffic not bound for your mail server. The expression would look like this:

```
tcpdump -w logfile gateway 192.168.0.1 and
host!=192.168.1.2
```

If you are looking for users using a particular application, such as a streaming video or an audio program, you can further specify that as long as you know its port number. If you know it uses the TCP port 1000, you can use the proto primitive to trap traffic using that protocol. For example:

```
tcpdump -w logfile gateway 192.168.0.1 and
host!=192.168.1.2
dst port 1000
```

For more complicated intrusion detection scenarios, you will be better off using one of the intrusion detection systems described in Chapter 7, but for a quick and dirty analysis, Tcpdump can be a very handy tool.

WinDump: An Ethernet Traffic Analyzer for Windows
WinDump
Author/primary contact: Loris Degioanni
Web site: windump.polito.it/install/default.htm
Platforms   Windows 95, 98, ME, NT4, 2000, XP
License: BSD
Version reviewed: 3.8 alpha
WinPcap mailing list:
www.mail-archive.com/winpcap-users@winpcap.polito.it/

Finally, there is a Tcpdump program for Windows. In fact, this is the actual UNIX Tcpdump ported over to the Windows platform, so all the functions and expressions work exactly the same.

Installing WinDump

Loris Degioanni was kind enough to do the porting work and made it a breeze to install—even easier than its UNIX counterpart.

1. Just like the UNIX Tcpdump, you first need to have the packet capture libraries installed before you can run WinDump. There is a special version for Windows called WinPcap. This is included on the CD-ROM in the Misc Folder. The latest version is also available at the program's Web site.
2. Install the WinPcap libraries by clicking on the file.
3. Download the WinDump executable and place it in the directory you want to run it from.
    No additional installation is necessary.

Using WinDump

Using WinDump is exactly the same as using Tcpdump from the command line. Just go to a command prompt in Windows and issue the command from the directory that the WinDump executable is in. All the commands and expressions work the same, but Table 6.5 lists a few commands specific to the Windows version.

The source code is also available on the Web site for those wishing to contribute or to make modifications of their own. A word of warning, though: this kind of Windows coding is only for the hard core and those truly knowledgeable about network protocols.

This is all you need to get going in either Windows or UNIX. If you want more than just a command line interface though, the next tool described offers a graphical interface for your sniffing activities.

Table 6.5 WinDump-Specific Commands

Commands	Descriptions
-B	Sets the driver buffer size in kilobytes for your capture session. If you are experiencing high rates of packet loss, you can try increasing this value a little. The default is 1MB (-B 1000)
-D	Prints a list of available network interfaces on your system. It shows the interface name, number, and description, if any. You can use these parameters to specify an interface to capture from using the Tcpdump -i switch.

Ethereal: A Network Protocol Analyzer for UNIX and Windows

Ethereal

Author/primary contact:	Gerald Combs
Web site:	www.ethereal.com
Platforms:	Most UNIX, Windows 95, 98, ME, NT4, 2000, XP
License:	GPL
Version reviewed:	0.10.2
Mailing lists:	

Ethereal-announce

General announcement list. Doesn't accept posts.
Subscribe at www.ethereal.com/mailman/listinfo/ethereal-announce.

Ethereal-users

General questions about using Ethereal. Post your newbie questions here.
Subscribe at www.ethereal.com/mailman/listinfo/ethereal-users.

Ethereal-dev

Development discussions.
Subscribe at www.ethereal.com/mailman/listinfo/ethereal-dev.

Ethereal-doc

For people writing Ethereal documentation or who want to become involved in writing documentation. Subscribe at www.ethereal.com/mailman/listinfo/ethereal-doc.

Ethereal-cvs

For monitoring changes to the Ethereal CVS tree, which maintains the very latest version of the code for developers. It doesn't accept posts, and any questions should be directed to either Ethereal-users or -dev depending on the question. Subscribe at www.ethereal.com/mailman/listinfo/ethereal-cvs.

Ethereal offers all the benefits of a command line tool like Tcpdump with a number of advantages. It has a user-friendly graphical interface, so you don't have to deal with learning all the command line parameters. It also offers many more analytical and statistical options. Some of the other benefits of Ethereal are:

- Cleaner output format. The output is much easier to read and understand than the raw packet captures of Tcpdump.
- Many more protocol formats are supported. Ethereal can interpret over 300 different network protocols, which covers just about every network type ever invented.

- More physical network formats are supported. This includes newer protocols such as IP over ATM and FDDI.
- Captured network data can be interactively browsed and sorted.
- Output can be saved as plain text or in PostScript format.
- A rich display filter mode. This includes the ability to highlight certain packets in color. There is a filter creation GUI to walk you through the process of creating filters easily.
- The ability to follow a TCP stream and view the content in ASCII. This can be invaluable when you need to read inter-server messages to track down e-mail or Web problems. You can follow the conversation between communicating nodes in order using this feature.
- The ability to work with a number of capture programs and libraries. Ethereal also works with dedicated hardware beyond libpcap. Some of the programs supported include Network Associate's Sniffer and Sniffer Pro; Novell's LANalyser; some Cisco, Lucent, and Toshiba devices; and some wireless sniffing gear such as Net-Stumbler and Kismet Wireless. Ethereal now works as a plug-in module for many of these programs and devices.
- The ability to save sessions in multiple formats. This is useful if you want to do additional analysis with different tools, including libcap (the default), Sun Snoop, Microsoft Network Monitor, and Network Associates' Sniffer.
- A command-line terminal mode. This is for those not graphically inclined, although a huge part of Ethereal's usefulness comes from its GUI tools.

Ethereal is so useful as a networking tool that it has been rated as number two among the most popular network security tools available by the security Web site Insecure.org. Ethereal has many uses beyond just security; in fact, you can also use it as a general network analysis tool.

Installing Ethereal for Linux

1. You need two prerequisites before loading Ethereal: the libpcap libraries and the GTK development libraries. If you have loaded the port scanners or vulnerability scanners from earlier chapters, you should be all set. If not, you will need to download the GTK libraries or install them off of your OS installation disks. You can get libpcap on the CD-ROM or at www.tcpdump.org. GTK is available at www.gtk.org.

2. Now, you have to decide whether to use an RPM or compile from the source code. There are many RPM packages for different versions of Linux. If one exists for your distribution, you can use that and skip the compile process. If there isn't an RPM version for your operating system, you need to compile it.

3. To compile Ethereal, first download and unpack the latest distribution. The default installation should work fine for most uses. Look at the INSTALL file if you want to set additional compile-time parameters.

4. Change to the install directory and type the usual:

```
./configure
make
make install
```

You can now run Ethereal by typing `./ethereal` at the command prompt or by clicking on the executable from X-Windows. You need to be the root user to run Ethereal in the X-windows environment. To run Ethereal in command-line mode, you can type `./tethereal`.

Installing Ethereal for Windows

1. You need to have the WinPcap libraries installed before running Ethereal. If you have already installed the port or vulnerability scanners from the previous chapters on your Windows system, then you already have these loaded and you can go to Step 2. Make sure your version of WinPcap is at least 2.3 or later. If you are running a machine with a multiprocessor or one of the newer Pentium processors with hyper-threading technology, you need to have WinPcap 3.0 or higher, and your results may be unpredictable as Ethereal doesn't work well with multiple processors.

2. The GTK tools for the graphical interface are included in the Ethereal installation package. Go to the Ethereal Web site and download a self-extracting install file. (I recommend you install the binary rather than messing with compilation on a Windows machine. This is much easier and doesn't require a Windows compiler.)

3. After you download the file, double-click on it. The installation program walks you through the install process. When it is done, it will put an icon on your desktop and you are ready to start using Ethereal.

Using Ethereal

Whether you are using the Windows or Linux version, almost all of the operations are the same and the interfaces look the same. When you bring up Ethereal, you will see a screen with three sections in it. These windows display the capture data and other information about your session. Figure 6.2 shows an example of this main window with a session in progress.

The top third of the screen is where the packet stream is displayed in order of receipt, although you can sort this in just about any way by clicking on the headings. Table 6.6 lists the items displayed for each packet or frame.

The next section of the screen goes into more detail on each packet that is highlighted. It is arranged in an order that basically conforms to the OSI model, so the first item listed

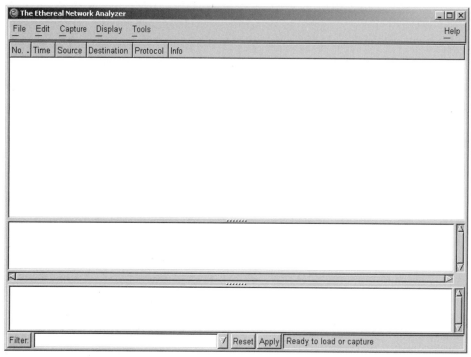

Figure 6.2 Ethereal Main Screen

Table 6.6 Packet Stream Data

Items	Descriptions
Packet number	Assigned by Ethereal.
Time	The time the packet was received, set from the elapsed time from the start of the capture session. Alternately, this can be configured to show the clock time, the clock time and date, or even the time between packets (this is helpful for network performance analysis).
Source address	Where the packet came from. This is an IP address on IP networks.
Destination address	Where the packet is going to, also usually an IP address.
Protocol	The level 4 protocol that the packet is using.
Info	Some summary information about the packet, usually a type field.

is detail on the data link layer, and so on. The little pluses can be expanded to show even more information on each level. It is amazing how much detail you can see on each packet. Ethereal is like an electron microscope for network packets!

The final section contains the actual packet contents, in both hexadecimal and translated into ASCII where possible. Binary files will still look like garbage, as will encrypted traffic, but anything in clear text will appear. This highlights the power (and danger) of having a sniffer on your network.

Starting a Capture Session

There are a lot of options and filters you can set. Begin by running a wide open capture session. Choose Start from the Capture menu, and the Capture Options window displays (see Figure 6.3).

Table 6.7 describes the options you can set before starting your session.

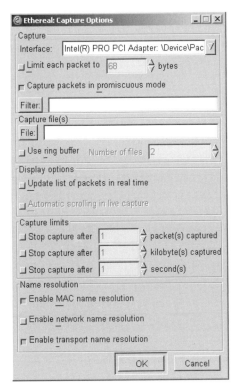

Figure 6.3 Ethereal Capture Options

Table 6.7 Ethereal Capture Options

Options	Describes
Interface	Picks the interface to capture from the pull-down menu. Ethereal automatically senses all the available interfaces and lists them. You can also choose to capture from all interfaces at once, just like Tcpdump.
Limit each packet to x bytes	Sets a maximum size for the packets captured. You can use this if you fear some of the packets may be very large and you don't want to overload your machine.
Capture packets in promiscuous mode	This is on by default. Turn this off if you want to capture traffic only to your sniffer machine.
Filter	Click the Filter button to create a filter using Tcpdump-style expressions. It will ask you to name the filter (which you can then use in future sessions) and enter the expression.
Capture file(s)	Click the File button if you want to read from a file rather than capture live data.
Display options	These are disabled by default, but enable them if you want to watch the packets scroll by in real time. If you are capturing on a busy network or your machine is slow, this is not recommended because it will cause the session to bog down and possibly drop packets. However, it is very useful if you want to "eyeball" the traffic to get a general idea of the nature of flow on the network as it goes by.
Capture limits	You have several more options here on when to end your session. Besides manually stopping it, you can have Ethereal stop after x number of packets or kilobytes of data have been captured, or after x number of seconds have elapsed.
Name resolution	You can specify whether you want Ethereal to resolve names at various levels of the network model. You can selectively resolve MAC address names, network names (SMB or hostnames), and/or transport layer names. Enabling all of these, especially DNS, can slow down your capture significantly.

Once you have set your options, click OK and your session will start. A window will appear that tracks the session statistics in real time (see Figure 6.4). If you set your session to show packets in real time, you will see them as they come across the wire in the window (see Figure 6.2).

You can stop your session at any time by clicking Stop in the statistic window or choosing Stop from the Capture menu. If you set a limit in the options, it will automatically stop when it reaches it. You can now analyze and manipulate your session results.

By clicking on the headings at the top of the window, you can resort the results by that heading, so you can sort the output by source address, destination, protocol, or the info fields. This helps to organize things if you are looking for a specific kind of traffic, for example, all the DNS queries or all the mail-related traffic. Of course, you could also write a filter to capture only this kind of traffic in the first place.

Display Options

Table 6.8 lists the commands on the Display menu that you can use to affect how the packets are displayed on the screen.

Ethereal Tools

There are several built-in analytical tools included with Ethereal. It is also built with a plug-in architecture so that other programs can interact with Ethereal or you can write your own. You can access these options under the Tools menu (see Table 6.9).

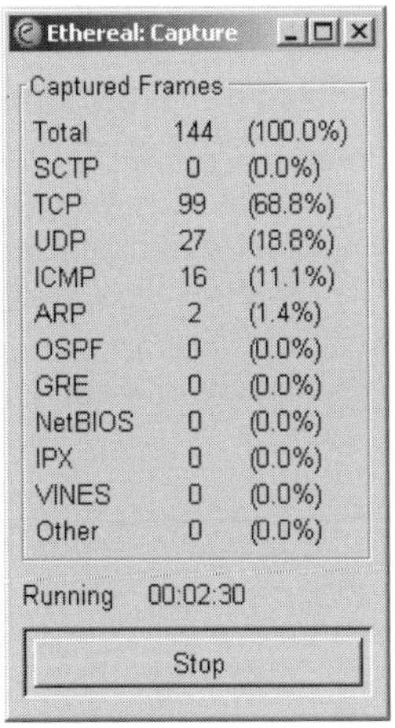

Figure 6.4 Ethereal Session Statistics Window

Table 6.8 Ethereal Display Menu Options

Menu Options	Descriptions
Options submenu	This where you can set some global settings, such as how the time field is calculated. You can also set automatic scrolling of traffic and name resolution to on since they are turned off by default.
Colorize display	You can select certain kinds of packet to shade different colors. This makes the display easier to read and pick out the items you are looking for.
Collapse/expand all	Shows either full detail on every item or just the top level.

Table 6.9 Ethereal Tools Menu Options

Options	Descriptions
Summary	Shows a listing of the top-level data on your captures session, such as time elapsed, packet count, average packet size, total bytes captured, and average Mps on the wire during the capture.
Protocol hierarchy statistics	Gives a statistical view of the traffic on your network. It shows what percentage of the capture session each type of packet makes up. You can collapse or expand the view to see major levels or minor protocols within a level.
Statistics	Contains a number of reports that are specific to certain kinds of protocols. Refer to the Ethereal documentation for more details on these tests.
Plugins	Shows the protocol analyzer plug-ins that you have loaded. These are decoders for newer protocols that can be added to Ethereal without a major version upgrade. And because it's a plug-in architecture, you can write your own.

Saving Your Ethereal Output

Once you have finished capturing and analyzing your Ethereal data, you may want to save it, either for analysis with additional tools or for presentation to other parties. Using the Save As option from the File menu, you can choose from a number of formats, including libpcap (the default), Sun Snoop, LANalyser, Sniffer, Microsoft Network Monitor, and Visual Networks traffic capture.

Ethereal Applications

Now that you understand the basics of Ethereal, here are some practical applications you can use it for.

Network Optimization   By running a wide-open network capture and then using the statistical reports, you can see how saturated your LAN is and what kinds of packets are making up most of the traffic. By looking at this, you may decide that it is time to move to a 100Mps switched network, or to segregate two departments into routed LANs versus one big network. You can also tell if you need to install a WINS server (too many SMB name requests being broadcast across the LAN) or if a particular server should be moved to a DMZ or a separate router port to take that traffic off the network.

Application Server Troubleshooting   Do you have a mail server that doesn't seem to be connecting? Having DNS problems? These application-level problems can be fiendishly difficult to troubleshoot. But if you have Ethereal, you can tap into the network and watch the inter-server communications. You can see the actual server messages for protocols like SMTP or HTTP and figure out where the problem is happening by watching the TCP stream.

Intrusion Detection Systems

In the last chapter you saw the power of a network sniffer and all of the useful things you can do with one. You can even use a sniffer to look for suspicious activities on your network. You can take this a step further with a type of software called an **intrusion detection system** (IDS). These programs are basically modified sniffers that see all the traffic on the network and actually try to sense potential bad network traffic and alert you when it appears. The primary way they do this is by examining the traffic coming through and trying to match it with a database of known bad activity, called **signatures**. This use of signatures is very similar to the way anti-virus programs work. Most types of attacks have a very distinctive look at the TCP/IP level. An IDS can define attacks based on the IP addresses, port numbers, content, and any number of criteria. There is another way of doing intrusion detection on a system level by checking the integrity of key files and making sure no changes are made to those files. And there are emerging technologies that merge the concept of intrusion detection and a firewall or take further action beyond mere detection (see the sidebar on "A New Breed of Intrusion Detection Systems"). However, in this chapter I focus on the two most popular ways to set up intrusion detection on your network and systems: network intrusion detection and file integrity checking.

Chapter Overview

Concepts you will learn:
- Types of intrusion detection systems
- Signatures for network intrusion detection systems
- False positives in network intrusion detection systems
- Proper intrusion detection system placement

- Tuning an intrusion detection system
- File integrity checking

Tools you will use:

Snort, Snort Webmin module, Snort for Windows, and Tripwire

A **Network Intrusion Detection System** (NIDS) can protect you from attacks that make it through your firewall onto your internal LAN. Firewalls can be misconfigured, allowing undesired traffic into your network. Even when operating correctly, firewalls usually leave in some application traffic that could be dangerous. Ports are often forwarded from the firewall to internal servers with traffic intended for a mail server or other public server. An NIDS can watch for this traffic and flag potentially dangerous packets. A properly configured NIDS can double-check your firewall rules and give you additional protection for your application servers.

While they are useful for protecting against outside attacks, one of the biggest benefits of an NIDS is to ferret out attacks and suspicious activity from internal sources. A firewall will protect you from many external attacks. However, once an attacker is on the local network, a firewall does you very little good. It only sees traffic traversing through it from the outside. Firewalls are mostly blind to activity on the local LAN. Think of an NIDS and firewall as complementary security devices, the strong door lock and alarm system of network security. One protects your perimeter; the other protects your interior (see Figure 7.1).

There is good reason to keep a close eye on your internal network traffic. FBI statistics show that over 70 percent of computer crime incidents come from an internal source. As much as we would like to think that our fellow employees wouldn't do anything to hurt us, this is sometimes not the case. Internal perpetrators aren't always moonlighting hackers. They can range from a disgruntled system administrator to a careless employee. The simple act of downloading a file or opening an e-mail attachment can load a Trojan horse that will create a hole in your firewall for all kinds of mischief. With an NIDS, you can catch this kind of activity as well as other computer shenanigans as they happen. A well-tuned NIDS can be the electronic "alarm system" for your network.

A New Breed of Intrusion Detection Systems

Anomalous Activity-Based IDS

Rather than using static signatures, which can only catch bad activity when it can be explicitly defined, these next-generation systems keep track of what normal levels are for different kinds of activity on your network. If it sees a sudden surge in FTP traffic, it will alert you to this. The problem with these kinds of systems is that they are very prone to false positives. False positives occur when an alert goes off, but the activity it is flagging is normal or allowed for your LAN. A person downloading a particularly large file would set off the alarm in the previous example.

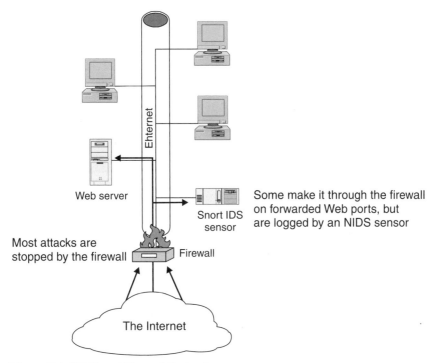

Figure 7.1 NIDS and Firewall Protection

Also, it takes time for an anomalous detection IDS to develop an accurate model of the network. Early on, the system generates so many alerts as to be almost useless. Additionally, these types of intrusion detection systems can be fooled by someone who knows your network well. If hackers are sufficiently stealthy and use protocols that are already in high use on your LAN, then they won't set off this kind of system. However, one big upside of this kind of system is that you don't have to continually download signature updates. As this technology matures and becomes more intelligent, this will probably become a popular way to detect intrusions.

Intrusion Prevention Systems

A new type of NIDS called an Intrusion Prevention System (IPS) is being trumpeted as the solution to enterprise security concerns. The concept behind these products is that they will take action upon alerts as they are generated. This can be either by working with a firewall or router to write custom rules on the fly, blocking activity from suspicious IP addresses, or actually interrogating or even counterattacking the offending systems.

While this new technology is constantly evolving and improving, it's a long way from providing the analysis and judgment of a human being. The fact remains that any system that is 100 percent dependant on a machine and software can always be outwitted by a dedicated human (although certain defeated chess grandmasters might beg to differ). An open source example of an IPS is Inline Snort by Jed Haile, a free module for the Snort NIDS discussed in this chapter.

NIDS Signature Examples

An NIDS operates by examining packets and comparing them to known signatures. A good example of a common attack that can be clearly identified by its signature is the cmd.exe attack that is used against the Internet Information Server (IIS), which is Microsoft's Web server. This attack is used by Internet worms and viruses such as Nimda and Code Red. In this case, the worm or human attacker attempts to execute a copy of cmd.exe, which is the Windows command line binary, in a writable directory using a buffer overflow in the IIS Web server module called Internet Server API (ISAPI). If successful, then the hacker or worm has access to a command line on that machine and can wreak considerable havoc. However, the command to copy this file is obvious; there is no reason for legitimate users to be executing this file over the network via IIS. So if you see this activity, then it's a good bet that it is an intrusion attempt. By examining the packet payload and searching for the words cmd.exe, an NIDS can identify this kind of attack. Listing 7.1 shows one of these packets. The hexadecimal contents are on the left and the ASCII translation is on the right.

Listing 7.1 The cmd.exe Execution Packet
```
length = 55

000 : 47 45 54 20 2F 73 63 72 69 70 74 73 2F 2E 2E 25  GET /
  scripts/..%
010 : 35 63 25 35 63 2E 2E 2F 77 69 6E 6E 74 2F 73 79  5c%5c../
  winnt/sy
020 : 73 74 65 6D 33 32 2F 63 6D 64 2E 65 78 65 3F 2F  stem32/
  cmd.exe?/
030 : 63 2B 64 69 72 0D 0A                             c+dir..
```

Another attack that is easy to identify by its signature is the .ida buffer overflow. The Code Red worm propagated using this method. It utilized a buffer overflow in the .ida extension for Microsoft's IIS Web server. This extension is installed by default but is often not needed. If you don't install the patch for this condition, it can allow direct access to your machine. Fortunately, an NIDS can quickly identify these packets by matching the GET /default.ida statement contained in them. You can see a partial listing of an .ida attack in Listing 7.2. This particular one also has the words Code Red II in it, which means it was generated by a Code Red worm trying to infect this machine. Even if your machines are fully patched and immune to these kinds of attacks, it is good to know where they are coming from and at what frequency.

Listing 7.2 Signature of an .ida Attack

```
length = 1414

000 : 47 45 54 20 2F 64 65 66 61 75 6C 74 2E 69 64 61   GET /
      default.ida
010 : 3F 58 58 58 58 58 58 58 58 58 58 58 58 58 58 58   ?XXXXXXXXXXXXXXX
020 : 58 58 58 58 58 58 58 58 58 58 58 58 58 58 58 58   XXXXXXXXXXXXXXXX
030 : 58 58 58 58 58 58 58 58 58 58 58 58 58 58 58 58   XXXXXXXXXXXXXXXX
040 : 58 58 58 58 58 58 58 58 58 58 58 58 58 58 58 58   XXXXXXXXXXXXXXXX
050 : 58 58 58 58 58 58 58 58 58 58 58 58 58 58 58 58   XXXXXXXXXXXXXXXX
060 : 58 58 58 58 58 58 58 58 58 58 58 58 58 58 58 58   XXXXXXXXXXXXXXXX
070 : 58 58 58 58 58 58 58 58 58 58 58 58 58 58 58 58   XXXXXXXXXXXXXXXX
080 : 58 58 58 58 58 58 58 58 58 58 58 58 58 58 58 58   XXXXXXXXXXXXXXXX
090 : 58 58 58 58 58 58 58 58 58 58 58 58 58 58 58 58   XXXXXXXXXXXXXXXX
0a0 : 58 58 58 58 58 58 58 58 58 58 58 58 58 58 58 58   XXXXXXXXXXXXXXXX
0b0 : 58 58 58 58 58 58 58 58 58 58 58 58 58 58 58 58   XXXXXXXXXXXXXXXX
0c0 : 58 58 58 58 58 58 58 58 58 58 58 58 58 58 58 58   XXXXXXXXXXXXXXXX
0d0 : 58 58 58 58 58 58 58 58 58 58 58 58 58 58 58 58   XXXXXXXXXXXXXXXX
0e0 : 58 58 58 58 58 58 58 58 58 58 58 58 58 58 58 58   XXXXXXXXXXXXXXXX
0f0 : 58 25 75 39 30 39 30 25 75 36 38 35 38 25 75 63   X%u9090%u6858%uc
100 : 62 64 33 25 75 37 38 30 31 25 75 39 30 39 30 25   bd3%u7801%u9090%
110 : 75 36 38 35 38 25 75 63 62 64 33 25 75 37 38 30   u6858%ucbd3%u780
120 : 31 25 75 39 30 39 30 25 75 36 38 35 38 25 75 63   1%u9090%u6858%uc
```

```
130 : 62 64 33 25 75 37 38 30 31 25 75 39 30 39 30 25
      bd3%u7801%u9090%
140 : 75 39 30 39 30 25 75 38 31 39 30 25 75 30 30 63
      u9090%u8190%u00c
150 : 33 25 75 30 30 30 33 25 75 38 62 30 30 25 75 35
      3%u0003%u8b00%u5
160 : 33 31 62 25 75 35 33 66 66 25 75 30 30 37 38 25
      31b%u53ff%u0078%
170 : 75 30 30 30 30 25 75 30 30 3D 61 20 20 48 54 54
      u0000%u00=a  HTT
180 : 50 2F 31 2E 30 0D 0A 43 6F 6E 74 65 6E 74 2D 74
      P/1.0..Content-t
190 : 79 70 65 3A 20 74 65 78 74 2F 78 6D 6C 0A 43 6F
      ype: text/xml.Co
1a0 : 6E 74 65 6E 74 2D 6C 65 6E 67 74 68 3A 20 33 33
      ntent-length: 33
1b0 : 37 39 20 0D 0A 0D 0A C8 C8 01 00 60 E8 03 00 00 79
      79 ........`....
1c0 : 00 CC EB FE 64 67 FF 36 00 00 64 67 89 26 00 00
      ....dg.6..dg.&..
1d0 : E8 DF 02 00 00 68 04 01 00 00 8D 85 5C FE FF FF
      .....h......\...
1e0 : 50 FF 55 9C 8D 85 5C FE FF FF 50 FF 55 98 8B 40
      P.U...\...P.U..@
1f0 : 10 8B 08 89 8D 58 FE FF FF FF 55 E4 3D 04 04 00
      .....X....U.=...
200 : 00 0F 94 C1 3D 04 08 00 00 0F 94 C5 0A CD 0F B6
      ....=...........
210 : C9 89 8D 54 FE FF FF 8B 75 08 81 7E 30 9A 02 00
      ...T....u..~0...
220 : 00 0F 84 C4 00 00 00 C7 46 30 9A 02 00 00 E8 0A
      ........F0......
230 : 00 00 00 43 6F 64 65 52 65 64 49 49 00 8B 1C 24
      ...CodeRedII...$
```

The Problem of NIDS False Positives

One of the main problems with intrusion detection systems is that they tend to generate a lot of false positives. A false positive occurs when the system generates an alert based on what it thinks is bad or suspicious activity but is actually normal traffic for that LAN. Generally, when you set up an NIDS with its default settings, it is going to look for anything and everything that is even slightly unusual. Most network intrusion detections systems have large default databases of thousands of signatures of possible suspicious activities. The IDS vendors have no way of knowing what your network traffic looks like, so they throw in everything to be on the safe side.

Common Causes of False Positives

Network Monitoring System Activity   Many companies use a Network Monitoring System (NMS) such as HP OpenView or WhatsUp Gold to keep track of the systems on their networks. They generate a lot of polling and discovery activity on your network. These systems usually use SNMP or some similar protocol to get the status, but they may also use pings and other more intrusive tests. By default, most detection systems see this activity as hostile or at least suspicious. An NMS on a large network can generate thousands of alerts per hour if the IDS is set to flag this kind of activity. You can avoid this by having your NIDS ignore activity to and from the IP of your NMS. You can also eliminate those NIDS alerts from the database if they are not something important for you to track.

Network Vulnerability Scanning/Port Scanners   If you are doing network vulnerability testing or port scanning using programs like Nessus and Nmap, then your NIDS is going to go nuts every time they run. These programs are designed to do exactly what hackers do. In fact, there is probably an alert for most Nessus plug-ins. Once again, you could disable reporting of the IP address of your Nessus or Nmap server within your NIDS. A better way to handle this is to shut down your IDS during your regularly scheduled scans. This way, the scanner box is still protected from attack when it is not scanning and your alert database isn't skewed with a lot of data from your own scanning activity.

User Activity   Most network intrusion detection systems are set up to flag various dangerous user activities, such as peer-to-peer file sharing, instant messaging, and so forth. However, if you allow this kind of activity either by formal policy or simply by not enforcing existing policies, then it will show up as alerts in your logs. This may make a good case for enforcing or creating policies against their use, because you can show how much bandwidth and time they are eating up, not to mention the security implications. However, if you intend to keep allowing this activity, you should comment out these rules so you won't fill up your logs with erroneous alerts.

Trojan Horse or Worm-Like Behavior   Modern viruses and virus-like software such as worms and Trojan horses are often network-aware. They attempt to perform various activities across the network, including infecting new machines and sending mass e-mails. These activities can be detected by an NIDS. However, these signatures can send alerts on normal activity as well. An example is the Nimda worm, which attempts to copy over numerous system files with certain extensions such as .eml. Unfortunately, Microsoft Exchange does the same thing when using its Web interface. So while being aware of Trojan-like activity on your network is valuable, you may want to turn off alerts that pick up known good activity on your LAN even when there is the potential for it to be bad traffic. This will help you to avoid being overwhelmed by false positives from your NIDS.

Long Basic Authentication Strings   This alert type looks for Web login strings that are overly long, because some exploits use this method to overflow a buffer and gain access. However, nowadays many Web sites cram a lot of information into this field and can trip off the NIDS unintentionally.

Database Authentication Activity   Some network intrusion detection systems look for administrative activity happening on a database. The theory here is that production databases should not have too much administrative activity going on, and this might be the sign of someone trying to tamper with a database. However, many databases are works-in-progress and have lots of administrative activity even while they are being used. This activity, though legitimate, will generate a lot of these types of alerts. If your databases are under constant development, then you should probably disable these alerts, at least until they are stabilized and put into production.

There are many other sources of false positives, depending on your network configuration and level of activity. An NIDS with default installations can generate hundreds of these false positive alerts in a single day. This can lead to a sense of despair for the system administrator; the resulting reaction is often that the alerts from these systems are soon ignored because of all the noise they generate. However, with a little work and using the techniques described in this chapter, an IDS can quickly become a helpful tool rather than the electronic version of the boy who cried wolf.

Getting the Most Out of Your IDS

To realize the true potential of an intrusion detection system, you need to do several things both before and after installation.

Proper System Configuration

If you just install an IDS and turn it loose with a default configuration, you will be quickly deluged with thousands of false positive alerts. While you can fine-tune your system after the fact, you will save a lot of time and effort by taking the time to carefully configure it beforehand. Don't just accept the default settings; customize these for your LAN.

Most intrusion detection systems group alerts into categories. Take a look at each group to see if it is relevant to your network. If there is a group of UNIX-based signatures but you don't have any UNIX systems on your network, you can probably safely turn off that whole batch of alerts. Some have policy-type alerts looking for things like instant messaging use or peer-to-peer software use. If you already have systems that filter these types of activities or you allow these activities, go ahead and deactivate them. You should go over the alert groups in detail. While you may want most Windows-based alerts, there will be some that are either irrelevant to your network or will cause false positives.

You can also exempt some hosts from examination. If your personal machine constantly does SNMP polls across your network or you are constantly logging in as administrator, it might generate more alerts than it is worth protecting. While this does lower the level of protection provided and might leave a critical machine unprotected, it may make your IDS more effective and be worth the risk. Taking a few hours up front to carefully configure your system before you activate it could save you a lot of time and frustration in the future. If you are going to the trouble and expense of running an IDS, it is worth taking the time to do it right.

IDS Tuning

Once it is up and running, even a meticulously configured IDS will start to generate alerts. Early on, if you take the time to analyze them and start to deactivate the rules that don't matter for your network, you can quickly lower the number of false positives your IDS is outputting. It will also give you insight as to how your network is working and what kind of traffic is going over it, which is helpful for any network manager. Plan some time each week to modify your IDS settings. Some systems make it relatively easy to mark an alert as false positive while others make you jump through some hoops. On average it takes a few months before an IDS is tuned to the point that it puts out useful alerts on actionable activity—and that's with a fairly dedicated fine-tuning effort.

IDS Analysis Tools

Intrusion detection systems typically offer administrators several different methods of being notified of an alert. At its most basic level, the alerts can simply be sent to a log file for later review. This is not really recommended, as it requires the administrator to be vigilant about reviewing the logs. If it is not monitored on a daily basis, then days or weeks can go by before discovering intrusion attempts. The other alternative is to send an e-mail or page the appropriate person whenever an alert is generated. However, even on a well-tuned system, it can become overwhelming to be receiving pages several times a day. Additionally, the e-mail alerts would not be in a format in which they can be compared to past alerts or analyzed in any way. The best way to handle IDS alerts is to port them immediately into a database to allow deeper analysis. There is an open source tool for intrusion detection systems called Analysis Console for Intrusion Detection (ACID). This tool is covered in more detail in Chapter 8.

Now that you know how Intrusion Detection Systems work, let's build one and put it to work.

Snort: An Open Source IDS for UNIX	
Snort	
Author/primary contact:	Martin Roesch
Web site:	www.snort.org
Platforms:	FreeBSD, Linux, Windows, and some UNIX
License:	GPL
Version reviewed:	2.1.1
Mailing lists:	
Snort-announcements	

Snort: An Open Source IDS for UNIX

General version and patch announcements. Not for discussion. Subscribe at lists.sourceforge.net/lists/listinfo/snort-announce.

Snort-users
General discussion of Snort. Newbies welcome. Subscribe at lists.source-forge.net/lists/listinfo/snort-users.

Snort-developers
For those developing or wishing to develop snort core code. Subscribe at lists.sourceforge.net/lists/listinfo/snort-developers.

Snort-sigs
For those developing or wishing to develop snort rules. Subscribe at lists.sourceforge.net/lists/listinfo/snort-sigs.

Snort-cvsinfo
CVS commits. Only for active developers wanting to be notified when the CVS tree is updated. No discussion allowed. Subscribe at lists.source-forge.net/lists/listinfo/snort-cvsinfo.

There is also an archive available on the Snort site of past posts. If you have a question, it is a good idea to check on there first to see if it has been answered previously. Chances are that someone else has had the problem before. Go to www.snort.org/lists.html.

There are local users groups that get together from time to time to talk about all things Snort. The list of user groups is at www.snort.org/user-groups.html.

There are about half a dozen major cities with active users groups and another dozen starting initial efforts. A form on the page lets you indicate interest in starting one if there isn't one in your area already.

Snort is Martin Roesch's baby, though it has grown far beyond his authorship and now counts some 30 plus developers in its core team, not including those writing rules and other parts of the software. As you can see from the lists above, there are many resources available for Snort. And these are just the free online resources. There are also several full-length books on the subject. This section, while not doing true justice to the subject, covers the basics and gets you up and running with Snort.

Snort is mostly a signature-based IDS, although with the addition of the Spade module Snort can now do anomalous activity detection. There are also add-on modules such as Inline Snort that allow Snort to act upon any alerts automatically.

Unique Features of Snort

- Open Source. Snort is open source and portable to just about any UNIX operating system. There are also versions of it available for Windows and other operating systems.
- Lightweight. Because the code runs so efficiently, it doesn't require a lot of hardware to run Snort (see the Hardware sidebar). This allows it to be able to analyze traffic on a 100Mbps network at near wire speed, which is pretty incredible when you think what it is doing with each packet.
- Snort custom rules. Snort offers an easy way to extend and customize the program by writing your own rules or signatures. There is lots of documentation to help you learn how to do this, not to mention the online forums and help lists.

Installing Snort

Snort is fairly straightforward to install.

1. As a prerequisite, you need the libpcap package installed. If you've loaded any of the previous packages from Chapters 4–6, you will already have libpcap installed. If not, you can download it from www.tcpdump.org.
2. Once you have those libraries loaded, simply take the file off the CD-ROM that accompanies this book or download the latest version from the Web site.
3. When it is on your machine, unzip it and issue the compile commands:

```
./configure
make
make install
```

Running Snort

Snort is run from the command line. You can run Snort in three different modes: packet sniffer, packet logger, and IDS mode. Most people run it in the latter to get the IDS benefits, but there are uses for the first two.

Packet Sniffer Mode In this mode, Snort acts just like a sniffer, showing you the unfiltered contents on the wire. Of course, if all you needed was a sniffer, you could just use Tcpdump or Ethereal. However, packet sniffer mode is good for making sure that everything is working correctly and Snort is seeing packets. Table 7.1 lists switches you can use when running Snort in this mode. You must include at least the -v command when using the packet sniffer mode, or else Snort defaults to running in one of the other modes (packet logging or intrusion detection) and expects other options.

You can test this by simply typing

```
snort -v
```

Table 7.1 Packet Sniffer Mode Options

Options	Descriptions
-v	Prints the packet headers of TCP/IP packets on the Ethernet to the screen.
-d	Same as above but also displays the application layer data.
-e	Same as above but also prints the data link layer.

or

```
snort -vde
```

at a command prompt. You will see output similar to the sniffers used in the previous chapter. Press Control+C to exit and you will see a summary of the packet sniffing session.

Hardware Requirement for Your NIDS

There are a couple of things to take into consideration when selecting the hardware to run your NIDS on. Because detection systems tend to be fairly processor- and disk-intensive, it is strongly recommended that you run the NIDS on a box dedicated solely to that purpose. However, being Linux-based, it still doesn't require much hardware compared to what an equivalent Windows machine would need. This assumes you are not running X-Windows, which can take a considerable amount of processor power and is not really needed for the Snort IDS.

To run Snort, you should have a 500MHz Intel processor, although I have run Snort boxes reliably on 266MHz PCs. If you are storing log files locally, you will also want at least several gigabytes of available hard drive space. A 100Mbps network card should be used to eliminate any bottlenecks if you are going to be sniffing on a 100Mbps network. The authors of Snort claim that the code will handle up to a saturated 100Mbps segment without dropping any packets, and I haven't seen anything to rebut these claims. However, if your network is that busy, you should probably up the hardware requirements a little to perhaps a 1GHz processor. Either way, these requirements should be easy to meet with all but the oldest machines.

Packet Logging Mode   This is similar to packet sniffer mode, but it lets you log sniffed packets to disk for future use and analysis, like the logging functionality found in the sniffers described previously. To run snort in packet logging mode, simply run it with the same command as packet sniffer mode (-v, -d, and/or -e) but add an additional switch, `-l` *logpath,* where you replace *logpath* with the path you want Snort to log the packets to. For example:

```
snort -vde -l /var/log/snort
```

This will create log files in the /var/log/snort directory. Make sure the directory you specify has been created or the program will not load properly. Snort logs packets by IP address and creates a separate directory for each IP logged. If you are logging traffic on a large local network with a lot of addresses, this can quickly get out of hand. Therefore you can use another setting to tell Snort to log packets relative to the home network you are on. You do this with the `-h` *homenet* command, where *homenet* is the IP address ranges in slash notation of your local network. This makes Snort put them in directories based on the nonlocal IP address in the packet, so you can see nonnative traffic easier. If both the destination and the source hosts are local, Snort puts it in the directory with the higher port number, ostensibly to pick the connecting host over a server host. If there is a tie, then Snort defaults to using the source address as the directory to put the packet data in. This may not seem important now, but when you are logging intrusion alerts, it is important to easily tell where the alert flagged traffic is coming from.

So the command line entry for packet logging mode now looks like this:

```
snort -vde -l /var/log/snort -h 192.168.1.0/24
```

This specifies an internal network in the range of 192.168.1.1–254.

You can also use the `-b` option to log all the data into a single binary file suitable for reading later with a packet sniffer such as Ethereal or Tcpdump. When logging this way, you don't need to specify your home network when using the `-b` switch, since it will be logging files sequentially into one big file. This method is a lot faster for logging busy networks or slower machines. It also facilitates analysis with more complex tools, which is necessary if you are going to be looking at a large amount of network capture data.

Intrusion Detection Mode This mode uses Snort to log packets that are suspicious or warrant some further attention. You need only one additional switch to the statement above to put Snort into this mode. This is the `-c` *configfile* switch, which tells Snort to use a configuration file to govern what packets it logs. The config file determines all the settings for Snort and is a very important file. Snort comes with a default config file, but you will want to make some changes to it before running it to reflect your environment. So by typing

```
snort -de -l /var/log/snort -h 192.168.1.0/24 -c /etc/
    snort/snort.conf
```

you will be running Snort in IDS mode using the default snort.conf configuration file. Be sure that the config file exists in the specified directory (/etc/snort/snort.conf) or change the path to reflect its location on your system.

Notice that I didn't use the `-v` switch for running Snort in IDS mode. When trying to compare all packets with signatures, forcing Snort to also write alerts to the screen may cause it to drop some packets, especially on busier networks. You can also leave off the `-e` switch to improve performance if you don't need to log the data link layers. If you leave off the −1 switch, Snort will default to using /var/log/snort as its logging directory. Again, make sure that the directory exists or Snort won't start. You could also use the −b switch if you wanted to log to a binary file for analysis with a separate program later. The command for running Snort in IDS mode now looks like this:

```
snort −h 192.168.1.0/24 −c /etc/snort/snort.conf
```

Snort Alert Modes   Now that you are logging alert packets, you need to decide how much detail you want and what format you want the alert data in. Table 7.2 lists options you can use from the command line using the −A switch.

There are also the syslog, smb, and database output options, but these don't use the −A switch from the command line. They use separate output modules and offer a wider variety of output options. These must be configured at compile time with switches added to the configure statement.

- SMB sends the alerts to the Windows pop-up service, so you can have your alerts visually popping up on your screen or the screen of a monitoring machine. However, you will want to have your IDS finely tuned before using this option, otherwise you will never get any work done with all the pop-ups displaying! Use the −enable-smbalerts statement in your configure statement when installing Snort to enable this alerting method. You then run snort with the following settings:

```
snort −c /etc/snort.conf −M workstations
```

where *workstations* is the Windows host name of the machine(s) to send the alerts to.

Table 7.2 Snort Alert Mode Options

Options	Descriptions
-A full	Full alert information including application data. This is the default alert mode and will be used when nothing is specified.
-A fast	Fast mode. Logs only the packet header information and the alert type. This is useful on very fast networks, but if you need more forensic information, you should use the full switch.
-A unsock	Sends the alert to a UNIX socket number that another program can be listening on.
-A none	Turns the alerts off.

- Syslog sends the alerts to a UNIX Syslog server. Syslog is a service running on a machine (usually UNIX) that can capture and store various log files. This helps consolidate logs for your network in a single place, as well as making it more difficult for a hacker to erase logs of an intrusion. This book doesn't cover the specifics of setting up a Syslog server, but if you have one Snort can send the alerts there if you include the -s switch in your command line argument. You can then specify the different Syslog formats within the configuration file, which is covered in the next section.
- Snort directly supports four kinds of database output through its output modules. The supported formats are MySQL, PostgreSQL, Oracle, and unixODBC. This should meet the needs of most database users. And of course if your database isn't supported, you can take on the project to write that module extension. The database output module requires both compile time parameters and settings within the configuration file. See the next section for more details.

Configuring Snort for Maximum Performance

Now that you have Snort up and running and know the basic commands, you need to edit the configuration file to make it a reliable IDS and get the results you want. The default configuration file is snort.conf and by default is at /etc/snort.conf. This file is where you do all of your setup and configuration of Snort. You can change the name of this file as long as you refer to its new file name and path after the -c switch when running Snort. Edit the file using vi, EMACS, or the text editor of your choice. A lot of lines in the file start with # and are followed by various comments. The # is a standard beginning for comment lines, and many languages, such as Perl and shell scripts, ignore lines starting with it. These are used to document a program or to disable old code. You will be using them later to fine-tune your rule set. But for now, the only lines that have any actual effect on the configuration are those without # signs at the beginning. The rest is just there for informational purposes. There are several steps to setting up your config file.

1. Set your home network.

   You need to tell Snort the addresses that represent your home network so it can correctly interpret attacks coming from outside your network. You do this with the statement

   ```
   var HOME_NET addresses
   ```

   where you replace *addresses* with the address space of your local network. If there are multiple networks, you can enter them all, separated by commas. You can also enter an interface name and have it use the IP address and net mask assigned to that interface as its HOME_NET. The format for doing this is

   ```
   var HOME_NET $interfacename
   ```

where you replace *interfacename* with the interface Snort is listening on such as
eth0 or eth1.

You can also define your external networks with a similar statement, replacing
HOME_NET with EXTERNAL_NET. The default entry for both of these variables is
any. You can leave it this way or define both. I recommend defining your internal
network but leaving external networks set as any.

2. Set up your internal servers.

In the configuration file you can define a number of servers, including Web, mail,
DNS, SQL, and Telnet. This will limit the false positive alerts for those services on
those machines.

You can also specify port numbers for those services, so unless the attack is on
the port you are using it doesn't register an alert. All of these configuration options
can help you reduce the number of false positives you get and alert you only to
information that has real value. There is also a section to add AIM servers to track
usage of AOL Instant Messenger. This is only applicable if you have the Chat rule
class enabled.

3. Configure the Snort decoders and preprocessors.

A number of switches and settings control the Snort decoders and preprocessors in
the config file. These routines run on the traffic before it passes through any rule
set, usually to format it properly or deal with a particular kind of traffic that is
easier to process upfront than using the rule sets. An example of this type of traffic
would be fragmented packets. Snort has a decoder that reassembles fragmented
packets. Many attacks attempt to hide their true nature by fragmenting the packets,
so this is a valuable feature.

Another decoder is for port scanning packets. Since these tend to come in
groups and in high volume, it is better to process them up front en mass than trying
to match each packet to a signature. This also makes the IDS more secure from
denial of service. The default settings for these subsystems should be fine, but as
you get more experienced with Snort, you can tweak these settings to get better
performance and results.

4. Configure the output modules.

This is an important step if you want to use a database to manage your output from
Snort. This is when you give the program directives on how to handle the alert
data. There are several output modules you can use depending on the format you
want the data in. They are Syslog, Database, and a new one called Unified, which
is a generic binary format useful for importing to various other programs. The general format for configuring the output modules is

```
output module_name: configuration options
```

where *module_name* is either alert_syslog, database, or alert_unified,
depending on the module you want to use.

The configuration options for each output module are as follows.

- Syslog

  For UNIX/Linux systems, you should use the following directive:

  ```
  output alert_syslog: LOG_AUTH LOG_ALERT
  ```

  For Windows system, you can use any of the following formats:

  ```
  output alert_syslog: LOG_AUTH LOG_ALERT
  output alert_syslog: host=hostname, LOG_AUTH LOG_ALERT
  output alert_syslog: host=hostname:port, LOG_AUTH
  LOG_ALERT
  ```

  where *hostname* and *port* are the IP address and port of your Syslog server.

- Database

  The general format for configuring database output is:

  ```
  output database: log, database_type, user=user_name
  password=password dbname=dbname host=database_address
  ```

  where you replace *database_type* with one of the valid databases for Snort (MySQL, postgresql, unixodbc, or mssql). You also replace *user_name* with a valid user name on the database box and *password* with the appropriate password. The *dbname* variable identifies the name of the database to log to. Finally, *database_address* is the IP address of your database server. It is not recommended that you try to run Snort and your database on the same server. In addition to being more secure to have your alert data on another box, Snort and a database running on the same machine will slow down performance considerably. While database configuration is not the subject of this book, the basic configuration of a MySQL database for Snort and other programs is discussed in Chapter 8.

- Unified

  This is a basic binary format for quick logging and storage for future use. The two arguments that are supported are *filename* and *limit*. Here is the format:

  ```
  output alert_unified: filename snort.alert, limit 128
  ```

5. Customize your rule sets.

   You can fine-tune Snort by adding or deleting rule sets. The snort.conf file lets you add or delete entire classes of rules. At the bottom of the file you will see all the alert rule sets listed. You can turn off a whole category of rules by commenting out that line by putting a # sign at the beginning. For example, you could turn off all the icmp-info rules to lower false positives on ping traffic or all the NetBIOS rules if you had no Windows machines on your network. There are also rule sets available publicly that have already been tuned for specific environments.

Once you are done making changes to your config file, save it, and then you are ready to run Snort.

Proper NIDS placement

When deciding where to place your NIDS on your network, you need to consider what you are trying to protect with your NIDS and how to maximize its effectiveness and interoperability with your other network protections. There are several possibilities where you can put your NIDS, and each has distinct advantages and disadvantages.

- On your local LAN behind your firewall. This is the most common configuration and offers the best protection from both outside and inside threats. By listening on the local wire, you can detect internal activity by your users, such as activity from workstation to workstation or illicit program use. It also backs up your firewall, detecting suspicious activity that somehow manages to make it through your firewall filters. In fact, an IDS can be used to test a firewall to see what it will let through.

    However, this will generate a lot of alerts based on Windows networking traffic, so be prepared to do a lot of tuning in this area. Also, if you are on a switched LAN, you will need the ability to mirror all ports to a monitor port in order to allow your IDS to listen to all LAN traffic.

- On your DMZ segment. You can put a Snort sensor on your DMZ network to track activity going to your public servers. Since these servers are the most exposed in your enterprise and usually represent valuable resources, it is a good idea to monitor them with an IDS. The problem you will have with this configuration is sorting through all the alerts. While all of them may be valid alerts, with the level of general attack traffic on the Internet these days, any public IP is generally attacked several times daily on a random basis. Reacting to and attempting to track down these alerts would be overkill and counterproductive.

    So how do you tell which ones are just worms bouncing off your server and which ones are actually getting away with something? One way is to reduce the number of signatures to a small number that go off only if the box actually got compromised, for example, rules specific to the applications running on that box, such as MySQL.rules or web-iis rules, or rules relating to administrative logon. You can eliminate most of the reconnaissance type alerts for activity such as ports scans, and so on.

- Between your ISP and your firewall. This would filter all the traffic going and coming to your LAN and DMZ. The good news is that you will catch anything attacking both your public servers and your internal LAN. The bad news is that you won't see any internal traffic, and the general alert volume may be quite high due to the general background attack traffic.

    Like the previous example, try to narrow down the alerts to the ones that really would show a problem for this network segment and leave those on. Also, you will have to put the sensor in line between your ISP and the firewall, which can create a traffic bottleneck and a single point of failure for your network traffic. A solution would be to install a small hub between the two links and hang the IDS off of that.

These are all valid ways to use an IDS. Of course, there is no reason you can't do all three as long as you have the hardware and time to manage it.

Disabling Rules in Snort

The easiest way to limit your alert traffic is to turn off rules that don't apply to your system. You can do this by going into your Snort box and finding the rules directory (usually under the directory you installed Snort in). In that directory there are many files with a .rules extension. Each of these contains many rules grouped by category. You can disable a whole class of rules by commenting it out in the configuration file, or you can disable individual rules if you still want the protection from the other rules in that class. You comment out a rule by finding it in the appropriate .rules files and placing a # in front of the line for that rule. Note that it is generally better to disable a single rule than a whole class of rules unless that whole class doesn't apply to you. Table 7.3 lists all the file names for Snort rule classes and describes them briefly.

Table 7.3 Snort Rule Classes File Names

Rule Classes	Descriptions
attack-responses.rule	These are alerts for common response packets after an attack is successful. They should rarely report false positives and should be left on in most cases.
backdoor.rule	These are common signs a backdoor or Trojan horse program is in use. They will rarely be false positive.
bad-traffic.rule	These rules represent nonstandard network traffic that should not typically be seen on most networks.
chat.rules	Look for standard sign-ons for many popular chat programs. If chat is allowed explicitly or implicitly, then these alerts should be turned off. Also, note that these are not silver bullets for chats and will not detect all types of chat traffic. Still, they can be helpful in ferreting out the worst offenders.

(continues)

Table 7.3 Snort Rule Classes File Names (*continued*)

Rule Classes	Descriptions
ddos.rule	Look for standard distributed denial of service types of attacks. On a DMZ and WAN, these alerts don't serve much purpose, because if you are under a distributed denial of service you will probably know it right away. However, they can be very useful inside the LAN to see if you have zombie machine participating unknowingly in a DDOS attack on another network.
dns.rules	Look for some standard exploits against DNS servers. If you aren't running your own DNS, you can turn these off.
dos.rules	Similar to the ddos.rule set above.
experimental.rules	These are turned off by default. These are generally used only for testing new rules until they are moved into one of the other categories.
exploit.rules	These are for standard exploit traffic and should always be enabled.
finger.rules	These rules flag traffic having to do with finger servers. If you are not running finger anywhere, you could probably turn these off. However, finger servers often are running hidden from the system administrator, so you could leave these on as they shouldn't generate false positives if you don't have any.
ftp.rules	Same as finger.rules but looking for FTP exploits. Again, there is no harm in leaving them enabled even if you don't have FTP servers since it will alert you to any rogue FTP servers you may have.
icmp-info.rules	These rules track the use of ICMP messages crossing your network, for example, pings. These are often the cause of false positives, and you may want to disable the whole lot unless you want to keep a close eye on ICMP traffic on your network. Another class for known bad ICMP traffic, icmp.rules catches ports scans and the like.
icmp.rules	Cover bad or suspicious ICMP traffic such as port scans, and are less likely to generate false positives. However, it is possible they will be triggered often on a busy network with lots of diagnostic services running.

Rule Classes	Descriptions
imap.rules	Rules regarding the use of Internet Message Access Protocol (IMAP) on your network.
info.rules	Trap miscellaneous error messages on your network from Web, FTP, and other servers.
local.rules	You add your own custom signatures for your network in this file. This file is empty by default. See the section at the end of the chapter for information on writing a custom Snort rule.
misc.rules	Rules that don't fit under one of the other categories or don't warrant their own sections are in this file. An example would be older alerts like Gopher server exploits.
multimedia.rules	Track usage of streaming video type software. If you allow streaming video applications or use video conferencing on your network, then you will want to disable these rules.
mysql.rules	Watch for administrator access and other important files in a MySQL database. If you don't run MySQL, then you can probably disable these alerts. Also, if your MySQL database is under development, these might trigger a lot of false positives.
Netbios.rules	This class of rules alerts you to various NetBIOS activity on your LAN. Some of them are obvious exploits. However, others, such as the NULL session alerts, may happen normally on a Windows LAN. You will have to play with this section to figure out the rules that are appropriate for your LAN.
nntp.rules	News server–related rules. If you don't run network news on your servers, you can probably turn these off.
oracle.rules	Oracle database server rules. Again, if you don't run it, turn it off.
other-ids.rules	These rules are related to exploits on other IDS manufacturers' boxes. Chances are that you don't have any NIDS on your LAN, but if you do, leave these on.

(continues)

Table 7.3 Snort Rule Classes File Names (*continued*)

Rule Classes	Descriptions
p2p.rules	Rules governing peer-to-peer file sharing software use. These rules will create alerts during normal use of these products, so if you allow this software then you will need to turn these off.
policy.rules	This file contains various alerts relating to allowed activity on the LAN, such as Go-to-my-pc and other programs. You should review these and enable only the ones that apply to your internal policies.
pop2.rules pop3.rules	Both files to mail servers. Most companies, if using POP, will be using a POP3 server. If you have either of these types of servers, leave these rules on; if not, disable them.
porn.rules	These are some rudimentary traps for pornography-related Web surfing. These are by no means a replacement for a good content-filtering system, but can catch some of the more egregious violators.
rpc.rules	This class handles remote procedure call (RPC) alerts. Even though you may not think you are running any of these services, they often run as part of other programs, so it is important to be aware when this is happening on your LAN. RPC can enable remote code execution and is often used in Trojans and exploits.
rservices.rules	Track use of various remote services programs, such as rlogin and rsh. These are insecure services in general, but if you have to use them, they can be tracked closely with this rule set.
scan.rules	Alert you to use of port scanning programs. Ports scans are a good indication of illicit activity. If you use port scanners, you will want to either turn off Snort during those times or disable the particular rule for your scanner machine.
shellcode.rules	This class looks for packets containing assembly code, low-level commands also known as shell code. These commands are often integral to many exploits such as buffer overflows. Catching a chunk of shell code flying by is often a pretty good indication that an attack is underway.
smtp.rules	Govern alerts for mail server use on the LAN. This section will need some fine-tuning, as many normal mail server activities will set off rules in this section.

Rule Classes	Descriptions
sql.rules	Rules for various SQL database programs. If you don't run any databases you can turn these off, but it's not a bad idea to leave them on just in case there are SQL databases running that you don't know about.
telnet.rules	Track Telnet use on the network. Telnet is often used on routers or other command line devices, so it is a good thing to track even if you don't run Telnet on your servers.
tftp.rules	TFTP (trivial FTP) is an alternate FTP server often run on routers. It can be used to upload new configurations and therefore is worth keeping an eye on.
virus.rules	Contain signatures of some common worms and viruses. This list is not complete and is not maintained regularly. It is not a replacement for virus scanning software but can catch some network-aware worms.
web-attacks.rules web-cgi.rules web-client.rules web-coldfusion.rules web-frontpage.rules web-iis.rules web-php.rules	All these classes refer to various kinds of suspicious Web activity. Some are generic, such as the web-attacks class. Others, like web-iis and web-frontpage, are specific to a particular Web server platform. However, even if you don't think you run a Microsoft Web server or use PHP, it is worth leaving them all running to uncover any of this kind of activity on your LAN you may be unaware of. You will have to do some fine-tuning of the rule sets, especially if your Web servers are in active development.
X11.rules	Track the use of the X11 graphical environment on your network.

Running Snort as a Service

If you are going to be running Snort on a server that is intended to be up 24/7, then you will want to run Snort immediately upon boot up so that if the box goes down, it will reload Snort and your IDS will continue to protect your LAN. One way to do this is to have a little script that runs Snort with the command line parameters in your startup routines. In Linux, you can place a line in the rc.local file in the /etc/rc.d directory with your command line arguments to run Snort. An example is:

```
snort -h 192.168.1.0/24 -c /etc/snort/snort.conf &
```

The & (ampersand) on the end means to run Snort as a background process. You can also run Snort as a service using the `service snort start` command.

Snort Webmin Interface: A Graphical Interface for Snort	
Snort Webmin Interface	
Author/primary contact:	Mike Baptiste/MSB Networks
Web site:	msnnetworks.net/snort/
Platforms:	Most Linux
License:	GPL
Version reviewed:	1.1

Doing all the configuration for Snort from the command line can get a little tedious. While there isn't a native graphical interface for Snort yet, there is a module for the popular Web management tool Webmin. This lets you do all of your fine-tuning and configuration from any Web browser. Some of the benefits of this system are:

- Form-based access to Snort configuration files
- User access levels that allow you to set up different users with different rights
- Point-and-click ability to enable and disable rule sets
- Status indicator for all rules and rule sets
- Embedded links to external database such as archNIDS, CVE, and Bugtraq
- Logging of changes
- International language capability
- Support for running Snort as a service using rc.d files
- Secure remote administration via SSL (if enabled)

Chapter 3 covered loading Webmin for your firewall administration. You can also use this add-on module to configure Snort. Refer back to Chapter 3 if you haven't loaded Webmin yet.

The Snort module requires version 0.87 of Webmin or later. You can use the Snort Webmin file on the CD-ROM, download the Snort module using the Webmin interface, or download the file separately and load it locally. The location to get the software is:

www.msbnetworks.com/snort/download/snort-1.1wbm

To load the Snort module from the Webmin interface, take the following steps.

1. Go into the Webmin main page. Log in using the username and password you set up when installing Webmin.
2. Click on the Webmin configuration tab. Click on Modules, and select either Local file or Ftp URL, depending on whether you have already downloaded it to your machine or want to have Webmin get it from the Web site.

3. Click on Install module, and it will install the Snort module file. The Snort module will appear as an icon on your Webmin main page. Click on this icon to display the Webmin Snort interface (see Figure 7.2).

Once you log onto the Snort page, you can see it has each major section of the config file, such as network settings, preprocessor settings, and your logging options, at the top of the screen. By clicking on any of the configuration options, you can enter your information in a form and Webmin will make the changes to the appropriate Snort configuration files.

All the rule sets are listed below that, and you can see which ones are enabled or disabled. Those with a check are currently enabled and those with an **X** mark are disabled. You can easily disable the entire rule set by double-clicking on the Action field. If you want to view that rule set and modify an individual rule, click on the blue underlined text and it will take you to the Edit Ruleset page (see Figure 7.3). Here you can see all the active rules within that set. You can also take actions on each rule such as disabling, enabling, or deleting it from the rule set. If there are any references to external databases within the alert, such as Common Vulnerability or Exploit (CVE) numbers, you can click a hyperlink to take you to more detail on what that alert does. Using this interface can make fine-tuning your alert rule set much easier.

With the Webmin Snort module, you can also control which users can access which settings (see Figure 7.4). On the Webmin users page you can set a variety of options for each user (assuming you are the administrator on Webmin). You can give certain users access to edit rules but not to edit configuration files. You can control which configuration files they can access. Or you can just let them view the files without editing or disabling them. As you can see, the Webmin Snort module gives you very granular access control so that you can delegate daily tuning duties to a lower-level technician while retaining configuration and change control.

> **Snort for Windows: An Open Source IDS for Windows**
>
> **Snort for Windows**
> Author/primary contact: Martin Roesch
> Ported by: Michael Davis and Chris Reid
> Web site: www.snort.org
> Platforms: Windows 2000, XP
> License: GPL
> Version reviewed: 2.0.0
> Other resources: See the listing in the section "Snort: An Open Source IDS for UNIX" earlier in this chapter.

For those of you who can't or won't install the UNIX version of Snort, thankfully there is a fully supported version for the Windows platform. While it is true that you will

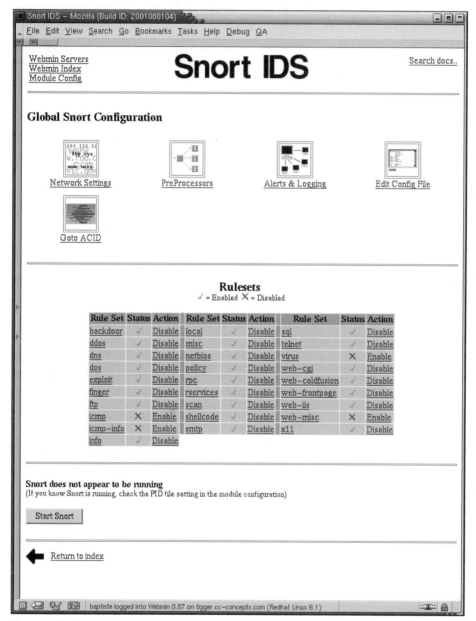

Figure 7.2 Webmin Snort Module

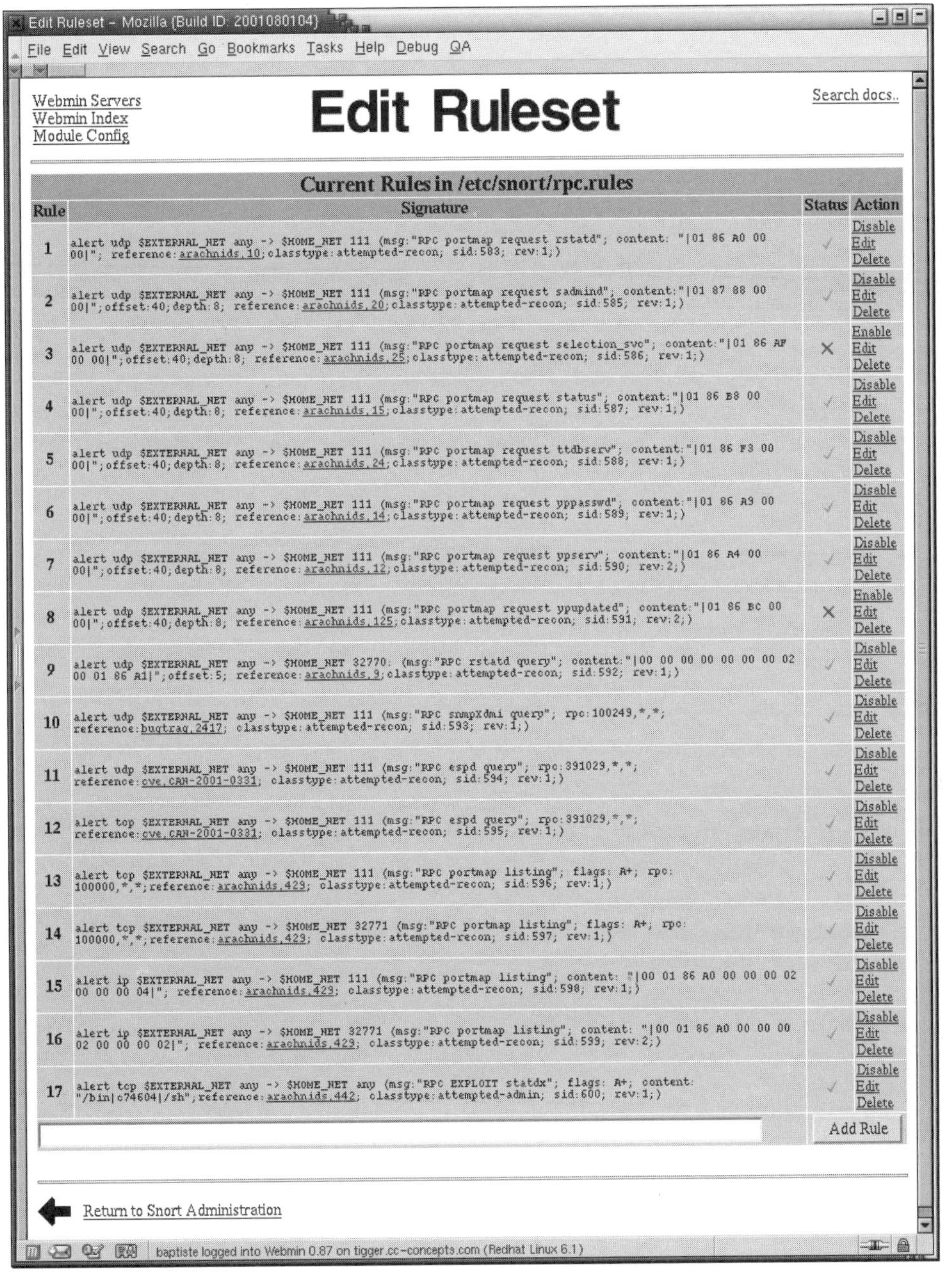

Figure 7.3 Webmin Snort Edit Ruleset Page

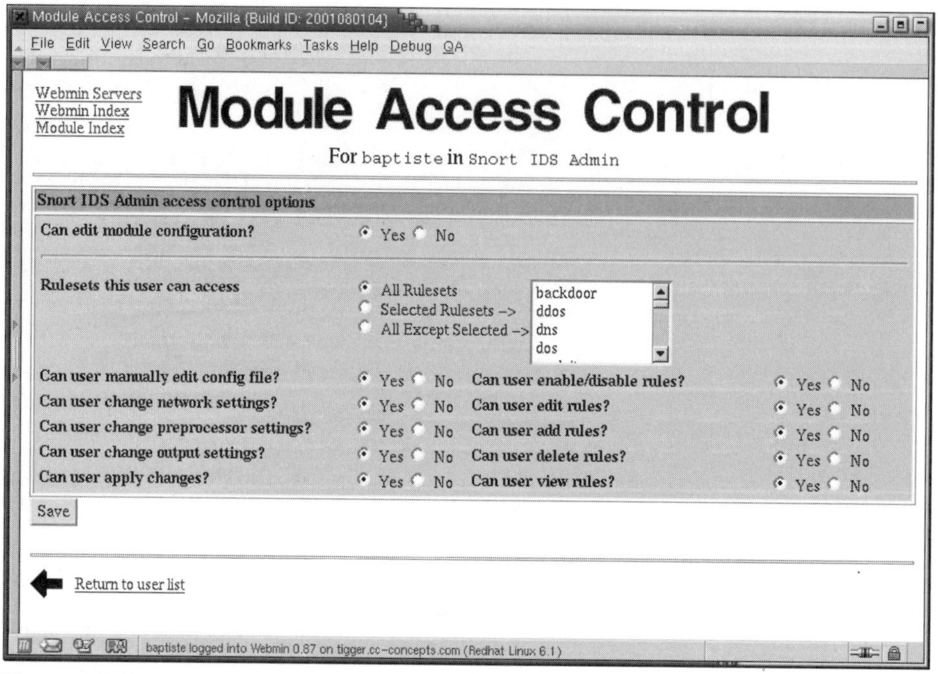

Figure 7.4 Webmin Snort Module Access Control

get more for your hardware dollar with the UNIX version, the Windows version is not just a side project—it is actually developed by the core Snort group and kept fairly current with the UNIX version. It also allows you to take advantage of point-and-click installation as well as some of the other niceties in Windows 2000 and XP such as built-in IPSec support. It's nice to see an open source project that realizes there are many Windows-only based companies that would still like to take advantage of this great open source IDS.

Requirements for Windows Snorting

Snort for Windows requires Windows 2000 or XP; it won't run on NT, 98, or 95. You will also need the WinPcap libraries installed. If you loaded them for a program described earlier in this book, such as Ethereal or WinDump, then you are all set. Otherwise, you can get them at:

> netgroup-serv.polito.it/winpcap

You will also want the MySQL database if you plan on importing your results into a database. Specific configuration of MySQL for this purpose is covered in Chapter 8.

You will need more powerful hardware for your Windows Snort box than the UNIX version to get similar performance. A 700MHz machine is the minimum, and you'll probably do better with a processor in the gigahertz range. You will also want to make sure your Windows server is locked down appropriately with a minimum of services running, taking extra care to uninstall processor hogs such as IIS. Use the Services window under Administrative tools to make sure you aren't running anything you absolutely don't need to.

Installing Snort for Windows

To get going with Snort for Windows, get the binary file from the book's CD-ROM or from www.snort.org. Double-click on it and it will automatically install for you. It prompts you to choose if you want certain database or add-on modules such as the flex-response module.

Setting Up Snort for Windows

The process for setting up the Windows version is very similar to the UNIX setup. All the config and rules files are in the same relative subdirectories as the UNIX version. Go into the Snort.conf file in the /etc subdirectories of your Snort installation. Make the changes and edits to the snort.conf file as suggested in the UNIX section. Then go into the rules files and make your changes there. Then you are ready to run Snort. Refer to the UNIX "Running Snort" section for more details on how to use Windows Snort, as all the commands are the same. Fine-tuning and placement rules of thumb are also the same as the native UNIX version.

Flamey the Tech Coders Corner:

Writing Custom Snort Rules

While the standard rule sets that Snort comes with provide adequate protection from known attack signatures, you can craft some custom rules specific to your network to get the most out of your IDS. You can write rules to:

- Track access to or from particular servers
- Look for certain file types or file names specific to your organization
- Watch for particular types of traffic that don't belong on your network

Snorts rule writing is fairly easy to learn and allows you to quickly add functionality to the program without a lot of programming knowledge. As you have seen, all the Snort rules are simply text statements within one of the rules files.

If you want to have Snort look for some unique behavior that would be suspicious on your network, you can code a rule quickly and be testing for behavior in short order. The format of a Snort rule is basically a single text line starting with an action (usually "alert") and followed by several arguments. In the newest version (2.0 and higher), you can add multiple lines simply by appending a / (slash) to the end of each line. You can also call other programs using an include statement for more complexity. But in its basic form, a Snort rule has two parts: a rule header and the rule options. Below is an example of a rule.

```
alert tcp any any 192.168.0.0/24 /
(content:"|00 05 A4 6F 2E|";msg:"Test Alert";)
```

The alert header is the part before the first parenthesis. This statement contains the action (alert in this case), the protocol, and destination and source addresses and ports. The action is what this rule will do if it is true. In this example, it will generate an alert. Other options for actions are Log, Pass, Activate, and Dynamic.

Log	Just log the packet.
Pass	Ignore the packet. This is the default action on packets that don't match the rule.
Activate	Alert, then activate a dynamic rule.
Dynamic	Remain idle until activated by a dynamic rule, then act as a log rule.

The protocols can be tcp, udp, icmp, or ip, which means any IP protocol. (In the future non-IP-based protocols such as IPX may be supported.) The source and destination ports are self-explanatory. The source address is first, listed in standard slash notation for IP ranges. You can also list multiple individual addresses and networks by separating them with a comma, no spaces, and encapsulating the statement in brackets, for example:

```
alert tcp any <> [192.168.1.1,192.168.1.5,192.168.1.10] 80 /
(content:"|00 05 A4 6F 2E|";msg:"Test Alert";)
```

This statement focuses on traffic coming from any addresses bound for the machines at 192.168.1.1, 192.168.1.5, and 192.168.1.10 on port 80. Assuming these are your Web servers, this would look for traffic going to them that contained the hex data in the content section.

The second part of a Snort alert is the alert options. This is where you specify further details about the kind of traffic you are looking for. You can search on the many fields in the TCP/IP header (see Chapter 6 for descriptions) or simply search the packet payload. Each option command should be followed by quotes and the value you are searching for. Multiple options can be added by separating them with a semicolon. The following are valid option commands.

msg	Provide the text description of an alert.
logto	Log the packet to a user-specified filename instead of the standard output file.
ttl	Test the IP header's TTL field value.
tos	Test the IP header's TOS field value.
id	Test the IP header's fragment ID field for a specific value.
ipoption	Watch the IP option fields for specific codes.
fragbits	Test the fragmentation bits of the IP header.
dsize	Test the packet's payload size against a value.
flags	Test the TCP flags for certain values.
seq	Test the TCP sequence number field for a specific value.
ack	Test the TCP acknowledgment field for a specific value.
itype	Test the ICMP type field against a specific value.
icode	Test the ICMP code field against a specific value.
icmp_id	Test the ICMP ECHO ID field against a specific value.
icmp_seq	Test the ICMP ECHO sequence number against a specific value.
content	Search for a pattern in the packet's payload.
content-list	Search for a set of patterns in the packet's payload.
offset	Modifier for the content option. Sets the offset to begin attempting a pattern match.
depth	Modifier for the content option. Sets the maximum search depth for a pattern match attempt.
nocase	Match the preceding content string with case insensitivity.
session	Dump the application layer information for a given session.
rpc	Watch RPC services for specific application/procedure calls.
resp	Active response. Closes the connection down (for example, take down connections).
react	Active response. Respond with a set of scripted behavior (for example, block certain Web sites).
reference	External attack reference IDs.
sid	Snort rule ID.
rev	Rule revision number.

classtype	Rule classification identifier.
priority	Rule severity identifier.
uricontent	Search for a pattern in the URI portion of a packet.
tag	Advanced logging actions for rules.
ip_proto	IP header's protocol value.
sameip	Determines if source IP equals the destination IP.
stateless	Valid regardless of stream state.
regex	Wildcard pattern matching.
byte_test	Numerical evaluation.
distance	Forcing relative pattern matching to skip a certain number of bytes into the packet.
byte_test	Numerical pattern testing.
byte_jump	Numerical pattern testing and offset adjustment.

See the man pages for details on each specific rule option. The following are some examples of using these options to create custom Snort rules.

Sample Custom Rule 1

Let's say you have a set of accounting servers that should never be accessed by anyone outside your network. You could write a Snort rule to flag traffic coming from any IP that was not on your home network going to these servers. Assuming your accounting servers are on the IP addresses 192.168.1.10, 192.168.1.11, and 192.168.1.12, and your home network is 192.168.2.0/24, the rule would look something like this:

```
alert tcp !192.168.1.0/24 any /
<>[192.168.1.10,192.168.1.11,192.168.1.12] any /
(msg:"Accounting Server Access from outside";)
```

The ! (exclamation mark) operator here is the NOT operator for Boolean operations. This basically says to issue an alert on any TCP traffic that is not coming from the 192.168.1.0/24 network that is bound for these servers. There are no options set other than `msg`, which is the label that shows up in the alert logs. This is because you are concerned with any traffic on any port. This would show you any access coming from the outside world to your accounting servers, because it assumes that any outside traffic to them should be considered bad.

Sample Custom Rule 2

Building off of the scenario described in rule example 1, assume you have to allow some outside access to these servers, but still want to make sure no one was copying certain files. Let's say there is a file called payroll.xls that has all of the payroll figures (a very sensitive file for both inside and outside the company). You could write a rule that looked for any traffic, internal or external, coming from these servers that contained those words. You could do this using the `content` option, which searches the actual content of the packet. This rule would look something like this:

```
alert tcp ![192.168.1.10,192.168.1.11,192.168.1.12] any <> /
[192.168.1.10,192.168.1.11,192.168.1.12] any
(content:"payroll.xls";/ msg:"Payroll File Access";)
```

Notice that the `!` operator again signifies that you want traffic from anywhere other than these servers, bound for these servers. This would avoid flagging server-to-server traffic. You also use `/` to continue the alert onto multiple lines, and the `content` option to search for the text `payroll.xls` in any packet. This way, that machine can still access the Internet but if that particular file is ever downloaded from it, you will be notified.

With all the other alert options, you can write rules to find just about any kind of traffic. If your rule is something that other companies would be able to use, you might want to submit it to the Snort developers list to have it incorporated into the official set of rules that is distributed. If you decide to do this, make sure you take advantage of all the documentation options such as `msg`, `sid`, `rev`, `class type`, and `priority`. Also, thoroughly test your rule to make sure it really catches all occurrences of the activity you are trying to trap and doesn't go off erroneously.

Host-Based Intrusion Detection

We have spent a lot of time on network-based intrusion detection. However, there are other ways of finding intrusion attempts. One alternative method is to load software to look for signs of intrusion on the system itself. If a machine has been exploited, often certain system files will be altered. For example, the password file may be changed, users may be added, system configuration files may be modified, or file permissions might be altered. Normally these system files shouldn't change much. By looking for modifications in these files, you can detect an intrusion or other unusual activity.

This method of intrusion detection can be much more accurate, producing fewer false positives since it doesn't go off unless a system is actually affected. It is a little more trouble to maintain since you have to load software on each system to be protected, but it might be well worth the time and effort to use both host-based and network-based intrusion detection to protect mission-critical systems.

Advantages of Host-Based Intrusion Detection Methods

- Fewer false positives
- Activities rather than signatures are tracked, so you don't need constant signature updates
- Less prone to being tricked
- Less tending and tuning needed

Disadvantages of Host-Based Intrusion Detection Methods

- Have to load and manage software on every box to be protected
- The alert comes after an attack has been successful; IDS sometimes provides earlier warning

Tripwire: A File-Integrity Checking Program

Tripwire
Author/primary contact: Dr. Eugene Spafford and Gene Kim
Web site: www.tripwire.org
Platforms: Most Linux
License: GPL
Version reviewed: V 2.3.47

Tripwire is another great example of open source software that has made the transition to a commercial platform. Tripwire was originally purely open source. Eventually, the founders formed a company to sell and support it commercially. However, they took the original code base and released it under the GPL license so that development could continue in the open source community. The open source version has been updated from version 2.2.1 released in October of 2000 to the current version of 2.3.

There are significant differences between the commercial and the open source versions. The biggest is that the commercial version isn't open source and supports more platforms. The open source version currently is available only on Linux, while the commercial version is available on several platforms including Windows. Another difference is that the commercial version comes with a program called twagent, which is a utility for managing multiple installations of Tripwire. The commercial version also has a nice GUI for managing your databases and configurations.

Both versions of Tripwire operate by creating a database of baseline attributes of important files you want to track, so you can check the actual attributes at any given time against the baseline to see if anything has changed. This is good for keeping track of your system's binary files. One of the favorite tricks of hackers once they've gotten into a system is to replace key binary files with trojanized versions of their own. That way, when you use commands like ls or ps, you don't see their illicit files or processes running. You can also use Tripwire during a forensic investigation to find out where an intruder has been; it's like following digital footprints.

Installing Tripwire

1. To install Tripwire, get the files from the CD-ROM, or download either the RPM or the tar files from the Tripwire Web site to compile from source.

   There are also RPMs available for some distributions (the RPMs for Mandrake and RedHat are on the CD-ROM). Just click on the RPM file to install the program. If you don't have an RPM for your operating system, you can download the source .tar file (or "tarball" as they are sometimes known) to compile it. Unzip the tar file and cd into the src directory.

2. From the src directory, type the following:

   ```
   make all
   ```

   This will compile Tripwire and get it ready for further configuration.

3. Open the install.cfg file and check to make sure all the defaults are correct for your system. This file governs where program files are installed and other system-level variables. Most of the defaults should be fine for most systems. Make sure your mail client is specified correctly.

4. Once you have your environment variables set, cd to the /etc/tripwire directory and type twinstall.sh.

   This displays the license agreement. You must type accept, and then the install script will copy the files to their appropriate places and prompt you for site and local pass-phrases. These are the passwords that will unlock your Tripwire database, so they are very important.

   Picking strong pass-phrases and keeping them in a safe place is important, as this will encrypt your databases and configuration files and keep them safe from tampering. If you lose these or forget them, you won't be able to use Tripwire when you need it most.

This completes the Tripware installation process.

Configuring Tripwire

The final step before running Tripwire is to set your policy. The policy file is a very important file for Tripwire operation: it tells Tripwire what files to keep an eye on and what level of detail to go into. You can find the main policy file, twpol.txt, in the main Tripwire directory. This is not the policy file itself but a copy of the encrypted version that the program actually uses. For better security, you should make a copy and delete the unencrypted copy, twpol.txt, once you have set and tested your policy.

The policy file contains some system variables at the top, and then it has a listing of various files and directories and the policy directives for them. These directives are represented by either code letters or variable names. They are called **property masks** and represent the properties that Tripwire is tracking. Table 7.4 lists the items that can be tracked for each file and their code letters.

Table 7.4 Tripwire Property Masks

Code Letters	Attributes Tracked
a	Last access time
b	Blocks allocated
c	Create/modify time
d	Device ID on which the integrated node (INode) resides
g	Group ID of the file owner
i	INode number
l	Whether the file is allowed to grow
m	Modification timestamp
n	INode reference count (number of links)
p	Read/write/execute permissions on the file and mode
s	File size
t	Type size
u	User ID of the file owner
c	CRC32 hash
h	Haval Hash
m	MD5 hash
s	SHA/SHS hash

Tripwire policies operate on the concept of ignore flags. You can configure Tripwire to keep track of or ignore different file properties. You use a + (plus sign) to track properties and a – (minus sign) to ignore them. The format for the policy file statement is as follows:

```
file/directory name -> property mask;
```

For example, this line in the policy file:

```
/etc/secretfile.txt -> +amcpstu;
```

would cause Tripwire to notify you any time the last access time, creation or modification time, permissions, ownership, or file size and type changed on the file secretfile.txt in /etc.

There are also several predefined property masks. Table 7.5 lists these template property masks and their effects.

These predefined variables fit the behavior of different sets of files. For instance, you may want to use $Readonly for your key configuration files since their access dates will be changing when programs use them, but you don't want the size or content to change. You could use $Growing for your log files, since they will be constantly growing (or should be anyways).

The policy configuration file also defines some variables that are combinations of the above presets with a few additions or subtractions. These give you a way to quickly set policies for various different classes of files. You can change them slightly if you want to ignore or examine more things. Listing 7.3 shows these variables from the policy file.

Table 7.5 Template Property Masks

Property Masks	Effects
$Readonly	+pinugtsdbmCM-rlasSH
$Dynamic	+pinugtd-srlbamcCMSH
$Growing	+pinugtdl-srbamcCMSH
$Device	+pugsdr-intlbamcCMSH
$IgnoreAll	-pinugtsdrlbamcCMSH
$IgnoreNone	+pinugtsdrlbamcCMSH

Listing 7.3 Property Mask Variables

```
SEC_CRIT    = $(IgnoreNone)-SHa ; # Critical files that cannot
                                     change
SEC_SUID    = $(IgnoreNone)-SHa ; # Binaries with the SUID or
                                     SGID flags set
SEC_BIN     = $(ReadOnly) ;     # Binaries that should not change
SEC_CONFIG  = $(Dynamic) ;      # Config files that are changed
                                  infrequently but accessed often
SEC_LOG     = $(Growing) ;      # Files that grow, but that should
                                  never change ownership
SEC_INVARIANT = +tpug ;          # Directories that should never
                                  change permission or ownership
SIG_LOW     = 33 ;          # Non-critical files that are of
                                  minimal security impact
SIG_MED     = 66 ;          # Non-critical files that are of
                                  significant security impact
SIG_HI      = 100 ;         # Critical files that are significant
                                  points of vulnerability
```

Below the property masks, policies are set for the various files and directories on the system. You can start with the default policy file and see how it works for you. Take time to peruse the file to see which files are being tracked. Once you are satisfied, save the file and exit. You are ready to run Tripwire.

Initializing Your Baseline Database

The first step in running Tripwire is to set up your baseline database. This creates the initial list of signatures against which the policies will be used. Remember, running this *after* you have suspect files on your system does you no good; you need to create your baseline database before you have any security problems, ideally just after your system is installed and configured. To establish your initial file database, use the following command:

```
tripwire -m i -v
```

The -m switch specifies which mode to run in, in this case i for initialize. The -v switch gives verbose output so you can see what's happening. Tripwire audits all the files specified in your policy file, creates the database in the ./database directory, and encrypts it using your site pass-phrase.

In order for Tripwire to be truly secure, you should make a copy of your baseline database to some secure offline media—floppy disk (if it will fit), CD, or tape. If you store it locally online, there is always a possibility that it could be altered, although Tripwire has some protections against this.

Checking File Integrity

This is the main mode you will run Tripwire in once you have set it up. It compares the current attributes of the files specified with the ones in the Tripwire database. The format is:

```
tripwire -m c file.txt
```

where you replace `file.txt` with the path to the file or directories you want checked. It will verify the attributes of that file according to the specifications of the policy file and return with a report of any changes.

Updating the Database

As you fine-tune your policy and make major system changes, you will want to update your database so it accurately reflects the valid state of those files. This is important so that not only will new files and directories be added to your database, but false positives will be eliminated. Do *not* update your database if there is any chance that your system has been compromised. This will invalidate those signatures and make your Tripwire database useless. You can update select directories; after all, some things like system binaries should rarely change. You update the Tripwire database using this command:

```
tripwire -m u -r path-to-report
```

You need to replace `path-to-report` with the name and path of the most recent report file. Running this command will show you all the changes that have occurred and which rules detected them. There will be an **x** in boxes by files in which Tripwire has detected changes. If you leave the **x** there, Tripwire will update the signature for that file when you exit the file. If you remove the **x**, Tripwire will assume that the original signature is correct and not update it. When you exit, Tripwire will perform these changes. You can specify `-c` in the command to skip doing the preview and to have Tripwire simply make the changes for the files it has detected.

Updating the Policy File

Over time, you will learn what rules are not generating valid alerts and will want to delete them or change the property masks on them. You may want to tighten property masks for some files as well. Make your changes to the Tripwire policy file, save it, and then issue the following command to have Tripwire update the policy file:

```
tripwire -m p policy-file.txt
```

where you replace `policy-file.txt` with the new policy file. Tripwire will ask for your local and site pass-phrases before updating the policy. Once you have your Tripwire policies sufficiently fine-tuned, you can create a cron job and have it run daily (or however often you want) to check your file systems looking for intruders.

Analysis and Management Tools

The tools discussed so far give you a lot of useful information to help you fix your network security problems. But the problem with these wonderful programs is that they can sometimes generate too much information. A single Nessus scan of a sizable network can generate a report that is hundreds of pages long. An active Snort sensor can output thousands of alerts a day. Even the lowly firewall might send out log notices on an hourly basis. Keeping track of all of this security information can be a full-time job. In fact, at larger companies, it often requires a small staff just to track and analyze the security data.

With all the data these tools generate, you can go from being uninformed to information overload very easily. This can be worse than being in the dark regarding your security situation. System administrators can suffer from "analysis paralysis"—feeling like they don't know where to start. For many overwhelmed technical managers, the solution is to do nothing at all, or to put the security issues on the back burner until they have time to deal with them. Of course, that time never seems to come.

Chapter Overview

Concepts you will learn:

- Managing server log files
- Using databases and Web servers for security data
- Analyzing IDS data
- Managing vulnerability scan data
- Running a vulnerability scan management system

Tools you will use:

Swatch, ACID, NPI, and NCC

To avoid this situation, you need tools to help organize your security data and prioritize the action items. Many commercial packages assist in this task, including HP Open-View, BMC NetPatrol, and NetIQ. Fortunately for the budget-impaired, there are also some great open source packages available.

While these open source applications are not strictly security tools in that they are not actively polling or protecting machines on your network, they are every bit as important as your network scanners and intrusion detection systems. Because if you can't see the forest for the trees, you are no better off than you were before.

One example of the challenges in analyzing security data is the server message logs. Most servers, UNIX and Windows alike, maintain logs on various activities going on in the system. Most of this activity is innocuous, like services starting up, user access, and so on. Linux, for example, keeps the system logs in the /var/log directory. Usually, there are two general logs—syslog and messages— along with several other more specific logs. These text files show you all the things going on in the background of the system. Listing 8.1 shows the typical contents of a Linux messages file.

Listing 8.1 Linux Messages File

```
Aug 17 04:02:06 earth syslogd 1.4.1: restart.

Aug 18 21:07:57 earth sshd(pam_unix)[17904]: session opened for
  user john by (uid=502)

Aug 18 21:12:39 earth su(pam_unix)[17960]: session opened for
  user root by john(uid=502)

Aug 18 21:12:52 earth su(pam_unix)[17960]: session closed for
  user root

Aug 18 21:13:44 earth sshd(pam_unix)[18008]: session opened for
  user john by (uid=502)

Aug 18 21:14:02 earth sshd(pam_unix)[18008]: session closed for
  user john

Aug 18 21:23:21 earth su(pam_unix)[18482]: session opened for
  user root by john(uid=502)

Aug 18 21:24:12 earth su(pam_unix)[18482]: session closed for
  user root

Aug 18 21:39:00 earth su(pam_unix)[10627]: session opened for
  user root by john(uid=502)
```

```
Aug 18 21:44:57 earth httpd: httpd shutdown succeeded

Aug 18 21:44:58 earth httpd: httpd: Could not determine the
   server's fully qualified domain name, using 127.0.0.1 for
   ServerName

Aug 18 21:45:00 earth httpd: httpd startup succeeded

Aug 19 23:39:02 earth sshd(pam_unix)[13219]: authentication
   failure; logname= uid=0 euid=0 tty=NODEVssh ruser=
   rhost=tayhou-tnt-9-216-40-228-250.isp.net user=john

Aug 22 10:31:14 earth sshd(pam_unix)[16205]: session opened for
   user tony by (uid=500)

Aug 22 10:31:20 earth su(pam_unix)[16240]: session opened for
   user root by tony(uid=500)
```

These messages are useful for debugging your system or troubleshooting a new program installation. You can see the details for each program or process that starts on your system. You can also see if there are any problems. In this example, you can see that the httpd process, the Web server, shut down. The next line says the problem is with the domain name set for the server. In this case, an IP address has been set incorrectly as the host name.

Log files also contain information that is of interest from a security standpoint. Certain activities are often the precursor of an attack in progress. Failed login attempts can be one of these signs. In Listing 8.1 you can see the user "john" had a failed login. It even tells where John was trying to log in from—an address owned by Isp.net. If it was just a single failed attempt and you knew John used Isp.net, then you would probably not worry about this entry. It was probably just John mistyping his password. However, if you saw multiple failed logins or this one was coming from an unfamiliar address, you would want to check into it further. Another sign of something going wrong is servers rebooting themselves at strange times. These are some of the things that can show up in logs files that would warrant your attention.

In an ideal world, you would review all your log files on a daily basis. Unfortunately, most of us don't have time to do this even weekly, if at all. There is just too much information in these files to easily be able to find the data that's important to us. Wouldn't it be great if there was a helper program that looked for these kinds of things and let us know when they came up, so we could react in a timely manner, rather than a few days or a week later? Well, as it happens, there is an open source program that does just that.

Swatch: A Log Monitoring Program

Swatch
Author/primary contact: Todd Atkins
Web site: swatch.sourceforge.net/
Platforms: Linux, most UNIX
License: GPL
Version reviewed: 3.0.8
Mailing lists:
Swatch-announce
Primarily for version updates and new releases. Does not take posts.
Subscribe at list.sourceforge.net/list/listinfo/swatch-announce.

Swatch-users
For general help, questions, and development information. Subscribe at
list.sourceforge.net/list/listinfo/swatch-users.

Swatch stands for Simple watcher or Syslog watcher, depending on whom you ask. Either way, Swatch is a helpful program that does your log watching and alerts you only when things that you are specifically looking for get logged. Swatch is a Perl program that regularly sweeps the main log files and looks for certain key words that you can define. It can be run in the background as a daemon or as a cron job. You can configure Swatch to notify you of any events in the messages or syslog log files that might indicate a security problem. However, Swatch can also be used to flag just about any kind of activity: a certain program being used, a certain user logging in, or anything that might appear in a log file. Swatch can also be configured to watch application-specific log files instead of the general log files that it does by default.

Returning to the security uses of Swatch, certain events that are logged have significance from a security standpoint. The default items that Swatch looks for are a good start.

- Bad logins. Criteria: The words `Invalid`, `Repeated`, or `Incomplete` appear in the messages file.
- System crashes. Criteria: The words `panic` or `halt` appear in the log files.
- System reboots. Criteria: The banner of your OS should only appear in the log files when you reboot.

Here are some other security-specific things that you might want to have Swatch look for.

- Snort or Nessus messages. If you are logging your Snort data to a syslog file, you can have Swatch search for occurrences of `snort`. This will appear every time a Snort alert is generated.

- Use of a text editor. This might indicate that someone is on your system trying to make changes to configuration files. Of course, if you are on the system a lot using a text editor, this alert might generate too many false positives.
- Uses of FTP, SSH, or Telnet. If someone is downloading or uploading files to your system, it could mean trouble. Also, if someone is logging in remotely, you will want to track this. However, if you are doing these activities frequently, it might create more noise that it is worth.

Note: By default, Swatch is configured to look for terms specific to the Sun operating system. While some of these may be common to Linux and other UNIX-based operating systems, others are not. For example, when looking for a reboot on a Mandrake Linux system, you will want to replace the search terms `Sun OS Release` with `Linux Mandrake Release`. If you are using a different OS, use the term from your OS reboot message. To find this, do a reboot and then look in the messages file for a unique statement to search for.

Installing Swatch

1. Swatch requires Perl 5 or higher. If you have a fairly new installation of Linux or BSD (less than a year old), then you should have a sufficiently current version.
2. Swatch also requires several Perl modules, which are add-on subprograms for the Perl language. These modules are Date::Calc, Date::HiRes, and Date::Format. The configuration process will tell you if you are missing these modules. To get them, you can check the Web site www.rpmfind.net to see if there is an RPM available for your distribution.

   If you used a Linux distribution, there is a good chance there are RPMs to load these modules on your distributions disks. If you don't have an RPM for the Perl modules, you can use the Comprehensive Perl Archive Network (CPAN) system for downloading the required modules. (The CPAN system is a way to auto download required Perl libraries without a lot of hassle.) To do this, type the following command:

   ```
   cpan -i module-name
   ```

   where you replace `module-name` with `Date::Calc` or whatever module you are trying to load. Make sure you get the spelling and capitalization right and use both colons. You will have to do this three times—once for each required module above. The CPAN system will take care of contacting the central CPAN servers, downloading the module, and installing it for you.

3. Download the tar file from the book's CD-ROM or the Sourceforge Web site and unzip it.

4. Since Swatch is a Perl program, the installation process is slightly different than the previous C-based programs. The sequence of commands to type is:

```
perl Makefile.PL
make
make test
make install
make realclean
```

Once those processes are done, Swatch is installed and ready to go.

Configuring and Running Swatch

Swatch is a command line utility and you start it by issuing a `swatch` command with various settings after it. Table 8.1 lists and describes the `swatch` options.

For example, running this command:

```
./swatch --config-file /home/john/my-swatch-config --
daemon
```

will run Swatch using the configuration file found at /home/john/my-swatch-config instead of the default config file. It will also run it as a background process or daemon. The above options may be issued alone or together.

Table 8.1 Swatch Command Options

Options	Descriptions
--config-file *filename*	Runs Swatch using the configuration *filename* indicated. The default is ./swatchrc if no option is given.
--restart-time *time*	Restarts Swatch at the indicated *time*. Also can be used with a + to have it restart at a given elapsed time after the current time. This can be used to have it refresh the view of the log file it has.
--input-record-separator	This statement followed by a regular expression tells Swatch to use the expression to delineate the boundaries between each input record and line in the log file. The default is a carriage return, but if your operating system uses something different, you can change it here.
--daemon	Runs Swatch as a system daemon. Accomplishes the same thing as running Swatch with the & (ampersand) switch.

Table 8.2 Swatch Log File Options

Options	Descriptions
--examine *file*	Makes Swatch do a complete pass through the indicated *file*. Use this when the file being examined is created anew each time.
--read-pipe *program*	Instead of reading a file, you can have Swatch read input directly piped from the indicated *program*.
--tail *file*	Reads only the newly added lines in *file*. This is the default operation for Swatch on log files, since new entries are usually appended to the end of an existing file. This is much faster than rereading a whole file every time, especially with log files that can get quite big, such as Web server logs.

Table 8.2 lists and describes some additional options that you can use to control how Swatch reads the log files. You can only use one of these switches at a time.

For example, running Swatch with this command:

```
./swatch --examine messages --daemon
```

has Swatch search the entire messages file every time it runs, rather than just checking for newly added lines.

Swatch normally scans the UNIX messages file or, if there is no messages file, it defaults to the syslog file. Using these switches in Table 8.2, you could have Swatch look at any log file you want, such as the security logs or even an application-specific log file like nessus.messages.

The Swatch Configuration File

The Swatch configuration file is where all the important settings are. In this file, called swatchrc by default, you tell the program what to look for in the log files and what to do if that shows up. Two sample swatchrc files are included with the program in the examples directory. The swatchrc.personal file is for use on a personal workstation, and swatchrc.monitor is for server monitoring. Listing 8.2 shows what the monitor version looks like.

Listing 8.2 The swatchrc Monitor Configuration File

```
#
# Swatch configuration file for constant monitoring
#
```

```
# Bad login attempts
watchfor   /INVALID|REPEATED|INCOMPLETE/
    echo
    bell 3
    exec "/usr/local/sbin/badloginfinger $0"

# Machine room temperature
watchfor   /WizMON/
    echo inverse
    bell

# System crashes and halts
watchfor   /(panic|halt)/
    echo
    bell
    mail
    exec "call_pager 3667615 0911"

# System reboots
watchfor   /SunOS Release/
    echo
    bell
    mail
exec "call_pager 3667615 0411"
```

As you can see in Listing 8.2, the basic format is a watchfor statement followed by a text statement between two slashes, and then one or more action commands. The text between the slashes is what Swatch looks for when it examines (tails) the log file. If the search text is found, then Swatch takes the actions below the statement. Table 8.3 lists and describes the action statements Swatch supports.

Table 8.3 Swatch Action Statements

Action Statements	Descriptions
echo *mode*	Makes the search text be echoed to the screen. The word *mode* is optional and indicates the color in which it is to be displayed. The default is your normal screen text color, but you can also use the following modes: blink, bold, underline, inverse, green, blue, red, yellow, black, magenta, cyan, white, or any of these choices followed by _h to use the highlighted colored version, for example black_h.
bell *number*	Rings the PC internal speaker the number of times indicated by *number*. The default if no number is given is 1.

Action Statements	Descriptions
exec *command*	Executes a command line parameter. You can use this to call any other program or script to do various things, for example, to send an SMB pop message to a particular workstation. This functionality greatly expands the things that Swatch can do. You can even configure this to call a script that would take further action conditionally, based on what was found in the log file.
pipe *command*	Passes along a command to another process.
mail addresses=*address1:address2: address3,subject=text*	Sends an e-mail using the Sendmail program to a single e-mail address or to multiple addresses separated by colons. Text appears as the subject line for your e-mail message. The alert text appears in the body of the e-mail.
write *user1:user2*	Causes the alert to be sent via the UNIX write command to a single user or a group of users.
throttle *hours:minutes:seconds*	Controls the number of times the alert is sent during a period of time for one watchfor statement. This keeps you from getting dozens of messages if a text string appears multiple times in the log file within the set time window.

As you can see, Swatch can notify you of flagged log events in several different ways. The easiest is to just have it beep or echo on the screen. If you are not around the server all the time, then you can have it e-mail you. If your pager or cell phone supports text messaging via e-mail, you could have it send the message directly to you. You can also write a script to have the server dial a pager number using the UNIX tip command.

Using Databases and Web Servers to Manage Your Security Data

Going beyond just checking server logs, you also want to be able to analyze the output of the security programs discussed earlier in this book. The best way to do this is to import the results into a database. The rest of the tools in this chapter are designed to let you import and view security data in a database. To use these tools you'll need a database program and a Web server running to review the results. Though there are other options supported, the database recommended for these programs is MySQL and the Web server is Apache with PHP. You should set up these programs before attempting to install any of these tools. The basic installation and configuration of each of these prerequisite servers are described briefly here.

Setting Up a MySQL Server

MySQL is an open source SQL-compliant database that is gaining acceptance in the corporate world for its power and flexibility. While this book does not intend to teach you all the ins and outs of running a MySQL database, the following information will help you set up and execute some basic administrative tasks on a MySQL database so you can use the analysis tools.

1. Download the latest version of MySQL from www.mysql.com or use an RPM from your OS and distribution disks. Make sure it is at least version 4.0 or later.

   Note: If you already have MySQL database version 4.0 or later installed, skip to Step 4.

2. Unpack the file and issue the usual compilation commands in the directory it creates:

   ```
   ./configure
   make
   make install
   ```

3. Run the install script located in the /scripts directory by typing:

   ```
   mysql_install_db
   ```

   This initializes your database program and gets it ready for use.

4. Create a MySQL user and group for the database to use to perform tasks. Do this by issuing the following commands:

   ```
   groupadd mysql
   useradd -g mysql mysql
   ```

5. Set the ownership and file permissions so that MySQL can operate using the following commands:

   ```
   chown -R root /usr/local/mysql
   chown -R mysql /usr/local/mysql/var
   chgrp -R mysql /usr/local/mysql
   cp /usr/local/mysql/support-files/my-medium.cnf /etc/
     my.cnf
   ```

6. Edit the file /etc/ld.so.conf and add the following lines:

   ```
   /usr/local/mysql/lib/mysql
    /usr/local/lib
   ```

7. Save the file.

8. As root, type:

   ```
   ldconfig -v
   ```

9. As root, set an admin user for the MySQL database by typing:

```
/usr/local/mysql/bin/mysqladmin -u root password 123456
```

where you replace *123456* with your password. Be sure to write down your password and keep it in a safe place.

When you are finished with this, change back to the user you logged in as by typing "exit" at the command line.

10. You will want to set up MySQL to start as a daemon and run all the time rather than having to start it manually. You can do this by placing the following line at the end of the rc.local file found in /etc/r.cd/.

```
mysqld -user=mysql &
```

This will start MySQL as a system process every time you reboot.

11. Finally, you will want to lock down MySQL so that it doesn't become a security hole on your system. By default, MySQL has pretty weak security. While MySQL security isn't the subject of this book, here are a few things you can do.

- Delete the standard users, unless you have a program that uses them.
- Make sure that the root user can only connect from a small number of hosts.
- Set up some rules on your firewall to only allow connections on a limited number of ports and from a limited number of machines to your MySQL server.
- Create system accounts for running programs. Don't use either the system root account or the MySQL root account (two different things) unless you absolutely have to (the NPI tool does require this, unfortunately). This chapter includes examples of application-specific accounts to create in each package description wherever possible.

MySQL is now ready to use. Type `mysql` at a command prompt and you will be prompted for a user name and password to enter the standard MySQL command line, where you can use standard SQL commands on your MySQL databases. See the sidebar for some basic MySQL commands.

Basic MySQL Commands

To log in to MySQL, type `mysql -u username -p password`, replacing *username* and *password* with the ones from the account on the MySQL database.

Note: This is different than your system login. This logs you into MySQL and puts you at the MySQL prompt `mysql>` where you can type commands. Be sure to put a semi-colon at the end of commands before pressing Enter to execute them.

The following are some basic commands to navigate and search a MySQL database.

`show databases;`	Displays all the databases available on that MySQL server.
`use database-name;`	Makes the *database-name* specified the active database so you can perform actions on it.
`show tables;`	Lists all the tables that exist in a database.
`select query from Tablename;`	Shows records that match the `query` in `Tablename`. There are a number of operands you can use in your `query` statement. Using an * (asterisk) as your query statement will list all records in that table.

Setting Up the Apache Web Server

The advanced analysis tools in this chapter require a Web server to act as both the configuration interface and the output mechanism. Again, this short section is not intended to be a comprehensive guide on how to run and operate a Web server; it is merely intended to get you up and running with what you need to use the security tools. If you intend to do use this server for more than ACID and NCC or to use it in high-volume environments, you should definitely do further reading on Web server administration. Running a Web server does involve some security issues, and you should make sure these servers are locked down, running minimal services, and keep them frequently patched. If you want to run IIS or an alternate Web server, it should work as long as it is compliant with PHP 4.0 or later.

1. Download the latest version of Apache from www.apache.org. If you can get it from your OS distribution disks or already have it installed, make sure you have at least version 1.3 or later.

   Note: If you already have Apache version 1.3 or later installed, skip to Step 3.

2. Unpack the program and issue the following commands:

   ```
   ./configure -prefix=/www -enable -so -activate-module-
   src/modules/php4/libphp4.a
   make
   make install
   ```

   These commands set the default directory to /www and enable the proper modules you will need.

3. Run the Web server by typing `apachectl start` at the command line. This starts the http daemon and sets it up to run as a system process.

   You can stop Apache at any time by issuing the same command with a `stop` parameter.

   Other Linux and UNIX variants may have different ways of handling starting and stopping. Consult your documentation or online resources on how to accomplish this.

4. Check your Web server installation by opening a Web browser and putting in the IP address of your server, or specify `localhost` if you are working directly on that machine. If it brings up a sample Apache Web page, then you have successfully installed your Web server. The root directory of your Web server, where you can put documents you want to be publicly viewable, is /usr/local/apache2/htdocs/ on a Mandrake Linux system; different distributions may vary slightly.

5. Next, set Apache to run automatically when the system is rebooted (you don't want to have to manually restart the Web server every time you reboot). To do this, go to the directory where all the startup scripts reside; on Mandrake Linux, this is the /etc/rc.d directory. Each rc. file represents a different run level. Add the following lines to the rc4.d and rc5.d files:

```
../init.d/httpd S85httpd
../init.d/httpd K85httpd
```

You can test this by rebooting your system and verifying that the httpd process displays when you the list processes running with the `ps -ax` command.

6. You should lock down Apache to prevent its abuse. Web servers are some of the most common targets for attackers, so if you are going to allow access to this machine from outside your network you need to make sure it is secure. The following are some basic tips for good Web server security.

- Run a vulnerability scanner against your Web server to make sure that it is all patched up and doesn't have any obvious security holes right after you have finished this installation and configuration process.
- Protect any non-public Web directories with some access control. The quickest and easiest way to do this is using .htaccess files.
- Encrypt communications from clients to the browser with SSL any time you are dealing with sensitive information (security data definitely counts in this category). If you are accessing your server from outside your local network, that is, across the Internet, consult your Web server documentation or the Internet on how to set this up.

Again, this isn't a comprehensive coverage of Web server security, but make sure you do these things before making your server public.

Setting Up PHP

PHP is a scripting language designed for use in Web pages. It is an interpreted language, which means it doesn't have to be compiled to work, so you can just insert your PHP script into a directory that recognizes PHP and it will run when accessed. This makes it easy to write code embedded into Web pages. Most current Web servers recognize PHP, though it may have to be configured on installation to do this.

Because of these features, PHP has become the language of choice for many Web-based applications. You will need it for the three remaining tools in this chapter (ACID, NPI, and NCC). PHP should have been installed as part of the configure directives in the

Apache instructions described earlier. To check if PHP is installed on your system and what version it is, type `php -v` at the command line. If it is there, you should get some output with the version number. However, if you were unable to install it as part of your Apache installation or you want to reload the latest version, use the following procedure.

1. Download the latest version of PHP from www.php.net or use the RPMs on your OS installation disks. If you use the ones provided with your OS, make sure that you have version 4.0 or later.
2. Unpack the distribution.
3. From the installed directory, run the following compile commands:

```
./configure -prefix=/www/php mysql=/usr/local/mysql
  -with-apxs2=/www/bin/apxs -with-zlib-dir=/usr/local
  -with-gd (all on one line)
make
make install
```

These configure statements enable several modules that are needed for the tools in this chapter.

4. Edit the Web server configuration file, httpd.conf, usually found in /www. Add the following lines, and then save the file.

```
LoadModule php4_module modules/libphp4.so
AddType application/x-httpd-php.php
```

5. To make sure PHP is running properly, use a text editor to create a small script file called test.php. Enter the following in the file and then save it.

```
<?php phpinfo(); ?>
```

This file is a short PHP script that will display some basic system information when run.

6. Copy the test file into the /www/htdocs directory. Type in the URL or IP address of your machine and then enter /test.php. You should see the PHP version displayed on a Web page. If you do, then your PHP-enabled Web server is ready to go.

ACID (Analysis Console for Intrusion Databases)

ACID
Author/primary contact: Roman Danyliw
Web site: www.andrew.cmu.edu/~rdanyliw/snort/
                         snortacid.html
Platforms: Most UNIX
License: GPL
Version reviewed: .9.6.b23
Mailing list:
Acidlab users list. Subscribe by sending an e-mail with the word "subscribe" in the body to acidlab-users@lists.sourceforge.net.

The Analysis Console for Intrusion Databases (ACID) is a program designed to make better use of data from intrusion detection devices. It was written by Roman Danyliw and others for the AirCERT program run by Carnegie Mellon University. They are part of the larger CERT (Computer Emergency Response Team) organization. CERT has been instrumental in protecting the Internet and the organizations using it for many years. CERT tracks incidents of computer crime and sends out notices to a mailing list whenever a large incident happens. The CERT mailing list is kind of an early warning system for any large outbreaks or attacks happening on the Internet. As such, it can be very useful to a system administrator. You can visit the CERT site and sign up for their mailing list at www.cert.org.

The AirCERT project is placing IDS sensors at various organizations and studying overall trends in intrusion activity and behavior. They wrote ACID to facilitate this process. Because they open sourced the code for the project, you can use it for your benefit without doing anything as part of AirCERT.

The idea behind ACID is to port all your intrusion detection data into a database where it can be sorted and organized by priority. ACID gives you a Web-based control panel of sorts to view and manipulate these results.

ACID uses just about any SQL database and any Web server, and supports multiple sensors for the input data. It also accepts both raw Snort alerts and syslog-compliant log files. ACID currently only works directly with one IDS, Snort, but you can import logs into the ACID database from any device that will output in a syslog-type format using a utility called Logsnorter, which is available on the ACID Web site.

ACID has quite a few prerequisite programs. Besides a database, a Web server, and PHP, which have been covered earlier in this chapter, you need the following libraries and subprograms.

ADOdb

This package provides the database abstraction layer so PHP can use a standard interface to a multitude of databases, including MySQL. Download it from http://php.weblogs.com/adodb, unpack it into your /www/htdocs or applicable Web root directory, and it should be ready to go. No further installation is needed.

PHPLOT

This package lets you create charts using ACID. If you want to use this capability, download the module from www.phplot.com. Unpack it in the /www/htdocs directory, and just like ADOdb, it should be ready to use.

JpGraph

This program upgrades PHP to do color graphs. You'll need it, along with PHPLOT above, if you want to be able to graph your Snort data. Download it from www.aditus.nu/jpgraph/

and unzip it into your Web root directory (for example, /www/htdocs). It will create its own subdirectory and be available when needed by ACID.

GD

This package has the image manipulation libraries for PHP, which are also needed for graphing. If you installed PHP according to the instructions given earlier in this chapter, then you should already have this utility. Otherwise, download it from www.boutell.com/gd/ and install it in your /www/php directory. If you didn't compile PHP with the commands given earlier, you also need to make sure you have the following libraries for GD.

- libpng. This provides PNG-format support for GD. You can get it at www.libpng.org/pub/png/ or from your OS distribution disks.
- libjpeg-6b. This is a JPEG library for PHP. You can get it at www.ijg.org/ or from your OS distribution disks.
- zlib. This provides compression support for GD. You can get it www.ijg.org/ or from your OS distribution disks.

Configuring Snort for MySQL

1. ACID assumes you have one or more Snort sensors up and running to feed it data. If you haven't already built your Snort sensors, refer back to Chapter 7. You must have your Snort sensors configured to log to a MySQL database. To do this, follow these steps when installing Snort.
   - When first compiling Snort, use the following configure statement:

     ```
     ./configure --with-mysql=/usr/local/mysql
     ```

     Make sure you specify the directory where MySQL is located on your machine.
   - Edit the configuration file, snort.conf. Find the commented out line that starts with #output database. Edit it as follows:

     ```
     output database: log,mysql,user=snort password=123456
        dbname=snort host=localhost
     ```

     Change the user *snort* and *password* to the correct database name and password you are going to use for ACID. ACID will create a database named "snort," although you can change this name by editing the ACID configuration file. If you are connecting to a local database, leave the host variable as *localhost*. If you are connecting to a database on a different machine, insert the IP address or hostname here.
2. Be sure to uncomment the line (delete the #), and then save the file.

This chapter assumes you will be installing ACID on a separate machine from your Snort sensor. Putting them on the same machine is not only a bad idea from a security standpoint, but will also bog down your Snort sensor to the point of making it unusable. The box running ACID should preferably be located at a separate site from the Snort sensors—this makes it harder for someone who hacks a Snort sensor to get to your logs. Figure 8.1 illustrates the elements of an ACID-Snort IDS.

Installing ACID

Once you have all the prerequisite programs loaded, you can finally install ACID.

1. Get the program file from the book's CD-ROM or download it from the ACID Web site.
2. Place the tar file in your /www/htdocs directory. Unzip it there and it will create its own directory.

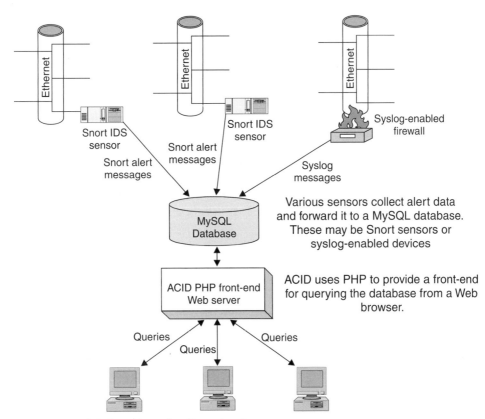

Figure 8.1 ACID-Snort Intrusion Detection System

3. Remove the remaining tar file, as anything left in your root /htdocs directory could be accessed by someone using the Web server.

Configuring ACID

1. Change directories to the /htdocs/www/acid directory.
2. Edit the acid_conf.php file. The lines starting with slashes and stars represent comments and instructions on how to complete the configuration. The lines starting with $ are variables and tell the program specific things about your system.
3. Change each of these $ statements with the parameters for your system. Table 8.4 lists the variables and information about and recommendations for each entry.

Table 8.4 Variables for Configuring ACID

Variable Names	Descriptions
$DBtype	The type of database ACID will be using. The default is mysql, but you can also put postgresql or mssql if you want to use either of those two databases.
$alert_dbname	The IDS that ACID is drawing from. Currently only the Snort native format, snort_log, is supported, though there are plans are for ACID to support other IDS types in the future.
$alert_host	The host on which the alert database is going to be stored. This can be an IP address or host name. If it's running on the same machine, it would be localhost. For better security or performance, you could run the database on a separate machine than the PHP Web server.
$alert_port	Port on which to access the database. If you are hosting it locally, just enter " " for this value.
$alert_user	The database user name that ACID will use to log the data. Make sure it matches the MySQL user name you created when you set up the database.
$alert_password	The password for the database user. Again, make sure it matches your MySQL password for that user.
$archive_dbname	The name of the database for Snort to archive to. The default of snort_archive is fine unless you are storing multiple databases on this machine and want more descriptive names.

Variable Names	Descriptions
$archive_host	The host where the archive database will be located. If it's on the same machine, this should be `localhost`.
$archive_port	The port to log into the database server. Use " " if you are logging locally.
$archive_user	The database user to log the archive data under. Typically the same value as $alert_user above, though you could create a separate user for logging the archives.
$archive_password	The password for the database user logging the archive data. Again, usually the same value as $alert_password.
$chartlib_path	Path to the charting modules. This should be `/www/htdocs/ jpgraph-1.11/src`.
$chart_file_format	The file format of chart graphics. The default is png. Other valid formats are jpg and gif.

4. After you have saved the file with these parameters, open a Web browser and enter the hostname or IP address of your Web server followed by `/acid/ acid_main.php`. For example:

```
http://localhost/acid/acid_main.php
```

This displays the ACID configuration page. From here on in, you can use the Web interface to finish configuring ACID.

5. Click on the Create ACID AG button. This will create a database for your Snort data. The default database name is "snort."

6. Go to http://localhost/acid and you will see the ACID main page for your Snort database (see Figure 8.2).

You have now finished configuring ACID and can start using it to manage your IDS systems.

Introduction to Using ACID

When you first log in, the ACID main page displays (see Figure 8.2). The top area of the main database view gives you overall statistics on the database you are viewing, including

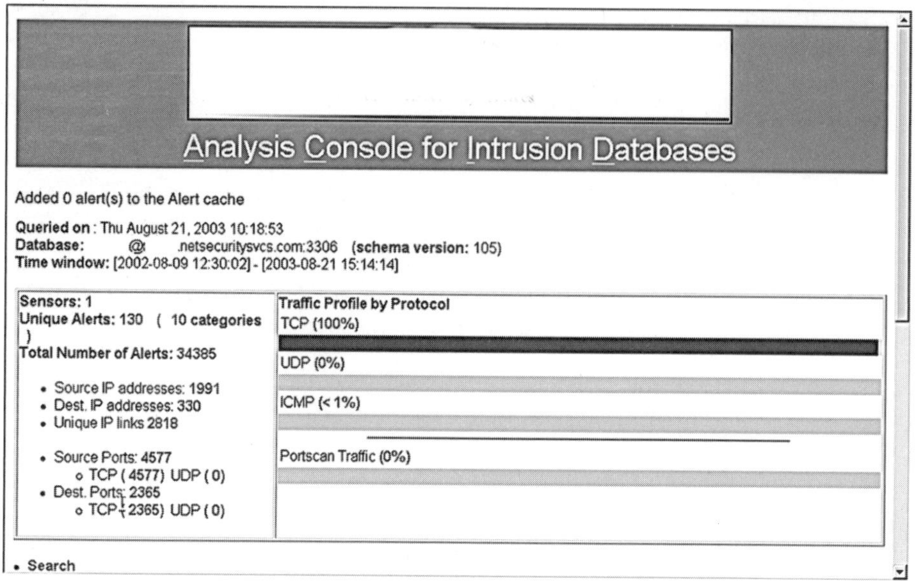

Analysis Console for Intrusion Databases

Added 0 alert(s) to the Alert cache

Queried on: Thu August 21, 2003 10:18:53
Database: @   .netsecuritysvcs.com:3306   **(schema version:** 105)
Time window: [2002-08-09 12:30:02] - [2003-08-21 15:14:14]

Sensors: 1
Unique Alerts: 130 (10 categories)
Total Number of Alerts: 34385

- Source IP addresses: 1991
- Dest. IP addresses: 330
- Unique IP links 2818

- Source Ports: 4577
    o TCP (4577) UDP (0)
- Dest. Ports: 2365
    o TCP (2365) UDP (0)

Traffic Profile by Protocol
TCP (100%)

UDP (0%)

ICMP (< 1%)

Portscan Traffic (0%)

- Search

Figure 8.2 Main ACID Interface

its name, the time frame of all the records contained in the database, and the date and time last queried.

The section below that has all the summary information on this particular alert group (AG). The AG is the sensor or group of sensors represented in this database. If you want to track different groups of sensors as an entity, such as for different customers or divisions, you need to create a separate database or AG for each one. This is also important when you are running reports and using the archival capabilities of ACID. You can only take search or query actions on an individual AG, not on multiple AGs, so make sure that your sensors are properly organized into distinct AGs. For most companies, it will be sufficient to have just one AG with all your sensors in it. But if you are a consulting company or have large operations with multiple divisions, you may want to put groups of sensors into different AGs so you can track them separately.

In the box on the left of the screen you can see the statistics on this AG: the total number of alerts, the number of unique alerts, and the number of different IP addresses appearing in the database, both by source IP and destination IP. If you have multiple sensors in your ACID network, you can click on the Sensors item to see them listed. You can narrow your search criteria down to the data from just one sensor. This main page also profiles your alert traffic graphically by each protocol and port scan traffic so you can get a flavor for what kind of traffic is being scanned by your NIDS sensor.

Using ACID to Tune and Manage Your NIDS

Before your NIDS can be useful at all, you must tune it to your network to eliminate false positive alerts. ACID can be invaluable in this effort. When you first turn on your NIDS, all of the alert signatures will be active and your database will begin to fill up with alert activity. Most of these alerts are going to be false positives at first. To make the alert data relevant to your network, you need to begin removing some of these signatures to eliminate much of the erroneous activity and to give you only data that is actionable.

Once you have a sufficient number of alerts in the database (at least a thousand on a busy network), you can start analyzing your alert data and eliminating some alert types. Watch your database carefully, as it may not take very long at all for it to fill up, especially with the default Snort rule list.

Open ACID and click on the Unique Alerts button. This shows the most recent alerts categorized by alert type (see Figure 8.3).

On this page, you see the following information on each alert type:

- Signature name
- Alert classification
- Total number of that type of alert in the database
- Sensor number that the alert came from

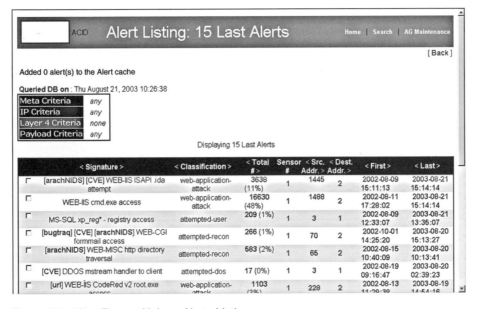

Figure 8.3 Most Recent Unique Alerts Listing

- The number of different source IP addresses associated with that alert
- The number of different destination IP addresses associated with that alert
- The time the alert came in

You can sort any of the columns by clicking on the little arrows at the top of the column. For example, you can sort by the number of alerts, then click on the largest offender. This narrows down the list to only that alert type. Scan the list and see if you can determine if this is really a security issue or a false positive. Are there any discernable patterns? Are they all coming from the same IP address? Are they all going to the same IP address? Are they happening at regular intervals or do they seem random? If this analysis doesn't lead to any conclusions, drill deeper by clicking on individual alerts. This lets you see the actual packet that set off the alert, and is very helpful from a forensic standpoint if you are actually being attacked and are trying to respond or pursue the attackers further.

Also, be forewarned: If sensitive data is crossing your network, you may inadvertently end up viewing it since you are capturing whole packets of data in the alerts. Make sure you are cleared to see this kind of data. It is also very important that your Snort database is properly secured, because anyone who breaks into your database machine would potentially have access to that sensitive information. Another solution to this is to turn down the level of detail captured in the alerts, though this may hinder your ability to use the alerts to track down the culprit.

In the example in Figure 8.3, Web-IIS cmd.exe is the most common alert. By clicking on the alert detail, you can see the actual packet that generated this alert (see Figure 8.4). The source IP is shown, along with all the TCP ports and settings.

Based on the host name, this packet came from an address in Japan (upper-level domain of .jp). You can use this to determine whether this is an address that should normally be accessing your network. You can also look lower and see the actual packet payload. The left side has the packet data in hexadecimal and the right side converts it to ASCII (if it is possible to display that way). This shows the actual commands the sender was trying to issue against your machine. From looking at these, it seems someone was trying to access the cmd.exe command; in other words, get a command line prompt. This is clearly an attack on your system. Unfortunately, this is probably a scripted attack done by an Internet worm, and these types of attacks happen dozens of times a day, as you can see from the large number of cmd.exe alerts in the database. Still, it's worth keeping an eye on, to see if that IP comes up consistently. You can at least file a complaint with the ISP and make sure the destination machine being attacked is secure against that exploit. You could also take further action against the IP address listed as the source, such as legal prosecution or civil action, if a successful break-in had occurred. At least you now know exactly what kinds of attacks are coming at your network and what they are trying to do. This will better enable you to proactively protect your network and react if it comes under attack.

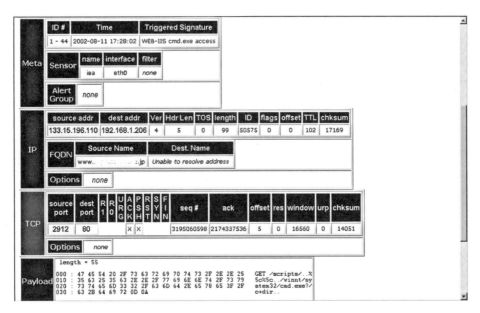

Figure 8.4 ACID Alert Detail

Other Ways to Analyze Alert Data Using ACID

Who's Being Attacked?   Using ACID, look up the most common IP destination addresses. This shows the IP addresses that are supposedly getting attacked the most, and therefore they are the machines to focus your security efforts on. This also helps you discern false positives from real ones, as you may find one particular machine generating a huge number of alerts from an application it is running. A sudden upsurge in alerts to a particular IP address could point you to an attack on that machine that is underway. Then you can batten down the hatches by running vulnerability scanners, checking patch levels, dropping packets from the offending source IP(s) at the router, and so on.

Who's Doing the Attacking?   Look at the IP source address that appears the most often. Go to the source IP list off the main page; this shows the IP and then the Fully Qualified Domain Name (FQDN). This tells you where the attack is coming from. Sorting by the number of alerts lets you see the worst offenders in terms of generating alerts. If the IP addresses with the most alerts are on your network, you may have an internal culprit or an application that is triggering an alert. Use the process discussed earlier to drill down to the alert detail level and analyze the alerts. If they are from external IP addresses, you will want to determine if this is legitimate traffic bound for your network or actual attacks. Look at the individual alerts to see what they are trying to do. Click on the IP address; this displays a page with additional information on the address and some options to analyze it further (see Figure 8.5). You can perform various functions on that address such as reverse

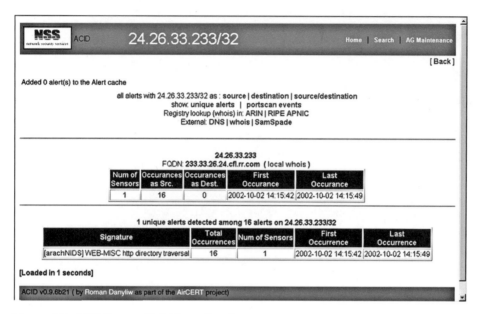

Figure 8.5 ACID Source IP Address Detail

DNS lookup, ARIN lookup, and even a Sam Spade search (similar to the tool studied in Chapter 2) from within ACID. The output of these functions should tell you what organization owns those IPs, any contact e-mails for their network operations center, and abuse e-mail contacts (if available). You can use these contacts to register a complaint about these activities. Also, if you see certain addresses showing up again and again, you can filter these IP addresses at your router or firewall.

What Service Is Being Attacked the Most?   By looking at the most common ports on which alerts are being received, you can see what services are being targeted. If you see a lot of Web-based alerts, you will want to pay closer attention to keeping your Web servers properly locked down. If the alerts show a lot of Windows NetBIOS activity, you will want to look at your Windows permissions and password policies. This will give you a good idea of what services to focus your attention on first.

Using ACID on a Daily Basis

Once you have ACID running and sufficiently tuned for your NIDS configuration, you should get in the habit of checking it at least once a day to see what new alerts have been generated. A good rule of thumb is to check first thing in the morning and again just before you go home. If you have after-hours personnel working, you could also add checking the ACID alert database to their routine.

When you log into the ACID database, you can go immediately to the Snapshot section (see Figure 8.6) and click on Most Recent Alerts to get a quick view of the most current activity. This shows you all the alerts in chronological order. If it is still generating too many alerts to be useful, in the Today's Alerts section select Unique. This shows you all the alerts from today grouped by alert type so you can see which ones are generating the most traffic. The Snapshot section options Last 24 Hours and Last 72 Hours are also useful. These let you search on the most frequent alerts, addresses, and ports during various periods.

Graphing ACID Data

If you are more of a visual person or you need something graphical to show management, ACID comes with the ability to create graphs and charts based on your alert database. This feature is still experimental, and you must have the PHP graphing modules listed at the beginning of this section. However, this does give you some nice options for outputting graphical summaries of Snort data. You can access the graph feature by clicking on Graph Alert Data just below the Alert statistics box off the main ACID screen. This displays the graphing options. You can arrange the data for your graph by:

- Time (hour, day, month) versus the number of alerts
- IP addresses (source or destination) versus the number of alerts
- TCP or UDP ports (source or destination) versus the number of alerts

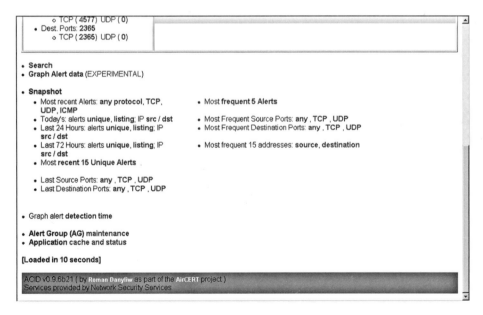

Figure 8.6 ACID Snapshot Section

Set your parameters using the pull-down boxes and click on Graph Data. Make sure you have filled in every box or you will get an error message. ACID generates and displays a graph. See Figure 8.7 for an example of an ACID graph

Maintaining Your ACID database

As your alert database grows, you will need to perform some maintenance on it periodically to keep it from getting too big and unwieldy. Also, your statistics and graphs will be more accurate if you archive your early alerts, which will contain many false positives. In addition, cleaning out your database from time to time will make your queries process faster.

To archive your alerts, use the query control at the bottom of the main screen. Create a query for the alerts you want to archive, for example, all the alerts generated last year. Then select Archive Alerts as the action for your query. You can selectively archive alerts by date, alert type, or other criteria. You can also choose to just copy the alerts into the archive or to remove them. The archived alerts will be placed in their own database with the name you set in the acid_conf.php file during configuration.

You should archive all of your alerts from the first few months of operation when you are fine-tuning the Snort sensor. After that, the data will have more relevance to actual attacks versus false positives. It is also a good idea to archive at least once a year or perhaps quarterly depending on the volume of alerts being logged. As a general rule of thumb, you don't want more than 100,000 alerts in your database at any given time.

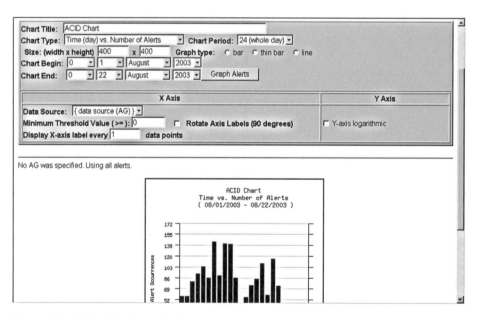

Figure 8.7 ACID Alert Data Graph

So, you now know how to build a complete Snort intrusion detection network, with multiple sensors logging into a database tool that can be used to analyze the data and do reporting. This will help you better use the intrusion detection data, make the most of your security efforts, and have some tangible reports and graphs to show management. Now, we will look at some tools that can help with your vulnerability scan data.

Flamey the Tech Tip:

Use Names Carefully!

Be careful when talking to your boss about using Snort and ACID at work. Make sure he or she understands that these are valuable management programs, not illegal controlled substances!

NPI (Nessus PHP Interface)

NPI
Author/primary contact: Kristofer T. Karas
Web site: http://enterprise.bidmc.harvard.edu/pub/
nessus-php/
Platforms: Most UNIX
License: GPL
Version reviewed: .01a

One problem when using the vulnerability scanner Nessus to scan medium- to large-size networks is that the reports can be quite intimidating. The Nessus reporting formats themselves are fine and the HTML is fairly easy to navigate, but when you have a couple of hundred pages of data to sort through, it can be hard to see the important data amongst all the noise. It would be nice to have something to organize the scan data any way you like. To really be able to analyze it, you need to get your data into a database versus the standard flat file format. You also want to be able to access the data easily, such as from a Web-based interface. With this capability, you could quickly get to the most important data and analyze scan results over time to see if your network was getting more secure or less secure.

Fortunately, several products integrate Nessus with a database. A few of the Nessus-to-database programs are NesQuik, Java Nessus Report Manager, and Nessus PHP Interface (NPI). I selected NPI for this book for a number of reasons. First, it is a truly open source product with no commercial ties. Also, it uses MySQL and PHP, which you have already used for other tools such as ACID. Using these applications, NPI offers the ability to port your Nessus data into a database and then view it with a Web browser

NPI, similar to ACID in its design, uses a MySQL database to store the results and a PHP-enabled Web server to view and query the results. Figure 8.8 illustrates the logical components of NPI. One difference between the Snort and Nessus architectures is that with Nessus there are two different parts generating the data: a client initiating the scans and a server running them. In some cases they might be on the same machine, but this figure shows two different physical servers. There is also database server to which the scan data is logged, and a Web server that provides the interface to the data. Again, the database and Web server could be on the same machine or two different boxes.

Figure 8.8 demonstates the flow of data and the logical parts in the NPI system. The Nessus client logs into the Nessus server to initiate a scan of a target. The data is stored on the client machine in the native Nessus .nbe format. Once you have the raw file, NPI runs a conversion script on the .nbe file and imports the data into a MySQL database. When the scan data is in the database, you can view and query the database using a Web-based PHP interface from any Web browser. This sounds like a much better way to analyze scan data, so let's get busy and set up NPI.

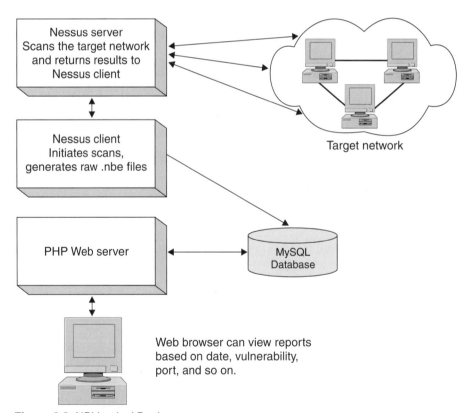

Figure 8.8 NPI Logical Design

Installing NPI

Before beginning to install NPI, you need to have your MySQL server and Apache Web server with PHP working. If you haven't already gotten these up and running, refer back to the appropriate sections earlier in this chapter. Once you have your SQL and Web servers ready, take these steps to install NPI.

1. Get the file from the book's CD-ROM, and unzip and untar the program. Place the contents in its own directory. The directory name doesn't matter as long as all the files are in the one directory. For example, /usr/local/nessus-php will work fine, assuming you have the permissions to write there.
2. Change into that directory and edit the file nsr-php using a text editor. This file contains variables (those lines that start with $) that allow the program to contact your MySQL server. Table 8.5 lists the variables you need to edit and recommendations for their values.

Table 8.5 NPI Variables for the MySQL Server

Variables	Descriptions
$db_host	Set this to the host on which the MySQL server will be running. If the MySQL server is running on the same machine as the Web server, then this is localhost. Otherwise enter the IP address or hostname of the MySQL machine.
$db_user	This is the username used to log into the MySQL database. This can be the same as the user name set up in the MySQL installation.
$db_pass	The password corresponding to the above user.
$db_database	This is the name of the database that is created to hold the NPI data. The default database name created by NPI is nessus, but you can change this to whatever you would like.
$db_suuser	This is the administrative user on the MySQL database. This is required by the nsr-php script. The default is root, which should work for most installations. Note that this is *not* the same as the root user on your operating system.
$db_supass	The MySQL root password corresponding to the $db_suuser account described above.
$your_domain	A list of domains that you want to be stripped out from the output. This will clean your reports up if you just want machine names to appear in the output rather than the full Internet host name. This is an optional variable.

3. Open the file nsr in a text editor and make the same entries in it as you did in Step 2 (see Table 8.5). Make sure that the path to the Nessus plug-ins directory is correct. In most installations they should be in the default location, which is /usr/local/lib/nessus/plugins. Check to make sure yours are there and if they are not, make the appropriate modification in the nsr file.

4. Edit the file nessusphp.inc, also changing the variables as in the above two steps.

5. Create your Nessus database. Do this by running the nsr-php script:

```
php nsr-php -b
```

This creates the MySQL database called nessus for your scan data. You can log into it and check to make sure the proper tables were created.

6. Verify that the database was properly created.

   a. Log into MySQL using the commands in the MySQL sidebar earlier in this chapter.

   b. Type show databases; (don't forget the semi-colon) at the MySQL command prompt. A list displays showing all the databases, and your newly created Nessus database should be one of them.

   c. Switch to that specific database using use NESSUS; and then type the show tables; command. You should get the results shown in Figure 8.9. This shows each of the three tables in the nessus database.

7. Copy the files in the /www subdirectory of your NPI install directory to your Web server's root directory. Create a new directory in your Web server's document root where your NPI files will reside. This is the location from which you will access your Nessus database. Issue the following commands from your nessus-php directory to do this and set the correct permissions for the files.

```
mkdir /usr/local/apache2/htdocs/nessus-php
mv ./www /usr/local/apache2/htdocs/nessus-php
chown -R www.www /usr/local/apache2/htdocs/nessus-php
chmod 755 /usr/local/apache2/htdocs/nessus-php/*
```

```
mysql> show tables;
+--------------------+
| Tables_in_nessus   |
+--------------------+
| report             |
| scans              |
| scripts            |
+--------------------+
3 rows in set (0.00 sec)
```

Figure 8.9 Output of the show tables; Command

Be sure to change the path to your Web document root if it is different from the example. You can change the name of the directory that the nessus-php files are in if you like. This example puts the NPI access page in /nessus-php off your Web document root. It also uses the same system user (www) for both the user and group that will access the MySQL database. For better security, set up a special user with only read access to the data. In that case you would change the www.www to the appropriate read-only user and group. You need to do this for the appropriate MySQL account as well.

You have now installed the NPI program.

Importing Nessus Scans into NPI

Now you are ready to import some Nessus scans into your database.

1. Run the nsr script on each native Nessus scan file to be imported. (Obviously, you must have some completed scan files available, saved in the native .nbe format.) NPI will also accept and convert the older Nessus format .nsr. Enter the following to run nsr from the command line:

    ```
    ./nsr /scans/scan.nbe
    ```

    Replace /scans/scan.nbe with your scan file name and path. This takes the raw Nessus file and imports it into your database. It also checks your Nessus plug-ins and creates entries in the database for any new plug-ins that may have been added.
2. You are now ready to view your Nessus scans in your database. Open a browser and enter the IP of your NPI Web server with the path to your Nessus-php index file, for example, http://localhost/nessus-php/. The results should appear in the NPI interface, fully searchable and sortable (see Figure 8.10).

Using NPI

You can now browse your scan data like any other database, sort it, and run queries to find specific vulnerabilities, hosts, or other criteria. There are quite a few way to analyze your Nessus data using NPI. You can sort by the:

- Host (IP address) with the most vulnerabilities
- Most common vulnerability
- Most common category of exploits
- Most exploitable service (port number)
- Scan date or date range
- CVE or CAN number

By creating queries with NPI, you can focus on areas that represent the greatest danger to your network and maximize the effects of your remediation activity. You can also

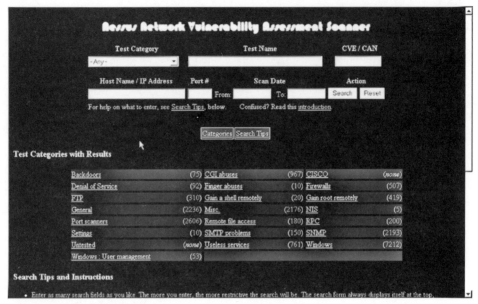

Figure 8.10 NPI Main Screen

quickly rule out certain alerts and/or machines. With NPI, you can manipulate your scan data any way you choose. One downside to the NPI tool is manually loading each scan file into the database. A script could easily be written to automate this process, but some associates and I decided to take it one step further.

The Birth of an Open Source Project

My consulting firm uses Nessus and Snort extensively. We use the ACID management tool to manage our network intrusion detection systems. We needed a similar tool to manage our Nessus scans. Even though NPI offered some very nice capabilities, it still didn't quite meet the needs of our organization. We wanted to be able to initiate scans from the Web interface, rather than just view the past results. We also found the need to do the manual importing of each scan arduous and time consuming. We have dozens of scans that need to be run at any given time, and because they typically belong to different organizations, they need to be tracked separately. What we really wanted was a tool that would manage our different scan's configurations, schedule them, run them automatically, and import the results into the appropriate database.

We were not able to find an open source tool that matched all these needs, so we were faced with the alternative of finding a commercial product to meet our needs or developing one in-house. However, even the commercial vulnerability scanners didn't quite offer what we needed in terms of scheduling and keeping track of different client's scans. Obviously writing a new vulnerability scanner from scratch would have been both cost and time prohibitive. So we explored the idea of developing our own add-on module to Nessus as an open source project. We went through a decision process to determine if it made sense. If you are thinking of writing your own open source program, you should do the same, taking the following factors into consideration.

Is There Something Already Out There?

First, search the Web to see if there is anything that already does what you need to do. Look at places like Sourceforge.net and Freshmeat.net, and use Google and other search engines. There is a good chance that something already exists to solve your problem. If you find something that is not quite exactly what you need, you could use it as a starter or a helper in building your program, as we did with NPI. Even if nothing exists, you might find some FAQs or sites with helpful information for your project. Also, during your explorations, you might find some people with the same problems willing to contribute to your project. Before you know it, you could have several programmers willing to help you.

Is There a Broader Need for Your Program?

If the problem you are solving is a specific niche problem for your company, it may not be worth going through the trouble to open source it. Drop a few messages on relevant message boards to see if there is any interest. If nobody else wants it, you may just want to keep it as an in-house development project. However, even in the smallest industries there are usually similar needs for applications, and the Internet has made the world a smaller place. Think of all the times you went searching for something obscure and found it, because someone on the Web thought it was worth releasing. So if there's any interest, make it open source!

Do You Have Permission to Release Code as Open Source?

If you are doing this as part of your duties for an employer, make sure they will allow you to release the source code. If it's part of a larger proprietary program, then it's doubtful that they will want it open sourced. However, if it's a stand-alone program and they see the benefits of peer review and additional contributors as well as free advertising, there is a good chance that your employer won't mind. Just check before you start posting code, if you value your job.

We went through this process and decided that for all the reasons above, it was worth developing our own add-on to Nessus as an open source project. We called this program Nessus Command Center (NCC) and this is the debut of that program in print.

Nessus Command Center (NCC)

Nessus Command Center (NCC)
Authors/primary contacts: Tony Howlett, Brian Credeur, Matt Sisk, Lorell Hathcock
Web site: www.netsecuritysvcs.com/ncc
Platforms: Linux, most UNIX
License: GPL
Version reviewed: .01b
Mailing list:
NCC Mailing list
General discussions and questions regarding NCC. Send an e-mail with the word "subscribe" in either the body or subject of the e-mail to ncc@netsecuritysvcs.com.

The genesis of NCC was our need to create a management tool to automate our scans and better analyze the results. The NPI tool described earlier does a pretty decent job of importing Nessus data into a database, but it doesn't address the scheduling issue and the interface left something to be desired. Rather than reinventing the wheel, we used parts of NPI for our Web interface and added on a management and scheduling module. Our goals in the project were as follows.

- A management platform for Nessus scanning. We needed a tool for keeping track of scans for different companies with different configurations and even different groups of companies. As a consulting firm, we deal with many different firms. We even have resellers ordering scans for companies using our infrastructure. We wanted a way to manage all these different entities and keep them separate, yet giving us a control panel to globally manage all of them easily.

- A scheduling database and interface for Nessus. The first goal was to develop a way to catalog our scan information, schedule the scans, and automatically run them. We wanted the ability to keep track of different entities, because the scans would belong to many different companies. There would be an administrator level for us to create and schedule the scans, and the possible capability in the future for clients to go in and modify certain parts of their scan configuration, such as time, hosts to scan, and so on. The database would need to have a Web-based interface, since we would have customers and agents outside our firewall accessing the system to configure their scans.

- A database interface for Nessus results. This goal was already partially achieved in the NPI program, but we wanted to improve the interface, which was rudimentary and didn't allow, for example, multiple users and levels of access. We planned to use NPI as our template for this part of the program. And given that NPI is GPL and our program would be GPL this wouldn't be a problem.

- A Web interface for setting all Nessus options. This was really an optional feature rather than a must-have for us. In studying the problem, we found that most of the scans we ran used only about five different configurations. However, it would be nice to be able to configure all the possible Nessus scan options right from the Web, without having the Nessus client loaded. This would allow us to input a scan directly from a customer's office or anywhere offsite. We looked around and found another open source project called Inprotect that was offering a Web interface for Nessus. The code was released under the GPL, so we could use this code as a guideline for our efforts in this area. Due to the more complicated nature of this task, we decided that this feature would not be in the beta release.

Platforms for NCC

From the very start, we decided we would write our program for the series of platforms known as **LAMP** (Linux, Apache, MySQL, and Perl).

- Linux: For obvious reasons, Linux offers the most portability and the lowest cost for entry. However, there is no reason why this system wouldn't run on other flavors of UNIX with some minor modifications. Also, it could be ported to a Windows-based programming platform, such as Perl for Windows.
- Apache: Again, we chose this because Apache is open source and is one of the most popular Web servers. It was also the most logical choice since we would be using it for our other tools. In addition, this system would also run on any PHP-compliant Web server including IIS.
- MySQL: There are several good open source databases including Postgresql and others. We chose MySQL because we were the most familiar with it and the licensing issues were the easiest to deal with. Like Apache, we were already using MySQL for our ACID databases.
- Perl: Again, there are lots of scripting languages, but we picked Perl because it is one of the most portable languages, doesn't requires any compiling, and is easily modifiable by third parties.

Based on this LAMP architecture, we set out to build a tool that would suit our purposes. We first wrote a project plan that detailed the work we would have to do. We then divided the tasks based on our different skill sets. We listed the programmatic elements that would be needed for our program, including Perl scripts, PHP scripts, MySQL scripts, and shell scripts, as well as text files for the documentation. Table 8.6 shows the project list with all of the pieces needed and what each one does.

Table 8.6 NCC Project Elements

Types	Items	Descriptions
Perl script	ncc.pl	Runs with cron and populates the queue table with scans ready to be run.
Perl script	ncc-client.pl	Removes scheduled scans from the queue, issues the command to run them, and then does the conversion to drop .nbe files into the MySQL database when they are done.
Perl script	ncc-daily.pl	Sends out daily summary e-mails and does clean up on the queue table.
PHP script	Main.php and other supporting php files, and so on	Interface to enter items into the schedule table; consists of multiple files.
PHP script	Reports.php	Interface to view MySQL database, modified versions of NPI; consists of multiple files.
MySQL database	NCC Database	Sample database for the scans; internal to MySQL database program.
MySQL script	ncc.mysql	Creates initial database.
Misc script	install.pl	Script to create the cron item, call MySQL script, copy executables to bin, and php file to Web.
Text file	ncc.ini	Environment variables for the Perl and PHP scripts; database names, file locations, e-mail to send notifies to, and so on.
Text file	INSTALL, README, and so on	Multiple files with installation instructions, operation instructions, and other pertinent data.

We also had to design a database schema with the tables that we would be populating with our program. The NPI program was a great help in this regard, although there were new tables relating to our scheduling that we needed to add.

While the dataflow was similar to that of NPI, there were some significant differences. We diagramed this so we could follow all the logical interactions between the systems. Figure 8.11 shows the logical layout of NCC.

We also created a Web site and a Sourceforge page for the project. The Web page is located at www.netsecuritysvcs.com/ncc. While we figured we had enough talent in our group to finish the project, it never hurts to let other people in the open source community know what you are working on. Also, once it was finished, we would need help in porting it to other platforms and adding new features.

So once all the preliminaries were taken care of, we got to work, usually holding weekly meetings to track the progress. Because this was not a full-time effort and we all had day jobs, it took about a year to complete the program, and even that was only a beta version. Still, we had something we could use, and now by leveraging the online community of developers, NCC can be extended and improved. Writing NCC as an open source

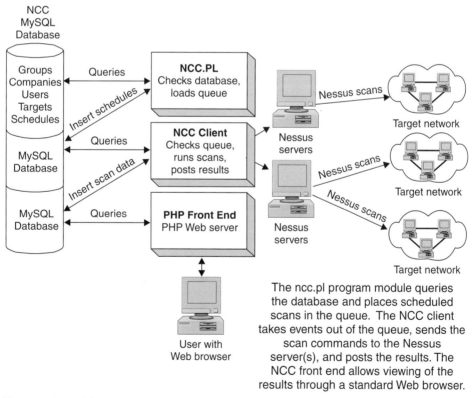

The ncc.pl program module queries the database and places scheduled scans in the queue. The NCC client takes events out of the queue, sends the scan commands to the Nessus server(s), and posts the results. The NCC front end allows viewing of the results through a standard Web browser.

Figure 8.11 NCC Logical Design

project certainly required a little more work on the front end than doing it as a private project because we had to do the research on existing programs and integrate the code bases, but we were able to leverage existing code bases, which cut our total development time down considerably. Also, we knew that if it became popular, it might get ported to other platforms or even used as the base for an even bigger program, which would only help us. All in all, the experience was a real win/win for my company and other users out there.

Installing NCC

NCC has requirements similar to those of the NPI tool described earlier in this chapter. You need a PHP-compliant Web server (such as Apache), MySQL database, and a Nessus server and client. NCC assumes you already have these installed and running. If you don't, refer to the sections earlier in this chapter on how to set up Apache and MySQL, and Chapter 5 for instructions on installing Nessus.

When these are in place you can install NCC.

1. Download the program or get it from the book's CD-ROM.
2. Unpack and unzip the program into its own directory, making sure the directory is in your path.
3. Change into the NCC directory and type ./install.pl. This runs the NCC installation script. (You don't have to compile NCC because it is programmed in interpreted languages such as Perl and PHP.)

   The install program first checks for the presence of the Perl modules required for NCC. If it doesn't find them, you have to load the appropriate module(s) either from your distribution disks or using the CPAN utilities described in the "Installing Swatch" section earlier in this chapter.
4. The program automatically initializes your database and copies all the files into the appropriate places. During the installation you are prompted for some input. Table 8.7 describes these installation settings.

Table 8.7 NCC Installation Settings

Settings	Descriptions
NCC user	This is a system account that NCC will run as. It is recommended that you create a special user account just for NCC.
Installation directory	You can choose one of the two standard locations, /usr/local/ncc or current, or you can specify your own.
NCC Administrator e-mail	The e-mail address of the NCC administrator who will get all the daily activity reports.

Settings	Descriptions
From address for results	The address that the reports will appear to come from (important for spam filters).
Name of MySQL server	Host name or IP address of your NCC MySQL server, which should be `localhost` if is running on the same machine.
Name of database for NCC	The name of the MySQL database that will be created by the install script. The default of ncc is fine for most installations.
MySQL user	A valid user on the MySQL system. You should create one specifically for NCC.
MySQL password	Password for the above user.
Nessus server	Host name or IP address of your Nessus server. This is `localhost` if you are running Nessus and NCC on the same machine.
Nessus port	The port to connect to on the Nessus server. The default of 1241 is correct unless you have changed this on your Nessus server.
Nessus username	A valid user on that Nessus server.
Nessus password	The password for the above user.
Nessus path	Path to the Nessus executables. The default is correct for the standard Nessus installation.
Temp directory	Where NCC will stage results from your scans before it imports them into the database. You can look here if you want to find the raw .nbe files that were used.

5. You will be prompted for the NCC admin user and password combination. This user will be an administrator of the entire program, so choose this login ID and password carefully.
6. Create a symbolic link from the place in your public Web directories that you want to access NCC. Point this to /html in the root NCC install directory. This will connect you to the main NCC page and to your public Web directories as well as protect the other NCC files from access.

7. You are now ready to run NCC. With the database and Web server running, open a Web browser and enter the host name of your NCC server along with the location you created above. For example, if you created the symlink in /ncc of your Web root directory and your NCC server is ncc.example.com, the URL would look like this:

http://ncc.example.com/ncc

If you were accessing it on the local machine, this would work:

http://localhost/ncc

This displays the NCC login page.

8. Log in with the user name and password you created during the installation process.

You can now begin using NCC to automate and schedule your scans.

Using NCC

After you have logged in, the NCC main screen displays (see Figure 8.12). This is where you manage all of your groups, companies, scan targets, and schedules.

NCC was designed to be modular and expandable. For example, you can use NCC to manage multiple scans within one company. However, if you are a consultant, you can

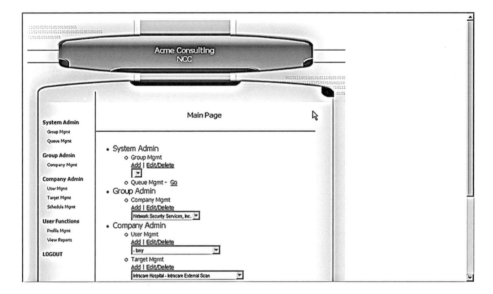

Figure 8.12 NCC Main Interface

create scans for multiple companies that have different profiles. Let's take it one step further and say that you want to run a security ASP. NCC lets you set up multiple groups, each with its own member companies for all of your individual agents and consultants selling security scans. (This group management feature will eventually allow for customizable interfaces and front ends, but this feature is not in the beta version.)

You can choose from four main options.

- System admin: These options are available only to the system administrator. This is where you create your groups and perform other system-level functions.
- Group admin: This option is available only to group administrators. These users may add, edit, or delete a group's company profiles. You would use this function if, for example, you were setting up different companies with a set of targets each could manage. Each group administrator will see only see the companies he or she has access to.
- Company admin: This is where you manage the users, target files, and schedules for each company. For example, you may want to have a lower-level system administrator start scans for one division but not for another. You can set those parameters here.
- User functions: This section is available to all users. Here individual users can edit their profile information and perform functions on their accounts such as changing their passwords. They can also access the data from scans that have run.

Let's take a simple example and walk through the steps of adding users, adding targets, and scheduling a scan. For simplicity, the example assumes you don't need multi-company and multi-group capabilities.

Adding Users

1. First, you should add a user (other than the system administration user you added earlier). Under Company Admin, click on Add user to add a user who can run scans.
2. Select the company they will belong to from the pull-down box and click on Add.
3. On the User Management screen, fill in the information on your new user (see Figure 8.13)

   You can select a user name and password here. The password will be starred out and stored as a MD5 hash rather than plain text. Also, select a user type here: System admin, Group admin, Company admin, and User. Note that you will only be able to create users that are at or below the user level you are logged on as. For example, company admins cannot create system admin level users.

   If you want to edit or delete an existing user, click on Edit/delete from the Main Screen under Company Management.
4. Click on Add, and NCC adds your user to the database. This person can now log on and add scans as part of the company they were added to.

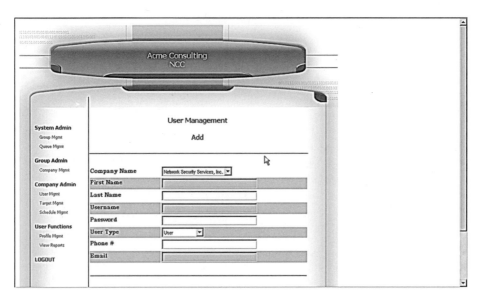

Figure 8.13 NCC User Management Screen

Adding Targets

NCC defines a **target** as any set of IP addresses and associated scan settings for those addresses. We made a conscious decision when designing the program to separate the target objects from the schedule objects. This allows the program to be much more modular and have greater flexibility. For example, you may want to schedule a certain scan to run at the beginning of each month. However, if a new vulnerability comes out, you might want to scan that target in the middle of the month, just once, to check your vulnerability. NCC allows you to add a one-time scan event to that target rather than changing your monthly scan and then having to change it back so that your monthly scan still runs.

1. To add a target, from the main screen under Company Admin click on Target Mgmt.
2. Pull down the context-sensitive menu to see all the targets that you have access to. If you are a group administrator, it will show you all the targets for every company that you are a member of.
3. Click on Add and the Target Management screen displays (see Figure 8.14).
   Here you can select the company you are adding this target for.
   Give the target a text description, such as DMZ Servers. This name will appear in the drop-down box, so make it specific enough that you can tell what it is.
4. Select a Scan type—whether your scan is of a single address, a subnet, or an address range.

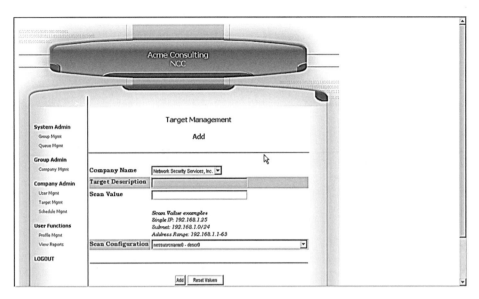

Figure 8.14 CC Target Management

5. Under Scan Value enter the IP address string that corresponds to your targets in Nessus-compliant syntax. Recall from Chapter 5 that the allowed formats for Nessus scan strings.

Single IP address	192.168.0.1
IPs separated by commas	192.168.0.1,192.168.0.2
IP ranges separated by dashes	192.168.0.1-192.168.0.254
Using standard slash notation	192.168.0.1/24 (a class C network of 256 addresses)
A host name	myhost.example.com
Any combination of the above separated by commas	192.168.0.1-192.168.0.254, 195.168.0.1/24,192.168.0.1-192.168.0.254

6. Select a scan configuration. The default is the Nessus default scan. There are up to four other scan types you can run. (Future versions will allow for uploading a custom configuration file and also pasting in a text file.)

7. Click on Add, and the target is added. You are now ready to schedule your scan.

Scheduling Your Scan

Once you have created one or more target objects, you can apply scan schedules to them.

1. On the main menu under Company Admin, click on Schedule Management. The Schedule Management screen displays (see Figure 8.15).

2. Select a company and a target within that company. Again, the pull-down menu selections available to you reflect the user level at which you logged in.

3. Select a scan date, time, how often it should run, and how many times to recur.

You can have the scan run one time, daily, weekly, monthly, bi-monthly, or quarterly. (Future versions will support custom recurrence strings in either cron or I-cal format.) You can also set the recurrence to happen only for a certain number of times, for example, for a customer who has signed a one-year contract for monthly scans. You can also choose to have it recur continuously, for example, for your own network's regular monthly scans.

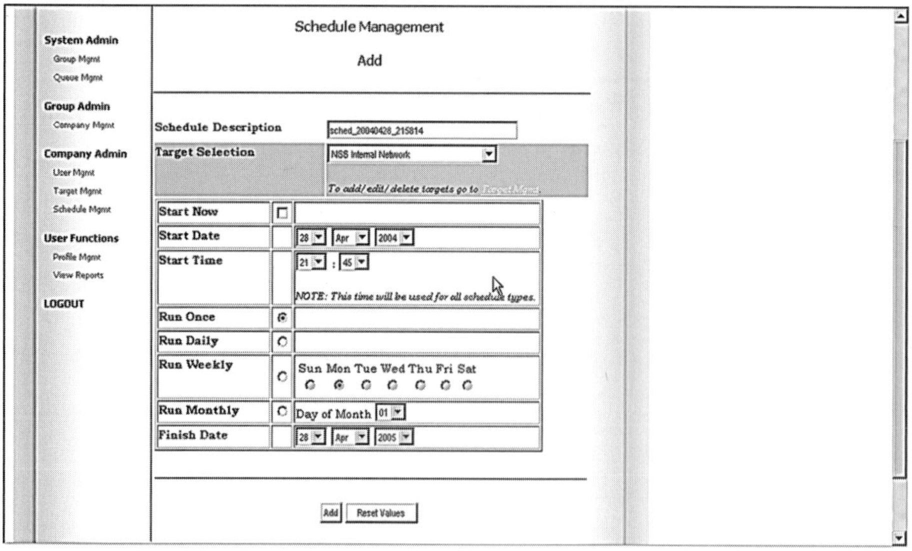

Figure 8.15 NCC Schedule Management Screen

4. Click on Add and your scan will be scheduled.

Now you can sit back and wait for the report. The user who created the scan will be notified by e-mail a day before the scan happens (except for daily scans, for which you are notified an hour beforehand), and another e-mail when the report is available to view.

5. Once your scan has run, you can view it by selecting View reports under User Functions on the main menu. This displays the NCC Scan database screen (see Figure 8.16)

This lets you browse the scan data and create custom reports.

You may notice this interface looks similar to the NPI interface reviewed earlier in this chapter. This is because we used the NPI code as a reference in creating this section. NPI is open source and GPL, so as long we were releasing our code GPL and included the copyright information, we were free to use this code. One of the great things about open source development is that it is perfectly acceptable to build on the successes of other people. And someone may build on your work to create something even better still. As long as it is open source, you have full access to any advances and improvements.

This may seem like a lot of work just to do a scan, and it is if you are only doing it once. But when you are managing dozens of scans with multiple users, then NCC is invaluable for keeping track of all this activity.

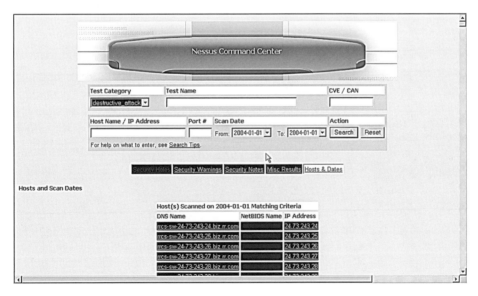

Figure 8.16 NCC Scan Database View

You now have the tools and the knowledge to create a complete intrusion detection and vulnerability scanning system with complex analytical functionality. By using these combinations of tools, you will be able to greatly increase the security of your internal network and external network servers. Together these tools can help you make the most of the time you spend on securing your network. Next, we are going to look at tools to help you keep your data secure inside and outside your network by using encryption tools.

Encryption Tools

So far, the tools discussed have been used for protecting your network and the machines that reside within that network. However, once that data passes outside the network boundaries, it is beyond the protection of the tools discussed thus far and is susceptible to potential capture by hostile entities. Most Internet applications today send their data in the clear, also known as **plain text**. This means that anyone viewing the packet can see your data. When your data crosses the Internet, it passes through different systems, many of which are out of your direct control and thus should be assumed to be nonfriendly. ISP routers and switches can be co-opted either from the inside or outside, and other mail and Web servers regularly handle your private data.

There is no way to avoid sending your data outside of your network. The biggest advantage of a global Internet is being able to share information with all of your business partners and customers in the outside world. You can't go back to the days of totally private networks. So, how do you protect your important data once it leaves the comfy and safe confines of your home network? Encryption is what most businesses rely on to make the Internet safe for their data, and it is an important tool you can use too for maintaining the integrity and confidentiality of your data on the Internet.

You may also want to protect your data from unauthorized viewers within your network, because certain information may not be for all eyes within the company. Finally, encrypting your important data can be a final line of defense against hackers. Even if they manage to break into your network and exploit the server, they still have to crack the encryption to get at your data.

Chapter Overview

Concepts you will learn:
- Symmetric and asymmetric encryption
- Different encryption algorithms
- Encryption applications
- Certificate authority security model
- Web of trust security model

Tools you will use:

PGP, GnuPG, OpenSSH, FreeS/WAN, and John the Ripper

There are many different protocols for encryption. Looking again at the OSI Reference Model (Figure 9.1), you can see that there are encryption tools that operate at several different levels of the network model. As you probably guessed, there are many excellent open source encryption tools available for just about every application, from encrypting single files to protecting all of your outbound Internet connections. In fact, the ready availability of high-quality encryption software has its roots in the open source movement.

OSI Layer	Layer Name	Encryption Standards
Layer 7	Application	PGP, GnuPG
Layer 6	Presentation	
Layer 5	Session	SSL, SSH
Layer 4	Transport	
Layer 3	Network	IPsec
Layer 2	Data Link	
Layer 1	Physical	

Figure 9.1 OSI Model and Encryption

Types of Encryption

There are two main ways to do encryption today. The first kind of encryption, called **symmetric cryptography** or **shared secret encryption**, has been used since ancient Egyptian times. This form of encryption uses a secret key, called the **shared secret**, to scramble the data into unintelligible gibberish. The person on the other end needs the shared secret (key) to unlock the data—the encryption algorithm. You can change the key and change the results of the encryption. It is called symmetric cryptography because the same key is used on both ends for both encryption and decryption (see Figure 9.2).

The problem with this method is that you have to communicate the secret key securely to your intended recipient. If your enemy intercepts the key, he can read the message. All kinds of systems were invented to try to get around this basic weakness, but the fact remained: you still had to communicate the secret key in some way to your intended recipient before you could commence secure communications.

A revolution in encryption was started when Whitfield Diffie, Martin Hellman, and Ralph Merkle invented Public Key cryptography. (Actually, there is some debate whether the British civil servant James Ellis really invented it earlier and kept it secret, but Diffie, Hellman, and Merkle were the first to go public with it in 1976.) They were trying to solve the age-old problem of key exchange. Diffie wondered how two individuals wanting to make a financial transaction over an electronic network could do so securely. He was thinking far ahead here, because the Internet was in its infancy at the time and e-commerce didn't yet exist. If big governments had problems dealing with the key exchange problem, how could the average person manage this? He wanted to come up with a system by which two parties could easily hold protected conversations and secure transactions without having to exchange keys every time. He knew that if he could solve the key exchange problem, it would be a huge advance in cryptography.

Diffie partnered with Martin Hellman and Ralph Merkle. It took them a few years, but finally they came up with a system called **public key encryption** (PKE), also known as **asymmetric cryptography**.

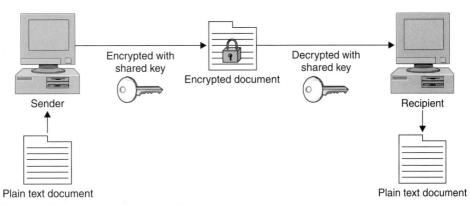

Figure 9.2 Symmetric Cryptography

Asymmetric cryptography uses encryption that splits the key into two smaller keys. One of the keys is made public and one is kept private. You encrypt a message with the recipient's public key. The recipient can then decrypt it with their private key. And they can do the same for you, encrypting a message with your public key so you can decrypt it with your private key (see Figure 9.3). The difference here is that you don't need someone's private key to send him or her a secure message. You use his or her public key, which doesn't have to be kept secure (in fact, it can be published like a phone number). By using your recipient's public key, you know that only that person can encrypt it using his or her private key. This system allows two entities to communicate securely without any prior exchange of keys.

Asymmetric cryptography is usually implemented by the use of one-way functions. In mathematic terms, these are functions that are easy to compute in one direction but very difficult to compute in reverse. This is what allows you to publish your public key, which is derived from your private key. It is very difficult to work backwards and determine the private key. A common one-way function used today is factoring large prime numbers. It is easy to multiply two prime numbers together and get a product. However, to determine which of the many possibilities are the two factors of the product is one of the great mathematical problems. If anyone were to invent a method for easily deducing factors of large prime numbers, it could make obsolete much of the public key encryption used today. Fortunately, other one-way functions work for this application, such as calculations on elliptical curves or computation of inverse logarithms over a finite field.

Soon after the paper by Diffie, Hellman, and Merkle was released, another group of three men developed a practical application of the theory. Their system for public key encryption was called RSA after their names: Ronald Rivest, Adi Shamir, and Leonard Adleman. They formed a company and began licensing their system. The adoption rate was slow and their company almost went out of business, until they cut a deal to take advantage of the growing Internet commerce field with a then little-known company

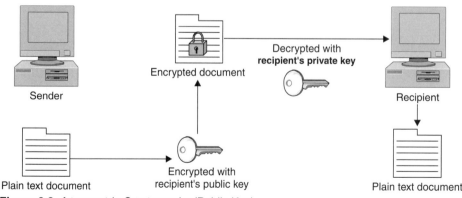

Encrypted document

Decrypted with
recipient's private key

Sender

Recipient

Plain text document

Encrypted with
recipient's public key

Plain text document

Figure 9.3 Asymmetric Cryptography (Public Key)

called Netscape. The rest is history, and RSA is now the most widely used public key encryption algorithm. Diffie and Hellman eventually released a practical application of their own, but it is usable only for key exchanges, whereas RSA can do authentication and nonrepudiation.

Public key encryption is now behind every Web server that offers you a secure purchase. Your transaction is encrypted without giving or taking a secret key, and it all happens in the background. All we know as users is that the little SSL lock symbol displays in our browser and we feel safer. Imagine the effects on Internet commerce if every time you wanted to buy something online you had to think of a secret key, encrypt the message, and then somehow communicate that key to the other party. Obviously, e-commerce could not exist as it does today without public key cryptography.

There are many different encryption algorithms, protocols, and applications based on these two main types of encryption. The following sections introduce some of these.

Encryption Algorithms

Today, strength of encryption is usually measured by key size. No matter how strong the algorithm, the encrypted data can be subject to brute force attacks in which all possible combinations of keys are tried. Eventually the encryption can be cracked. For most modern ciphers with decent key lengths, the time to crack them with brute force them is measured in millennia. However, an undisclosed flaw in an algorithm or an advance in computer technology or mathematical methods could sharply decrease these times.

Generally, the thinking is that the key length should be suitable for keeping the data secure for a reasonable amount of time. If the item is very topical, such as battlefield communications or daily stock information, then a cipher that protects it for a matter of weeks or months is just fine. However, something like your credit card number or national security secrets need to be kept secure for a longer period, effectively forever. So using weaker encryption algorithms or shorter key lengths for some things is okay, as long as the information usefulness to an outsider expires in a short amount of time.

Data Encryption Standard (DES)   DES is the original standard that the U.S. government began promoting for both government and business use. Originally thought to be practically unbreakable in the 1970s, the increase in power and decrease in cost of computing has made its 56-bit key functionally obsolete for highly sensitive information. However, it is still used in many commercial products and is considered acceptable for lower security applications. It also is used in products that have slower processors, such as smart cards and appliance devices that can't process a larger key size.

TripleDES   TripleDES, or 3DES as it is sometimes written, is the newer, improved version of DES, and its name implies what it does. It runs DES three times on the data in three phases: encrypt, decrypt, and then encrypt again. It actually doesn't give a threefold increase in the strength of the cipher (because the first encryption key is used twice to encrypt the data and then a second key is used to encrypt the results of that process), but it still gives an effective key length of 168 bits, which is plenty strong for almost all uses.

RC4, RC5, and RC6   This is an encryption algorithm developed by Ronald Rivest, one of the developers of RSA, the first commercial application of public key cryptography. Improvements have been made over time to make it stronger and fix minor issues. The current version, RC6, allows up to a 2,040-bit key size and variable block size up to 128 bits.

AES   When the U.S. government realized that DES would eventually reach the end of its useful life, it began a search for a replacement. The National Institute of Standards and Technology (NIST), a government standards body, announced an open competition for a new algorithm that would become the new government standard. There were many competitors including RC6, Blowfish by renowned cryptographer Bruce Schneier, and other worthy algorithms. They settled on AES, which is based on an algorithm called Rijndael, designed by two Belgian cryptographers. This is significant because they used an open competition to decide on the standard. Also, selecting an algorithm by two non-American developers with no significant commercial interests helped to legitimize this selection worldwide. AES is rapidly becoming the new standard for encryption. It offers up to a 256-bit cipher key, which is more than enough power for the foreseeable future. Typically, AES is implemented in either 128- or 192-bit mode for performance considerations.

Encryption Applications

Hashes   Hashes are a special use of one-way functions to provide authentication and verification using encryption. A hash function takes a file and puts it through a function so that it produces a much smaller file of a set size. By hashing a file, you produce a unique fingerprint of it. This gives you a way to make sure that the file has not been altered in any way. By hashing a suspect file and comparing the hash to the known good hash, you can tell if any changes have been made. It is unlikely that a file with a different structure would produce an identical hash. Even changing one character changes the hash significantly. The chances of two different files producing the same hash are infinitesimal.

Hashes are often provided on downloaded versions of software to make sure you are getting the real thing. This is important, especially with open source software, where it may have been passed around quite a bit or downloaded from another site. The official Web site will usually post the correct hash of the latest version. If the two don't match, then you know some changes have been made, possibly without the permission or knowledge of the software developers. The most popular hashing algorithm is called MD5.

Digital Certificates   Digital certificates are the "signature" of the Internet commerce world. These use a combination of encryption types to provide authentication. They prove that who you are connecting to is really who they say they are. Simply put, a certificate is a "certification" of where the information is coming from. A certificate contains the public key of the organization encrypted with either its private key or the private key of a signing authority. Using a signing or certificate authority is considered the more secure method of the two. If you can decrypt the certificate with their public key, then you can reasonably assume the Web site belongs to that organization.

Certificates are usually tied to a particular domain. They can be issued by a central entity, called a Certificate Authority (CA), or created and signed locally as described above. There are several of these organizations, the biggest of which is VeriSign, the company that also runs the domain names system. They have sanctioned many other companies to offer certificates under their authority. Getting a certificate from VeriSign or one of the companies it authorizes is like having someone vouch for you. Generally, they will not issue you a certificate until they verify the information you are putting in the certificate, either by phone or via some kind of paper documentation, such as a corporate charter. Once they "certify" you, they will take this information, including the URLs you are going to use the certificate for, and digitally "sign" it by encrypting it with their private key. Then a Web server or other program can use this certificate. When outside users receive some data, such as a Web page from the server, and it has a certificate attached, they can use public key cryptography to decrypt the certificate and verify your identity. Certificates are used most often at e-commerce Web sites, but they can also be used for any form of communications. SSH and Nessus both can use certificates for authentication. VPNs also can use certificates for authentication instead of passwords.

Encryption Protocols

IPsec   It's a well-known fact that the IP protocol as designed originally was not very secure. IP version 4 (IPv4), which is what most of the world uses for IP communications, doesn't provide any kind of authentication or confidentiality. Packet payloads are sent in the clear, and packet headers can easily be modified since they are not verified at the destination. Many Internet attacks rely on this basic insecurity in the Internet infrastructure. A new IP standard, called IPv6, was developed to provide authentication and confidentiality via encryption. It also expanded the IP address space by using a 128-bit address rather than the 32-bit currently used and improved on a number of other things as well.

Fully implementing the IPv6 standard would require wide-scale hardware upgrades, so IPv6 deployment has been pretty slow. However, an implementation of security for IP, called IPsec, was developed that wouldn't require major changes in the addressing scheme. Hardware vendors have jumped on this, and IPsec has gradually become a de facto standard for creating Internet VPNs.

IPsec is not a specific encryption algorithm, but rather a framework for encrypting and verifying packets within the IP protocol. IPsec can use different algorithms and can be implemented in whole or just partially. A combination of public key and private key cryptography is used to encrypt the packet contents, and hashes add authentication as well. This function is called **Authentication Header** (AH). With AH, a hash is made of the IP header and passed along. When the packet arrives at the destination, a new hash is made of each header. If it doesn't compare to the one sent, then you know the header has been altered somehow in transit. This provides a high level of assurance that the packet came from where it says it does. You may choose to do encryption of the packet payload but not do AH, as this can slow down the throughput. AH can also get fouled up in some environments with NAT or firewalls. There are also different two operation modes you can run IPsec in: tunnel mode or transport mode.

In **tunnel mode**, the entire packet—header and all—is encapsulated and encrypted, placed in another packet, and forwarded to a central VPN processor. The endpoints decrypt the packets and then forward them to the correct IP. A benefit of this method is that outsiders can't even tell what the final destination is for the encrypted packet. Another advantage is that the VPN can be controlled and administered from a few central points. The downside is that this requires dedicated hardware at both ends to do the tunneling.

In **transport mode**, only the packet payloads are encrypted; the headers are sent intact. This makes deployment a little easier and requires less infrastructure. You can still do AH when using transport mode and verify the source address of the packets

Point-to-Point Tunneling Protocol (PPTP)   PPTP is a standard that was developed by Microsoft, 3Com, and other large companies to provide encryption. Microsoft has added it to Windows 98 and later releases. This made it seem a likely candidate to be the major standard for widespread encryption technology. However, some major flaws were discovered in PPTP, which limited its acceptance. When Microsoft bundled IPsec with Windows 2000, it seemed a tacit admission that IPsec had won as the new encryption standard. However, PPTP is still a useful and inexpensive protocol for setting up VPNs between older Windows PCs.

Layer Two Tunneling Protocol (L2TP)   This is another industry-developed protocol, and is endorsed by Microsoft and Cisco. Although used frequently in hardware-based encryption devices, its use in software is relatively limited.

Secure Socket Layer (SSL)   This protocol was designed specifically for use on the Web, although it can be used for almost any type of TCP communications. Netscape originally developed it for their browser to help stimulate e-commerce. SSL provides data encryption, authentication on both ends, and message integrity using certificates. Most of the time, SSL is used when connecting to a Web server so that we know the information we send it is being protected along the way. Most people don't even realize that SSL is running in the background. Usually it only authenticates one end, the server side, since most end users don't have certificates.

Encryption Applications

Phil Zimmerman is a programmer who was heavily involved with human rights. He was concerned that the growing use of computers and communication networks would make it easier for the state security agencies of repressive regimes to intercept and gather information on dissidents. Phil wanted to write some software that would help these people keep their information private and safe from the eyes of the brutal regimes that ruled them. This software could quite literally save people's lives. He also didn't entirely trust his own government not to observe his personal data as it traveled across interconnected networks. He knew how easy it would be for the government to build systems to search every line of every e-mail for certain key words. He wanted to provide people with a way to protect and guarantee their constitutional right to privacy.

He called his software Pretty Good Privacy (PGP), as he felt it did a good enough job to protect the data from smaller countries' intelligence forces. However, the U.S. information security agency, NSA, didn't see it that way. Zimmerman was investigated for violating federal munitions export laws for allowing his software to be downloaded out of the country.

He originally intended on founding a company to sell his innovation. However, when the government came after him, he freely distributed the software over the Internet to get it widely distributed. He did subsequently form a company to market commercial versions of the software, but there are open source implementations of PGP all over the Internet. Some of them are more popular than others, and some are for niche applications such as e-mail encryption. The next section reviews the official PGP Corporation freeware version as well as a full open source version. You can find a list of all the implementations of PGP at www.cypherspace.org/openpgp/.

PGP Freeware: A Public Key Encryption Tool

PGP Freeware
Author/primary contact: Phil Zimmerman
Web site: www.pgp.com
Platforms: Multiple platforms including all Windows and Linux
License: Freeware for noncommercial use
Version reviewed: 8.0.2
Other resources:
www.pgpi.com
Mailing lists:
PGP Freeware Help Team
IETF OpenPGP working group
PGP users mailing list
PGP/MIME working group
PGPi developers mailing list
PGPi translators mailing list
Pgplib developers mailing list
All these lists can be accessed and subscribed to at
www.pgpi.org/links/mailinglists/en/.

P G P F r e e w a r e : A P u b l i c K e y E n c r y p t i o n T o o l

USENET Newsgroups:
Alt.security.pgp
Comp.security.pgp.announce
Comp.security.pgp.discuss
Comp.security.pgp.resources
Comp.security.pgp.tech

MIT maintains the official freeware version of PGP. Since it is licensed from Phil Zimmerman and PGP Corporation, you can be reasonably sure of its integrity and validity. The downside of the PGP freeware is that it is licensed for personal use only, so you can use it for your personal e-mail or for educational purposes if you are student. If you are going to use this version of PGP, make sure that you carefully read the license and understand it. While this version of PGP is open source and freeware, there are considerable restrictions on what you can use it for. Remember, open source doesn't always mean free. If you want the best of both worlds, both the most current version and ease of use and support, you should look into buying a full license from PGP Corporation. It runs about $125 for a single user, and has a discount for volume purchases. If you can't or won't pay, then the next tool, GnuPG, which is a fully free implementation of PGP, may be of more interest to you

The official PGP from PGP Corporation does have some excellent features.

- A built-in VPN client, IPsec 3DES VPN, which can be used to communicate securely with anyone who has PGP 8.0 or later.
- The ability to build self-decrypted archives to send PGP messages to someone who doesn't have PGP software loaded.
- Deleted file wiping, which is the ability to permanently delete a file by overwriting the data on the disk multiple times.
- Free space wiping, which is the same concept as deleted file wiping, but for your disk free space that may contain traces of old data.
- Integrated command line support for those familiar with old-style commands.
- Plug-ins for major e-mail programs, including Outlook, Eudora, and Claris Emailer (paid version only).
- Proxy support, which is useful for users behind a proxy firewall (paid version only).
- PGPDisk, which lets you encrypt a whole volume or subvolume of your disk so that encryption and decryption of your data happens automatically (paid version only).

Before you install and begin using PGP, you should understand a little about how it works and the principles behind it. This section is not meant to give you detailed training and understanding of cryptography or PGP; you can refer to the many books on those subjects. But you should come out of this chapter being able to encrypt and decrypt messages using PGP.

Caution: If you implement PGP improperly, it can provide little or no protection at all. You can also irrevocably lose your data if you are not careful with your decryption keys (see the sidebar "Don't Lose Your Keys!!").

PGP is considered a **hybrid cryptosystem**, which means that it uses a combination of symmetric and asymmetric encryption to accomplish its function. Public key encryption takes a lot more processing power than shared secret encryption because public key encryption typically uses complex math involving prime numbers. PGP uses only public key encryption to create a session key, which is then used to encrypt the whole message using traditional symmetric cryptography. Most public key cryptosystems use this method to improve performance.

Rather than type in your whole private key each time you use PGP, which would take quite some time and be very prone to error, your private key is stored on your hard drive in encrypted form. To unlock your key, you type in a **pass-phrase** each time you use PGP. This is like a password, only generally it is longer and made up of several words, preferably with numbers and letters. This pass-phrase is very important to remember, because if you ever lose or forget it, you won't be able to recover the data you encrypted with PGP.

Installing PGP and Generating Your Public/Private Key Pair

1. First, download the PGP program file from the Web site.
2. Click on this self-extracting zip file, and it will automatically begin the installation process.
3. You have the option of purchasing a full license or evaluating the product. Click on Purchase Now if you want to get a full version, authorized for commercial use. Otherwise click on Later to use the freeware version.
4. The install program then guides you through the process of generating your public/private key pair. This process is *very* important as it is the heart of the protection that PGP provides.
5. The program prompts you for your name, organization, and e-mail address.
   You don't have to enter an e-mail address, but if you don't, your public key won't be associated with your e-mail address on the key server, and it may be hard for someone who is trying to send you a PGP-encrypted message to find your public key if they don't already have it.
6. Next, the program asks for your pass-phrase.
   This is what allows you to use the keys on your disk. *Do not* enter a normal password here such as single word or set of letters. This will seriously degrade the security of your keys. Use a series of words, with a combination of letters and numbers. This will make it easier to remember, but make sure you use something complex. A good example of a complex pass-phrase with numbers, uppercase and lower case letters, and symbols is `one+one=Two`.
   Note: Do not use this example, and no…that is not my personal pass-phrase.
   After you enter your pass-phrase, the rest of the program will load, and the installation will be complete.

If you want to delete PGP from your computer, you must use the uninstaller function provided. Simply removing the files will not work properly as PGP makes significant changes to your registry and other core windows settings.

Flamey the Tech Tip:

Don't Lose Your Keys!!

Losing your keys for PGP is kind of like losing your house keys or car keys, except it's a whole lot worse. Imagine if, when you lost your physical keys, your car or house was forever inaccessible. Well, that's exactly what will happen to your encrypted data if you lose your private key. And because your private key is usually encrypted on your disk using your pass-phrase, losing your pass-phrase has the same effect.

Make sure you back up the private key folder on your computer (you do regular backups of your data, right?). If you have a problem remembering passwords, write down your pass-phrase and store it somewhere safe (this would not be on a sticky note taped to your monitor).

Remember, if you lose one of these two items, your data will be gone forever; not even the NSA can recover it. Sound extreme? If it were easy to recover your data, then it would be easy for an outsider to do the same. So, mind your Ps (pass-phrases) and Ks (keys).

Using PGP

You access PGP from your Programs menu under Start. There are several available options, including PGPMail and the documentation. The PGP freeware version has great documentation, including a 70-plus page introduction to cryptography. It is a good primer for those new to cryptography. PGP also has a huge user's guide.

When you start PGPMail, a small tool bar displays on your screen. This can be minimized to a small icon on your system tray when you are not using it. This simple interface offers your several options: PGPKeys, Encrypt, Sign, Encrypt and Sign, Decrypt/Verify, Wipe, and FreeSpace wipe. The specific functions of each item are covered next.

PGPKeys   You use the PGPKeys section to manage both your own public and private keys and the public keys of others you wish to communicate with (see Figure 9.4). The PGP program creates two directories for keys on your disk. These directories are called **key rings**, as they contain all the keys that you need to use PGP, both public and private. The file **pubring** found in your main PGP directory contains your public key as well as others of people you want to send encrypted files to. The file **secring** contains your private key, usually in encrypted format. It normally contains only one private key, but you can maintain more than one private key. For example, you can have one for your business e-mail and another for your private correspondence. Just remember, items encrypted with

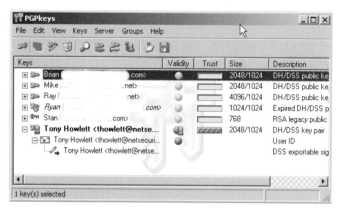

Figure 9.4 PGPKeys Screen

a specific public key are not decryptable with anything other than that specific matching private key.

You can also create new key pairs here, and revoke pairs of keys you are no longer using. You can upload your public key to one of several public key servers. This allows someone who has never talked to you to find your key on a public key server and send you a PGP message. Many folks who use PGP are in the habit of putting their public key in the signature line on their e-mails so correspondents can easily send them a PGP-encrypted message.

Another way to help to verify the legitimacy of a person's key is have it signed by other people's keys. This is a way of validating that someone's public key is a match to that person. You should only sign public keys of people that you personally know well and have verified that the key is correct. You should also get your friends and associates to sign your keys. This circle of key signing creates a nonhierarchical trust model called a **web of trust**. The nice thing about this model is that it doesn't require a central authority to make it work. For more details on how this web of trust works, see the GnuPG section later in this chapter.

To add other users' keys to your public key ring, you can either import them directly from a file or do a search of public key servers. By selecting Search on the Servers menu or clicking on the magnifying glass icon and typing in part of a name or some identifying text, you can see what keys on the public key servers match your request. Drag and drop the appropriate selection from the results to the main PGPKey screen and that person's public key will be available for using in your PGP messages. You can also view the specific properties of any key, including the signers of that key, size of the key (in bits), and the method (usually DH for Diffie-Hellman). Finally, you can import or export your key rings if you have moved computers or need to restore from a backup.

Encrypt The Encrypt function is pretty straightforward. First, a dialog box lets you pick the file to encrypt. Once you select a file, PGP prompts you to select the recipient's public key from your key ring. If you don't have it yet, do a search on the public key servers for it as described above and add it to your list. Select the public key of your intended recipient and drag and drop the key from the box on top down to the recipient list.

The check boxes on the lower left have several important options (see Figure 9.5). One of the most important is Wipe Original. Click on this if you are encrypting this file to keep on your hard disk. Otherwise, PGP will simply create a new encrypted file and leave the original in plain text in the same directory for viewing. Remember, though, if you do this and lose your keys, that file is gone forever.

Another important option is Conventional Encryption. If you select this, public key encryption will not be used. Instead, standard shared secret encryption will be employed and you will have to pick a pass-phrase in order to encrypt the data. This pass-phrase will then have to be passed securely to your intended party on the other end. This method defeats the main benefit of PGP, but it may be necessary if you don't have the recipient's public key. If the recipient doesn't have PGP software, select the Self-Decrypting Archive file option. This creates a file that will decrypt itself when the person receiving the file clicks on it. Of course, your recipient will still have to know the pass-phrase you used to create the file.

Sign   The Sign function lets you sign a file with your public key, thereby allowing someone to verify that it hasn't changed since you signed it. This uses a hash function to summarize the file in a digest format and then encrypt it with your private key. This is the reverse of normal public key encryption. The recipient can take the signature and attempt to decrypt it with your public key. If the hashes match, then he or she knows that the contents haven't changed since you signed it. This is a useful function if you are more con-

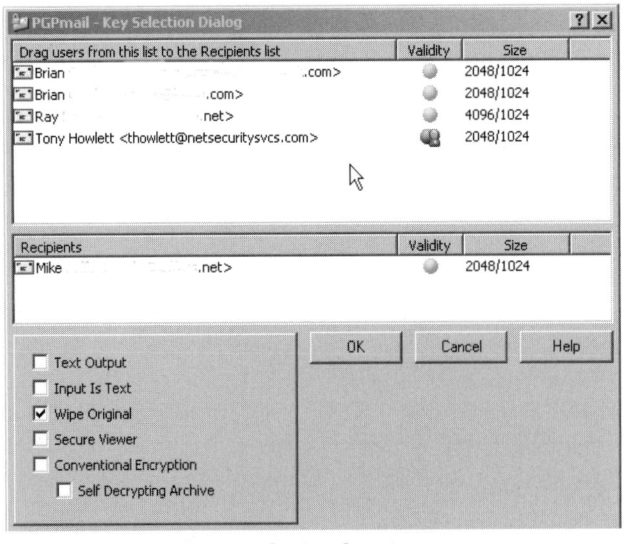

Figure 9.5 PGP Encrypt Option Screen

cerned about the integrity of the file than the confidentiality of the information. An example would be a lengthy contract that has been heavily edited. You could sign it digitally and be sure that no one could change it after you looked at it. Signing can also be used to provide what is known as **nonrepudiation**, that is, if you sign a document, it can be proven that you did it, unless someone got hold of your private keys. This is akin to the validity of your physical signature except the ability to forge a digital signature is significantly harder than a traditional signature.

Encrypt and Sign   This function performs both of the Encrypt and Sign functions above, providing strong confidentiality, integrity, and nonrepudiation.

Decrypt/Verify   You use the Decrypt/Verify function to reverse the PGP encryption process. After you select the file to decrypt, it prompts you for your pass-phrase to use your private key on your disk. If entered correctly, it asks you for a new file name to decrypt the file into. You can also use this function to verify that a signature is valid.

Wipe   The Wipe function permanently removes a file from your hard disk. This process is much more final that the Windows Delete function. The problem with Windows (and most operating systems) is that it doesn't actually remove the data from your hard disk when you delete a file—it just removes the file's listing in the file system index. The data is still sitting there on the disk platters. It can be viewed with a low-level disk editor or recovered using readily available utilities like Norton or DD (DD is demonstrated in Chapter 11). The Wipe function actually overwrites the data multiple times on the disk with random zeros and ones. The default for this activity is three times, which is fine for most uses. You may want to increase this to at least ten if you are using this for highly sensitive data, since specialists in data recovery can actually recover data even when it has been overwritten several times. You can increase the passes made, up to 28 times, at which point not even the NSA could get the file back. Note that if you are deleting large files with lots of passes your disk will turn for a quite a while. This is very disk-intensive activity.

Freespace Wipe   Freespace Wipe performs the same function as the Wipe function, but on the free space on your disk. You should do this occasionally because old files that you deleted but didn't wipe may still exist. Also, programs regularly create temp files that may contain copies of sensitive data. They are deleted by the operating system when you close the program but they still exist on your disk. Freespace Wipe sanitizes your entire hard disk. You can also schedule this function to do automatic regular wipes of your hard drive.

PGP Options

There are a number of global options you can set in PGP. From the PGPKeys main menu, under File choose Edit to display the PGP Options dialog box (see Figure 9.6). Table 9.1 lists the tabs and gives an overview of each.

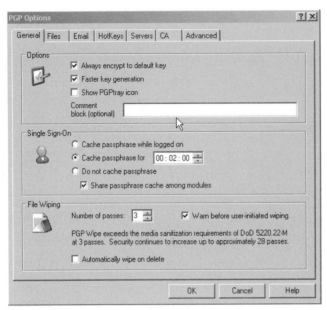

Figure 9.6 PGP Options Dialog Box

Table 9.1 Tabs in the PGP Options Dialog Box

Tabs	Descriptions
General	You can set up PGP to remember your pass-phrase for a certain amount of time after using it so you don't have to keep entering it every time you decrypt a file or sign a document. The default is two minutes. You can also increase the default number of passes for the Wipe function and make Windows automatically wipe a file when it is deleted. Use this setting with care if you want to be able to recover deleted files.
Files	You can change the default directory for your public and private key rings here.
Email	On this tab you can set various options for handling encrypted e-mail, including automatically decrypting PGP messages, always signing your outgoing e-mail, and so forth.
HotKeys	Here you can quickly access main PGP functions via hotkeys. Some are already preset for you. For example, you can purge your pass-phrase cache by pressing the F12 key.

Tabs	Descriptions
Servers	This is where you set the servers to search for public keys. There are two main servers listed, one in the U.S. and one in Europe, but you can add others.
CA	If you want to use digital certificates, you set your certificate authority and various settings here.
Advanced	This tab contains options for the encryption process. You can select the algorithm you want to use for the asymmetric part of the encryption process (AES is the default). You can also set your options for backing up your key rings. The default is to always create a backup file of each key ring whenever you close the program. However, you should remove the backup file periodically to a secure storage, either burned onto a CD-ROM or to a floppy disk. This will protect your keys if the hard drive crashes or the computer is stolen.

This should give you enough information to start with PGP and protect your files and communications. Again, this is meant to be a quick overview of the PGP product. Please read the ample documentation if you intend to be a heavy PGP user. If you need additional functionality or commercial use, consider upgrading to the commercial version.

If you don't want to agree to all the limitations of the PGP freeware license but want to use PGP, there is another option, the GNU version of PGP, which is described next.

GNU Privacy Guard (GnuPG): A GPL Implementation of PGP

GNU Privacy Guard (GnuPG)
Author/Primary Contact: Matthew Skala, Michael Roth, Niklas Hernaeus, Rémi Guyomarch, Werner Koch, and others
Web site: www.gnupg.org
Platforms: Linux, Windows, BSD, and Mac
License: GPL
Version reviewed: 1.2.4
Other resources: www.pgpi.com
Mailing lists:
PGP Freeware help team
IETF OpenPGP working group
PGP users mailing list

GNU Privacy Guard (GnuPG): A GPL Implementation of PGP

PGP/MIME working group
PGPi developers mailing list
PGPi translators mailing list
Pgplib developers mailing list
All these lists can be accessed and subscribed to at
www.pgpi.org/links/mailinglists/en/.
Newsgroups:
Alt.security.pgp
Comp.security.pgp.announce
Comp.security.pgp.discuss
Comp.security.pgp.resources
Comp.security.pgp.tech

GNU Privacy Guard (GnuPG) is based on the OpenPGP standard and is an answer to the commercial and restrictive freeware license versions of PGP. Of course, as with most things from GNU, the name is a play on words (it's the inverse of PGP). The big upside of the GNU version is that you can use it for any application, personal or commercial. Also, since its license is GPL, you can extend it or graft it onto any application you like. The downside is that it is a command line tool, so it doesn't come with some of the nice add-ons that the commercial version of PGP offers. If cost is an issue and you don't mind learning to use the commands, then GnuPG is for you. A word of warning, though: GnuPG is probably not the best choice for nontechnical users, unless you add your own front end or some user-friendly scripts (there are several available on the Internet).

Installing GnuPG

Many current versions of Linux and BSD ship with GPG already installed, so you can check to see if you already have it by typing `gpg --version` at the command line. If you get a listing of the program information, you can skip this section and start using GnuPG.

Also, check your distribution disks to see if you have an RPM file to automatically install it. If you want the latest version, there are RPMs for many distributions on the Web site. If there is an RPM for your OS, download it and simply click on it to install the program. If you can't find an RPM, you can download the .tar files from the book's CD-ROM or from the official Web site and compile them manually with the following instructions.

1. Unpack it and then type the usual compile commands:

```
./configure
make
make install
```

The program creates a directory structure in your user directory under /.gnupg where your keys and other information will be stored.

2. (Optional) Type `make clean` after installing GnuPG to get rid of any binary files or temporary files created by the configure process.

Creating Key Pairs

Once you have the program installed, the first thing you need to do is to create your public-private key pair. If you already have a key and want to import it onto this system, use the command:

```
gpg --import path/filename
```

where you replace `path/filename` with the path and file to your keys. You must do separate statements for your public and private key rings. The file format of the key rings is generally pubring.pkr and secring.skr.

Otherwise, follow this procedure.

1. Type `gpg --gen-key`. This starts the process and prompts you for several items.

2. GnuPG asks you for the bit size of your keys. The default is 1,024, which is generally considered sufficient for strong public key cryptography. You can increase it to as high as 2,048 for stronger security.

3. Generally, you never want your keys to expire, but if you have a special case where you will only be using this key for a limited time, you can set when it should expire.

4. GnuPG prompts for your name and e-mail address. This is important, because this is how your public key will be indexed on the public key servers.

5. Finally, GnuPG asks for a pass-phrase. Pass-phrases should be sufficiently long and complex, yet something you can easily remember. (See the description of pass-phrases earlier in this chapter in the PGP section.) Once you enter your pass-phrase twice, GnuPG will generate your keys. This may take a minute. During this process, you should move your mouse around a bit. GnuPG takes random signals from the keyboard and mouse to generate entropy for its random number generator.

   Note: Once again, just like with PGP or any strong encryption product, maintain backup copies of your key pairs in a safe place and don't lose them or your encrypted data will be lost forever.

Creating a Revocation Certificate

Once you've created your keys, you can also create a revocation certificate. This is used if you lose your keys or if someone gains access to your private key. You can then use this certificate to revoke your key from the public key servers. You can still decrypt messages you have received using the old public key (assuming you didn't lose it) but no one will be able to encrypt messages anymore with the bad public keys.

To create your revocation certificate, type:

```
gpg -output revoke.asc -gen-revoke user
```

where you replace *user* with a unique phrase from that user on your secret key ring. This generates a file called revoke.asc. You should remove this from your hard drive and store it somewhere safe. You do not want to leave it in the same place as your private key, the theory being if someone has access to your private key material, they could also keep you from revoking it.

Publishing Your Public Key

You will want to place your public key on a key server so people can easily find your public key to send messages to you. To do this, use this command:

```
gpg -keyserver server -send-key user
```

where you replace *server* with the name of a public key server and *user* with the e-mail address of the key you want to publish. You can use any public PGP key server since they all sync up on a regular basis. You can choose any one of them and your public key will propagate across the servers. There are many public key servers, including:

- certserver.pgp.com
- pgp.mit.edu
- usa.keyserver.net

Encrypting Files with GnuPG

To encrypt a file you use the --encrypt command. The format is as follows:

```
gpg --output file.gpg --encrypt --recipient
    friend@example.com
    file.doc [All on one line]
```

where you replace *file.gpg* with the resulting filename you want, *friend@example.com* with the e-mail address of the user you are sending it to, and *file.doc* with the file you want to encrypt. Note that you must have the recipient's public key on your key ring in order to do this.

You can also use GnuPG to encrypt files with simple symmetric cryptography. You might use this for local files you want to protect or for someone for whom you don't have a public key. To do this, use the --symmetric command in this format:

```
gpg --output file.gpg --symmetric file.doc
```

where you replace *file.gpg* with the output file you want and *file.doc* with the name of the file you want to encrypt.

Decrypting Files

To use GnuPG to decrypt files you have received, use the following command:

```
gpg --output file.doc --decrypt file.gpg
```

where *file.doc* is the resulting file name you want and *file.gpg* is the encrypted file. You must have the private key for the user it was encrypted for on your secret ring. This prompts you for the pass-phrase, and once you have entered it correctly, GnuPG produces the decrypted file.

Signing Files

As mentioned earlier, another use of GnuPG and PGP is signing documents to verify their integrity. You can do this by issuing the following command:

```
gpg --output signed.doc --sign unsigned.doc
```

Replace *signed.doc* with the resulting output filename you want and *unsigned.doc* with the file you want signed. This command signs and encrypts the document and produces the output file signed.doc. When it is decrypted, GnuPG will also verify the document. You can verify a file with the following command:

```
gpg --verify signed.doc
```

where *signed.doc* is the encrypted file you want to verify. You can also create signatures separate from the file if you want users without GnuPG to be able to access them but still want to include the signature. There are two commands for this. The command

```
gpg --clearsign file.doc
```

creates a text addendum to the file with the signature. If you don't want to alter the file, you can create a separate signature file with the command

```
gpg --output sig.doc --detached-sig file.doc
```

The PGP/GnuPG Web of Trust Model

As mentioned earlier, rather than use a hieratical trust system like digital certificates and their central certificate authority, PGP and GnuPG use a web of trust model. By signing the keys of people you know, you can verify that their key is worthy of trust. And if they sign other people's keys who you don't know directly, you create a chain of trust. The model is based on the idea of "any friend of yours is a friend of mine." Granted this model doesn't work perfectly; someone far down the trust chain could turn out to be a bad apple and get away with stuff for a while. But the idea behind this system is that it spreads organically and doesn't require any infrastructure. Because of this, it can't be dismantled or co-opted on a large scale easily. The way you establish this web of trust is by signing people's keys and having them sign yours. In the example in Figure 9.7, Tony can implicitly trust Jane, Joe, John, and Eve's keys even though he doesn't know them directly.

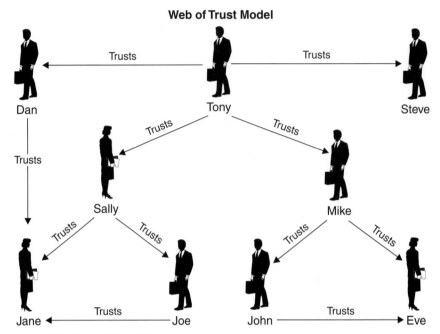

Figure 9.7 Web of Trust Model

Signing Keys and Managing Your Key Trusts

In GnuPG you sign keys and manage your key trusts by going into key edit mode with the following command:

```
gpg --edit-key friend@example.org
```

where *friend@example.org* matches the e-mail address of the key you want to sign or manage and must be one of the keys on your public ring. It prints out basic information on the key. Within this mode, type `fpr` to print the fingerprint of that key. Just like humans, the key fingerprint is a specific identifier of that key. Make sure that this is the person's key by comparing it with him or her either on the phone or by some other manner. You can also check to see who else has signed this key by typing `check`. This prints a list of other signers of this key and may help you decide the validity of the key.

When you are sure that this is the person's key, type `sign`. This signs that person's key so that anyone looking at it knows that you trust him or her. In this mode you can also edit the trust levels of the different keys in your ring. Enter this mode from within key edit mode by typing `trust`. This displays the following menu.

1 = Don't know

2 = I do NOT trust

3 = I trust marginally

4 = I trust fully

s = Please show me more information

m = Back to the main menu

Pick one of the items and that key will be marked as such by you. This is another way you can communicate to yourself and others about which users have your highest level of trust and which ones you barely know.

This should give you a good introduction to the world of PGP and GnuPG. Again, this chapter is not intended to be the conclusive source on these, and you should refer to their respective Web sites and the other listed sources to read further on these revolutionary programs.

PGP and GnuPG are great for encrypting files. However, what if you want to encrypt all communications between two points? PGP is not really viable for this function (the newly included VPN client with the commercial version not withstanding). An open source tool for creating these standing connections where everything is encrypted on the fly is discussed next.

OpenSSH: A Free Suite of Session Encryption Tools

OpenSSH (Server)
Author/primary contact: Tatu Ylönen (original author) and others
Web site: www.openssh.org
Platforms: BSD, Linux, and most UNIX
License: BSD
Version reviewed: 2.1.1p4
Mailing lists:

Announcement list
A read-only list that contains general announcements of new version releases, bug fixes, and so on. Subscribe at
www.mindrot.org/mailman/listinfo/openssh-unix-announce.

General SSH users list
Questions and general discussion on SSH usage. Subscribe by sending an empty message to secureshell-subscribe@securityfocus.com.
To unsubscribe to the list, send an empty message to
secureshell-unsubscribe@securityfocus.com.
There is also an archive of this list at
http://marc.theaimsgroup.com/?l=secure-shell&r=1&w=2.

Developers list
Discussions on SSH development and coding. Subscribe at
www.mindrot.org/mailman/listinfo/openssh-unix-dev.

Most of the file and communication utilities used on the Internet today hark back to the days when the Internet was a small and safe place. One of the most common tools used, other than a Web browser, is Telnet. This utility is used for remote terminal access to all types of servers, routers, firewalls, and other devices. The big downside of Telnet is that it sends its transmissions in the clear, so if you are using Telnet to log into a system over the Internet, someone could capture your traffic, including your passwords. You may think finding your password in the stream of data would be like finding a needle in a haystack, but hackers have written programs that run on top of sniffers to search for common login terms and catalog the results. This is also true of other remote tools such as FTP, TFTP, and RCP.

SSH fixes this problem by using both public key and symmetric cryptography to encrypt your session starting from the first keystroke. This way, all anyone listening to your connection gets is random noise. SSH not only provides confidentiality for your data by using encryption, but it also provides strong authentication that foils spoofing and other identity-type attacks. It does this by using digital certificates to authenticate users. Don't confuse SSH with SSL, the Web encryption standard. Though they both do the same thing, SSH works with any protocol, whereas SSL is primarily designed for Web communications.

SSH also includes SCP, which is a secure replacement for RCP, the remote copying tool, and SFTP, a secure replacement for FTP. SSH can also be used to tunnel other protocols, such as HTTP and SMTP, between machines. Several applications are discussed at the end of this section. Using this suite of programs instead of their older counterparts ensures that your remote communications to servers aren't being read. Eliminating the use Telnet and FTP on your network may be difficult, but the more you do it, the more secure you will be.

In order to use SSH, you must have a SSH server running on the machine you want to connect to and a SSH client on the machine you are connecting to. Regular FTP and Telnet clients won't connect to a SSH server. The client is built into most current Linux operating systems, although you may have to select this option when installing your OS. (See Chapter 2 for information on the SSH client.) The SSH server is usually optional and you have to select it when you install your OS. To determine if it is already installed, type `ps` and see if the sshd process is running. If not, you will have to install the server to allow connections to your machine via SSH.

Installing and Starting the OpenSSH Server

1. First, download and unzip the package from the Web site or the book's CD-ROM.

2. Issue the usual Linux compile commands:

```
/.configure
make
make install
```

This builds and installs the SSH programs. The binaries and associated libraries will be located in /usr/local/bin (on the Mandrake Linux system, other distributions may vary). The system daemons are found in /usr/local/sbin, and the config files are in /usr/local/etc/ssh or /etc/ssh, depending on your install.

You can choose an alternative install path by using

```
--prefix=filepath
```

where *filepath* is replaced with your desired alternate location.

3. Once OpenSSH is installed, check the configuration file located in /etc/ssh to make sure it matches your system parameters. The configuration file for the server piece is sshd_config. You can use a text editor such as vi or EMACS to make your changes. A few items to check are:

- Port: The port that SSH listens to for incoming connections. This defaults to 22. If you change this, people attempting to connect to you will have to manually change the port number on their SSH clients.
- Protocols: This tells the server what SSH protocols to accept. The default is to accept both SSH1 and SSH2 type connections. For slightly better security, you could change this to accept only SSH2, but this will keep some older clients from connecting.
- Hostkey: This gives the location of the keys used to generate key-based authentication of a user when connecting to a separate machine. These are not the same as the server keys that are generated on install.

4. Before you can use the SSH server, you must generate its various keys. You do this by typing the following command:

```
ssh make-host-key
```

You will get something like the following response.

```
Generating public/private rsa key pair.
Enter file in which to save the key (/home/me/.ssh/
id_rsa):

Created directory '/home/me/.ssh'.

Enter passphrase (empty for no passphrase):

Enter same passphrase again:

Your identification has been saved in
/home/me/.ssh/id_rsa.
Your public key has been saved in
/home/me/.ssh/id_rsa.pub.
The key fingerprint is
:f6:41:99:d8:a5:d1:fb:e7:93:86:7e:e6:4f:01:d9:5b
```

The fingerprint provides a unique identifier for your server's keys.

5. You can now start the SSH server at the command line by typing `sshd &`.
This runs sshd, the server daemon, in the background and listens continuously for connections. If you want to run sshd automatically when you reboot (which is preferable), place that line at the end of the rc.local file in your /etc/rc.d/ directory (on Mandrake Linux, or in the corresponding start-up file for your distribution).

Remember, to connect to your server via SSH you need to be running a compatible version of the SSH on the client end. Instructions on the installation and use of the SSH client are in Chapter 2.

Port Forwarding with OpenSSH

While SSH was primarily intended for Telnet-like command line interaction, it can also be used to set up a secure tunnel between two machines for any application. You can create a secure connection between two servers with the built-in port forwarding capability in SSH. For this to work, you must have SSH running on both ends of the connection. You can do with any service on any port with the following statement issued on the client end.

```
ssh -L local_port:local_host:remote_port remote_hostname
    -N &
```

where you replace:

- `local_port` with a random high number port chosen by you to make the new encrypted connection
- `local_host` with your local machine
- `remote_port` with the port of the service you want to tunnel on the remote end
- `remote_hostname` with the IP address or host name of the server on the other end of the connection

The `-L` option tells SSH to listen on the `local_port` on `local_host` and forward any connections to the `remote_port` on the `remote_host`. The `-N` option tells SSH not to try to log in, just to keep the connection open for forwarded traffic. The `&` runs the task in the background, so it will run as a system process and you can do other things on the machine. If the machine is rebooted, you will have to enter the command again unless you put it in the start-up script.

Using this method, you do not need a login on the remote end to establish the encrypted connection to the remote server. You will need appropriate credentials for anything you want to do over the forwarded port if they are required.

The following are two examples to show how this works.

Example 1: Creating an Encrypted E-mail Connection with OpenSSH   Normally, e-mail is sent over port 25 unencrypted. Let's say you want to encrypt this connection instead. The way to do this is to use SSH to set up an encrypted tunnel for any traffic bound for port 25 traffic on your mail server. Using the above format and assuming your mail server has IP address 192.168.1.2, the correct command would be:

```
ssh -L 5000:localhost:25 192.168.1.2 -N &
```

This sets up port 5000 on your local machine as the port that would tunnel the mail port (25) to your remote mail server. So if you set up your mail client to connect to local-host:5000 instead of the default mail port, SSH will automatically forward the traffic to port 25 on your mail server using SSH to encrypt it. Now, you can receive and send mail to this machine without worry of having your mail read off of the wire.

Example 2: Creating a Secure Web Connection
What if you want to connect your Web server for a secure transaction? If the server wasn't set up to do SSL, you could still use SSH to securely tunnel your Web traffic to the server. If your Web server is located at 192.168.1.3, the command string looks like this:

```
ssh -L 5000:localhost:80 192.168.1.3 -N &
```

Now you can connect by entering `localhost:5000` in your Web browser, and you will actually be forwarded via a secure tunnel to port (80) on the remote machine. You can port forward several different ports on the same machine. For example:

```
ssh -L 5000:localhost:5000:25 -L 5001:localhost:80
    192.168.1.2 -N &
```

will forward all traffic on port 5000 locally to the mail port on 192.168.1.2, and all traffic to port 5001 to port 80 on the remote machine. Of course, this example assumes you have a mail account on the remote server.

As you can see, SSH works great for creating a secure connection between two machines for just about any protocol. However, what if you want to encrypt all traffic, regardless of what port or service? In this case, setting up a virtual private network makes more sense.

Virtual Private Networks

Companies used to create private networks using expensive point-to-point data lines from the phone company to keep their information safe. These lines cost thousands of dollars per month per location and linked only two sites at a time. Companies often ended up with a spider web of expensive communication lines connecting their sites. With the advent of the commercial Internet, people immediately saw its potential for interoffice communications. Unfortunately, the open nature of the Internet presented a major security risk. This is where encryption came to the rescue. By using encryption technology, companies can create a Virtual Private Network (VPN) and harness the low-cost Internet for their corporate communications, safely and securely. Their data is encapsulated in a "tunnel" of encryption, so any parties intercepting the packets in between cannot recover any usable data.

There are many vendors selling dedicated hardware devices to do virtual public networks. However, there is an open source solution that will let you set up your own VPN with nothing more than a couple of extra PCs.

FreeS/WAN: Open Source IPsec VPN Software	
FreeS/WAN	
Author/primary contact:	John Gilmore
Web site:	www.freeswan.org/
Platforms:	Most Linux
License:	GPL
Version reviewed:	2.02
Mailing lists:	
Announce	Read-only, for major announcements.
Briefs	Summary of activity on other lists.
Users	The main list for user questions and discussion.
Users-moderated	A moderated less-trafficked version of the above.
Design	Discussion by developers only.
Distros	Linux Distribution Maintainers Forum.
Bugs	To report any bugs found in FreeS/WAN.
For instructions on subscribing to any of the above lists, see www.freeswan.org/mail.html.	
Posts from an older list are currently archived at www.sandelman.ottawa.33on.ca/linux-ipsec/.	

The FreeS/WAN project is sponsored and managed by John Gilmore. John is a legendary name in coder and net-libertarian circles. He is one of the founders of the Electronic Freedom Foundation, which was an early proponent of free strong encryption. After making his fortune in several Silicon Valley start-ups, most notably Sun Microsystems, he now dedicates his time to various projects, many of them open source software–related.

The FreeS/WAN project started as an effort to have everyone encrypting his or her communications. While it hasn't quite had this effect yet, it does offer users of Linux a cost-effective way to set up a VPN. It also allows you to connect to other devices using IPsec, since the IPsec protocol is a widespread standard. Some vendors may not stick precisely to the standard, so your results may vary when using other equipment or software for one of the ends. Check the FreeS/WAN Web site for a list of compatibility with other vendor's implementations.

Using IPsec, everything is encrypted at the IP level, regardless of the application or port. This is what makes IPsec the most popular system for creating secure communications. FreeS/WAN also can use what is called **opportunistic encryption**, which means it will use encryption to communicate with hosts that support IPsec, and will use regular IP communications for those that don't. So if you run FreeS/WAN on your firewall box, you can have an automatic VPN to sites running IPsec and still interoperate with other sites that don't.

You need two machines to act as your gateways. To use FreeS/WAN, these machines must be UNIX boxes, preferably Linux. If you want to set up an IPsec connection between Windows systems, you can use the built-in IPsec support (Windows 2000 and later) and don't need FreeS/WAN. Supposedly, the newest Linux kernel is going to have IPsec integrated into it. But even when it does, FreeS/WAN will still have an application for communicating with older versions and using the opportunistic encryption feature. The FreeS/WAN team is also working on interoperability with the upcoming Linux kernel IPsec support.

Installing and Starting FreeS/WAN

FreeS/WAN comes preinstalled on many Linux distributions. To see if you have FreeS/WAN installed, type `ipsec verify` at the command line. If you get a "file not found" response, then you don't have it preloaded. Even if you don't have the RPMs, you can get the source code from the book's CD-ROM or you can download the latest version to take advantage of the latest cryptographic protocols and features. Follow these instructions to compile FreeS/WAN from source code.

1. Download the latest package from the Web site and unzip it, or copy the file from the CD-ROM.
2. Run the following commands as root from the FreeS/WAN directory to compile and install the package:

   ```
   Make oldmod
   Make minstall
   ```

3. Once FreeS/WAN is installed, you need to reboot your system for the changes to take effect.
4. When your system comes back up, use the `verify ipsec` at the command line to check your install. You should see a message something like this:

   ```
   Checking your system to see if IPsec got installed and
   started correctly
     Version check and ipsec on-path              [OK]
     Checking for KLIPS support in kernel          [OK]
     Checking for RSA private key (/etc/ipsec.secrets)  [OK]
     Checking that pluto is running                [OK]
     . . .
   ```

5. If you see this, you can start the IPsec service using this command:

```
service start ipsec
```

The IPsec service runs in the background. You are now ready to initiate IPsec sessions.

Using FreeS/WAN

There are several ways to use FreeS/WAN. One is for a gateway-to-gateway permanent connection, which is called **peer-to-peer** mode. This mode is appropriate if you have two offices wanting to communicate securely over the Internet. The second method is called **road warrior** mode, where you have remote users wanting to connect securely to your LAN. Finally, you can operate in **Opportunistic Encryption** (OE) mode, in which it connects with encryption to any hosts or gateways that are capable of it. The following procedures describe how to set up each one.

Peer-to-Peer Mode   FreeS/WAN uses the names **Right** and **Left** to refer to the two machines you are connecting via IPsec. This doesn't have anything to do with direction or location; it just makes it easier to refer to the different sides of the IPsec connection. Just pick one to be your Left machine and one to be your Right machine.

1. First, get on one machine that you are going to call the Right machine. Type the following command to get its public key:

   ```
   ipsec showhostkey --right
   ```

   FreeS/WAN shows you some information about the IPsec on that machine, including its public key. After the equals sign will be a long list of seemingly random digits. This is the key. Copy this number down or use the copy function in your text editor.
2. Now get the public key from the Left machine by using the same command, except use the `--left` switch in the command.
3. Go to /etc/freeswan and edit the file ipsec.conf (some distributions may store this file in /etc). Table 9.2 lists and describes the parameters you need to set in the `conn net-to-net` section.
4. Leave the rest of the settings as is and save the file.
5. Copy this file onto the other machine in the same place.
6. Use the `verify ipsec` command described earlier to be sure that the IPsec service is running on both machines
7. To start up the IPsec connection, type:

   ```
   ipsec auto --up net-to-net
   ```

   You should see the message `IPsec SA established`. If you don't, check your settings or consult the man pages for troubleshooting information.

Table 9.2 FreeS/WAN Parameters

Parameters	Description
Left	The IP address of your Left IPsec gateway.
Leftsubnet	The range of IPs behind the Left gateway.
Leftid	The host name in a fully qualified domain name format and with an @ in front of it. For example, @gateway.example.com.
Leftrsasigkey	The key you copied earlier from the Left machine.
Leftnexthop	The default gateway for the Left machine. The default setting should work in most cases.
Right	Same as Left above but for the Right machine
Rightsubnet	Same as Leftsubnet above but for the Right machine.
Rightid	Same as Leftid above but for the Right machine.
Rightrsasigkey	Same as Leftrsasigkey above but for the Right machine.
Rightnexthop	Same as Leftnexthop above but for the Right machine.
Auto	The default setting of add authorizes the connection but doesn't start it up when the system is booted. If you want it to start automatically, change this to start.

If you are running a firewall with NAT, you may have to write a special rule in your firewall so that it doesn't translate the network address of that machine. Many newer firewall models automatically recognize IPsec packets and pass them through unchanged so this extra step is unnecessary.

8. To test your connection, try pinging an internal address on the other side of the remote gateway. If you get a successful response, then you have an IPsec tunnel up and running.

9. If you really want to verify that the packets are being encrypted, use a packet sniffer such as Tcpdump or Ethereal to see if you can read any of the packets. If the sniffer identifies the packets as ESP packets (ESP is one of the IPsec subprotocols)

and the packet payloads come up looking like gibberish, then all is working correctly.

10. If you want to add multiple net-to-net connections, you can just add another section with a new title such as conn office1-to-office2. You can also rename the original net-to-net connection name as long as it is the same in the ipsec config files on both machines.

Road Warrior Mode   This procedure is fairly similar to the last one, with a few exceptions. In this mode, the Right machine is the local machine on your IPsec gateway and the Left machine is your remote user.

1. On your remote machine, edit the same /etc/freeswan/ipsec.conf file using the following template. It looks similar to the net-to-net configuration with a few differences.

```
conn road
  left=%defaultroute
  leftnexthop=%defaultroute
  leftid=@tonyslaptop.example.com
  leftrsasigkey=0sAQPIPN9uI...
  right=192.0.2.2
  rightsubnet=10.0.0.0/24
  rightid=@gateway.example.com
  rightrsasigkey=0sAQOnwiBPt...
  auto=add
```

The remote configuration uses %defaultroute to pick up your dynamic IP.

2. The Right side should contain the information for the gateway. Get on the gateway machine and use this template for that ipsec.conf file.

```
conn road
  left=192.0.2.2
  leftid=gateway@example.com
  leftsubnet=192.0.2.1/24
  leftrsasigkey=0sAQOnwiBPt...
  rightnexthop=%defaultroute
  right=%any
  rightid=tonyslaptop@example.com
  rightrsasigkey=0sAQPIPN9uI...
  auto=add
```

Notice the entries are reversed on the gateway, using left for the Local machine and right for the remote. Also, the right IP is defined as %any. This is a wildcard that allows any IP address, since you won't learn it until the remote user tries to connect.

3. Save this file.

4. You are ready to connect. Make sure that IPsec is up and running on the gateway machine, and then type the following command on the remote user end:

```
ipsec auto --start road
```

This should initiate the connection as before. If you don't get the message `Ipsec SA established`, check your settings or refer to the troubleshooting section on the FreeS/WAN Web site.

5. Test and verify the connection in the same manner as the net-to-net procedure.

6. You can set up multiple remote connections as in the previous procedure and rename them whatever makes sense to you.

Opportunistic Encryption If you want to do this with FreeS/WAN, your gateway box must not be behind a firewall doing NAT (the change in the IP address in the headers messes up the IPsec header verification mode). It is preferable to have a static IP address on your gateway box. There are two ways to do OE: full or partial. In the full OE you can initiate outward IPsec connections and other IPsec hosts can initiate OE sessions with your gateway. In partial mode, your gateway must always initiate the connection. Both OE modes require you to have access to the DNS record for the hostname you want set up.

Setting Up a Partial Opportunistic Encryption (initiate only)

1. First, edit the DNS record for the host name that you intend to use to add an entry for your key. The DNS record must match the ID you use in the ipsec.conf file. In the Road Warrior example earlier, that was `gateway.example.com`. Issue the following command on your gateway machine to create this record:

```
ipsec showhostkey --txt @gateway_hostname
```

Replace `gateway_hostname` with your hostname, such as `gateway.example.com`.

It produces a text file with a text record containing your key and formatted in the proper DNS syntax.

2. Insert this record into the zone file for that domain as a forward TXT record.
Note: If you aren't sure how to edit DNS records, have your DNS administrator help you. Making a mistake with a DNS record can easily take your whole domain down.

Also, keep in mind that the changes will take a while to propagate across the Internet. Depending on where you are querying from, this process might take as long as 48 hours.

3. You can check to see if the change has taken place yet with the following query:

```
ipsec verify --host gateway.example.com
```

It should respond with an OK statement for the forward record.

The reverse record lookup will fail, but this is acceptable as long as you don't want to do a full OE. Remember that even though you can correctly query the DNS server, the other end of your connection may not be able to yet. Have them run the verify command as well.

4. Once both sides can see the DNS record, then all you should have to do is restart your IPsec service by typing:

```
service ipsec restart
```

When it comes back up, you should be ready to go.

This is all that is required, since FreeS/WAN will automatically configure the connection using the DNS record information when it comes up.

Setting Up Full Opportunistic Encryption
In order to do full OE, you must have a static IP on the gateway and have full control of the DNS record for that IP. FreeS/WAN OE uses a reverse DNS lookup to verify the public key of any machine attempting to connect. The instructions are exactly the same as for partial OE, except that you also create a reverse DNS record for your gateway host name. Create the text file the same way as above and after adding it as a forward record, add it as a reverse record tying it back to your static IP address. Again, if you are unsure of how to edit a DNS file, get some help. DNS is not something to monkey around with lightly. Once both records are visible from the Internet, you should be able to restart your IPsec service and establish connections with IPsec OE compliant hosts.

Password Crackers   You have learned how to protect your information various ways using encryption, and how to encrypt files, sessions, and whole connections with other sites. The next section looks at a tool to help you make sure your password files are safe. This tool is a password encryption cracker. It does the reverse of all the tools in this chapter in that it tries to decrypt the password file without any keys. It is primarily to be used on password files to make sure you don't have passwords that are easy to crack.

Most passwords these days are not stored in plain text on the server. They are stored as hashes of the password so that the clear text password is not being passed across the network. On some operating systems, however, this hashing system is weak and the encryption is easily cracked. Worst case, if someone captures a password file, he or she can run a brute force attack on the hashes, discovering some passwords. This takes advantage of the tendency of most people to use simple passwords. You can limit this ability in most operating systems, but even then, people will figure out ways to get around the limitations in the interest of making their life simpler. Testing your password files with password crackers is the only way to know for sure how safe your users' passwords are.

John the Ripper: A Password Cracking Tool	
John the Ripper	
Author/primary contact:	Solar Designer
Web site:	www.openwall.com/john
Platforms:	Windows and most UNIX
License:	Freeware, BSD-like
Version reviewed:	1.6

John the Ripper was designed by the enigmatic Solar Designer to help system administrators flush out weak passwords, mostly on UNIX systems. John uses a text password file and checks the hash for each word in the file against the password file. It even tries variations on dictionary words such as cat1, cat2, and so on. It also uses some randomizing techniques after it runs out of words to keep on trying as long as you want to let it run. It comes with a basic word file and you can also download various custom word files for different operating systems or create your own.

It is available for both UNIX and Windows. Since it is a command line tool only, the basic operations are the same for both operating systems. The separate installation processes are covered here.

Windows Installation

1. Download the Windows binary package from the Web site or the book's CD-ROM and unzip the file into its own directory.
2. There is no real Windows setup process here. Just put the files where you want them to reside and run them from that directory with the proper commands. You may want to add that directory to your system path if you want to be able to run John the Ripper from any directory. Otherwise, change to the john/run directory to access the binaries and run the program.

UNIX Installation

1. Download and untar the source code files from the Web site or the book's CD-ROM.
2. Issue the following command from the src directory it created:

   ```
   make
   ```

   This displays a list of systems supported.

   Note: If your system is not listed, substitute the command `make generic` in the next step (this should work most of the time).
3. Issue the following command substituting your supported system type for *system*:

   ```
   make system
   ```

   This builds the program and puts the main binary programs in the john/run directory.
4. Change into that directory and you are ready to run John the Ripper.

Using John the Ripper

1. First, you need to have a copy of the password file.
   On most UNIX systems the password hashes aren't stored in the main password file but are kept in a file called the shadow password file (called shadow on Linux systems). This protects the password hashes from being viewed easily, since the main user password file has to be accessible to various other parts of the operating system and so has to be world-readable.

The password hash file looks something like Listing 9.1.

Listing 9.1 Sample Password Hash File

```
root:$1$%8_pwš/,$3ABCmAmVVtBbgXc1EpAZ7.:12080:0:99999:7:::
bin:*:12080:0:99999:7:::
daemon:*:12080:0:99999:7:::
adm:*:12080:0:99999:7:::
lp:*:12080:0:99999:7:::
sync:*:12080:0:99999:7:::
apache:!!:12080:0:99999:7:::
postfix:!!:12080:0:99999:7:::
mysql:!!:12080:0:99999:7:::
tony:$1$™bFÌb/_R$6RFzrkqq6nY4zTkmWQ8xV0:12080:0:99999:7:::
```

The seemingly list of random characters after the account name is the hash of the password. That is what John the Ripper goes to work on.

2. The text file `password` in your John the Ripper directory contains the default word list. You can add to this list if you have some custom passwords you want it to try or replace it with your own word list.

3. To run John the Ripper, type the following command:

   ```
   john password_filename
   ```

   Replace `password_filename` with the filename of the password file you want to test.

   John the Ripper shows you any passwords it is able to crack on the screen as it tries. Most of the word lists will be run through in a few minutes. This is long enough for most purposes, but if you want to let it run longer to really test your passwords, you can run the process in the background.

   You can also interrupt the testing process and return to it later. Press CTRL+C once to stop the testing and save the results in a file called john.pot. Note that pressing CTRL+C *twice* will abort the search and not save your results.

4. You can view the passwords retrieved thus far by typing:

   ```
   john -show password_file
   ```

5. If you want to back up a cracking session, use the following command:

   ```
   john -restore
   ```

And that's about all there is to it. Happy password cracking (only your own password files, please!). If you find weak passwords, you can go to those people and have them change them or institute policies on the server that require stronger passwords.

Wireless Tools

Until recently, network administrators mostly only had to worry about securing physical, fixed information technology assets. This includes servers, routers, and firewalls: the things that make up our wire-line networks. However, with the advent of inexpensive wireless network equipment, there is a whole new spectrum (no pun intended) of security problems to contend with.

This new technology has helped to lower the cost of deploying networks, brought access to places it wasn't before, and made the term "mobile computing" truly a reality. It has also drastically changed the network security perimeter for companies of all sizes. Traditionally, corporate networks were connected to the outside world in only a few places (see Figure 10.1). This allowed network managers to concentrate on protecting these limited access points. You could put firewalls and other defenses at these crucial choke points. The inside of the network was largely treated as trusted because there was no way to get there other than through the protected points.

Chapter Overview

Concepts you will learn:
- Wireless LAN terms
- The 802.11 protocols
- Weaknesses of wireless LANs
- Wireless assessment equipment

Tools you will use:

NetStumbler, StumbVerter, Kismet Wireless, and AirSnort

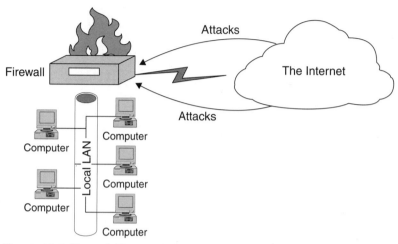

Figure 10.1 Network Threats Before Wireless Networking

Now the advancing march of technology has moved the security bar up a notch again. With a wireless LAN deployed, your new security perimeter becomes literally the air around you. Wireless attackers or eavesdroppers can come from any direction. If you have wireless access deployed, anyone with a $50.00 card can potentially listen in on your network wire without ever stepping foot on your premises. Figure 10.2 shows the new network security perimeter with wireless technology. As you can see, if you are using wireless for part of your network, your security threats go up considerably. But before you can properly secure your wireless network, you need to understand how wireless local area networks function and what their basic weaknesses are.

Manufacturers of wireless LAN equipment have lowered the prices so much that it is now a feasible alternative for home networks. Rather than wiring your house for Ethernet to connect your PCs, you can buy a wireless base station and a couple of wireless cards and use the Internet from any room in your house (or outside for that matter). Many business conventions now offer free wireless Internet access to their attendees via wireless stations. There are grassroots campaigns to create free Internet access for neighborhoods outside the reach of DSL or cable by using public wireless access points. Wide deployment of wireless LAN technology is definitely here to stay, and sooner or later you will probably have to deal with it.

Wireless LAN Technology Overview

The most popular protocol for wireless LAN technology today is by far the 802.11 series, commonly known as **Wi-Fi**. The 802.11 wireless standards are basically an extension of the Ethernet protocol, which is why it interoperates so well with wired Ethernet networks. It uses the frequencies of 2.4GHz for 802.11b and 802.11g and 5GHz for 802.11a to

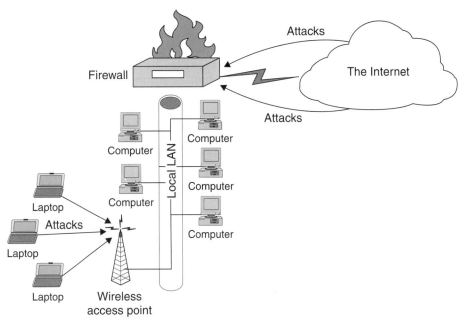

Figure 10.2 Network Threats with Wireless Networking

broadcast data signals. These frequencies are general-use spectrum, so you don't have to apply for a license from the FCC to use them. The downside of this is that other consumer devices can use these wavelengths too. Some cordless phones and microwaves are also on the 2.4GHz band, so if you have these devices or other Wi-Fi networks in your area, you may encounter some interference.

This wavelength is perfect for the short range that Wi-Fi is intended for. Its design parameters allow for about 150 feet indoors and over 800 feet outdoors under normal conditions. However, with a high-power antenna and line of sight, you can get up to a 20-mile range, which makes it attractive for office-to-office communications within a city (this assumes you are not in very mountainous terrain and you have access to a rooftop at least several floors up). Table 10.1 describes the four flavors of the 802.11 wireless standard that have emerged.

Wi-Fi Terms

A Wi-Fi wireless network can operate in one of two modes. **Ad-hoc mode** allows you to directly connect two nodes together. This is useful if you want to connect some PCs together and don't need access to a LAN or to the Internet. **Infrastructure mode** lets you set up a base station, known as an **access point** (AP), and connect it to your LAN. All of the wireless nodes connect to the LAN through this point. This is the most common configuration in corporate networks, as it allows the administrator to control wireless access at

Table 10.1 802.11 Wireless Standards

Standards	Descriptions
802.11a	This version of the standard uses the 5 GHz wavelength, which is a less crowded spectrum and is less likely to have interference problems. The theoretical potential for this technology is 54Mps, which is a huge amount of bandwidth, but most applications in the field do not get that nearly that much.
802.11b	This is currently the most popular wireless standard. It uses the 2.4 GHz wavelength, which Bluetooth and other consumer devices also use. It offers up to 11Mps of bandwidth, although practical applications under less than optimal conditions usually yield about half of that.
802.11g	A newer release, this standard provides up to 54Mps bandwidth, but in the same 2.4GHz spectrum as 11b. It is also backwardly compatible with 11b hardware.
802.11i	This new protocol is basically an extension of 802.11b with fixes to the encryption protocol to make it much more secure. It has just recently been approved by the IEEE, and products using it should be available in late 2004.

one point. Each wireless access point and card has a number assigned to it called a **Basic Station System ID** (BSSID). This is the MAC address for the access point's wireless side. The access point also has a **Station Set Identifier** (SSID), which defines the name of the wireless network that all the nodes associate with. This name is not necessarily unique to that access point. In fact, most manufacturers assign a default SSID to APs so they are usable right out of the box. The access point's SSID is needed to connect to the network. Some base stations have additional functionality, including routers and built-in DHCP servers. There are even some integrated units that act as a wireless access point, firewall, and router for home and small business users.

You set up a wireless network node by installing a wireless **network interface card** (NIC) in a computer. A wireless NIC comes in several forms: It can be a card that goes in a PC slot, a PCMCIA card, an external USB device, and now even a compact flash format for the smaller slots in handheld computers. An 802.11 wireless network in infrastructure mode has an access point that acts as your bridge between the wired Ethernet LAN and one or more wireless endpoints. The access point sends out "beacon" broadcasts frequently to let any wireless node in the area know that it is there. The beacon broadcasts act like a lighthouse, inviting any wireless nodes in the area to log on. These beacon signals are part of the problem with Wi-Fi. It is impossible turn off these signals completely, which makes it hard to hide the fact that you have a wireless network in your office. Anyone with a wireless card can at least see your beacon signals if they are in range, although some sets allow you to limit the amount of information that goes out in these broadcasts.

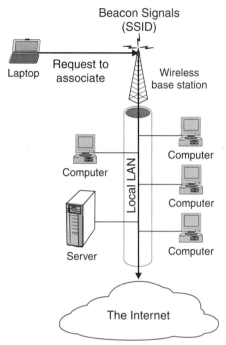

Figure 10.3 Wireless Network Operation

These signals contain basic information about the wireless access point, usually including its SSID (see Figure 10.3). If the network isn't using any encryption or other protections, then this is all that is required for someone to access to the network. However, even on an encrypted wireless network, the SSID is often transmitted in the clear and the encrypted packets may still be sniffed out of the air and subject to cracking attempts.

Dangers of Wireless LANs

While they offer flexibility and functionality that a wired LAN can't offer, they also introduce some unique challenges and dangers to the security-minded network administrator. Here are some things to consider when adding wireless LANs to your infrastructure.

Eavesdropping

The easiest thing for a hacker to do to a wireless network is to gather packets using a wireless sniffer. There is very little you can do about this, barring encircling your building in lead shielding! The designers of wireless networks did think about this, and built into the design an encryption standard called **Wired Equivalent Privacy** (WEP) so that the data could be encrypted. Unfortunately, a fundamental flaw in the way the algorithm works makes it potentially crackable (one of the tools later in this chapter demonstrates this). So even with WEP running, any data that travels over a wireless network is potentially subject to inspection by outsiders. Someone could listen over your wireless link, sniffing for logins, passwords, or any other data.

Access to Wireless PCs

A wireless link gives potential attackers a vector into a machine on your network. Besides the access points, machines with wireless cards can sometimes be seen from the outside. Using this mode of access, they can launch attacks against a machine that is probably not protected by your firewall and may not be locked down like your perimeter defenses or public servers.

Access to the LAN

This is probably the biggest danger that wireless networks present. If hackers can get access to your LAN via a wireless access point, they often have the keys to your kingdom. Most LANs run an unrestricted DHCP server, so hackers can get a valid IP address and begin exploring your network. They can then run vulnerability scanners or port scanners such as Nessus and Nmap to find machines of interest and to find holes to exploit.

Anonymous Internet Access

Even if hackers are not interested in what is on your LAN, they can use your bandwidth for other nefarious uses. By logging onto your network and then accessing the Internet, they can hack and do whatever damage they wish to do without it being traceable back to them. Any attacks or mischief perpetrated from this connection will be traced to your network. The authorities will come knocking on *your* door, not theirs. This method of hacking will become more common as hackers realize how hard it is to trace attacks originating in this manner. There is little chance of catching someone coming from a wireless network unless you have expensive triangulation equipment in place beforehand. Unsecured wireless LANs offer hackers the best anonymous access there is.

802.11-Specific Vulnerabilities

In addition to the basic insecurities of wireless LANs, there are some problems specific to the 802.11 standard. Some of these are due to the manufacturer's bad design or default configurations. Other issues are due to problems with the standard's overall design.

Default SSIDs   Each Wi-Fi base station has a specific identifier that you must know to log onto the network. This provides some level of security if it is implemented properly. Unfortunately, many people fail to change the default SSID set by the manufacturer. It is easy to find networks with the manufacturer's default SSID, such as linksys, default, and so on. When hackers see this, they can assume that the administrator didn't spend much time setting up and securing the wireless network.

Beacon Broadcast   Beacon broadcasts are an inherent problem with wireless networks. The base station must regularly broadcast its existence so end user radios can find and negotiate a session, and because the legitimate user devices have not been authenticated yet, this signal must be broadcast in the clear. This signal can be captured by anyone, and at a minimum they then know that you have a wireless LAN. Many models let you turn off the SSID portion of this broadcast to at least make it a little harder for wireless eavesdroppers, but the SSID is still sent when a station is connecting, so there is nonetheless a small window of vulnerability.

Unencrypted Communications by Default   Most wireless LAN devices today offer the option of turning on the built-in wireless encryption standard WEP. The problem is this usually has to be turned on manually. Most manufacturers ship their equipment with it off by default. Many administrators are in a hurry to set up a wireless network and don't take the time to enable this important feature. If a nontechnical person is setting up the network, the chances are almost nil that the encryption will get turned on. There is also the issue of sharing the secret key with all your users, since WEP uses a single key among all users. This can be an administrative nightmare if you have a lot of users connecting wirelessly.

Weaknesses of WEP   Even when the built-in encryption is used, the signal is still at risk of being read. There are some fundamental weaknesses in the implementation of the encryption algorithm in WEP that allows it to be broken after a certain amount of traffic is intercepted. These weaknesses have to do with the way the keys are scheduled. WEP uses weak initialization vectors (IVs) at a high enough rate that it eventually becomes possible to crack the key. Once the encryption is broken, not only can attackers read all the traffic traversing the wireless network, they can probably log on to the network. So while WEP offers some basic protection against casual eavesdroppers, any serious interloper is going to have software to potentially crack the encryption.

The "War-Driving" Phenomenon

Searching for unsecured wireless LANs has become a popular pastime among hackers and wireless hobbyists. This practice, akin to earlier hackers mass dialing or **war dialing** random banks of telephone numbers to find active modems, has become known as **war driving**. Mostly what wireless hackers do is drive around with a wireless card and some software waiting to pick up a signal from a network. The software can log the exact location of the wireless network via GPS, as well as lots of other information such as if it is encrypted or not. If the wireless LAN doesn't have encryption or other protections turned on, war drivers can surf the Internet or explore the local LAN over the wireless link. There is not a high skill level required to do this, so it appeals to all levels of the hacker ranks.

Companies using wireless LANs in dense environments around their offices or near major roads and freeways are at the most risk from this kind of activity. This would include offices in urban environments and downtown areas where there are a lot of high rises. Wireless networks using 802.11b have an effective distance of a couple hundred yards. This can easily bridge the space between two buildings or several floors in a high rise. In a crowded downtown area, it is not uncommon to find several unprotected wireless LANs inside a building. From a security standpoint, tall buildings tend to be one of the worst places to run a wireless LAN. The typical glass-windowed building allows the signals from your LAN to travel quite a distance. If other buildings are nearby, it is almost a sure thing that they will be able to pick up some of your signals. Even worse are tall buildings around a residential area. Imagine teenagers and other ne'er-do-wells scanning for available wireless LANs from the comfort of their bedrooms in suburbia.

A recent study found that over 60% of wireless LANs are completely unsecured. War drivers have even taken to posting the wireless access points they find to online databases with maps so anyone can find open wireless LANs just about anywhere in the country. They categorize them by equipment type, encrypted or not, and so forth. If you have a wireless LAN in a major metropolitan area, its a good chance that it is cataloged in a system like this, just waiting for an opportunistic hacker in your area with some time on his hands. The following are some of the online databases you can check to see if your company's wireless LANs are already cataloged.

- www.shmoo.com/gawd/
- www.netstumbler.com/nation.php

Note that most sites will remove your company's name from the listing if you request it.

Performing a Wireless Network Security Assessment

It would be easy for me to tell you that due to the security dangers of wireless networking, you should just not allow any wireless access on your network. However, that would be analogous to telling you to stick your head in the sand and hope the problem will go away. Wireless access is not going away. It is one of the hottest areas for growth and investment in the technology area. Vendors are churning out wireless adapters for all kinds of devices at a scary and ever-cheaper rate. Many retail companies such as McDonald's and Starbucks are installing wireless access points in their stores to attract customers. Intel Centrino laptops have a wireless radio built right in. Your users will come to expect the freedom that wireless LAN technology brings. They will want to be able to log on with their wireless-enabled laptops anytime, anywhere. This means that you are going to have to deal with your wireless security sooner or later. The tools in this chapter will help you assess your wireless network security and take steps to improve it if need be. It will also help you to deploy a wireless LAN solution more securely if you are doing it for the first time.

Equipment Selection

To perform wireless network security assessments, you will need at a minimum a wireless network card, a machine to run it on, and some software.

Wireless Cards Most of the software covered in this chapter is free, but you will have to buy at least one wireless network card. There are many different manufacturers to choose from and prices are quite competitive. Expect to pay from $40 to $80 for a basic card. You will want to carefully research your choice of manufacturers and models because not all cards work with all wireless software packages.

There are basically three different chipsets for 802.11b devices. The Prism II chipset by Intersil is probably the most common and is used by Linksys, the largest manufacturer of consumer wireless cards. The Lucent Hermes chipset is used in the WaveLAN and ORiNOCO cards and tends to be in higher-end corporate equipment. Cisco has its own proprietary chip, which has some special security features. The Prism II cards will work on Kismet wireless, the Linux software reviewed in this chapter, but not on the Windows platform. D-Link cards work with Windows but not with the Windows security toolkits that are commonly available. Also, models of particular manufacturers can be important. The older Linksys USB cards used a different chipset and do not work on well Linux.

To add to this confusion, some of the newer protocols aren't supported yet by many packages. The current versions of the software packages reviewed in this chapter don't support the newer 802.11g standard. The major vendors have yet to release their interface code for software developers to write to. Once they do, the drivers should become available shortly thereafter. You should check the respective software Web sites before purchasing your equipment for supported cards and protocols. For purposes of these reviews, I used the ORiNOCO Gold PCMCIA card, which works well with both the Windows and Linux software.

Hardware and Software In terms of hardware to load the software on, just about any decently powered machine will do. The UNIX software ran fine for me on a PII 300 with 64MB of ram. The Windows software should also run on a system like this. You should definitely load the software on a laptop since you are going to be mobile with it. There is a Palm OS version of Kismet Wireless and a Pocket PC version of NetStumbler available, so you can even put them on palmtops. There are now wireless cards available for both major platforms (Palm and Pocket PC) of the smaller handheld computers that can take advantage of this software.

You should also make sure you have plenty of hard disk space available if you intend to attempt cracking WEP keys. This requires anywhere from 500MB to several gigabytes of space. Be careful not to leave the machine unattended if you are sniffing wireless data and don't have a lot of extra space—you could easily fill up your hard drive and crash the computer.

If you are auditing your wireless perimeter and want to know exact locations, you may also consider getting a small handheld GPS receiver. Make sure your GPS device has an NMEA-compatible serial cable to interface with your laptop. With this hardware, you can log the exact points from which your wireless access points are available. The products covered in this chapter have the capability to take GPS data directly from the receivers and integrate it into the output. Finally, if you can spring for GPS-compatible mapping software such as Microsoft MapPoint, you can draw some really nice maps of your assessment activity.

Antennas   For wireless sniffing around the office, the built-in antennas on most cards work just fine. However, if you really want to test your wireless vulnerability outdoors, you will want an external antenna that lets you test the extreme range of your wireless network. After all, the bad guys can fashion homemade long-range antennas with a Pringles can and some PVC. You can buy inexpensive professional-grade wireless antennas from several outfits. I bought a bundle that came with the ORiNOCO card and an external antenna suitable for mounting on the top of a car.

This is another reason you need to choose your wireless card carefully. Some cards allow external antennas to be attached but others do not. You should be sure the card(s) you purchase have a port for one if you intend to do wireless assessments. Cards known to allow external antennas are the ORiNOCO mentioned earlier as well as the Cisco, Samsung, and Proxim cards.

Now that you have the background and the gear, let's check out some free software that will let you get out there and do some wireless assessments (on your own network, of course!).

NetStumbler: A Wireless Network Discovery Program for Windows	
NetStumbler	
Author/primary contact:	Marius Milner
Web site:	www.netstumbler.org /
Platform:	Windows
License:	Freeware
Version reviewed:	0.3.30z
NetStumbler forums:	http://forums.netstumbler.com/

NetStumbler is probably the most popular tool used for wireless assessments, mainly because it is free and it works on the Windows platform. In fact, it is so popular that its name has become synonymous with war driving, as in "I went out NetStumbling last night." I guess the author so-named it because he "accidentally" stumbled on wireless networks while using it.

NetStumbler isn't considered truly open source since the author doesn't currently make the source available. However, it is freeware and it is worth mentioning since it's the most widely used tool on the Windows platform. There are many open source add-ons available for it (one of these is discussed later in this chapter). It also has a very open source mentality in terms of its user community and Web site. The Web site is highly informative and has lots of good resources for wireless security beyond just the program. There is also a mapping database where other NetStumblers enter access points that they found while using the program. If your company's wireless network is in the database and you want it removed, they will be happy to do that for you.

Installing NetStumbler

1. Before installing NetStumbler, make sure you have the correct drivers installed for your wireless card. On newer versions of Windows, such as 2000 and XP, this is usually pretty straightforward. Install the software that came with your card and the system should automatically recognize the card and let you configure it. Support for Windows 95 and 98 can be dicey. Check your card's documentation for specifics.
2. Once your card is up and working, verify it by attempting to access the Internet through a wireless access point. If you can see the outside world, then you are ready to start installing NetStumbler.

3. The NetStumbler installation process is as easy as installing any Windows program. Download the file from the book's CD-ROM or www.netstumbler.org and unzip it into its own directory.
4. Execute the setup file in its directory and the normal Windows installation process begins.

When the installation is complete, you are ready to start Netstumbling.

Using NetStumbler

When you start NetStumbler , the main screen displays (see Figure 10.4).

In the MAC column, you can see a list of access points NetStumbler has detected. The network icons to the left of the MAC address are lit up green if they are currently in range. The icon turns yellow and then red as you pass out of range. Inactive network icons are gray. The graphic also shows a little lock in the circle if that network is encrypted. This gives you a quick way to see which networks are using WEP. NetStumbler gathers additional data on any point that it detects. Table 10.2 lists the data fields it displays and what they signify.

As you go about your network auditing, the main NetStumbler screen fills up with the wireless networks that you find. You will probably be surprised at the number of networks that show up around your office. And you will be even more surprised at how many have encryption turned off and are using default SSIDs.

The left side of the screen displays the different networks detected. You can organize them using different filters. You can view them by channel, SSID, and several other criteria. You can set up filters to show only those with encryption on or off, those that are

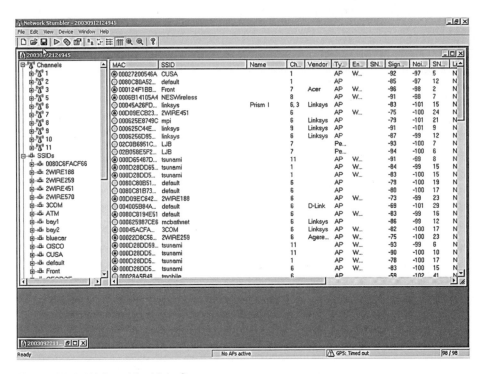

Figure 10.4 NetStumbler Main Screen

Table 10.2 NetStumbler Data Fields

Data Fields	Descriptions
MAC	The BSSID or MAC address of the base station. This is a unique identifier assigned by the manufacturer, and it comes in handy when you have a lot of stations with the same manufacturer default SSID such as linksys.
SSID	The Station Set Identifier that each access point is set up with. This defines each wireless network. You need this to log on to any wireless network, and Net-Stumbler gladly gathers it for you from the beacon signal. As noted in the MAC field description, this is not necessarily a unique ID since other base stations may have the same SSID. This could be a problem if two companies in the same building are using default SSIDs. Employees may end up using another company's network or Internet connection if it is not set up correctly with a unique SSID.
Name	The descriptive name, if any, on the access point. Sometimes the manufacturer fills this in. The network owner can also edit it; for example, Acme Corp Wireless Network. Leaving this name blank might be a good idea if you don't want people knowing your access point belongs to you when they are war driving around.

Data Fields	Descriptions
Channel	The channel the base station is operating on. If you are having interference problems, changing this setting on your access point might eliminate them. Most of the manufacturers use a default channel. For example, Linksys APs default to 6.
Vendor	NetStumbler tries to identify the manufacturer and model of the wireless equipment found using the BSSID.
Type	This tells you whether you found an access point, a network node, or some other type of device. Generally you will be finding access points that are signified by AP. Wireless nodes show up on here as Peer. This is why, even without a wireless network set up, having wireless cards in your PC can be risky. Many laptops now come with built-in wireless radios, so you may want to disable these before they are initially deployed if the users are not going to be using them.
Encryption	This shows what kind of encryption the network is running, if any. This is very important; if the network isn't encrypted, outsiders can pull your network traffic right out of the air and read it. They can also log onto your network if other protections aren't in place.
SNR	Signal-to-Noise ratio. This tells you how much other interference and noise is present at the input of the wireless card's receiver.
Signal	The signal power level at the input to the receiver.
Noise	The noise power level at the input to the receiver.
Latitude	Exact latitude coordinates if you are using a GPS receiver with NetStumbler.
Longitude	Exact longitude coordinates if you are using a GPS receiver with NetStumbler.
First seen	The time, based on your system clock, when the network's beacon was first sensed.
Last seen	NetStumbler updates this each time you enter an access point's zone of reception.
Beacon	How often the beacon signal is going out, in milliseconds.

access points or peers (in ad-hoc mode), those that are CF pollable (provide additional information when requested), and any that are using default SSIDs.

On the bar along the bottom of the main screen you can see the status of your wireless network card. If it is functioning properly, you will see the icon blinking every second or so and how many active access points you can see at that moment. If there is a problem with the interface between your network card and the software, you will see it here. On the far right of the bottom bar is your GPS location if you are using a GPS device.

The blinking indicates how often you are polling for access points. NetStumbler is an active network-scanning tool, so it is constantly sending out "Hello" packets to see if any wireless networks will answer. Other wireless tools, such as the Kismet tool discussed later in this chapter, are passive tools in that they only listen for the beacon signals. The downside of the active tools is that they can miss some access points that are configured not to answer polls. The upside of an active scanning tool is that some access points send out beacon signals so infrequently on their own that you would never see them with a passive tool. Also, keep in mind that active polling can set off wireless intrusion detection systems. However, very few organizations run wireless detection systems, and if you are using NetStumbler only as an assessment tool for your own network, then being stealthy shouldn't be that important to you.

If you click on an individual network in this mode it shows a graph of the signal-to-noise ratios over the times that you saw the network. This lets you see how strong the signal is in different areas (see Figure 10.5).

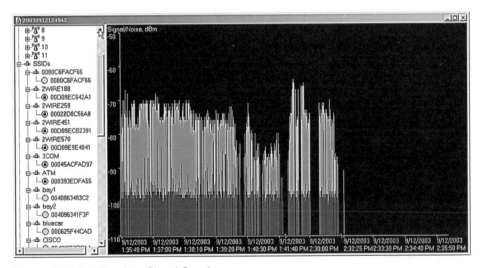

Figure 10.5 NetStumbler Signal Graph

NetStumbler Options

Under the View menu, select the Options submenu to display the dialog box for setting NetStumbler options. Table 10.3 lists the tabs and the choices available.

Tips for Effective—and Ethical—Wireless Auditing

Get Permission

Make sure you have permission from management to do your wireless assessment. If you are an outside consultant, you should have a letter of permission or engagement signed by upper management. If the company does not own the building, get management to clear it with building security so you have permission to be on the premises.

Determine Your Wireless Perimeter

Walk the entire perimeter and find out how far your signal goes. (A good rule of thumb is to go only in publicly accessible places that wireless crackers or war drivers would have access to.) If possible, get a map and mark your wireless perimeter on it.

Table 10.3 NetStumbler Options

Tabs	Descriptions
General	Set the rate of polling for your access points. You can also set it to auto-adjust based on your speed if using GPS. There is an option to automatically reconfigure your card when a new network is found, but you probably don't want to do this in a busy area—if there are a lot of access points around, your card will be changing configuration every few seconds and it will slow your computer down. Also, the software may end up configuring your card for a foreign network and you could be trespassing inadvertently. Not cool! (See the sidebar on "Tips for Effective—and Ethical—Wireless Auditing".)
GPS	Set up your GPS receiver to interface with NetStumbler. I used a Meridian handheld GPS with a serial cable. All I had to do was set the right port and communication settings and NetStumbler started importing the data right away.
Scripting	Set up to call external scripts. You can use Visual Basic or any number of Windows-based languages to do additional things based on the NetStumbler output. External programs can also use this functionality.
MIDI	You can configure NetStumbler to play the signal-to-noise ratio as a Midi file. I'm not sure why you'd want to do this as it could get noisy in an area with a lot of networks, but I guess you could use it to home in on a elusive signal by sound.

Start outside what you think is a reasonable reception range and work your way in. Make a broad circle around your business premises and work your way in to find out how far out the signal goes. Then go back and make a broader circle to see if any pockets of reception extend out farther.

Sometimes quirks in the landscape or manufactured objects can cause weird extensions of the signal: it can be reflected or focused by buildings, billboards, trees, and other objects. Assume the war drivers take advantage of this.

Once you've established the perimeter, you can evaluate the pockets of reception and take steps to eliminate or reduce them. Sometimes you can decrease the distance the signal goes by moving your access points to an interior room or to the other side of the building. As mentioned earlier, many units let you adjust the signal strength to limit radiation from the building.

Flamey the Tech Tip:

Be a Good Wireless Network Neighbor

When auditing your own network, it is likely that you will come across other wireless access points and nodes in the nearby area or building. Some of them will be unsecured.

Be a good neighbor and let them know that they have an unsecured access point. They may not even be aware of the dangers this poses.

Be a good neighbor and don't attempt to surf their network to demonstrate how bad their security is. Not only is this very bad behavior, but it could get you put in jail if you are caught. So resist the temptation and be a good wireless network neighbor.

Use an External Antenna

Using a card that supports the addition of an external antenna extends your range dramatically. These cards don't cost much more than the cheapest wireless NICs. The consumer varieties, such as Linksys or D-Link, generally don't support this, but it is worth paying an extra $100.00 for a better card. If you are really strapped, there are Web sites that tell how to make a homemade antenna for your card. Assume that your opponents will be able to find these sites too and will have at least as good an antenna as yours.

Audit Under Optimal Conditions

Rain, humidity, and smog can affect wireless transmission. The wavelength that 802.11b operates on resonates in water, and that can dull a signal in a rainstorm or even when there is a lot of moisture in the air. Tree leaves, due to their high water content, have the same effect. Your results in the winter may be different from those in the summer. Pick a clear, dry day to test to optimize your results.

Saving NetStumbler Sessions

NetStumbler automatically starts saving your session each time you open it. This lets you examine your NetStumbler sessions at another time. By default, sessions are saved in a native NetStumbler format. You can also save the sessions as text for importing into a spreadsheet or word processor and in the wi-scan format, which is a budding file standard for wireless sniffing logs. You can also export them in a number of formats.

NetStumbler assigns a unique number that is a combination of the date and time for each session at the top of the window (see Figure 10.5). This is helpful for tracking your sessions and results. You can change this name to something more descriptive if you like.

Now that you have a lot of data about your wireless perimeter, you may want to produce some reports, either for management or for a customer if you are doing this as a consultant. If you have been collecting GPS data, you can create some nice maps with the Microsoft MapPoint program and the open source tool discussed next.

StumbVerter: A Map Conversion Program for NetStumbler

StumbVerter
Author/primary contact: Michael Puchol; Sonic Security
Web site: www.sonar-security.com/
Platform: Windows
License: Freeware (GPL-like)
Version reviewed: 1.5
Mailing list:
Send a blank e-mail to stumbverter-subscribe@c2security.org.

StumbVerter is a neat little program that takes the output from NetStumbler and converts it into input for the Microsoft MapPoint program. It has functionality beyond the basic NetStumbler program, including:

- Access points shown as little beacons on the map.
- Beacons displayed in various in sizes and colors depending on the APs strength and WEP mode.
- Balloons for logging notes and other information.
- Navigational information such as speed, heading, and distance to the nearest known AP.
- An antenna comparison tool.

You must have a legal license for Microsoft MapPoint 2002 software to use Stumb-Verter. I know this is getting away from the idea of free software, but the functionality this adds is well worth the extra $200.00 that MapPoint will set you back. And of course, the StumbVerter software itself is freeware. Several projects are underway to develop a program to convert NetStumbler files into something free, such as a MapQuest or Map-Blast map (but none of these were far enough along as of publication to include). At any rate, if you have to present reports to management, the color maps will definitely help your case.

Installing StumbVerter

1. Make sure you have Microsoft MapPoint and NetStumbler installed before attempting to install StumbVerter. It will not load correctly without these two programs. If you just installed these, reboot your computer.
2. You must also be operating with a GPS receiver and logging that information into NetStumbler. In order for StumbVerter to be able to do anything the data, it must have the GPS coordinates of the wireless networks. This is how it figures out where to put the graphics.

3. Download StumbVerter from the book's CD-ROM or the Web site and unzip it.
4. Double-click on the setup file and it will install it on your system.

Once you have all these installed, you can start working with NetStumbler and StumbVerter.

Using StumbVerter

1. To use StumbVerter, you need some data to map. So go out with NetStumbler and collect some data on your wireless networks.
2. Save the session in NetStumbler and export it in text summary format.
3. Start StumbVerter by double-clicking its icon on your desktop.
4. On the menu at the top of the screen, click on Map, select Create New, then pick your region.
5. Once the map loads, click on Import and select the .nsi file that represents the Net-Stumbler session you want to map. StumbVerter displays the logged data graphically as a map (see Figure 10.6)

Green towers represent encrypted access points; red towers represent unencrypted access points. The signal strength is shown by the waves coming out of the top of the icon: the more waves, the stronger the signal.

If you single-click on a specific access point, the map centers on that point and shows you the informational balloon. Initially, this shows the network's SSID. Double-clicking on it shows all the notes associated with that AP and lets you add comments.

The View menu has several options for manipulating and cleaning up your map. For example, you can remove the Points Of Interest (POIs) that MapPoint inserts, unless you

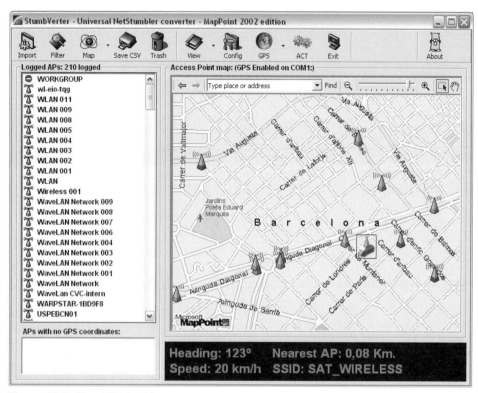

Figure 10.6 StumbVerter Map

want these for illustrative purposes. You can hide certain informational balloons if you want to show only the APs. You can also use the drawing tools to add any text, graphics, or other items to the map. When you are ready to save your map, you can either save it as a native MapPoint file or choose the CSV option if you want to save it in a text format suitable for importing into other programs.

The antenna comparison feature is useful for comparing several external antennas or different cards with built-in antennas to see which ones work best. You can import up to three different NetStumbler files, and StumbVerter grades them against the same access points and shows you the results side by side (see Figure 10.7). This can be helpful in deciding what card to use or which antennas work best if you are making one yourself.

Now that you know about some great Windows tools, I will switch platforms and talk about Linux tools. While the Windows tools are easier to install and use, there are some things that the Windows tools don't do yet, such as passive scanning and WEP cracking attempts.

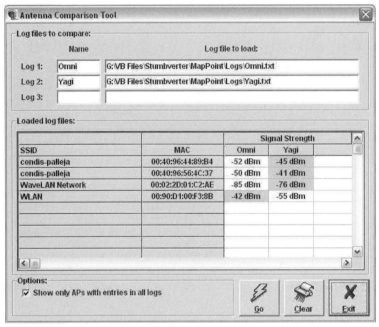

Figure 10.7 StumbVerter Antenna Comparison Screen

Kismet Wireless: A Wireless Network Discovery Program for Linux

Kismet Wireless

Author/primary contact: Mike Kershaw

Web site: www.kismetwireless.net/

Platforms: Most Linux

License: GPL

Version reviewed: .4.0.1

Mailing lists:

wireless@kismetwireless.net

Primarily for Kismet usage, suggestions, discussion, announcements of new features, and so on. Subscribe by sending an e-mail with "subscribe" in the body to wireless-subscribe@kismetwireless.net.

There is also an archive of past discussions at

www.kismetwireless.net/archive.php.

wireless-security@kismetwireless.net

A mailing list for discussion of wireless security, vulnerabilities, and other topics not directly related to Kismet. Subscribe by sending an e-mail with "subscribe" in the body to wireless-security-subscribe@kismetwireless.net.

Kismet Wireless is one of the leading wireless sniffers for the Linux operating system. There are several programs, including AeroSniff and Prism2Dump, that work well on Linux as well. I chose to review Kismet because of its growing support base and add-on modules in addition to its support for a wide variety of wireless hardware. It is also a client-server tool like Nessus, which gives it even more flexibility.

Another nice thing about using the Linux platform is that you can run WEPcrack and AirSnort, which are Linux-only programs right now. As of publication, there weren't any really good WEP testing open source software available for the Windows platform, though I expect this to change.

Kismet has some features that go beyond the basic functionality of a program like NetStumbler. Kismet works with a number of other programs and can be designed to gather weak encryption keys for cracking attempts by external programs. You can even run Kismet in IDS mode to look for intrusion attempts coming from your wireless network.

Installing Your Network Interface Card and Drivers

Before loading Kismet, you should make sure your card supports it. Kismet currently works with the following wireless cards:

- D-Link
- Linksys (PCI and PCMCIA only)
- RangeLan
- Cisco Aeronet
- ORiNOCO

Theoretically, Kismet should work with any card that uses the Prism II and Hermes chipsets or ones that can be put into rf_mon or Monitor mode, but your results may vary. I recommend that you stick with one of the above cards for the fewest problems.

Now the fun really begins. There are several steps to getting your Linux system ready to be a wireless sniffer. These steps will vary slightly depending if you have a different hardware and software configuration than the procedure. Check the documentation on the Kismet Web site to see if there are specific instructions for your hardware.

1. Start by making sure your PCMCIA drivers are up to date (assuming your card uses the PCMCIA card slot). If you have installed a fairly recent version Linux, then you are probably okay. This installation example uses Mandrake Linux 9.1.
2. If you need the latest drivers, go to www.rpmfind.com and search for the file pcmcia-cs for your distribution. Run the RPM and it will install the latest drivers.
3. Make sure you have all the correct wireless drivers loaded for your card.
   Wireless drivers for Linux are not quite as well supported as those for Windows and don't usually have a nice graphical interface to install them. (Hopefully this will change as vendors add support for Linux and someone produces RPMs for installing the drivers.)

I had to "roll my own" drivers, and the experience was less than fun. If possible, pick one of the supported cards; there are detailed instructions and lots of information online about them. With the ORiNOCO card, I compiled the driver located on the disk that came with the card. The latest driver is also available at www.orinocowireless.com, and several other sites offer cards based on this chipset.

If you are using a Prism II card, you need the Linux wlan-ng drivers. They are available at www.linux-wlan.org/.

4. Install the drivers and any patches needed for your card to operate in the Monitor mode required by wireless sniffers. This mode is similar to the Promiscuous mode on Ethernet cards that sets the card to listen to the airwaves without associating it to a particular access point.

The following instructions are for the ORiNOCO card, which required the Monitor mode patch. Consult your documentation or the Internet for other cards.

a. Download the file or copy it from the book's CD-ROM.

b. To being the installation process, type:

```
make config
```

The configuration script asks you some basic questions about your system. The defaults are generally the correct setting.

c. Type the following commands as root:

```
./Build
./Install
```

d. With the ORiNOCO card, you also have to install a patch on top of this in order for it to work in Monitor mode. This may not be necessary with other cards. You can get the patch from airsnort.shmoo.com/orinocoinfo.html.

e. If you need to patch your driver, download the patch file, otherwise go to Step 5.

f. Untar it, and type the following commands:

```
patch –p0 < patchfile.diff
```

where you replace *patchfile.diff* with the name of the current patch file. It should write over any files that are not updated. If the -p0 switch doesn't work, try -p1.

5. Next, go into the wireless configuration file and edit the setup parameters. This file is found in /etc/pcmcia/config.opts.

• If you are going to be using this card with Kismet, leave these parameters blank.

• If you want to use it to access your local access point, enter the appropriate settings for your network in this file, such as SSID and so on.

6. You can now reboot your system with your wireless card in the slot.
When it comes up you should hear two beeps. This indicates that the network card was recognized and configured.

If you don't hear the beeps, refer back to your card's documentation and make sure you followed all the steps correctly.

7. Type `ifconfig` at the command prompt. You should see a wlan01 interface. If you don't see this interface, refer back to your card's documentation and make sure you followed all the steps correctly.

8. One you have the drivers loaded, make sure your wireless card is actually working. You should be able to get Internet access or ping a network machine on the wired LAN. If you can't, then you need to refer back to your card's installation instructions. The card must be functional before loading the Kismet software.

9. You also need to have a recent libpcap library available so the operating system can read packets directly from your card. Many of the tools described earlier in this book use this driver, but if you haven't loaded it yet, download it from the book's CD-ROM or www.tcpdump.org and install it.

You have now finished installing your network interface card and the drivers you need to run Kismet.

Installing Kismet

If you made it through all that unscathed, you are ready to actually load the program.

1. Download Kismet from the book's CD-ROM or the Web site.
2. Unpack the distribution.
3. Enter the following command with any appropriate configure statement(s) listed in Table 10.4 to compile Kismet:

```
./configure
```

Table 10.4 Kismet Configuration Switches

Switches	Descriptions
--disable-curses	Disables the curses user interface.
--disable-panel	Disables ncurses panel extensions.
--disable-gps	Disables GPS support.
--disable-netlink	Disables Linux NetLink socket capture (prism2/orinoco patched).
--disable-wireless	Disables Linux kernel wireless extensions.

(continues)

Table 10.4 Kismet Configuration Switches (*continued*)

Switches	Descriptions
--disable-pcap	Disables `libpcap` capture support.
--enable-syspcap	Uses system `libpcap` (not recommended).
--disable-setuid	Disables `suid` capabilities (not recommended).
--enable-wsp100	Enables WSP100 remote sensor capture device.
--enable-zaurus	Enables some extra stuff (like piezzo buzzer) for Zaurus PDA.
--enable-local-dumper	Forces the use of local dumper code even if Ethereal is present.
--with-ethereal=DIR	Supports Ethereal wiretap for logs.
--without-ethereal	Disables support for Ethereal wiretap
--enable-acpi	Enables Linux kernel ACPI support.

These are compile-time switches you can enter with your configure statement to enable or disable certain functions.

4. Once the configuration process completes, run the following commands as root to finish the compilation process and install the program:

```
make dep
make
make install
```

5. Once Kismet is installed, find the file kismet.conf, which should be in /usr/local/ etc by default. This is where you set up your logging and interface preferences. Table 10.5 describes the parameters you can set.

6. Next, edit the file kismet_ui.conf, also found in /user/local/etc. This sets certain interface settings. Table 10.6 lists the options.

7. Save these two files.

You are ready to start using Kismet to audit your wireless network.

Table 10.5 Kismet Logging and Interface Options

Parameters	Descriptions
Capture source	Defines what interfaces Kismet will listen on. Normally your main wireless interface (wlan0) should already be set up here. If you want to add additional interfaces, do it in the format: `source=type,` `interface,name`. For example, `source=prism2,wlan0,Prism` directs Kismet to listen on wlan0 for a prism2 type card. This shows up as `Prism` in your logs.
Fuzzy encryption	Shows any identified packets as unencrypted for those stations using undefined or proprietary encryption methods. Generally leave this off unless your card is reporting known encrypted networks as unencrypted.
Filtering packet logs	Limits what packets get logged. Use the `noiselog` option to drop any packets that seem to be broken or fragmented due to noise. In a crowded area with lots of interference or when using a card that does not have an external antenna, this can keep your log size down. The `beaconlog` option drops all but the first beacon packet from a particular access point. The `phylog` setting drops any physical layer packets that are sometimes picked up. You can use any combination of these settings.
Decrypt WEP keys	Decrypts intercepted data packets on the fly. You must first, however, have the key, which can sometimes be obtained using AirSnort (described later in this chapter). Each access point needs a separate statement in the format `bssid:key` where `bssid` is the MAC address of the access point and `key` is the key for that access point.
Using an external IDS	Sends packets to an external instruction detection system for further analysis. You specify a `FIFO` pipe in this statement and then direct your NIDS to read from the pipe name.

Table 10.6 Kismet Interface Settings

Settings	Descriptions
Columns	Changes what columns appear in the Kismet interface and in what order. Change the value of `columns` or `clientcolumns` to what you want to see. A complete listing of the columns available is in the Kismet man pages.
Colors	Changes the colors of any of the elements of the display. Change the `colorxxx` setting to the color code you want. You will have to play with it a bit to get the colors right. (I found the defaults to be acceptable except for printing, and changed those to a more printer-friendly color.)

Using Kismet Wireless

Start Kismet by running the executable file from the command line or from an X-Windows terminal that supports the Curses toolkit. The main interface displays (see Figure 10.8). Kismet immediately starts reporting any wireless networks in your area and information on them.

The interface is divided into three main sections. The Network List section on the left shows all the currently active wireless networks that Kismet can see and some basic information on them: the SSID of the network (if available), the type (access point versus

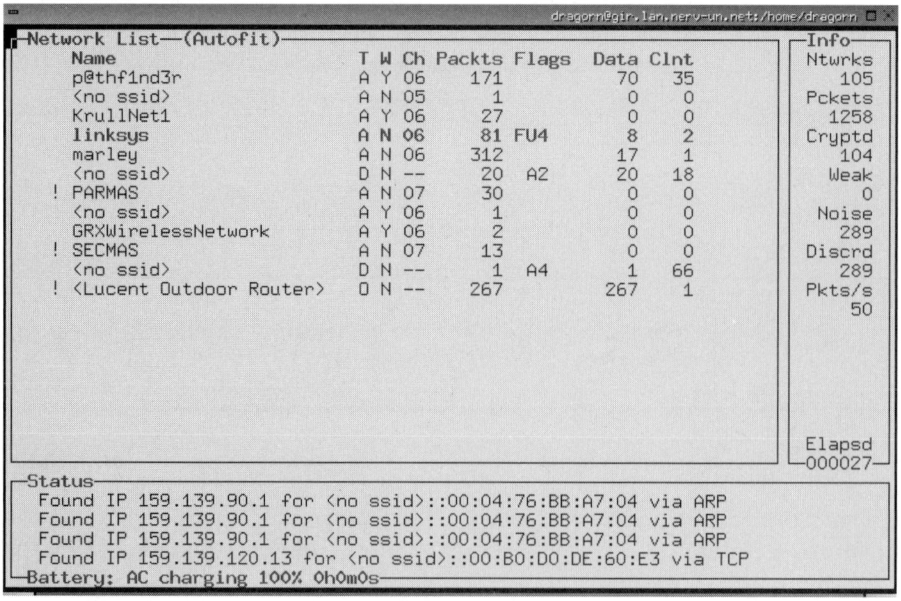

Figure 10.8 Kismet Wireless Main Screen

node), whether or not it is encrypted using WEP, the channel it is broadcasting on, the number of packets intercepted so far, any flags on the data, and the amount of data going through the network. The display is color coded with active networks appearing in red and ones that are no longer active in black.

The Info box on the right shows overall statistics for this capture session, including the total number of networks sensed, the total number of packets, the number of packets that were encrypted, weak networks perceived, packets with a high noise level, packets that were discarded, and the average number of packets per second.

The Status box on the bottom contains a scrolling view of events as they happen. Messages pop up when new networks appear or other events happen.

Because Kismet is a command line tool, albeit with a GUI, it uses key commands to control its functions. Table 10.7 lists the key commands available from the main screen.

Table 10.7 Kismet Key Commands

Key Commands	Descriptions
a	Shows statistics about packet counts and channel allocation.
c	Opens a client pop-up window to display clients in the selected network.
d	Instructs the server to start extracting printable strings from the packet stream and displays them.
e	Opens a pop-up window on Kismet servers. This lets you simultaneously monitor two or more Kismet servers on different hosts (remember, it's a client-server architecture).
f	Follows the estimated center of a network and displays a compass.
g	Groups currently tagged networks.
h	Gets a listing of possible commands.
i	Displays detailed information about the current network or group.
l	Shows signal/power/noise levels if the card reports them.

(continues)

Table 10.7 Kismet Key Commands (*continued*)

Key Commands	Descriptions
m	Mutes sound and speech if they are enabled (or turns them on if they were previously silenced). You must have sound or speech enabled in your configuration to be able to use them.
n	Renames the selected network or group.
p	Displays packet types as they are received.
r	Displays a bar graph of the packet rate.
s	Sorts the network list differently.
t	Tags (or untags) the current network.
u	Ungroups the current network.
w	Displays all previous alerts and warnings.
z	Zooms the network display panel to full screen (or returns it to normal size if it is already zoomed).

As noted above, you can expand views of information on each network detected to show all the details on a particular access point by entering i at the command line. Figure 10.9 illustrates this output.

You can also expand the network box to full screen and see additional information on each network, such as the manufacturer of the equipment detected using the z command. This may make it easier to organize your access points into groups if you are trying to track a particular set of APs and want to be able to filter the others out. Do this with the g and u commands to group and ungroup, respectively.

The sound feature is handy—it beeps when you detect new networks. You can toggle that option off using the m command if you are going in and out of many network's reception areas. Otherwise you get a cacophony of beeps!

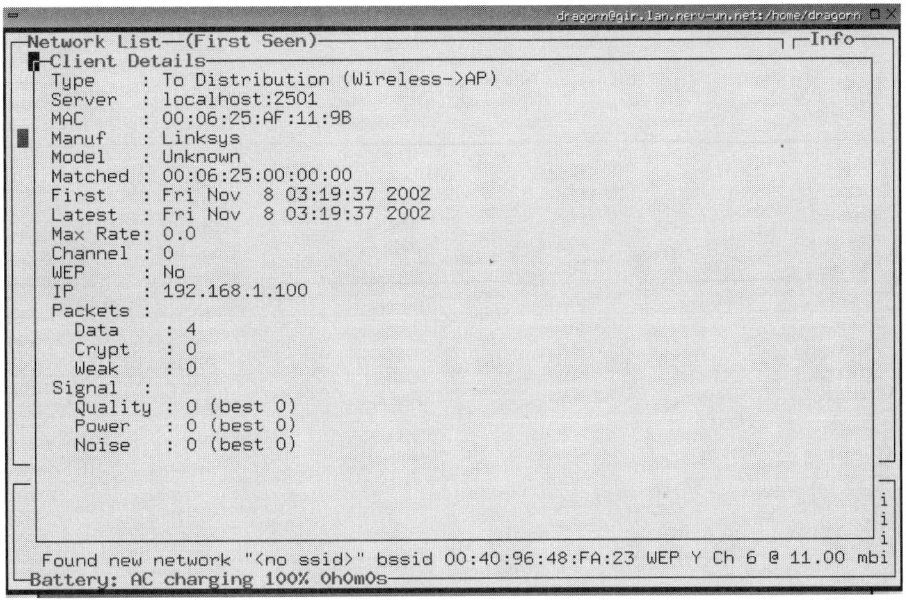

```
                                          dragorn@gir.lan.nerv-un.net:/home/dragorn  □ ✕
 ┌Network List──(First Seen)──────────────────────────────────────┐ ┌Info─
 ┃─Client Details──────
 ┃   Type     : To Distribution (Wireless->AP)
 ┃   Server   : localhost:2501
 ┃   MAC      : 00:06:25:AF:11:9B
 ┃  Manuf    : Linksys
 ┃   Model    : Unknown
 ┃   Matched  : 00:06:25:00:00:00
 ┃   First    : Fri Nov  8 03:19:37 2002
 ┃   Latest   : Fri Nov  8 03:19:37 2002
 ┃   Max Rate: 0.0
 ┃   Channel : 0
 ┃   WEP      : No
 ┃   IP       : 192.168.1.100
 ┃   Packets :
 ┃     Data    : 4
 ┃     Crypt   : 0
 ┃     Weak    : 0
 ┃   Signal  :
 ┃     Quality : 0 (best 0)
 ┃     Power   : 0 (best 0)
 ┃     Noise   : 0 (best 0)
 ┗─
                                                                     i
                                                                     i
                                                                     i
  Found new network "<no ssid>" bssid 00:40:96:48:FA:23 WEP Y Ch 6 @ 11.00 mbi
 ─Battery: AC charging 100% 0h0m0s──
```

Figure 10.9 Kismet Network Detail Screen

Kismet GPS Support

Kismet has the ability to record GPS data if you have a GPS receiver plugged into your machine. You need the GPS daemon software GPSD for Kismet to read it. You can get GPSD at http://russnelson.com/gpsd/. You must enable GPS support when compiling Kismet using the compile-time parameters in Table 10.4. Kismet then automatically picks up the coordinates of any networks sensed and logs them.

You can take this one step further and map these coordinates just like with the Windows program. Kismet comes with a built in program called GPSMAP that automatically plots the data collected onto maps in .gps format. The downside is you have to provide your own GPS-calibrated map. There is an open source mapping program for Linux called GPSDrive, which you can download from http://gpsdrive.kraftvoll.at/index.shtml.

Kismet IDS

You can also set up Kismet as a wireless IDS. Kismet will intercept incoming signals and detect wireless traffic that is known to be associated with war driving or other suspicious wireless activity. It detects about 10 different kinds of traffic, including NetStumbler polls and activity from Airjack and other wireless hacking tools. Currently this IDS capability is fairly limited, but expect it to expand in the future. And, since it's open source, you can always expand it yourself by writing your own alerts. You can also pipe your Kismet data through a traditional IDS such as Snort for more detailed analysis. The IDS feature is set in kismet.conf and is turned off by default. You can also set up Kismet to gather known cryptographically weak keys for a program such as AirSnort, the next tool in this chapter, which analyzes wireless packets and attempts to crack the WEP encryption.

AirSnort: A WEP Encryption Key Recovery Program	
AirSnort	
Original authors/primary contacts:	Jeremy Bruestle and Blake Hegerle
Web site:	http://schmoo.airsnort.org
Platforms:	Most Linux
License:	GPL
Version reviewed:	2.4.22

The authors developed AirSnort as a practical application to demonstrate the weakness in the WEP, the wireless encryption protocol. A paper entitled "Weaknesses in the Key Scheduling Algorithm of RC4," written by the cryptographic experts Fluhrer, Martin, and Shamir, detailed a theoretical weakness in the WEP algorithm, describing how some of the Initialization Vectors (IVs) were weak. Packets encrypted with these weak IVs could be collected and eventually enough data would be present to extrapolate the shared secret key. This allowed the packets to be easily decrypted. Two tools were released shortly thereafter, AirSnort and WEPCrack, that employed the described weakness to recover WEP keys, effectively cracking WEP. They are both good tools, but AirSnort has some additional functionality as a wireless sniffer. AirSnort is now an open source project hosted on SourceForge.net and has been extended and improved considerably since its release. Given that there are no real alternatives under Windows for doing this, AirSnort and WEPCrack are currently the only viable alternatives for testing your WEP.

Uses for AirSnort

Why use AirSnort on your wireless network? Some might say there is no legitimate use for the program and its only purpose is as a hacker's tool. However, I believe that the only way to know what the exposure on your wireless network is for *you* to do what the hackers do to see if your encryption is crackable and the amount of time it takes to do it. AirSnort lets you do just that.

By attempting to crack your wireless encryption, you can see if it is crackable. If you are using standard WEP, then it is merely a matter of time. It is a mathematical certainty that it can be cracked at some point using this tool. The question is, how long does it take? If it's a very long time, you can reasonably assume you are pretty safe. If the traffic level on your wireless LAN is small, then it might take days or even weeks. This puts your network out of the realm of practicality of most casual hackers. However, if it's a busy network, then someone might be able to pick up enough packets to break it in a few hours or a day.

Knowing this will help you to better protect your network. It can justify putting in further protections, such as better physical controls or limiting the traffic on that network. It also might justify upgrading your wireless equipment. Cisco Aeronet gear uses a variation of WEP called LEAP to improve and fix the weakness with the original WEP protocol. A wireless network using that protocol should be uncrackable, at least with readily available tools. You may find that your traffic level doesn't make it practical to crack your encryption. Either way, you'll sleep better at night knowing.

Installing AirSnort

Getting the drivers and software working for AirSnort can be quite a chore. Its requirements closely match those of the Kismet program. Refer back to the "Installing Your Network Interface Card and Drivers" section and follow that procedure. Finally, when all the moons align and you get all these things in order, you are ready to install the program. This is the easy part.

1. Download the program file from the book's CD-ROM or the official Web site and unzip it.
2. Change to the directory where you unzipped the file and run the script

   ```
   ./autogen.sh
   ```

3. Become root and then run

   ```
   make
   ```

The program will be built for you automatically. If this completes without errors, you have successfully installed AirSnort.

Running AirSnort

AirSnort has three primary executable files.

- **airsnort** does the work of collecting the packets from some source, usually your wireless network card.
- **gencases** sorts through the captured data for weak keys.
- **decrypt** does offline decryption attempts for files loaded from another source.

AirSnort accept files from other wireless sniffers as along as they are saved in pcap format. Kismet, our Linux wireless tool of choice, will specifically pull out interesting packets for AirSnort ahead of time, saving this step.

You don't have to do all the data collection at once. AirSnort can save a session and let you open it later and add to it. This makes AirSnort a particularly dangerous tool to wireless networks, because someone doesn't have to spend a single uninterrupted session near your facility to collect enough packets to crack your network. They can split their collection activities into smaller, less noticeable time increments, assuming the target network doesn't change its keys often.

Once you have AirSnort installed, you can start it by typing `airsnort` at the command line. The interface is simplicity itself: it is a single screen that shows the interesting packets and the total number of encrypted and unencrypted packets. The top section shows you settings such as NIC card type and so forth. On the left, you can change some settings, such as the **breadth**— the number of guessing attempts AirSnort will make for each key byte—for either 40-bit or 128-bit decryption attempts. The default is 3 for 40-bit encryption and 2 for 128-bit encryption. If you don't have a lot of data or you have a lot of excess processing power, you can try increasing this slightly, but don't go much more than 4 or 5.

After that, it is time to just sit back and collect packets. Don't expect to be able to crack WEP keys in just a few moments. For AirSnort to work properly, it needs approximately 1,500 to 4,500 packets with weak keys. This amounts to between 100MB and 500MB of data. On a moderately busy network, it might take a day or more to collect this much data. On slower networks it could take much longer and on busier networks much less. Expect it to take at least a couple of hours but probably longer. Of course, all of this is based on a little luck too, so your results may vary from an hour to never. Generally, you want to spend about as much time collecting data as you think the average outsider might be able to spend undetected. And of course, AirSnort's resume session feature could make this time window much shorter since they could use multiple collection sessions.

When a successful crack of the WEP key has occurred, it appears in both plain text and the original hexadecimal on the far left of the display and the capture session ends. Happy WEP cracking!

What do you do if you find your WEP keys? Well, don't panic, because most casual hackers won't go to the trouble. However, you should think about taking steps to increase the security of your wireless network to make it harder for outsiders to collect this data. There are a number of steps you can take, ranging from replacing your equipment to reconfiguring and changing your AP position. You will have to decide based on the sensitivity of the data on your network which ones are appropriate.

Steps for More Secure Wireless LANs

The chances are that eventually you will have to implement wireless technology. Even if you don't, you should still occasionally audit your network and make sure someone isn't running a rogue wireless access point. While running any wireless access is a risk, you can lessen your exposure by taking the following preventative measures.

Turn On WEP

By encrypting your data you are requiring hackers to spent a lot more time and effort to get to your wireless data and network. This will discourage casual hackers and make the serious ones have to hang around your area for a day or so, increasing the chances that they will be noticed by security personnel or vigilant employees.

Use Wireless Equipment with an Improved Encryption Protocol

As mentioned earlier, Cisco equipment uses an improved version of WEP call LEAP, which so far has proven impervious to cracking attempts. There is also a new standard, 802.11i, which permanently fixes the problems with WEP. Unfortunately, 802.11i has only recently been approved as a standard and equipment based on it should be available soon. If you can get them, do so. The pricing shouldn't be any different than the older 802.11a and 802.11b gear.

Require Wireless Users to Come in Via a VPN Tunnel

This step adds a mostly insurmountable hurdle for would-be wireless intruders. Even if they manage to crack your WEP encryption, they then have to tackle the VPN encryption. Some vendors (such as SonicWALL with its Wi-FiSec feature) have added this capability into their equipment. The downsides are that there is an additional layer of complexity for your users and this makes it harder to support "guest" users, as they would need VPN client software loaded as well as the WEP key to access the WLAN.

Treat Your Wireless Network as Untrusted

Since you cannot control what traffic is coming across the air to access points, you shouldn't treat it any differently than the public side of your firewall. If you can afford it, place a firewall between your wireless network and your LAN (see Chapter 3 for some open source options) or place it on your DMZ. Then you can filter certain kinds of attack packets, limit types of traffic, and track any activity coming from that interface.

Audit Your Wireless Perimeter on a Regular Basis

This is especially important if you are in one of those dense areas mentioned earlier. Test to see how far away your signal can be picked up and if your network is overlapping nearby ones. Even if you don't officially allow wireless access, you should do this periodically to locate any rogue or "unofficial" access points. Wireless has become so cheap and easy to set up that unthinking or uncaring managers will often go to the local electronics store and set up an access point for some temporary purpose, such as a demo in an unwired conference room, opening up your network to wireless attack. Additionally, remember that a lot of new PCs, especially laptops, are coming with Wi-Fi cards built-in, and enabling them is easy to do. You may be running wireless on your network without realizing it. A wireless audit is the only way to find out.

Move Your Access Points

Sometimes just by moving the base station into an interior room you can decrease the broadcast of your wireless network signal considerably. Use your wireless audit results to figure out which access points are problematic. Play around with placement so you get optimal reception inside the building but minimal reception outside the building. For example, if your building has a large parking lot in front and a wooded lot in back, moving the base station to the back of the building will probably still allow most internal people to reach it, but will limit the radiation of the signal to an area that is not easily accessible by war drivers.

Configure Your Wireless Network Properly

There are many features and settings you can use to increase your security considerably. Not all equipment supports these options, but here are some things you can do.

- Turn off the SSID broadcast. Doing this requires a user to know the SSID to establish a session with the base station. This acts as a weak password. However, if an eavesdropper manages to crack your encryption, he or she will be able to gain the SSID easily.
- Restrict access by MAC address. This makes it more difficult for someone to gain access to your network via a wireless base station. In most access points, you can restrict access to certain hardware MAC addresses. This is a fairly strong method of authentication, since only people with the correct serialized network card can gain access. However, it may be cumbersome for administrators to keep track of authorized NIC cards and it doesn't allow for instant access for a new user in your office. Also, if the attacker knows one of the authorized MAC addresses, it is possible to forge this address on his or her card and masquerade as that user.

Train Your Staff

As with all computer security, the human element can be your weakest or strongest point. Make sure security guards, receptionists, and other personnel know how to look for suspicious behavior associated with war driving. For example, if they see someone sitting in your parking lot for long periods of time, possibly with a strange antenna on their roof, then it might be likely he or she is targeting your wireless network.

Also, develop and get approval on a company-wide policy for deploying wireless LANs. Make sure managers know that they can't set up a wireless LAN themselves; that they need to go through you for an official connection. Make them understand how they are putting the whole company at risk with this behavior. Sometimes a demonstration is the best way to get the danger of this across. An informed workforce can be your best defense.

## CHAPTER 11

Forensic Tools

All of the tools and techniques described in this book so far will make your network very secure if implemented properly and maintained vigilantly. But even if you do everything right, no network is 100 percent secure. If attackers are dedicated enough or lucky enough, sometimes they can break in anyway. An outsider can take advantage of a zero-day exploit that isn't published yet or catch you in the window of opportunity between exploit announcement and patching. A tricky insider can use physical means to break in, such as gaining physical access to a server or stealing a password. Or they might use social engineering to bypass all your security measures by getting an overly helpful employee to give them access. So what do you do if in spite of all your preparations your network or systems get compromised?

Assuming you still have a job, it's not the end of the world. Even the largest companies in the world with huge security staffs get hacked, so it is nothing to be ashamed of. However, now it is time to pick up the pieces, figure out how they got in, patch up the holes, and if necessary, track down the perpetrators and take further action. A number of open source tools can help you in this endeavor. They are called **forensic** tools since you are trying to determine what happened based on the evidence you have available to you.

Chapter Overview

Concepts you will learn:
- Uses for forensic tools
- Incident response concepts
- Preparing for forensic investigation
- Tenets of good forensic investigation

Tools you will use:
Fport, lsof, DD, UNIX and Windows log files, Sleuth Kit, Autopsy Forensic Browser, and
The Forensic Toolkit

Uses for Computer Forensic Tools

After an attack on your system, you are going to want to figure out how it was done so you
can prevent it from happening again. If they managed to get past your existing electronic
defenses, then obviously there is a hole in your armor somewhere. It may not immediately
be obvious where this hole is, especially if they were good about covering up their tracks.
Forensic tools can help you retrace their digital footsteps and find the holes so you can
patch them up.

Cleaning Up and Rebuilding

If the attackers did damage, you need to figure out exactly what they did so you know how
extensive the damage is and can rebuild appropriately. You don't want to miss any hacked
servers or backdoor accounts they may have left behind. Using forensic tools can help you
figure out where the bodies are buried, so to speak. If the attacker deleted files, you may be
able to recover some of them using forensic tools.

Criminal Investigation

If the damage done by an attacker is severe enough, you may want to consider pressing
criminal charges. Simple Web defacings or intrusions usually aren't worth pursuing due to
the high costs involved. However, if your infrastructure or corporate reputation was significantly damaged, then you may want to file criminal charges against your attacker. Your
insurance company may require that you file a police report in order to make a claim.
Forensic tools will help you identify your attackers so you can report them and provide the
evidence to prosecute them.

There are a few things you should consider before proceeding down this path. For
small damages, you can file a report with your local police department. Be aware that they
often do not have the resources to properly pursue computer crime at the local level and
you may end up doing most of the investigative work. You can use the tools in this chapter
to help with the effort. Just be careful that you don't contaminate the evidence so that it is
not useful in a court of law (see the sidebar on computer forensics).

If the damages are large enough or involve a federal crime (such as interstate or international commerce), you can take your case to the FBI. You can find contact information
for your local FBI field office in your telephone book or on the Web at www.fbi.gov. If the
case involves the violation of federal law or material dollar damages of over $25,000, they
will probably take your case. Otherwise, they might refer you to local law authorities. If
you can show some involvement with terrorism, interstate fraud (such as stealing credit

card numbers or identity theft), or some other element that is high on their radar screen, you might get them involved for lesser amounts. Garden-variety hacking attacks will probably not be investigated heavily; there are too many incidents reported daily for the FBI to give any real attention to anything that isn't a significant case.

If you do succeed in having criminal charges filed against your attacker, proper forensic analysis becomes all the more important. There is a heavy burden of proof in computer criminal cases. Tying a certain act that was performed by a user ID to a specific person is quite difficult in a court of law. Usually prosecutors have to prove that the person was actually at his or her keyboard using that account while the attack was taking place. Otherwise, there are many defenses available to the accused, such as "Someone else used my password," "I was hacked," and so on. There is also close attention paid to the chain of custody of any evidence collected. This refers to who has had access to the data and could have changed or altered it along the way. In a case like this, defer to the authorities, who may want to use their own data collection techniques. You may also want to use a third party who does this professionally to assist in your interaction with law enforcement.

Flamey the Tech Tip:

A Little Knowledge Can Be Dangerous!

If you are thinking about pressing criminal charges, it is important that you do *not* use the tools in this book right away. Other than your lockdown and recovery activity, you shouldn't tamper with the evidence in any way if possible. An unskilled person using these tools can wipe out evidence or make it unusable in court. Imagine a neophyte gumshoe wandering around a murder scene. Not good! Get the law enforcement professionals involved, and then you can help them, if directed, with the tools and knowledge from this chapter.

Careers in Computer Forensics

The growth of computer crime has created the budding field of computer forensics. There are many career options available for those interested in a career in computer forensics. The need has never been greater for computer-savvy cops. There are several areas to look into if you are interested in this field.

Local Law Enforcement

Police departments in large cities usually have a computer crime division. This may require a degree with a major or minor in law enforcement or a similar field. Sometimes, though, departments are so strapped for technical talent that they are willing to overlook police experience for technical know-how.

Federal Law Enforcement

The ultimate computer forensic positions are with the FBI. Here you would get to work on high-profile cases of national or international importance. Usually the FBI hires from within its own ranks, although they do make an occasional exception for someone of particular talent or prestige. Working with the FBI would give you the chance to truly have an impact on computer crime.

Armed Forces

If you are of a military bent, all of the armed forces have computer crime staffs, most notably the Air Force's Office of Special Investigation. The OSI, while focused on crimes and incidents within the armed forces, often become involved in civilian matters due to the overlap of computer crime incidents.

Department of Homeland Security

There are lots of new positions and departments being created as part of the Department of Homeland Security. Taking a position in law enforcement or the military may require you to take a lower salary than your commercial counterparts. However, many find these positions more fulfilling. There are also large companies that employ full-time computer forensics staffs. Civil experience can also greatly enhance your resume if you want to go into private practice or join a company's computer forensic department.

Civil Action

If you find that pursuing criminal charges is unwarranted, you may still want to file a civil lawsuit to punish your hacker. Sometimes this is the only way you can get someone to stop his or her attacks. If the assailant is coming from another company, either sanctioned, in the case of corporate espionage, or unsanctioned, in the case of a wayward employee, you may have cause to file a lawsuit and collect significant damages. Although the burden of proof is less in the civil courts, you still have to be able to substantiate your case. The tools in this chapter will help you to do so. However, if the case is big enough and the stake large enough, you should still probably hire a computer forensic expert rather than try to do it yourself.

Internal Investigations

If you suspect your intrusion may be from an internal source, it is imperative that you track down this huge source of business liability. An internal hacker can do volumes more damage than an outsider because they often know the personnel, systems, and information that could cause the most damage to a company if revealed or compromised. By using these forensic tools, you can track them down. If disciplinary action is warranted, you will have the evidence to back it up. In this litigious age, you don't want to get sued by a former employee for wrongful termination.

ISP Complaints

If you decide not to pursue criminal or civil action or if the person assaulting your network is still doing it, you will want to file a complaint with his ISP and try to at least get him shut down. Often, this is the only real recourse that doesn't cost a lot of money for companies hit by a hacker attack. Using the forensic tools in this chapter, you can follow the perpetrator's trails, at least as far as his or her ISP. Once you have tracked the attacker this far, you can make a formal complaint with the ISP, asking them to take further action. Most ISPs have acceptable use policies for their users, which of course don't include hacking. If you can show them sufficient evidence, they will usually take action, ranging from a warning to terminating that user's account. Because of privacy concerns, they will not usually disclose any personal information about the user unless required to by a subpoena, but some ISPs are more helpful than others in this area. Most of the major providers have a special abuse e-mail address that you can send your messages to.

You should make sure you have gathered sufficient information so they can find your assailant. This would include IP addresses tied to specific times. Most ISPs gives out dynamic IP addresses, which change every time someone logs on. Without time information to match to their logs, they probably won't be able to help you. If possible, give them multiple access times so they can correlate the user from several data points, as their log files might be out of sync with yours and the times won't exactly match. Also include any other data you might have such as logs of commands used, places they copied files to, and so on. The ISP may be a victim too and will want this data to investigate further.

Building an Incident Response Plan

Just like you have a plan for back-up and disaster recovery (you do, don't you?), you should have a plan for response to computer crime incidents. This will help you take the right steps, both in advance of an incident and after it, to make sure you have the right groundwork laid and don't shoot yourself in the foot. This is a large subject area and there are whole books on the subject, but basically you want to document a process for dealing with incidents so you can proceed without uncertainty when something happens.

With input from upper management, build a map that lays out your actions if certain things occur. Make sure you have the proper approvals from upper management to do certain things like involve law enforcement, or your job could be at risk. In larger companies this will probably involve lawyers and the public relations department, and this may quickly be taken out of your hands, which is fine as long as you understand your role in the process and that is clear to everyone. This action plan might look something like this in its basic form.

1. Contain the problem. Make sure that your assailants can't do any more damage.
2. Start any preliminary recovery/restore operations, making sure to preserve any evidence properly.

3. Assess the damage. Try to quickly determine monetary amounts of loss either in hard or soft dollars. Management tends to react quicker when presented with dollars and cents.

4. Report the problem to upper management for either referral to law enforcement or internal investigation.

5. Decide whether to do the investigation in house or bring in third-party professionals.

6. Proceed with internal investigation or assist law enforcement officials.

Preparing for Good Forensic Data

As with anything, taking the proper steps to prepare before disaster strikes can make your job significantly easier. If you have poor logging and auditing practices in place, this will make your forensic job more difficult if not impossible. While no one likes to plan for disaster, taking these steps can help you pick up the pieces afterwards.

Log Granularity

If you have the disk space and the processor time available, turn your logging up to the highest detail level that is reasonable on your servers. This provides a lot more information in case you need to reconstruct something from the logs and is useful for troubleshooting server problems as well. You will probably want to play with the settings to find the level of log detail that makes sense for you. In Windows, you can adjust your logging granularity by going to Event Viewer in Administrative Tools. Click on the properties of each log type (application, security, system) and you can set the logging level of each item.

Run a Central Log Server

Keeping all your log files locally on each server is a liability from several standpoints. If attackers manage to co-opt a machine, they will have access to the log files to either change them or erase them totally. Utilities are available to help intruders selectively wipe logs files of their activity. At least if they are on another server, the invader has to hack yet another machine to get to them. The popular log server utility **syslog** is a good tool for this, and most servers, routers, firewalls, and other devices support this format. From a management standpoint, it is a lot easier to have all your logs on one server for reviewing them on a regular basis, and you know they are all synchronized to the same clock. This leads us to the next point.

Time Sync Your Servers

You should have all of your servers getting their time from a central timeserver rather than relying on the internal clocks. PC clocks are notoriously inaccurate and are subject to drift.

You can use the Network Time Protocol (NTP) to get your time from a central server, subscribe to atomic clocks on the Internet, or run your own internal timeserver to ensure that you are getting the correct time. This way, log times will be the same from one server to another so you can correctly follow a sequence of log events. There is nothing more frustrating than trying to put together an attack from logs that have multiple disparate clock settings. Using a public timeserver is highly recommended. Most of these are free and use atomic clocks for the greatest accuracy. This way your logs are more likely to match external log files such as an ISP's files. Public time clocks are available at the following Web sites:

- clock.isc.org
- clock.via.net
- clock.sgi.net
- ttp.nasa.gov
- tick.gpsclock.org

Where to Look for Forensic Data

There are the obvious places to look for information after a computer attack. The machine or machines that were exploited are the first place to start. Log file and key system files often hold clues as to methods and identity. You should also consult any intrusion detection systems you have in place. These tools may be what alerted you to the incident in the first place. Tools like Tripwire (described in Chapter 7) can be invaluable in determining what was done and if a system has been compromised.

However, important information is often located in the least likely places, such as a user's directory in the case of an exploited account or temporary directories created by your assailant. If possible, quarantine the entire system to go through it with a fine-tooth comb. The tools described later in this chapter will help expedite this process.

Also, don't limit yourself to the suspect computers. Often you will want to look somewhere other than the machine(s) in question to find information on your attackers. While they might wipe the local logs on the exploited machine, you can sometimes find their tracks on nearby servers or devices. An attack is rarely successful the first time it is tried. Usually an attacker has to try multiple machines to find one that is vulnerable. This activity shows on the log files of neighboring machines. You can find evidence of reconnaissance scans on other machines. Also, you can find signs of unusual activity on your router and firewalls. Check the logs around the time of the break-in (here is where synchronized log files really make a difference). You might look at your public Web server logs around the time of the break-in. When hackers find a vulnerable server, they will often go to the Web site associated with that domain name to see whom they have hacked. Try to find IP addresses that match between logs.

Tenets of Good Forensic Analysis

When doing forensic analysis on information systems, there are different methods and techniques to use and a variety of software tools to help you. However, there are some basic guidelines that you should always follow if possible.

Operate on a Disconnected System

If possible, completely disconnect the system in question from the network while gathering your data. If the system is connected, you could be dealing with a moving target while collecting the data. Log files can fill up, parts of the disk can get overwritten, and services could die or be shut down. Worst case, if your attackers still have access to the system (and you never can be absolutely sure of this), they might discover your work and take evasive action.

If the system has been taken down by an attack, you might be under considerable pressure to bring it back online as fast as possible. For production systems still up and running, there also might be resistance to taking them offline. It may not be politically popular, but at a minimum, try to take the system offline while you collect your data. Wait until after hours if you have to and advertise it as a system maintenance window. Make a copy of the information in question (the whole hard drive if possible). Then you can return the system to production and minimize users' downtime while you do your work. Which leads to the next point.

Use a Copy of the Evidence

Use data imaging software, such as the dd tool presented later in this chapter, to make a copy of the evidence to work on. If you plan to pursue any legal action, criminal or civil, make two copies and seal one in a tamper-proof container. This protects your chain of custody and makes your case less assailable by charges of tainted evidence. Also, if you accidentally make a mistake and delete some important evidence, you can always return to your known good copy. If possible, take these initial steps in the presence of another witness. It is even better if he or she is an impartial third party. Attach a paper log with the creator's name, date, and time, and then log each time it changes hands with dates and signatures.

Use Hashes to Provide Evidence of Integrity

When making your copies of the data and producing other evidentiary files, it is worthwhile to create a MD5 hash of the data and record it. Some of these tools, such as The Coroner's Toolkit (see the section on Sleuth Kit later in this chapter), will do this for you automatically. You can also use one of the encryption tools mentioned in Chapter 9, such as PGP or GnuPG. Again, if the authenticity of your findings is challenged, you can prove that the copy you worked on was electronically exactly the same as the one on the machine attacked. This also helps you verify differences between files and if any changes were made by system-level utilities.

Use Trusted Boot Media and Executables

Whenever examining a system, it is good practice to boot using a trusted media, such as a boot floppy or CD-ROM. You can create one of these during the OS installation process. Some of these tools create their own bootable environment. This is especially important if you are working on the exploited system. If the attack has managed to compromise the system's binary files using a root kit, then any results you obtain from the utilities on that hard disk should be suspect. In addition to possibly writing over file dates and other crucial data, the attacker may have left certain time bombs or daemons running that could cause further damage or erase evidence.

You can create an incident response disk that includes all of the programs you would need on a bootable CD-ROM. You will need one for Windows and one for UNIX if you are in a mixed environment.

Forensic Analysis Tools

One issue computer investigators face is that normal file utilities can irrevocably change files, effectively "polluting" the crime scene as well as deleting evidence you need. For example, viewing files with a regular editor changes things like the timestamp. Imagine someone tromping through a real crime scene in dirty boots and moving objects all over the house. This is the same as rummaging through your system without the proper tools. Not only will you have eliminated your chance of being able to take any criminal or civil action, but you may also erase the attacker's digital trail. Hackers often use tools that hide processes and files from normal system utilities, so you need special tools that operate outside of the normal operating system to look beyond what the operating system thinks it sees.

The following sections review tools for both Linux and Windows. First we will look at a few of the investigation tools on operating systems, then at full-featured toolkits for deeper analysis. Keep in mind that using operating system-based tools may return false or bogus data if your OS has truly been compromised.

Fport: A Process Identification Tool for Windows

Fport
Author/primary contact: Foundstone, Inc.
Web site: www.foundstone.com/index.htm?subnav=resources/
navigation.htm&subcontent=/resources/freetools.htm

Platforms:	Windows NT, 2000, XP
License:	Freeware
Version reviewed:	2.0

This little system add-on can be useful when investigating a machine for suspicious activity. Often a memory-resident virus or Trojan horse will show up as a process running under a strange name or on an unusual port. Fport looks for open TCP or UDP network ports and prints them out along with the associated process id (PID), process name, and path. It is similar to the native Windows netstat command except that it provides a little more information and allows you to format it different ways for analysis. This can help you track down suspicious programs that are opening up network ports on your machine. This behavior is the hallmark of a Trojan horse.

Of course, every process you don't recognize isn't necessarily an evil program, but you should understand what weird-looking services are doing. The most obvious ones will have nonstandard paths (other than the Windows system directories and such). Also, strange or hacker-like names are a dead giveaway.

The program is designed and offered by Foundstone Corporation, a security software and consulting company. They offer several other free security tools and their Web site is worth a look. While Fport is not purely open source (only the binaries are distributed), it is freeware and there are few limitations on its use for commercial purposes.

Installing Fport

Download the zip file from the Foundstone Web site and unzip it into its own directory. There will be two files, the Fport executable and a short README file.

Using Fport

Fport can help you figure out if a machine has been tampered with and where the intruder is coming from. You need to run Fport on a system that is live, that is, up and running; you can't run Fport on static data.

Running Fport is about as simple as it comes. From the directory the executable is in, type `fport`. It prints a listing of all the ports open at that moment and their associated applications (see Listing 11.1).

Listing 11.1 Fport Display

```
Port v2.0 - TCP/IP Process to Port Mapper
Copyright 2000 by Foundstone, Inc.
http://www.foundstone.com


Pid   Process        Port  Proto Path
940   svchost     -> 135   TCP   C:\WINDOWS\system32\svchost.exe

4     System      -> 139   TCP

4     System      -> 445   TCP
1348  WCESCOMM    -> 990   TCP   C:\Program Files\Microsoft
                                    ActiveSync\WCESCOMM.EXE
```

4072	WCESMgr	->	999	TCP	C:\Program Files\Microsoft ActiveSync\WCESMgr.exe
1032	svchost	->	1025	TCP	C:\WINDOWS\System32\svchost.exe
1032	svchost	->	1031	TCP	C:\WINDOWS\System32\svchost.exe
1032	svchost	->	1034	TCP	C:\WINDOWS\System32\svchost.exe
4	System	->	1042	TCP	
4072	WCESMgr	->	2406	TCP	C:\Program Files\Microsoft ActiveSync\WCESMgr.exe
2384	websearch	->	3008	TCP	C:\Program Files\websearch\websearch.exe
1144		->	54321	TCP	C:\Temp\cmd.exe
4072	WCESMgr	->	5678	TCP	C:\Program Files\Microsoft ActiveSync\WCESMgr.exe
2384	websearch	->	8755	TCP	C:\Program Files\websearch\websearch.exe
136	javaw	->	8765	TCP	C:\WINDOWS\System32\javaw.exe
1348	WCESCOMM	->	123	UDP	C:\Program Files\Microsoft ActiveSync\WCESCOMM.EXE
2384	websearch	->	123	UDP	C:\Program Files\websearch\websearch.exe
940	svchost	->	135	UDP	C:\WINDOWS\system32\svchost.exe
1144		->	137	UDP	
1032	svchost	->	1026	UDP	C:\WINDOWS\System32\svchost.exe

By looking at this listing, you can see what appear to be normal services and programs running, until about half way down where you can see that cmd.exe is running from the temp directory. This is the command prompt binary and it has no business being in a temp directory. Also, the fact that the service has no name should arouse suspicion. Finally, the incoming port number doesn't match any known services. In fact, if you look it up in a database of known Trojan horses on the Internet (www.simovits.com/trojans/

Table 11.1 Fport Sorting Options

Options	Descriptions
-a	Sorts the output by application name.
-ap	Sorts the output by application path.
-i	Sorts the output by Process ID (PID).
-p	Sorts the output by port.

trojans.html), it matches the port number of a documented Trojan horse. There is strong evidence that this system has been exploited. At this point, you have to decide if it is worth taking the system down to do further forensic analysis of the system.

Table 11.1 lists a few options you can run with Fport to sort the output. You can also use the –h option to display short help descriptions.

If you have a lot of processes, you can use these switches to look at all the high port numbers running, which is typically where malware runs. You can also sort by application path or name to find nonstandard applications running.

lsof: A Port and Process Identification Tool for UNIX
lsof
Author/primary contact: Ray Shaw
Web site   http://freshmeat.net/projects/lsof/
Platforms: Linux and most UNIX
License: GPL
Version reviewed: 4.68
Mirror sites (these allow anonymous FTP without reverse DNS):
thewiretapped.net/pub/security/host-security/lsof
ftp.tau.ac.il/pub/unix/admin/

This tool is similar to the Fport tool for Windows just discussed. The lsof tool (LiSt Open Files) associates open files with processes and users. It is like the netstat command, but in addition it reports the network port the service is using. This is important when trying to track down an active program on the network. Often the only way to find these elusive bugs is to watch for what network ports they open up.

The lsof tool is being preinstalled on some UNIX and Linux distributions and is available in RPM form on the installation disks of others such as Mandrake and RedHat Linux. To see if you have it preinstalled, type `lsof` and see if you get any response.

Installing lsof

1. Download the tar file from the book's CD-ROM or the official Web site.
   If the IP address you are downloading from doesn't have a reverse DNS record, the main FTP site will not allow you to connect to it. Try one of the alternate mirror sites listed.
2. Unzip the tar file.
3. You will see some text files and another tar file, something like lsof_4.68_src. This file has the sources in it. Untar this file and enter that directory.
4. Before you start the compilation process, you need to know the abbreviation code for your UNIX dialect. Since the lsof program is designed to be portable to just about any version of UNIX, you must tell it what flavor of UNIX you are running so the configure routine can set it up for your system.

   To find out the codes for the different versions of UNIX, type

   ```
   ./configure -h
   ```

   For example, the code for Linux is `linux` (easy enough, right?).
5. When you are ready, type the following command:

   ```
   ./Configure unix_dialect_code
   ```

   where you replace `unix_dialect_code` with the code for your specific system, for example, `linux`. This configures the program for compilation.
6. When the configuration is finished, type:

   ```
   make
   ```

7. This finishes the build process.

You are now ready to start using lsof.

Using lsof

The lsof program has many uses, and has extensive man pages and several README files for the different applications. However, this section concentrates only on a few specific commands that are useful for forensic research.

If you want to see all of the open files on your system at any given moment and the processes associated with them, type:

```
lsof -n
```

The -n option tells lsof *not* to attempt to do a DNS record on any IP addresses connecting to your machine. This speeds up the process considerably. The output will look something like Listing 11.2

Listing 11.2 lsof –n output

```
COMMAND      PID    USER    FD    TYPE    DEVICE      SIZE      NODE
xfs          903     xfs    0r    DIR       3,1       4096         2
atd          918  daemon   rtd    DIR       3,1       4096         2
atd          918  daemon   txt    REG       3,6      14384    273243
/usr/sbin/atd
sshd         962    root    cwd   DIR       3,1       4096         2
sshd         962    root    rtd   DIR       3,1       4096         2
sshd         962    root    txt   REG       3,6     331032    274118
/usr/sbin/sshd
dhcpcd       971    root    cwd   DIR       3,1       4096         2
dhcpcd       971    root    rtd   DIR       3,1       4096         2
dhcpcd       971    root    txt   REG       3,1      31576     78314
/sbin/dhcpcd
xinetd      1007    root    cwd   DIR       3,1       4096         2
5u   IPv4          1723          TCP 127.0.0.1:1024  (LISTEN)
xinetd      1007    root     8u   unix 0xc37a8540              1716
rwhod       1028    root    cwd   DIR       3,1       4096     61671
/var/spool/rwho
rwhod       1028    root    rtd   DIR       3,1       4096     61671
/var/spool/rwho
rwhod       1028     tim    cwd   DIR       3,1       4096     61671
/var/spool/rwho
crond       1112    root    cwd   DIR       3,1       4096        14
/var/spool
crond       1112    root    1w   FIFO       0,5                 1826
            1112    root    2w   FIFO              0,5     1827     pipe
nessusd     1166    root    cwd   DIR       3,1       4096         2
nessusd     1166    root    rtd   DIR       3,1       4096         2
nessusd     1166    root    txt   REG       3,6    1424003    323952
init           1    root    cwd   DIR       3,1       4096         2
init           1    root    rtd   DIR       3,1       4096         2
init           1    root    txt   REG       3,1      31384     75197
```

The connections in this listing look normal. The connection via the rwho service might give you pause. You would want to make sure that a valid user on your system is using this command legitimately. If this account belonged to a nontechnical secretary type, you might want to investigate this further.

You can also use lsof to look for a specific file. If you want to see if anyone was accessing your password file, you could use the following command:

```
lsof path/filename
```

Replace `path/filename` with the specific path and filename you are interested in, in this case, /etc/passwd. You have to give lsof the whole path for it to find the file.

Another way to use lsof is to have it list all the open socket files. This shows if there is a server listening that you don't know about. The format of this command is:

```
lsof -i
```

This produces output similar to Listing 11.3. You can see all the programs you are running, including sshd and nessusd, which are the daemons for Nessus and SSH. You can even see the individual connections to these services. It looks like someone is using the Nessus server at the moment. Checking the IP address, you can see that it is an internal user. In fact, it is your own machine! So there is nothing to worry about this time.

Listing 11.3 lsof –i Output

```
COMMAND   PID USER    FD     TYPE DEVICE SIZE NODE NAME
portmap   733 rpc     3u     IPv4   1417      UDP  *:sunrpc
portmap   733 rpc     4u     IPv4   1426      TCP  *:sunrpc (LISTEN)
sshd      962 root    3u     IPv4   1703      TCP  *:ssh (LISTEN)
xinetd   1007 root    5u     IPv4   1728      TCP
localhost.localdomain:1024 (LISTEN)
rwhod    1028 root    3u     IPv4   1747      UDP  *:who
nessusd  1166 root    4u     IPv4   1971      TCP  *:1241 (LISTEN)
nessusd  1564 root    5u     IPv4   1972      TCP  192.168.1.101:1241-
>192.168.1.2:1994 (ESTABLISHED)
```

You can specify a particular IP address or host to look for by putting an @ (at sign) and the address after the -i switch. For example:

```
lsof -i@192.168.1.0/24
```

shows any connections coming from within your network, assuming your internal network is 192.168.1.0/24.

Reviewing Log Files

You should also peruse your log files when you are looking for signs of trouble. The Windows log files can be found under Event Viewer in Administrative Tools. Under Linux and BSD-variant UNIX, log files are found in the /var/log/ directory. Other UNIX variants may have these files also though their location may be different. Table 11.2 lists the major Unix log files and their functions.

These files may be located in a slightly different location or may not exist on other versions of UNIX. Also, programs often create their own log files, which may be kept in the /var directory. You can use a text editor to view these files and search for certain text strings or number (such as IP addresses and user names).

Table 11.3 lists several operating system-level commands you can use on Linux and UNIX systems to scan these files quickly.

Table 11.2 UNIX Log Files

Log Files	Descriptions
/var/log/messages	Stores general system messages.
/var/log/secure	Stores authentication and security messages.
/var/log/wtmp	Stores a history of past logins and logouts.
/var/run/utmp	Stores a dynamic list of who is currently logged in.
/var/log/btmp	For Linux only. Stores any failed or bad logins.

Table 11.3 Linux and UNIX Scanning Commands

Commands	Descriptions
users	Shows the users currently on the system from the utmp file.
w	Shows users on the system with details such as where they logged in from (local or remote), IP address if they logged in remotely, and what commands they are executing. This command is highly useful for catching intruders in the act.
last	Shows the most recent contents of the wtmp file. This can also be quite useful in seeing who is logging onto your system, at what hours, and for how long. Listing 11.4 shows an example of this output.
lastb	For Linux only. This does the same thing as last but for btmp, the bad login log file. This can be the first place an intruder shows up with multiple failed login attempts.

Listing 11.4 Output from the last command
```
tony     pts/0        10.1.1.1      Sun Sep  5 23:06   still logged in
tony     pts/0        10.1.1.1      Sun Sep  5 22:44 - 23:04  (00:20)
tony     pts/0        10.1.1.1      Sun Sep  5 21:08 - 21:16  (00:07)
tony     pts/0        10.1.1.1      Sun Sep  5 20:20 - 20:36  (00:16)
reboot   system boot 2.4.18-14      Sun Sep  5 17:32 (05:34)
```

```
tony     tty1                        Sun Sep  5 17:29 - down(00:01)
tony     pts/2       10.1.1.1        Sat Sep  4 23:02 - 23:34 (00:32)
tony     pts/2       10.1.1.1        Sat Sep  4 22:36 - 22:36 (00:00)
hank     pts/0       10.1.1.200      Sat Sep  4 12:13 - 12:22 (00:08)
hank     pts/0       adsl-66-141-23-1 Fri Sep  3 23:53 - 23:53(00:00)
hank     pts/0       192.168.1.100   Fri Sep  3 14:47 - 14:47(00:00)
tony     pts/3       192.168.1.139   Fri Sep  3 09:59 - down (00:01)
larry    pts/3       adsl-65-67-132-2 Thu Sep  2 22:59 - 23:11(00:12)
tony     pts/3        10.1.1.1       Thu Sep  2 21:33 - 21:49  (00:16)
brian    pts/3       adsl-65-68-90-12 Thu Sep  2 18:23 - 18:31(00:07)
hank     pts/5       192.168.1.139   Thu Sep  2 14:29 - 15:35 (01:06)
sam      pts/        dialup-207-218-2 Wed Sep  1 22:24 - 00:40(02:16)
```

Keep in mind that if your system has been compromised, these programs may have been replaced with trojanized copies. A program like Tripwire (see Chapter 7) can help you determine if your system binaries have been tampered with. You should make known good copies of these binary files so you can execute from secure boot media instead of using the ones on the system. Also, remember that attackers will often selectively edit your log files to remove any trace of their actions. However, if they simply delete the log file, you may be able to recover it. You should also check all the log files as some neophytes only delete some of them.

Making Copies of Forensic Evidence

If you have verified that your system has been attacked or exploited, the first thing to do is take immediate action to stop the attack or limit that machine's exposure. Ideally, this would mean disconnecting the machine from the network to conduct further analysis. If this is not possible, you will still want to disable any suspect accounts, kill any rogue processes, and possibly block offending IP addresses at the firewall while you figure out what is going on.

Once you have eliminated the immediate danger, you should make a copy of any important data to look at offline per the tenet of good forensic analysis described earlier. You don't want to use your tools on live data. To do this, make a perfect copy of the data. This requires creating an image of the data rather than just copying it. You don't want to use the operating system's built-in copy functions because this might change file dates and insert other unwanted information. There are special tools for making these mirror-image copies. Unfortunately, there are not any good open source alternatives for the Windows platform right now (anyone want to sign up for a good Windows open source project?). The most popular program for Windows is Norton Ghost by Symantec, which retails for about $50.00. Under UNIX, there is an excellent open source program for doing this: dd, which stands for data dump.

dd: A Disk and File Replication Tool

dd	
Authors/primary contacts:	Paul Rubin, David MacKenzie, and Stuart Kem
Web site:	http://mirrors.kernel.org/gnu/fileutils/
Platforms:	Most Linux and UNIX
License:	GPL
Version reviewed:	N/A
Other resources:	
Type man dd at the command prompt.	

You can use the dd tool to literally read blocks of data right off the hard disk and make exact copies of it. It goes directly to the media rather than using the file system, so it can capture deleted data and other things that a file system can't see. It can be used to make bit-wise copies of your data on a UNIX file system. Because UNIX treats devices as files, you can take a whole hard drive and replicate it this way by simply copying the device file with a tool like dd.

Installing dd

You shouldn't have to install dd on most UNIX operating systems because it is a part of any UNIX file system. Type man dd to verify that you have it. If for some reason you don't have it, you can get it from the book's CD-ROM or as part of the GNU file utilities at the site above.

Using dd

There are two ways to use dd. One way is to make a **bit-wise** copy, that is, copy the data bit by bit. This creates a mirror image of the data on another hard disk or partition. The other way is to create a single large file. This is sometimes convenient for analysis and portability purposes. You can easily make a hash of the file for verification purposes. This file is often referred to as an **evidence file**, and many forensic programs are designed to use these files as input.

The basic format of the dd command is as follows:

```
dd -if=input_file -of=output_file options
```

where you replace *input_file* with the device file you want to copy, *output_file* with the filename you want to copy it to, and *options* with any dd options you want to use. The dd tool has many options, and Table 11.4 lists the basic ones.

So, if you want to copy the hard drive device /dev/hdc onto another hard drive, device hdd using dd, you could use the following command:

```
dd -if=dev/hdc of=/dev/hdd bs=1024
conv=noerror,notrunc,sync
```

Table 11.4 Basic dd Options

Options	Descriptions
bs=	Block size. The size of the blocks, in bytes, to copy at a time.
count=	Block count. How many blocks to copy. This is useful if you don't want to copy the whole file system if you have a very large hard drive or partition or limited space on your target media.
skip=	Skip x number of blocks before starting the copy. Again, this is useful for copying only a part of a file system.
conv=	Specifies any of several suboptions: notrunc—Won't truncate the output if an error occurs. This is recommended in most cases. noerror—Won't stop reading the input file in case of an error such as problems with the physical media. Also recommended. sync—Requires the noerror command before it. If an error occurs, this will place zeros in its place, maintaining the sequential continuity of the data.

This copies the contents of the device at /dev/hdc (probably your primary hard drive) to the device at /dev/hdd (probably your secondary hard drive). Make sure you understand which drives relate to which devices. As the sidebar on dd explains, a mistake here can be very costly!

Flamey the Tech Tip:

Be Very Careful with dd!

Do not use a low-level disk tool like dd lightly. One wrong command could easily erase your whole hard drive. Be particularly careful about the input and the output sources. Getting them mixed up can mean overwriting your evidence–or worse. Don't play with dd unless you have at least a basic understanding of hard-disk terms like blocks and sectors. Unlike user-friendly Windows, dd won't prompt you twice if you are about to do something stupid. So, like a good carpenter, read the manual twice . . . execute once. . . .

If you want to create a single big evidence file instead, you can use the following command to copy the file onto a new device.

```
dd if=/dev/hdc of=/mnt/storage/evidence.bin
```

You will probably want to mount a new device to capture this file. It should preferably be brand new media so as not to taint the evidence with old data. Remember, even deleted data will show up with these tools. If you can't use fresh media, make sure it is truly wiped clean with a disk utility. The dd tool has this capability. Read the man pages for more information on this option.

When you have all your evidence gathered, you are ready to analyze it further with a forensic toolkit. There are many excellent, professional-grade commercial toolkits. There are also some very good free toolkits available both for Windows and UNIX.

The Sleuth Kit/Autopsy Forensic Browser: A Collection of Forensic Tools for UNIX

The Sleuth Kit and Autopsy Forensic Browser
Author/primary contact: Brian Carrier
Web site: www.sleuthkit.org/sleuthkit/index.php
Platforms: Most UNIX
License: IBM Public License
Version reviewed: 1.70
Mailing lists:
The Sleuth Kit User's list
General questions and discussion on Sleuth Kit. Subscribe at
http://lists.sourceforge.net/lists/listinfo/sleuthkit-users
The Sleuth Kit Informer list
A monthly newsletter with news and tricks and tips. Subscribe at
www.sleuthkit.org/informer/index.php.
The Sleuth Kit Developer's list
For developers' questions and discussion. Subscribe at: http://lists.source-forge.net/lists/listinfo/sleuthkit-developers.
The Sleuth Kit Announcement list
A read-only list with major announcements or releases of Sleuth Kit and Autopsy Forensic Browser. Subscribe at
http://lists.sourceforge.net/lists/listinfo/sleuthkit-announce.
The Coroner's Toolkit (TCT) list
Information on TCT, which Sleuth Kit is based on. Subscribe at www.porcupine.org/forensics/tct.html#mailing_list.

The Sleuth Kit by Brian Carrier is a compilation of various forensic tools that run under UNIX. It includes parts of the popular Coroner's Toolkit by Dan Farmer as well as other contributions, and works with the Autopsy Forensic Browser, which is a nifty Web interface for Sleuth Kit. It is designed to work with data files such as those output by disk utilities like dd. It is quite feature rich; in fact, it has more depth than some of the commercial programs available. Some of the key functions are:

- Tracking of separate cases and multiple investigators
- Viewing allocated and deleted files and directories
- Accessing low-level file system structures
- Generating a timeline of file activity
- Sorting by file categories and checking extensions
- Searching image data by keywords
- Identifying graphic images and creating thumbnails
- Looking up hash databases, including the forensic standards NIST NSRL and Hash Keeper
- Creating investigator notes
- Generating reports

Installing Sleuth Kit

1. Download and unzip the file from the book's CD-ROM or the Web site.
2. In the directory, type:

   ```
   make
   ```

   The program automatically configures and compiles itself. It may prompt you with a few questions during the installation process.

Installing Autopsy Forensic Browser

This program is the graphical interface counterpart to Sleuth Kit. Using it with Sleuth Kit will make your life a whole lot easier and allow you to produce some nice graphical output. You can still use the Sleuth Kit command line tools separately if you want to.

1. Make sure you have Sleuth Kit installed before you start to install Autopsy.
2. Get the Autopsy file from the Web site or from the book's CD-ROM in the /autopsy directory.
3. Untar and unzip it with the usual `tar -zxvf` command.
4. Have the path to the Sleuth Kit program directory handy and think about where you want to put your "evidence locker"—the special directory where all your Sleuth Kit case data will reside.
5. Type the `make` command. This installs the program, and prompts you for your evidence locker directory and the directory that Sleuth Kit is installed in.

Using Sleuth Kit and Autopsy Forensic Browser

1. To start the server program, type `./autopsy &` from the /autopsy directory. This runs the server in the background on port 9999.
2. Make a note of the URL that is displayed when it starts up. You will need this to log into the server.

3. To connect to the server, open a browser and enter the URL you copied from the location window in Step 2. It will look something like this:

```
http://localhost:9999/654378938759042387490587/autopsy
```

The number between the slashes changes each time you run Sleuth Kit. Once you enter the URL, the main screen displays (see Figure 11.1).

Creating and Logging Into a Case

The Sleuth Kit with Autopsy Forensic Browser lets you monitor separate cases so you can track different incidents and customers. You will need to create a case for evidence files before you can work on them.

1. From the main screen, click on Create Case.
   The Create a New Case screen displays (see Figure 11.2).
2. Enter a case name. This will be the same directory that your evidence data is stored in. This directory is created under your main evidence locker directory specified at installation.

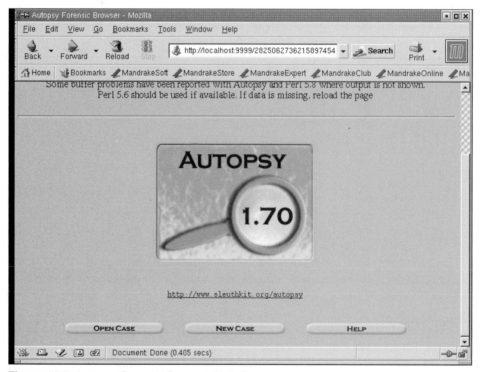

Figure 11.1 Autopsy Forensic Browser Main Screen

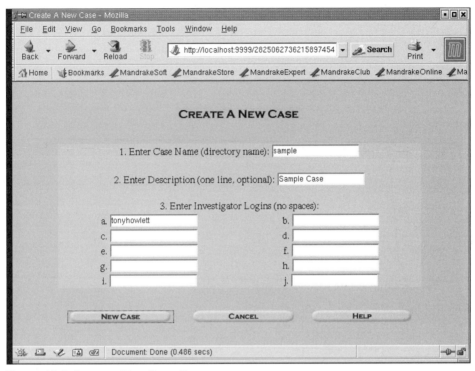

Figure 11.2 Create a New Case Screen

3. If you want, you can give the case a full name to better describe it.

4. You must create at least one investigator ID to have access to that case.

You can see the power of this program here. This feature allows you to have multiple people working on the case and track each one's access and actions. Click on New Case to finalize your input.

5. Once your case is created, the Case Gallery displays. This shows all the cases you have created. You can see the details on each case, including which investigators are working on them. Select your new case, click on OK, and log into your newly created case.

You have now created a case and are logged in and ready to start working on it.

Adding a Host

Once you have logged into your case, you need to define at least one host that you are going to examine. This host represents the specific machine you are investigating.

1. From the Case Gallery, click on Add Host. The Add a New Host Screen displays (see Figure 11.3).
2. Enter a host name.
3. If you want, enter a short description of the host.
4. Enter a time zone and clock skew, which is any variance from the time stamp on the main case file so Sleuth Kit tracks it separately in terms of any timestamps. This can be very important when reviewing multiple servers with different clock times.
5. If you want, add the optional information requested.
6. Click on Add Host to add the host and go back to the Case Gallery.
7. Follow this procedure for each host you have data on.

Adding an Image

You now need to add any data images for the hosts you have created. Use the copy of data you created using dd, Norton Ghost, or some other data replication utility.

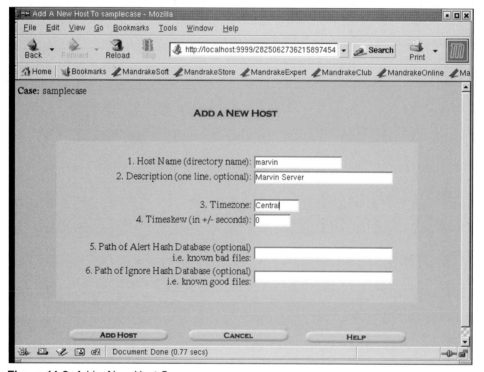

Figure 11.3 Add a New Host Screen

1. Select the host from the Host Gallery screen and click OK.
2. Click on Add Image. The Add a New Image screen displays (see Figure 11.4).
3. Enter the location and details of your image file. You have the option of copying the file into that host directory in your evidence locker or just creating a symbolic link to it. Be careful when moving your image files around too much, especially larger files, as this can cause data loss if a problem occurs during transfer.
4. Choose the file system type. This determines how Sleuth Kit looks at the data in the image.
5. Sleuth Kit automatically creates a hash file for you. You can check the validity of the hash against the data in the file at any time. This vastly increases the legitimacy of your efforts in a court of law.
6. You can add multiple images to each host. For example, you might have had to break a large drive up into several image files. Click on Add Image to add the image and return to the Main Case Gallery.

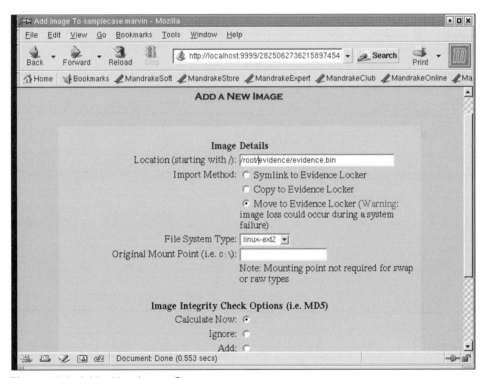

Figure 11.4 Add a New Image Screen

Analyzing Your Data

Now you are finally ready to begin your analysis. This may seem like a lot of setup work, but you will appreciate Sleuth Kit when you have a large number of images to manipulate or when you have to be able to produce a certain piece of data quickly. Go to the Image Gallery and click on the image you want to analyze. Table 11.5 lists the types of analysis you can perform on data images.

Sleuth Kit with Autopsy Forensic Browser gives you a powerful tool for organizing and analyzing forensic data that is on par with any professional lab in the country. This section has covered some of the basic functions, but whole books could be written about this great tool. Many commands and functions are not covered here. Read the online manual and other resources on the Web site for more details. The site also offers a monthly newsletter with interesting articles and tips for those in the forensic field.

Table 11.5 Sleuth Kit Analysis Types

Analysis Types	Descriptions
File Analysis	Shows the image as files and directories that the file system would see. Using this, you can also see files and folders that might normally be hidden by the operating system.
Keyword Search	Lets you search the entire image for certain keywords. This is useful if you are after a certain program file or even the mention of particular thing. Lawyers often use this type of feature when searching for incriminating evidence of wrongdoing on a person's hard drive. It can help find a needle in a haystack quite quickly (see Figure 11.5).
File Type	Sorts all the files by type or searches for a specific file type. This comes in handy if you are looking for all instances of a particular type of file, such all JPEGs or all MP3 files.
Image Details	Displays all the details on the image you are examining. This can be useful in data recovery jobs when you need to know where the data is physically laid out.
MetaData	Shows you the underlying directory and file structures in your image. This can be used to find deleted content and see other items the file system doesn't normally show you.
Data Unit	Lets you delve deeper into any file you have found and look at the actual file content, either in ASCII or hex.

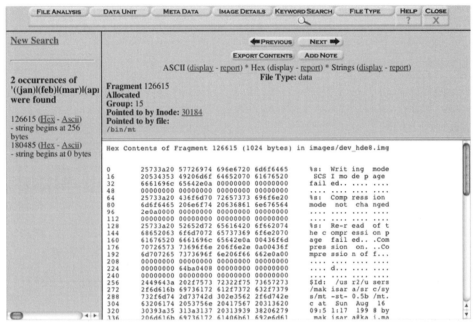

Figure 11.5 Results of Keyword Search

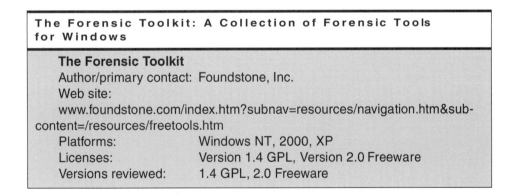

The Forensic Toolkit is another great free program from the folks at Foundstone. This collection of tools can help you examine Window-based file systems and gather information for your forensic investigation. Version 1.4 of the program is fully open source licensed under the GPL. Version 2.0 is freeware and is usable for commercial purposes, but it has limitations on adding or changing the program and is not currently available in source form.

Note that these tools work only on NTFS file systems. If you want to examine any FAT32 partitions, you will have to use different tools.

Installing Forensic Toolkit

1. Download the appropriate file from the Web site (either version 1.4 or 2.0, depending on whether you want the full open source version or not).

2. Unzip the file into its own directory. This completes the installation.

Using Forensic Toolkit

The tools consist of various command line utilities that generate various statistics and information on the file system in question. To execute a command, open up a command line window and type it (you must be in the appropriate directory). The following sections describe the individual tools.

Afind   This utility searches for files by their access time. It does this without modifying any file access information, as the normal Windows utilities do. The basic format is:

```
afind search_directory options
```

where you replace *search_directory* with the directory to search and replace *options* with the appropriate search options. Table 11.6 lists the basic options.

Hfind   This tool finds hidden files in the Windows operating system. It shows files that have the hidden attribute bit turned on and those hidden using the Windows NT special directory/system attribute method. The format is:

```
hfind path
```

Table 11.6 Basic Afind Search Options

Options	Descriptions
-f *filename*	Gives the access time information for *filename*.
-s *X*	Finds files that were accessed within *X* seconds.
-m *X*	Finds files that were accessed within *X* minutes.
-d *X*	Finds files that were accessed within *X* days.
-a *d/m/y-h:m:s*	Finds files that were accessed after the date and time indicated.

where *path* is replaced with the path you want to search. It lists the hidden files and their last date and time of access. Be careful of searching the whole hard drive as this could take a while.

Sfind This tool finds hidden datastreams on the hard disk. These are different from hidden files in that they won't be seen on the hard disk when you click on the option to view hidden files. Hidden datastreams are an NTFS feature that allows certain programs to access alternate datastreams. The files are linked to a parent file, which is visible, but may not be deleted when the file system deletes the parent file. They may be used to hide data or malware. The format of the sfind command is:

        sfind *path*

where *path* is the path you want to search. Again, this may take quite some time if you are searching the root directory of a large drive.

FileStat This command creates a full listing of file attributes, including security information. It only works on one file at a time. You can pipe the output into a text file for further processing. This command generates quite a lot of information, including a lot of file descriptor information you don't normally see. Listing 11.5 shows a sample of this information for a file called test.txt.

Listing 11.5 FileStat Output

```
Creation Time - 01/10/2004   03:18:40
Last Mod Time - 01/10/2004   03:18:40
Last Access Time - 01/10/2004   03:18:40
Main File Size - 11
File Attrib Mask - Arch
Dump complete...Dumping C:\temp\test.txt...
SD is valid.
SD is 188 bytes long.
SD revision is 1 == SECURITY_DESCRIPTOR_REVISION1
SD's Owner is Not NULL
SD's Owner-Defaulted flag is FALSE
  SID = TONYVPRDESKTOP/Tony Howlett    S-1-5-21--1816634606
SD's Group-Defaulted flag is FALSE
  SID = TONYVPRDESKTOP/None    S-1-5-21--181663460--953405037-
SD's DACL is Present
SD's DACL-Defaulted flag is FALSE
    ACL has 4 ACE(s), 112 bytes used, 0 bytes free
    ACL revision is 2 == ACL_REVISION2
  SID = BUILTIN/Administrators    S-1-5-32-544
    ACE 0 is an ACCESS_ALLOWED_ACE_TYPE
    ACE 0 size = 24
    ACE 0 flags = 0x00
    ACE 0 mask = 0x001f01ff -R -W -X -D -DEL_CHILD
    -CHANGE_PERMS -TAKE_OWN
```

```
   SID = NT AUTHORITY/SYSTEM    S-1-5-18
     ACE 1 is an ACCESS_ALLOWED_ACE_TYPE
     ACE 1 size = 20
     ACE 1 flags = 0x00
     ACE 1 mask = 0x001f01ff -R -W -X -D -DEL_CHILD -CHANGE_PERMS -
TAKE_OWN
   SID = TONYVPRDESKTOP/Tony Howlett    S-1-5-21--181663460-
     ACE 2 is an ACCESS_ALLOWED_ACE_TYPE
     ACE 2 size = 36
     ACE 2 flags = 0x00
     ACE 2 mask = 0x001f01ff -R -W -X -D -DEL_CHILD -CHANGE_PERMS -
TAKE_OWN
   SID = BUILTIN/Users    S-1-5-32-545
     ACE 3 is an ACCESS_ALLOWED_ACE_TYPE
     ACE 3 size = 24
     ACE 3 flags = 0x00
     ACE 3 mask = 0x001200a9 -R -X
SD's SACL is Not Present
Stream 1:
  Type: Security
  Stream name = ?? ??Size: 188

Stream 2:
  Type: Data
  Stream name = ?? ??Size: 11

Stream 3:
  Type: Unknown
  Stream name = ?? ??Size: 64
```

Hunt   This tool can be used to generate a lot of information on a system using the Windows NULL session capabilities. Depending on the permissiveness of your system, it could generate significant information such as users lists, shares, and services running. The command takes the following format:

```
        hunt system_name
```

where *system_name* represents the proper Windows host name of the system you want to run hunt on. Listing 11.6 represents an example of this output.

Listing 11.6 Hunt Output

```
share = IPC$ - Remote IPC

share = print$ - Printer Drivers

share = SharedDocs -
```

```
share = Printer3 - Acrobat Distiller

share = Printer2 - Acrobat PDFWriter

User = Administrator, , , Built-in account for administering the
  computer/domain

Admin is TONYVPRDESKTOP\Administrator
User = Howlett, , ,

User = Guest, , , Built-in account for guest access to the
  computer/domain

User = HelpAssistant, Remote Desktop Help Assistant Account,
  Account for Providing Remote Assistance

User = SUPPORT_388945a0, CN=Microsoft
  Corporation,L=Redmond,S=Washington,C=US, , This is a vendor's
  account for the Help and Support Service

User = Tony Howlett,
```

In this listing you can see two users you don't normally see in the User Accounts section on your Windows system: the HelpAssistant and SUPPORT users. These are system-level users for internal programs (the Remote assistance features and the annoying Notify Support feature that pops up every time a program bombs out). Other hidden users concealed by a skilled intruder could be revealed using this tool.

This chapter is not meant to be a comprehensive listing of all possible forensic tools, but these tools should give you enough to get started with basic forensic activity on just about any system. If you are doing this as a career or have an involved investigation, there are many other tools available. For a good listing of open source forensic tools, visit www.opensourceforensics.org/.

More on Open Source Software

You know now how to keep your data safe inside and outside your network and how to detect and investigate attacks on your systems and networks. This book has reviewed dozens of open source security tools covering just about every aspect of information security. However, this just scratches the surface of what is available. For each category, I tried to pick the best tool (in my opinion) to showcase, but there were often scores of others to choose from. In addition, there are open source software alternatives for just about every type of application you can think of, including word processors, network management, multimedia, and more. The list goes on and on.

This final chapter gives you some resources for further investigation of open source security tools and how to get involved in the open source community.

Open Source Resources

If you want to further explore the world of open source software, check out the many resources on the Internet.

USENET Newsgroups

USENET is a network of servers that hosts discussion lists on subjects as varied as politics, hobbies, and of course computers. These forums are called **newsgroups** and they act as a sort of community bulletin boards for people interested in particular topics. USENET got its start as a technical discussion group, and there are still a wide variety of groups covering technical subjects. Although spammers and the use of Web-based forums have dulled the effectiveness of USENET, there are still a number of active USENET newsgroups related to open source.

You need a USENET newsreader to access USENET. Most modern browsers have one built in. In Internet Explorer, from the Tools menu choose Mail and News, and then select Read News. You also need a valid USENET News Server to subscribe to. ISPs used to provide this service as part of their standard offering and many still do. If yours doesn't, there are public USENET servers you can connect to. Check out www.newzbots.com to find public USENET feeds. Once you've subscribed to a server, here are a few of the general groups that might be of interest. There are many others related to specific operating systems or programs.

- comp.sci.opensource
- comp.os.linux.advocacy
- comp.os.unix.bsd.freebsd.misc
- comp.os.unix.bsd.openbsd.misc

You can also go to the Google Groups site (click on Groups at www.google.com). In addition to having access to current postings and groups, it houses the former Dejanews site, which was an archive of USENET news discussions going to back to 1992. However, the use of USENET is declining and many forums are moving to Web-based forums or moderated mailing lists to cut down on the noise-to-signal ratio in the postings.

Mailing Lists

There are many mailing lists related to open source. Most are specific to a particular program. They are used to provide support and collaboration on the project. Check the Web site or documentation for your program to find out if it has a mailing list and how to subscribe. The tools discussed in this book have pertinent mailing lists shown at the beginning of each tool section. There are also some general discussion lists.

- Linux general discussion: http://computers.rootsweb.com/
  To subscribe, send an e-mail to
  LINUX-L-request@COMPUTERS.rootsweb.com
  and put SUBSCRIBE on the Subject line.
- BSD mailing list archive: http://www.hu.freebsd.org/hu/arch/

Web Sites

There are tons of Web sites about open source software. Any project of a decent size will have a Web site dedicated to it. There are also some good general information sites. The following are great sites to start if you are just getting into open source.

SourceForge   SourceForge (sourceforge.net) is a great Web site for support and information on open source projects (see Figure 12.1). It is run by the Open Source Development Network, which funds the site with ads and by selling its open source development

Figure 12.15 SourceForge Web Site

software. SourceForge provides a forum for discussing open source software and has many resources for open source projects. If you have a budding open source program, SourceForge will provide you with a home page, forums, project management tools, a place to store your program for download, and many other resources. This is all provided for free, although there are some strings attached to your use of them.

It is also a great place to look through the over 80,000 open source software projects cataloged there, and they are searchable by category and platform. Granted that some of them are probably half-baked ideas with minimal support, but there are also thousands of full-featured, time-tested programs. You can get involved with any of the projects or get feedback or support there. SourceForge attracts hundred of thousands of users and creators of the latest open source software. If you are starting up a project, it's a great place to look for recruits.

Slashdot   Slashdot (www.slashdot.org) is a site for news on all things open source. It is written and maintained by and for hardcore coders, mostly open source based. Go there to get the latest scuttlebutt, rumors, and breaking news as well as all kinds of interesting articles and opinions. It is part geek shoptalk, part hard news and articles, and part satire and commentary. In fact, it has become part of the techie lexicon to say a site has been "slash-dotted" when it receives an overwhelming amount of traffic from being mentioned on the site.

Freshmeat   Freshmeat (www.freshmeat.net) is a no-nonsense site for discussing and developing open source software. It is kind of a combination of Slashdot and SourceForge but on a smaller scale. This might be a plus for some who are intimidated by Source-Forge's size and the number of options and resources. It also has articles and discussion groups as well as directly offering many projects for download.

Open Source Initiative   The Open Source Initiative (www.opensource.org) is an organization dedicated to promoting and refining the concept of open source software development. It offers a formal definition of what open source software should consist of and offers certification of such status, even though many people may claim this is a moving target and open source by definition is constantly changing and indefinable. Only a handful of programs so far bear their approval seal, but they are some of the bigger ones such as the Apache Web server and the Sendmail program. I feel that it's a move in the right direction for the future of open source: Only once the open source world organizes itself and agrees to certain standards will it gain a significant foothold in corporate America. Standardization promotes adoption.

Free Software Foundation   This site (www.fsf.org) is the home base for one of the two major camps in the open source world. The FSF houses the GNU project as well as their official software products. It is also the place to find the GPL license and learn all about how it works. Some might see their view of advocating that all software should be free as radical, but they have certainly provided the base for much of the open source software available today.

There are many, many other sites on open source software, and new ones are being established all the time. Use your favorite search engine and enter the terms "open source security" or "open source software" and see where it takes you.

Joining the Open Source Movement

Once you've used the open source security tools in this book and benefited from them, you may feel like you want to get more involved. In most cases, the software is free and you are not obligated to do anything in return for the benefit you receive. However, a lot of time and effort went into building and maintaining the software you are using, all of it by volunteers. The only way that open source continues to work and grow is by the collective effort. This may sound vaguely socialist to some, especially to employees of commercial software concerns, but it is not that different from your local PTA or little league baseball organization. It is the people involved who make open source software great.

In doing so, you will not only help keep open source alive and growing, but also meet friends who have the same interests, make valuable business contacts in your field, and learn a lot in the process about project management, working with others, and of course technical knowledge and experience.

You don't have to be a coding guru to contribute. The key to helping the open source movement prosper is just to participate. There are a number of ways you can get involved, ranging from taking a few hours of your time to this work becoming a second job.

Bug Finder/Beta Tester

Even if you are just a user and have no interest in coding, you can help your favorite open source security tool. Most major projects have bug tracking mailing lists, and some have more complicated systems for reporting issues. If you are working with the program and find something that doesn't work right, report it and see if it can be fixed. In the process of getting your problem fixed, you'll help the developers track down bugs and improve the program. Of course, you will want to make sure that the problem you are having is a software bug and not an installation error on your part, but the people on the lists are usually more than happy to set you straight.

To report bugs properly, make sure that you gather all the environmental variables and try to duplicate the problem to figure out under exactly what conditions the error happens. Things like operating system, version of the program, settings, hardware, and so on are all important. Also make sure you have any error messages, log files, or core dumps for the developers to analyze.

You can also be a beta tester of the latest code. Some projects offer you the ability to run either "stable" or "experimental" code. While most users will use the stable code, you can be a trailblazer and try the experimental or beta versions. Keep in mind that there may be hiccups while using this software, for example, sometimes the new code will break things that worked before. If you are going to run beta code, you will probably want to run it on a test machine before putting it into production.

Other projects may distribute beta code to a limited list of testers. They will want the first users of the code to be experienced users who know they are using beta software. That way, they can rule out the usual newbie mistakes and have users who understand how the software works and can accurately describe their problems. So, you probably shouldn't volunteer to be a beta user until you have some experience with the software. When you are ready, ask the key developers to be put on this list. This way you can help improve the software for future users. The side benefit of this is that you will be the first to get cutting-edge features and you can be instrumental in deciding what new features get added.

Participate in Discussion Groups and Support Other Users

Most open source projects have a mailing list for discussion and technical questions. You should subscribe to this list even if you don't plan on participating right away. You don't have to be an active poster to the list to gain some benefits. It's okay to just "lurk" and read the questions and answers that are posted. I have learned a lot of things about the software that I never would have found out, just by casually following the mailing list discussions. A word of warning, though: Some of these lists are very active and have dozens of messages posted a day. This can be overwhelming for some, especially if you are already over-worked like most system administrators. But even reading only an occasional message that interests you can be of value. If you feel you are getting too much e-mail, consider sub-scribing to a "digest" version of the list, which is a single message you get daily or weekly that contains a compilation of all the messages posted. This way you only get one message and can sort through it when you have the time. Still, make sure you understand how to unsubscribe from a list before subscribing so you can get off the list easily if the volume is too much for you to handle.

Most open source mailing lists use a software package called Major Domo to manage their lists (this is also an open source project!). The standard commands for subscribing and unsubscribing on this kind of system are as follows.

- Subscribe: Send a message to the list manager address (usually found on the Web site) with the word "Subscribe" in the subject and body of your message. You may get a message to confirm that you do want to be on the list. Once you reply, you'll start getting messages.
- Unsubscribe: Send a message to the list manager address, and put the word "Unsubscribe" in the subject and body of the message.

Mailing lists can be operated as moderated or unmoderated forums. In the unmoderated format, anyone can post anything and the messages go up immediately. This is the best kind of list for getting information quickly. However, many unmoderated lists quickly fill up with off-topic conversations, arguments, and flame-wars. That's why most lists are now moderated, which means that a person, the list moderator, must review each post, decide if it's relevant to the list charter, and approves it to be posted. This makes for a much lower message volume that is always relevant, but it may mean your posts for help on a subject are delayed for several days until the moderator gets around to it. And moderators will usually shut down list activity for holidays (moderators deserve holidays too), so getting answers during a holiday may be spotty.

Once you are confident that you can hang with the big dogs, begin making some posts, answer some easy questions, and provide an opinion here or there. This will take the load off of more technical developers by having others answer basic questions, and it will also provide a wider base of knowledge for the whole project. After all, you may have experience with a specific configuration or platform that no one else has—you may be operating in an unusual environment or you might have a different take on a particular question or issue. Chances are that someone out there can use your help. You will feel good about helping others and you'll be amazed at how thankful and gracious the people you help will be. If only your internal users could be so nice and grateful!

Provide Resources to the Project

Here is something you can do even if you don't have programming abilities or much experience with the software. Open source projects generally don't have any revenue to support any expenses incurred in the development and maintenance of the software. While most of the labor is provided by the volunteers, there are still the issues of where to host the Web site for the project, what hardware to put it on, and many others. Again, the participants usually donate most of this. If you have an old machine that could be used as a Web server, let the key people know. You'd be surprised what an old machine can do running Linux and Apache. If your company is amenable to it, see if you could offer to host the project Web site on company bandwidth. Your company might not want to do it if it's a big project, but for small projects just getting off the ground bandwidth utilization will probably be minimal and most of it will be during non-office hours. If you have Web design skills, offer to put up a Web site. If your personal ISP provides free Web site space, offer to use that for the project. A nonprofit endeavor usually falls under your terms of service for personal Web space. Finally, some open source packages even accept good old green backs as a "donation" for using the software. You might be able to convince your company to put up a few bucks as an alternative to paying retail for off-the-shelf software. Anything you can think of will usually come in handy for an open source project. Graphic design skill to design a logo, e-mail accounts to support the mailing lists, legal help in crafting the licenses—all these things represent creative ways to help your favorite open source project.

Patronize Companies That Use or Support Open Source Products

While you don't have to spend your budget dollars on the software, you do spend money on other things. When buying hardware, software, or services, make it a point to give vendors who use or support open source software special consideration. After all, if companies can be commercially viable by using open source software as a key part of their offerings, it only strengthens the cause. Companies such as Sun, IBM, and Dell are heavily promoting open source.

More Open Source Security Tools

You should now understand the basic concepts of information security and how to apply them to your company using open source security tools. Using the programs and information in this book, you can make your systems and network much more secure from the dangers of computer crime. We have covered programs that will bring greater confidentiality, integrity, and availability to your networks, systems, and data, all for a price that should fit into everyone's budget.

Hopefully, you understand that good information security is more than just programs and technology. It is also about processes and people. It takes a combination of good people, processes, and technology to truly secure your network. Open source security tools can give you best-of-breed software to build a solid foundation for information security.

The open source movement is growing every day, increasing its visibility and legitimacy. I hope that this book encourages you to become more involved and contribute to the effort of creating quality security tools using the open source framework. It is a lot of fun, you will learn a lot, and you will feel good about making the Internet and networks more secure. Perhaps a future edition of this book will feature an open source security tool written by you.

Open Source Licenses

This appendix contains both the GNU General Public License and the BSD Open Source License. You can get these on the Web from www.gnu.org/licenses/gpl.html and www.opensource.org/licenses/bsd-license.php, respectively.

The GNU General Public License (GPL)

GNU GENERAL PUBLIC LICENSE
Version 2, June 1991

Copyright (C) 1989, 1991 Free Software Foundation, Inc.
59 Temple Place, Suite 330, Boston, MA 02111-1307 USA
Everyone is permitted to copy and distribute verbatim copies
of this license document, but changing it is not allowed.

Preamble

The licenses for most software are designed to take away your
freedom to share and change it. By contrast, the GNU General Public
License is intended to guarantee your freedom to share and change free
software—to make sure the software is free for all its users. This
General Public License applies to most of the Free Software
Foundation's software and to any other program whose authors commit to
using it. (Some other Free Software Foundation software is covered by
the GNU Library General Public License instead.) You can apply it to
your programs, too.

When we speak of free software, we are referring to freedom, not
price. Our General Public Licenses are designed to make sure that you
have the freedom to distribute copies of free software (and charge for
this service if you wish), that you receive source code or can get it
if you want it, that you can change the software or use pieces of it
in new free programs; and that you know you can do these things.

To protect your rights, we need to make restrictions that forbid
anyone to deny you these rights or to ask you to surrender the rights.
These restrictions translate to certain responsibilities for you if you
distribute copies of the software, or if you modify it.

For example, if you distribute copies of such a program, whether
gratis or for a fee, you must give the recipients all the rights that
you have. You must make sure that they, too, receive or can get the
source code. And you must show them these terms so they know their
rights.

We protect your rights with two steps: (1) copyright the software, and
(2) offer you this license which gives you legal permission to copy,
distribute and/or modify the software.

Also, for each author's protection and ours, we want to make certain
that everyone understands that there is no warranty for this free
software. If the software is modified by someone else and passed on, we
want its recipients to know that what they have is not the original, so
that any problems introduced by others will not reflect on the original
authors' reputations.

Finally, any free program is threatened constantly by software
patents. We wish to avoid the danger that redistributors of a free
program will individually obtain patent licenses, in effect making the
program proprietary. To prevent this, we have made it clear that any
patent must be licensed for everyone's free use or not licensed at all.

The precise terms and conditions for copying, distribution and
modification follow.

GNU GENERAL PUBLIC LICENSE
TERMS AND CONDITIONS FOR COPYING, DISTRIBUTION AND MODIFICATION

0. This License applies to any program or other work which contains
a notice placed by the copyright holder saying it may be distributed

under the terms of this General Public License. The "Program", below, refers to any such program or work, and a "work based on the Program" means either the Program or any derivative work under copyright law: that is to say, a work containing the Program or a portion of it, either verbatim or with modifications and/or translated into another language. (Hereinafter, translation is included without limitation in the term "modification".) Each licensee is addressed as "you".

Activities other than copying, distribution and modification are not covered by this License; they are outside its scope. The act of running the Program is not restricted, and the output from the Program is covered only if its contents constitute a work based on the Program (independent of having been made by running the Program). Whether that is true depends on what the Program does.

1. You may copy and distribute verbatim copies of the Program's source code as you receive it, in any medium, provided that you conspicuously and appropriately publish on each copy an appropriate copyright notice and disclaimer of warranty; keep intact all the notices that refer to this License and to the absence of any warranty; and give any other recipients of the Program a copy of this License along with the Program.

You may charge a fee for the physical act of transferring a copy, and you may at your option offer warranty protection in exchange for a fee.

2. You may modify your copy or copies of the Program or any portion of it, thus forming a work based on the Program, and copy and distribute such modifications or work under the terms of Section 1 above, provided that you also meet all of these conditions:

a) You must cause the modified files to carry prominent notices stating that you changed the files and the date of any change.

b) You must cause any work that you distribute or publish, that in whole or in part contains or is derived from the Program or any part thereof, to be licensed as a whole at no charge to all third parties under the terms of this License.

c) If the modified program normally reads commands interactively when run, you must cause it, when started running for such interactive use in the most ordinary way, to print or display an announcement including an appropriate copyright notice and a

notice that there is no warranty (or else, saying that you provide
a warranty) and that users may redistribute the program under
these conditions, and telling the user how to view a copy of this
License. (Exception: if the Program itself is interactive but
does not normally print such an announcement, your work based on
the Program is not required to print an announcement.)

These requirements apply to the modified work as a whole. If
identifiable sections of that work are not derived from the Program,
and can be reasonably considered independent and separate works in
themselves, then this License, and its terms, do not apply to those
sections when you distribute them as separate works. But when you
distribute the same sections as part of a whole which is a work based
on the Program, the distribution of the whole must be on the terms of
this License, whose permissions for other licensees extend to the
entire whole, and thus to each and every part regardless of who wrote it.

Thus, it is not the intent of this section to claim rights or contest
your rights to work written entirely by you; rather, the intent is to
exercise the right to control the distribution of derivative or
collective works based on the Program.

In addition, mere aggregation of another work not based on the Program
with the Program (or with a work based on the Program) on a volume of
a storage or distribution medium does not bring the other work under
the scope of this License.

  3. You may copy and distribute the Program (or a work based on it,
under Section 2) in object code or executable form under the terms of
Sections 1 and 2 above provided that you also do one of the following:

  a) Accompany it with the complete corresponding machine-readable
  source code, which must be distributed under the terms of Sections
  1 and 2 above on a medium customarily used for software interchange; or,

  b) Accompany it with a written offer, valid for at least three
  years, to give any third party, for a charge no more than your
  cost of physically performing source distribution, a complete
  machine-readable copy of the corresponding source code, to be
  distributed under the terms of Sections 1 and 2 above on a medium
  customarily used for software interchange; or,

c) Accompany it with the information you received as to the offer to distribute corresponding source code. (This alternative is allowed only for noncommercial distribution and only if you received the program in object code or executable form with such an offer, in accord with Subsection b above.)

The source code for a work means the preferred form of the work for making modifications to it. For an executable work, complete source code means all the source code for all modules it contains, plus any associated interface definition files, plus the scripts used to control compilation and installation of the executable. However, as a special exception, the source code distributed need not include anything that is normally distributed (in either source or binary form) with the major components (compiler, kernel, and so on) of the operating system on which the executable runs, unless that component itself accompanies the executable.

If distribution of executable or object code is made by offering access to copy from a designated place, then offering equivalent access to copy the source code from the same place counts as distribution of the source code, even though third parties are not compelled to copy the source along with the object code.

4. You may not copy, modify, sublicense, or distribute the Program except as expressly provided under this License. Any attempt otherwise to copy, modify, sublicense or distribute the Program is void, and will automatically terminate your rights under this License. However, parties who have received copies, or rights, from you under this License will not have their licenses terminated so long as such parties remain in full compliance.

5. You are not required to accept this License, since you have not signed it. However, nothing else grants you permission to modify or distribute the Program or its derivative works. These actions are prohibited by law if you do not accept this License. Therefore, by modifying or distributing the Program (or any work based on the Program), you indicate your acceptance of this License to do so, and all its terms and conditions for copying, distributing or modifying the Program or works based on it.

6. Each time you redistribute the Program (or any work based on the Program), the recipient automatically receives a license from the original licensor to copy, distribute or modify the Program subject to these terms and conditions. You may not impose any further

restrictions on the recipients' exercise of the rights granted herein.
You are not responsible for enforcing compliance by third parties to
this License.

7. If, as a consequence of a court judgment or allegation of patent
infringement or for any other reason (not limited to patent issues),
conditions are imposed on you (whether by court order, agreement or
otherwise) that contradict the conditions of this License, they do not
excuse you from the conditions of this License. If you cannot
distribute so as to satisfy simultaneously your obligations under this
License and any other pertinent obligations, then as a consequence you
may not distribute the Program at all. For example, if a patent
license would not permit royalty-free redistribution of the Program by
all those who receive copies directly or indirectly through you, then
the only way you could satisfy both it and this License would be to
refrain entirely from distribution of the Program.

If any portion of this section is held invalid or unenforceable under
any particular circumstance, the balance of the section is intended to
apply and the section as a whole is intended to apply in other
circumstances.

It is not the purpose of this section to induce you to infringe any
patents or other property right claims or to contest validity of any
such claims; this section has the sole purpose of protecting the
integrity of the free software distribution system, which is
implemented by public license practices. Many people have made
generous contributions to the wide range of software distributed
through that system in reliance on consistent application of that
system; it is up to the author/donor to decide if he or she is willing
to distribute software through any other system and a licensee cannot
impose that choice.

This section is intended to make thoroughly clear what is believed to
be a consequence of the rest of this License.

8. If the distribution and/or use of the Program is restricted in
certain countries either by patents or by copyrighted interfaces, the
original copyright holder who places the Program under this License
may add an explicit geographical distribution limitation excluding
those countries, so that distribution is permitted only in or among
countries not thus excluded. In such case, this License incorporates
the limitation as if written in the body of this License.

9. The Free Software Foundation may publish revised and/or new versions of the General Public License from time to time. Such new versions will be similar in spirit to the present version, but may differ in detail to address new problems or concerns.

Each version is given a distinguishing version number. If the Program specifies a version number of this License which applies to it and "any later version", you have the option of following the terms and conditions either of that version or of any later version published by the Free Software Foundation. If the Program does not specify a version number of this License, you may choose any version ever published by the Free Software Foundation.

10. If you wish to incorporate parts of the Program into other free programs whose distribution conditions are different, write to the author to ask for permission. For software which is copyrighted by the Free Software Foundation, write to the Free Software Foundation; we sometimes make exceptions for this. Our decision will be guided by the two goals of preserving the free status of all derivatives of our free software and of promoting the sharing and reuse of software generally.

NO WARRANTY

11. BECAUSE THE PROGRAM IS LICENSED FREE OF CHARGE, THERE IS NO WARRANTY FOR THE PROGRAM, TO THE EXTENT PERMITTED BY APPLICABLE LAW. EXCEPT WHEN OTHERWISE STATED IN WRITING THE COPYRIGHT HOLDERS AND/OR OTHER PARTIES PROVIDE THE PROGRAM "AS IS" WITHOUT WARRANTY OF ANY KIND, EITHER EXPRESSED OR IMPLIED, INCLUDING, BUT NOT LIMITED TO, THE IMPLIED WARRANTIES OF MERCHANTABILITY AND FITNESS FOR A PARTICULAR PURPOSE. THE ENTIRE RISK AS TO THE QUALITY AND PERFORMANCE OF THE PROGRAM IS WITH YOU. SHOULD THE PROGRAM PROVE DEFECTIVE, YOU ASSUME THE COST OF ALL NECESSARY SERVICING,REPAIR OR CORRECTION.

12. IN NO EVENT UNLESS REQUIRED BY APPLICABLELAW OR AGREED TO IN WRITING WILL ANY COPYRIGHT HOLDER, OR ANY OTHER PARTY WHO MAY MODIFY AND/OR REDISTRIBUTE THE PROGRAM AS PERMITTED ABOVE, BE LIABLE TO YOU FOR DAMAGES,INCLUDING ANY GENERAL, SPECIAL, INCIDENTAL OR CONSEQUENTIAL DAMAGES ARISING OUT OF THE USE OR INABILITY TO USE THE PROGRAM (INCLUDING BUT NOT LIMITED TO LOSS OF DATA OR DATA BEING RENDERED INACCURATE OR LOSSES SUSTAINED BY YOU OR THIRD PARTIES OR A FAILURE OF THE PROGRAM TO OPERATE WITH ANY OTHER PROGRAMS), EVEN IF SUCH HOLDER OR OTHER PARTY HAS BEEN ADVISED OF THE POSSIBILITY OF SUCH DAMAGES.

END OF TERMS AND CONDITIONS

How to Apply These Terms to Your New Programs

If you develop a new program, and you want it to be of the greatest
possible use to the public, the best way to achieve this is to make it
free software which everyone can redistribute and change under these terms.

To do so, attach the following notices to the program. It is safest
to attach them to the start of each source file to most effectively
convey the exclusion of warranty; and each file should have at least
the "copyright" line and a pointer to where the full notice is found.

<one line to give the program's name and a brief idea of what it does.>
Copyright (C) <year> <name of author>

This program is free software; you can redistribute it and/or modify
it under the terms of the GNU General Public License as published by
the Free Software Foundation; either version 2 of the License, or
(at your option) any later version.

This program is distributed in the hope that it will be useful,
but WITHOUT ANY WARRANTY; without even the implied warranty of
MERCHANTABILITY or FITNESS FOR A PARTICULAR PURPOSE. See the
GNU General Public License for more details.

You should have received a copy of the GNU General Public License
along with this program; if not, write to the Free Software
Foundation, Inc., 59 Temple Place, Suite 330, Boston, MA 02111-1307USA.

Also add information on how to contact you by electronic and paper mail.

If the program is interactive, make it output a short notice like this
when it starts in an interactive mode:

Gnomovision version 69, Copyright (C) year name of author
Gnomovision comes with ABSOLUTELY NO WARRANTY; for details type
'show w'.
This is free software, and you are welcome to redistribute it
under certain conditions; type 'show c' for details.

The hypothetical commands 'show w' and 'show c' should show the appropriate parts of the General Public License. Of course, the commands you use may be called something other than 'show w' and 'show c'; they could even be mouse-clicks or menu items—whatever suits your program.

You should also get your employer (if you work as a programmer) or your school, if any, to sign a "copyright disclaimer" for the program, if necessary. Here is a sample; alter the names:

> Yoyodyne, Inc., hereby disclaims all copyright interest in the program 'Gnomovision' (which makes passes at compilers) written by James Hacker.

<signature of Ty Coon>, 1 April 1989
Ty Coon, President of Vice

This General Public License does not permit incorporating your program into proprietary programs. If your program is a subroutine library, you may consider it more useful to permit linking proprietary applications with the library. If this is what you want to do, use the GNU Library General Public License instead of this License.

The BSD Open Source License

The following is a BSD license template. To generate your own license, change the values of OWNER, ORGANIZATION and YEAR from their original values as given here, and substitute your own.

> *Note*: The advertising clause in the license appearing on BSD Unix files was officially rescinded by the Director of the Office of Technology Licensing of the University of California on July 22 1999. He states that clause 3 is "hereby deleted in its entirety."

> Note the new BSD license is thus equivalent to the MIT License, except for the no-endorsement final clause.

<OWNER> = Regents of the University of California
<ORGANIZATION> = University of California, Berkeley
<YEAR> = 1998

In the original BSD license, both occurrences of the phrase "COPYRIGHT HOLDERS AND CONTRIBUTORS" in the disclaimer read "REGENTS AND CONTRIBUTORS".

Here is the license template:

Copyright (c) <YEAR>, <OWNER>
All rights reserved.

Redistribution and use in source and binary forms, with or without modification, are permitted provided that the following conditions are met:

- Redistributions of source code must retain the above copyright notice, this list of conditions and the following disclaimer.
- Redistributions in binary form must reproduce the above copyright notice, this list of conditions and the following disclaimer in the documentation and/or other materials provided with the distribution.
- Neither the name of the <ORGANIZATION> nor the names of its contributors may be used to endorse or promote products derived from this software without specific prior written permission.

THIS SOFTWARE IS PROVIDED BY THE COPYRIGHT HOLDERS AND CONTRIBUTORS "AS IS" AND ANY EXPRESS OR IMPLIED WARRANTIES, INCLUDING, BUT NOT LIMITED TO, THE IMPLIED WARRANTIES OF MERCHANTABILITY AND FITNESS FOR A PARTICULAR PURPOSE ARE DISCLAIMED. IN NO EVENT SHALL THE COPYRIGHT OWNER OR CONTRIBUTORS BE LIABLE FOR ANY DIRECT, INDIRECT, INCIDENTAL, SPECIAL, EXEMPLARY, OR CONSEQUENTIAL DAMAGES (INCLUDING, BUT NOT LIMITED TO, PROCUREMENT OF SUBSTITUTE GOODS OR SERVICES; LOSS OF USE, DATA, OR PROFITS; OR BUSINESS INTERRUPTION) HOWEVER CAUSED AND ON ANY THEORY OF LIABILITY, WHETHER IN CONTRACT, STRICT LIABILITY, OR TORT (INCLUDING NEGLIGENCE OR OTHERWISE) ARISING IN ANYWAY OUT OF THE USE OF THIS SOFTWARE, EVEN IF ADVISED OF THE POSSIBILITY OF SUCH DAMAGE.

Basic Linux/UNIX Commands

The tables in this appendix list some basic Linux/UNIX commands to get you up and running. There may be slight differences in syntax from distribution to distribution, and there are many, many more commands. Check your user manuals, online resources, or simply type man `command` at the prompt for more information on any command, where you replace `command` with any Linux/UNIX command.

Table B.1 File System Navigation Commands

Commands	Descriptions
cd *path/directory-name*	Changes the directory to the specified directory.
ls	Shows a short version of the file listing of the current directory.
ls –l	Shows the file listing with more information.
pwd	Shows the name of the directory you are in.

Table B.2 File Viewing Commands

Commands	Descriptions
cat *file-name*	Shows the content of the file you specify on screen.
less *file-name*	Opens the file to view in a read-only mode (Linux systems only).
pico *file-name*	Opens the file in a text editor.

Table B.3 Directory and File Manipulation Commands

Commands	Descriptions
cp –r *source-dir dest-dir*	Copies a whole directory's contents to *dest-dir*.
cp *source-file dest-file*	Copies a file named *source-file* to a file named *dest-file*.
mkdir *dir-name*	Makes a new directory with the name *dir-name*.
mv *path/source-file path/ dest-file*	Moves a file from *source-file* to *dest-file* in the appropriate paths.
rm *file-name**	Removes a one or more files matching the wildcard statement using * (asterisk).
rmdir *dir-name*	Removes a directory. Will not remove non-empty directories.
rmdir –rf *dir-name*	Removes the directory and all subdirectories and files under it.

Table B.4 Miscellaneous Commands

Commands	Descriptions
date	Shows system time and date. It is important to make sure this is the correct time and date.
df	Checks file system's capacity.
du	Shows disk usage.
grep *string*	Searches for a string when used with other commands. For example, `ls	grep Tony` will list all files with Tony in their name in the directory you issue the command in.
printenv	Shows all the environment variables for the current user (terminal, shell, text editor preferences, and so on).
ps	Shows running processes owned by current user.
ps –ax	Shows all running process.
w	Shows logged in users.

Well-Known TCP/IP Port Numbers

This appendix lists the well-known TCP/IP port numbers. This listing is maintained by IANA, and you can find the most recent version at www.iana.org/assignments/port-numbers.

```
(last updated 2003-10-20)

The port numbers are divided into three ranges: the Well Known Ports,
the Registered Ports, and the Dynamic and/or Private Ports.

The Well Known Ports are those from 0 through 1023.

The Registered Ports are those from 1024 through 49151

The Dynamic and/or Private Ports are those from 49152 through 65535


### UNASSIGNED PORT NUMBERS SHOULD NOT BE USED.  THE IANA WILL ASSIGN
THE NUMBER FOR THE PORT AFTER YOUR APPLICATION HAS BEEN APPROVED ###


WELL KNOWN PORT NUMBERS

The Well Known Ports are assigned by the IANA and on most systems can
only be used by system (or root) processes or by programs executed by
privileged users.

Ports are used in the TCP [RFC793] to name the ends of logical
connections which carry long term conversations.  For the purpose of
providing services to unknown callers, a service contact port is
defined.  This list specifies the port used by the server process as
```

its contact port. The contact port is sometimes called the
"well-known port".

To the extent possible, these same port assignments are used with the
UDP [RFC768].

The range for assigned ports managed by the IANA is 0-1023.

Port Assignments:

```
Keyword            Decimal    Description                     References
-------            -------    -----------                     ----------
                   0/tcp      Reserved
                   0/udp      Reserved
#                             Jon Postel <postel@isi.edu>
tcpmux             1/tcp      TCP Port Service Multiplexer
tcpmux             1/udp      TCP Port Service Multiplexer
#                             Mark Lottor <MKL@nisc.sri.com>
compressnet        2/tcp      Management Utility
compressnet        2/udp      Management Utility
compressnet        3/tcp      Compression Process
compressnet        3/udp      Compression Process
#                             Bernie Volz <VOLZ@PROCESS.COM>
#                  4/tcp      Unassigned
#                  4/udp      Unassigned
rje                5/tcp      Remote Job Entry
rje                5/udp      Remote Job Entry
#                             Jon Postel <postel@isi.edu>
#                  6/tcp      Unassigned
#                  6/udp      Unassigned
echo               7/tcp      Echo
echo               7/udp      Echo
#                             Jon Postel <postel@isi.edu>
#                  8/tcp      Unassigned
#                  8/udp      Unassigned
discard            9/tcp      Discard
discard            9/udp      Discard
#                             Jon Postel <postel@isi.edu>
#                  10/tcp     Unassigned
#                  10/udp     Unassigned
systat             11/tcp     Active Users
systat             11/udp     Active Users
#                             Jon Postel <postel@isi.edu>
#                  12/tcp     Unassigned
#                  12/udp     Unassigned
daytime            13/tcp     Daytime (RFC 867)
daytime            13/udp     Daytime (RFC 867)
#                             Jon Postel <postel@isi.edu>
#                  14/tcp     Unassigned
#                  14/udp     Unassigned
#                  15/tcp     Unassigned [was netstat]
```

```
#                15/udp     Unassigned
#                16/tcp     Unassigned
#                16/udp     Unassigned
qotd             17/tcp     Quote of the Day
qotd             17/udp     Quote of the Day
#                           Jon Postel <postel@isi.edu>
msp              18/tcp     Message Send Protocol
msp              18/udp     Message Send Protocol
#                           Rina Nethaniel <---none--->
chargen          19/tcp     Character Generator
chargen          19/udp     Character Generator
ftp-data         20/tcp     File Transfer [Default Data]
ftp-data         20/udp     File Transfer [Default Data]
ftp              21/tcp     File Transfer [Control]
ftp              21/udp     File Transfer [Control]
#                           Jon Postel <postel@isi.edu>
ssh              22/tcp     SSH Remote Login Protocol
ssh              22/udp     SSH Remote Login Protocol
#                           Tatu Ylonen <ylo@cs.hut.fi>
telnet           23/tcp     Telnet
telnet           23/udp     Telnet
#                           Jon Postel <postel@isi.edu>
                 24/tcp     any private mail system
                 24/udp     any private mail system
#                           Rick Adams <rick@UUNET.UU.NET>
smtp             25/tcp     Simple Mail Transfer
smtp             25/udp     Simple Mail Transfer
#                           Jon Postel <postel@isi.edu>
#                26/tcp     Unassigned
#                26/udp     Unassigned
nsw-fe           27/tcp     NSW User System FE
nsw-fe           27/udp     NSW User System FE
#                           Robert Thomas <BThomas@F.BBN.COM>
#                28/tcp     Unassigned
#                28/udp     Unassigned
msg-icp          29/tcp     MSG ICP
msg-icp          29/udp     MSG ICP
#                           Robert Thomas <BThomas@F.BBN.COM>
#                30/tcp     Unassigned
#                30/udp     Unassigned
msg-auth         31/tcp     MSG Authentication
msg-auth         31/udp     MSG Authentication
#                           Robert Thomas <BThomas@F.BBN.COM>
#                32/tcp     Unassigned
#                32/udp     Unassigned
dsp              33/tcp     Display Support Protocol
dsp              33/udp     Display Support Protocol
#                           Ed Cain <cain@edn-unix.dca.mil>
#                34/tcp     Unassigned
#                34/udp     Unassigned
                 35/tcp     any private printer server
```

```
                     35/udp     any private printer server
#                               Jon Postel <postel@isi.edu>
#                    36/tcp     Unassigned
#                    36/udp     Unassigned
time                 37/tcp     Time
time                 37/udp     Time
#                               Jon Postel <postel@isi.edu>
rap                  38/tcp     Route Access Protocol
rap                  38/udp     Route Access Protocol
#                               Robert Ullmann <ariel@world.std.com>
rlp                  39/tcp     Resource Location Protocol
rlp                  39/udp     Resource Location Protocol
#                               Mike Accetta <MIKE.ACCETTA@CMU-CS-A.EDU>
#                    40/tcp     Unassigned
#                    40/udp     Unassigned
graphics             41/tcp     Graphics
graphics             41/udp     Graphics
name                 42/tcp     Host Name Server
name                 42/udp     Host Name Server
nameserver           42/tcp     Host Name Server
nameserver           42/udp     Host Name Server
nicname              43/tcp     Who Is
nicname              43/udp     Who Is
mpm-flags            44/tcp     MPM FLAGS Protocol
mpm-flags            44/udp     MPM FLAGS Protocol
mpm                  45/tcp     Message Processing Module [recv]
mpm                  45/udp     Message Processing Module [recv]
mpm-snd              46/tcp     MPM [default send]
mpm-snd              46/udp     MPM [default send]
#                               Jon Postel <postel@isi.edu>
ni-ftp               47/tcp     NI FTP
ni-ftp               47/udp     NI FTP
#                               Steve Kille <S.Kille@isode.com>
auditd               48/tcp     Digital Audit Daemon
auditd               48/udp     Digital Audit Daemon
#                               Larry Scott <scott@zk3.dec.com>
tacacs               49/tcp     Login Host Protocol (TACACS)
tacacs               49/udp     Login Host Protocol (TACACS)
#                               Pieter Ditmars <pditmars@BBN.COM>
re-mail-ck           50/tcp     Remote Mail Checking Protocol
re-mail-ck           50/udp     Remote Mail Checking Protocol
#                               Steve Dorner <s-dorner@UIUC.EDU>
la-maint             51/tcp     IMP Logical Address Maintenance
la-maint             51/udp     IMP Logical Address Maintenance
#                               Andy Malis <malis_a@timeplex.com>
xns-time             52/tcp     XNS Time Protocol
xns-time             52/udp     XNS Time Protocol
#                               Susie Armstrong <Armstrong.wbst128@XEROX>
domain               53/tcp     Domain Name Server
domain               53/udp     Domain Name Server
#                               Paul Mockapetris <PVM@ISI.EDU>
```

```
xns-ch           54/tcp     XNS Clearinghouse
xns-ch           54/udp     XNS Clearinghouse
#                           Susie Armstrong <Armstrong.wbst128@XEROX>
isi-gl           55/tcp     ISI Graphics Language
isi-gl           55/udp     ISI Graphics Language
xns-auth         56/tcp     XNS Authentication
xns-auth         56/udp     XNS Authentication
#                           Susie Armstrong <Armstrong.wbst128@XEROX>
                 57/tcp     any private terminal access
                 57/udp     any private terminal access
#                           Jon Postel <postel@isi.edu>
xns-mail         58/tcp     XNS Mail
xns-mail         58/udp     XNS Mail
#                           Susie Armstrong <Armstrong.wbst128@XEROX>
                 59/tcp     any private file service
                 59/udp     any private file service
#                           Jon Postel <postel@isi.edu>
                 60/tcp     Unassigned
                 60/udp     Unassigned
ni-mail          61/tcp     NI MAIL
ni-mail          61/udp     NI MAIL
#                           Steve Kille <S.Kille@isode.com>
acas             62/tcp     ACA Services
acas             62/udp     ACA Services
#                           E. Wald <ewald@via.enet.dec.com>
whois++          63/tcp     whois++
whois++          63/udp     whois++
#                           Rickard Schoultz <schoultz@sunet.se>
covia            64/tcp     Communications Integrator (CI)
covia            64/udp     Communications Integrator (CI)
#                           Dan Smith <dan.smith@den.galileo.com>
tacacs-ds        65/tcp     TACACS-Database Service
tacacs-ds        65/udp     TACACS-Database Service
#                           Kathy Huber <khuber@bbn.com>
sql*net          66/tcp     Oracle SQL*NET
sql*net          66/udp     Oracle SQL*NET
#                           Jack Haverty <jhaverty@ORACLE.COM>
bootps           67/tcp     Bootstrap Protocol Server
bootps           67/udp     Bootstrap Protocol Server
bootpc           68/tcp     Bootstrap Protocol Client
bootpc           68/udp     Bootstrap Protocol Client
#                           Bill Croft <Croft@SUMEX-AIM.STANFORD.EDU>
tftp             69/tcp     Trivial File Transfer
tftp             69/udp     Trivial File Transfer
#                           David Clark <ddc@LCS.MIT.EDU>
gopher           70/tcp     Gopher
gopher           70/udp     Gopher
#                           Mark McCahill <mpm@boombox.micro.umn.edu>
netrjs-1         71/tcp     Remote Job Service
netrjs-1         71/udp     Remote Job Service
netrjs-2         72/tcp     Remote Job Service
```

```
netrjs-2          72/udp    Remote Job Service
netrjs-3          73/tcp    Remote Job Service
netrjs-3          73/udp    Remote Job Service
netrjs-4          74/tcp    Remote Job Service
netrjs-4          74/udp    Remote Job Service
#                           Bob Braden <Braden@ISI.EDU>
                  75/tcp    any private dial out service
                  75/udp    any private dial out service
#                           Jon Postel <postel@isi.edu>
deos              76/tcp    Distributed External Object Store
deos              76/udp    Distributed External Object Store
#                           Robert Ullmann <ariel@world.std.com>
                  77/tcp    any private RJE service
                  77/udp    any private RJE service
#                           Jon Postel <postel@isi.edu>
vettcp            78/tcp    vettcp
vettcp            78/udp    vettcp
#                           Christopher Leong <leong@kolmod.mlo.dec.com>
finger            79/tcp    Finger
finger            79/udp    Finger
#                           David Zimmerman <dpz@RUTGERS.EDU>
http              80/tcp    World Wide Web HTTP
http              80/udp    World Wide Web HTTP
www               80/tcp    World Wide Web HTTP
www               80/udp    World Wide Web HTTP
www-http          80/tcp    World Wide Web HTTP
www-http          80/udp    World Wide Web HTTP
#                           Tim Berners-Lee <timbl@W3.org>
hosts2-ns         81/tcp    HOSTS2 Name Server
hosts2-ns         81/udp    HOSTS2 Name Server
#                           Earl Killian <EAK@MORDOR.S1.GOV>
xfer              82/tcp    XFER Utility
xfer              82/udp    XFER Utility
#                           Thomas M. Smith <Thomas.M.Smith@lmco.com>
mit-ml-dev        83/tcp    MIT ML Device
mit-ml-dev        83/udp    MIT ML Device
#                           David Reed <--none--->
ctf               84/tcp    Common Trace Facility
ctf               84/udp    Common Trace Facility
#                           Hugh Thomas <thomas@oils.enet.dec.com>
mit-ml-dev        85/tcp    MIT ML Device
mit-ml-dev        85/udp    MIT ML Device
#                           David Reed <--none--->
mfcobol           86/tcp    Micro Focus Cobol
mfcobol           86/udp    Micro Focus Cobol
#                           Simon Edwards <--none--->
                  87/tcp    any private terminal link
                  87/udp    any private terminal link
#                           Jon Postel <postel@isi.edu>
kerberos          88/tcp    Kerberos
```

```
kerberos          88/udp     Kerberos
#                            B. Clifford Neuman <bcn@isi.edu>
su-mit-tg         89/tcp     SU/MIT Telnet Gateway
su-mit-tg         89/udp     SU/MIT Telnet Gateway
#                            Mark Crispin <MRC@PANDA.COM>
########## PORT 90 also being used unofficially by Pointcast #########
dnsix             90/tcp     DNSIX Securit Attribute Token Map
dnsix             90/udp     DNSIX Securit Attribute Token Map
#                            Charles Watt <watt@sware.com>
mit-dov           91/tcp     MIT Dover Spooler
mit-dov           91/udp     MIT Dover Spooler
#                            Eliot Moss <EBM@XX.LCS.MIT.EDU>
npp               92/tcp     Network Printing Protocol
npp               92/udp     Network Printing Protocol
#                            Louis Mamakos <louie@sayshell.umd.edu>
dcp               93/tcp     Device Control Protocol
dcp               93/udp     Device Control Protocol
#                            Daniel Tappan <Tappan@BBN.COM>
objcall           94/tcp     Tivoli Object Dispatcher
objcall           94/udp     Tivoli Object Dispatcher
#                            Tom Bereiter <--none--->
supdup            95/tcp     SUPDUP
supdup            95/udp     SUPDUP
#                            Mark Crispin <MRC@PANDA.COM>
dixie             96/tcp     DIXIE Protocol Specification
dixie             96/udp     DIXIE Protocol Specification
#                 Tim Howes <Tim.Howes@terminator.cc.umich.edu>
swift-rvf         97/tcp     Swift Remote Virtural File Protocol
swift-rvf         97/udp     Swift Remote Virtural File Protocol
#                            Maurice R. Turcotte
#                 <mailrus!uflorida!rm1!dnmrt%rmatl@uunet.UU.NET>
tacnews           98/tcp     TAC News
tacnews           98/udp     TAC News
#                            Jon Postel <postel@isi.edu>
metagram          99/tcp     Metagram Relay
metagram          99/udp     Metagram Relay
#                            Geoff Goodfellow <Geoff@FERNWOOD.MPK.CA.US>
newacct          100/tcp     [unauthorized use]
hostname         101/tcp     NIC Host Name Server
hostname         101/udp     NIC Host Name Server
#                            Jon Postel <postel@isi.edu>
iso-tsap         102/tcp     ISO-TSAP Class 0
iso-tsap         102/udp     ISO-TSAP Class 0
#                            Marshall Rose <mrose@dbc.mtview.ca.us>
gppitnp          103/tcp     Genesis Point-to-Point Trans Net
gppitnp          103/udp     Genesis Point-to-Point Trans Net
acr-nema         104/tcp     ACR-NEMA Digital Imag. & Comm. 300
acr-nema         104/udp     ACR-NEMA Digital Imag. & Comm. 300
#                            Patrick McNamee <--none--->
cso              105/tcp     CCSO name server protocol
```

```
cso             105/udp    CCSO name server protocol
#                          Martin Hamilton <martin@mrrl.lut.as.uk>
csnet-ns        105/tcp    Mailbox Name Nameserver
csnet-ns        105/udp    Mailbox Name Nameserver
#                          Marvin Solomon <solomon@CS.WISC.EDU>
3com-tsmux      106/tcp    3COM-TSMUX
3com-tsmux      106/udp    3COM-TSMUX
#                          Jeremy Siegel <jzs@NSD.3Com.COM>
##########      106        Unauthorized use by insecure poppassd protocol
rtelnet         107/tcp    Remote Telnet Service
rtelnet         107/udp    Remote Telnet Service
#                          Jon Postel <postel@isi.edu>
snagas          108/tcp    SNA Gateway Access Server
snagas          108/udp    SNA Gateway Access Server
#                          Kevin Murphy <murphy@sevens.lkg.dec.com>
pop2            109/tcp    Post Office Protocol - Version 2
pop2            109/udp    Post Office Protocol - Version 2
#                          Joyce K. Reynolds <jkrey@isi.edu>
pop3            110/tcp    Post Office Protocol - Version 3
pop3            110/udp    Post Office Protocol - Version 3
#                          Marshall Rose <mrose@dbc.mtview.ca.us>
sunrpc          111/tcp    SUN Remote Procedure Call
sunrpc          111/udp    SUN Remote Procedure Call
#                          Chuck McManis <cmcmanis@freegate.net>
mcidas          112/tcp    McIDAS Data Transmission Protocol
mcidas          112/udp    McIDAS Data Transmission Protocol
#                          Glenn Davis <support@unidata.ucar.edu>
ident           113/tcp
auth            113/tcp    Authentication Service
auth            113/udp    Authentication Service
#                          Mike St. Johns <stjohns@arpa.mil>
audionews       114/tcp    Audio News Multicast
audionews       114/udp    Audio News Multicast
#                          Martin Forssen <maf@dtek.chalmers.se>
sftp            115/tcp    Simple File Transfer Protocol
sftp            115/udp    Simple File Transfer Protocol
#                          Mark Lottor <MKL@nisc.sri.com>
ansanotify      116/tcp    ANSA REX Notify
ansanotify      116/udp    ANSA REX Notify
#                          Nicola J. Howarth <njh@ansa.co.uk>
uucp-path       117/tcp    UUCP Path Service
uucp-path       117/udp    UUCP Path Service
sqlserv         118/tcp    SQL Services
sqlserv         118/udp    SQL Services
#                          Larry Barnes <barnes@broke.enet.dec.com>
nntp            119/tcp    Network News Transfer Protocol
nntp            119/udp    Network News Transfer Protocol
#                          Phil Lapsley <phil@UCBARPA.BERKELEY.EDU>
cfdptkt         120/tcp    CFDPTKT
cfdptkt         120/udp    CFDPTKT
#                          John Ioannidis <ji@close.cs.columbia.ed>
```

```
erpc             121/tcp    Encore Expedited Remote Pro.Call
erpc             121/udp    Encore Expedited Remote Pro.Call
#                           Jack O'Neil <---none--->
smakynet         122/tcp    SMAKYNET
smakynet         122/udp    SMAKYNET
#                           Pierre Arnaud <pierre.arnaud@iname.com>
ntp              123/tcp    Network Time Protocol
ntp              123/udp    Network Time Protocol
#                           Dave Mills <Mills@HUEY.UDEL.EDU>
ansatrader       124/tcp    ANSA REX Trader
ansatrader       124/udp    ANSA REX Trader
#                           Nicola J. Howarth <njh@ansa.co.uk>
locus-map        125/tcp    Locus PC-Interface Net Map Ser
locus-map        125/udp    Locus PC-Interface Net Map Ser
#                           Eric Peterson <lcc.eric@SEAS.UCLA.EDU>
nxedit           126/tcp    NXEdit
nxedit           126/udp    NXEdit
#                           Don Payette <Don.Payette@unisys.com>
###########Port 126 Previously assigned to application below#######
#unitary         126/tcp    Unisys Unitary Login
#unitary         126/udp    Unisys Unitary Login
#                           <feil@kronos.nisd.cam.unisys.com>
###########Port 126 Previously assigned to application above#######
locus-con        127/tcp    Locus PC-Interface Conn Server
locus-con        127/udp    Locus PC-Interface Conn Server
#                           Eric Peterson <lcc.eric@SEAS.UCLA.EDU>
gss-xlicen       128/tcp    GSS X License Verification
gss-xlicen       128/udp    GSS X License Verification
#                           John Light <johnl@gssc.gss.com>
pwdgen           129/tcp    Password Generator Protocol
pwdgen           129/udp    Password Generator Protocol
#                           Frank J. Wacho <WANCHO@WSMR-SIMTEL20.ARMY.MIL>
cisco-fna        130/tcp    cisco FNATIVE
cisco-fna        130/udp    cisco FNATIVE
cisco-tna        131/tcp    cisco TNATIVE
cisco-tna        131/udp    cisco TNATIVE
cisco-sys        132/tcp    cisco SYSMAINT
cisco-sys        132/udp    cisco SYSMAINT
statsrv          133/tcp    Statistics Service
statsrv          133/udp    Statistics Service
#                           Dave Mills <Mills@HUEY.UDEL.EDU>
ingres-net       134/tcp    INGRES-NET Service
ingres-net       134/udp    INGRES-NET Service
#                           Mike Berrow <---none--->
epmap            135/tcp    DCE endpoint resolution
epmap            135/udp    DCE endpoint resolution
#                           Joe Pato <pato@apollo.hp.com>
profile          136/tcp    PROFILE Naming System
profile          136/udp    PROFILE Naming System
#                           Larry Peterson <llp@ARIZONA.EDU>
netbios-ns       137/tcp    NETBIOS Name Service
```

```
netbios-ns        137/udp    NETBIOS Name Service
netbios-dgm       138/tcp    NETBIOS Datagram Service
netbios-dgm       138/udp    NETBIOS Datagram Service
netbios-ssn       139/tcp    NETBIOS Session Service
netbios-ssn       139/udp    NETBIOS Session Service
#                            Jon Postel <postel@isi.edu>
emfis-data        140/tcp    EMFIS Data Service
emfis-data        140/udp    EMFIS Data Service
emfis-cntl        141/tcp    EMFIS Control Service
emfis-cntl        141/udp    EMFIS Control Service
#                            Gerd Beling <GBELING@ISI.EDU>
bl-idm            142/tcp    Britton-Lee IDM
bl-idm            142/udp    Britton-Lee IDM
#                            Susie Snitzer <---none--->
imap              143/tcp    Internet Message Access Protocol
imap              143/udp    Internet Message Access Protocol
#                            Mark Crispin <MRC@CAC.Washington.EDU>
uma               144/tcp    Universal Management Architecture
uma               144/udp    Universal Management Architecture
#                            Jay Whitney <jw@powercenter.com>
uaac              145/tcp    UAAC Protocol
uaac              145/udp    UAAC Protocol
#                            David A. Gomberg <gomberg@GATEWAY.MITRE.ORG>
iso-tp0           146/tcp    ISO-IP0
iso-tp0           146/udp    ISO-IP0
iso-ip            147/tcp    ISO-IP
iso-ip            147/udp    ISO-IP
#                            Marshall Rose <mrose@dbc.mtview.ca.us>
jargon            148/tcp    Jargon
jargon            148/udp    Jargon
#                            Bill Weinman <wew@bearnet.com>
aed-512           149/tcp    AED 512 Emulation Service
aed-512           149/udp    AED 512 Emulation Service
#                            Albert G. Broscius <broscius@DSL.CIS.UPENN.EDU>
sql-net           150/tcp    SQL-NET
sql-net           150/udp    SQL-NET
#                            Martin Picard <<---none--->
hems              151/tcp    HEMS
hems              151/udp    HEMS
bftp              152/tcp    Background File Transfer Program
bftp              152/udp    Background File Transfer Program
#                            Annette DeSchon <DESCHON@ISI.EDU>
sgmp              153/tcp    SGMP
sgmp              153/udp    SGMP
#                            Marty Schoffstahl <schoff@NISC.NYSER.NET>
netsc-prod        154/tcp    NETSC
netsc-prod        154/udp    NETSC
netsc-dev         155/tcp    NETSC
netsc-dev         155/udp    NETSC
#                            Sergio Heker <heker@JVNCC.CSC.ORG>
sqlsrv            156/tcp    SQL Service
```

```
sqlsrv          156/udp     SQL Service
#                           Craig Rogers <Rogers@ISI.EDU>
knet-cmp        157/tcp     KNET/VM Command/Message Protocol
knet-cmp        157/udp     KNET/VM Command/Message Protocol
#                           Gary S. Malkin <GMALKIN@XYLOGICS.COM>
pcmail-srv      158/tcp     PCMail Server
pcmail-srv      158/udp     PCMail Server
#                           Mark L. Lambert <markl@PTT.LCS.MIT.EDU>
nss-routing     159/tcp     NSS-Routing
nss-routing     159/udp     NSS-Routing
#                           Yakov Rekhter <Yakov@IBM.COM>
sgmp-traps      160/tcp     SGMP-TRAPS
sgmp-traps      160/udp     SGMP-TRAPS
#                           Marty Schoffstahl <schoff@NISC.NYSER.NET>
snmp            161/tcp     SNMP
snmp            161/udp     SNMP
snmptrap        162/tcp     SNMPTRAP
snmptrap        162/udp     SNMPTRAP
#                           Marshall Rose <mrose@dbc.mtview.ca.us>
cmip-man        163/tcp     CMIP/TCP Manager
cmip-man        163/udp     CMIP/TCP Manager
cmip-agent      164/tcp     CMIP/TCP Agent
cmip-agent      164/udp     CMIP/TCP Agent
#                           Amatzia Ben-Artzi <---none--->
xns-courier     165/tcp     Xerox
xns-courier     165/udp     Xerox
#                           Susie Armstrong <Armstrong.wbst128@XEROX.COM>
s-net           166/tcp     Sirius Systems
s-net           166/udp     Sirius Systems
#                           Brian Lloyd <brian@lloyd.com>
namp            167/tcp     NAMP
namp            167/udp     NAMP
#                           Marty Schoffstahl <schoff@NISC.NYSER.NET>
rsvd            168/tcp     RSVD
rsvd            168/udp     RSVD
#                           Neil Todd <mcvax!ist.co.uk!neil@UUNET.UU.NET>
send            169/tcp     SEND
send            169/udp     SEND
#                           William D. Wisner <wisner@HAYES.FAI.ALASKA.EDU>
print-srv       170/tcp     Network PostScript
print-srv       170/udp     Network PostScript
#                           Brian Reid <reid@DECWRL.DEC.COM>
multiplex       171/tcp     Network Innovations Multiplex
multiplex       171/udp     Network Innovations Multiplex
cl/1            172/tcp     Network Innovations CL/1
cl/1            172/udp     Network Innovations CL/1
#                           Kevin DeVault <<---none--->
xyplex-mux      173/tcp     Xyplex
xyplex-mux      173/udp     Xyplex
#                           Bob Stewart <STEWART@XYPLEX.COM>
mailq           174/tcp     MAILQ
```

```
mailq          174/udp      MAILQ
#                           Rayan Zachariassen <rayan@AI.TORONTO.EDU>
vmnet          175/tcp      VMNET
vmnet          175/udp      VMNET
#                           Christopher Tengi <tengi@Princeton.EDU>
genrad-mux     176/tcp      GENRAD-MUX
genrad-mux     176/udp      GENRAD-MUX
#                           Ron Thornton <thornton@qm7501.genrad.com>
xdmcp          177/tcp      X Display Manager Control Protocol
xdmcp          177/udp      X Display Manager Control Protocol
#                           Robert W. Scheifler <RWS@XX.LCS.MIT.EDU>
nextstep       178/tcp      NextStep Window Server
nextstep       178/udp      NextStep Window Server
#                           Leo Hourvitz <leo@NEXT.COM>
bgp            179/tcp      Border Gateway Protocol
bgp            179/udp      Border Gateway Protocol
#                           Kirk Lougheed <LOUGHEED@MATHOM.CISCO.COM>
ris            180/tcp      Intergraph
ris            180/udp      Intergraph
#                           Dave Buehmann <ingr!daveb@UUNET.UU.NET>
unify          181/tcp      Unify
unify          181/udp      Unify
#                           Mark Ainsley <ianaportmaster@unify.com>
audit          182/tcp      Unisys Audit SITP
audit          182/udp      Unisys Audit SITP
#                           Gil Greenbaum <gcole@nisd.cam.unisys.com>
ocbinder       183/tcp      OCBinder
ocbinder       183/udp      OCBinder
ocserver       184/tcp      OCServer
ocserver       184/udp      OCServer
#                           Jerrilynn Okamura <--none--->
remote-kis     185/tcp      Remote-KIS
remote-kis     185/udp      Remote-KIS
kis            186/tcp      KIS Protocol
kis            186/udp      KIS Protocol
#                           Ralph Droms <rdroms@NRI.RESTON.VA.US>
aci            187/tcp      Application Communication Interface
aci            187/udp      Application Communication Interface
#                           Rick Carlos <rick.ticipa.csc.ti.com>
mumps          188/tcp      Plus Five's MUMPS
mumps          188/udp      Plus Five's MUMPS
#                           Hokey Stenn <hokey@PLUS5.COM>
qft            189/tcp      Queued File Transport
qft            189/udp      Queued File Transport
#                           Wayne Schroeder <schroeder@SDS.SDSC.EDU>
gacp           190/tcp      Gateway Access Control Protocol
gacp           190/udp      Gateway Access Control Protocol
#                           C. Philip Wood <cpw@LANL.GOV>
prospero       191/tcp      Prospero Directory Service
prospero       191/udp      Prospero Directory Service
#                           B. Clifford Neuman <bcn@isi.edu>
```

```
osu-nms         192/tcp     OSU Network Monitoring System
osu-nms         192/udp     OSU Network Monitoring System
#                           Doug Karl <KARL-D@OSU-20.IRCC.OHIO-STATE.EDU>
srmp            193/tcp     Spider Remote Monitoring Protocol
srmp            193/udp     Spider Remote Monitoring Protocol
#                           Ted J. Socolofsky <Teds@SPIDER.CO.UK>
irc             194/tcp     Internet Relay Chat Protocol
irc             194/udp     Internet Relay Chat Protocol
#                           Jarkko Oikarinen <jto@TOLSUN.OULU.FI>
dn6-nlm-aud     195/tcp     DNSIX Network Level Module Audit
dn6-nlm-aud     195/udp     DNSIX Network Level Module Audit
dn6-smm-red     196/tcp     DNSIX Session Mgt Module Audit Redir
dn6-smm-red     196/udp     DNSIX Session Mgt Module Audit Redir
#                           Lawrence Lebahn <DIA3@PAXRV-NES.NAVY.MIL>
dls             197/tcp     Directory Location Service
dls             197/udp     Directory Location Service
dls-mon         198/tcp     Directory Location Service Monitor
dls-mon         198/udp     Directory Location Service Monitor
#                           Scott Bellew <smb@cs.purdue.edu>
smux            199/tcp     SMUX
smux            199/udp     SMUX
#                           Marshall Rose <mrose@dbc.mtview.ca.us>
src             200/tcp     IBM System Resource Controller
src             200/udp     IBM System Resource Controller
#                           Gerald McBrearty <---none--->
at-rtmp         201/tcp     AppleTalk Routing Maintenance
at-rtmp         201/udp     AppleTalk Routing Maintenance
at-nbp          202/tcp     AppleTalk Name Binding
at-nbp          202/udp     AppleTalk Name Binding
at-3            203/tcp     AppleTalk Unused
at-3            203/udp     AppleTalk Unused
at-echo         204/tcp     AppleTalk Echo
at-echo         204/udp     AppleTalk Echo
at-5            205/tcp     AppleTalk Unused
at-5            205/udp     AppleTalk Unused
at-zis          206/tcp     AppleTalk Zone Information
at-zis          206/udp     AppleTalk Zone Information
at-7            207/tcp     AppleTalk Unused
at-7            207/udp     AppleTalk Unused
at-8            208/tcp     AppleTalk Unused
at-8            208/udp     AppleTalk Unused
#                           Rob Chandhok <chandhok@gnome.cs.cmu.edu>
qmtp            209/tcp     The Quick Mail Transfer Protocol
qmtp            209/udp     The Quick Mail Transfer Protocol
#                           Dan Bernstein <djb@silverton.berkeley.edu>
z39.50          210/tcp     ANSI Z39.50
z39.50          210/udp     ANSI Z39.50
#                           Mark H. Needleman <markn@sirsi.com>
914c/g          211/tcp     Texas Instruments 914C/G Terminal
914c/g          211/udp     Texas Instruments 914C/G Terminal
#                           Bill Harrell <---none--->
```

```
anet              212/tcp      ATEXSSTR
anet              212/udp      ATEXSSTR
#                              Jim Taylor <taylor@heart.epps.kodak.com>
ipx               213/tcp      IPX
ipx               213/udp      IPX
#                              Don Provan <donp@xlnvax.novell.com>
vmpwscs           214/tcp      VM PWSCS
vmpwscs           214/udp      VM PWSCS
#                              Dan Shia <dset!shia@uunet.UU.NET>
softpc            215/tcp      Insignia Solutions
softpc            215/udp      Insignia Solutions
#                              Martyn Thomas <---none--->
CAIlic            216/tcp      Computer Associates Int'l License Server
CAIlic            216/udp      Computer Associates Int'l License Server
#                              Chuck Spitz <spich04@cai.com>
dbase             217/tcp      dBASE Unix
dbase             217/udp      dBASE Unix
#                              Don Gibson
#                              <sequent!aero!twinsun!ashtate.A-T.COM!dong@uunet.UU.NET>
mpp               218/tcp      Netix Message Posting Protocol
mpp               218/udp      Netix Message Posting Protocol
#                              Shannon Yeh <yeh@netix.com>
uarps             219/tcp      Unisys ARPs
uarps             219/udp      Unisys ARPs
#                              Ashok Marwaha <---none--->
imap3             220/tcp      Interactive Mail Access Protocol v3
imap3             220/udp      Interactive Mail Access Protocol v3
#                              James Rice <RICE@SUMEX-AIM.STANFORD.EDU>
fln-spx           221/tcp      Berkeley rlogind with SPX auth
fln-spx           221/udp      Berkeley rlogind with SPX auth
rsh-spx           222/tcp      Berkeley rshd with SPX auth
rsh-spx           222/udp      Berkeley rshd with SPX auth
cdc               223/tcp      Certificate Distribution Center
cdc               223/udp      Certificate Distribution Center
#                              Kannan Alagappan <kannan@sejour.enet.dec.com>
########## Possible Conflict of Port 222 with "Masqdialer"#############
### Contact for Masqdialer is Charles Wright <cpwright@villagenet.com>###
masqdialer        224/tcp      masqdialer
masqdialer        224/udp      masqdialer
#                              Charles Wright <cpwright@villagenet.com>
#                 225-241      Reserved
#                              Jon Postel <postel@isi.edu>
direct            242/tcp      Direct
direct            242/udp      Direct
#                              Herb Sutter <HerbS@cntc.com>
sur-meas          243/tcp      Survey Measurement
sur-meas          243/udp      Survey Measurement
#                              Dave Clark <ddc@LCS.MIT.EDU>
inbusiness        244/tcp      inbusiness
inbusiness        244/udp      inbusiness
#                              Derrick Hisatake <derrick.i.hisatake@intel.com>
```

```
link              245/tcp    LINK
link              245/udp    LINK
dsp3270           246/tcp    Display Systems Protocol
dsp3270           246/udp    Display Systems Protocol
#                            Weldon J. Showalter <Gamma@MINTAKA.DCA.MIL>
subntbcst_tftp    247/tcp    SUBNTBCST_TFTP
subntbcst_tftp    247/udp    SUBNTBCST_TFTP
#                            John Fake <fake@us.ibm.com>
bhfhs             248/tcp    bhfhs
bhfhs             248/udp    bhfhs
#                            John Kelly <johnk@bellhow.com>
#                 249-255    Reserved
#                            Jon Postel <postel@isi.edu>
rap               256/tcp    RAP
rap               256/udp    RAP
#                            J.S. Greenfield <greeny@raleigh.ibm.com>
set               257/tcp    Secure Electronic Transaction
set               257/udp    Secure Electronic Transaction
#                            Donald Eastlake <dee3@torque.pothole.com>
yak-chat          258/tcp    Yak Winsock Personal Chat
yak-chat          258/udp    Yak Winsock Personal Chat
#                            Brian Bandy <bbandy@swbell.net>
esro-gen          259/tcp    Efficient Short Remote Operations
esro-gen          259/udp    Efficient Short Remote Operations
#                            Mohsen Banan <mohsen@rostam.neda.com>
openport          260/tcp    Openport
openport          260/udp    Openport
#                            John Marland <jmarland@dean.openport.com>
nsiiops           261/tcp    IIOP Name Service over TLS/SSL
nsiiops           261/udp    IIOP Name Service over TLS/SSL
#                            Jeff Stewart <jstewart@netscape.com>
arcisdms          262/tcp    Arcisdms
arcisdms          262/udp    Arcisdms
#                            Russell Crook (rmc@sni.ca)
hdap              263/tcp    HDAP
hdap              263/udp    HDAP
#                            Troy Gau <troy@zyxel.com>
bgmp              264/tcp    BGMP
bgmp              264/udp    BGMP
#                            Dave Thaler <thalerd@eecs.umich.edu>
x-bone-ctl        265/tcp    X-Bone CTL
x-bone-ctl        265/udp    X-Bone CTL
#                            Joe Touch <touch@isi.edu>
sst               266/tcp    SCSI on ST
sst               266/udp    SCSI on ST
#                            Donald D. Woelz <don@genroco.com>
td-service        267/tcp    Tobit David Service Layer
td-service        267/udp    Tobit David Service Layer
td-replica        268/tcp    Tobit David Replica
td-replica        268/udp    Tobit David Replica
#                            Franz-Josef Leuders <development@tobit.com>
```

```
#                  269-279      Unassigned
http-mgmt          280/tcp      http-mgmt
http-mgmt          280/udp      http-mgmt
#                               Adrian Pell
#                               <PELL_ADRIAN/HP-UnitedKingdom_om6@hplb.hpl.hp.com>
personal-link      281/tcp      Personal Link          .
personal-link      281/udp      Personal Link
#                               Dan Cummings <doc@cnr.com>
cableport-ax       282/tcp      Cable Port A/X
cableport-ax       282/udp      Cable Port A/X
#                               Craig Langfahl
#                               <Craig_J_Langfahl@ccm.ch.intel.com>
rescap             283/tcp      rescap
rescap             283/udp      rescap
#                               Paul Hoffman <phoffman@imc.org>
corerjd            284/tcp      corerjd
corerjd            284/udp      corerjd
#                               Chris Thornhill <cjt@corenetworks.com>
#                  285          Unassigned
fxp                286/tcp      FXP Communication
fxp                286/udp      FXP Communication
#                               James Darnall <james_r_darnall@sbcglobal.net>
k-block            287/tcp      K-BLOCK
k-block            287/udp      K-BLOCK
#                               Simon P Jackson <jacko@kring.co.uk>
#                  288-307      Unassigned
novastorbakcup     308/tcp      Novastor Backup
novastorbakcup     308/udp      Novastor Backup
#                               Brian Dickman <brian@novastor.com>
entrusttime        309/tcp      EntrustTime
entrusttime        309/udp      EntrustTime
#                               Peter Whittaker <pww@entrust.com>
bhmds              310/tcp      bhmds
bhmds              310/udp      bhmds
#                               John Kelly <johnk@bellhow.com>
asip-webadmin      311/tcp      AppleShare IP WebAdmin
asip-webadmin      311/udp      AppleShare IP WebAdmin
#                               Ann Huang <annhuang@apple.com>
vslmp              312/tcp      VSLMP
vslmp              312/udp      VSLMP
#                               Gerben Wierda <Gerben_Wierda@RnA.nl>
magenta-logic      313/tcp      Magenta Logic
magenta-logic      313/udp      Magenta Logic
#                               Karl Rousseau <kr@netfusion.co.uk>
opalis-robot       314/tcp      Opalis Robot
opalis-robot       314/udp      Opalis Robot
#                               Laurent Domenech, Opalis <ldomenech@opalis.com>
dpsi               315/tcp      DPSI
dpsi               315/udp      DPSI
#                               Tony Scamurra <Tony@DesktopPaging.com>
```

```
decauth           316/tcp    decAuth
decauth           316/udp    decAuth
#                            Michael Agishtein <misha@unx.dec.com>
zannet            317/tcp    Zannet
zannet            317/udp    Zannet
#                            Zan Oliphant <zan@accessone.com>
pkix-timestamp    318/tcp    PKIX TimeStamp
pkix-timestamp    318/udp    PKIX TimeStamp
#                            Robert Zuccherato
                             <robert.zuccherato@entrust.com>
ptp-event         319/tcp    PTP Event
ptp-event         319/udp    PTP Event
ptp-general       320/tcp    PTP General
ptp-general       320/udp    PTP General
#                            John Eidson <eidson@hpl.hp.com>
pip               321/tcp    PIP
pip               321/udp    PIP
#                            Gordon Mohr <gojomo@usa.net>
rtsps             322/tcp    RTSPS
rtsps             322/udp    RTSPS
#                            Anders Klemets <anderskl@microsoft.com>
#                 323-332    Unassigned
texar             333/tcp    Texar Security Port
texar             333/udp    Texar Security Port
#                            Eugen Bacic <ebacic@texar.com>
#                 334-343    Unassigned
pdap              344/tcp    Prospero Data Access Protocol
pdap              344/udp    Prospero Data Access Protocol
#                            B. Clifford Neuman <bcn@isi.edu>
pawserv           345/tcp    Perf Analysis Workbench
pawserv           345/udp    Perf Analysis Workbench
zserv             346/tcp    Zebra server
zserv             346/udp    Zebra server
fatserv           347/tcp    Fatmen Server
fatserv           347/udp    Fatmen Server
csi-sgwp          348/tcp    Cabletron Management Protocol
csi-sgwp          348/udp    Cabletron Management Protocol
mftp              349/tcp    mftp
mftp              349/udp    mftp
#                            Dave Feinleib <davefe@microsoft.com>
matip-type-a      350/tcp    MATIP Type A
matip-type-a      350/udp    MATIP Type A
matip-type-b      351/tcp    MATIP Type B
matip-type-b      351/udp    MATIP Type B
#                            Alain Robert <arobert@par.sita.int>
# The following entry records an unassigned but widespread use
bhoetty           351/tcp    bhoetty (added 5/21/97)
bhoetty           351/udp    bhoetty
#                            John Kelly <johnk@bellhow.com>
dtag-ste-sb       352/tcp    DTAG (assigned long ago)
```

```
dtag-ste-sb      352/udp     DTAG
#                            Ruediger Wald <wald@ez-darmstadt.telekom.de>
# The following entry records an unassigned but widespread use
bhoedap4         352/tcp     bhoedap4 (added 5/21/97)
bhoedap4         352/udp     bhoedap4
#                            John Kelly <johnk@bellhow.com>
ndsauth          353/tcp     NDSAUTH
ndsauth          353/udp     NDSAUTH
#                            Jayakumar Ramalingam <jayakumar@novell.com>
bh611            354/tcp     bh611
bh611            354/udp     bh611
#                            John Kelly <johnk@bellhow.com>
datex-asn        355/tcp     DATEX-ASN
datex-asn        355/udp     DATEX-ASN
#                            Kenneth Vaughn <kvaughn@mail.viggen.com>
cloanto-net-1    356/tcp     Cloanto Net 1
cloanto-net-1    356/udp     Cloanto Net 1
#                            Michael Battilana <mcb-iana@cloanto.com>
bhevent          357/tcp     bhevent
bhevent          357/udp     bhevent
#                            John Kelly <johnk@bellhow.com>
shrinkwrap       358/tcp     Shrinkwrap
shrinkwrap       358/udp     Shrinkwrap
#                            Bill Simpson <wsimpson@greendragon.com>
nsrmp            359/tcp     Network Security Risk Management Protocol
nsrmp            359/udp     Network Security Risk Management Protocol
#                            Eric Jacksch <jacksch@tenebris.ca>
scoi2odialog     360/tcp     scoi2odialog
scoi2odialog     360/udp     scoi2odialog
#                            Keith Petley <keithp@sco.COM>
semantix         361/tcp     Semantix
semantix         361/udp     Semantix
#                            Semantix <xsSupport@semantix.com>
srssend          362/tcp     SRS Send
srssend          362/udp     SRS Send
#                            Curt Mayer <curt@emergent.com>
rsvp_tunnel      363/tcp     RSVP Tunnel
rsvp_tunnel      363/udp     RSVP Tunnel
#                            Andreas Terzis <terzis@cs.ucla.edu>
aurora-cmgr      364/tcp     Aurora CMGR
aurora-cmgr      364/udp     Aurora CMGR
#                            Philip Budne <budne@auroratech.com>
dtk              365/tcp     DTK
dtk              365/udp     DTK
#                            Fred Cohen <fc@all.net>
odmr             366/tcp     ODMR
odmr             366/udp     ODMR
#                            Randall Gellens <randy@qualcomm.com>
mortgageware     367/tcp     MortgageWare
mortgageware     367/udp     MortgageWare
#                            Ole Hellevik <oleh@interlinq.com>
```

```
qbikgdp            368/tcp    QbikGDP
qbikgdp            368/udp    QbikGDP
#                             Adrien de Croy <adrien@qbik.com>
rpc2portmap        369/tcp    rpc2portmap
rpc2portmap        369/udp    rpc2portmap
codaauth2          370/tcp    codaauth2
codaauth2          370/udp    codaauth2
#                             Robert Watson <robert@cyrus.watson.org>
clearcase          371/tcp    Clearcase
clearcase          371/udp    Clearcase
#                             Dave LeBlang <leglang@atria.com>
ulistproc          372/tcp    ListProcessor
ulistproc          372/udp    ListProcessor
#                             Anastasios Kotsikonas <tasos@cs.bu.edu>
legent-1           373/tcp    Legent Corporation
legent-1           373/udp    Legent Corporation
legent-2           374/tcp    Legent Corporation
legent-2           374/udp    Legent Corporation
#                             Keith Boyce <---none--->
hassle             375/tcp    Hassle
hassle             375/udp    Hassle
#                             Reinhard Doelz <doelz@comp.bioz.unibas.ch>
nip                376/tcp    Amiga Envoy Network Inquiry Proto
nip                376/udp    Amiga Envoy Network Inquiry Proto
#                             Heinz Wrobel <hwrobel@gmx.de>
tnETOS             377/tcp    NEC Corporation
tnETOS             377/udp    NEC Corporation
dsETOS             378/tcp    NEC Corporation
dsETOS             378/udp    NEC Corporation
#                             Tomoo Fujita <tf@arc.bs1.fc.nec.co.jp>
is99c              379/tcp    TIA/EIA/IS-99 modem client
is99c              379/udp    TIA/EIA/IS-99 modem client
is99s              380/tcp    TIA/EIA/IS-99 modem server
is99s              380/udp    TIA/EIA/IS-99 modem server
#                             Frank Quick <fquick@qualcomm.com>
hp-collector       381/tcp    hp performance data collector
hp-collector       381/udp    hp performance data collector
hp-managed-node 382/tcp    hp performance data managed node
hp-managed-node 382/udp    hp performance data managed node
hp-alarm-mgr       383/tcp    hp performance data alarm manager
hp-alarm-mgr       383/udp    hp performance data alarm manager
#                             Frank Blakely <frankb@hpptc16.rose.hp.com>
arns               384/tcp    A Remote Network Server System
arns               384/udp    A Remote Network Server System
#                             David Hornsby <djh@munnari.OZ.AU>
ibm-app            385/tcp    IBM Application
ibm-app            385/udp    IBM Application
#                             Lisa Tomita <---none--->
asa                386/tcp    ASA Message Router Object Def.
asa                386/udp    ASA Message Router Object Def.
#                             Steve Laitinen <laitinen@brutus.aa.ab.com>
```

```
aurp              387/tcp    Appletalk Update-Based Routing Pro.
aurp              387/udp    Appletalk Update-Based Routing Pro.
#                            Chris Ranch <cranch@novell.com>
unidata-ldm       388/tcp    Unidata LDM
unidata-ldm       388/udp    Unidata LDM
#                            Glenn Davis <support@unidata.ucar.edu>
ldap              389/tcp    Lightweight Directory Access Protocol
ldap              389/udp    Lightweight Directory Access Protocol
#                            Tim Howes <Tim.Howes@terminator.cc.umich.edu>
uis               390/tcp    UIS
uis               390/udp    UIS
#                            Ed Barron <---none--->
synotics-relay    391/tcp    SynOptics SNMP Relay Port
synotics-relay    391/udp    SynOptics SNMP Relay Port
synotics-broker   392/tcp    SynOptics Port Broker Port
synotics-broker   392/udp    SynOptics Port Broker Port
#                            Illan Raab <iraab@synoptics.com>
meta5             393/tcp    Meta5
meta5             393/udp    Meta5
#                            Jim Kanzler <jim.kanzler@meta5.com>
embl-ndt          394/tcp    EMBL Nucleic Data Transfer
embl-ndt          394/udp    EMBL Nucleic Data Transfer
#                            Peter Gad <peter@bmc.uu.se>
netcp             395/tcp    NETscout Control Protocol
netcp             395/udp    NETscout Control Protocol
#                            Anil Singhal <---none--->
netware-ip        396/tcp    Novell Netware over IP
netware-ip        396/udp    Novell Netware over IP
mptn              397/tcp    Multi Protocol Trans. Net.
mptn              397/udp    Multi Protocol Trans. Net.
#                            Soumitra Sarkar <sarkar@vnet.ibm.com>
kryptolan         398/tcp    Kryptolan
kryptolan         398/udp    Kryptolan
#                            Peter de Laval <pdl@sectra.se>
iso-tsap-c2       399/tcp    ISO Transport Class 2 Non-Control over TCP
iso-tsap-c2       399/udp    ISO Transport Class 2 Non-Control over UDP
#                            Yanick Pouffary <pouffary@taec.enet.dec.com>
work-sol          400/tcp    Workstation Solutions
work-sol          400/udp    Workstation Solutions
#                            Jim Ward <jimw@worksta.com>
ups               401/tcp    Uninterruptible Power Supply
ups               401/udp    Uninterruptible Power Supply
#                            Charles Bennett <chuck@benatong.com>
genie             402/tcp    Genie Protocol
genie             402/udp    Genie Protocol
#                            Mark Hankin <---none--->
decap             403/tcp    decap
decap             403/udp    decap
nced              404/tcp    nced
nced              404/udp    nced
ncld              405/tcp    ncld
```

```
ncld            405/udp    ncld
#                          Richard Jones <---none--->
imsp            406/tcp    Interactive Mail Support Protocol
imsp            406/udp    Interactive Mail Support Protocol
#                          John Myers <jgm+@cmu.edu>
timbuktu        407/tcp    Timbuktu
timbuktu        407/udp    Timbuktu
#                          Marc Epard <marc@netopia.com>
prm-sm          408/tcp    Prospero Resource Manager Sys. Man.
prm-sm          408/udp    Prospero Resource Manager Sys. Man.
prm-nm          409/tcp    Prospero Resource Manager Node Man.
prm-nm          409/udp    Prospero Resource Manager Node Man.
#                          B. Clifford Neuman <bcn@isi.edu>
decladebug      410/tcp    DECLadebug Remote Debug Protocol
decladebug      410/udp    DECLadebug Remote Debug Protocol
#                          Anthony Berent <anthony.berent@reo.mts.dec.com>
rmt             411/tcp    Remote MT Protocol
rmt             411/udp    Remote MT Protocol
#                          Peter Eriksson <pen@lysator.liu.se>
synoptics-trap  412/tcp    Trap Convention Port
synoptics-trap  412/udp    Trap Convention Port
#                          Illan Raab <iraab@synoptics.com>
smsp            413/tcp    Storage Management Services Protocol
smsp            413/udp    Storage Management Services Protocol
#                          Murthy Srinivas <murthy@novell.com>
infoseek        414/tcp    InfoSeek
infoseek        414/udp    InfoSeek
#                          Steve Kirsch <stk@infoseek.com>
bnet            415/tcp    BNet
bnet            415/udp    BNet
#                          Jim Mertz <JMertz+RV09@rvdc.unisys.com>
silverplatter   416/tcp    Silverplatter
silverplatter   416/udp    Silverplatter
#                          Peter Ciuffetti <petec@silverplatter.com>
onmux           417/tcp    Onmux
onmux           417/udp    Onmux
#                          Stephen Hanna <hanna@world.std.com>
hyper-g         418/tcp    Hyper-G
hyper-g         418/udp    Hyper-G
#                          Frank Kappe <fkappe@iicm.tu-graz.ac.at>
ariel1          419/tcp    Ariel 1
ariel1          419/udp    Ariel 1
#                          Joel Karafin <jkarafin@infotrieve.com>
smpte           420/tcp    SMPTE
smpte           420/udp    SMPTE
#                          Si Becker <71362.22@CompuServe.COM>
ariel2          421/tcp    Ariel 2
ariel2          421/udp    Ariel 2
ariel3          422/tcp    Ariel 3
ariel3          422/udp    Ariel 3
#                          Joel Karafin <jkarafin@infotrieve.com>
```

```
opc-job-start      423/tcp     IBM Operations Planning and Control Start
opc-job-start      423/udp     IBM Operations Planning and Control Start
opc-job-track      424/tcp     IBM Operations Planning and Control Track
opc-job-track      424/udp     IBM Operations Planning and Control Track
#                              Conny Larsson  <cocke@VNET.IBM.COM>
icad-el            425/tcp     ICAD
icad-el            425/udp     ICAD
#                              Larry Stone   <lcs@icad.com>
smartsdp           426/tcp     smartsdp
smartsdp           426/udp     smartsdp
#                              Alexander Dupuy <dupuy@smarts.com>
svrloc             427/tcp     Server Location
svrloc             427/udp     Server Location
#                              <veizades@ftp.com>
ocs_cmu            428/tcp     OCS_CMU
ocs_cmu            428/udp     OCS_CMU
ocs_amu            429/tcp     OCS_AMU
ocs_amu            429/udp     OCS_AMU
#                              Florence Wyman <wyman@peabody.plk.af.mil>
utmpsd             430/tcp     UTMPSD
utmpsd             430/udp     UTMPSD
utmpcd             431/tcp     UTMPCD
utmpcd             431/udp     UTMPCD
iasd               432/tcp     IASD
iasd               432/udp     IASD
#                              Nir Baroz <nbaroz@encore.com>
nnsp               433/tcp     NNSP
nnsp               433/udp     NNSP
#                              Rob Robertson <rob@gangrene.berkeley.edu>
mobileip-agent     434/tcp     MobileIP-Agent
mobileip-agent     434/udp     MobileIP-Agent
mobilip-mn         435/tcp     MobilIP-MN
mobilip-mn         435/udp     MobilIP-MN
#                              Kannan Alagappan <kannan@sejour.lkg.dec.com>
dna-cml            436/tcp     DNA-CML
dna-cml            436/udp     DNA-CML
#                              Dan Flowers <flowers@smaug.lkg.dec.com>
comscm             437/tcp     comscm
comscm             437/udp     comscm
#                              Jim Teague <teague@zso.dec.com>
dsfgw              438/tcp     dsfgw
dsfgw              438/udp     dsfgw
#                              Andy McKeen <mckeen@osf.org>
dasp               439/tcp     dasp      Thomas Obermair
dasp               439/udp     dasp      tommy@inlab.m.eunet.de
#                              Thomas Obermair <tommy@inlab.m.eunet.de>
sgcp               440/tcp     sgcp
sgcp               440/udp     sgcp
#                              Marshall Rose <mrose@dbc.mtview.ca.us>
decvms-sysmgt      441/tcp     decvms-sysmgt
```

```
decvms-sysmgt     441/udp     decvms-sysmgt
#                             Lee Barton <barton@star.enet.dec.com>
cvc_hostd         442/tcp     cvc_hostd
cvc_hostd         442/udp     cvc_hostd
#                             Bill Davidson <billd@equalizer.cray.com>
https             443/tcp     http protocol over TLS/SSL
https             443/udp     http protocol over TLS/SSL
#                             Kipp E.B. Hickman <kipp@mcom.com>
snpp              444/tcp     Simple Network Paging Protocol
snpp              444/udp     Simple Network Paging Protocol
#                             [RFC1568]
microsoft-ds      445/tcp     Microsoft-DS
microsoft-ds      445/udp     Microsoft-DS
#                             Pradeep Bahl <pradeepb@microsoft.com>
ddm-rdb           446/tcp     DDM-Remote Relational Database Access
ddm-rdb           446/udp     DDM-Remote Relational Database Access
ddm-dfm           447/tcp     DDM-Distributed File Management
ddm-dfm           447/udp     DDM-Distributed File Management
#                             Steven Ritland <srr@us.ibm.com>
ddm-ssl           448/tcp     DDM-Remote DB Access Using Secure Sockets
ddm-ssl           448/udp     DDM-Remote DB Access Using Secure Sockets
#                             Steven Ritland <srr@us.ibm.com>
as-servermap      449/tcp     AS Server Mapper
as-servermap      449/udp     AS Server Mapper
#                             Barbara Foss <BGFOSS@rchvmv.vnet.ibm.com>
tserver           450/tcp     Computer Supported Telecomunication Applications
tserver           450/udp     Computer Supported Telecomunication Applications
#                             Harvey S. Schultz <harvey@acm.org>
sfs-smp-net       451/tcp     Cray Network Semaphore server
sfs-smp-net       451/udp     Cray Network Semaphore server
sfs-config        452/tcp     Cray SFS config server
sfs-config        452/udp     Cray SFS config server
#                             Walter Poxon <wdp@ironwood.cray.com>
creativeserver    453/tcp     CreativeServer
creativeserver    453/udp     CreativeServer
contentserver     454/tcp     ContentServer
contentserver     454/udp     ContentServer
creativepartnr    455/tcp     CreativePartnr
creativepartnr    455/udp     CreativePartnr
#                             Jesus Ortiz <jesus_ortiz@emotion.com>
macon-tcp         456/tcp     macon-tcp
macon-udp         456/udp     macon-udp
#                             Yoshinobu Inoue
#                             <shin@hodaka.mfd.cs.fujitsu.co.jp>
scohelp           457/tcp     scohelp
scohelp           457/udp     scohelp
#                             Faith Zack <faithz@sco.com>
appleqtc          458/tcp     apple quick time
appleqtc          458/udp     apple quick time
#                             Murali Ranganathan
#                             <murali_ranganathan@quickmail.apple.com>
```

```
ampr-rcmd          459/tcp    ampr-rcmd
ampr-rcmd          459/udp    ampr-rcmd
#                             Rob Janssen <rob@sys3.pe1chl.ampr.org>
skronk             460/tcp    skronk
skronk             460/udp    skronk
#                             Henry Strickland <strick@yak.net>
datasurfsrv        461/tcp    DataRampSrv
datasurfsrv        461/udp    DataRampSrv
datasurfsrvsec     462/tcp    DataRampSrvSec
datasurfsrvsec     462/udp    DataRampSrvSec
#                             Diane Downie <downie@jibe.MV.COM>
alpes              463/tcp    alpes
alpes              463/udp    alpes
#                             Alain Durand <Alain.Durand@imag.fr>
kpasswd            464/tcp    kpasswd
kpasswd            464/udp    kpasswd
#                             Theodore Ts'o <tytso@MIT.EDU>
urd                465/tcp    URL Rendesvous Directory for SSM
igmpv3lite         465/udp    IGMP over UDP for SSM
#                             Toerless Eckert <eckert@cisco.com>
digital-vrc        466/tcp    digital-vrc
digital-vrc        466/udp    digital-vrc
#                             Peter Higginson <higginson@mail.dec.com>
mylex-mapd         467/tcp    mylex-mapd
mylex-mapd         467/udp    mylex-mapd
#                             Gary Lewis <GaryL@hq.mylex.com>
photuris           468/tcp    proturis
photuris           468/udp    proturis
#                             Bill Simpson <Bill.Simpson@um.cc.umich.edu>
rcp                469/tcp    Radio Control Protocol
rcp                469/udp    Radio Control Protocol
#                             Jim Jennings +1-708-538-7241
scx-proxy          470/tcp    scx-proxy
scx-proxy          470/udp    scx-proxy
#                             Scott Narveson <sjn@cray.com>
mondex             471/tcp    Mondex
mondex             471/udp    Mondex
#                             Bill Reding <redingb@nwdt.natwest.co.uk>
ljk-login          472/tcp    ljk-login
ljk-login          472/udp    ljk-login
#                             LJK Software, Cambridge, Massachusetts
#                             <support@ljk.com>
hybrid-pop         473/tcp    hybrid-pop
hybrid-pop         473/udp    hybrid-pop
#                             Rami Rubin <rami@hybrid.com>
tn-tl-w1           474/tcp    tn-tl-w1
tn-tl-w2           474/udp    tn-tl-w2
#                             Ed Kress <eskress@thinknet.com>
tcpnethaspsrv      475/tcp    tcpnethaspsrv
tcpnethaspsrv      475/udp    tcpnethaspsrv
#                             Charlie Hava <charlie@aladdin.co.il>
```

```
tn-tl-fd1       476/tcp    tn-tl-fd1
tn-tl-fd1       476/udp    tn-tl-fd1
#                          Ed Kress <eskress@thinknet.com>
ss7ns           477/tcp    ss7ns
ss7ns           477/udp    ss7ns
#                          Jean-Michel URSCH <ursch@taec.enet.dec.com>
spsc            478/tcp    spsc
spsc            478/udp    spsc
#                          Mike Rieker <mikea@sp32.com>
iafserver       479/tcp    iafserver
iafserver       479/udp    iafserver
iafdbase        480/tcp    iafdbase
iafdbase        480/udp    iafdbase
#                          ricky@solect.com <Rick Yazwinski>
ph              481/tcp    Ph service
ph              481/udp    Ph service
#                          Roland Hedberg <Roland.Hedberg@umdac.umu.se>
bgs-nsi         482/tcp    bgs-nsi
bgs-nsi         482/udp    bgs-nsi
#                          Jon Saperia <saperia@bgs.com>
ulpnet          483/tcp    ulpnet
ulpnet          483/udp    ulpnet
#                          Kevin Mooney <kevinm@bfs.unibol.com>
integra-sme     484/tcp    Integra Software Management Environment
integra-sme     484/udp    Integra Software Management Environment
#                          Randall Dow <rand@randix.m.isr.de>
powerburst      485/tcp    Air Soft Power Burst
powerburst      485/udp    Air Soft Power Burst
#                          <gary@airsoft.com>
avian           486/tcp    avian
avian           486/udp    avian
#                          Robert Ullmann
#                          <Robert_Ullmann/CAM/Lotus.LOTUS@crd.lotus.com>
saft            487/tcp    saft Simple Asynchronous File Transfer
saft            487/udp    saft Simple Asynchronous File Transfer
#                          Ulli Horlacher <framstag@rus.uni-stuttgart.de>
gss-http        488/tcp    gss-http
gss-http        488/udp    gss-http
#                          Doug Rosenthal <rosenthl@krypton.einet.net>
nest-protocol   489/tcp    nest-protocol
nest-protocol   489/udp    nest-protocol
#                          Gilles Gameiro <ggameiro@birdland.com>
micom-pfs       490/tcp    micom-pfs
micom-pfs       490/udp    micom-pfs
#                          David Misunas <DMisunas@micom.com>
go-login        491/tcp    go-login
go-login        491/udp    go-login
#                          Troy Morrison <troy@graphon.com>
ticf-1          492/tcp    Transport Independent Convergence for FNA
ticf-1          492/udp    Transport Independent Convergence for FNA
ticf-2          493/tcp    Transport Independent Convergence for FNA
```

```
ticf-2            493/udp    Transport Independent Convergence for FNA
#                            Mamoru Ito <Ito@pcnet.ks.pfu.co.jp>
pov-ray           494/tcp    POV-Ray
pov-ray           494/udp    POV-Ray
#                            POV-Team Co-ordinator
#                            <iana-port.remove-spamguard@povray.org>
intecourier       495/tcp    intecourier
intecourier       495/udp    intecourier
#                            Steve Favor <sfavor@tigger.intecom.com>
pim-rp-disc       496/tcp    PIM-RP-DISC
pim-rp-disc       496/udp    PIM-RP-DISC
#                            Dino Farinacci <dino@cisco.com>
dantz             497/tcp    dantz
dantz             497/udp    dantz
#                            Richard Zulch <richard_zulch@dantz.com>
siam              498/tcp    siam
siam              498/udp    siam
#                            Philippe Gilbert <pgilbert@cal.fr>
iso-ill           499/tcp    ISO ILL Protocol
iso-ill           499/udp    ISO ILL Protocol
#                            Mark H. Needleman <markn@sirsi.com>
isakmp            500/tcp    isakmp
isakmp            500/udp    isakmp
#                            Mark Schertler <mjs@tycho.ncsc.mil>
stmf              501/tcp    STMF
stmf              501/udp    STMF
#                            Alan Ungar <aungar@farradyne.com>
asa-appl-proto    502/tcp    asa-appl-proto
asa-appl-proto    502/udp    asa-appl-proto
#                            Dennis Dube <ddube@modicon.com>
intrinsa          503/tcp    Intrinsa
intrinsa          503/udp    Intrinsa
#                            Robert Ford <robert@intrinsa.com>
citadel           504/tcp    citadel
citadel           504/udp    citadel
#                            Art Cancro <ajc@uncnsrd.mt-kisco.ny.us>
mailbox-lm        505/tcp    mailbox-lm
mailbox-lm        505/udp    mailbox-lm
#                            Beverly Moody <Beverly_Moody@stercomm.com>
ohimsrv           506/tcp    ohimsrv
ohimsrv           506/udp    ohimsrv
#                            Scott Powell <spowell@openhorizon.com>
crs               507/tcp    crs
crs               507/udp    crs
#                            Brad Wright <bradwr@microsoft.com>
xvttp             508/tcp    xvttp
xvttp             508/udp    xvttp
#                            Keith J. Alphonso <alphonso@ncs-ssc.com>
snare             509/tcp    snare
snare             509/udp    snare
#                            Dennis Batchelder <dennis@capres.com>
```

```
fcp             510/tcp    FirstClass Protocol
fcp             510/udp    FirstClass Protocol
#                          Mike Marshburn <paul@softarc.com>
passgo          511/tcp    PassGo
passgo          511/udp    PassGo
#                          John Rainford <jrainford@passgo.com>
exec            512/tcp    remote process execution;
#                          authentication performed using
#                          passwords and UNIX login names
comsat          512/udp
biff            512/udp    used by mail system to notify users
#                          of new mail received; currently
#                          receives messages only from
#                          processes on the same machine
login           513/tcp    remote login a la telnet;
#                          automatic authentication performed
#                          based on priviledged port numbers
#                          and distributed data bases which
#                          identify "authentication domains"
who             513/udp    maintains data bases showing who's
#                          logged in to machines on a local
#                          net and the load average of the
#                          machine
shell           514/tcp    cmd
#                          like exec, but automatic authentication
#                          is performed as for login server
syslog          514/udp
printer         515/tcp    spooler
printer         515/udp    spooler
videotex        516/tcp    videotex
videotex        516/udp    videotex
#                          Daniel Mavrakis <system@venus.mctel.fr>
talk            517/tcp    like tenex link, but across
#                          machine - unfortunately, doesn't
#                          use link protocol (this is actually
#                          just a rendezvous port from which a
#                          tcp connection is established)
talk            517/udp    like tenex link, but across
#                          machine - unfortunately, doesn't
#                          use link protocol (this is actually
#                          just a rendezvous port from which a
#                          tcp connection is established)
ntalk           518/tcp
ntalk           518/udp
utime           519/tcp    unixtime
utime           519/udp    unixtime
efs             520/tcp    extended file name server
router          520/udp    local routing process (on site);
#                          uses variant of Xerox NS routing
#                          information protocol - RIP
ripng           521/tcp    ripng
```

```
ripng            521/udp     ripng
#                            Robert E. Minnear <minnear@ipsilon.com>
ulp              522/tcp     ULP
ulp              522/udp     ULP
#                            Max Morris <maxm@MICROSOFT.com>
ibm-db2          523/tcp     IBM-DB2
ibm-db2          523/udp     IBM-DB2
#                            Juliana Hsu <jhsu@ca.ibm.com>
ncp              524/tcp     NCP
ncp              524/udp     NCP
#                            Don Provan <donp@sjf.novell.com>
timed            525/tcp     timeserver
timed            525/udp     timeserver
tempo            526/tcp     newdate
tempo            526/udp     newdate
#                            Unknown
stx              527/tcp     Stock IXChange
stx              527/udp     Stock IXChange
custix           528/tcp     Customer IXChange
custix           528/udp     Customer IXChange
#                            Ferdi Ladeira <ferdi.ladeira@ixchange.com>
irc-serv         529/tcp     IRC-SERV
irc-serv         529/udp     IRC-SERV
#                            Brian Tackett <cym@acrux.net>
courier          530/tcp     rpc
courier          530/udp     rpc
conference       531/tcp     chat
conference       531/udp     chat
netnews          532/tcp     readnews
netnews          532/udp     readnews
netwall          533/tcp     for emergency broadcasts
netwall          533/udp     for emergency broadcasts
mm-admin         534/tcp     MegaMedia Admin
mm-admin         534/udp     MegaMedia Admin
#                            Andreas Heidemann <a.heidemann@ais-gmbh.de>
iiop             535/tcp     iiop
iiop             535/udp     iiop
#                            Jeff M.Michaud <michaud@zk3.dec.com>
opalis-rdv       536/tcp     opalis-rdv
opalis-rdv       536/udp     opalis-rdv
#                            Laurent Domenech <ldomenech@opalis.com>
nmsp             537/tcp     Networked Media Streaming Protocol
nmsp             537/udp     Networked Media Streaming Protocol
#                            Paul Santinelli Jr. <psantinelli@narrative.com>
gdomap           538/tcp     gdomap
gdomap           538/udp     gdomap
#                            Richard Frith-Macdonald
                             <richard@brainstorm.co.uk>
apertus-ldp      539/tcp     Apertus Technologies Load Determination
apertus-ldp      539/udp     Apertus Technologies Load Determination
uucp             540/tcp     uucpd
```

```
uucp             540/udp    uucpd
uucp-rlogin      541/tcp    uucp-rlogin
uucp-rlogin      541/udp    uucp-rlogin
#                           Stuart Lynne <sl@wimsey.com>
commerce         542/tcp    commerce
commerce         542/udp    commerce
#                           Randy Epstein <repstein@host.net>
klogin           543/tcp
klogin           543/udp
kshell           544/tcp    krcmd
kshell           544/udp    krcmd
appleqtcsrvr     545/tcp    appleqtcsrvr
appleqtcsrvr     545/udp    appleqtcsrvr
#                           Murali Ranganathan
#                           <Murali_Ranganathan@quickmail.apple.com>
dhcpv6-client    546/tcp    DHCPv6 Client
dhcpv6-client    546/udp    DHCPv6 Client
dhcpv6-server    547/tcp    DHCPv6 Server
dhcpv6-server    547/udp    DHCPv6 Server
#                           Jim Bound <bound@zk3.dec.com>
afpovertcp       548/tcp    AFP over TCP
afpovertcp       548/udp    AFP over TCP
#                           Leland Wallace <randall@apple.com>
idfp             549/tcp    IDFP
idfp             549/udp    IDFP
#                           Ramana Kovi <ramana@kovi.com>
new-rwho         550/tcp    new-who
new-rwho         550/udp    new-who
cybercash        551/tcp    cybercash
cybercash        551/udp    cybercash
#                           Donald E. Eastlake 3rd <dee@cybercash.com>
devshr-nts       552/tcp    DeviceShare
devshr-nts       552/udp    DeviceShare
#                           Benjamin Rosenberg <brosenberg@advsyscon.com>
pirp             553/tcp    pirp
pirp             553/udp    pirp
#                           D. J. Bernstein <djb@silverton.berkeley.edu>
rtsp             554/tcp    Real Time Stream Control Protocol
rtsp             554/udp    Real Time Stream Control Protocol
#                           Rob Lanphier <robla@prognet.com>
dsf              555/tcp
dsf              555/udp
remotefs         556/tcp    rfs server
remotefs         556/udp    rfs server
openvms-sysipc   557/tcp    openvms-sysipc
openvms-sysipc   557/udp    openvms-sysipc
#                           Alan Potter <potter@movies.enet.dec.com>
sdnskmp          558/tcp    SDNSKMP
sdnskmp          558/udp    SDNSKMP
teedtap          559/tcp    TEEDTAP
teedtap          559/udp    TEEDTAP
```

```
#                              Mort Hoffman <hoffman@mail.ndhm.gtegsc.com>
rmonitor      560/tcp          rmonitord
rmonitor      560/udp          rmonitord
monitor       561/tcp
monitor       561/udp
chshell       562/tcp          chcmd
chshell       562/udp          chcmd
nntps         563/tcp          nntp protocol over TLS/SSL (was snntp)
nntps         563/udp          nntp protocol over TLS/SSL (was snntp)
#                              Kipp E.B. Hickman <kipp@netscape.com>
9pfs          564/tcp          plan 9 file service
9pfs          564/udp          plan 9 file service
whoami        565/tcp          whoami
whoami        565/udp          whoami
streettalk    566/tcp          streettalk
streettalk    566/udp          streettalk
banyan-rpc    567/tcp          banyan-rpc
banyan-rpc    567/udp          banyan-rpc
#                              Tom Lemaire <toml@banyan.com>
ms-shuttle    568/tcp          microsoft shuttle
ms-shuttle    568/udp          microsoft shuttle
#                              Rudolph Balaz <rudolphb@microsoft.com>
ms-rome       569/tcp          microsoft rome
ms-rome       569/udp          microsoft rome
#                              Rudolph Balaz <rudolphb@microsoft.com>
meter         570/tcp          demon
meter         570/udp          demon
meter         571/tcp          udemon
meter         571/udp          udemon
sonar         572/tcp          sonar
sonar         572/udp          sonar
#                              Keith Moore <moore@cs.utk.edu>
banyan-vip    573/tcp          banyan-vip
banyan-vip    573/udp          banyan-vip
#                              Denis Leclerc <DLeclerc@banyan.com>
ftp-agent     574/tcp          FTP Software Agent System
ftp-agent     574/udp          FTP Software Agent System
#                              Michael S. Greenberg <arnoff@ftp.com>
vemmi         575/tcp          VEMMI
vemmi         575/udp          VEMMI
#                              Daniel Mavrakis <mavrakis@mctel.fr>
ipcd          576/tcp          ipcd
ipcd          576/udp          ipcd
vnas          577/tcp          vnas
vnas          577/udp          vnas
ipdd          578/tcp          ipdd
ipdd          578/udp          ipdd
#                              Jay Farhat <jfarhat@ipass.com>
decbsrv       579/tcp          decbsrv
decbsrv       579/udp          decbsrv
#                              Rudi Martin
                               <movies::martin"@movies.enet.dec.com>
```

```
sntp-heartbeat   580/tcp      SNTP HEARTBEAT
sntp-heartbeat   580/udp      SNTP HEARTBEAT
#                             Louis Mamakos <louie@uu.net>
bdp              581/tcp      Bundle Discovery Protocol
bdp              581/udp      Bundle Discovery Protocol
#                             Gary Malkin <gmalkin@xylogics.com>
scc-security     582/tcp      SCC Security
scc-security     582/udp      SCC Security
#                             Prashant Dholakia <prashant@semaphorecom.com>
philips-vc       583/tcp      Philips Video-Conferencing
philips-vc       583/udp      Philips Video-Conferencing
#                             Janna Chang <janna@pmc.philips.com>
keyserver        584/tcp      Key Server
keyserver        584/udp      Key Server
#                             Gary Howland <gary@systemics.com>
imap4-ssl        585/tcp      IMAP4+SSL (use 993 instead)
imap4-ssl        585/udp      IMAP4+SSL (use 993 instead)
#                             Terry Gray <gray@cac.washington.edu>
#                Use of 585 is not recommended, use 993 instead
password-chg     586/tcp      Password Change
password-chg     586/udp      Password Change
submission       587/tcp      Submission
submission       587/udp      Submission
#                             Randy Gellens <randy@qualcomm.com>
cal              588/tcp      CAL
cal              588/udp      CAL
#                             Myron Hattig <Myron_Hattig@ccm.jf.intel.com>
eyelink          589/tcp      EyeLink
eyelink          589/udp      EyeLink
#                             Dave Stampe <dstampe@psych.toronto.edu>
tns-cml          590/tcp      TNS CML
tns-cml          590/udp      TNS CML
#                             Jerome Albin <albin@taec.enet.dec.com>
http-alt         591/tcp      FileMaker, Inc. - HTTP Alternate (see Port 80)
http-alt         591/udp      FileMaker, Inc. - HTTP Alternate (see Port 80)
#                             Clay Maeckel <clay_maeckel@filemaker.com>
eudora-set       592/tcp      Eudora Set
eudora-set       592/udp      Eudora Set
#                             Randall Gellens <randy@qualcomm.com>
http-rpc-epmap   593/tcp      HTTP RPC Ep Map
http-rpc-epmap   593/udp      HTTP RPC Ep Map
#                             Edward Reus <edwardr@microsoft.com>
tpip             594/tcp      TPIP
tpip             594/udp      TPIP
#                             Brad Spear <spear@platinum.com>
cab-protocol     595/tcp      CAB Protocol
cab-protocol     595/udp      CAB Protocol
#                             Winston Hetherington
smsd             596/tcp      SMSD
smsd             596/udp      SMSD
#                             Wayne Barlow <web@unx.dec.com>
```

```
ptcnameservice   597/tcp    PTC Name Service
ptcnameservice   597/udp    PTC Name Service
#                           Yuri Machkasov <yuri@ptc.com>
sco-websrvrmg3   598/tcp    SCO Web Server Manager 3
sco-websrvrmg3   598/udp    SCO Web Server Manager 3
#                           Simon Baldwin <simonb@sco.com>
acp              599/tcp    Aeolon Core Protocol
acp              599/udp    Aeolon Core Protocol
#                           Michael Alyn Miller <malyn@aeolon.com>
ipcserver        600/tcp    Sun IPC server
ipcserver        600/udp    Sun IPC server
#                           Bill Schiefelbein <schief@aspen.cray.com>
syslog-conn      601/tcp    Reliable Syslog Service
syslog-conn      601/udp    Reliable Syslog Service
#                           RFC 3195
xmlrpc-beep      602/tcp    XML-RPC over BEEP
xmlrpc-beep      602/udp    XML-RPC over BEEP
#                           RFC3529 <ftp://ftp.isi.edu/in-notes/rfc3529.txt>
                            March 2003
idxp             603/tcp    IDXP
idxp             603/udp    IDXP
#                           RFC-ietf-idwg-beep-idxp-07.txt
tunnel           604/tcp    TUNNEL
tunnel           604/udp    TUNNEL
#                           RFC-ietf-idwg-beep-tunnel-05.txt
soap-beep        605/tcp    SOAP over BEEP
soap-beep        605/udp    SOAP over BEEP
#                           RFC3288 <ftp://ftp.isi.edu/in-notes/rfc3288.txt>
                            April 2002
urm              606/tcp    Cray Unified Resource Manager
urm              606/udp    Cray Unified Resource Manager
nqs              607/tcp    nqs
nqs              607/udp    nqs
#                           Bill Schiefelbein <schief@aspen.cray.com>
sift-uft         608/tcp    Sender-Initiated/Unsolicited File Transfer
sift-uft         608/udp    Sender-Initiated/Unsolicited File Transfer
#                           Rick Troth <troth@rice.edu>
npmp-trap        609/tcp    npmp-trap
npmp-trap        609/udp    npmp-trap
npmp-local       610/tcp    npmp-local
npmp-local       610/udp    npmp-local
npmp-gui         611/tcp    npmp-gui
npmp-gui         611/udp    npmp-gui
#                           John Barnes <jbarnes@crl.com>
hmmp-ind         612/tcp    HMMP Indication
hmmp-ind         612/udp    HMMP Indication
hmmp-op          613/tcp    HMMP Operation
hmmp-op          613/udp    HMMP Operation
#                           Andrew Sinclair <andrsin@microsoft.com>
sshell           614/tcp    SSLshell
sshell           614/udp    SSLshell
#                           Simon J. Gerraty <sjg@quick.com.au>
```

```
sco-inetmgr      615/tcp    Internet Configuration Manager
sco-inetmgr      615/udp    Internet Configuration Manager
sco-sysmgr       616/tcp    SCO System Administration Server
sco-sysmgr       616/udp    SCO System Administration Server
sco-dtmgr        617/tcp    SCO Desktop Administration Server
sco-dtmgr        617/udp    SCO Desktop Administration Server
#                           Christopher Durham <chrisdu@sco.com>
dei-icda         618/tcp    DEI-ICDA
dei-icda         618/udp    DEI-ICDA
#                           David Turner <digital@Quetico.tbaytel.net>
compaq-evm       619/tcp    Compaq EVM
compaq-evm       619/udp    Compaq EVM
#                           Jem Treadwell <Jem.Treadwell@compaq.com>
sco-websrvrmgr   620/tcp    SCO WebServer Manager
sco-websrvrmgr   620/udp    SCO WebServer Manager
#                           Christopher Durham <chrisdu@sco.com>
escp-ip          621/tcp    ESCP
escp-ip          621/udp    ESCP
#                           Lai Zit Seng <lzs@pobox.com>
collaborator     622/tcp    Collaborator
collaborator     622/udp    Collaborator
#                           Johnson Davis <johnsond@opteamasoft.com>
asf-rmcp         623/tcp    ASF Remote Management and Control Protocol
asf-rmcp         623/udp    ASF Remote Management and Control Protocol
#                           Carl First <Carl.L.First@intel.com>
cryptoadmin      624/tcp    Crypto Admin
cryptoadmin      624/udp    Crypto Admin
#                           Tony Walker <tony@cryptocard.com>
dec_dlm          625/tcp    DEC DLM
dec_dlm          625/udp    DEC DLM
#                           Rudi Martin <Rudi.Martin@edo.mts.dec.com>
asia             626/tcp    ASIA
asia             626/udp    ASIA
#                           Michael Dasenbrock <dasenbro@apple.com>
passgo-tivoli    627/tcp    PassGo Tivoli
passgo-tivoli    627/udp    PassGo Tivoli
#                           Chris Hall <chall@passgo.com>
qmqp             628/tcp    QMQP
qmqp             628/udp    QMQP
#                           Dan Bernstein <djb@cr.yp.to>
3com-amp3        629/tcp    3Com AMP3
3com-amp3        629/udp    3Com AMP3
#                           Prakash Banthia <prakash_banthia@3com.com>
rda              630/tcp    RDA
rda              630/udp    RDA
#                           John Hadjioannou <john@minster.co.uk>
ipp              631/tcp    IPP (Internet Printing Protocol)
ipp              631/udp    IPP (Internet Printing Protocol)
#                           Carl-Uno Manros <manros@cp10.es.xerox.com>
bmpp             632/tcp    bmpp
bmpp             632/udp    bmpp
#                           Troy Rollo <troy@kroll.corvu.com.au>
```

```
servstat          633/tcp   Service Status update (Sterling Software)
servstat          633/udp   Service Status update (Sterling Software)
#                           Greg Rose <Greg_Rose@sydney.sterling.com>
ginad             634/tcp   ginad
ginad             634/udp   ginad
#                           Mark Crother <mark@eis.calstate.edu>
rlzdbase          635/tcp   RLZ DBase
rlzdbase          635/udp   RLZ DBase
#                           Michael Ginn <ginn@tyxar.com>
ldaps             636/tcp   ldap protocol over TLS/SSL (was sldap)
ldaps             636/udp   ldap protocol over TLS/SSL (was sldap)
#                           Pat Richard <patr@xcert.com>
lanserver         637/tcp   lanserver
lanserver         637/udp   lanserver
#                           Chris Larsson <clarsson@VNET.IBM.COM>
mcns-sec          638/tcp   mcns-sec
mcns-sec          638/udp   mcns-sec
#                           Kaz Ozawa <k.ozawa@cablelabs.com>
msdp              639/tcp   MSDP
msdp              639/udp   MSDP
#                           Dino Farinacci <dino@cisco.com>
entrust-sps       640/tcp   entrust-sps
entrust-sps       640/udp   entrust-sps
#                           Marek Buchler <Marek.Buchler@entrust.com>
repcmd            641/tcp   repcmd
repcmd            641/udp   repcmd
#                           Scott Dale <scott@Replicase.com>
esro-emsdp        642/tcp   ESRO-EMSDP V1.3
esro-emsdp        642/udp   ESRO-EMSDP V1.3
#                           Mohsen Banan <mohsen@neda.com>
sanity            643/tcp   SANity
sanity            643/udp   SANity
#                           Peter Viscarola <PeterGV@osr.com>
dwr               644/tcp   dwr
dwr               644/udp   dwr
#                           Bill Fenner <fenner@parc.xerox.com>
pssc              645/tcp   PSSC
pssc              645/udp   PSSC
#                           Egon Meier-Engelen <egon.meier-engelen@dlr.de>
ldp               646/tcp   LDP
ldp               646/udp   LDP
#                           Bob Thomas <rhthomas@cisco.com>
dhcp-failover     647/tcp   DHCP Failover
dhcp-failover     647/udp   DHCP Failover
#                           Bernard Volz <volz@ipworks.com>
rrp               648/tcp   Registry Registrar Protocol (RRP)
rrp               648/udp   Registry Registrar Protocol (RRP)
#                           Scott Hollenbeck <shollenb@netsol.com>
cadview-3d        649/tcp   Cadview-3d - streaming 3d models over the
                            internet
```

```
cadview-3d       649/udp    Cadview-3d - streaming 3d models over the
                            internet
#                           David Cooper <david.cooper@oracle.com>
obex             650/tcp    OBEX
obex             650/udp    OBEX
#                           Jeff Garbers <FJG030@email.mot.com>
ieee-mms         651/tcp    IEEE MMS
ieee-mms         651/udp    IEEE MMS
#                           Curtis Anderson <canderson@turbolinux.com>
hello-port       652/tcp    HELLO_PORT
hello-port       652/udp    HELLO_PORT
#                           Patrick Cipiere <Patrick.Cipiere@UDcast.com>
repscmd          653/tcp    RepCmd
repscmd          653/udp    RepCmd
#                           Scott Dale <scott@tioga.com>
aodv             654/tcp    AODV
aodv             654/udp    AODV
#                           Charles Perkins <cperkins@eng.sun.com>
tinc             655/tcp    TINC
tinc             655/udp    TINC
#                           Ivo Timmermans <itimmermans@bigfoot.com>
spmp             656/tcp    SPMP
spmp             656/udp    SPMP
#                           Jakob Kaivo <jkaivo@nodomainname.net>
rmc              657/tcp    RMC
rmc              657/udp    RMC
#                           Michael Schmidt <mmaass@us.ibm.com>
tenfold          658/tcp    TenFold
tenfold          658/udp    TenFold
#                           Louis Olszyk <lolszyk@10fold.com>
#                659        Removed (2001-06-06)
mac-srvr-admin   660/tcp    MacOS Server Admin
mac-srvr-admin   660/udp    MacOS Server Admin
#                           Forest Hill <forest@apple.com>
hap              661/tcp    HAP
hap              661/udp    HAP
#                           Igor Plotnikov <igor@uroam.com>
pftp             662/tcp    PFTP
pftp             662/udp    PFTP
#                           Ben Schluricke <support@pftp.de>
purenoise        663/tcp    PureNoise
purenoise        663/udp    PureNoise
#                           Sam Osa <pristine@mailcity.com>
asf-secure-rmcp  664/tcp    ASF Secure Remote Management and Control
                            Protocol
asf-secure-rmcp  664/udp    ASF Secure Remote Management and Control
                            Protocol
#                           Carl First <Carl.L.First@intel.com>
sun-dr           665/tcp    Sun DR
sun-dr           665/udp    Sun DR
#                           Harinder Bhasin <Harinder.Bhasin@Sun.COM>
```

```
mdqs              666/tcp
mdqs              666/udp
doom              666/tcp      doom Id Software
doom              666/udp      doom Id Software
#                              <ddt@idcube.idsoftware.com>
disclose          667/tcp      campaign contribution disclosures - SDR
                               Technologies
disclose          667/udp      campaign contribution disclosures - SDR
                               Technologies
#                              Jim Dixon  <jim@lambda.com>
mecomm            668/tcp      MeComm
mecomm            668/udp      MeComm
meregister        669/tcp      MeRegister
meregister        669/udp      MeRegister
#                              Armin Sawusch <armin@esd1.esd.de>
vacdsm-sws        670/tcp      VACDSM-SWS
vacdsm-sws        670/udp      VACDSM-SWS
vacdsm-app        671/tcp      VACDSM-APP
vacdsm-app        671/udp      VACDSM-APP
vpps-qua          672/tcp      VPPS-QUA
vpps-qua          672/udp      VPPS-QUA
cimplex           673/tcp      CIMPLEX
cimplex           673/udp      CIMPLEX
#                              Ulysses G. Smith Jr. <ugsmith@cesi.com>
acap              674/tcp      ACAP
acap              674/udp      ACAP
#                              Chris Newman <chris.newman@sun.com>
dctp              675/tcp      DCTP
dctp              675/udp      DCTP
#                              Andre Kramer <Andre.Kramer@ansa.co.uk>
vpps-via          676/tcp      VPPS Via
vpps-via          676/udp      VPPS Via
#                              Ulysses G. Smith Jr. <ugsmith@cesi.com>
vpp               677/tcp      Virtual Presence Protocol
vpp               677/udp      Virtual Presence Protocol
#                              Klaus Wolf <wolf@cobrow.com>
ggf-ncp           678/tcp      GNU Generation Foundation NCP
ggf-ncp           678/udp      GNU Generation Foundation NCP
#                              Noah Paul <noahp@altavista.net>
mrm               679/tcp      MRM
mrm               679/udp      MRM
#                              Liming Wei <lwei@cisco.com>
entrust-aaas      680/tcp      entrust-aaas
entrust-aaas      680/udp      entrust-aaas
entrust-aams      681/tcp      entrust-aams
entrust-aams      681/udp      entrust-aams
#                              Adrian Mancini <adrian.mancini@entrust.com>
xfr               682/tcp      XFR
xfr               682/udp      XFR
#                              Noah Paul <noahp@ultranet.com>
corba-iiop        683/tcp      CORBA IIOP
```

```
corba-iiop        683/udp     CORBA IIOP
corba-iiop-ssl    684/tcp     CORBA IIOP SSL
corba-iiop-ssl    684/udp     CORBA IIOP SSL
#                             Henry Lowe <lowe@omg.org>
mdc-portmapper    685/tcp     MDC Port Mapper
mdc-portmapper    685/udp     MDC Port Mapper
#                             Noah Paul <noahp@altavista.net>
hcp-wismar        686/tcp     Hardware Control Protocol Wismar
hcp-wismar        686/udp     Hardware Control Protocol Wismar
#                             David Merchant <d.f.merchant@livjm.ac.uk>
asipregistry      687/tcp     asipregistry
asipregistry      687/udp     asipregistry
#                             Erik Sea <sea@apple.com>
realm-rusd        688/tcp     REALM-RUSD
realm-rusd        688/udp     REALM-RUSD
#                             Jerry Knight <jknight@realminfo.com>
nmap              689/tcp     NMAP
nmap              689/udp     NMAP
#                             Peter Dennis Bartok <peter@novonyx.com>
vatp              690/tcp     VATP
vatp              690/udp     VATP
#                             Atica Software <comercial@aticasoft.es>
msexch-routing    691/tcp     MS Exchange Routing
msexch-routing    691/udp     MS Exchange Routing
#                             David Lemson <dlemson@microsoft.com>
hyperwave-isp     692/tcp     Hyperwave-ISP
hyperwave-isp     692/udp     Hyperwave-ISP
#                             Gerald Mesaric <gmesaric@hyperwave.com>
connendp          693/tcp     connendp
connendp          693/udp     connendp
#                             Ronny Bremer <rbremer@future-gate.com>
ha-cluster        694/tcp     ha-cluster
ha-cluster        694/udp     ha-cluster
#                             Alan Robertson <alanr@unix.sh>
ieee-mms-ssl      695/tcp     IEEE-MMS-SSL
ieee-mms-ssl      695/udp     IEEE-MMS-SSL
#                             Curtis Anderson <ecanderson@turbolinux.com>
rushd             696/tcp     RUSHD
rushd             696/udp     RUSHD
#                             Greg Ercolano <erco@netcom.com>
uuidgen           697/tcp     UUIDGEN
uuidgen           697/udp     UUIDGEN
#                             James Falkner <james.falkner@sun.com>
olsr              698/tcp     OLSR
olsr              698/udp     OLSR
#                             Thomas Clausen <thomas.clausen@inria.fr>
accessnetwork     699/tcp     Access Network
accessnetwork     699/udp     Access Network
#                             Yingchun Xu <Yingchun_Xu@3com.com>
epp               700/tcp     Extensible Provisioning Protocol
epp               700/udp     Extensible Provisioning Protocol
#                             RFC-ietf-provreg-epp-tcp-06.txt
```

```
#                701-703    Unassigned
elcsd            704/tcp    errlog copy/server daemon
elcsd            704/udp    errlog copy/server daemon
agentx           705/tcp    AgentX
agentx           705/udp    AgentX
#                           Bob Natale <natale@acec.com>
silc             706/tcp    SILC
silc             706/udp    SILC
#                           Pekka Riikonen <priikone@poseidon.pspt.fi>
borland-dsj      707/tcp    Borland DSJ
borland-dsj      707/udp    Borland DSJ
#                           Gerg Cole <gcole@corp.borland.com>
#                708        Unassigned
entrust-kmsh     709/tcp    Entrust Key Management Service Handler
entrust-kmsh     709/udp    Entrust Key Management Service Handler
entrust-ash      710/tcp    Entrust Administration Service Handler
entrust-ash      710/udp    Entrust Administration Service Handler
#                           Peter Whittaker <pww@entrust.com>
cisco-tdp        711/tcp    Cisco TDP
cisco-tdp        711/udp    Cisco TDP
#                           Bruce Davie <bsd@cisco.com>
#                712-728    Unassigned
netviewdm1       729/tcp    IBM NetView DM/6000 Server/Client
netviewdm1       729/udp    IBM NetView DM/6000 Server/Client
netviewdm2       730/tcp    IBM NetView DM/6000 send/tcp
netviewdm2       730/udp    IBM NetView DM/6000 send/tcp
netviewdm3       731/tcp    IBM NetView DM/6000 receive/tcp
netviewdm3       731/udp    IBM NetView DM/6000 receive/tcp
#                           Philippe Binet  (phbinet@vnet.IBM.COM)
#                732-740    Unassigned
netgw            741/tcp    netGW
netgw            741/udp    netGW
#                           Oliver Korfmacher (okorf@netcs.com)
netrcs           742/tcp    Network based Rev. Cont. Sys.
netrcs           742/udp    Network based Rev. Cont. Sys.
#                           Gordon C. Galligher <gorpong@ping.chi.il.us>
#                743        Unassigned
flexlm           744/tcp    Flexible License Manager
flexlm           744/udp    Flexible License Manager
#                           Matt Christiano
#                           <globes@matt@oliveb.atc.olivetti.com>
#                745-746    Unassigned
fujitsu-dev      747/tcp    Fujitsu Device Control
fujitsu-dev      747/udp    Fujitsu Device Control
ris-cm           748/tcp    Russell Info Sci Calendar Manager
ris-cm           748/udp    Russell Info Sci Calendar Manager
kerberos-adm     749/tcp    kerberos administration
kerberos-adm     749/udp    kerberos administration
rfile            750/tcp
loadav           750/udp
kerberos-iv      750/udp    kerberos version iv
#                           Martin Hamilton <martin@mrrl.lut.as.uk>
```

```
pump              751/tcp
pump              751/udp
qrh               752/tcp
qrh               752/udp
rrh               753/tcp
rrh               753/udp
tell              754/tcp       send
tell              754/udp       send
#                               Josyula R. Rao <jrrao@watson.ibm.com>
#                 755-756       Unassigned
nlogin            758/tcp
nlogin            758/udp
con               759/tcp
con               759/udp
ns                760/tcp
ns                760/udp
rxe               761/tcp
rxe               761/udp
quotad            762/tcp
quotad            762/udp
cycleserv         763/tcp
cycleserv         763/udp
omserv            764/tcp
omserv            764/udp
webster           765/tcp
webster           765/udp
#                               Josyula R. Rao <jrrao@watson.ibm.com>
#                 766           Unassigned
phonebook         767/tcp       phone
phonebook         767/udp       phone
#                               Josyula R. Rao <jrrao@watson.ibm.com>
#                 768           Unassigned
vid               769/tcp
vid               769/udp
cadlock           770/tcp
cadlock           770/udp
rtip              771/tcp
rtip              771/udp
cycleserv2        772/tcp
cycleserv2        772/udp
submit            773/tcp
notify            773/udp
rpasswd           774/tcp
acmaint_dbd       774/udp
entomb            775/tcp
acmaint_transd    775/udp
wpages            776/tcp
wpages            776/udp
#                               Josyula R. Rao <jrrao@watson.ibm.com>
multiling-http    777/tcp       Multiling HTTP
multiling-http    777/udp       Multiling HTTP
#                               Alejandro Bonet <babel@ctv.es>
```

```
#                778-779     Unassigned
wpgs             780/tcp
wpgs             780/udp
#                            Josyula R. Rao <jrrao@watson.ibm.com>
#                781-785     Unassigned
#                786         Unassigned (Removed 2002-05-08)
#                787         Unassigned (Removed 2002-10-08)
#                788-799     Unassigned
mdbs_daemon      800/tcp
mdbs_daemon      800/udp
device           801/tcp
device           801/udp
#                802-809     Unassigned
fcp-udp          810/tcp     FCP
fcp-udp          810/udp     FCP Datagram
#                            Paul Whittemore <paul@softarc.com>
#                811-827     Unassigned
itm-mcell-s      828/tcp     itm-mcell-s
itm-mcell-s      828/udp     itm-mcell-s
#                            Miles O'Neal <meo@us.itmasters.com>
pkix-3-ca-ra     829/tcp     PKIX-3 CA/RA
pkix-3-ca-ra     829/udp     PKIX-3 CA/RA
#                            Carlisle Adams <Cadams@entrust.com>
#                830-846     Unassigned
dhcp-failover2   847/tcp     dhcp-failover 2
dhcp-failover2   847/udp     dhcp-failover 2
#                            Bernard Volz <volz@ipworks.com>
gdoi             848/tcp     GDOI
gdoi             848/udp     GDOI
#                            RFC-ietf-msec-gdoi-07.txt
#                849-859     Unassigned
iscsi            860/tcp     iSCSI
iscsi            860/udp     iSCSI
#                            RFC-draft-ietf-ips-iscsi-20.txt
#                861-872     Unassigned
rsync            873/tcp     rsync
rsync            873/udp     rsync
#                            Andrew Tridgell <tridge@samba.anu.edu.au>
#                874-885     Unassigned
iclcnet-locate   886/tcp     ICL coNETion locate server
iclcnet-locate   886/udp     ICL coNETion locate server
#                            Bob Lyon <bl@oasis.icl.co.uk>
iclcnet_svinfo   887/tcp     ICL coNETion server info
iclcnet_svinfo   887/udp     ICL coNETion server info
#                            Bob Lyon <bl@oasis.icl.co.uk>
accessbuilder    888/tcp     AccessBuilder
accessbuilder    888/udp     AccessBuilder
#                            Steve Sweeney <Steven_Sweeney@3mail.3com.com>
# The following entry records an unassigned but widespread use
cddbp            888/tcp     CD Database Protocol
#                            Steve Scherf <steve@moonsoft.com>
#
```

```
#                       889-899     Unassigned
omginitialrefs          900/tcp     OMG Initial Refs
omginitialrefs          900/udp     OMG Initial Refs
#                                   Christian Callsen
                                    <Christian.Callsen@eng.sun.com>
smpnameres              901/tcp     SMPNAMERES
smpnameres              901/udp     SMPNAMERES
#                                   Leif Ekblad <leif@rdos.net>
ideafarm-chat           902/tcp     IDEAFARM-CHAT
ideafarm-chat           902/udp     IDEAFARM-CHAT
ideafarm-catch          903/tcp     IDEAFARM-CATCH
ideafarm-catch          903/udp     IDEAFARM-CATCH
#                                   Wo'o Ideafarm <1@ideafarm.com>
#                       904-910     Unassigned
xact-backup             911/tcp     xact-backup
xact-backup             911/udp     xact-backup
#                                   Bill Carroll <billc@xactlabs.com>
apex-mesh               912/tcp     APEX relay-relay service
apex-mesh               912/udp     APEX relay-relay service
apex-edge               913/tcp     APEX endpoint-relay service
apex-edge               913/udp     APEX endpoint-relay service
#                                   [RFC3340]
#                       914-988     Unassigned
ftps-data               989/tcp     ftp protocol, data, over TLS/SSL
ftps-data               989/udp     ftp protocol, data, over TLS/SSL
ftps                    990/tcp     ftp protocol, control, over TLS/SSL
ftps                    990/udp     ftp protocol, control, over TLS/SSL
#                                   Christopher Allen <ChristopherA@consensus.com>
nas                     991/tcp     Netnews Administration System
nas                     991/udp     Netnews Administration System
#                                   Vera Heinau <heinau@fu-berlin.de>
#                                   Heiko Schlichting <heiko@fu-berlin.de>
telnets                 992/tcp     telnet protocol over TLS/SSL
telnets                 992/udp     telnet protocol over TLS/SSL
imaps                   993/tcp     imap4 protocol over TLS/SSL
imaps                   993/udp     imap4 protocol over TLS/SSL
ircs                    994/tcp     irc protocol over TLS/SSL
ircs                    994/udp     irc protocol over TLS/SSL
#                                   Christopher Allen <ChristopherA@consensus.com>
pop3s                   995/tcp     pop3 protocol over TLS/SSL (was spop3)
pop3s                   995/udp     pop3 protocol over TLS/SSL (was spop3)
#                                   Gordon Mangione <gordm@microsoft.com>
vsinet                  996/tcp     vsinet
vsinet                  996/udp     vsinet
#                                   Rob Juergens <robj@vsi.com>
maitrd                  997/tcp
maitrd                  997/udp
busboy                  998/tcp
puparp                  998/udp
garcon                  999/tcp
applix                  999/udp     Applix ac
```

```
puprouter        999/tcp
puprouter        999/udp
cadlock2         1000/tcp
cadlock2         1000/udp
#                1001-1009    Unassigned
#                1008/udp     Possibly used by Sun Solaris????
surf             1010/tcp     surf
surf             1010/udp     surf
#                             Joseph Geer <jgeer@peapod.com>
#                1011-1022    Reserved
                 1023/tcp     Reserved
                 1023/udp     Reserved
#                             IANA <iana@iana.org>
```

General Permission and Waiver Form

Port Scanning and Vulnerability Testing

General Permission and Waiver

The terms of this agreement cover all services performed by _____ ("The Consultant") for _____ ("The Client"), in relation to port scanning or vulnerability testing client network or computer systems with the following hostnames or IP addresses _____ (attach list if too long). By signing below, the Client agrees to the following terms and conditions:

1. The Client hereby grants the Consultant and its agents permission to access or attempt to access the servers and network devices necessary to perform various port scanning and vulnerability testing services. The individual signing this agreement warrants that they are an officer of the client company, or are authorized by an officer to give such permission.

2. The Client agrees that it is responsible for properly backing up any systems to be surveyed. While the tests performed are generally passive and non-intrusive, there is the risk of systems being crashed or data loss. Client should maintain regular backups of their data. The Client agrees to indemnify and hold harmless The Consultant and its agents for any inadvertent or coincidental loss of data, service, business or productivity due to this activity.

3. The Client shall be responsible for taking action on any security flaws or holes identified by the services. The Consultant is not responsible under this contract for putting these remedies in place.

4. This agreement shall be subject to and governed by the laws of the State of ____. The parties agree that for venue purposes any and all lawsuits, disputes, causes of action and/or arbitration shall be in _____ County, __.

Warranties

1. The Consultant shall not be liable for any delay of performance of the service, or any damages suffered by Client as a result of such delay, when such delay is directly or indirectly caused by or results from any act of God or other intervening external cause, accident, governmental laws or regulations, labor disputes, civil disorder, transportation delays, or any other cause beyond the reasonable control of the Consultant or the Client.

2. THE CONSULTANT MAKES NO WARRANTY, EXPRESSED OR IMPLIED, INCLUDING WARRANTIES OF MERCHANTABILITY OR FITNESS FOR ANY PARTICULAR PURPOSE, WITH RESPECT TO THE SERVICE. CLIENT AGREES THAT THE CONSULTANT SHALL HAVE NO LIABILITY FOR DAMAGES, INCLUDING BUT NOT LIMITED TO INDIRECT, INCIDENTAL, CONSEQUENTIAL OR SPECIAL DAMAGES, INCLUDING LOSS OF BUSINESS.

AGREED: _____ Date: _____

CLIENT NAME: _____

CLIENT TITLE: _____

Nessus Plug-ins

This appendix lists all of the Nessus Plug-ins, which plug-in family they belong to, and their corresponding Common Vulnerability and Exploit (CVE) and BugTraq numbers if appropriate. Please note that this list is in constant flux. Check the Nessus Web site at www.nessus.org for the most current list and updated information.

Nessus Plug-ins Updated 1/12/2004

Family	Plug-in Name	CVE ID Number(s)	BugTraq ID Number(s)
Backdoors	Cart32 ChangeAdmin-Password	CAN-2000-0429	1153
Backdoors	Trin00 for Windows Detect	CAN-2000-0138	
Backdoors	NetSphere Backdoor	CAN-1999-0660	
Backdoors	Finger backdoor	CAN-1999-0660	
Backdoors	RemoteNC detection		
Backdoors	Check for VNC		
Backdoors	Desktop Orbiter Server Detection		
Backdoors	PC Anywhere		
Backdoors	Trinity v3 Detect	CAN-2000-0138	

Family	Plug-in Name	CVE ID Number(s)	BugTraq ID Number(s)
Backdoors	mstream handler Detect	CAN-2000-0138	
Backdoors	4553 Parasite Mothership Detect		
Backdoors	Lion worm		
Backdoors	Bugbear.B worm		
Backdoors	CodeRed version X detection	CVE-2001-0500	2880
Backdoors	lovgate virus is installed		
Backdoors	CDK Detect	CAN-1999-0660	
Backdoors	DeepThroat	CAN-1999-0660	
Backdoors	WinSATAN		
Backdoors	mstream agent Detect	CAN-2000-0138	
Backdoors	Trojan horses		
Backdoors	SubSeven	CAN-1999-0660	
Backdoors	Shaft Detect	CAN-2000-0138	2189
Backdoors	Check for VNC HTTP		
Backdoors	Bugbear.B web backdoor		
Backdoors	RemotelyAnywhere SSH detection		
Backdoors	alya.cgi		
Backdoors	JRun Sample Files	CVE-2000-0539	1386
Backdoors	NetBus 2.x	CAN-1999-0660	
Backdoors	GirlFriend	CAN-1999-0660	
Backdoors	TFN Detect	CAN-2000-0138	
Backdoors	NetBus 1.x	CAN-1999-0660	7538
Backdoors	Bugbear worm	CVE-2001-0154	
Backdoors	radmin detection		

Family	Plug-in Name	CVE ID Number(s)	BugTraq ID Number(s)
Backdoors	Dansie Shopping Cart backdoor	CVE-2000-0252	1115
Backdoors	Kuang2 the Virus	CAN-1999-0660	
Backdoors	Stacheldraht Detect	CAN-2000-0138	
Backdoors	PC Anywhere TCP		
Backdoors	Portal of Doom	CAN-1999-0660	
Backdoors	Wollf backdoor detection		
Backdoors	BackOrifice	CAN-1999-0660	
Backdoors	Alcatel OmniSwitch 7700/ 7800 switches backdoor	CAN-2002-1272	
Backdoors	IIS Possible Compromise		
Backdoors	GateCrasher	CAN-1999-0660	
Backdoors	FsSniffer Detection		
Backdoors	MPEi/X Default Accounts		
Backdoors	Remote PC Access Server Detection		
Backdoors	RemotelyAnywhere WWW detection		
Backdoors	SyGate Backdoor	CVE-2000-0113	952
Backdoors	Trin00 Detect	CAN-2000-0138	
Backdoors	Fluxay Sensor Detection		
CGI abuses	bttlxeForum SQL injection	CAN-2003-0215	
CGI abuses	rpm_query CGI	CVE-2000-0192	1036
CGI abuses	WebsitePro buffer overflow	CAN-2000-0623	1492
CGI abuses	Ocean12 Database Download		7328

Family	Plug-in Name	CVE ID Number(s)	BugTraq ID Number(s)
CGI abuses	AtomicBoard file reading		8236
CGI abuses	ftp.pl shows the listing of any dir	CVE-2000-0674	1471
CGI abuses	php file upload	CVE-2000-0860	1649
CGI abuses	cgitest.exe buffer overrun	CVE-2002-0128	3885
CGI abuses	Webfroot Shoutbox Directory Traversal		7717
CGI abuses	ServletExec 4.1 / JRun ISAPI DoS	CAN-2002-0894, CVE-2000-0681	4796, 1570
CGI abuses	IkonBoard arbitrary command execution		7361
CGI abuses	AutomatedShops WebC.cgi buffer overflows		7268
CGI abuses	typo3 arbitrary file reading		6993, 6988, 6986, 6985, 6984, 6983, 6982
CGI abuses	alibaba.pl	CAN-1999-0885	770
CGI abuses	Sambar Web Server CGI scripts	CAN-2000-0213	1002
CGI abuses	pals-cgi	CAN-2001-0216	2372
CGI abuses	iiprotect bypass		7661
CGI abuses	Turba Path Disclosure		
CGI abuses	sglMerchant Information Disclosure Vulnerability	CAN-2001-1019	3309
CGI abuses	VP-ASP SQL Injection		4861
CGI abuses	multihtml cgi	CVE-2000-0912	
CGI abuses	Coppermine Gallery SQL injection		7471
CGI abuses	Outlook Web anonymous access	CVE-2001-0660	3301

Family	Plug-in Name	CVE ID Number(s)	BugTraq ID Number(s)
CGI abuses	ibillpm.pl		3476
CGI abuses	jj cgi	CVE-1999-0260	2002
CGI abuses	e107 database dump		8273
CGI abuses	Oracle 9iAS access to SOAP documentation		
CGI abuses	view_source	CVE-1999-0174	2251
CGI abuses	TrendMicro Emanager software check	CAN-2001-0958	3327
CGI abuses	texi.exe information disclosure		7105
CGI abuses	Check for bdir.htr files		
CGI abuses	Check for IIS .cnf file leakage		4078
CGI abuses	test-cgi	CVE-1999-0070	2003
CGI abuses	testcgi.exe Cross Site Scripting		7214
CGI abuses	gallery code injection	CVE-2001-1234	3397
CGI abuses	PHPix directory traversal vulnerability	CVE-2000-0919	1773
CGI abuses	Avenger's News System Command Execution	CAN-2002-0307	4147
CGI abuses	Neoteris IVE XSS	CAN-2003-0217	
CGI abuses	Netscape Administration Server admin password		1579
CGI abuses	IIS .IDA ISAPI filter applied	CVE-2001-0500	2880
CGI abuses	Oracle 9iAS DAD Admin interface		
CGI abuses	directory pro web traversal	CAN-2001-0780	2793

Family	Plug-in Name	CVE ID Number(s)	BugTraq ID Number(s)
CGI abuses	UploadLite cgi		7051
CGI abuses	InterScan VirusWall Remote Configuration Vulnerability	CAN-2001-0432	2579
CGI abuses	Bonsai Mutiple Flaws	CAN-2003-0152, CAN-2003-0153, CAN-2003-0154, CAN-2003-0155	
CGI abuses	gallery code injection (2)		8814
CGI abuses	Mantis Detection		
CGI abuses	PHP-Nuke security vulnerability (bb_smilies.php)	CAN-2001-0320	
CGI abuses	eLDAPo cleartext passwords		7535
CGI abuses	php socket_iovec_alloc() integer overflow	CAN-2003-0172	7187, 7197, 7198, 7199, 7210, 7256, 7259
CGI abuses	Mnogosearch overflows		
CGI abuses	OpenBB SQL injection		7401, 7404, 7405
CGI abuses	Agora CGI Cross Site Scripting	CVE-2001-1199	3702
CGI abuses	admin.cgi overflow	CAN-2002-0199	3934
CGI abuses	Super Guestbook config disclosure		7319
CGI abuses	WebLogic management servlet		7122, 7124, 7130, 7131
CGI abuses	GroupWise Web Interface 'HTMLVER' hole	CAN-2002-0341	
CGI abuses	phpMyAdmin multiple flaws		7965, 7964, 7963, 7962

Family	Plug-in Name	CVE ID Number(s)	BugTraq ID Number(s)
CGI abuses	auktion.cgi	CAN-2001-0212	2367
CGI abuses	MSQL CGI overflow	CVE-1999-0753	591
CGI abuses	Simple File Manager File-name Script Injection		7035
CGI abuses	Sambar sendmail /session/ sendmail		
CGI abuses	Poll It v2.0 cgi	CVE-2000-0590	1431
CGI abuses	Netscape Server ? PageServices bug	CVE-1999-0269	
CGI abuses	empower cgi path	CAN-2001-0224	2374
CGI abuses	CERN httpd problem	CAN-2000-0079	936
CGI abuses	ICECast FileSystem disclosure		5189
CGI abuses	Adcycle Password Disclosure	CAN-2000-1161	1969
CGI abuses	album.pl Command Execution		7444
CGI abuses	tektronix's _ncl_items.shtml	CAN-2001-0484	2659
CGI abuses	ht://Dig's htsearch potential exposure/dos	CVE-2001-0834	3410
CGI abuses	UltraSeek 3.1.x Remote DoS	CVE-2000-1019	1866
CGI abuses	Novell Web Server NDS Tree Browsing	CAN-1999-1020	484
CGI abuses	WebSphere Cross Site Scripting		2401
CGI abuses	paFileDB XSS		6021
CGI abuses	Coppermine Gallery Remote Command Execution		7300

Family	Plug-in Name	CVE ID Number(s)	BugTraq ID Number(s)
CGI abuses	sojourn.cgi	CVE-2000-0180	1052
CGI abuses	printenv		
CGI abuses	Beanwebb's guestbook		7232, 7231
CGI abuses	Ocean12 Guestbook XSS		7329
CGI abuses	IMP SQL injection		
CGI abuses	TalentSoft Web+ Input Validation Bug Vulnerability	CVE-2000-0282	1102
CGI abuses	Xoops path disclosure	CAN-2002-0216, CAN-2002-0217	3977, 3978, 3981, 5785, 6344, 6393
CGI abuses	Directory listing through Sambar's search.dll	CAN-2000-0835	1684
CGI abuses	store.cgi	CAN-2001-0305	2385
CGI abuses	ttCMS code injection		7542, 7543, 7625
CGI abuses	Philboard database access		
CGI abuses	Non-Existant Page Physical Path Disclosure Vulnerability		4261
CGI abuses	webdriver		2166
CGI abuses	SLMail WebMail overflows		
CGI abuses	whois_raw	CAN-1999-1063	304
CGI abuses	Extent RBS ISP	CVE-2000-1036	1704
CGI abuses	Cobalt siteUserMod cgi	CVE-2000-0117	951
CGI abuses	cpanel remote command execution		6882
CGI abuses	ddicgi.exe vulnerability	CAN-2000-0826	1657
CGI abuses	myPHPcalendar injection		
CGI abuses	AspUpload vulnerability	CAN-2001-0938	

Family	Plug-in Name	CVE ID Number(s)	BugTraq ID Number(s)
CGI abuses	Microsoft Frontpage 'authors' exploits		
CGI abuses	FormHandler.cgi	CAN-1999-1051	799
CGI abuses	TextPortal Default Passwords		7673
CGI abuses	/scripts/repost.asp		
CGI abuses	ht://Dig's htsearch reveals web server path	CAN-2000-1191	
CGI abuses	ASP.NET Cross Site Scripting	CAN-2003-0223	
CGI abuses	Auction Deluxe XSS	CAN-2002-0257	4069
CGI abuses	KW whois	CVE-2000-0941	1883
CGI abuses	Owl Login bypass		
CGI abuses	IIS directory traversal	CVE-2000-0884	1806
CGI abuses	Cobalt RaQ2 cgiwrap	CVE-1999-1530, CVE-2000-0431	777, 1238
CGI abuses	PHP-Nuke is installed on the remote host	CAN-2001-0292, CAN-2001-0320, CAN-2001-0854, CAN-2001-0911, CAN-2001-1025, CAN-2002-0206, CAN-2002-0483, CAN-2002-1242	6446, 6465, 6503, 6750, 6887, 6890, 7031, 7060, 7078, 7079
CGI abuses	PHP-Nuke Gallery Add-on File View	CVE-2001-0900	
CGI abuses	PHP Ashnews code injection		8241
CGI abuses	shtml.exe reveals full path	CAN-2000-0413	1174
CGI abuses	webspirs.cgi	CAN-2001-0211	2362

Family	Plug-in Name	CVE ID Number(s)	BugTraq ID Number(s)
CGI abuses	Ultimate PHP Board admin_ip.php code injection		7678
CGI abuses	WebSite pro reveals the physical file path of web directories	CAN-2000-0066	932
CGI abuses	glimpse	CVE-1999-0147	2026
CGI abuses	WebLogic source code disclosure	CVE-2000-0682	1518
CGI abuses	Poster version.two privilege escalation		
CGI abuses	mod_ssl off by one	CVE-2002-0653	5084
CGI abuses	Sun's Java Web Server remote command execution	CAN-2000-0629	1459
CGI abuses	Apache 2.0.39 Win32 directory traversal	CAN-2002-0661	5434
CGI abuses	quickstore traversal	CAN-1999-0607, CAN-2000-1188	
CGI abuses	EZShopper 3.0	CAN-2000-0187	1014
CGI abuses	Oracle 9iAS mod_plsql Buffer Overflow	CAN-2001-1216	3726
CGI abuses	TalentSoft Web+ version detection		
CGI abuses	mod_ssl overflow	CVE-2002-0082	4189
CGI abuses	viewpage.php arbitrary file reading		7191
CGI abuses	gallery xss		8288
CGI abuses	Dune Web Server Overflow		7945
CGI abuses	Apache Tomcat Directory Listing and File disclosure	CAN-2003-0042	6721

Family	Plug-in Name	CVE ID Number(s)	BugTraq ID Number(s)
CGI abuses	args.bat	CAN-1999-1180	
CGI abuses	SimpleBBS users disclosure		7045
CGI abuses	Web Wiz Forums database disclosure		7380
CGI abuses	Redhat Stronghold File System Disclosure	CAN-2001-0868	
CGI abuses	bigconf	CVE-1999-1550	778
CGI abuses	Interactive Story Directory Traversal Vulnerability	CVE-2001-0804	3028
CGI abuses	MyAbraCadaWeb Cross Site Scripting		7126, 7127
CGI abuses	AltaVista Intranet Search	CVE-2000-0039	896
CGI abuses	JServ Cross Site Scripting		
CGI abuses	infosrch.cgi	CVE-2000-0207	1031
CGI abuses	Oracle 9iAS Globals.jsa access	CAN-2002-0562	4034
CGI abuses	/scripts directory browsable		
CGI abuses	Reading CGI script sources using /cgi-bin-sdb	CVE-2000-0868	1658
CGI abuses	PHP-Nuke' opendir	CVE-2001-0321	
CGI abuses	guestbook tr3 password storage		7167
CGI abuses	IIS dangerous sample files		
CGI abuses	Read any file thanks to ~nobody/		
CGI abuses	IBM-HTTP-Server View Code		3518

Family	Plug-in Name	CVE ID Number(s)	BugTraq ID Number(s)
CGI abuses	MacOS X Finder reveals contents of Apache Web files		3325
CGI abuses	uploader.exe	CVE-1999-0177	
CGI abuses	Microsoft Frontpage XSS	CAN-2000-0746	1594, 1595
CGI abuses	bizdb1-search.cgi located	CVE-2000-0287	1104
CGI abuses	nph-publish.cgi	CVE-1999-1177, CVE-2001-0400	
CGI abuses	MPC SoftWeb Guestbook database disclosure		7390, 7389
CGI abuses	YaBB	CVE-2000-0853	1668
CGI abuses	Pi3Web tstisap.dll overflow	CAN-2001-0302	2381
CGI abuses	GTcatalog password disclosure		
CGI abuses	Apache Tomcat /servlet Cross Site Scripting	CAN-2002-0682	5193
CGI abuses	Sambar XSS		7209
CGI abuses	PDGSoft Shopping cart vulnerability	CAN-2000-0401	1256
CGI abuses	php POST file uploads	CVE-2002-0081	4183
CGI abuses	AnyForm	CVE-1999-0066	719
CGI abuses	ows-bin	CVE-2000-0169	1053
CGI abuses	Cognos Powerplay WE Vulnerability		491
CGI abuses	PHP3 Physical Path Disclosure Vulnerability		
CGI abuses	DCP-Portal Code Injection		6525
CGI abuses	rot13sj.cgi		

Family	Plug-in Name	CVE ID Number(s)	BugTraq ID Number(s)
CGI abuses	/cgi-bin directory browsable ?		
CGI abuses	CVSWeb 1.80 gives a shell to cvs committers	CVE-2000-0670	1469
CGI abuses	Netauth	CVE-2000-0782	1587
CGI abuses	DB4Web TCP relay		
CGI abuses	ad.cgi	CAN-2001-0025	2103
CGI abuses	Sambar /sysadmin directory 2		2255
CGI abuses	perlcal	CVE-2001-0463	2663
CGI abuses	WihPhoto file reading		
CGI abuses	readmsg.php detection	CAN-2001-1408	
CGI abuses	CuteNews code injection		
CGI abuses	php log	CVE-2000-0967	1786
CGI abuses	Zope ZClass permission mapping bug	CVE-2001-0567	
CGI abuses	Netscape Server ?wp bug	CVE-2000-0236	1063
CGI abuses	imagemap.exe	CVE-1999-0951	739
CGI abuses	Synchrologic User account information disclosure		
CGI abuses	phorum's common.cgi		1985
CGI abuses	NetCommerce SQL injection	CVE-2001-0319	2350
CGI abuses	Snitz Forums 2000 Password Reset and XSS		7381, 7922, 7925
CGI abuses	Allaire JRun directory browsing vulnerability		3592
CGI abuses	MS Site Server Information Leak		3998

Family	Plug-in Name	CVE ID Number(s)	BugTraq ID Number(s)
CGI abuses	KF Web Server /%00 bug		
CGI abuses	BEA WebLogic Scripts Server scripts Source Disclosure (3)	CVE-2000-0683	1517
CGI abuses	Pages Pro CD directory traversal		
CGI abuses	paFileDB SQL injection		7183
CGI abuses	Post-Nuke information disclosure (2)		
CGI abuses	htdig	CVE-1999-0978, CVE-2000-0208	1026
CGI abuses	ustorekeeper	CAN-2001-0466	2536
CGI abuses	ttforum multiple flaws		7543, 7542
CGI abuses	Resin traversal	CAN-2001-0304	2384
CGI abuses	WebCalendar file reading		8237
CGI abuses	RDS / MDAC Vulnerability Content-Type overflow	CAN-2002-1142	
CGI abuses	Zope DocumentTemplate package problem	CVE-2000-0483	1354
CGI abuses	openwebmail command execution	CAN-2002-1385	6425, 6232
CGI abuses	counter.exe vulnerability	CAN-1999-1030	267
CGI abuses	PGPMail.pl detection	CAN-2001-0937	
CGI abuses	Psunami.CGI Command Execution		6607
CGI abuses	AnalogX web server traversal	CVE-2000-0664	1508
CGI abuses	paFileDB command execution		8271
CGI abuses	ProductCart SQL Injection		8103, 8105, 8108, 8112

Family	Plug-in Name	CVE ID Number(s)	BugTraq ID Number(s)
CGI abuses	SquirrelMail's Cross Site Scripting	CAN-2002-1276, CAN-2002-1341	7019, 6302
CGI abuses	technote's main.cgi	CAN-2001-0075	2156
CGI abuses	Webfroot shoutbox file inclusion		
CGI abuses	AnalogX web server traversal	CVE-2000-0664	1508
CGI abuses	Oracle 9iAS web admin	CAN-2002-0561	4292
CGI abuses	BEA WebLogic Scripts Server scripts Source Disclosure (2)		2527
CGI abuses	IIS .HTR ISAPI filter applied	CVE-2002-0071	4474
CGI abuses	PIX Firewall Manager Directory Traversal	CVE-1999-0158	691
CGI abuses	MailMax Web Path Disclosure		
CGI abuses	Bypass Axis Storpoint CD authentication	CVE-2000-0191	1025
CGI abuses	DB4Web directory traversal		
CGI abuses	ion-p.exe vulnerability	CAN-2002-1559	6091
CGI abuses	YaBB SE command execution	CAN-2000-1176	7399, 6674, 6663, 6591, 1921
CGI abuses	P-Synch multiple issues		7740, 7745, 7747
CGI abuses	htgrep	CAN-2000-0832	
CGI abuses	Directory listing through WebDAV	CVE-2000-0869	1656
CGI abuses	JRun directory traversal		3666
CGI abuses	IIS phonebook	CVE-2000-1089	2048

Family	Plug-in Name	CVE ID Number(s)	BugTraq ID Number(s)
CGI abuses	b2 cafelog code injection	CVE-2002-0734	4673, 7738, 7782, 7783, 7786
CGI abuses	pagelog.cgi	CAN-2000-0940	1864
CGI abuses	webdist.cgi	CVE-1999-0039	374
CGI abuses	SilverStream directory listing		
CGI abuses	Oracle 9iAS default error information disclosure	CVE-2001-1372	3341
CGI abuses	PHP4 Physical Path Disclosure Vulnerability	CAN-2002-0249	4056
CGI abuses	Upload cgi		
CGI abuses	wwwboard passwd.txt	CVE-1999-0953	649
CGI abuses	Philboard philboard_ admin.ASP Authenti- cation Bypass		7739
CGI abuses	mmstdod.cgi	CVE-2001-0021	2063
CGI abuses	php IMAP overflow		6557
CGI abuses	Achievo code injection		5552
CGI abuses	Oracle XSQL Stylesheet Vulnerability	CVE-2001-0126	2295
CGI abuses	/iisadmpwd/aexp2.htr	CVE-1999-0407, CAN-2002-0421	2110
CGI abuses	CVS/Entries		
CGI abuses	Oracle 9iAS SOAP con- figuration file retrieval	CAN-2002-0568	4290
CGI abuses	AlienForm CGI script	CAN-2002-0934	4983
CGI abuses	Advanced Poll info.php		7171
CGI abuses	MediaHouse Statistic Server Buffer Overflow	CVE-1999-0931	734

Family	Plug-in Name	CVE ID Number(s)	BugTraq ID Number(s)
CGI abuses	DCP-Portal Path Disclosure	CAN-2002-0282	4113
CGI abuses	IIS possible DoS using ExAir's query	CVE-1999-0449	193
CGI abuses	SIX Webboard's generate.cgi	CAN-2001-1115	3175
CGI abuses	IMail account hijack		
CGI abuses	Bugzilla Multiple Flaws	CAN-2003-0012, CAN-2003-0013, CAN-2002-1198, CAN-2002-1197, CAN-2002-1196	6501, 6502, 6257, 5844, 5842, 4964
CGI abuses	Tomcat's snoop servlet gives too much information	CAN-2000-0760	1532
CGI abuses	MiniVend Piped command	CVE-2000-0635	1449
CGI abuses	phpMyExplorer dir traversal	CAN-2001-1168	3266
CGI abuses	formmail.pl	CVE-1999-0172	2079
CGI abuses	Zope Invalid Query Path Disclosure		7999, 8000, 8001
CGI abuses	phpPgAdmin arbitrary files reading	CAN-2001-0479	2640
CGI abuses	php safemode	CVE-2001-1246	2954
CGI abuses	Oracle 9iAS mod_plsql directory traversal	CAN-2001-1217	3727
CGI abuses	webwho plus	CVE-2000-0010	892
CGI abuses	PlusMail vulnerability	CAN-2000-0074	2653
CGI abuses	p-news Admin Access		
CGI abuses	Dumpenv	CAN-1999-1178	

Family	Plug-in Name	CVE ID Number(s)	BugTraq ID Number(s)
CGI abuses	Alexandria-dev upload spoofing		7223, 7224, 7225
CGI abuses	way-board	CAN-2001-0214	2370
CGI abuses	Web server traversal		
CGI abuses	Oracle 9iAS SOAP Default Configuration Vulnerability	CVE-2001-1371	4289
CGI abuses	Vignette StoryServer TCL code injection		7683, 7685, 7690, 7691, 7692
CGI abuses	Stronghold Swish		4785
CGI abuses	IIS 5 .printer ISAPI filter applied	CVE-2001-0241	
CGI abuses	Post-Nuke Rating System Denial Of Service		7702
CGI abuses	Allaire JRun Directory Listing	CVE-2000-1050	1830
CGI abuses	IMP_MIME_Viewer_html class XSS vulnerabilities		
CGI abuses	MRTG mrtg.cgi File Disclosure	CAN-2002-0232	4017
CGI abuses	phf	CVE-1999-0067	629
CGI abuses	WebStores 2000 browse_item_details.asp SQL injection		7766
CGI abuses	Lotus Notes ?OpenServer Information Disclosure		
CGI abuses	php-proxima file reading		
CGI abuses	AN-HTTPd tests CGIs	CVE-1999-0947	762
CGI abuses	ezPublish Directory Cross Site Scripting		7616
CGI abuses	Authentication bypassing in Lotus Domino		4022

Family	Plug-in Name	CVE ID Number(s)	BugTraq ID Number(s)
CGI abuses	counter.php file overwrite		
CGI abuses	cgiforum	CVE-2000-1171	1963
CGI abuses	Unify eWave ServletExec 3.0C file upload	CVE-2000-1024	1876
CGI abuses	Super-M Son hServer Directory Traversal		7717
CGI abuses	Savant original form CGI access	CVE-2000-0521	1313
CGI abuses	NetTools command execution	CVE-2001-0899	
CGI abuses	BadBlue Directory Traversal Vulnerability		3913
CGI abuses	Domino traversal	CVE-2001-0009	2173
CGI abuses	info2www	CVE-1999-0266	1995
CGI abuses	Cafe Wordpress SQL injection		
CGI abuses	Post-Nuke information disclosure		
CGI abuses	WebChat XSS		7190
CGI abuses	mod_gzip running		
CGI abuses	IIS 5.0 Sample App vulnerable to cross-site scripting attack		
CGI abuses	No 404 check		
CGI abuses	Web-ERP Configuration File Remote Access		6996
CGI abuses	php 4.3.0	CAN-2003-0097	
CGI abuses	axis2400 webcams		6987, 6980
CGI abuses	guestbook.pl	CAN-1999-1053	776

Family	Plug-in Name	CVE ID Number(s)	BugTraq ID Number(s)
CGI abuses	N/X Web Content Management code injection		6500
CGI abuses	/perl directory browsable ?	CVE-2000-0883	1678
CGI abuses	Basit cms Cross Site Scripting Bugs		7139
CGI abuses	Sambar webserver pagecount hole	CVE-2001-1010	3091
CGI abuses	Novell Groupwise WebAcc Information Disclosure		3436
CGI abuses	phpping code execution		
CGI abuses	icat	CAN-1999-1069	2126
CGI abuses	Nuked-klan Cross Site Scripting Bugs		6916, 6917
CGI abuses	SimpleChat information disclosure		7168
CGI abuses	Forum51/Board51/News51 Users Disclosure		8126, 8127, 8128
CGI abuses	OneOrZero SQL injection		7609, 7611
CGI abuses	Sambar CGIs path disclosure		
CGI abuses	Master Index directory traversal vulnerability	CVE-2000-0924	1772
CGI abuses	Spyke Flaws		
CGI abuses	php.cgi	CAN-1999-0238	2250
CGI abuses	Apache::ASP source.asp	CVE-2000-0628	1457
CGI abuses	Apache Remote Command Execution via .bat files	CVE-2002-0061	4335
CGI abuses	IIS Service Pack - 404		

Family	Plug-in Name	CVE ID Number(s)	BugTraq ID Number(s)
CGI abuses	anacondaclip CGI vulnerability	CVE-2001-0593	2512
CGI abuses	iXmail arbitrary file upload		8046, 8048
CGI abuses	sdbsearch.cgi	CVE-2001-1130	
CGI abuses	iiprotect sql injection		7675
CGI abuses	Oracle XSQL Sample Application Vulnerability		
CGI abuses	mod_gzip format string attack		
CGI abuses	WordPress code/sql injection		7785
CGI abuses	IMP Session Hijacking Bug	CVE-2001-0857	3525
CGI abuses	GroupWise Web Interface 'HELP' hole	CVE-1999-1005, CVE-1999-1006	879
CGI abuses	ColdFusion Vulnerability	CAN-1999-0455, CAN-1999-0477	115
CGI abuses	mod_gzip format string attack		
CGI abuses	msmmask.exe		
CGI abuses	ttawebtop	CVE-2001-0805	2890
CGI abuses	Tomcat's /admin is world readable	CVE-2000-0672	1548
CGI abuses	Htmlscript	CVE-1999-0264	2001
CGI abuses	VChat information disclosure		7186, 7188
CGI abuses	CgiMail.exe vulnerability	CVE-2000-0726	1623
CGI abuses	GTcatalog code injection		6998
CGI abuses	Roxen counter module		

Family	Plug-in Name	CVE ID Number(s)	BugTraq ID Number(s)
CGI abuses	IIS possible DoS using ExAir's search	CVE-1999-0449	193
CGI abuses	RedHat 6.0 cachemgr.cgi	CVE-1999-0710	2059
CGI abuses	IIS IDA/IDQ Path Disclosure	CAN-2000-0071	1065
CGI abuses	HSWeb document path	CAN-2001-0200	2336
CGI abuses	PCCS-Mysql User/ Password Exposure	CVE-2000-0707	1557
CGI abuses	Apache Tomcat DOS Device Name XSS		5194
CGI abuses	commerce.cgi	CAN-2001-0210	2361
CGI abuses	WEB-INF folder accessible		5119
CGI abuses	Oracle 9iAS OWA UTIL access	CAN-2002-0560	4294
CGI abuses	Oracle XSQLServlet XSQLConfig.xml File	CAN-2002-0568	4290
CGI abuses	cc_guestbook.pl XSS		7237
CGI abuses	Apache Directory Listing	CVE-2001-0731	3009
CGI abuses	websendmail	CVE-1999-0196	2077
CGI abuses	ShowCode possible	CAN-1999-0736	167
CGI abuses	smb2www remote command execution	CAN-2002-1342	6313
CGI abuses	Oracle 9iAS Dynamic Monitoring Services	CAN-2002-0563	4293
CGI abuses	php 4.2.x malformed POST	CAN-2002-0986	5278
CGI abuses	Apache Tomcat DOS Device Name XSS		5194
CGI abuses	nph-test-cgi	CVE-1999-0045	686

Family	Plug-in Name	CVE ID Number(s)	BugTraq ID Number(s)
CGI abuses	Webnews.exe vulner-ability	CVE-2002-0290	4124
CGI abuses	Post-Nuke SQL injection		7697
CGI abuses	Infinity CGI Exploit Scanner		7910, 7911, 7913
CGI abuses	Hidden WWW server name		
CGI abuses	Tomcat 4.x JSP Source Exposure		
CGI abuses	PHP-Nuke copying files security vulnerability (admin.php)	CVE-2001-1032	3361
CGI abuses	A1Stats Traversal	CAN-2001-0561	2705
CGI abuses	ColdFusion Debug Mode		
CGI abuses	CWmail.exe vulnerability	CAN-2002-0273	4093
CGI abuses	PayPal Store Front code injection		8791
CGI abuses	osCommerce Cross Site Scripting Bugs		7156, 7151, 7153, 7158, 7155
CGI abuses	StellarDocs Path Disclosure		8385
CGI abuses	vpopmail.php command execution		7063
CGI abuses	Mantis Multiple Flaws	CAN-2002-1110, CAN-2002-1111, CAN-2002-1112, CAN-2002-1113, CAN-2002-1114	5563, 5565, 5509, 5504, 5510, 5514, 5515
CGI abuses	Xoops XSS		7356
CGI abuses	DCP-Portal Cross Site Scripting Bugs		7144, 7141

Family	Plug-in Name	CVE ID Number(s)	BugTraq ID Number(s)
CGI abuses	cgiWebupdate.exe vulnerability	CAN-2001-1150	3216
CGI abuses	Basilix includes download	CAN-2001-1044	2198
CGI abuses	idq.dll directory traversal	CAN-2000-0126	968
CGI abuses	fpcount.exe overflow	CAN-1999-1376	
CGI abuses	Codebrws.asp Source Disclosure Vulnerability	CAN-1999-0739	
CGI abuses	Webcart misconfiguration	CAN-1999-0610	2281
CGI abuses	miniPortail Cookie Admin Access	CAN-2003-0272	
CGI abuses	Justice guestbook		7233, 7234
CGI abuses	Hosting Controller vulnerable ASP pages	CAN-2002-0466	3808
CGI abuses	FAQManager Arbitrary File Reading Vulnerability		3810
CGI abuses	Kebi Academy Directory Traversal		7125
CGI abuses	phptonuke directory traversal		
CGI abuses	Buffer overflow in WebSitePro webfind.exe	CVE-2000-0622	1487
CGI abuses	mod_python handle abuse	CVE-2002-0185	4656
CGI abuses	webgais	CVE-1999-0176	2058
CGI abuses	GOsa code injection		
CGI abuses	ShopPlus Arbitrary Command Execution	CAN-2001-0992	
CGI abuses	Kietu code injection		
CGI abuses	Pod.Board Forum_Details.PHP Cross Site Scripting		7933

Family	Plug-in Name	CVE ID Number(s)	BugTraq ID Number(s)
CGI abuses	WebAdmin detection		
CGI abuses	php < 4.3.3		8201
CGI abuses	textcounter.pl	CVE-1999-1479	2265
CGI abuses	Carello detection		
CGI abuses	popper_mod	CVE-2002-0513, CAN-2002-0513	4412
CGI abuses	WebActive world read-able log file	CVE-2000-0642	1497
CGI abuses	Count.cgi	CVE-1999-0021	128
CGI abuses	SunSolve CD CGI user input validation	CAN-2002-0436	4269
CGI abuses	JWalk server traversal		7160
CGI abuses	ASP source using %2e trick	CAN-1999-0253	1814
CGI abuses	TrueGalerie admin access		7427
CGI abuses	webcart.cgi		3453
CGI abuses	IIS Remote Command Execution	CVE-2001-0507, CVE-2001-0333	2708
CGI abuses	viralator	CAN-2001-0849	
CGI abuses	Lotus Domino admini-stration databases	CAN-2000-0021, CAN-2002-0664	881
CGI abuses	bb-hostsvc.sh	CVE-2000-0638	1455
CGI abuses	ScozBook flaws		7235, 7236
CGI abuses	Nuked-Klan function execution		6916, 6917, 6697, 6699, 6700
CGI abuses	mod_frontpage installed	CAN-2002-0427	4251
CGI abuses	IIS XSS via 404 error	CVE-2002-0148, CAN-2002-0150	4483
CGI abuses	SQL injection in phpBB		7979

Family	Plug-in Name	CVE ID Number(s)	BugTraq ID Number(s)
CGI abuses	Bugzilla XSS and insecure temporary filenames		7412
CGI abuses	Handler	CVE-1999-0148	380
CGI abuses	nsiislog.dll DoS	CAN-2003-0227, CAN-2003-0349	8035
CGI abuses	Web Wiz Site News database disclosure		
CGI abuses	pfdispaly	CVE-1999-0270	
CGI abuses	Zope Image updating Method	CVE-2000-0062	922
CGI abuses	Post-Nuke Multiple XSS		7898, 7901
CGI abuses	dcforum	CVE-2001-0436	2728
CGI abuses	Home Free search.cgi directory traversal	CAN-2000-0054	921
CGI abuses	ctss.idc check		
CGI abuses	CVSWeb detection		
CGI abuses	Cross-Referencing Linux (lxr) file reading		7062
CGI abuses	Oracle 9iAS Jsp Source File Reading	CAN-2002-0562	4034
CGI abuses	Basilix webmail dummy request vulnerability	CAN-2001-1045	2995
CGI abuses	mailnews.cgi	CAN-2001-0271	2391
CGI abuses	Zope installation path disclose		5806
CGI abuses	Windmail.exe allows any user to execute arbitrary commands	CAN-2000-0242	1073
CGI abuses	tst.bat CGI vulnerability	CAN-1999-0885	770

Family	Plug-in Name	CVE ID Number(s)	BugTraq ID Number(s)
CGI abuses	MacOS X Finder reveals contents of Apache Web directories		3316
CGI abuses	Directory Manager's edit_image.php	CVE-2001-1020	3288
CGI abuses	mod_ssl wildcard DNS cross site scripting vulnerability	CAN-2002-1157	6029
CGI abuses	calendar_admin.pl	CVE-2000-0432	1215
CGI abuses	ezPublish config disclosure		7349, 7347
CGI abuses	ImageFolio Default Password		
CGI abuses	Netscape FastTrack 'get'	CVE-1999-0239	481
CGI abuses	StockMan Shopping Cart Path disclosure		
CGI abuses	Power Up Information Disclosure	CAN-2001-1138	3304
CGI abuses	texi.exe path disclosure	CAN-2002-0266	4035
CGI abuses	Cold Fusion Administration Page Overflow	CVE-2000-0538	1314
CGI abuses	spin_client.cgi buffer overrun		
CGI abuses	wwwwais	CAN-2001-0223	
CGI abuses	ServletExec 4.1 ISAPI Physical Path Disclosure	CVE-2002-0892	4793
CGI abuses	Wordit Logbook		7043
CGI abuses	csSearch.cgi	CVE-2002-0495	4368
CGI abuses	iXmail SQL injection		8047
CGI abuses	netscape publishingXpert 2 PSUser problem	CVE-2000-1196	

Family	Plug-in Name	CVE ID Number(s)	BugTraq ID Number(s)
CGI abuses	ClearTrust XSS		7108
CGI abuses	zentrack files reading		
CGI abuses	pmachine cross site scripting		7980, 7981
CGI abuses	zentrack code injection		
CGI abuses	JBoss source disclosure		7764
CGI abuses	Ecartis Username Spoofing	CAN-2003-0162	6971
CGI abuses	SunONE Application Server source disclosure		
CGI abuses	Various dangerous cgi scripts	CAN-1999-1072, CAN-2002-0749, CAN-2001-0135, CAN-2002-0955, CAN-2001-0562, CAN-2002-0346, CVE-2000-0923, CVE-2001-0123	
CGI abuses	Unprotected SiteScope Service		
CGI abuses	RDS / MDAC Vulnerability (msadcs.dll) located	CVE-1999-1011	529
CGI abuses	iPlanet Directory Server traversal	CVE-2000-1075	1839
CGI abuses	vpasswd.cgi		
CGI abuses	Zope DoS	CVE-2000-0483	1354
CGI abuses	Check for dangerous IIS default files	CAN-1999-0737	
CGI abuses	Apache Tomcat Trouble-Shooter Servlet Installed		4575
CGI abuses	hsx directory traversal	CAN-2001-0253	2314

Family	Plug-in Name	CVE ID Number(s)	BugTraq ID Number(s)
CGI abuses	ASP/ASA source using Microsoft Translate f: bug	CVE-2000-0778	1578
CGI abuses	myphpPageTool code injection		
CGI abuses	IIS Global.asa Retrieval		
CGI abuses	Unpassworded iiprotect administrative interface		
CGI abuses	JRun's viewsource.jsp	CVE-2000-0539	1386
CGI abuses	ActiveState Perl directory traversal		
CGI abuses	AutomatedShops WebC.cgi installed		
CGI abuses	Mambo Site Server Cookie Validation		6926
CGI abuses	ActivePerl perlIS.dll Buffer Overflow	CVE-2001-0815	3526
CGI abuses	ASP.NET path disclosure		
CGI abuses	Bandmin XSS	CAN-2003-0416	7729
CGI abuses	IIS possible DoS using ExAir's advsearch	CVE-1999-0449	193
CGI abuses	Roxen Server /%00/ bug	CVE-2000-0671	1510
CGI abuses	Alchemy Eye HTTP Command Execution	CAN-2001-0871	3599
CGI abuses	myguestbk admin access		7213
CGI abuses	Checks for listrec.pl	CAN-2001-0997	
CGI abuses	phpinfo.php		
CGI abuses	TMax Soft Jeus Cross Site Scripting		7969
CGI abuses	ROADS' search.pl	CVE-2001-0215	2371

Family	Plug-in Name	CVE ID Number(s)	BugTraq ID Number(s)
CGI abuses	ServletExec 4.1 ISAPI File Reading	CAN-2002-0893	4795
CGI abuses	GeekLog SQL vulns	CAN-2002-0962, CVE-2002-0096, CVE-2002-0097	7742, 7744, 6601, 6602, 6603, 6604
CGI abuses	Campas	CVE-1999-0146	1975
CGI abuses	CSNews.cgi vulnerability	CVE-2002-0923	4994
CGI abuses	zml.cgi Directory Traversal	CAN-2001-1209	3759
CGI abuses	VirusWall's catinfo overflow	CAN-2001-0432	2579
CGI abuses	Macromedia ColdFusion MX Path Disclosure Vulnerability		7443
CGI abuses	Invision PowerBoard code injection		6976, 7204
CGI abuses	processit		
CGI abuses	ideabox code injection		7488
CGI abuses	biztalk server flaws	CAN-2003-0117, CAN-2003-0118	7469, 7470
CGI abuses	overflow.cgi detection		
CGI abuses	HappyMall Command Execution	CAN-2003-0243	
CGI abuses	Bugzilla Detection		
CGI abuses	phpMyAdmin arbitrary files reading	CAN-2001-0478	2642
CGI abuses	BLnews code injection		7677
CGI abuses	CGIEmail's CGICso (Send CSO via CGI) Command Execution Vulnerability		6141

Family	Plug-in Name	CVE ID Number(s)	BugTraq ID Number(s)
CGI abuses	Savant cgitest.exe buffer overflow		
CGI abuses	OmniHTTPd visadmin exploit	CAN-1999-0970	1808
CGI abuses	ArGoSoft Mail Server multiple flaws		7608, 7610, 5906, 5395, 5144
CGI abuses	Faxsurvey	CVE-1999-0262	2056
CGI abuses	AN HTTPd count.pl file truncation		7397
CGI abuses	BadBlue invalid null byte vulnerability	CAN-2002-1021	5226
CGI abuses	WebLogic clear-text passwords		
CGI abuses	get32.exe vulnerability	CAN-1999-0885	770
CGI abuses	IIS ASP.NET Application Trace Enabled		
CGI abuses	Tests for Nimda Worm infected HTML files		
CGI abuses	php4 multiple flaws	CAN-2003-0442	8693, 8696
CGI abuses	XMB Cross Site Scripting	CAN-2002-0316, CAN-2003-0375	4944, 8013
CGI abuses	w3-msql overflow	CVE-2000-0012	898
CGI abuses	Horde and IMP test disclosure		
CGI abuses	EZsite Forum Discloses Passwords to Remote Users		
CGI abuses	directory.php	CAN-2002-0434	4278
CGI abuses	ping.asp		
CGI abuses	Oracle 9iAS mod_plsql cross site scripting		

Family	Plug-in Name	CVE ID Number(s)	BugTraq ID Number(s)
CGI abuses	readfile.tcl		
CGI abuses	Awol code injection	CVE-2001-1048	3387
CGI abuses	Web mirroring		
CGI abuses	Mambo Site Server 4.0.10 XSS		7135
CGI abuses	phpWebSite multiple flaws		
CGI abuses	OmniPro HTTPd 2.08 scripts source full disclosure		2788
CGI abuses	CGIEmail's Cross Site Scripting Vulnerability (cgicso)		
CGI abuses	IIS perl.exe problem	CAN-1999-0450	194
CGI abuses	Instaboard SQL injection		7338
CGI abuses	vBulletin's Calender Command Execution Vulnerability	CVE-2001-0475	2474
CGI abuses	smb2www installed		
CGI abuses	PHP Rocket Add-in File Traversal	CAN-2001-1204	3751
CGI abuses	sendtemp.pl	CAN-2001-0272	2504
CGI abuses	IIS 5.0 Sample App reveals physical path of web root		
CGI abuses	SWC Overflow		
CGI abuses	SilverStream database structure		
CGI abuses	Jakarta Tomcat Path Disclosure	CAN-2000-0759	1531
CGI abuses	ASP source using %20 trick	CAN-2001-1248	2975

Family	Plug-in Name	CVE ID Number(s)	BugTraq ID Number(s)
CGI abuses	perl interpreter can be launched as a CGI	CAN-1999-0509	
CGI abuses	lednews XSS		7920
CGI abuses	Siteframe Cross Site Scripting Bugs		7140, 7143
CGI abuses	newdsn.exe check	CVE-1999-0191	1818
CGI abuses	ASP source using ::$DATA trick	CVE-1999-0278	149
CGI abuses	htimage.exe overflow	CAN-2000-0256	1117
CGI abuses	IIS : Directory listing through WebDAV	CVE-2000-0951	1756
CGI abuses	Microsoft Frontpage dvwssr.dll backdoor	CVE-2000-0260	1109
CGI abuses	Unknown CGIs arguments torture		
CGI abuses	mailreader.com directory traversal and arbitrary command execution		6055, 6058, 5393
CGI abuses	SQLQHit Directory Structure Disclosure	CAN-2001-0986	3339
CGI abuses	ColdFusion Path Disclosure	CVE-2002-0576	4542
CGI abuses	Zeus Admin Interface XSS		7751
CGI abuses	wrap	CVE-1999-0149	373
CGI abuses	ezPublish Cross Site Scripting Bugs	CAN-2003-0310	7137, 7138
CGI abuses	Vignette StoryServer Information Disclosure	CAN-2002-0385	
CGI abuses	Shells in /cgi-bin	CAN-1999-0509	

Family	Plug-in Name	CVE ID Number(s)	BugTraq ID Number(s)
CGI abuses	E-Shopping Cart Arbitrary Command Execution (WebDiscount)	CAN-2001-1014	3340
CGI abuses	ndcgi.exe vulnerability	CAN-2001-0922	
CGI abuses	PHP Mail Function Header Spoofing Vulnerability	CAN-2002-0985	5562
CGI abuses	Rich Media E-Commerce Stores Sensitive Information Insecurely		4172
CGI abuses	Passwordless frontpage installation		
CGI abuses	myServer 0.4.3 Directory Traversal Vulnerability		
CGI abuses	SquirrelMail's Multiple Flaws		7952
CGI abuses	PT News Unauthorized Administrative Access		7394
CGI abuses	BroadVision Physical Path Disclosure Vulnerability	CAN-2001-0031	2088
CGI abuses	FastCGI Echo.exe Cross Site Scripting		
CGI abuses	VsSetCookie.exe vulnerability	CAN-2002-0236	3784
CGI abuses	/doc/packages directory browsable ?	CVE-2000-1016	1707
CGI abuses	OfficeScan configuration file disclosure		3438
CGI abuses	guestbook.cgi	CVE-1999-0237	776
CGI abuses	php.cgi buffer overrun	CVE-1999-0058	712
CGI abuses	/doc directory browsable ?	CVE-1999-0678	318

Family	Plug-in Name	CVE ID Number(s)	BugTraq ID Number(s)
CGI abuses	PHPAdsNew code injection	CVE-2001-1054	3392
CGI abuses	myphpnuke code injection		
CGI abuses	Backup CGIs download		
CGI abuses	Lotus Domino XSS	CVE-2001-1161	2962
CGI abuses	wpoison (nasl version)		
CGI abuses	Microsoft's Index server reveals ASP source code	CVE-2000-0302, CVE-2000-0097	1084
CGI abuses	IIS XSS via error		5900
CGI abuses	E-Theni code injection		6970
CGI abuses	AdMentor Login Flaw	CAN-2002-0308	4152
CGI abuses	DBMan CGI server information leakage	CVE-2000-0381	1178
CGI abuses	Anti Nessus defenses		
CGI abuses	news desk	CAN-2001-0231	2172
CGI abuses	bb-hist.sh	CAN-1999-1462	142
CGI abuses	BEA WebLogic Scripts Server scripts Source Disclosure		2527
CGI abuses	Sambar /cgi-bin/mailit.pl installed ?		
CGI abuses	webchat code injection		7000
CGI abuses	StockMan Shopping Cart Command Execution		7485
CGI abuses	PHP.EXE / Apache Win32 Arbitrary File Reading Vulnerability		3786
CGI abuses	/iisadmin is world readable	CAN-1999-1538	189

Family	Plug-in Name	CVE ID Number(s)	BugTraq ID Number(s)
CGI abuses	Snitz Forums Cmd execution		
CGI abuses	Oracle 9iAS Java Process Manager	CAN-2002-0563	4293
CGI abuses	WebSpeed remote configuration	CVE-2000-0127	969
CGI abuses	mod_survey ENV tags SQL injection		7192
CGI abuses	XMB SQL Injection		7406
CGI abuses	pmachine code injection		7919
CGI abuses	Snapstream PVS web directory traversal	CVE-2001-1108	3100
CGI abuses	MS Personal Web-Server …	CVE-1999-0386	
CGI abuses	Domino HTTP server exposes the set up of the filesystem	CAN-2000-0021	881
CGI abuses	http TRACE XSS attack		
CGI abuses	Lotus Domino Banner Information Disclosure Vulnerability	CAN-2002-0245	4049
CGI abuses	Resin DOS device path disclosure		5252
CGI abuses	Sambar default CGI info disclosure		7207, 7208
CGI abuses	PHPay Information Disclosure		7313, 7310, 7309
CGI abuses	Microsoft IIS UNC Mapped Virtual Host Vulnerability	CVE-2000-0246	1081
CGI abuses	ncbook/book.cgi	CAN-2001-1114	3178

Family	Plug-in Name	CVE ID Number(s)	BugTraq ID Number(s)
CGI abuses	WF-Chat User Account Disclosure		7147
CGI abuses	ODBC tools check		
CGI abuses	Zeus shows the content of the cgi scripts	CVE-2000-0149	977
CGI abuses	Excite for WebServers	CVE-1999-0279	2248
CGI abuses	iPlanet Search Engine File Viewing	CAN-2002-1042	5191
CGI abuses	Finger cgi		
CGI abuses	Microsoft Frontpage exploits	CAN-2000-0114	
CISCO	CSCdi36962		
CISCO	CSCdy03429	CVE-2002-0813	5328
CISCO	CSCdy38035		
CISCO	ATA-186 password circumvention / recovery	CAN-2002-0769	4711
CISCO	CSCdz39284, CSCdz41124		6904
CISCO	CSCdw67458	CAN-2002-0012, CAN-2002-0013	4088
CISCO	CSCds66191	CVE-2001-0041	2072
CISCO	CSCdw19195		
CISCO	CSCdx17916, CSCdx61997		
CISCO	CSCdi34061	CVE-1999-0162	
CISCO	CSCdv48261		
CISCO	CSCea42030	CAN-2003-0216	
CISCO	Cisco IOS HTTP Configuration Arbitrary Administrative Access	CVE-2001-0537	2936

Family	Plug-in Name	CVE ID Number(s)	BugTraq ID Number(s)
CISCO	CSCdu81936	CVE-2001-0895	3547
CISCO	CSCdu82823		
CISCO	CSCdx54675		
CISCO	CSCdt46181	CVE-2001-1183	3022
CISCO	GSR ICMP unreachable	CVE-2001-0861, CVE-2001-0862, CVE-2001-0863, CVE-2001-0864, CVE-2001-0865, CVE-2001-0866, CVE-2001-0867	3534, 3535, 3536, 3537, 3538, 3539, 3540
CISCO	CSCds07326	CVE-2001-0750	2804
CISCO	CSCdt62732	CVE-2001-0429	2604
CISCO	Multiple SSH vulnerabilities	CAN-2001-0572	
CISCO	CSCdx92043	CAN-2002-1222	6823
CISCO	CSCdt93866	CVE-2001-0414	2540
CISCO	CSCdx39981		
CISCO	CSCdv66718	CAN-2002-1092	
CISCO	CSCdu15622	CAN-2002-1093	
CISCO	Cisco Aironet Telnet DoS	CVE-2002-0545	4461
CISCO	CSCdw50657		
CISCO	CSCdt56514		
CISCO	cisco 675 http DoS		
CISCO	CISCO IOS Interface blocked by IPv4 Packet	CAN-2003-0567	8211
CISCO	CSCdea77143, CSCdz15393, CSCdt84906		

Family	Plug-in Name	CVE ID Number(s)	BugTraq ID Number(s)
CISCO	GSR ACL pub	CVE-2000-0700	1541
CISCO	Cisco password not set	CAN-1999-0508	
CISCO	CSCdu35577		
CISCO	CSCdp35794	CVE-2000-0700	1541
CISCO	CISCO Secure ACS Management Interface Login Overflow	CAN-2003-0210	7413
CISCO	CSCdx07754, CSCdx24622, CSCdx24632		
CISCO	Cisco Catalyst Web Execution	CVE-2000-0945	1846
CISCO	CSCdu20643	CVE-2002-0339	4191
CISCO	CSCdw33027	CVE-2002-1024	5114
CISCO	CSCdy26428	CAN-2002-1222	5976
CISCO	CSCds04747	CAN-2001-0328	2682
CISCO	CSCdt65960	CVE-2001-0757	2874
CISCO	CSCdv88230, CSCdw22408		
CISCO	CSCdv85279, CSCdw59394	CVE-2002-1024	5114
CISCO	CSCdz60229, CSCdy87221, CSCdu75477	CAN-2002-1357, CAN-2002-1358, CAN-2002-1359, CAN-2002-1360	6397
CISCO	CSCdp58462		6895
Default Unix Accounts	Unpassworded backdoor account	CVE-1999-0502	
Default Unix Accounts	Default password (ibmdb2) for db2as	CAN-2001-0051	

Family	Plug-in Name	CVE ID Number(s)	BugTraq ID Number(s)
Default Unix Accounts	Unpassworded hax0r account	CVE-1999-0502	
Default Unix Accounts	Unpassworded jill account	CVE-1999-0502	
Default Unix Accounts	Unpassworded root account	CVE-1999-0502	
Default Unix Accounts	Unpassworded toor account	CVE-1999-0502	
Default Unix Accounts	Unpassworded OutOfBox account	CVE-1999-0502	
Default Unix Accounts	Default password (ibmdb2) for db2fenc1	CAN-2001-0051	
Default Unix Accounts	Unpassworded date account	CVE-1999-0502	
Default Unix Accounts	Unpassworded sync account	CVE-1999-0502	
Default Unix Accounts	Unpassworded 4Dgifts account	CVE-1999-0502	
Default Unix Accounts	Unpassworded lp account	CVE-1999-0502	
Default Unix Accounts	Unpassworded friday account	CVE-1999-0502	
Default Unix Accounts	Default password (lrkr0x) for gamez	CVE-1999-0502	
Default Unix Accounts	Default password (db2as) for db2as	CAN-2001-0051	
Default Unix Accounts	Default password (wh00t!) for root	CVE-1999-0502	
Default Unix Accounts	Unpassworded EZsetup account	CVE-1999-0502	
Default Unix Accounts	Default password (manager) for system	CVE-1999-0502	
Default Unix Accounts	Default password (D13HH[) for root	CVE-1999-0502	

Family	Plug-in Name	CVE ID Number(s)	BugTraq ID Number(s)
Default Unix Accounts	Default password (D13hh[) for root	CVE-1999-0502	
Default Unix Accounts	Default password (db2fenc1) for db2fenc1	CAN-2001-0051	
Default Unix Accounts	Default password (satori) for rewt	CVE-1999-0502	
Default Unix Accounts	Unpassworded tutor account	CVE-1999-0502	
Default Unix Accounts	Default password (db2inst1) for db2inst1	CAN-2001-0051	
Default Unix Accounts	Default password (ibmdb2) for db2inst1	CAN-2001-0051	
Default Unix Accounts	Unpassworded demos account	CVE-1999-0502	
Default Unix Accounts	Default password (guest) for guest	CVE-1999-0502	
Default Unix Accounts	Default password (wank) for wank	CVE-1999-0502	
Default Unix Accounts	Default password (root) for root	CVE-1999-0502	
Default Unix Accounts	Default password (glftpd) for glftpd	CVE-1999-0502	
Default Unix Accounts	Unpassworded StoogR account	CVE-1999-0502	
Default Unix Accounts	Unpassworded jack account	CVE-1999-0502	
Default Unix Accounts	Unpassworded guest account	CVE-1999-0502	
Denial of Service	Eicon Diehl LAN ISDN modem DoS	CAN-1999-1533	665
Denial of Service	Netscape Enterprise Server DoS	CVE-1999-0752	516

Family	Plug-in Name	CVE ID Number(s)	BugTraq ID Number(s)
Denial of Service	SMB null param count DoS	CAN-2002-0724	5556
Denial of Service	GoodTech ftpd DoS	CAN-2001-0188	2270
Denial of Service	IIS FrontPage DoS	CVE-2001-0096	2144
Denial of Service	ping of death		
Denial of Service	DoSable Oracle Web-Cache server	CAN-2002-0102	3760
Denial of Service	3com RAS 1500 DoS		7175
Denial of Service	jolt2	CVE-2000-0482	1312
Denial of Service	mod_jk chunked encoding DoS		6320
Denial of Service	Hyperbomb	CVE-1999-1336	
Denial of Service	Linksys Gozila CGI denial of service		
Denial of Service	spank.c		
Denial of Service	Ascend Kill	CVE-1999-0060	714
Denial of Service	SLMail denial of service	CAN-1999-0231	
Denial of Service	WinLogon.exe DoS	CVE-2000-0377	1331
Denial of Service	Cisco DoS	CVE-1999-0430	705
Denial of Service	FTP Windows 98 MS/DOS device names DOS		
Denial of Service	Marconi ASX DoS	CAN-2001-0270	2400
Denial of Service	GAMSoft TelSrv 1.4/1.5 Overflow	CVE-2000-0665	1478
Denial of Service	DB2 DOS	CAN-2001-1143	3010
Denial of Service	WINS UDP flood denial	CVE-1999-0288	298
Denial of Service	IIS 5.0 WebDav Memory Leakage		2736

Family	Plug-in Name	CVE ID Number(s)	BugTraq ID Number(s)
Denial of Service	FTP Serv-U 2.5e DoS	CVE-2000-0837	
Denial of Service	Oracle Web Server denial of Service	CAN-1999-1068	
Denial of Service	D-Link router overflow		
Denial of Service	IIS Malformed Extension Data in URL	CVE-2000-0408	1190
Denial of Service	Bonk	CAN-1999-0258	
Denial of Service	UDP null size going to SNMP DoS	CVE-2000-0221	1009
Denial of Service	Microsoft Media Server 4.1 - DoS	CVE-2000-0211	1000
Denial of Service	Proxomitron DoS		7954
Denial of Service	Checkpoint Firewall-1 UDP denial of service		1419
Denial of Service	Cassandra NNTP Server DoS	CVE-2000-0341	1156
Denial of Service	Too long line		
Denial of Service	Exchange Malformed MIME header	CVE-2000-1006	1869
Denial of Service	HTTP unfinished line denial		5664
Denial of Service	BadBlue invalid GET DoS	CAN-2002-1023	5187
Denial of Service	Microsoft Frontpage DoS	CAN-2000-0709	1608
Denial of Service	NAI PGP Cert Server DoS	CAN-2000-0543	1343
Denial of Service	Ken! DoS	CVE-2000-0262	1103
Denial of Service	AnalogX denial of service by long CGI name	CAN-2000-0473	1349
Denial of Service	MDaemon Worldclient crash	CAN-1999-0844	823

Family	Plug-in Name	CVE ID Number(s)	BugTraq ID Number(s)
Denial of Service	Novell FTP DoS		7072
Denial of Service	FTP ServU CWD overflow	CVE-1999-0219	269
Denial of Service	Webseal denial of service	CAN-2001-1191	3685
Denial of Service	BIND9 DoS	CAN-2002-0400	4936
Denial of Service	WindowsNT DNS flood denial	CVE-1999-0275	
Denial of Service	Teardrop	CAN-1999-0015	124
Denial of Service	Polycom ViaVideo denial of service		5962
Denial of Service	SLMail:27 denial of service	CAN-1999-0231	
Denial of Service	Trend Micro OfficeScan Denial of service	CAN-2000-0203	1013
Denial of Service	Crash SMC AP		
Denial of Service	WebSphere Host header overflow	CAN-2002-1153	5749
Denial of Service	Mercur WebView Web-Client	CAN-2000-0239	1056
Denial of Service	Domino HTTP Denial	CVE-2000-0023	881
Denial of Service	l2tpd DoS		
Denial of Service	Xeneo Web Server 2.2.9.0 DoS		
Denial of Service	Orange DoS	CAN-2001-0647	2432
Denial of Service	WebShield	CVE-2000-0738, CAN-2000-1130	1589, 1993
Denial of Service	DoSable squid proxy server	CVE-2001-0843	3354
Denial of Service	Dragon FTP overflow	CAN-2000-0479	1352

Family	Plug-in Name	CVE ID Number(s)	BugTraq ID Number(s)
Denial of Service	myServer DoS		6359, 7770, 7917, 8010, 8120
Denial of Service	NetGear ProSafe VPN Login DoS		7166
Denial of Service	Linux 2.1.89 - 2.2.3 : 0 length fragment bug	CAN-1999-0431	2247
Denial of Service	SNMP bad length field DoS (2)	CAN-2002-0012	4088
Denial of Service	HTTP Windows 98 MS/ DOS device names DOS	CVE-2001-0386, CVE-2001-0493, CAN-2001-0391, CVE-2001-0558, CAN-2002-0200, CVE-2000-0168, CAN-2003-0016, CAN-2001-0602	2622, 2704, 3929, 1043, 2575
Denial of Service	Nestea	CAN-1999-0257	7219
Denial of Service	ICQ Denial of Service attack	CAN-2000-0564	1463
Denial of Service	Generic flood		
Denial of Service	MacOS X Directory Service DoS		7323
Denial of Service	WebServer 4D GET Buffer Overflow		7479
Denial of Service	Axent Raptor's DoS	CVE-1999-0905	736
Denial of Service	Notes MTA denial	CAN-1999-0284	
Denial of Service	SNMP bad length field DoS	CAN-2002-0013	
Denial of Service	WindowsNT PPTP flood denial	CAN-1999-0140	2111
Denial of Service	Linux 2.4 NFSv3 DoS	-2228	8298
Denial of Service	RealServer Ramgen crash (ramcrash)	CVE-2000-0001	888

Family	Plug-in Name	CVE ID Number(s)	BugTraq ID Number(s)
Denial of Service	SalesLogix Eviewer WebApp crash	CVE-2000-0278	1089
Denial of Service	LiteServe URL Decoding DoS		
Denial of Service	IIS propfind DoS	CVE-2001-0151	2453
Denial of Service	IPSEC IKE check		
Denial of Service	Xeneo web server %A DoS	CAN-2002-1248	
Denial of Service	NT IIS Malformed HTTP Request Header DoS Vulnerability	CVE-1999-0867	579
Denial of Service	MDaemon crash	CAN-1999-0284	
Denial of Service	Sambar web server DOS	CVE-2002-0128	3885
Denial of Service	HTTP method overflow	CAN-2002-1061	5319
Denial of Service	CP syslog overflow		7159
Denial of Service	MS RPC Services null pointer reference DoS		6005
Denial of Service	IIS 'GET ../../'	CAN-1999-0229	2218
Denial of Service	Sedum DoS	CAN-2001-0282	2413
Denial of Service	Savant DoS		2468
Denial of Service	Worldspan gateway DOS	CAN-2002-1029	5169
Denial of Service	Wingate POP3 USER overflow	CVE-1999-0494	
Denial of Service	IIS FTP server crash	CVE-1999-0349	192
Denial of Service	MDaemon Webconfig crash	CAN-1999-0844	820
Denial of Service	cisco http DoS	CVE-2000-0380	1154
Denial of Service	Nortel Contivity DoS	CVE-2000-0063	938

Family	Plug-in Name	CVE ID Number(s)	BugTraq ID Number(s)
Denial of Service	Jigsaw webserver MS/DOS device DoS	CAN-2002-1052	5258
Denial of Service	LinkSys EtherFast Router Denial of Service Attack		8834
Denial of Service	rfparalyze	CVE-2000-0347	1163
Denial of Service	stream.c	CVE-1999-0770	549
Denial of Service	IIS 5.0 PROPFIND Vulnerability	CVE-2001-0151	2453
Denial of Service	Oracle webcache admin interface DoS	CAN-2002-0386	3765
Denial of Service	Dragon telnet overflow	CAN-2000-0480	1352
Denial of Service	Eserv Memory Leaks		
Denial of Service	RealServer denial of Service	CVE-2000-0272	1128
Denial of Service	Novell Border Manager	CVE-2000-0152	
Denial of Service	AppSocket DoS		
Denial of Service	Pi3Web Webserver v2.0 Denial of Service	CAN-2003-0276	
Denial of Service	HP Instant TopTools DoS	CAN-2003-0169	
Denial of Service	Quake3 Arena 1.29 f/g DOS	CAN-2001-1289	3123
Denial of Service	Firewall/1 UDP port 0 DoS	CVE-1999-0675	576
Denial of Service	smad		
Denial of Service	Desktop Orbiter Remote Reboot		
Denial of Service	OShare	CVE-1999-0357	
Denial of Service	Pi3Web Webserver v2.0 Buffer Overflow	CAN-2002-0142	3866

Family	Plug-in Name	CVE ID Number(s)	BugTraq ID Number(s)
Denial of Service	Netscape Enterprise '../' buffer overflow	CVE-2001-0252	2282
Denial of Service	Abyss httpd crash		7287
Denial of Service	Wingate denial of service	CVE-1999-0290	
Denial of Service	pimp	CVE-1999-0918	514
Denial of Service	HotSync Manager Denial of Service attack	CAN-2000-0058	920
Denial of Service	Infinite HTTP request		2465
Denial of Service	WinSyslog (DoS)		
Denial of Service	AnalogX denial of service	CVE-2000-0243	1076
Denial of Service	Land	CVE-1999-0016	2666
Denial of Service	SMTP antivirus scanner DoS		3027
Denial of Service	Winnuke	CVE-1999-0153	2010
Denial of Service	Chameleon SMTPd overflow	CAN-1999-0261	2387
Denial of Service	AnalogX SimpleServer: WWW DoS	CVE-2002-0968	5006
Denial of Service	GroupWise buffer overflow	CVE-2000-0146	972
Denial of Service	Interscan 3.32 SMTP Denial	CAN-1999-1529	787
Denial of Service	rfpoison	CVE-1999-0980	754
Denial of Service	CISCO view-source DoS	CVE-2000-0984	1838
Denial of Service	Imail Host: overflow	CVE-2000-0825	2011
Denial of Service	FTgate DoS		
Denial of Service	MDaemon DELE DoS	CAN-2002-1539	6053
Denial of Service	Cisco VoIP phones DoS	CAN-2002-0882	4794

Family	Plug-in Name	CVE ID Number(s)	BugTraq ID Number(s)
Denial of Service	Yahoo Messenger Denial of Service attack	CAN-2000-0047	
Denial of Service	DB2 discovery service DOS		
Denial of Service	IIS FrontPage ISAPI Denial of Service	CAN-1999-1376, CVE-2000-0226, CVE-2002-0072	4479
Denial of Service	MDaemon DoS	CAN-1999-0846	
Denial of Service	Cajun p13x DoS		
Denial of Service	Livingston Portmaster crash	CVE-1999-0218	2225
Denial of Service	Lotus /./ database lock	CVE-2001-0954	3656
Denial of Service	+ + + ATH0 modem hangup	CAN-1999-1228	
Denial of Service	EMule DoS		7189
Denial of Service	Argosoft DoS		
Denial of Service	mod_access_referer 1.0.2 NULL pointer dereference		7375
Denial of Service	LabView web server DoS	CVE-2002-0748	4577
Denial of Service	Shambala web server DoS	CAN-2002-0876	4897
Denial of Service	iParty	CAN-1999-1566	
Denial of Service	vxworks ftpd buffer over-flow Denial of Service		6297, 7480
Denial of Service	Microsoft's SQL TCP/IP denial of service	CVE-1999-0999	817
Denial of Service	Lotus Domino SMTP bounce DoS	CAN-2000-1203	3212
Denial of Service	SuSE's identd overflow	CVE-1999-0746	587
Denial of Service	SunKill	CVE-1999-0273	

Family	Plug-in Name	CVE ID Number(s)	BugTraq ID Number(s)
Denial of Service	MSDTC denial of service by flooding with nul bytes	CAN-2002-0224	4006
Denial of Service	Annex DoS	CAN-1999-1070	
Denial of Service	Check for RealServer DoS	CVE-2000-0474	1288
Denial of Service	BlackIce DoS (ping flood)	CVE-2002-0237	4025
Denial of Service	MAILsweeper Power-Point DoS		7562
Denial of Service	Xerver web server DOS	CAN-2002-0448	4254
Denial of Service	RPC DCOM Interface DoS	CAN-2003-0605	8234
Denial of Service	WebSphere Edge caching proxy denial of service	CAN-2002-1169	6002
Denial of Service	HTTP negative Content-Length DoS		
Denial of Service	pnserver crash	CAN-1999-0271	
Denial of Service	BFTelnet DoS	CVE-1999-0904	771
Denial of Service	Tomcat servlet engine MD/DOS device names denial of service		
Denial of Service	Personal Web Sharing overflow		84, 2715
Finger abuses	Solaris finger disclosure		3457
Finger abuses	akfingerd		6323
Finger abuses	Finger redirection check	CAN-1999-0105, CVE-1999-0106	
Finger abuses	Cfinger's search.**@host feature	CVE-1999-0259	
Finger abuses	cfinger's version		
Finger abuses	in.fingerd pipe	CVE-1999-0152	

Family	Plug-in Name	CVE ID Number(s)	BugTraq ID Number(s)
Finger abuses	Finger zero at host feature	CAN-1999-0197	
Finger abuses	FreeBSD 4.1.1 Finger	CVE-2000-0915	1803
Finger abuses	Finger dot at host feature	CAN-1999-0198	
Finger abuses	cfingerd format string attack	CAN-1999-0243, CVE-1999-0708, CAN-2001-0609	2576
Firewalls	L2TP detection		
Firewalls	RADIUS server detection	CAN-2001-1377, CAN-2000-0321, CAN-2001-0534, CAN-2001-1081, CAN-2001-1376, CAN-2001-1377	7892, 5103, 4230, 3530, 3529, 2994, 2989, 2991, 6261, 3532
Firewalls	CheckPoint Firewall-1 Telnet Authentication Detection		
Firewalls	Remote host replies to SYN+FIN		7487
Firewalls	Checkpoint Firewall open Web adminstration		
Firewalls	Usable remote proxy		
Firewalls	Checkpoint SecuRemote information leakage	CVE-2001-1303	3058
Firewalls	Checkpoint FW-1 identification		
Firewalls	icmp timestamp request	CAN-1999-0524	
Firewalls	UDP packets with source port of 53 bypass firewall rules		7436
Firewalls	Kerio personal Firewall buffer overflow		7180
Firewalls	StoneGate client authentication detection		

Family	Plug-in Name	CVE ID Number(s)	BugTraq ID Number(s)
Firewalls	CheckPoint Firewall-1 Web Authentication Detection		
Firewalls	Passwordless Wingate installed	CVE-1999-0291	
Firewalls	Source routed packets		
Firewalls	BenHur Firewall active FTP firewall leak		5279
Firewalls	Proxy accepts gopher:// requests	CAN-2002-0371	
Firewalls	PIX's smtp content filtering	CVE-2000-1022	1698
Firewalls	icmp netmask request	CAN-1999-0524	
Firewalls	Proxy accepts CONNECT requests		
Firewalls	Raptor Weak ISN	CAN-2002-1463	
Firewalls	Proxy accepts POST requests		
Firewalls	Checkpoint SecureRemote detection		
Firewalls	IBM Tivoli Relay Overflow		7154, 7157
Firewalls	Raptor FW version 6.5 detection		
Firewalls	Usable remote proxy on any port		
FTP	WS_FTP SITE CPWD Buffer Overflow	CAN-2002-0826	5427
FTP	TypSoft FTP STOR/ RETR DoS	CAN-2001-1156	3409
FTP	.forward in FTP root		

Family	Plug-in Name	CVE ID Number(s)	BugTraq ID Number(s)
FTP	WFTP 2.41 rc11 multiple DoS	CAN-2000-0647	
FTP	wu-ftpd buffer overflow	CVE-1999-0368, CVE-1999-0878, CVE-1999-0879, CVE-1999-0950	2242
FTP	NiteServer FTP directory traversal		6648
FTP	SunFTP Buffer Overflow	CVE-2000-0856	1638
FTP	FTP bounce check	CVE-1999-0017	
FTP	Windows Administrator NULL FTP password		
FTP	SunFTP directory traversal	CAN-2001-0283	
FTP	Platinum FTP Server		
FTP	Solaris FTPd tells if a user exists		2564
FTP	FTP site exec	CVE-1999-0080, CVE-1999-0955	2241
FTP	ProFTPd buffer overflow	CAN-1999-0911	612
FTP	War FTP Daemon Directory Traversal	CVE-2001-0295	2444
FTP	proftpd 1.2.0preN check	CVE-1999-0368	2242
FTP	CrobFTP format string		7776
FTP	BSD ftpd Single Byte Buffer Overflow	CVE-2001-0053	2124
FTP	proftpd mod_sql injection		7974
FTP	hpux ftpd REST vulnerability		
FTP	FTPd tells if a user exists		

Family	Plug-in Name	CVE ID Number(s)	BugTraq ID Number(s)
FTP	ST FTP traversal		7674
FTP	NB1300 router default FTP account		7359
FTP	AIX FTPd buffer overflow	CVE-1999-0789	679
FTP	Passwordless Zaurus FTP server		5200
FTP	HP-UX ftpd glob() Expansion STAT Buffer Overflow	CAN-2001-0248	2552
FTP	hpux ftpd PASS vulnerability	CVE-2000-0699	1560
FTP	NGC ActiveFTP Denial of Service		7900
FTP	Multiple WarFTPd DoS		2698
FTP	.rhosts in FTP root		
FTP	Serv-U path disclosure	CAN-2000-0176, CVE-1999-0838	1016, 859
FTP	wu-ftpd SITE NEWER vulnerability	CVE-1999-0880	
FTP	Broker FTP files listing	CAN-2001-0450	301
FTP	GuildFTPd Directory Traversal	CAN-2001-0767	2789
FTP	Ftp PASV denial of service	CVE-1999-0079	271
FTP	Guild FTPd tells if a given file exists	CVE-2000-0640	1452
FTP	proftpd exhaustion attack		6341
FTP	bftpd chown overflow	CAN-2001-0065, CVE-2000-0943	2120

Family	Plug-in Name	CVE ID Number(s)	BugTraq ID Number(s)
FTP	MS FTPd DoS	CVE-2002-0073, CVE-2002-0073	4482
FTP	Serv-U Directory traversal	CVE-2001-0054	2052
FTP	EFTP installation directory disclosure	CAN-2001-1109	3333
FTP	ftp 'glob' overflow	CAN-2001-0247	2548
FTP	proftpd mkdir buffer overflow	CAN-1999-0911	612
FTP	Ftp PASV on connect crashes the FTP server	CVE-1999-0075	
FTP	webweaver FTP DoS		7425
FTP	EFTP tells if a given file exists	CAN-2001-1109	3333
FTP	Anonymous FTP enabled	CAN-1999-0497	
FTP	wu-ftpd glob vulnerability (2)	CAN-2001-0935	
FTP	FTPD glob Heap Corruption	CAN-2001-0249, CVE-2001-0550	2550, 3581
FTP	Generic FTP traversal	CVE-2001-0680, CAN-2001-1335, CAN-2001-0582	2618, 2786
FTP	Debian proftpd 1.2.0 runs as root	CVE-2001-0456	
FTP	wu-ftpd fb_realpath() off-by-one overflow	CAN-2003-0466	8315
FTP	War FTP Daemon USER/ PASS Overflow	CVE-1999-0256	
FTP	EFTP carriage return DoS	CVE-2000-0871	1677
FTP	ftpd strtok() stack overflow	CAN-2001-0325	2342
FTP	Writeable FTP root	CAN-1999-0527	

Family	Plug-in Name	CVE ID Number(s)	BugTraq ID Number(s)
FTP	Linux FTP backdoor	CAN-1999-0452	
FTP	proftpd 1.2.0rc2 format string vuln	CVE-2001-0318	
FTP	wu-ftpd PASV format string	CVE-2001-0187	2296
FTP	ftp USER, PASS or HELP overflow	CAN-2000-0133, CVE-2000-0943, CAN-2002-0126, CVE-2000-0870, CVE-2000-1035, CVE-2000-1194, CAN-2000-1035	961, 1858, 3884, 7251, 7278, 7307
FTP	ProFTPd pre6 buffer overflow	CAN-1999-0911	612
FTP	vxworks ftpd buffer overflow		6297
FTP	FTP Service Allows Any Username		
FTP	bftpd format string vulnerability		
FTP	VisNetic and Titan FTP Server traversal		7718
FTP	FTP CWD ~root	CVE-1999-0082	
FTP	vftpd buffer overflow	CAN-1999-1058	818
FTP	War FTP Daemon CWD/ MKD Buffer Overflow	CVE-2000-0131	966
FTP	PFTP login check		
FTP	ftp writeable directories	CAN-1999-0527	
FTP	BlackMoon FTP user disclosure		
FTP	ProFTPd ASCII upload overflow		8679

Family	Plug-in Name	CVE ID Number(s)	BugTraq ID Number(s)
FTP	BSD ftpd setproctitle() format string	CAN-2000-0574	1425
FTP	SmallFTP traversal		
FTP	Windows NT ftp 'guest' account	CAN-1999-0546	
FTP	WS FTP overflows	CAN-2001-1021	
FTP	WFTP login check	CAN-1999-0200	
FTP	FTP real path	CVE-1999-0201	
FTP	WFTP RNTO DoS	CAN-2000-0648	1456
FTP	wu-ftpd SITE EXEC vulnerability	CVE-2000-0573, CVE-1999-0997	1387, 2240, 726
Gain a shell remotely	/bin/login overflow exploitation	CVE-2001-0797	3681
Gain a shell remotely	SSH 3 Allowed-Authentication		4810
Gain a shell remotely	MCMS : Buffer overflow in Profile Service	CAN-2002-0620, CVE-2002-0621, CVE-2002-0622, CVE-2002-0623, CVE-2002-0050	
Gain a shell remotely	Multiple vulnerabilities in CUPS	CAN-2002-1383, CAN-2002-1366, CAN-2002-1367, CAN-2002-1368, CAN-2002-1384, CAN-2002-1369, CAN-2002-1372	
Gain a shell remotely	rsh on finger output		
Gain a shell remotely	OpenSSL overflow via invalid certificate passing	CAN-2003-0543, CAN-2003-0544, CAN-2003-0545	8732
Gain a shell remotely	ipop2d buffer overflow	CVE-1999-0920	283

Family	Plug-in Name	CVE ID Number(s)	BugTraq ID Number(s)
Gain a shell remotely	Omron WorldView Wnn Overflow	CAN-2000-0704	1603
Gain a shell remotely	Canna Overflow	CVE-2000-0584	1445
Gain a shell remotely	MailMax IMAP overflows (2)		7327
Gain a shell remotely	iWS shtml overflow	CVE-2000-1077	1848
Gain a shell remotely	Cyrus IMAP pre-login buffer overrun		
Gain a shell remotely	Shell Command Execution Vulnerability		
Gain a shell remotely	libgtop_daemon format string	CAN-2001-0927	
Gain a shell remotely	gnocatan multiple buffer overflows		
Gain a shell remotely	shtml.exe overflow	CAN-2002-0692	5804
Gain a shell remotely	SSH Secure-RPC Weak Encrypted Authentication	CVE-2001-0259	2222
Gain a shell remotely	OpenSSL overflow (generic test)	CAN-2002-0656, CAN-2002-0655, CAN-2002-0657, CAN-2002-0659, CVE-2001-1141	5363
Gain a shell remotely	tanned format string vulnerability		6553
Gain a shell remotely	qpopper euidl problem	CVE-2000-0320	1133
Gain a shell remotely	Netscape Enterprise 'Accept' buffer overflow	CVE-1999-0751	631
Gain a shell remotely	OpenSSH 2.5.x -> 2.9.x adv.option	CVE-2001-0816	3369

Family	Plug-in Name	CVE ID Number(s)	BugTraq ID Number(s)
Gain a shell remotely	PostgreSQL multiple flaws	CAN-2002-1402, CAN-2002-1401, CAN-2002-1400, CAN-2002-1397, CAN-2002-1399	6610, 6614, 5527, 5497, 6615, 6611, 6612, 6613, 7075
Gain a shell remotely	MySQL double free()	CAN-2003-0073	6718
Gain a shell remotely	CesarFTP multiple overflows	CAN-2001-0826	7950, 7946
Gain a shell remotely	BitKeeper remote command execution		
Gain a shell remotely	mod_mylo overflow		8287
Gain a shell remotely	uw-imap buffer overflow after logon	CAN-2000-0284	1110
Gain a shell remotely	NAI Management Agent overflow	CVE-2000-0447	1254
Gain a shell remotely	Lotus Domino Vulner-abilities	CAN-2003-0123, CAN-2001-1311	7038, 7039
Gain a shell remotely	qpopper LIST buffer overflow	CAN-2000-0096	948
Gain a shell remotely	wsmp3d command execution	CAN-2003-0338	
Gain a shell remotely	LPRng malformed input	CVE-2000-0917	1712
Gain a shell remotely	IMAP4rev1 buffer over-flow after logon	CAN-1999-1224	
Gain a shell remotely	Oracle LINK overflow	CAN-2003-0222	7453
Gain a shell remotely	iPlanet Application Server Buffer Overflow	CAN-2002-0387	7082
Gain a shell remotely	multiple MySQL flaws	CAN-2002-1373, CAN-2002-1374, CAN-2002-1375, CAN-2002-1376	6368, 6370, 6373, 6374, 6375

Family	Plug-in Name	CVE ID Number(s)	BugTraq ID Number(s)
Gain a shell remotely	PKCS 1 Version 1.5 Session Key Retrieval	CVE-2001-0361	2344
Gain a shell remotely	FakeBO buffer overflow		
Gain a shell remotely	Batalla Naval Overflow		
Gain a shell remotely	Apache < 2.0.44 DOS device name	CAN-2003-0016	
Gain a shell remotely	Magic WinMail Format string	CAN-2003-0391	7667
Gain a shell remotely	MySQL password handler overflaw	CAN-2003-0780	8590
Gain a shell remotely	SSH Insertion Attack	CVE-1999-1085	
Gain a shell remotely	IMAP4buffer overflow in the BODY command	CVE-2002-0379	4713
Gain a shell remotely	rwhois format string attack	CAN-2001-0838	
Gain a shell remotely	qpopper Qvsnprintf buffer overflow	CAN-2003-0143	7058
Gain a shell remotely	Apache chunked encoding	CVE-2002-0392	5033
Gain a shell remotely	rwhois format string attack (2)	CAN-2001-0913	
Gain a shell remotely	scp File Create/Overwrite	CVE-2000-0992	1742
Gain a shell remotely	Kerio WebMail interface flaws		7966, 7967, 7968
Gain a shell remotely	Quicktime/Darwin Remote Admin Exploit	CAN-2003-0050, CAN-2003-0051, CAN-2003-0052, CAN-2003-0053, CAN-2003-0054, CAN-2003-0055	6954, 6955, 6956, 6957, 6958, 6960, 6990
Gain a shell remotely	Gauntlet overflow	CVE-2000-0437	1234
Gain a shell remotely	netscape imap buffer over-flow after logon	CVE-2000-0961	1721

Family	Plug-in Name	CVE ID Number(s)	BugTraq ID Number(s)
Gain a shell remotely	Oops buffer overflow	CAN-2001-0029	2099
Gain a shell remotely	SSH Overflow	CVE-1999-0834	843
Gain a shell remotely	Helix RealServer Buffer Overrun	CAN-2003-0725	
Gain a shell remotely	SSH 3.0.0	CVE-2001-0553	3078
Gain a shell remotely	Apache-SSL overflow	CVE-2002-0082	4189
Gain a shell remotely	OpenSSH < 3.0.1	CVE-2002-0083	3560, 4560, 4241
Gain a shell remotely	MDaemon IMAP CREATE overflow		7446
Gain a shell remotely	MailMax IMAP overflows	CVE-1999-0404	7326
Gain a shell remotely	OpenSSH 2.3.1 authentication bypass vulnerability		2356
Gain a shell remotely	SSH Kerberos issue	CVE-2000-0575	1426
Gain a shell remotely	mod_ntlm overflow / format string bug		7393, 7388
Gain a shell remotely	rsh with null username	CVE-1999-0180	
Gain a shell remotely	OpenSSH Client Unauthorized Remote Forwarding	CVE-2000-1169	1949
Gain a shell remotely	SSH1 SSH Daemon Logging Failure	CAN-2001-0471	2345
Gain a shell remotely	ActiveSync packet overflow		7150
Gain root remotely	mountd overflow	CVE-1999-0002	
Gain root remotely	Imap buffer overflow	CVE-1999-0005	130
Gain root remotely	Microsoft RPC Interface Buffer Overrun (823980)	CAN-2003-0352	8205
Gain root remotely	Samba trans2open buffer overflow	CAN-2003-0201, CAN-2003-0196	7294

Family	Plug-in Name	CVE ID Number(s)	BugTraq ID Number(s)
Gain root remotely	INN version check	CVE-1999-0705, CVE-1999-0043, CVE-1999-0247	616
Gain root remotely	Linux nfs-utils xlog() off-by-one overflow	CAN-2003-0252	8179
Gain root remotely	Format string on HTTP method name		
Gain root remotely	EFTP buffer overflow	CAN-2001-1112	3330
Gain root remotely	SimpleServer remote execution		3112
Gain root remotely	Alibaba 2.0 buffer overflow	CAN-2000-0626	1482
Gain root remotely	BIND iquery overflow	CVE-1999-0009	134
Gain root remotely	Too long OPTIONS parameter		
Gain root remotely	OpenSSH < 3.7.1	CAN-2003-0693, CAN-2003-0695	8628
Gain root remotely	Samba Fragment Reassembly Overflow	CAN-2003-0085, CAN-2003-0086	7106, 7107
Gain root remotely	Buffer overflow in Microsoft Telnet	CVE-2002-0020	4061
Gain root remotely	BrowseGate HTTP headers overflows	CVE-2000-0908	1702
Gain root remotely	SSH Multiple Vulns	CAN-2002-1357, CAN-2002-1358, CAN-2002-1359, CAN-2002-1360	
Gain root remotely	Samba Remote Arbitrary File Creation	CVE-2001-1162	2928
Gain root remotely	MDBMS overflow	CVE-2000-0446	1252
Gain root remotely	lsh overflow		8655

Family	Plug-in Name	CVE ID Number(s)	BugTraq ID Number(s)
Gain root remotely	RealServer G2 buffer overrun	CAN-1999-0271	
Gain root remotely	Oracle9iAS too long URL	CVE-2001-0836	3443
Gain root remotely	Webalizer Cross Site Scripting Vulnerability	CAN-2001-0835	3473
Gain root remotely	Multiple IRC daemons format string attack		8038
Gain root remotely	Imail's imap buffer overflow	CAN-1999-1557	502
Gain root remotely	l2tpd < 0.68 overflow	CVE-2002-0872, CVE-2002-0873	
Gain root remotely	HTTP negative Content-Length buffer overflow		
Gain root remotely	Solaris lpd remote command execution		3274
Gain root remotely	Webserver4everyone too long URL		
Gain root remotely	IIS : WebDAV Overflow (MS03-007)	CAN-2003-0109	7116
Gain root remotely	dwhttpd format string		5384
Gain root remotely	Various pop3 overflows	CAN-2002-0799, CVE-1999-0822	789, 790, 830, 894, 942, 1965, 2781, 2811, 4055, 4295, 4614
Gain root remotely	IIS buffer overflow	CVE-1999-0874	307
Gain root remotely	OpenSSH < 2.1.1 UseLogin feature	CVE-2000-0525	1334
Gain root remotely	BIND 4.x resolver overflow	CAN-2002-0684	7228
Gain root remotely	INN version check (2)	CVE-2000-0472	1316

Family	Plug-in Name	CVE ID Number(s)	BugTraq ID Number(s)
Gain root remotely	OpenSSH Channel Code Off by 1	CVE-2002-0083	4241
Gain root remotely	Buffer overflow in FreeBSD 2.x lpd	CVE-1999-0299	
Gain root remotely	OpenSSH UseLogin Environment Variables	CVE-2001-0872	3614
Gain root remotely	SOCKS4A hostname overflow	CAN-2002-1001	5138
Gain root remotely	HTTP 1.0 header overflow		
Gain root remotely	X Font Service Buffer Overflow	CAN-2002-1317	
Gain root remotely	IIS ASP ISAPI filter Overflow	CVE-2002-0079, CAN-2002-0079, CAN-2002-0147, CVE-2002-0149	4485
Gain root remotely	snmpXdmid overflow	CVE-2001-0236	2417
Gain root remotely	PPTP overflow	CAN-2003-0213	7316
Gain root remotely	HTTP version number overflow		
Gain root remotely	rsync modules		
Gain root remotely	SSH setsid() vulnerability		
Gain root remotely	Microsoft RPC Interface Buffer Overrun (KB824146)	CAN-2003-0715, CAN-2003-0528, CAN-2003-0605	8458
Gain root remotely	rlogin -froot	CVE-1999-0113	458
Gain root remotely	XMail APOP Overflow	CAN-2000-0841	1652
Gain root remotely	Buffer overflow in AIX lpd	CAN-2001-0671	
Gain root remotely	TESO in.telnetd buffer overflow	CVE-2001-0554	3064

Family	Plug-in Name	CVE ID Number(s)	BugTraq ID Number(s)
Gain root remotely	ePolicy orchestrator format string	CAN-2002-0690	7111
Gain root remotely	Too long authorization		
Gain root remotely	yppasswdd overflow	CVE-2001-0779	2763
Gain root remotely	mibiisa overflow	CVE-2002-0797, CAN-2002-0796	4933, 4932
Gain root remotely	IIS .HTR overflow	CVE-2002-0364, CAN-2002-0071, CAN-2002-0364	4855
Gain root remotely	BIND vulnerable to overflows	CVE-2001-0010, CVE-2001-0011, CVE-2001-0012, CVE-2001-0013	2302
Gain root remotely	Too long POST command		
Gain root remotely	ICEcap default password	CVE-2000-0350	1216
Gain root remotely	BIND vulnerable	CVE-1999-0833, CVE-1999-0837, CVE-1999-0848, CVE-1999-0849	788
Gain root remotely	SysV /bin/login buffer overflow (telnet)	CVE-2001-0797	3681, 7481
Gain root remotely	Delegate overflow	CVE-2000-0165	808
Gain root remotely	Knox Arkeia buffer overflow	CAN-1999-1534	661
Gain root remotely	Netwin's Dmail ETRN overflow	CVE-2000-0490	1297
Gain root remotely	Samba Unicode Buffer Overflow	CVE-1999-0182	
Gain root remotely	Abyss httpd overflow		8062, 8064
Gain root remotely	ICECast Format String	CVE-2001-0197	2264
Gain root remotely	PXE server overflow		7129

Family	Plug-in Name	CVE ID Number(s)	BugTraq ID Number(s)
Gain root remotely	NSM format strings vulnerability		
Gain root remotely	Buffer overflow in BSD in.lpd	CVE-2001-0670, CAN-1999-0061	3252
Gain root remotely	dtspcd overflow	CVE-2001-0803	3517
Gain root remotely	Header overflow against HTTP proxy	CAN-2002-0133	3904
Gain root remotely	OpenSSH AFS/Kerberos ticket/token passing	CVE-2002-0575, CAN-2002-0575	4560
Gain root remotely	NT IIS 5.0 Malformed HTTP Printer Request Header Buffer Overflow Vulnerability	CVE-2001-0241	2674
Gain root remotely	Unreal Engine flaws		6770, 6771, 6772, 6773, 6774, 6775
Gain root remotely	Rockliffe's MailSite overflow	CVE-2000-0398	1244
Gain root remotely	pam_smb / pam_ntdom overflow	CAN-2000-0843	1666
Gain root remotely	OpenLink web config buffer overflow	CVE-1999-0943	
Gain root remotely	MonkeyWeb POST with too much data	CAN-2003-0218	
Gain root remotely	DHCP server overflow / format string bug	CAN-2003-0026, CAN-2002-0702, CAN-2003-0039	4701, 6627, 6628
Gain root remotely	Boozt index.cgi overflow		6281
Gain root remotely	thttpd 2.04 buffer overflow	CVE-2000-0359	1248
Gain root remotely	Samba Buffer Overflow		5587
Gain root remotely	rsync array overflow	CAN-2002-0048	3958
Gain root remotely	Generic format string		

Family	Plug-in Name	CVE ID Number(s)	BugTraq ID Number(s)
Gain root remotely	rpc.nisd overflow	CVE-1999-0008	104
Gain root remotely	BIND vulnerable to cached RR overflow	CAN-2002-1219	
Gain root remotely	irix rpc.passwd overflow	CAN-2002-0357	4939
Gain root remotely	Portable SSH OpenSSH < 3.7.1p2	CAN-2003-0786, CAN-2003-0787	8677
Gain root remotely	uw-imap buffer overflow	CVE-1999-0005	130
Gain root remotely	IIS ISAPI Overflow	CVE-2001-0544, CVE-2001-0545, CVE-2001-0506, CVE-2001-0507, CVE-2001-0508, CVE-2001-0500	2690, 3190, 3194, 3195
Gain root remotely	IRIX Objectserver	CVE-2000-0245	1079
Gain root remotely	SSH1 CRC-32 compensation attack	CVE-2001-0144	2347
Gain root remotely	remwatch	CAN-1999-0246	
Gain root remotely	Xitami Web Server buffer overflow		
Gain root remotely	Samba TNG multiple flaws	CAN-2003-0085	7206, 7106
Gain root remotely	Gnu Cfserv remote buffer overflow	CAN-2003-0849	8699
Gain root remotely	Imail's imonitor buffer overflow	CVE-1999-1046, CVE-2000-0056	502, 504, 506, 914
Gain root remotely	qpopper buffer overflow	CVE-1999-0006	133
Gain root remotely	sadmind command execution	CAN-2003-0722	8615
Gain root remotely	rpc.walld format string	CVE-2002-0573	4639
Gain root remotely	SysV /bin/login buffer overflow (rlogin)	CVE-2001-0797	3681

Family	Plug-in Name	CVE ID Number(s)	BugTraq ID Number(s)
Gain root remotely	Too long URL	CVE-2000-0002, CVE-2000-0065, CAN-2001-1250	2979, 6994, 7067, 7280
Gain root remotely	HTTP User-Agent overflow	CVE-2001-0836	3443, 3449, 7054
Gain root remotely	HTTP 1.1 header overflow		
Gain root remotely	Piranha's RH6.2 default password	CAN-2000-0248	1148
Gain root remotely	SOCKS4 username overflow		
Gain root remotely	Communigate Pro overflow	CVE-1999-0865	860
Gain root remotely	ntpd overflow	CVE-2001-0414	2540
Gain root remotely	Avirt gateway insecure telnet proxy	CAN-2002-0134	3901
Gain root remotely	IRCd OperServ Raw Join DoS		8131
Gain root remotely	fakeidentd overflow		5351
Gain root remotely	Oracle Application Server Overflow	CAN-2001-0419	2569
Gain root remotely	Netware Perl CGI overflow	CAN-2003-0562	
Gain root remotely	ePolicy orchestrator multiple issues	CAN-2003-0148, CAN-2003-0149, CAN-2003-0616	
Gain root remotely	HTTP header overflow	CVE-2000-0182	
Gain root remotely	Usermin Session ID Spoofing	CAN-2003-0101	6915
Gain root remotely	klogind overflow	CVE-2001-0035	
Gain root remotely	Xtramail pop3 overflow	CAN-1999-1511	791

Family	Plug-in Name	CVE ID Number(s)	BugTraq ID Number(s)
Gain root remotely	BIND 9 overflow	CAN-2002-0684	
Gain root remotely	Netware Perl CGI overflow	CAN-2003-0562	
Gain root remotely	iPlanet unauthorized sensitive data retrieval	CVE-2001-0327	
Gain root remotely	iPlanet chunked encoding	CVE-2002-0845	5433
Gain root remotely	SCO i2odialogd buffer overrun	CVE-2000-0026	
Gain root remotely	IIS FrontPage DoS II	CVE-2001-0341	2906
Gain root remotely	Tinyproxy heap overflow	CVE-2001-0129	2217
Gain root remotely	lpd, dvips and remote command execution	CVE-2001-1002	3241
Gain root remotely	cachefsd overflow	CAN-2002-0084, CVE-2002-0033	4631
Gain root remotely	Rover pop3 overflow	CVE-2000-0060	894
Gain root remotely	SmartServer pop3 overflow		790
Gain root remotely	OpenSSH <= 3.3	CVE-2002-0639, CVE-2002-0640, CAN-2002-0639, CAN-2002-0640	5093
Gain root remotely	Buffer overflow in Solaris in.lpd	CVE-2001-0353	2894
Gain root remotely	HTTP Cookie overflow		
Gain root remotely	BIND Buffer overflows in the DNS stub resolver library	CAN-2002-0029	6186
Gain root remotely	vpopmail input validation bug	CVE-2000-0583	1418
Gain root remotely	xfstt possible code execution	CAN-2003-0581	8182

Family	Plug-in Name	CVE ID Number(s)	BugTraq ID Number(s)
Gain root remotely	Webmin Session ID Spoofing	CAN-2003-0101	6915
Gain root remotely	apcupsd overflows	CVE-2001-0040, CAN-2003-0098, CAN-2003-0099	2070, 6828, 7200
General	Oracle Web Administration Server Detection		
General	SHOUTcast Server DoS detector vulnerability	CAN-2001-1304	
General	Compaq WBEM Server Detection		
General	Amanda client version		
General	SMTP Server type and version		
General	Detect talkd server port and protocol version	CVE-1999-0048	
General	Formmail Version Information Disclosure	CAN-2001-0357	
General	MySQL Server version		
General	clarkconnectd detection		6934
General	PHP-Nuke sql_debug Information Disclosure		3906
General	Oracle Applications One-Hour Install Detect		
General	DCShop exposes sensitive files	CAN-2001-0821	2889
General	Access Point detection		
General	robot(s).txt exists on the Web Server		
General	HealthD detection		

Family	Plug-in Name	CVE ID Number(s)	BugTraq ID Number(s)
General	Oracle Jserv Executes outside of doc_root	CAN-2001-0307	
General	WWW fingerprinting		
General	News Server type and version		
General	LinuxConf grants network access	CAN-2000-0017	
General	Enhydra Multiserver Default Password		
General	A CVS pserver is running		
General	Determine which version of BIND name daemon is running		
General	F5 Device Default Support Password		
General	WhatsUp Gold Default Admin Account		
General	Kerberos IV cryptographic weaknesses	CAN-2003-0138	7113
General	Mediahouse Statistics Web Server Detect	CVE-2000-0776	1568
General	SHOUTcast Server logfiles XSS		
General	FTP Server type and version		
General	Ultraseek Web Server Detect		
General	IRC daemon identification		
General	Network Chemistry Wireless Sensor Detection		
General	DNS AXFR	CAN-1999-0532	

Family	Plug-in Name	CVE ID Number(s)	BugTraq ID Number(s)
General	Determine if Bind 9 is running		
General	SSH protocol version 1 enabled		
General	TTL Anomaly detection		
General	HTTP Server type and version		
General	Linksys Router Default Password		
General	Cobalt Web Administration Server Detection		
General	BIND vulnerable to DNS storm	CAN-2002-1221, CAN-2002-1219, CAN-2002-1220	6159, 6160, 6161
General	Amanda Index Server version		
General	NetGear Router Default Password		
General	Relative IP Identification number change		
General	Useable remote name server	CVE-1999-0024	678
General	POP3 Server type and version		
General	SSL ciphers		
General	UDDI detection		
General	DNS Server Detection		
General	vqServer administrative port	CVE-2000-0766	1610
General	SiteScope Web Managegment Server Detect		

Family	Plug-in Name	CVE ID Number(s)	BugTraq ID Number(s)
General	A Nessus Daemon is running		
General	Unconfigured web server		
General	S-HTTP detection		
General	AOLserver Default Password		
General	a tftpd server is running		
General	Detect Server type and version via Telnet		
General	OS fingerprint	CAN-1999-0454	
General	NetCharts Server Default Password		
General	Shopping Cart Arbitrary Command Execution (Hassan)	CAN-2001-0985	3308
General	SiteScope Web Administration Server Detection		
General	Compaq Web-based Management Login		
General	Compaq Web Based Management Agent Proxy Vulnerability		
General	Detect SWAT server port	CVE-2000-0935	1872
General	Misc information on News server		
General	SCO OpenServer multiple vulnerabilities	CAN-2002-0164, CAN-2002-0158	4396
General	McAfee myCIO detection		
General	WebDAV enabled		
General	NTP read variables		

Family	Plug-in Name	CVE ID Number(s)	BugTraq ID Number(s)
General	Detect presence of PGP-Net server and its version		
General	Sun JavaServer Default Admin Password		
General	redhat Interchange		5453
General	WorldClient for Mdaemon Server Detection		
General	Predictable TCP sequence number	CVE-1999-0077	
General	Apache Tomcat Default Accounts		
General	AFS client version		
General	Unprotected Netware Management Portal		
General	SWAT allows user names to be obtained by brute force	CVE-2000-0938	
General	CVS pserver double free() bug	CAN-2003-0015	6650
General	HTTP version spoken		
General	Apache Auth Module SQL Insertion Attack	CAN-2001-1379	3253
General	RTSP Server type and version		
General	VisualRoute Web Server Detection		
General	Tripwire for Webpages Detection		
General	Microsoft Exchange Public Folders Information Leak	CVE-2001-0660	3301

Family	Plug-in Name	CVE ID Number(s)	BugTraq ID Number(s)
General	Detect the presence of Napster		
General	Cisco IDS Device Manager Detection		
General	NetInfo daemon		
General	Notes detection		
General	DHCP server info gathering		
General	SSH protocol versions supported		
General	IRCXPro Default Admin password		
General	Sun Cobalt Adaptive Fire-wall Detection		
General	Delta UPS Daemon Detection		
General	iPlanet Application Server Detection		
General	Dropbear SSH server for-mat string vulnerability		8439
General	Leafnode denials of service		6490
General	Standard & Poors detection	CAN-2000-0109	1080
General	apcnisd detection		
General	Netscape Enterprise Default Administrative Password		
General	Kerberos 5 issues	CAN-2003-0072, CAN-2003-0082, CAN-2003-0059, CAN-2003-0060, CAN-2002-0036	7184, 7185, 6714, 6713, 6712

Family	Plug-in Name	CVE ID Number(s)	BugTraq ID Number(s)
General	Public CVS pserver		
General	Obtain /etc/passwd using NetInfo		2953
General	HTTP TRACE		
General	IMAP Banner		
General	Private IP address leaked in HTTP headers	CAN-2000-0649	1499
General	SSH Server type and version		
General	The remote BIND has dynamic updates enabled		
Misc.	Brute force login (Hydra)	CAN-1999-0502, CAN-1999-0505, CAN-1999-0516, CAN-1999-0518	
Misc.	Identifies unknown services with 'HELP'		
Misc.	Citrix published applications		5817
Misc.	BGP detection		
Misc.	SheerDNS directory traversal		7336, 7335
Misc.	Nortel Networks password-less router (user level)		
Misc.	AppleShare IP Server status query		
Misc.	WebLogic Server host-name disclosure		7257
Misc.	Netgear ProSafe Router password disclosure		7270, 7267

Family	Plug-in Name	CVE ID Number(s)	BugTraq ID Number(s)
Misc.	Proxy Web Server Cross Site Scripting		7596
Misc.	Passwordless HP LaserJet	CAN-1999-1061	
Misc.	PPTP detection and versioning		
Misc.	Apache < 2.0.45	CAN-2003-0132	7254, 7255
Misc.	Motorola Vanguard with No Password		
Misc.	IPSwitch IMail SMTP Buffer Overflow		2651
Misc.	Oracle tnslsnr security		
Misc.	OSPF detection		
Misc.	Netscape /.perf accessible		
Misc.	Directory Scanner		
Misc.	Shiva LanRover Blank Password		
Misc.	Axis Camera Default Password		
Misc.	SOCKS server detection		
Misc.	Airport Administrative Port	CAN-2003-0270	
Misc.	TinyWeb 1.9		8810
Misc.	Passwordless Alcatel ADSL Modem		
Misc.	URLScan Detection		
Misc.	EGP detection		
Misc.	icmp leak		
Misc.	Apache UserDir Sensitive Information Disclosure	CAN-2001-1013	3335

Family	Plug-in Name	CVE ID Number(s)	BugTraq ID Number(s)
Misc.	OpenSSL password interception	CAN-2003-0078, CAN-2003-0131, CVE-1999-0428	6884, 7148
Misc.	Nortel/Bay Networks default password		
Misc.	Apache < 1.3.28	CAN-2003-0460, CAN-2002-0061	8226
Misc.	QMTP		
Misc.	Tektronix /ncl_items.html	CAN-1999-1508	806
Misc.	xtel detection		
Misc.	TCP Chorusing	CAN-1999-1201	225
Misc.	Apache /server-status accessible		
Misc.	Default password router Zyxel	CAN-1999-0571	3161
Misc.	Pocsag password	CVE-2000-0225	1032
Misc.	RIP detection		
Misc.	Oracle tnslsnr version query	CVE-2000-0818	1853
Misc.	Linksys Router default password		
Misc.	Cisco 675 passwordless router	CVE-1999-0889	
Misc.	Cayman DSL router one char login		3017
Misc.	ShareMailPro Username Identification		7658
Misc.	Unknown services banners		
Misc.	Apache < 2.0.46	CAN-2003-0245, CAN-2003-0189	7723, 7725

Family	Plug-in Name	CVE ID Number(s)	BugTraq ID Number(s)
Misc.	Apache < 2.0.48	CVE-2002-0061	
Misc.	Apache < 1.3.27	CAN-2002-0839, CAN-2002-0840, CAN-2002-0843	5847, 5884, 5995, 5996
Misc.	Alcatel PABX 4400 detection		
Misc.	Netscape Messenging Server User List	CVE-2000-0960	1787
Misc.	Portable OpenSSH PAM timing attack	CAN-2003-0190	7482, 7467, 7342
Misc.	Etherleak	CAN-2003-0001	6535
Misc.	RealServer Memory Content Disclosure	CVE-2000-1181	1957
Misc.	Shiva Integrator Default Password		
Misc.	LCDproc server detection		
Misc.	List of printers is available through CUPS		
Misc.	OpenSSH Reverse DNS Lookup bypass	CAN-2003-0386	7831
Misc.	Nortel/Bay Networks/ Xylogics Annex default password		
Misc.	Cabletron Web View Administrative Access		
Misc.	XTramail control denial	CAN-1999-1511	791
Misc.	3Com Superstack II switch with default password		
Misc.	Apache < 2.0.46 on OS/2	CAN-2003-0134	7332
Misc.	AirConnect Default Password		

Family	Plug-in Name	CVE ID Number(s)	BugTraq ID Number(s)
Misc.	X Server	CVE-1999-0526	
Misc.	12Planet Chat Server ClearText Password		7354
Misc.	hp jetdirect vulnerabilities		7070
Misc.	Apache /server-info accessible		
Misc.	Kerberos PingPong attack	CVE-1999-0103	
Misc.	Sambar Transmits Passwords in PlainText		
Misc.	RedHat 6.2 inetd	CVE-2001-0309	2395
Misc.	BIND vulnerable to ZXFR bug	CVE-2000-0887	1923
Misc.	Webserver 4D Cleartext Passwords		
Misc.	WebLogic Certificates Spoofing		
Misc.	Traceroute		
Misc.	Nortel Baystack switch password test		
Misc.	HP LaserJet display hack		
Misc.	RIP poisoning		
Misc.	Tomcat /status information disclosure		
Misc.	qpopper options buffer overflow	CVE-2001-1046	2811
Misc.	Apache < 2.0.43	CAN-2002-1156, CAN-2003-0083	6065
Misc.	12Planet Chat Server Path Disclosure		7355
Misc.	3Com hub		

Family	Plug-in Name	CVE ID Number(s)	BugTraq ID Number(s)
Misc.	irix performance copilot	CVE-2000-0283, CVE-2000-1193	1106, 4642
Misc.	Apache < 2.0.47	CAN-2003-0192, CAN-2003-0253, CAN-2003-0254	8134, 8135, 8137, 8138
Misc.	LCDproc buffer overflow	CAN-2000-0295	1131
Misc.	Alcatel ADSL modem with firewalling off		2568
Misc.	xtelw detection		
Misc.	Check open ports		
Misc.	Web Server Cross Site Scripting		5305, 7353, 7344, 8037
Misc.	Nortel Networks passwordless router (manager level)		
Misc.	Find if IIS server allows BASIC and/or NTLM authentication	CAN-2002-0419	
Misc.	Passwordless Cayman DSL router	CAN-1999-0508	
Misc.	HP LaserJet direct print	CAN-1999-1062	
Misc.	Services		
Misc.	NAI Management Agent leaks info	CVE-2000-0448	1253
Netware	Novell NetWare HTTP POST Perl Code Execution Vulnerability	CAN-2002-1436, CAN-2002-1437, CAN-2002-1438	5520
Netware	Netware NDS Object Enumeration		
NIS	bootparamd service	CAN-1999-0647	
NIS	NIS server	CAN-1999-0620	

Family	Plug-in Name	CVE ID Number(s)	BugTraq ID Number(s)
Peer-To-Peer File Sharing	Web Server hosting copyrighted material		
Peer-To-Peer File Sharing	WinMX P2P check		
Peer-To-Peer File Sharing	Trillian is installed		5677, 5733, 5755, 5765, 5769, 5775, 5776, 5777, 5783
Peer-To-Peer File Sharing	mldonkey telnet		
Peer-To-Peer File Sharing	mldonkey www		
Peer-To-Peer File Sharing	Kazaa is installed	CAN-2002-0314, CAN-2002-0315	3135, 4121, 4122, 5317, 6435, 6747
Peer-To-Peer File Sharing	eDonkey detection		
Peer-To-Peer File Sharing	ICQ is installed	CAN-1999-1418, CAN-1999-1440, CAN-2000-0046, CAN-2000-0564, CVE-2000-0552, CAN-2001-0367, CVE-2002-0028, CAN-2001-1305	
Peer-To-Peer File Sharing	SMB share hosting copyrighted material		
Peer-To-Peer File Sharing	LimeWire is installed		
Peer-To-Peer File Sharing	shareaza P2P check		
Peer-To-Peer File Sharing	WinMX is installed		
Peer-To-Peer File Sharing	Gnutella servent detection		

Family	Plug-in Name	CVE ID Number(s)	BugTraq ID Number(s)
Peer-To-Peer File Sharing	Kazaa / Morpheus Client Detection		
Peer-To-Peer File Sharing	FTP server hosting copyrighted material		
Peer-To-Peer File Sharing	Overnet P2P check		
Peer-To-Peer File Sharing	XoloX is installed		
Peer-To-Peer File Sharing	Kazaa P2P check	CAN-2003-0397	
Port scanners	Exclude toplevel domain wildcard host		
Port scanners	Ping the remote host		
Port scanners	SYN Scan		
Port scanners	scan for LaBrea tarpitted hosts		
Port scanners	tcp connect() scan		
Remote file access	MySQL various flaws	CVE-2000-0045, CAN-2001-1275, CVE-2001-0407	2380, 2522
Remote file access	3com RAS 1500 configuration disclosure		7176
Remote file access	thttpd directory traversal thru Host:	CAN-2002-1562	
Remote file access	McAfee myCIO Directory Traversal	CVE-2001-1144	3020
Remote file access	TFTP get file	CAN-1999-0498	
Remote file access	WebLogic Server DoS	CAN-2001-0098	2138
Remote file access	FileMakerPro Detection		7315
Remote file access	Check for Apache Multiple / vulnerability	CVE-2000-0505	1284

Family	Plug-in Name	CVE ID Number(s)	BugTraq ID Number(s)
Remote file access	WebSite 1.0 buffer overflow	CVE-1999-0178	2078
Remote file access	Office files list		
Remote file access	sawmill password	CAN-2000-0589	1403
Remote file access	MySQL mysqld Privilege Escalation Vulnerability	CAN-2003-0150	7052
Remote file access	thttpd ssi file retrieval	CVE-2000-0900	1737
Remote file access	ipop2d reads arbitrary files		1484
Remote file access	Anaconda remote file retrieval	CVE-2000-0975	2338
Remote file access	NFS cd ..	CVE-1999-0166	
Remote file access	BadBlue Remote Administrative Interface Access		
Remote file access	MultiTech Proxy Server Default Password		7203
Remote file access	NFS export	CAN-1999-0554, CAN-1999-0548	
Remote file access	Sambar Default Accounts		
Remote file access	eXtropia Web Store remote file retrieval	CVE-2000-1005	1774
Remote file access	Web Shopper remote file retrieval	CVE-2000-0922	1776
Remote file access	Boa file retrieval	CVE-2000-0920	1770
Remote file access	Eserv traversal	CAN-1999-1509	773
Remote file access	Lotus Domino 6.0 vulnerabilities		6870, 6871
Remote file access	Mountable NFS shares	CVE-1999-0170, CVE-1999-0211, CAN-1999-0554	

Family	Plug-in Name	CVE ID Number(s)	BugTraq ID Number(s)
Remote file access	thttpd flaw	CAN-1999-1457	
Remote file access	Misconfigured Gnutella		
Remote file access	AliBaba path climbing	CAN-1999-0776	270
Remote file access	Atrium Mercur Mailserver	CVE-2000-0318	1144
Remote file access	MetaInfo servers		110
Remote file access	Unpassworded MySQL		
Remote file access	MySQLs accepts any password	CVE-2000-0148	975
Remote file access	Apache < 2.0.44 file reading on Win32	CAN-2003-0017	
Remote file access	WebLogic Server /%00/ bug		2513
Remote file access	The ACC router shows configuration without authentication	CVE-1999-0383	183
Remote file access	Test Microsoft IIS Source Fragment Disclosure	CVE-2000-0457, CVE-2000-0630	1193, 1488
Remote file access	Netscape Enterprise INDEX request problem	CAN-2001-0250	2285
Remote file access	NFS fsirand	CVE-1999-0167	
Remote file access	LDAP allows anonymous binds	CVE-1999-0385	503
Remote file access	Unpassworded PostgreSQL		
Remote file access	iPlanet Certificate Management Traversal	CVE-2000-1075	1839
Remote file access	Linux TFTP get file	CVE-1999-0183	
Remote file access	The remote portmapper forwards NFS requests	CVE-1999-0168	
Remote file access	vqServer web traversal vulnerability	CVE-2000-0240	1067

Family	Plug-in Name	CVE ID Number(s)	BugTraq ID Number(s)
Remote file access	Informix traversal	CAN-2001-0924	3575
Remote file access	sawmill allows the reading of the first line of any file	CVE-2000-0588	1402
Remote file access	CommunigatePro Hijacking		
Remote file access	FTPGate traversal		
Remote file access	mod_auth_any command execution	CAN-2003-0084	7448
Remote file access	BadBlue Administrative Actions Vulnerability		7387
Remote file access	NetBeans Java IDE	CAN-1999-1527	816
Remote file access	LocalWeb2000 remote read	CVE-2001-0189	2268, 4820, 7947
Remote file access	Insecure Napster clone	CAN-2000-0412	1186
Remote file access	iChat	CVE-1999-0897	
Remote file access	Test HTTP dangerous methods		
Remote file access	Eserv Directory Index		7669
Remote file access	LDAP allows null bases		
Remote file access	Lotus Domino ?open Vulnerability		
RPC	rexd service	CVE-1999-0627	37
RPC	keyserv service		
RPC	sadmin service	CVE-1999-0977	866, 8615
RPC	ypxfrd service		
RPC	rstatd service	CAN-1999-0624	
RPC	etherstatd service		
RPC	rquotad service	CAN-1999-0625	

Family	Plug-in Name	CVE ID Number(s)	BugTraq ID Number(s)
RPC	statd service	CVE-1999-0018, CVE-1999-0019, CVE-1999-0493	127, 450
RPC	ypbind service	CVE-1999-0312	52
RPC	statmon service		
RPC	X25 service	CAN-1999-0648	
RPC	rje mapper service		
RPC	sprayd service	CAN-1999-0613	
RPC	amd service	CVE-1999-0704	614
RPC	automountd service	CVE-1999-0210, CVE-1999-0704	235, 614
RPC	format string attack against statd	CVE-2000-0666, CAN-2000-0800	1480
RPC	fam service	CVE-1999-0059	353
RPC	snmp service	CAN-1999-0615	
RPC	walld service	CVE-1999-0181	
RPC	Sun portmap xdrmem_ getbytes() overflow	CAN-2003-0028	7123
RPC	tooltalk format string	CAN-2002-0677, CVE-2001-0717, CVE-2002-0679	3382
RPC	dmisd service	CVE-2002-0391	5356
RPC	nlockmgr service	CVE-2000-0508	1372
RPC	showfhd service		
RPC	database service		
RPC	alis service		
RPC	rusersd service	CVE-1999-0626	
RPC	nfsd service	CVE-1999-0832, CAN-2002-0830	782

Family	Plug-in Name	CVE ID Number(s)	BugTraq ID Number(s)
RPC	rpcinfo -p		
RPC	llockmgr service		
RPC	tooltalk service	CVE-1999-0003, CVE-1999-0693	122
RPC	yppasswd service		
RPC	rusersd output	CVE-1999-0626	
RPC	ypupdated service	CVE-1999-0208	
RPC	Sun rpc.cmsd overflow	CVE-2002-0391	5356
RPC	sunlink mapper service		
RPC	3270 mapper service		
RPC	Kcms Profile Server	CVE-2001-0595	2605
RPC	selection service		
RPC	nibindd is running		
RPC	nsed service		
RPC	RPC portmapper	CAN-1999-0632, CVE-1999-0189	205
RPC	tfsd service		
RPC	sched service		
RPC	nsemntd service		
Settings	SMTP settings		
Settings	SMB Scope		
Settings	Libwhisker options		
Settings	NIDS evasion		
Settings	Login configurations		
Settings	cgibin() in the KB		
Settings	HTTP NIDS evasion		

Family	Plug-in Name	CVE ID Number(s)	BugTraq ID Number(s)
Settings	HTTP login page		
SMTP problems	Sendmail ETRN command DOS	CVE-1999-1109	
SMTP problems	TFS SMTP 3.2 MAIL FROM overflow	CAN-1999-1516	
SMTP problems	Sendmail 8.8.8 to 8.12.7 Double Pipe Access Validation Vulnerability	CAN-2002-1165	5845
SMTP problems	Imate HELO overflow	CVE-2000-0507	1286
SMTP problems	Sendmail Parsing Redirection DOS	CVE-1999-0393	
SMTP problems	Sendmail Local Starvation and Overflow	CVE-1999-0131	717
SMTP problems	SMTP too long line		
SMTP problems	Xtramail MTA 'HELO' denial	CAN-1999-1511	791
SMTP problems	Sendmail remote header buffer overflow	CAN-2002-1337, CVE-2001-1349	6991
SMTP problems	Sendmail mailing to programs	CAN-1999-0163	
SMTP problems	eXtremail format strings	CAN-2001-1078	2908
SMTP problems	MS SMTP DoS	CVE-2002-0055	4204
SMTP problems	Sendmail's from piped program	CVE-1999-0203	2308
SMTP problems	Sendmail 'decode' flaw	CVE-1999-0096	
SMTP problems	Sendmail 8.11 local overflow	CVE-2001-0653	3163
SMTP problems	Generic SMTP overflows		
SMTP problems	Lotus MAIL FROM overflow	CVE-2000-0452	1229

Family	Plug-in Name	CVE ID Number(s)	BugTraq ID Number(s)
SMTP problems	Sendmail 8.7.*/8.8.* local overflow	CVE-1999-0130	716
SMTP problems	Sendmail Group Permissions Vulnerability	CVE-1999-0129	715
SMTP problems	MS SMTP Authorization bypass	CVE-2002-0054	4205
SMTP problems	Sendmail mime overflow	CVE-1999-0206	
SMTP problems	Sendmail long debug local overflow	CVE-1999-1309	
SMTP problems	Buffer Overrun in ITHouse Mail Server v1.04	CVE-2000-0488	1285
SMTP problems	smtpscan		
SMTP problems	Postfix Multiple Vulnerabilities	CAN-2003-0540, CAN-2003-0468	8361, 8362
SMTP problems	Lotus Domino SMTP overflow	CVE-2000-1047	1905
SMTP problems	Sendmail 8.6.9 ident	CVE-1999-0204	2311
SMTP problems	poprelayd & sendmail authentication problem	CVE-2001-1075	2986
SMTP problems	SLMail MTA 'HELO' denial	CAN-1999-0284	
SMTP problems	Sendmail -bt option		
SMTP problems	ISMail overflow		
SMTP problems	Exchange XEXCH50 Remote Buffer Overflow	CAN-2003-0714	8838
SMTP problems	Sendmail buffer overflow due to type conversion	CAN-2003-0161	7230
SMTP problems	Sendmail DNS Map TXT record overflow	CVE-2002-0906	5122
SMTP problems	Sendmail mailing to files		

Family	Plug-in Name	CVE ID Number(s)	BugTraq ID Number(s)
SMTP problems	Exim Heap Overflow	CAN-2003-0743	8518
SMTP problems	Sendmail redirection check		
SMTP problems	HELO overflow	CAN-1999-0098	
SMTP problems	Sendmail prescan() overflow	CAN-2003-0694	8641
SMTP problems	SMTP Authentication Error	CVE-2001-0504	2988
SMTP problems	Sendmail mail.local DOS	CVE-2000-0319	1146
SMTP problems	SLMail SMTP overflows		
SMTP problems	BaSoMail SMTP Command HELO overflow		7726
SMTP problems	EXPN and VRFY commands	CAN-1999-0531	
SMTP problems	Sendmail custom configuration file	CAN-2001-0713	3377
SMTP problems	Cmail's MAIL FROM overflow	CAN-1999-1521	633
SMTP problems	IMC SMTP EHLO Buffer Overrun	CVE-2002-0698	5306
SMTP problems	Sendmail Forward File Privilege Escalation Vulnerability		7033
SMTP problems	Sendmail 8.8.3 and 8.8.4 mime conversion overflow	CVE-1999-0047	685
SMTP problems	Sendmail queue manipulation & destruction	CAN-2001-0714	3378
SMTP problems	Mail relaying (thorough test)		
SMTP problems	Sendmail DEBUG	CVE-1999-0095	1

Family	Plug-in Name	CVE ID Number(s)	BugTraq ID Number(s)
SMTP problems	NTMail3 spam feature	CVE-1999-0819	
SMTP problems	CSM Mail server MTA 'HELO' denial	CVE-2000-0042	895
SMTP problems	EXPN overflow		2412
SMTP problems	Mail relaying	CAN-1999-0512, CAN-2002-1278, CAN-2003-0285	8196
SMTP problems	Sendmail debug mode leak	CAN-2001-0715	3898
SNMP	Obtain processes list via SNMP		
SNMP	SNMP VACM		2427
SNMP	Discover HP JetDirect EWS Password via SNMP	CAN-2002-1048	7001
SNMP	Enumerate Lanman shares via SNMP	CAN-1999-0499	
SNMP	Default community names of the SNMP Agent	CAN-1999-0517, CAN-1999-0186, CAN-1999-0254, CAN-1999-0516	177, 7081, 7212, 7317
SNMP	Obtain OS type via SNMP		
SNMP	Obtain network interfaces list via SNMP		
SNMP	Enumerate Lanman users via SNMP		
SNMP	Enumerate Lanman services via SNMP		
SNMP	D-Link DSL Broadband Modem		7212
SNMP	An SNMP Agent is running		

Family	Plug-in Name	CVE ID Number(s)	BugTraq ID Number(s)
SNMP	Obtain Cisco type via SNMP		
Useless services	X Display Manager Control Protocol (XDMCP)		
Useless services	rexecd	CAN-1999-0618	
Useless services	Systat	CVE-1999-0103	
Useless services	rsh	CAN-1999-0651	
Useless services	Finger	CVE-1999-0612	
Useless services	Telnet	CAN-1999-0619	
Useless services	Echo port open	CVE-1999-0103, CAN-1999-0635	
Useless services	Check for Webmin		
Useless services	rlogin	CAN-1999-0651	
Useless services	Chargen	CVE-1999-0103	
Useless services	Quote of the day	CVE-1999-0103	
Useless services	GameSpy detection		6636
Useless services	Identd enabled	CAN-1999-0629	
Useless services	Check for a Citrix server		7276
Useless services	Windows Terminal Service Enabled	CAN-2001-0540	7258
Useless services	netstat	CAN-1999-0650	
Useless services	Daytime	CVE-1999-0103	
Useless services	Writesrv		
Useless services	Discard port open	CAN-1999-0636	
Useless services	xtux server detection	CVE-2002-0431	4260
Windows	SMB Registry : SQL7 Patches	CVE-2002-0642	5205

Family	Plug-in Name	CVE ID Number(s)	BugTraq ID Number(s)
Windows	Multiple ICQ Vulnerabilities	CAN-2003-0235, CAN-2003-0236, CAN-2003-0237, CAN-2003-0238, CAN-2003-0239	7461, 7462, 7463, 7464, 7465, 7466
Windows	Visual Basic for Application Overflow	CAN-2003-0347	8534
Windows	Domain account lockout vulnerability		1973
Windows	Certificate Validation Flaw Could Enable Identity Spoofing (Q328145)	CAN-2002-1183, CAN-2002-0862	5410
Windows	DirectX MIDI Overflow (819696)	CAN-2003-0346	7370
Windows	Cumulative Patch for Internet Information Services (Q327696)	CVE-2002-0147, CVE-2002-0149, CVE-2002-0150, CAN-2002-0224, CAN-2002-0869, CAN-2002-1182, CAN-2002-1180, CAN-2002-1181	4474
Windows	SMB get domain SID	CVE-2000-1200	959
Windows	CuteFTP multiple flaws		6786, 6642
Windows	RPC Endpoint Mapper can Cause RPC Service to Fail	CVE-2001-0662	3313
Windows	SMB Registry : is the remote host a PDC/BDC	CAN-1999-0659	
Windows	Buffer Overrun in Messenger Service (828035)	CAN-2003-0717	8826
Windows	scan for UPNP hosts	CVE-2001-0876	3723
Windows	Incomplete TCP/IP packet vulnerability	CAN-2000-1039	2022

Family	Plug-in Name	CVE ID Number(s)	BugTraq ID Number(s)
Windows	WinAMP3 buffer overflow		6515
Windows	Opening Group Policy Files (Q318089)	CVE-2002-0051	4438
Windows	SMB Registry : Classic Logon Screen		
Windows	NetBIOS Name Server Protocol Spoofing patch	CVE-2000-0673	1514
Windows	Possible RPC Interface compromise	CAN-2003-0528	
Windows	Buffer overrun in NT kernel message handling	CAN-2003-0112	7370
Windows	SMB Registry : Do not show the last user name		
Windows	Telnet Client NTLM Authentication Vulnerability	CVE-2000-0834	1683
Windows	Flaw in Windows Function may allow DoS (823803)	CAN-2003-0525	
Windows	SmartFTP Overflow		
Windows	Flaw in message handling through utility mgr	CAN-2003-0350	8205
Windows	The ScriptLogic service is running		7477, 7575
Windows	Relative Shell Path patch	CVE-2000-0663	1507
Windows	Quicktime player buffer overflow	CAN-2003-0168	7247
Windows	SMB accessible registry	CAN-1999-0562	
Windows	SMB NativeLanMan		
Windows	scan for UPNP/Tcp hosts		

Family	Plug-in Name	CVE ID Number(s)	BugTraq ID Number(s)
Windows	XML Core Services patch (Q318203)	CVE-2002-0057	3699
Windows	Windows Messenger is installed	CAN-1999-1484, CAN-2002-0228, CAN-2002-0472	668, 4028, 4316, 4675, 4827
Windows	Using NetBIOS to retrieve information from a Windows host	CAN-1999-0621	
Windows	Blackmoon FTP stores passwords in cleartext	CAN-2003-0342	7646
Windows	Unchecked buffer in Windows Shell	CVE-2002-0070	4248
Windows	Vulnerability in Authenticode Verification Could Allow Remote Code Execution (823182)	CAN-2003-0660	
Windows	Drag And Zip Overflow		
Windows	SMB use domain SID to enumerate users	CVE-2000-1200	959
Windows	Microsoft's SQL Overflows	CAN-2002-1137, CAN-2002-1138, CAN-2002-0649, CVE-2002-0650, CAN-2002-1145, CAN-2002-0644, CAN-2002-0645, CAN-2002-0721	5310, 5311
Windows	Flaw in SMB Signing Could Enable Group Policy to be Modified (329170)	CAN-2002-1256	
Windows	SMB Registry : Winlogon caches passwords		
Windows	Flaw in RPC Endpoint Mapper (MS03-010)	CAN-2002-1561	

Family	Plug-in Name	CVE ID Number(s)	BugTraq ID Number(s)
Windows	Unchecked Buffer in XP upnp	CVE-2001-0876	3723
Windows	SMB on port 445		
Windows	SMB log in as users	CAN-1999-0504, CAN-1999-0506	
Windows	FlashFXP Overflow		7857, 7859
Windows	DrWeb Folder Name Overflow		7022
Windows	SMB Windows9x password verification vulnerability	CVE-2000-0979	1780
Windows	Unprotected PC Anywhere Service		
Windows	Cumulative Patch for Internet Information Services (Q11114)	CAN-2003-0224, CAN-2003-0225, 2003-0226	7731, 7735, 7733
Windows	SMB Registry : permissions of keys that can lead to admin	CAN-1999-0589	
Windows	Malformed RPC Packet patch	CAN-2000-0544	1304
Windows	IrDA access violation patch	CVE-2001-0659	3215
Windows	CesarFTP stores passwords in cleartext	CAN-2003-0329	
Windows	IRCXPro Clear Text Passwords		7792
Windows	Unchecked buffer in Locate Service	CAN-2003-0003	
Windows	Buffer Overflow in Windows Troubleshooter ActiveX Control (826232)	CAN-2003-0661	

Family	Plug-in Name	CVE ID Number(s)	BugTraq ID Number(s)
Windows	Yahoo!Messenger is installed	CAN-2002-0320, CAN-2002-0321, CAN-2002-0031, CVE-2002-0032, CAN-2002-0322	2299, 4162, 4163, 4164, 4173, 4837, 4838, 5579, 6121
Windows	Buffer overrun in Windows Shell (821557)	CAN-2003-0351	
Windows	Unchecked Buffer in PPTP Implementation Could Enable DOS Attacks (Q329834)	CAN-2002-1214	
Windows	SMB Registry : permissions of winlogon	CAN-1999-0589	
Windows	Flaw in Certificate Enrollment Control (Q323172)	CAN-2002-0699	
Windows	Local Security Policy Corruption	CVE-2000-0771	1613
Windows	Buffer overrun in RPC Interface (823980)	CAN-2003-0352	
Windows	IE VBScript Handling patch (Q318089)	CVE-2002-0052	4158
Windows	NT IP fragment reassembly patch not applied (jolt2)	CVE-2000-0305	1236
Windows	PFTP clear-text passwords		
Windows	SMB log in	CAN-1999-0504, CAN-1999-0506, CVE-2000-0222, CAN-1999-0505, CAN-2002-1117	490
Windows	Opera remote heap corruption vulnerability		7450
Windows	Word can lead to Script execution on mail reply	CVE-2002-1056	4397

Family	Plug-in Name	CVE ID Number(s)	BugTraq ID Number(s)
Windows	The remote host is infected by a virus		
Windows	SMB Registry : No dial in		
Windows	The alerter service is running	CAN-1999-0630	
Windows	NTLMSSP Privilege Escalation	CVE-2001-0016	2348
Windows	Microsoft ISA Server DNS - Denial Of Service (MS03-009)	CAN-2003-0011	7145
Windows	Cumulative patch for Windows Media Player	CVE-2002-0372, CVE-2002-0373, CAN-2002-0615	5107, 5109, 5110
Windows	Malformed PPTP Packet Stream vulnerability	CVE-2001-0017	2368
Windows	CA Unicenter's Transport Service is running		
Windows	Microsoft ISA Server Winsock Proxy DoS (MS03-012)	CAN-2003-0110	7314
Windows	SMB Registry : permissions of WinVNC's key	CVE-2000-1164	1961
Windows	Cumulative VM update	CAN-2002-0058, CVE-2002-0078	4228, 4392
Windows	Unchecked buffer in ASP.NET worker process	CVE-2002-0369	4958
Windows	Unchecked Buffer in XP Redirector (Q810577)	CAN-2003-0004	
Windows	SMB Registry : permissions of HKLM	CAN-1999-0589	
Windows	NT ResetBrowser frame & HostAnnouncement flood patc	CVE-2000-0404	1262

Family	Plug-in Name	CVE ID Number(s)	BugTraq ID Number(s)
Windows	Windows Media Player Library Access	CAN-2003-0348	8034
Windows	Windows Debugger flaw can Lead to Elevated Privileges (Q320206)	CVE-2002-0367	4287
Windows	Unchecked buffer in MDAC Function	CVE-2002-0695, CVE-2003-0353, 2002-0695, CAN-2003-0353	5372
Windows	Multiple flaws in the Opera web browser		7056, 6962, 6811, 6814, 6754, 6755, 6756, 6757, 6759, 6218
Windows	Buffer Overrun in Messenger Service (real test)	CAN-2003-0717	8826
Windows	SMB get host SID	CVE-2000-1200	959
Windows	Windows Network Manager Privilege Elevation (Q326886)	CVE-2002-0720	5480
Windows	Microsoft SQL TCP/IP listener is running	CAN-1999-0652	
Windows	Windows RAS overflow (Q318138)	CVE-2002-0366	4852
Windows	Detect CIS ports		
Windows	Webserver file request parsing	CVE-2000-0886	1912
Windows	RealPlayer PNG deflate heap corruption	CAN-2003-0141	7177
Windows	Unchecked Buffer in Windows Help(Q323255)	CAN-2002-0693, CAN-2002-0694	
Windows	Flaw in WinXP Help center could enable file deletion	CAN-2002-0974	5478

Family	Plug-in Name	CVE ID Number(s)	BugTraq ID Number(s)
Windows	Unchecked buffer in Network Share Provider (Q326830)	CAN-2002-0724	5556
Windows	Gator/GAIN Spyware Installed		
Windows	WM_TIMER Message Handler Privilege Elevation (Q328310)	CAN-2002-1230	5927
Windows	Java Media Framework (JMF) Vulnerability		
Windows	ARCserve hidden share	CAN-2001-0960	3343
Windows	SMB Registry : permissions of the SNMP key	CAN-2001-0046	2066
Windows	Cumulative patches for Excel and Word for Windows	CVE-2002-0616, CVE-2002-0617, CVE-2002-0618, CVE-2002-0619	4821
Windows	SMB Registry : permissions of the Microsoft Transaction Server key	CAN-2001-0047	2065
Windows	scriptlogic logging share		7476
Windows	NetBIOS Name Service Reply Information Leakage	CAN-2003-0661	8532
Windows	SMB log in with W32/ Deloder passwords		
Windows	DCE Services Enumeration		
Windows	Flaw in Microsoft VM (816093)	CAN-2003-0111	

Family	Plug-in Name	CVE ID Number(s)	BugTraq ID Number(s)
Windows	Microsoft's SQL Version Query	CAN-2000-1081, CVE-2000-0202, CVE-2000-0485, CAN-2000-1087, CAN-2000-1088, CAN-2002-0982, CAN-2001-0542, CVE-2001-0344	4135, 4847, 5014, 5205
Windows	Opera web browser HREF overflow	CAN-2003-0870	
Windows	Microsoft's SQL Hello Overflow	CAN-2002-1123	5411
Windows	SMB shares enumeration		
Windows	SMB Registry : value of SFCDisable		
Windows	Gupta SQLBase EXECUTE buffer overflow		6808
Windows	Buffer Overrun In HTML Converter Could Allow Code Execution (823559)	CAN-2003-0469	
Windows	Unchecked Buffer in ntdll.dll (Q815021)	CAN-2003-0109	7116
Windows	SMB enum services		
Windows	Cumulative Patch for MS SQL Server (815495)	CAN-2003-0230, CAN-2003-0231, CAN-2003-0232	8274, 8275, 8276
Windows	Windows Media Player Skin Download Overflow	CAN-2003-0228	

Family	Plug-in Name	CVE ID Number(s)	BugTraq ID Number(s)
Windows	IE 5.01 5.5 6.0 Cumulative patch	CAN-2003-0838, CAN-2003-0809, CAN-2003-0530, CAN-2003-0531, CAN-2003-0113, CAN-2003-0114, CAN-2003-0115, CAN-2003-0116	3578, 8556, 8565
Windows	Microsoft's SQL version less than or equal to 7	CAN-2000-0199	1055
Windows	SMB Registry : Autologon		
Windows	Unchecked buffer in SQLXML	CVE-2002-0186, CVE-2002-0187, CAN-2002-0186, CAN-2002-0187	5004, 5005
Windows	MS SQL7.0 Service Pack may leave passwords on system	CVE-2000-0402	1281
Windows	SMB Registry : permissions of Schedule	CAN-1999-0589	
Windows	Unchecked Buffer in XP Shell Could Enable System Compromise (329390)	CAN-2002-1327	
Windows	Still Image Service Privilege Escalation patch	CVE-2000-0851	1651
Windows	SMB Registry : permissions of the RAS key	CAN-2001-0045	2064
Windows	Word Macros may run automatically	CAN-2003-0664, CAN-1999-0354	8533
Windows	MS SQL Installation may leave passwords on system	CAN-2002-0643	

Family	Plug-in Name	CVE ID Number(s)	BugTraq ID Number(s)
Windows	DBTools DBManager Information Disclosure		7040
Windows	Winreg registry key write-able by non-admins	CVE-2002-0049	4053
Windows	Citrix redirection bug		
Windows	Microsoft's SQL Blank Password	CAN-2000-1209	1281
Windows	Buffer Overrun in the ListBox and in the ComboBox (824141)	CAN-2003-0659	
Windows	SMB Request Handler Buffer Overflow	CAN-2003-0345	8152
Windows	Malformed request to index server	CVE-2001-0244, CVE-2001-0245	2709
Windows	Winsock Mutex vulnerability	CVE-2001-0006	2303
Windows	CA Unicenter's File Transfer Service is running		
Windows	Trusting domains bad verification	CVE-2002-0018	3997
Windows	SMB Registry : XP Service Pack version	CAN-1999-0662	
Windows	Security issues in the remote version of Flash-Player		7005
Windows	Flaw in Windows Script Engine (Q814078)	CAN-2003-0010	7146
Windows	SMB Registry : NT4 Service Pack version	CAN-1999-0662	
Windows	SMB LanMan Pipe Server browse listing		

Family	Plug-in Name	CVE ID Number(s)	BugTraq ID Number(s)
Windows	Service Control Manager Named Pipe Imperson-ation patch	CVE-2000-0737	1535
Windows	SMB Registry : Win2k Service Pack version	CAN-1999-0662	7930, 8090, 8128, 8154
Windows	LPC and LPC Ports Vulnerabilities patch		1743
Windows	AOL Instant Messenger is Installed		
Windows	MUP overlong request kernel overflow Patch (Q311967)	CVE-2002-0151	4426
Windows	Malformed request to domain controller	CVE-2001-0502	2929
Windows	The messenger service is running	CAN-1999-0630	
Windows	SMB shares access	CAN-1999-0519, CAN-1999-0520	8026
Windows	SMB fully accessible registry		
Windows	SMB use host SID to enumerate local users	CVE-2000-1200	959
Windows	FTP Voyager Overflow		7862
Windows	Exchange 2000 Exhaust CPU Resources (Q320436)	CAN-2002-0368	
Windows	The remote host is infected by msblast.exe		
Windows	Checks for MS HOTFIX for snmp buffer overruns	CAN-2002-0053	

Family	Plug-in Name	CVE ID Number(s)	BugTraq ID Number(s)
Windows	Flaw in Microsoft VM Could Allow Code Execution (810030)	CAN-2002-1257, CAN-2002-1258, CAN-2002-1183, CAN-2002-0862	
Windows	Microsoft RDP flaws could allow sniffing and DOS(Q324380)	CAN-2002-0863	5410
Windows	Microsoft's SQL Server Brute Force		
Windows	SMB Registry : missing winreg		
Windows	Detect the HTTP RPC endpoint mapper		
Windows	SMB Registry : permissions of keys that can change common paths	CAN-1999-0589	
Windows	LeapFTP Overflow		
Windows	Microsoft Shlwapi.dll Malformed HTML form tag DoS		7402
Windows	Unchecked Buffer in Decompression Functions(Q329048)	CAN-2002-0370, CAN-2002-1139	
Windows	Microsoft's SQL UDP Info Query		
Windows : User management	Local users information : Never changed password		
Windows : User management	Users in the 'Backup Operator' group		
Windows : User management	Obtains the lists of users groups		
Windows : User management	Users information : automatically disabled accounts		

Family	Plug-in Name	CVE ID Number(s)	BugTraq ID Number(s)
Windows : User management	Local users information : automatically disabled accounts		
Windows : User management	Guest belongs to a group		
Windows : User management	Local users information : User has never logged on		
Windows : User management	Users information : Passwords never expires		
Windows : User management	Local users information : disabled accounts		
Windows : User management	Obtains local user information		
Windows : User management	Users in the Admin group		
Windows : User management	Users in the 'Replicator' group		
Windows : User management	Local users information : Can't change password		
Windows : User management	Users in the 'Print Operator' group		
Windows : User management	Users information : disabled accounts		
Windows : User management	Users in the 'System Operator' group		
Windows : User management	Users information : Can't change password		
Windows : User management	Local users information : Passwords never expires		
Windows : User management	Users in the Domain Admin group		

Family	Plug-in Name	CVE ID Number(s)	BugTraq ID Number(s)
Windows : User management	Users information : User has never logged in		
Windows : User management	Obtains the lists of users aliases		
Windows : User management	Obtains user information		
Windows : User management	Users information : Never changed password		
Windows : User management	Users in the 'Account Operator' group		

References

Web Sites

ACID: http://acidlab.sourceforge.net

AirSnort: http://airsnort.shmoo.com

Bastille Linux: www.bastille-linux.org

CERT: www.cert.org

Ethereal: www.ethereal.com

FBI: www.fbi.gov

Foundstone: www.foundstone.com

FreeS/WAN www.freeswan.org

GNU Project www.gnu.org

GPG www.gnupg.org

John the Ripper: www.openwall.com/john

Iptables: www.netfilter.org

Kismet Wireless: www.kismetwireless.net

lsof: http://freshmeat.net/projects/lsof

NCC: www.netsecuritysvcs.com/ncc

Nessus: www.nessus.org

NessusWX: nessuswx.nessus.org

NetStumbler: www.netstumbler.com

Nlog: www.secureaustin.com/nlog

Nmap: www.insecure.org/nmap

NPI Website,

Open Source Windows Forensics Tools: www.opensourceforensics.org/tools/windows.html

OpenSSH: www.openssh.org

PGP: www.pgp.com

PuTTY: www.chiark.greenend.org.uk/~sgtatham/putty

Sam Spade for Windows: www.samspade.org/ssw

Sleuth Kit: www.sleuthkit.org

SmoothWall Express: www.smoothwall.org

Snort: www.snort.org

Snort Webmin Module: http://msbnetworks.net/snort

SourceForge: www.sourceforge.net

StumbVerter: www.sonar-security.com

Swatch: swatch.sourceforge.net

Tcpdump, Windump: www.tcpdump.org

Tripwire: www.tripwire.org

Turtle Firewall: www.turtlefirewall.com

Books and Articles

Caswell, Brian, Jay Beale, James C. Foster, and Jeffrey Posluns. 2003. *Snort 2.0 Intrusion Detection*. Rockland, MA: Syngress.

Cisco Internetwork Basics: www.idevelopment.info/data/Networking/Networking_Basics/BASICS_Understanding_OSI_Model.shtml

Drummond, Richard. 1993. *Data Communications for the Office*. New York: Bantam Professional Books.

EMACS quick reference: http://seamons.com/emacs/

Hafner, Katie and John Markoff. 1991. *Cyberpunk: Outlaws and Hackers on the Computer Frontier*. New York: Simon and Schuster.

Introduction to Cryptography, Network Associates: www.pgpi.org/doc/pgpintro/

Krutz, Ronald L.and Russell Dean Vines. 2001. *The CISSP Prep Guide*. New York: John Wiley & Sons.

Lammle, Todd. 2003. CCNA Cisco Certified Network Associate Study Guide, Fourth Edition. Location: San Francisco: Sybex.

Levy, Steven. 2002. *Crypto: How the Code Rebels Beat the Government Saving Privacy in the Digital Age*. New York: Penguin Putnam Inc.

Marcus, J. Scott. 1999. *Designing Wide Area Networks and Internetworks: A Practical Guide*. Boston: Addison-Wesley.

The OSI Model: www.wdsd.org/strut/OSI/osimodel.html

Scambray, Joel, Stuart McClure, and George Kurtz. 2001. *Hacking Exposed*, Second Edition. New York: McGraw Hill.

Schneier, Bruce. 1995. *Applied Cryptography: Protocols, Algorithms, and Source Code in C*, Second Edition. Hoboken, NJ: John Wiley & Sons.

Schultz, E. Eugene. 2000. *Windows NT/2000 Network Security*. New York: MacMillan Technical Publishing.

Singh, Simon. 2000. *The Code Book: The Science of Secrecy from Ancient Egypt to Quantum Cryptography*. London: Anchor Books.

Smith, Richard E. 2001. *Authentication: From Passwords to Public Keys*. Boston: Addison-Wesley.

Stanger, James, Patrick T. Lane, and Edgar Danielyan. 2001. *Hackproofing Linux*. Rockland, MA: Syngress.

Torvalds, Linus and David Diamond. 2002. *Just for Fun: The Story of an Accidental Revolutionary*. New York: HarperBusiness.

Index

M

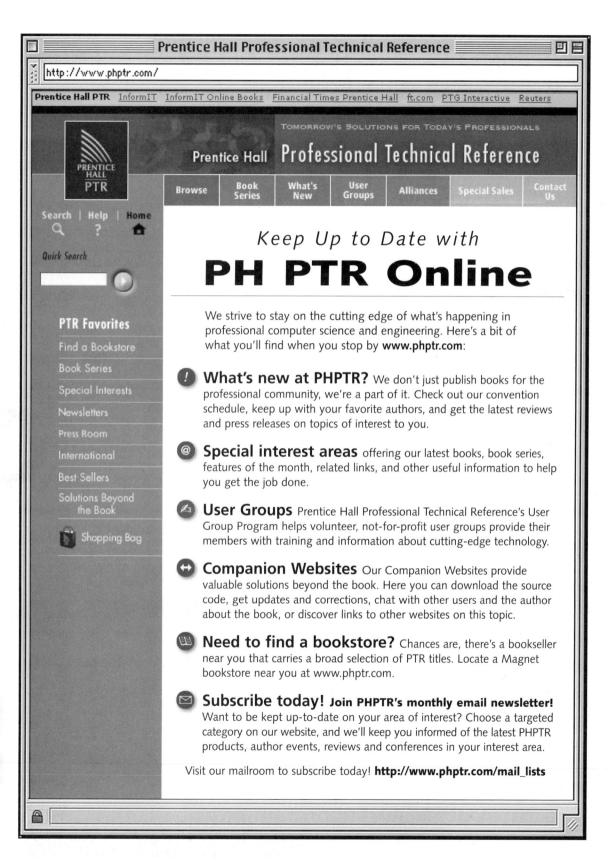

CD-ROM Warranty

Pearson Technology Group warrants the enclosed CD-ROM to be free of defects in materials and faulty workmanship under normal use for a period of ninety days after purchase (when purchased new). If a defect is discovered in the CD-ROM during this warranty period, a replacement CD-ROM can be obtained at no charge by sending the defective CD-ROM, postage prepaid, with proof of purchase to:

For use on both the PC running Windows 98 or above and most Linux and BSD distributions.

More information and updates are available at:

http://www.phptr.com/parens

Most tools on this CD-ROM copyrighted under GNU or BSD licenses. See the following for details.

GNU General Public Licence

BSD License